Purch...
april...

Rachel likes to buy
books @ school when
she subs.

FIX-IT
Has Miriam's
easy meatballs

and

FORGET-IT™
COOKBOOK
Feasting with your Slow Cooker

FIX-IT
and
FORGET-IT™
COOKBOOK

Feasting with your slow cooker

Dawn J. Ranck
Phyllis Pellman Good

Good Books
Intercourse, PA 17534
800/762-7171 • www.goodbks.com

Cover design and illustrations by Cheryl Benner
Design by Dawn J. Ranck

FIX-IT AND FORGET-IT™ COOKBOOK: FEASTING WITH YOUR SLOW COOKER
Copyright © 2000 by Good Books, Intercourse, PA 17534

Publishing History
Original Paperback Edition published 2000.
Hardcover Gift Edition published 2001.
Comb-bound Paperback Edition published 2001.
Special edition published 2005.

International Standard Book Number: 1-56148-491-1 (special edition)
International Standard Book Number: 1-56148-317-6 (paperback edition)
International Standard Book Number: 1-56148-338-9 (hardcover gift edition)
International Standard Book Number: 1-56148-339-7 (comb-bound paperback edition)
Library of Congress Catalog Card Number: 00-052110

Printed in Canada

Library of Congress Cataloging-in-Publication Data
Ranck, Dawn J.
    Fix-it and forget-it cookbook : feasting with your slow cooker / Dawn J. Ranck,
Phyllis Pellman Good.
        p.cm.
    Includes index.
    1. Electric cookery, Slow. I. Good, Phyllis Pellman II. Title.
TX827.R35 2000
641.5'884--dc21   00-052110

Table of Contents

About This Cookbook

Slow Cookers have long ago proven to be the efficient friend of those cooks who are gone all day, but want to offer substantial home-cooked food to their households.

Slow Cookers have aged, but they haven't faded. Instead, they've shown themselves to be first-rate adaptable appliances. They handle dried beans famously well, pleasing the growing numbers of vegetarians. They do their job whatever their size—1-quart, 3-quart, 6-quart, or in between. Little ones work well for singles or doubles—or cook the vegetables while the beef stew burbles away in a bigger Cooker, sharing the counter-space.

And Slow Cookers are mobile tools. You can prepare a dish one evening, store the filled "lift-out" vessel in the frig overnight, and then place it into its electric holder in the morning as you do your dash to the door. Or you can tote the whole works to a buffet or carry-in meal, doing no damage to the quality of its contents.

Slow Cookers prefer cheap cuts of meat. Tell that to your favorite graduate student, or newly independent young adult, or to the parents of a growing brood.

The recipes in this collection are tried and true favorites from heavy-duty Cooker-users. We've weeded out a lot of duplicates and still have 800 plus for you to try. There's tempting variety among the recipes, and many that differ only by a tantalizing ingredient or two.

What's more, you'll find helpful Tips spread among the recipes— the kind of pointers that you usually learn only after a long acquaintance with a Slow Cooker. These Tips tell you how to maximize the usefulness of your Cooker, plus how to realize top flavor from the food you prepare in it.

May the *Fix-It and Forget-It Cookbook* help make your meal preparations less harried and your dinners more satisfying!

— *Dawn J. Ranck and Phyllis Pellman Good*

Appetizers, Snacks, and Spreads

Quick and Easy Nacho Dip

Kristina Shull
Timberville, VA

Makes 10-15 servings

1 lb. ground beef
dash of salt
dash of pepper
dash of onion powder
2 garlic cloves, minced,
    optional
2 16-oz. jars salsa (as hot
    or mild as you like)
15-oz. can refried beans
1½ cups sour cream
3 cups shredded cheddar
    cheese, divided
tortilla chips

1. Brown ground beef.
Drain. Add salt, pepper,
onion powder, and minced
garlic.
2. Combine beef, salsa,
beans, sour cream, and 2
cups cheese in slow cooker.

3. Cover. Heat on Low 2
hours. Just before serving
sprinkle with 1 cup cheese.
4. Serve with tortilla chips.

Southwest Hot Chip Dip

Annabelle Unternahrer
Shipshewana, IN

Makes 15-20 servings

1 lb. ground beef,
    browned, crumbled fine,
    and drained
2 15-oz. cans refried beans
2 10-oz. cans diced
    tomatoes and chilies
1 pkg. taco seasoning
1 lb. Velveeta cheese,
    cubed
tortilla chips

1. Combine ground beef,
beans, tomatoes, and taco seasoning in slow cooker.

2. Cover. Cook on Low 3-4
hours, or on High 1½ hours.
3. Add cheese. Stir occa-
sionally. Heat until cheese is
melted.
4. Serve with tortilla chips.

Note:
Serve as a main dish alongside a soup.

5

Hot Refried Bean Dip

Sharon Anders
Alburtis, PA

*Makes 1½ quarts,
or 12-20 servings*

15-oz. can refried beans,
  drained and mashed
½ lb. ground beef
3 Tbsp. bacon drippings
1 lb. American cheese,
  cubed
1-3 Tbsp. taco sauce
1 Tbsp. taco seasoning
dash garlic salt
tortilla chips

1. In skillet, brown beans
and ground beef in bacon
drippings. Pour into slow
cooker.
2. Stir in cheese, taco
sauce, taco seasoning, and
garlic salt.
3. Cover. Cook on High 45
minutes, or until cheese is
melted, stirring occasionally.
Turn to Low until ready to
serve, up to 6 hours.

Chili-Cheese Taco Dip

Kim Stoltzfus
New Holland, PA

Makes 10-12 servings

1 lb. ground beef
1 can chili, without beans
1 lb. mild Mexican
  Velveeta cheese, cubed
taco *or* tortilla chips

1. Brown beef, crumble
into small pieces, and drain.
2. Combine beef, chili, and
cheese in slow cooker.
3. Cover. Cook on Low 1-
1½ hours, or until cheese is
melted, stirring occasionally
to blend ingredients.
4. Serve warm with taco or
tortilla chips.

Hamburger Cheese Dip

Julia Lapp
New Holland, PA

Makes 8-10 servings

1 lb. ground beef, browned
  and crumbled into small
  pieces
½ tsp. salt
½ cup chopped green
  peppers
¾ cup chopped onion
8-oz. can tomato sauce
4-oz. can green chilies,
  chopped
1 Tbsp. Worcestershire
  sauce
1 Tbsp. brown sugar
1 lb. Velveeta cheese,
  cubed
1 Tbsp. paprika
red pepper to taste
tortilla chips

1. Combine beef, salt,
green peppers, onion, tomato
sauce, green chilies,
Worcestershire sauce, and
brown sugar in slow cooker.
2. Cover. Cook on Low 2-3
hours. During the last hour
stir in cheese, paprika, and
red pepper.
3. Serve with tortilla chips.

Variation:
Prepare recipe using only
⅓-½ lb. ground beef.

Leave the lid on while the slow cooker cooks. The steam
that condenses on the lid helps cook the food from the top.
Every time you take the lid off, the cooker loses steam. After
you put the lid back on, it takes one to 20 minutes to regain
the lost steam and temperature. That means it takes longer
for the food to cook.
Pam Hochstedler
Kalona, IA

Chili-Cheese Dip

Ruth Hofstetter
Versailles, Missouri
Paula King
Harrisonburg, VA

Makes 10 servings

1 lb. ground beef,
   browned, crumbled fine,
   and drained.
2 lbs. Velveeta cheese,
   cubed
10-oz. can tomatoes with
   chilies
1 tsp. Worcestershire sauce
1/2 tsp. chili powder
tortilla *or* corn chips

1. Combine all ingredients
except chips in slow cooker.
Mix well.
2. Cover. Cook on High 1
hour, stirring occasionally
until cheese is fully melted.
3. Serve immediately, or
turn to Low for serving up to
6 hours later.
4. Serve with tortilla or
corn chips.

Variation:
For a thicker dip, make a
smooth paste of 2 Tbsp. flour
mixed with 3 Tbsp. cold
water. Stir into hot dip.

Michelle's Taco Dip

Michelle Strite
Harrisonburg, VA

Makes 6-8 servings

1 1/2 lbs. ground beef,
   browned, crumbled fine,
   and drained
1 pkg. taco seasoning mix
10-oz. jar salsa
1 lb. Velveeta cheese,
   cubed
1/4 cup chopped onion
tortilla chips

1. Combine all ingredients
except chips in slow cooker.
2. Cover. Heat on Low for
2-3 hours.
3. Serve with tortilla chips.

Variation:
The recipe can be made
with half the amount of meat
called for, if you prefer.

Karen's Nacho Dip

Karen Stoltzfus
Alto, MI

Makes 10-12 servings

1 lb. ground beef
2 lbs. American cheese,
   cubed
16-oz. jar salsa (mild,
   medium, *or* hot,
   whichever you prefer)
1 Tbsp. Worcestershire
   sauce
tortilla *or* corn chips

1. Brown beef, crumble
into small pieces, and drain.
2. Combine beef, cheese,
salsa, and Worcestershire
sauce in slow cooker.
3. Cover. Cook on High 1
hour, stirring occasionally
until cheese is fully melted.
4. Serve immediately, or
turn to Low for serving up to
6 hours later.

Mexican Chip Dip Ole'

Joy Sutter
Iowa City, IA

Makes 10-12 servings

2 lbs. ground turkey
1 large onion, chopped
15-oz. can tomato sauce
4-oz. can green chilies, chopped
3-oz. can jalapeno peppers, chopped
2 lbs. Velveeta cheese, cubed
tortilla chips

1. Brown turkey and onion. Drain.
2. Add tomato sauce, chilies, jalapeno peppers, and cheese. Pour into slow cooker.
3. Cover. Cook on Low 4 hours, or High 2 hours.
4. Serve warm with tortilla chips.

Barbara's Chili Cheese Dip

Barbara Shie
Colorado Springs, CO

Makes 8-10 servings

1 lb. ground beef
1 lb. Velveeta cheese, cubed
8-oz. can green chilies and tomato sauce
2 tsp. Worcestershire sauce
½ tsp., or more, chili powder
¼ cup salsa with jalapeno peppers
tortilla *or* corn chips

1. Brown ground beef, crumble fine, and drain.
2. Combine all ingredients except chips in slow cooker. Stir well.
3. Cover. Cook on High 1 hour, stirring until cheese is melted. Serve immediately, or turn on Low for serving up to 6 hours later.
4. Serve with tortilla or corn chips.

Note:
Serve over rice, noodles, or baked potatoes as a main dish, making 4-5 servings.

Pizza Fondue

Lisa Warren
Parkesburg, PA

Makes 8-12 servings

1 lb. ground beef
2 cans pizza sauce with cheese
8 oz. grated cheddar cheese
8 oz. grated mozzarella cheese
1 tsp. dried oregano
½ tsp. fennel seed, optional
1 Tbsp. cornstarch
tortilla chips

1. Brown beef, crumble fine, and drain.
2. Combine all ingredients except tortilla chips in slow cooker.
3. Cover. Heat on Low 2-3 hours.
4. Serve with tortilla chips.

Super Bowl Super Dip

Colleen Heatwole
Burton, MI

*Makes 4-5 cups,
or approximately 12 servings*

1 lb. ground beef
1 lb. Mexican Velveeta
cheese spread
8-oz. salsa (mild, medium,
or hot)
tortilla chips

1. Brown ground beef,
crumble into fine pieces, and
drain. Place in slow cooker.
Add cheese.
2. Cover. Cook on High for
45 minutes, stirring occasionally until cheese melts.
3. Add salsa. Reduce heat
to Low and cook until heated
through.
4. Serve warm with tortilla
chips.

Hamburger Hot Dip

Janice Martins
Fairbank, IA

Makes 6 cups dip

1 lb. ground beef
1 medium onion, chopped
fine
1/2 tsp. salt
1/4 tsp. pepper
8-oz. jar salsa
14-oz. can nacho cheese
soup
8 slices Velveeta cheese
nacho chips

1. Brown ground beef and
onions in saucepan. Drain.
Season with salt and pepper.
2. Combine all ingredients
in slow cooker.
3. Cover. Cook on Low 4
hours. Stir occasionally.
4. Serve with nacho chips.

Chili Con Queso Cheese Dip

Melanie Thrower
McPherson, KS

Makes 8 servings

1 lb. ground beef
1/2 cup chopped onion
1 cup Velveeta cheese,
cubed
10-oz. can diced tomatoes
and green chilies
1 can evaporated milk
2 Tbsp. chili powder
tortilla chips

1. Brown ground beef and
onion. Crumble beef into fine
pieces. Drain.
2. Combine all ingredients
except tortilla chips in slow
cookers.
3. Cover. Heat on Low 1-2
hours, until cheese is melted.
4. Serve with tortilla chips.

Good 'n' Hot Dip

Joyce B. Suiter
Garysburg, NC

Makes 30-50 servings

1 lb. ground beef
1 lb. bulk sausage
10¾-oz. can cream of
   chicken soup
10¾-oz. can cream of
   celery soup
24-oz. jar salsa (use hot for
   some zing)
1 lb. Velveeta cheese,
   cubed
chips

1. Brown beef and
sausage, crumbling into small
pieces. Drain.
2. Combine meat, soups,
salsa, and cheese in slow
cooker.
3. Cover. Cook on High 1
hour. Stir. Cook on Low until
ready to serve.
4. Serve with chips.

Cheese Queso Dip

Janie Steele
Moore, OK

Makes about 2 quarts dip

2-lbs. Velveeta cheese,
   cubed
10-oz. can diced tomatoes
   and chilies
1 lb. bulk sausage,
   browned, crumbled fine,
   and drained
tortilla chips

1. Combine cheese, toma-
toes, and sausage in slow
cooker.
2. Cover. Heat on Low 1-2
hours.
3. Serve with tortilla chips.

Hot Cheese and Bacon Dip

Lee Ann Hazlett
Freeport, IL

Makes 6-8 servings

16 slices bacon, diced
2 8-oz. pkgs. cream cheese,
   cubed and softened
4 cups shredded mild
   cheddar cheese
1 cup half-and-half
2 tsp. Worcestershire sauce
1 tsp. dried minced onion
½ tsp. dry mustard
½ tsp. salt
2-3 drops Tabasco

1. Brown and drain bacon.
Set aside.
2. Mix remaining ingredi-
ents in slow cooker.
3. Cover. Cook on Low 1
hour, stirring occasionally
until cheese melts.
4. Stir in bacon.
5. Serve with fruit slices or
French bread slices. (Dip fruit
in lemon juice to prevent
browning.)

Championship Bean Dip

Renee Shirk
Mt. Joy, PA
Ada Miller
Sugarcreek, OH

Makes 4½ cups dip

15-oz. can refried beans
1 cup picante sauce
1 cup (4 oz.) shredded
  Monterey Jack cheese
1 cup (4 oz.) shredded
  cheddar cheese
3/4 cup sour cream
3-oz. pkg. cream cheese,
  softened
1 Tbsp. chili powder
1/4 tsp. ground cumin
tortilla chips
salsa

1. In a bowl, combine all ingredients except chips and salsa. Transfer to slow cooker.
2. Cover. Cook on High 2 hours, or until heated through, stirring once or twice.
3. Serve with tortilla chips and salsa.

Refried Bean Dip

Maryann Markano
Wilmington, DE

Makes 6 servings

20-oz. can refried beans
1 cup shredded cheddar
  cheese
1/2 cup chopped green
  onions
1/4 tsp. salt
2-4 Tbsp. bottled taco
  sauce (depending upon
  how spicy a dip you
  like)
tortilla chips

1. Combine beans, cheese, onions, salt, and taco sauce in slow cooker.
2. Cover. Cook on Low 2-2½ hours, or cook on High 30 minutes and then on Low 30 minutes.
3. Serve with tortilla chips.

Jeanne's Chile Con Queso

Jeanne Allen
Rye, CO

Makes 15-20 servings

40-oz. can chili without
  beans
2-lbs. Velveeta cheese,
  cubed
16-oz. jar picante sauce
  (mild, medium, *or* hot,
  whichever you prefer)
tortilla chips

1. Combine all ingredients except chips in slow cooker.
2. Cover. Cook on Low 1-2 hours, until cheese is melted. Stir.
3. Serve with tortilla chips.

A slow cooker is great for taking food to a potluck supper, even if you didn't prepare it in the cooker.
Irma H. Schoen
Windsor, CT

Maryann's Chili Cheese Dip

Maryann Westerberg
Rosamond, CA

Makes about 10 servings

2 lbs. Velveeta cheese,
cubed
16-oz. can chili without
beans
10-oz. can diced tomatoes
with chilies, drained
10¾-oz. can cream of
mushroom soup
tortilla chips

1. Combine cheese and
chili in slow cooker. Heat on
Low until cheese melts, stirring occasionally.
2. Add tomatoes and soup.
3. Cover. Cook on Low 2
hours. Stir before serving.
4. Serve with tortilla chips.

Tina's Cheese Dip

Tina Houk
Clinton, MO

Makes 12 servings

2 8-oz. pkgs. cream cheese,
softened
3 15½-oz. cans chili
2 cups shredded cheddar
or mozzarella cheese
tortilla chips

1. Spread cream cheese in
bottom of slow cooker.
2. Spread chili on top of
cream cheese.
3. Top with shredded
cheese.
4. Cover. Cook on Low
1-1½ hours, until shredded
cheese is melted. Stir.
5. Serve with tortilla chips.

Cheese Spread

Barbara Kuhns
Millersburg, OH

*Makes approximately
12-15 servings*

1 lb. white American
cheese, cubed
1½ cups milk
crackers

1. Combine cheese and
milk in slow cooker.
2. Cover. Cook on Low
about 2 hours, or until cheese
is melted, stirring occasionally.
3. Serve on crackers.

Mexicana Dip

Julia B. Boyd
Memphis, TN
Sue Williams
Gulfport, MS

Makes 10-12 servings

2 lbs. American, *or*
Velveeta cheese, cubed
10-oz. can tomatoes with
green chilies
tortilla chips, corn chips,
or potato chips

1. Combine cheese and
tomatoes in slow cooker.
2. Cover. Cook on Low
2-3 hours, stirring until
cheese is melted. If mixture is
too thick, add a little milk.
3. Serve as a dip, or pour
over platter of favorite chips.

Variation:
Stir in ½ lb. browned bulk
sausage, crumbled into small
pieces.

Jane Steele
Moore, OK

Marilyn's Chili Con Queso

Marilyn Mowry
Irving, TX

Makes 2 cups dip

1 Tbsp. chopped green peppers
1 Tbsp. chopped celery
1 Tbsp. chopped onions
2 Tbsp. diced tomatoes
2 tsp. chopped jalapeno pepper
1/2 cup water
3/4 cup heavy cream
8 oz. Velveeta cheese, cubed
2 oz. cheddar cheese, shredded
tortilla chips

1. Place first 5 ingredients in slow cooker. Add water.
2. Cover. Cook on High 1 hour, or until vegetables are tender.
3. Stir in cream and cheeses.
4. Reduce heat to Low. Cook until cheese is melted. Serve immediately, or keep warm on Low for hours.
5. Serve with tortilla chips.

Chili Con Queso Dip

Jenny R. Unternahrer
Wayland, IA

Makes approximately 12 servings

1 lb. Velveeta cheese, cubed
1 cup salsa (mild, medium, *or* hot, whichever you prefer)
1 cup sour cream
tortilla chips

1. Combine cheese, salsa, and sour cream in slow cooker.
2. Cover. Heat on Low, stirring occasionally until cheese melts and dip is well blended, about 1-1½ hours.
3. Serve with tortilla chips.

Short-Cut Fondue Dip

Jean Butzer
Batavia, NY

Makes 8-10 servings

2 10¾-oz. cans condensed cheese soup
2 cups grated sharp cheddar cheese
1 Tbsp. Worcestershire sauce
1 tsp. lemon juice
2 Tbsp. dried chopped chives
celery sticks
cauliflower florets
corn chips

1. Combine soup, cheese, Worcestershire sauce, lemon juice, and chives in slow cooker.
2. Cover. Heat on Low 2-2½ hours. Stir until smooth and well blended.
3. Serve warm dip with celery sticks, cauliflower, and corn chips.

Chili Verde con Queso Dip

Bonita Ensenberger
Albuquerque, NM

Makes 1 quart (8-10 servings)

2 10¾-oz. cans cheddar
  cheese soup
7-oz. can chopped green
  chilies
1 garlic clove, minced
½ tsp. dried cilantro leaves
½ tsp. ground cumin
corn chips

1. Mix together all ingredients except corn chips in slow cooker.
2. Cover. Cook on Low 1-1½ hours. Stir well. Cook an additional 1½ hours.
3. Serve with corn chips.

Variation:

Make this a main dish by serving over baked potatoes.

Lilli's Nacho Dip

Lilli Peters
Dodge City, KS

Makes 10 servings

3-lbs. Velveeta cheese,
  cubed
10¾-oz. can cream of
  chicken soup
2 4-oz. cans chopped green
  chilies and juice
tortilla chips

1. Place cheese in slow cooker. Cook on Low until cheese melts, stirring occasionally.
2. Add soup and chilies. Stir. Heat on Low 1 hour.
3. Pour over tortilla chips just before serving.

Note:

If you want to speed up the process, melt the cheese in the microwave. Heat on High for 1½ minutes, stir, and continue heating at 1½-minute intervals as long as needed.

Variations:

1. Instead of using 2 4-oz. cans chilies, use 10-oz. can tomatoes and chilies.
2. For a heartier dip, add ½-1 lb. bulk sausage, browned, crumbled into small pieces, and drained.

Reuben Spread

Clarice Williams
Fairbank, IA
Julie McKenzie
Punxsutawney, PA

Makes 5 cups spread

½ lb. corned beef,
  shredded *or* chopped
16-oz. can sauerkraut, well
  drained
1-2 cups shredded Swiss
  cheese
1-2 cups shredded cheddar
  cheese
1 cup mayonnaise
snack rye bread
Thousand Island dressing,
  optional

1. Combine all ingredients except bread and Thousnd Island dressing in slow cooker. Mix well.
2. Cover. Cook on High 1-2 hours until heated through, stirring occasionally.
3. Turn to Low and keep warm in cooker while serving. Put spread on bread slices. Top individual servings with Thousand Island dressing, if desired.

Note:

Low-fat cheese and mayonnaise are not recommended for this spread.

Variation:

Use dried beef instead of corned beef.

Cheesy New Orleans Shrimp Dip

Kelly Evenson
Pittsboro, NC

Makes 3-4 cups dip

1 slice bacon
3 medium onions, chopped
1 garlic clove, minced
4 jumbo shrimp, peeled and deveined
1 medium tomato, peeled and chopped
3 cups Monterey Jack cheese, shredded
4 drops Tabasco sauce
1/8 tsp. cayenne pepper
dash of black pepper
chips

1. Cook bacon until crisp. Drain on paper towel. Crumble.
2. Saute onion and garlic in bacon drippings. Drain on paper towel.
3. Coarsely chop shrimp.
4. Combine all ingredients except chips in slow cooker.
5. Cover. Cook on Low 1 hour, or until cheese is melted. Thin with milk if too thick. Serve with chips.

Broccoli Cheese Dip

Carla Koslowsky
Hillsboro, KS

Makes 6 cups dip

1 cup chopped celery
1/2 cup chopped onion
10-oz. pkg. frozen chopped broccoli, cooked
1 cup cooked rice
10¾-oz. can cream of mushroom soup
16-oz. jar cheese spread, *or* 15 slices American cheese, melted and mixed with 2/3 cup milk
snack breads or crackers

1. Combine all ingredients in slow cooker.
2. Cover. Heat on Low 2 hours.
3. Serve with snack breads or crackers.

Roasted Pepper and Artichoke Spread

Sherril Bieberly
Salina, KS

Makes 3 cups, or about 12 servings

1 cup grated Parmesan cheese
1/2 cup mayonnaise
8-oz. pkg. cream cheese, softened
1 garlic clove, minced
14-oz. can artichoke hearts, drained and chopped finely
1/3 cup finely chopped roasted red bell peppers (from 7¼-oz. jar)
crackers, cut-up fresh vegetables, *or* snack-bread slices

1. Combine Parmesan cheese, mayonnaise, cream cheese, and garlic in food processor. Process until smooth. Place mixture in slow cooker.
2. Add artichoke hearts and red bell pepper. Stir well.
3. Cover. Cook on Low 1 hour. Stir again.
4. Use as spread for crackers, cut-up fresh vegetables, or snack-bread slices.

The great thing about using a slow cooker in hot weather is that it doesn't heat up your kitchen like an oven does.
Carol Peachey
Lancaster, PA

Baked Brie with Cranberry Chutney

Amymarlene Jensen
Fountain, CO

Makes 8-10 servings

1 cup fresh, *or* dried,
  cranberries
1/2 cup brown sugar
1/3 cup cider vinegar
2 Tbsp. water, *or* orange
  juice
2 tsp. minced crystallized
  ginger
1/4 tsp. cinnamon
1/8 tsp. ground cloves
oil
8-oz. round of Brie cheese
1 Tbsp. sliced almonds,
  toasted
crackers

1. Mix together cranberries, brown sugar, vinegar, water or juice, ginger, cinnamon, and cloves in slow cooker.
2. Cover. Cook on Low 4 hours. Stir once near the end to see if it is thickening. If not, remove top, turn heat to High and cook 30 minutes without lid.
3. Put cranberry chutney in covered container and chill for up to 2 weeks. When ready to serve, bring to room temperature.
4. Brush ovenproof plate with vegetable oil, place unpeeled Brie on plate, and bake uncovered at 350° for 9 minutes, until cheese is soft and partially melted. Remove from oven.

5. Top with at least half the chutney and garnish with almonds. Serve with crackers.

Artichokes

Susan Yoder Graber
Eureka, IL

Makes 4 servings

4 artichokes
1 tsp. salt
2 Tbsp. lemon juice
melted butter

1. Wash and trim artichokes by cutting off the stems flush with the bottoms of the artichokes and by cutting 3/4-1 inch off the tops. Stand upright in slow cooker.
2. Mix together salt and lemon juice and pour over artichokes. Pour in water to cover 3/4 of artichokes.
3. Cover. Cook on Low 8-10 hours, or High 2-4 hours.
4. Serve with melted butter. Pull off individual leaves and dip bottom of each into butter. Using your teeth, strip the individual leaf of the meaty portion at the bottom of each leaf.

Curried Almonds

Barbara Aston
Ashdown, AR

Makes 4 cups nuts

2 Tbsp. melted butter
1 Tbsp. curry powder
1/2 tsp. seasoned salt
1 lb. blanched almonds

1. Combine butter with curry powder and seasoned salt.
2. Pour over almonds in slow cooker. Mix to coat well.
3. Cover. Cook on Low 2-3 hours. Turn to High. Uncover cooker and cook 1-1 1/2 hours.
4. Serve hot or cold.

Chili Nuts

Barbara Aston
Ashdown, AR

Makes 5 cups nuts

1/4 cup melted butter
2 12-oz. cans cocktail
  peanuts
1 5/8-oz. pkg. chili
  seasoning mix

1. Pour butter over nuts in slow cooker. Sprinkle in dry chili mix. Toss together.
2. Cover. Heat on Low 2-2 1/2 hours. Turn to High. Remove lid and cook 10-15 minutes.
3. Serve warm or cool.

All-American Snack

Doris M. Coyle-Zipp
South Ozone Park, NY
Melissa Raber, Millersburg, OH
Ada Miller, Sugarcreek, OH
Nanci Keatley, Salem, OR

Makes 3 quarts snack mix

3 cups thin pretzel sticks
4 cups Wheat Chex
4 cups Cheerios
12-oz. can salted peanuts
1/4 cup melted butter, *or*
   margarine
1 tsp. garlic powder
1 tsp. celery salt
1/2 tsp. seasoned salt
2 Tbsp. grated Parmesan
   cheese

1. Combine pretzels, cereal, and peanuts in large bowl.
2. Melt butter. Stir in garlic powder, celery salt, seasoned salt, and Parmesan cheese. Pour over pretzels and cereal. Toss until well mixed.
3. Pour into large slow cooker. Cover. Cook on Low 2½ hours, stirring every 30 minutes. Remove lid and cook another 30 minutes on Low.
4. Serve warm or at room temperature. Store in tightly covered container.

Variations:
1. Use 3 cups Wheat Chex (instead of 4 cups) and 3 cups Cheerios (instead of 4 cups). Add 3 cups Corn Chex.
   Marcia S. Myer
   Manheim, PA

2. Alter the amounts of pretzels, cereal, and peanuts to reflect your preferences.

Hot Caramel Dip

Marilyn Yoder
Archbold, OH

Makes about 3 cups dip

1/2 cup butter
1/2 cup light corn syrup
1 cup brown sugar
1 can sweetened
   condensed milk
apple slices

1. Mix together all ingredients except apples in saucepan. Bring to boil.
2. Pour into crockpot. Set on Low.
3. Dip fresh apple slices into hot caramel.

Variation:
   Add 1/2 cup peanut butter to dip.

Rhonda's Apple Butter

Rhonda Burgoon
Collingswood, NJ

Makes about 2 pints apple butter

4 lbs. apples
2 tsp. cinnamon
1/2 tsp. ground cloves

1. Peel, core, and slice apples. Place in slow cooker.
2. Cover. Cook on High 2-3 hours. Reduce to Low and cook 8 hours. Apples should be a rich brown and be cooked down by half.
3. Stir in spices. Cook on High 2-3 hours with lid off. Stir until smooth.
4. Pour into freezer containers and freeze, or into sterilized jars and seal.

Shirley's Apple Butter

Shirley Sears
Tiskilwa, IL

Makes 6-10 pints apple butter

4 qts. finely chopped tart
 apples
2¾ cups sugar
2¾ tsp. cinnamon
¼ tsp. ground cloves
⅛ tsp. salt

1. Pour apples into slow cooker.
2. Combine remaining ingredients. Drizzle over apples.
3. Cover. Cook on High 3 hours, stirring well with a large spoon every hour. Reduce heat to Low and cook 10-12 hours, until butter becomes thick and dark in color. Stir occasionally with strong wire whisk for smooth butter.
4. Freeze or pour into sterilized jars and seal.

Kelly's Apple Butter

Kelly Evenson
Pittsboro, NC

Makes 4-5 pints apple butter

4 lbs. cooking apples
2 cups cider
3 cups sugar
2 tsp. cinnamon
1 tsp. ground cloves,
 optional
⅛ tsp. allspice

1. Stem, core, and quarter apples. Do not peel.
2. Combine apples and cider in large slow cooker.
3. Cover. Cook on Low 10 hours.
4. Stir in sugar and spices. Continue cooking 1 hour. Remove from heat and cool thoroughly. Blend to mix in skins.
5. Freeze in pint containers, or pour into hot sterilized jars and seal.

Charlotte's Apple Butter

Charlotte Fry
St. Charles, MO

Makes 5 pints apple butter

3 quarts Jonathan, *or*
 Winesap, apples
2 cups apple cider
2½ cups sugar
1 tsp. star anise, optional
2 Tbsp. lemon juice
2 sticks cinnamon

1. Peel, core, and chop apples. Combine with apple cider in large slow cooker.
2. Cover. Cook on Low 10-12 hours.
3. Stir in sugar, star anise, lemon juice, and stick cinnamon.
4. Cover. Cook on High 2 hours. Stir. Remove lid and cook on High 2-4 hours more, until thickened.
5. Pour into sterilized jars and seal.

Dolores' Apple Butter

Dolores Metzler
Mechanicsburg, PA

Makes 3 quarts apple butter

3 quarts unsweetened
  applesauce
3 cups sugar (or sweeten to
  taste)
2 tsp. cinnamon
1 tsp., *or* less, ground
  cloves

1. Combine all ingredients
in large slow cooker.
2. Cover. Cook on High 8-
10 hours. Remove lid during
last 4 hours. Stir occasionally.

Ann's Apple Butter

Ann Bender
Ft. Defiance, VA

Makes 2 pints apple butter

7 cups unsweetened
  applesauce
2-3 cups sugar, depending
  upon the sweetness of
  the applesauce and your
  own preference
2 tsp. cinnamon
1 tsp. ground nutmeg
1/4 tsp. allspice

1. Combine all ingredients in
slow cooker.
2. Put a layer of paper
towels under lid to prevent
condensation from dripping
into apple butter. Cook on
High 8-10 hours. Remove lid
during last hour. Stir occasionally.

Variation:
  Use canned peaches,
pears, or apricots in place of
applesauce.

Anna's Slow-Cooker Apple Butter

Anna Musser
Manheim, PA

Makes 6 pints apple butter

1 cup cider, *or* apple juice
2 1/2 quarts unsweetened
  applesauce
2-3 cups sugar, depending
  upon the sweetness of
  the applesauce and your
  own preference
1 tsp. vinegar
1 tsp. cinnamon
1/2 tsp. allspice

1. Boil cider until 1/2 cup
remains.
2. Combine all ingredients
in slow cooker.
3. Cover. Cook on High 12-
16 hours, until apple butter
has cooked down to half the
original amount. Put in containers and freeze.

Marilyn's Slow-Cooker Apple Butter

Marilyn Yoder
Archbold, OH

Makes 80 servings

2 qts. unsweetened
  applesauce
2-4 cups sugar, depending
  upon sweetness of
  applesauce and your
  preference
1/2 tsp. ground cloves
2 Tbsp. lemon juice
1/4 heaping cup red hot
  candies

1. Combine all ingredients
in slow cooker.
2. Vent lid. Cook on Low
8-10 hours, stirring about
every hour. Apple butter
thickens as it cooks, so cook
longer to make it thicker.

Dianna's Apple Butter

Dianna Milhizer
Springfield, VA

Makes 6 pints apple butter

1 bushel red tart apples (Winesap, Rome, *or* Macintosh)
1 quart "raw" honey *or* least-processed honey available
1/2 cup cinnamon sticks
1 Tbsp. salt

1. Peel, core, and slice apples.
2. Combine all ingredients in large slow cooker. If apples don't fit, continue to add them as butter cooks down.
3. Cover. Cook on High 8 hours. Stir. Remove lid and let butter cook down on Low 8 additional hours. Consistency should be thick and creamy.
4. Freeze, or pack into sterilized jars and seal.

Lilli's Apple Butter

Lilli Peters
Dodge City, KS

Makes about 2 pints apple butter

7 cups unsweetened applesauce
2 cups apple cider
1 1/2 cups honey
1 tsp. cinnamon
1/2 tsp. ground cloves
1/2 tsp. allspice

1. Combine all ingredients in slow cooker. Mix well with whisk.
2. Cook on Low 14-15 hours.

Peach or Apricot Butter

Charlotte Shaffer
East Earl, PA

Makes 6 8-oz. jars butter

4 1-lb. 13-oz. cans peaches, *or* apricots
2 3/4-3 cups sugar
2 tsp. cinnamon
1 tsp. ground cloves

1. Drain fruit. Remove pits. Puree in blender. Pour into slow cooker.
2. Stir in remaining ingredients.

3. Cover. Cook on High 8-10 hours. Remove cover during last half of cooking. Stir occasionally.

Note:
Spread on bread, or use as a topping for ice cream or toasted pound cake.

Pear Butter

Dorothy Miller
Gulfport, MI

Makes 6 pints pear butter

8 cups pear sauce
3 cups brown sugar
1 Tbsp. lemon juice
1 Tbsp. cinnamon

1. Combine all ingredients in slow cooker.
2. Cover. Cook on High 10-12 hours.

Note:
To make pear sauce, peel, core, and slice 12 large pears. Place in slow cooker with 3/4 cup water. Cover and cook on Low 8-10 hours, or until very soft. Stir to blend.

Breakfast Foods

Welsh Rarebit

Sharon Timpe
Mequon, WI

Makes 6-8 servings

12-oz. can beer
1 Tbsp. dry mustard
1 tsp. Worcestershire sauce
1/2 tsp. salt
1/8 tsp. black, *or* white, pepper
1 lb. American cheese, cubed
1 lb. sharp cheddar cheese, cubed
English muffins, *or* toast
bacon, cooked until crisp
tomato slices

1. In slow cooker, combine beer, mustard, Worcestershire sauce, salt, and pepper.
2. Cover and cook on High 1-2 hours, until mixture boils.
3. Add cheese, a little at a time, stirring constantly until all the cheese melts.
4. Heat on High 20-30 minutes with cover off, stirring frequently.
5. Serve hot over toasted English muffins or over toasted bread cut into triangles. Garnish with strips of crisp bacon and tomato slices.

Note:
This is a good dish for brunch with fresh fruit, juice, and coffee. Also makes a great lunch or late-night light supper. Serve with a tossed green salad, especially fresh spinach and orange slices with a vinaigrette dressing.

One hour on High equals about 2 to 2½ hours on Low.
Rachel Kauffman
Alto, MI

Cheese Souffle Casserole

Iva Schmidt
Fergus Falls, MN

Makes 6 servings

8 slices bread (crusts removed), cubed *or* torn into squares
2 cups (8 oz.) grated cheddar, Swiss, *or* American, cheese
1 cup cooked, chopped ham
4 eggs
1 cup light cream, *or* milk
1 cup evaporated milk
1/4 tsp. salt
1 Tbsp. parsley
paprika

1. Lightly grease slow cooker. Alternate layers of bread and cheese and ham.
2. Beat together eggs, milk, salt, and parsley. Pour over bread in slow cooker.
3. Sprinkle with paprika.
4. Cover and cook on Low 3-4 hours. (The longer cooking time yields a firmer, dryer dish.)

Breakfast Casserole

Shirley Hinh
Wayland, IA

Makes 8-10 servings

6 eggs, beaten
1 lb. little smokies (cocktail wieners), *or* 1 1/2 lbs. bulk sausage, browned and drained
1 1/2 cups milk
1 cup shredded cheddar cheese
8 slices bread, torn into pieces
1 tsp. salt
1/2 tsp. dry mustard
1 cup shredded mozzarella cheese

1. Mix together all ingredients except cheese. Pour into greased slow cooker.
2. Sprinkle mozzarella cheese over top.
3. Cover and cook 2 hours on High, and then 1 hour on Low.

Egg and Cheese Bake

Evie Hershey
Atglen, PA

Makes 6 servings

3 cups toasted bread cubes
1 1/2 cups shredded cheese
fried, crumbled bacon, *or* ham chunks, optional
6 eggs, beaten
3 cups milk
3/4 tsp. salt
1/4 tsp. pepper

1. Combine bread cubes, cheese, and meat in greased slow cooker.
2. Mix together eggs, milk, salt, and pepper. Pour over bread.
3. Cook on Low 4-6 hours.

Egg and Broccoli Casserole

Joette Droz
Kalona, IA

Makes 6 servings

24-oz. carton small-curd cottage cheese
10-oz. pkg. frozen chopped broccoli, thawed and drained
2 cups (8 oz.)shredded cheddar cheese
6 eggs, beaten
1/3 cup flour
1/4 cup melted butter, *or* margarine
3 Tbsp. finely chopped onion
1/2 tsp. salt
shredded cheese, optional

1. Combine first 8 ingredients. Pour into greased slow cooker.
2. Cover and cook on High 1 hour. Stir. Reduce heat to Low. Cover and cook 2½-3 hours, or until temperature reaches 160° and eggs are set.
3. Sprinkle with cheese and serve.

Creamy Old-Fashioned Oatmeal

Mary Wheatley
Mashpee, MA

Makes 4 servings

1 1/3 cups dry old-fashioned rolled oats
2 1/2 cups, plus 1 Tbsp., water
dash of salt

1. Mix together cereal, water, and salt in slow cooker.
2. Cook on Low 6 hours.

Note:
The formula is this: for one serving, use 1/3 cup dry oats and 2/3 cup water, plus a few grains salt. Multiply by the number of servings you need.

Variation:
Before cooking, stir in a few chopped dates or raisins for each serving, if you wish.
Cathy Boshart
Lebanon, PA

Baked Oatmeal

Ellen Ranck
Gap, PA

Makes 4-6 servings

1/3 cup oil
1/2 cup sugar
1 large egg, beaten
2 cups dry quick oats
1 1/2 tsp. baking powder
1/2 tsp. salt
3/4 cup milk

1. Pour the oil into the slow cooker to grease bottom and sides.
2. Add remaining ingredients. Mix well.
3. Bake on Low 2½-3 hours.

Apple Oatmeal

Frances B. Musser
Newmanstown, PA

Makes 4-5 servings

2 cups milk
2 Tbsp. honey
1 Tbsp. butter (no
    substitute!)
1/4 tsp. salt
1/2 tsp. cinnamon
1 cup dry old-fashioned
    oats
1 cup chopped apples
1/2 cup chopped walnuts
2 Tbsp. brown sugar

1. Mix together all ingredients in greased slow cooker.
2. Cover. Cook on Low 5-6 hours.
3. Serve with milk or ice cream.

Variation:
Add 1/2 cup light or dark raisins to mixture.
Jeanette Oberholtzer
Manheim, PA

Don't peek. It takes 15-20 minutes for the cooker to regain lost steam and return to the right temperature.
Janet V. Yocum
Elizabethtown, PA

Breads

Healthy Whole Wheat Bread

Esther Becker
Gordonville, PA

Makes 8 servings

2 cups warm reconstituted
    powdered milk
2 Tbsp. vegetable oil
1/4 cup honey, *or* brown
    sugar
3/4 tsp. salt
1 pkg. yeast
2 1/2 cups whole wheat
    flour
1 1/4 cups white flour

1. Mix together milk, oil,
honey or brown sugar, salt,
yeast, and half the flour in
electric mixer bowl. Beat
with mixer for 2 minutes.
Add remaining flour. Mix
well.
2. Place dough in well-
greased bread or cake pan
that will fit into your cooker.

Cover with greased tin foil.
Let stand for 5 minutes. Place
in slow cooker.
3. Cover cooker and bake
on High 2 1/2-3 hours. Remove
pan and uncover. Let stand
for 5 minutes. Serve warm.

Corn Bread From Scratch

Dorothy M. Van Deest
Memphis, TN

Makes 6 servings

1 1/4 cups flour
3/4 cup yellow cornmeal
1/4 cup sugar
4 1/2 tsp. baking powder
1 tsp. salt
1 egg, slightly beaten
1 cup milk
1/3 cup melted butter, *or* oil

1. In mixing bowl sift
together flour, cornmeal,
sugar, baking powder, and
salt. Make a well in the center.
2. Pour egg, milk, and butter into well. Mix into the dry
mixture until just moistened.
3. Pour mixture into a
greased 2-quart mold. Cover
with a plate. Place on a trivet
or rack in the bottom of slow
cooker.
4. Cover. Cook on High 2-3
hours.

Broccoli Corn Bread

Winifred Ewy
Newton, KS

Makes 8 servings

1 stick margarine, melted
10-oz. pkg. chopped
  broccoli, cooked and
  drained
1 onion, chopped
1 box corn bread mix
4 eggs, well beaten
8 oz. cottage cheese
1¼ tsp. salt

1. Combine all ingredients. Mix well.
2. Pour into greased slow cooker. Cook on Low 6 hours, or until toothpick inserted in center comes out clean.
3. Serve like spoon bread, or invert the pot, remove bread, and cut into wedges.

Lemon Bread

Ruth Ann Gingrich
New Holland, PA

Makes 6 servings

½ cup shortening
¾ cup sugar
2 eggs, beaten
1⅔ cups flour
1⅔ tsp. baking powder
½ tsp. salt
½ cup milk
½ cup chopped nuts
grated peel from 1 lemon

Glaze:
¼ cup powdered sugar
juice of 1 lemon

1. Cream together shortening and sugar. Add eggs. Mix well.
2. Sift together flour, baking powder, and salt. Add flour mixture and milk alternately to shortening mixture.
3. Stir in nuts and lemon peel.
4. Spoon batter into well-greased 2-pound coffee can and cover with well-greased tin foil. Place in cooker set on High for 2-2¼ hours, or until done. Remove bread from coffee can.
5. Mix together powdered sugar and lemon juice. Pour over loaf.
6. Serve plain or with cream cheese.

Old-Fashioned Gingerbread

Mary Ann Westerberg
Rosamond, CA

Makes 6-8 servings

½ cup butter, softened
½ cup sugar
1 egg
1 cup light molasses
2½ cups flour
1½ tsp. baking soda
1 tsp. ground cinnamon
2 tsp. ground ginger
½ tsp. ground cloves
½ tsp. salt
1 cup hot water
warm applesauce, optional
whipped cream, optional
nutmeg, optional

1. Cream together butter and sugar. Add egg and molasses. Mix well.
2. Stir in flour, baking soda, cinnamon, ginger, cloves, and salt. Mix well.
3. Add hot water. Beat well.
4. Pour batter into greased and floured 2-pound coffee can.
5. Place can in cooker. Cover top of can with 8 paper towels. Cover cooker and bake on High 2½-3 hours.
6. Serve with applesauce. Top with whipped cream and sprinkle with nutmeg.

A slow cooker provides enough warmth to a raise dough.
Donna Barnitz
Jenks, OK

Soups, Stews, and Chilis

Nancy's Vegetable Beef Soup

Nancy Graves
Manhattan, KS

Makes 6-8 servings

2-lb. roast cut into bite-
sized pieces, *or* 2 lbs.
stewing meat
15-oz. can corn
15-oz. can green beans
1-lb. bag frozen peas
40-oz. can stewed tomatoes
5 beef bouillon cubes
Tabasco to taste
2 tsp. salt

1. Combine all ingredients
in slow cooker. Do not drain
vegetables.
2. Add water to fill slow
cooker to within 3 inches of
top
3. Cover. Cook on Low 8
hours, or until meat is tender
and vegetables are soft.

Variation:
Add 1 large onion, sliced,
2 cups sliced carrots, and ¾
cup pearl barley to mixture
before cooking.

Frances' Hearty Vegetable Soup

Frances Schrag
Newton, KS

Makes 10 servings

1 lb. round steak, cut into
½-inch pieces
14½-oz. can diced
tomatoes
3 cups water
2 potatoes, peeled and
cubed
2 onions, sliced
3 celery ribs, sliced
2 carrots, sliced
3 beef bouillon cubes
½ tsp. dried basil
½ tsp. dried oregano

1 tsp. salt
¼ tsp. pepper
1½ cups frozen mixed
vegetables, *or* your
choice of frozen
vegetables

1. Combine first 3 ingredients in slow cooker.
2. Cover. Cook on High 6
hours.
3. Add remaining ingredi-
ents. Cover and cook on High
2 hours more, or until meat
and vegetables are tender.

Variation:
Cut salt back to ½ tsp.
Increase dried basil to 1 tsp.
and dried oregano to 1 tsp.
Tracy Clark
Mt. Crawford, VA

Anona's Beef Vegetable Soup

Anona M. Teel
Bangor, PA

Makes 6 servings

1-1½-lb. soup bone
1 lb. stewing beef cubes
1½ qts. cold water
1 Tbsp. salt
¾ cup diced celery
¾ cup diced carrots
¾ cup diced potatoes
¾ cup diced onion
1 cup frozen mixed
    vegetables of your
    choice
1-lb. can tomatoes
⅛ tsp. pepper
1 Tbsp. chopped dried
    parsley

1. Put all ingredients in slow cooker.
2. Cover. Cook on Low 8-10 hours. Remove bone before serving.

"Absent Cook" Stew

Kathy Hertzler
Lancaster, PA

Makes 5-6 servings

2 lbs. stewing beef, cubed
2-3 carrots, sliced
1 onion, chopped
3 large potatoes, cubed
3 ribs celery, sliced
10¾-oz. can tomato soup
1 soup can water
1 tsp. salt
dash of pepper
2 Tbsp. vinegar

1. Combine all ingredients in slow cooker.
2. Cover. Cook on Low 10-12 hours.

Kim's Vegetable Beef Soup

Kim McEuen
Lincoln University, PA

Makes 8-10 servings

1-2 lbs. beef shanks, *or*
    short ribs
1-lb. can tomatoes
2 carrots, sliced
3 ribs celery, sliced
2 medium onions, chopped
2 medium potatoes,
    chopped
3 cups water
1 tsp. salt
4-6 whole peppercorns
5 beef bouillon cubes
10-oz. pkg. frozen mixed
    vegetables, *or* its
    equivalent of your
    favorite frozen, fresh, *or*
    canned vegetables

1. Combine all ingredients in slow cooker. Mix well.
2. Cover. Cook on Low 12-14 hours, or High 4-6 hours.

Note:
I have a scrap vegetable container which I keep in the freezer. When I have too much of a fresh vegetable I throw it in this container and freeze it. When the container gets full, I make soup.

Variation:
To increase the proportion of vegetables, add another 10-oz. pkg. of vegetables.

You may want to revise herb amounts when using a slow cooker. Whole herb and spices increase their flavoring power, while ground spices tend to lose some flavor. It's a good idea to season to taste before serving.
Irma H. Schoen
Windsor, CT

Lilli's Vegetable Beef Soup

Lilli Peters
Dodge City, KS

Makes 10-12 servings

3 lbs. stewing meat, cut in 1-inch pieces
2 Tbsp. oil
4 potatoes, cubed
4 carrots, sliced
3 ribs celery, sliced
14-oz. can diced tomatoes
14-oz. can Italian tomatoes, crushed
2 medium onions, chopped
2 wedges cabbage, sliced thinly
2 beef bouillon cubes
2 Tbsp. fresh parsley
1 tsp. seasoned salt
1 tsp. garlic salt
1/2 tsp. pepper
water

1. Brown meat in oil in skillet. Drain.
2. Combine all ingredients except water in large slow cooker. Cover with water.
3. Cover. Cook on Low 8-10 hours.

Ruby's Vegetable Beef Soup

Ruby Stoltzfus
Mount Joy, PA

Makes 8-10 servings

1 lb. beef cubes
1 cup beef broth
1 1/2 cups chopped cabbage
1 1/2 cups stewed tomatoes, undrained
1 1/2 cups frozen, *or* canned, corn
1 1/2 cups frozen peas
1 1/2 cups frozen green beans
1 1/2 cups sliced carrots
3/4 tsp. salt
1/4-1/2 tsp. pepper

1. Combine all ingredients in slow cooker.
2. Cover. Cook on Low 6-8 hours, or High 3-4 hours.

Jeanne's Vegetable Beef Borscht

Jeanne Heyerly
Chenoa, IL

Makes 8 servings

1 lb. beef roast, cooked and cubed
half a head of cabbage, sliced thin
3 medium potatoes, diced
4 carrots, sliced
1 large onion, diced
1 cup tomatoes, diced
1 cup corn
1 cup green beans
2 cups beef broth
2 cups tomato juice
1/4 tsp. garlic powder
1/4 tsp. dill seed
2 tsp. salt
1/2 tsp. pepper
water
sour cream

1. Mix together all ingredients except water and sour cream. Add water to fill slow cooker three-quarters full.
2. Cover. Cook on Low 8-10 hours.
3. Top individual servings with sour cream.

Variation:
Add 1 cup diced cooked red beets during the last half hour of cooking.

Sharon's Vegetable Soup

Sharon Wantland
Menomonee Falls, WI

Makes 6-8 servings

46-oz. can tomato juice
5 beef bouillon cubes
4 celery ribs, sliced
4 large carrots, sliced
1 onion, chopped
one-quarter head of
  cabbage, chopped
1-lb. can green beans
2 cups water
1 lb. beef stewing meat,
  browned
4-oz. can sliced
  mushrooms

1. Combine all ingredients in slow cooker.
2. Cover. Cook on Low 8 hours, or until meat and vegetables are tender.

Winter's Night Beef Soup

Kimberly Jensen
Bailey, CO

Makes 8-12 servings

1 lb. boneless chuck, cut in
  1/2-inch cubes
1-2 Tbsp. oil
28-oz. can tomatoes
2 tsp. garlic powder
2 carrots, sliced
2 ribs celery, sliced
4 cups water
1/2 cup red wine
1 small onion, coarsely
  chopped
4 beef bouillon cubes
1 tsp. pepper
1 tsp. dry oregano
1/2 tsp. dry thyme
1 bay leaf
1/4-1/2 cup couscous

1. Brown beef cubes in oil in skillet.
2. Place vegetables in bottom of slow cooker. Add beef.
3. Combine all other ingredients in separate bowl except couscous. Pour over ingredients in slow cooker.
4. Cover. Cook on Low 6 hours. Stir in couscous. Cover and cook 30 minutes.

Variation:
  Add zucchini or mushrooms to the rest of the vegetables before cooking.

Old-Fashioned Vegetable Beef Soup

Pam Hochstedler
Kalona, IA

Makes 8-10 servings

1-2 lbs. beef short ribs
2 qts. water
1 tsp. salt
1 tsp. celery salt
1 small onion, chopped
1 cup diced carrots
1/2 cup diced celery
2 cups diced potatoes
1-lb. can whole kernel
  corn, undrained
1-lb. can diced tomatoes
  and juice

1. Combine meat, water, salt, celery salt, onion, carrots, and celery in slow cooker.
2. Cover. Cook on Low 4-6 hours.
3. Debone meat, cut into bite-sized pieces, and return to pot.
4. Add potatoes, corn, and tomatoes.
5. Cover and cook on High 2-3 hours.

Texican Chili

Becky Oswald
Broadway, VA

Makes 15 servings

8 bacon strips, diced
2½ lbs. beef stewing meat, cubed
28-oz. can stewed tomatoes
14½-oz. can stewed tomatoes
2 8-oz. cans tomato sauce
16-oz. can kidney beans, rinsed and drained
2 cups sliced carrots
1 medium onion, chopped
1 cup chopped celery
½ cup chopped green pepper
¼ cup minced fresh parsley
1 Tbsp. chili powder
1 tsp. salt
½ tsp. ground cumin
¼ tsp. pepper

1. Cook bacon in skillet until crisp. Drain on paper towel.
2. Brown beef in bacon drippings in skillet.
3. Combine all ingredients in slow cooker.
4. Cover. Cook on Low 9-10 hours, or until meat is tender. Stir occasionally.

Forgotten Minestrone

Phyllis Attig
Reynolds, IL

Makes 8 servings

1 lb. beef stewing meat
6 cups water
28-oz. can tomatoes, diced, undrained
1 beef bouillon cube
1 medium onion, chopped
2 Tbsp. minced dried parsley
1½ tsp. salt
1½ tsp. dried thyme
½ tsp. pepper
1 medium zucchini, thinly sliced
2 cups finely chopped cabbage
16-oz. can garbanzo beans, drained
1 cup uncooked small elbow, *or* shell, macaroni
¼ cup grated Parmesan cheese

1. Combine beef, water, tomatoes, bouillon, onion, parsley, salt, thyme, and pepper.
2. Cover. Cook on Low 7-9 hours, or until meat is tender.
3. Stir in zucchini, cabbage, beans, and macaroni. Cover and cook on High 30-45 minutes, or until vegetables are tender.
4. Sprinkle individual servings with Parmesan cheese.

Slow-Cooker Minestrone

Dorothy Shank
Sterling, IL

Makes 8 servings

3 cups water
1½ lbs. stewing meat, cut into bite-sized pieces
1 medium onion, diced
4 carrots, diced
14½-oz. can tomatoes
2 tsp. salt
10-oz. pkg. frozen mixed vegetables, *or* your choice of frozen vegetables
1 Tbsp. dried basil
½ cup dry vermicelli
1 tsp. dried oregano
grated Parmesan cheese

1. Combine all ingredients except cheese in slow cooker. Stir well.
2. Cover. Cook on Low 10-12 hours, or on High 4-5 hours.
3. Top individual servings with Parmesan cheese.

Hearty Alphabet Soup

Maryann Markano
Wilmington, DE

Makes 5-6 servings

1/2 lb. beef stewing meat, *or* round steak, cubed
14 1/2-oz. can stewed tomatoes
8-oz. can tomato sauce
1 cup water
1 envelope dry onion soup mix
10-oz. pkg. frozen vegetables, partially thawed
1/2 cup uncooked alphabet noodles

1. Combine meat, tomatoes, tomato sauce, water, and soup mix in slow cooker.
2. Cover. Cook on Low 6-8 hours. Turn to High.
3. Stir in vegetables and noodles. Add more water if mixture is too dry and thick.
4. Cover. Cook on High 30 minutes, or until vegetables are tender.

Hamburger Vegetable Soup

Donna Conto
Saylorsburg, PA

Makes 6-8 servings

1/2 lb. ground beef, browned
6 beef bouillon cubes, crushed
16-oz. can tomatoes
1 large onion, diced
3/4 cup sliced celery
1 medium carrot, diced
1 garlic clove, minced
1 bay leaf
1/2 tsp. salt
1/8 tsp. pepper
10-oz. pkg. frozen peas
3 Tbsp. chopped parsley

1. Combine all ingredients except peas and parsley in slow cooker.
2. Cover. Cook on Low 5 hours.
3. Stir in peas during last hour.
4. Garnish with parsley before serving.

Vegetable Beef Soup

Ruth Ann Swartzendruber
Hydro, OK

Makes 4-5 servings

1 lb. ground beef, browned and drained
2 cups tomato juice
2 cups beef broth
1 lb. frozen mixed vegetables, *or* your choice of vegetables

1. Combine all ingredients in slow cooker.
2. Cover. Cook on High 3 hours, and then on Low 3-4 hours.

Quick and Easy Italian Vegetable Beef Soup

Lisa Warren
Parkesburg, PA

Makes 8-10 servings

1 lb. ground beef, *or*
  turkey, browned and
  drained
3 carrots, sliced
4 potatoes, peeled and
  cubed
1 small onion, diced
1 tsp. garlic powder
1 tsp. Italian seasoning
3/4 tsp. salt
1/4 tsp. pepper
15-oz. can diced Italian
  tomatoes, *or* 2 fresh
  tomatoes, chopped
6-oz. can Italian-flavored
  tomato paste
4 1/2 cups water
1 quart beef broth

1. Combine all ingredients
in slow cooker.
2. Cover. Cook on High 6-8
hours, or until potatoes and
carrots are tender.

Spicy Beef Vegetable Stew

Melissa Raber
Millersburg, OH

Makes 12 servings

1 lb. ground beef
1 cup chopped onions
30-oz. jar meatless
  spaghetti sauce
3 1/2 cups water
1 lb. frozen mixed
  vegetables
10-oz. can diced tomatoes
  with green chilies
1 cup sliced celery
1 tsp. beef bouillon
  granules
1 tsp. pepper

1. Cook beef and onion in
skillet until meat is no longer
pink. Drain. Transfer to slow
cooker.
2. Stir in remaining ingredients.
3. Cover. Cook on Low 8
hours.

Hearty Beef and Cabbage Soup

Carolyn Mathias
Williamsville, NY

Makes 8 servings

1 lb. ground beef
1 medium onion, chopped
40-oz. can tomatoes
2 cups water
15-oz. can kidney beans
1 tsp. salt
1/2 tsp. pepper
1 Tbsp. chili powder
1/2 cup chopped celery
2 cups thinly sliced
  cabbage

1. Saute beef in skillet.
Drain.
2. Combine all ingredients
except cabbage in slow
cooker.
3. Cover. Cook on Low 3
hours. Add cabbage. Cook on
High 30-60 minutes longer.

I find that adding 1/4-1/2 cup of a burgundy or Chablis
wine to most soup and stew recipes brings out the flavor of
the other seasonings.

Joyce Kant
Rochester, NY

Hamburger Soup with Barley

Becky Oswald
Broadway, VA

Makes 10 servings

1 lb. ground beef
1 medium onion, chopped
3 14½-oz. cans beef
    consomme
28-oz. can diced, *or*
    crushed, tomatoes
3 carrots, sliced
3 celery ribs, sliced
8 Tbsp. barley
1 bay leaf
1 tsp. dried thyme
1 Tbsp. dried parsley
1 tsp. salt
½ tsp. pepper

1. Brown beef and onion in skillet. Drain.
2. Combine all ingredients in slow cooker.
3. Cover. Cook on High 3 hours, or Low 6-8 hours.

Vegetable Soup with Potatoes

Annabelle Unternahrer
Shipshewana, IN

Makes 6-8 servings

1 lb. hamburger, browned
    and drained
2 15-oz. cans diced
    tomatoes
2 carrots, sliced *or* cubed
2 onions, sliced *or* cubed
2 potatoes, diced
1-2 garlic cloves, minced
12-oz. can V-8 vegetable
    juice
1½-2 cups sliced celery
2 tsp. beef stock
    concentrate, *or* 2 beef
    bouillon cubes
2-3 cups vegetables
    (cauliflower, peas, corn,
    limas, *or* your choice of
    leftovers from your
    freezer)

1. Combine all ingredients in slow cooker.
2. Cover. Cook on Low 12 hours, or High 4-6 hours.

Note:
If using leftover vegetables that are precooked, add during last hour if cooking on Low, or during last half hour if cooking on High.

Variation:
Use 3 cups pre-cooked dried beans or lentils instead of hamburger.

Vegetable Potato Beef Soup

Beth Shank
Wellman, IA

Makes 6-8 servings

1½ cups sliced carrots
1½ cups cubed potatoes
1 cup sliced celery
½ cup chopped onion
2 cups water
1¼ lbs. ground beef,
    browned and drained
2 tsp. salt
5 cups tomato juice
1 Tbsp. brown sugar

1. Combine vegetables and water in microwave-safe container. Cover and microwave on High 18-20 minutes. Do not drain. Place vegetables in slow cooker.
2. Combine all ingredients in slow cooker.
3. Cover. Cook on Low 6-8 hours, or until vegetables are done.

Variation:
Add 15-oz. can green beans, drained, *or* 15-oz. can lima beans, drained.

Hamburger Lentil Soup

Juanita Marner
Shipshewana, IN

Makes 8 servings

1 lb. ground beef
1/2 cup chopped onions
4 carrots, diced
3 ribs celery, diced
1 garlic clove, minced, *or* 1 tsp. garlic powder
1 qt. tomato juice
1 Tbsp. salt
2 cups dry lentils, washed with stones removed
1 qt. water
1/2 tsp. dried marjoram
1 Tbsp. brown sugar

1. Brown ground beef and onion in skillet. Drain.
2. Combine all ingredients in slow cooker.
3. Cover. Cook on Low 8-10 hours, or High 4-6 hours.

Vegetable Soup with Noodles

Glenda S. Weaver
New Holland, PA

Makes 6 servings

1 pint water
2 beef bouillon cubes
1 onion, chopped
1 lb. ground beef
1/4 cup ketchup
1 tsp. salt
1/8 tsp. celery salt
1/2 cup uncooked noodles
12-16 oz. pkg. frozen mixed vegetables, *or* vegetables of your choice
1 pint tomato juice

1. Dissolve bouillon cubes in water.
2. Brown onion and beef in skillet. Drain.
3. Combine all ingredients in slow cooker.
4. Cover. Cook on Low 6 hours, or on High 2-3 hours, until vegetables are tender.

Steak Soup

Ilene Bontrager
Arlington, KS
Deb Unternahrer
Wayland, IA

Makes 10-12 servings

2 lbs. coarsely ground chuck, browned and drained
5 cups water
1 large onion, chopped
4 ribs celery, chopped
3 carrots, sliced
2 14 1/2-oz. cans diced tomatoes
10-oz. pkg. frozen mixed vegetables
5 Tbsp. beef-based granules, *or* 5 beef bouillon cubes
1/2 tsp. pepper
1/2 cup melted butter
1/2 cup flour
2 tsp. salt

1. Combine chuck, water, onion, celery, carrots, tomatoes, mixed vegetables, beef granules, and pepper in slow cooker.
2. Cover. Cook on Low 8-12 hours, or High 4-6 hours.
3. One hour before serving, turn to High. Make a paste of melted butter and flour. Stir until smooth. Pour into slow cooker and stir until well blended. Add salt.
4. Cover. Continue cooking on High until thickened.

Dottie's Creamy Steak Soup

Debbie Zeida
Mashpee, MA

Makes 4-6 servings

1 lb. ground beef
half a large onion, chopped
12-oz. can V-8 vegetable juice
2-3 medium potatoes, diced
10³/4-oz. can cream of mushroom soup
10³/4-oz. can cream of celery soup
16-oz. pkg. frozen mixed vegetables, *or* your choice of frozen vegetables
2 tsp. salt
¹/2-³/4 tsp. pepper

1. Saute beef and onions in skillet. Drain.
2. Combine all ingredients in slow cooker.
3. Cover. Cook on Low 8-10 hours.

Taco Soup with Black Beans

Alexa Slonin
Harrisonburg, VA

Makes 6-8 servings

1 lb. ground beef, browned and drained
28-oz. can crushed tomatoes
15¹/4-oz. can corn, undrained
15-oz. can black beans, undrained
15¹/2-oz. can red kidney beans, undrained
1 envelope dry Hidden Valley Ranch Dressing mix
1 envelope dry taco seasoning
1 small onion, chopped
tortilla, *or* corn, chips
shredded cheese
sour cream

1. Combine all ingredients except chips, shredded cheese, and sour cream in slow cooker.
2. Cover. Cook on Low 4-6 hours.
3. Garnish individual servings with chips, cheese, and sour cream.

Taco Soup with Pinto Beans

Janie Steele
Moore, OK

Makes 10-12 servings

1 lb. ground beef
1 large onion, chopped
3 14-oz. cans pinto beans
14-oz. can tomatoes with chilies
14¹/2-oz. can chopped tomatoes
15-oz. can tomato sauce
1 pkg. dry Hidden Valley Ranch Dressing mix
1 pkg. dry taco seasoning
15¹/4-oz. can corn, drained

1. Brown beef and onions in skillet. Drain.
2. Combine all ingredients in slow cooker.
3. Cover. Cook on Low 4 hours, or until ingredients are heated through.

Sante Fe Soup with Melted Cheese

Carla Koslowsky
Hillsboro, KS

Makes 8 servings

1 lb. Velveeta cheese, cubed
1 lb. ground beef, browned and drained
15¼-oz. can corn, undrained
15-oz. can kidney beans, undrained
14½-oz. can diced tomatoes with green chilies
14½-oz. can stewed tomatoes
2 Tbsp. dry taco seasoning
corn chips, *or* soft tortillas

1. Combine all ingredients except chips or tortillas in slow cooker.
2. Cover. Cook on High 3 hours.
3. Serve with corn chips as a side, or dip soft tortillas in individual servings in soup bowls.

Taco Soup with Whole Tomatoes

Marla Folkerts
Holland, OH

Makes 6-8 servings

1 lb. ground beef
½ cup chopped onions
28-oz. can whole tomatoes with juice
14-oz. can kidney beans with juice
17-oz. can corn with juice
8-oz. can tomato sauce
1 pkg. dry taco seasoning
1-2 cups water
salt to taste
pepper to taste
1 cup grated cheddar cheese
taco, *or* corn, chips

1. Brown beef and onions in skillet. Drain.
2. Combine all ingredients except cheese and chips in slow cooker.
3. Cover. Cook on Low 4-6 hours.
4. Ladle into bowls. Top with cheese and serve with chips.

Taco Soup with Pork and Beans

Beth Shank
Wellman, IA

Makes 6 servings

1 lb. ground beef
half a small onion, finely diced
1 envelope dry taco seasoning
2 Tbsp. brown sugar
⅛ tsp. red cayenne pepper
15-oz. can kidney beans, drained
15-oz. can whole kernel corn, drained
15-oz. can pork and beans
46-oz. can tomato juice
taco chips, crushed
shredded cheese
sour cream

1. Brown bccf and onion in skillet. Drain. Place in slow cooker.
2. Stir in taco seasoning, brown sugar, and pepper. Add beans, corn, pork and beans, and tomato juice. Mix well.
3. Cover. Cook on Low 4-6 hours.
4. Garnish individual servings with taco chips, cheese, and dollop of sour cream.

Taco Soup with Pizza Sauce

Barbara Kuhns
Millersburg, OH

Makes 8-10 servings

2 lbs. ground beef, browned
1 small onion, chopped and sauteed in ground beef drippings
3/4 tsp. salt
1/2 tsp. pepper
1 1/2 pkgs. dry taco seasoning
1 qt. pizza sauce
1 qt. water
tortilla chips
shredded mozzarella cheese
sour cream

1. Combine ground beef, onion, salt, pepper, taco seasoning, pizza sauce, and water in 5-quart, or larger, slow cooker.
2. Cover. Cook on Low 3-4 hours.
3. Top individual servings with tortilla chips, cheese, and sour cream.

Variation:
Add 15-oz. can black beans and 4-oz. can chilies to mixture before cooking. (Be sure to use one very large cooker, or two medium-sized cookers.)

Easy Chili

Sheryl Shenk
Harrisonburg, VA

Makes 10-12 servings

1 lb. ground beef
1 onion, chopped
1 green pepper, chopped
1 1/2 tsp. salt
1 Tbsp. chili powder
2 tsp. Worcestershire sauce
29-oz. can tomato sauce
3 16-oz. cans kidney beans, drained
14 1/2-oz. can crushed, *or* stewed, tomatoes
6-oz. can tomato paste
2 cups grated cheddar cheese

1. Brown meat in skillet. Add onion and green pepper halfway through browning process. Drain. Pour into slow cooker.
2. Stir in remaining ingredients except cheese.
3. Cover. Cook on High 3 hours, or Low 7-8 hours.
4. Serve in bowls topped with cheddar cheese.

Note:
This chili can be served over cooked rice.

Berenice's Favorite Chili

Berenice M. Wagner
Dodge City, KS

Makes 6 servings

2 16-oz. cans red kidney beans, drained
2 14 1/2-oz. cans diced tomatoes
2 lbs. coarsely ground beef, browned and drained
2 medium onions, coarsely chopped
1 green pepper, coarsely chopped
2 garlic cloves, minced
2-3 Tbsp. chili powder
1 tsp. pepper
2 1/2 tsp. salt

1. Combine all ingredients in slow cooker in order listed. Stir once.
2. Cover. Cook on Low 10-12 hours, or High 5-6 hours.

Variations:
1. Top individual servings with green onion, sour cream, and cheese.
Judy Govotsus
Monrovia, MD

2. Increase proportion of tomatoes in chili by adding 8-oz. can tomato sauce before cooking.
Bernice A. Esau
North Newton, KS

Slow-Cooker Chili

Wanda S. Curtin
Bradenton, FL
Ann Sunday McDowell
Newtown, PA

Makes 10 servings

2 lbs. ground beef,
   browned and drained
2 16-oz. cans red kidney
   beans, drained
2 14½-oz. cans diced
   tomatoes, drained
2 medium onions, chopped
2 garlic cloves, crushed
2-3 Tbsp. chili powder
1 tsp. ground cumin
1 tsp. black pepper
1 tsp. salt

1. Combine all ingredients
in slow cooker.
2. Cover. Cook on Low 8-
10 hours.

Note:
Use leftovers over lettuce
and other fresh garden vegetables to make a taco salad.

Variations:
1. For more flavor, add
cayenne pepper or a jalapeno
pepper before cooking.
   Dorothy Shank
   Sterling, IL

2. Add 1 cup chopped
green peppers before cooking.
   Mary V. Warye
   West Liberty, OH

Trail Chili

Jeanne Allen
Rye, CO

Makes 8-10 servings

2 lbs. ground beef
1 large onion, diced
28-oz. can diced tomatoes
2 8-oz. cans tomato puree
1, *or 2*, 16-oz. cans kidney
   beans, undrained
4-oz. can diced green
   chilies
1 cup water
2 garlic cloves, minced
2 Tbsp. mild chili powder
2 tsp. salt
2 tsp. ground cumin
1 tsp. pepper

1. Brown beef and onion
in skillet. Drain. Place in
slow cooker on High.
2. Stir in remaining ingredients. Cook on High 30 minutes.
3. Reduce heat to Low.
Cook 4-6 hours.

Note:
Top individual servings
with shredded cheese. Serve
with taco chips.

Judy's Chili Soup

Judy Buller
Bluffton, OH

Makes 6 servings

1 lb. ground beef
1 onion, chopped
10¾-oz. can condensed
   tomato soup
16-oz. can kidney beans,
   drained
1 qt. tomato juice
⅛ tsp. garlic powder
1 Tbsp. chili powder
½ tsp. pepper
½ tsp. ground cumin
½ tsp. salt

1. Brown hamburger and
onion in skillet. Drain.
2. Combine all ingredients
in slow cooker. Mix well.
3. Cover. Cook on Low 7-8
hours.

Variation:
Use ground venison
instead of ground beef.

Colleen's Favorite Chili

Colleen Heatwole
Burton, MI

Makes 6-8 servings

2 medium onions, coarsely chopped
1-1½ lbs. ground beef, browned and drained
2 garlic cloves, minced fine, *or* ½ tsp. garlic powder
¾ cup finely diced green peppers
2 14½-oz. cans diced tomatoes, *or* 1 quart home-canned tomatoes
30-32 oz. beans—kidney, *or* pinto, *or* mixture of the two
8-oz. can tomato sauce
¼ tsp. beaumonde spice, optional
1 tsp. ground cumin
½ tsp. pepper
1 tsp. seasoned salt
1 Tbsp., or more, chili powder
1 tsp. dried basil

1. Combine all ingredients in slow cooker.
2. Cover. Cook on Low 8-12 hours, or High 5-6 hours.

Variations:
1. Add 1 Tbsp. brown sugar to mixture before cooking.
2. Put in another 1 lb. beans and then decrease ground beef to 1 lb.

Chili Con Carne

Donna Conto
Saylorsburg, PA

Makes 8 servings

1 lb. ground beef
1 cup chopped onions
¾ cup chopped green peppers
1 garlic clove, minced
14½-oz. can tomatoes, cut up
16-oz. can kidney beans, drained
8-oz. can tomato sauce
2 tsp. chili powder
½ tsp. dried basil

1. Brown beef, onion, green pepper, and garlic in saucepan. Drain.
2. Combine all ingredients in slow cooker.
3. Cover. Cook on Low 5-6 hours.
4. Serve in bread bowl.

Variation:
Add 16-oz. can pinto beans, ¼ tsp. salt, and ¼ tsp. pepper in Step 2.
Alexa Slonin
Harrisonburg, VA

Quick and Easy Chili

Nan Decker
Albuquerque, NM

Makes 4 servings

1 lb. ground beef
1 onion, chopped
16-oz. can stewed tomatoes
11½-oz. can Hot V-8 juice
2 15-oz. cans pinto beans
¼ tsp. cayenne pepper
½ tsp. salt
1 Tbsp. chili powder
sour cream
chopped green onions
grated cheese
sliced ripe olives

1. Crumble ground beef in microwave-safe casserole. Add onion. Microwave, covered, on High 15 minutes. Drain. Break meat into pieces.
2. Combine all ingredients in slow cooker.
3. Cook on Low 4-5 hours.
4. Garnish with sour cream, chopped green onions, grated cheese, and sliced ripe olives.

Cindy's Chili
Cindy Krestynick
Glen Lyon, PA

Makes 4-6 servings

1 lb. ground beef, browned
  and drained
3 15½-oz. cans chili beans
  (hot *or* mild)
28-oz. can stewed
  tomatoes, chopped
1 rib celery, chopped
4 cups tomato juice
½ tsp. garlic salt
½ tsp. chili powder
¼ tsp. pepper
¼ tsp. Tabasco sauce

1. Combine all ingredients
in large slow cooker.
2. Cover. Cook on Low 4-6
hours.

Ed's Chili
Marie Miller
Scotia, NY

Makes 4-6 servings

1 lb. ground beef
1 pkg. dry taco seasoning
  mix
half a 12-oz. jar salsa
16-oz. can kidney beans,
  undrained
15-oz. can black beans,
  undrained
14½-oz. can diced
  tomatoes, undrained
pinch of sugar
shredded cheese
chopped onions
sour cream
diced fresh tomatoes
guacamole
sliced black olives

1. Brown ground beef in
skillet. Drain.
2. Combine first 7 ingredients in slow cooker.
3. Cover. Heat on High
until mixture comes to boil.
Reduce heat to Low. Simmer
1½ hours.
4. To reduce liquids, continue cooking uncovered.
5. Top individual servings
with choice of shredded
cheese, onions, a dollop of
sour cream, fresh diced tomatoes, guacamole, and sliced
olives.

Pirate Stew
Nancy Graves
Manhattan, KS

Makes 4-6 servings

¾ cup sliced onion
1 lb. ground beef
¼ cup uncooked, long
  grain rice
3 cups diced raw potatoes
1 cup diced celery
2 cups canned kidney
  beans, drained
1 tsp. salt
⅛ tsp. pepper
¼ tsp. chili powder
¼ tsp. Worcestershire
  sauce
1 cup tomato sauce
½ cup water

1. Brown onions and
ground beef in skillet. Drain.
2. Layer ingredients in
slow cooker in order given.
3. Cover. Cook on Low 6
hours, or until potatoes and
rice are cooked.

Variation:
Add a layer of 2 cups
sliced carrots between pota-
toes and celery.
  Katrine Rose
  Woodbridge, VA

Corn Chili

Gladys Longacre
Susquehanna, PA

Makes 4-6 servings

1 lb. ground beef
1/2 cup chopped onions
1/2 cup chopped green
  peppers
1/2 tsp. salt
1/8 tsp. pepper
1/4 tsp. dried thyme
14 1/2-oz. can diced
  tomatoes with Italian
  herbs
6-oz. can tomato paste,
  diluted with 1 can water
2 cups frozen whole kernel
  corn
16-oz. can kidney beans
1 Tbsp. chili powder
sour cream
shredded cheese

1. Saute ground beef,
onions, and green peppers in
deep saucepan. Drain and
season with salt, pepper, and
thyme.
2. Stir in tomatoes, tomato
paste, and corn. Heat until
corn is thawed. Add kidney
beans and chili powder. Pour
into slow cooker.
3. Cover. Cook on Low 5-6
hours.
4. Top individual servings
with dollops of sour cream,
or sprinkle with shredded
cheese.

White Bean Chili

Tracey Stenger
Gretna, LA

Makes 10-12 servings

1 lb. ground beef, browned
  and drained
1 lb. ground turkey,
  browned and drained
3 bell peppers, chopped
2 onions, chopped
4 garlic cloves, minced
2 14 1/2-oz. cans chicken, *or*
  vegetable, broth
15 1/2-oz. can butter beans,
  rinsed and drained
15-oz. can black-eyed peas,
  rinsed and drained
15-oz. can garbanzo beans,
  rinsed and drained
15-oz. can navy beans,
  rinsed and drained
4-oz. can chopped green
  chilies
2 Tbsp. chili powder
3 tsp. ground cumin
2 tsp. dried oregano
2 tsp. paprika
1 1/2-2 tsp. salt
1/2 tsp. pepper

1. Combine all ingredients
in slow cooker.
2. Cover. Cook on Low 8-
10 hours.

Lotsa-Beans Chili

Jean Weller
State College, PA

Makes 12-15 servings

1 lb. ground beef
1 lb. bacon, diced
1/2 cup chopped onions
1/2 cup brown sugar
1/2 cup sugar
1/2 cup ketchup
2 tsp. dry mustard
1 tsp. salt
1/2 tsp. pepper
2 15-oz. cans green beans,
  drained
2 14 1/2-oz. cans baked
  beans
2 15-oz. cans butter beans,
  drained
2 16-oz. cans kidney beans,
  rinsed and drained

1. Brown ground beef and
bacon in slow cooker. Drain.
2. Combine all ingredients
in slow cooker.
3. Cover. Cook on High 1
hour. Reduce heat to Low
and cook 7-8 hours.

Dorothea's Slow-Cooker Chili

Dorothea K. Ladd
Ballston Lake, NY

Makes 6-8 servings

1 lb. ground beef
1 lb. bulk pork sausage
1 large onion, chopped
1 large green pepper, chopped
2-3 ribs celery, chopped
2 15½-oz. cans kidney beans
29-oz. can tomato puree
6-oz. can tomato paste
2 cloves garlic, minced
2 Tbsp. chili powder
2 tsp. salt

1. Brown ground beef and sausage in skillet. Drain.
2. Combine all ingredients in slow cooker.
3. Cover. Cook on Low 8-10 hours.

Variations:

1. For extra flavor, add 1 tsp. cayenne pepper.
2. For more zest, use mild or hot Italian sausage instead of regular pork sausage.
3. Top individual servings with shredded sharp cheddar cheese.

Chili for Twenty

Janie Steele
Moore, OK

Makes 15-20 servings

4 lbs. ground beef
3 onions, finely chopped
3 green peppers, finely chopped
2 garlic cloves, minced
4 16-oz. cans Italian-style tomatoes
4 16-oz. cans kidney beans, drained
10-oz. can diced tomatoes and chilies
2 6-oz. cans tomato paste
1 cup water
1 Tbsp. salt
1 tsp. pepper
3 whole cloves
2 bay leaves
2 Tbsp. chili powder

1. Brown meat, onions, and peppers in soup pot on top of stove. Drain.
2. Combine all ingredients in large bowl. Divide among several medium-sized slow cookers.
3. Cover. Cook on Low 3-4 hours.

Crab Soup

Susan Alexander
Baltimore, MD

Makes 10 servings

1 lb. carrots, sliced
½ bunch celery, sliced
1 large onion, diced
2 10-oz. bags frozen mixed vegetables, *or* your choice of frozen vegetables
12-oz. can tomato juice
1 lb. ham, cubed
1 lb. beef, cubed
6 slices bacon, chopped
1 tsp. salt
¼ tsp. pepper
1 Tbsp. Old Bay seasoning
1 lb. claw crabmeat

1. Combine all ingredients except seasonings and crabmeat in large slow cooker. Pour in water until cooker is half-full.
2. Add spices. Stir in thoroughly. Put crab on top.
3. Cover. Cook on Low 8-10 hours.
4. Stir well and serve.

Special Seafood Chowder

Dorothea K. Ladd
Ballston Lake, NY

Makes 8-10 servings

1/2 cup chopped onions
2 Tbsp. butter
1 lb. fresh *or* frozen cod, *or* haddock
4 cups diced potatoes
15-oz. can creamed corn
1/2 tsp. salt
dash pepper
2 cups water
1 pint half-and-half

1. Saute onions in butter in skillet until transparent but not brown.
2. Cut fish into 3/4-inch cubes. Combine fish, onions, potatoes, corn, seasonings, and water in slow cooker.
3. Cover. Cook on Low 6 hours, until potatoes are tender.
4. Add half-and-half during last hour.

Variation:
To cut milk fat, use 1 cup half-and-half and 1 cup skim milk, instead of 1 pint half-and-half.

Manhattan Clam Chowder

Joyce Slaymaker
Strasburg, PA
Louise Stackhouse
Benton, PA

Makes 8 servings

1/4 lb. salt pork, *or* bacon, diced and fried
1 large onion, chopped
2 carrots, thinly sliced
3 ribs celery, sliced
1 Tbsp. dried parsley flakes
1-lb. 12-oz. can tomatoes
1/2 tsp. salt
2, *or* 3, 8-oz. cans clams with liquid
2 whole peppercorns
1 bay leaf
1 1/2 tsp. dried crushed thyme
3 medium potatoes, cubed

1. Combine all ingredients in slow cooker.
2. Cover. Cook on Low 8-10 hours.

Rich and Easy Clam Chowder

Rhonda Burgoon
Collingswood, NJ

Makes 4-5 servings

3 10 3/4-oz. cans cream of potato soup
2 10 3/4-oz. cans New England clam chowder
1/2 cup butter
1 small onion, diced
1 pint half-and-half
2 6 1/2-oz. cans clams, chopped

1. Combine all ingredients in slow cooker.
2. Cover. Cook on Low 2-4 hours.

Chicken Clam Chowder

Irene Klaeger
Inverness, Fl

Makes 10-12 servings

1 lb. bacon, diced
1/4 lb. ham, cubed
2 cups chopped onions
2 cups diced celery
1/2 tsp. salt
1/4 tsp. pepper
2 cups diced potatoes
2 cups cooked, diced chicken
4 cups chicken broth
2 bottles clam juice, *or* 2 cans clams with juice
1-lb. can whole kernel corn with liquid
3/4 cup flour
4 cups milk
4 cups shredded cheddar, *or* Jack, cheese
1/2 cup whipping cream (not whipped)
2 Tbsp. fresh parsley

1. Saute bacon, ham, onions, and celery in skillet until bacon is crisp and onions and celery are limp. Add salt and pepper.
2. Combine all ingredients in slow cooker except flour, milk, cheese, cream, and parsley.
3. Cover. Cook on Low 6-8 hours, or on High 3-4 hours.
4. Whisk flour into milk. Stir into soup, along with cheese, whipping cream, and parsley. Cook one more hour on High.

Chicken Broth

Ruth Conrad Liechty
Goshen IN

Makes about 6 cups broth

bony chicken pieces from 2 chickens
1 onion, quartered
3 whole cloves, optional
3 ribs celery, cut up
1 carrot, quartered
1 1/2 tsp. salt
1/4 tsp. pepper
4 cups water

1. Place chicken in slow cooker.
2. Stud onion with cloves. Add to slow cooker with other ingredients.
3. Cover. Cook on High 4-5 hours.
4. Remove chicken and vegetables. Discard vegetables. Debone chicken. Cut up meat and add to broth. Use as stock for soups.

Chicken Noodle Soup

Beth Shank
Wellman, IA

Makes 6-8 servings

5 cups hot water
2 Tbsp. chicken bouillon granules, *or* 2 chicken bouillon cubes
46-oz. can chicken broth
2 cups cooked chicken
1 tsp. salt
4 cups "homestyle" noodles, uncooked
1/3 cup thinly sliced celery, lightly pre-cooked in microwave
1/3 cup shredded, *or* chopped, carrots

1. Dissolve bouillon in water. Pour into slow cooker.
2. Add remaining ingredients. Mix well.
3. Cover. Cook on Low 4-6 hours.

Brown Jug Soup

Dorothy Shank
Sterling, IL

Makes 10-12 servings

10½-oz. can chicken broth
4 chicken bouillon cubes
1 qt. water
2 cups (3-4 ribs) diced
   celery
2 cups (2 medium-sized)
   diced onions
4 cups (4 large) diced
   potatoes
3 cups (8 medium-sized)
   diced carrots
10-oz. pkg. frozen whole
   kernel corn
2 10¾-oz. cans cream of
   chicken soup
½ lb. Velveeta cheese,
   cubed

1. Combine all ingredients
except cheese in slow cooker.
2. Cover. Cook on Low
10-12 hours, or until vegetables are tender.
3. Just before serving, add
cheese. Stir until cheese is
melted. Serve.

Chicken Corn Soup

Eleanor Larson
Glen Lyon, PA

Makes 4-6 servings

2 whole boneless skinless
   chicken breasts, cubed
1 onion, chopped
1 garlic clove, minced
2 carrots, sliced
2 ribs celery, chopped
2 medium potatoes, cubed
1 tsp. mixed dried herbs
⅓ cup tomato sauce
12-oz. can cream-style corn
14-oz. can whole kernel
   corn
3 cups chicken stock
¼ cup chopped Italian
   parsley
1 tsp. salt
¼ tsp. pepper

1. Combine all ingredients
except parsley, salt, and pepper in slow cooker.
2. Cover. Cook on Low 8-9
hours, or until chicken is tender.
3. Add parsley and seasonings 30 minutes before serving.

Chili, Chicken, Corn Chowder

Jeanne Allen
Rye, CO

Makes 6-8 servings

¼ cup oil
1 large onion, diced
1 garlic clove, minced
1 rib celery, finely chopped
2 cups frozen, *or* canned,
   corn
2 cups cooked, deboned,
   diced chicken
4-oz. can diced green
   chilies
½ tsp. black pepper
2 cups chicken broth
salt to taste
1 cup half-and-half

1. In saucepan, saute
onion, garlic, and celery in oil
until limp.
2. Stir in corn, chicken,
and chilies. Saute for 2-3 minutes.
3. Combine all ingredients
except half-and-half in slow
cooker.
4. Cover. Heat on Low 4
hours.
5. Stir in half-and-half
before serving. Do not boil,
but be sure cream is heated
through.

Slow cookers come in a variety of sizes, from 2- to 8-
quarts. The best size for a family of four or five is a 5-6
quart-size.

Dorothy M. Van Deest
Memphis, TN

White Chili

Esther Martin
Ephrata, PA

Makes 8 servings

3 15-oz. cans Great
  Northern beans, drained
8 oz. cooked and shredded
  chicken breasts
1 cup chopped onions
1½ cups chopped yellow,
  red, *or* green bell
  peppers
2 jalapeno chili peppers,
  stemmed, seeded, and
  chopped (optional)
2 garlic cloves, minced
2 tsp. ground cumin
½ tsp. salt
½ tsp. dried oregano
3½ cups chicken broth
sour cream
shredded cheddar cheese
tortilla chips

1. Combine all ingredients
except sour cream, cheddar
cheese, and chips in slow
cooker.

2. Cover. Cook on Low 8-
10 hours, or High 4-5 hours.

3. Ladle into bowls and
top individual servings with
sour cream, cheddar cheese,
and chips.

White Chili Speciality

Barbara McGinnis
Jupiter, FL

Makes 8-10 servings

1 lb. large Great Northern
  beans, soaked overnight
2 lbs. boneless, skinless
  chicken breasts, cut up
1 medium onion, chopped
2 4½-oz. cans chopped
  green chilies
2 tsp. cumin
½ tsp. salt
14½-oz. can chicken broth
1 cup water

1. Put soaked beans in
medium-sized saucepan and
cover with water. Bring to
boil and simmer 20 minutes.
Discard water.

2. Brown chicken, if
desired, in 1-2 Tbsp. oil in
skillet.

3. Combine pre-cooked
and drained beans, chicken,
and all remaining ingredients
in slow cooker.

4. Cover. Cook on Low 10-
12 hours, or High 5-6 hours.

Chicken Tortilla Soup

Becky Harder
Monument, CO

Makes 6-8 servings

4 chicken breast halves
2 15-oz. cans black beans,
  undrained
2 15-oz. cans Mexican
  stewed tomatoes, *or*
  Rotel tomatoes
1 cup salsa (mild, medium,
  or hot, whichever you
  prefer)
4-oz. can chopped green
  chilies
14½-oz. can tomato sauce
tortilla chips
2 cups grated cheese

1. Combine all ingredients
except chips and cheese in
large slow cooker.

2. Cover. Cook on Low 8
hours.

3. Just before serving,
remove chicken breasts and
slice into bite-sized pieces.
Stir into soup.

4. To serve, put a handful
of chips in each individual
soup bowl. Ladle soup over
chips. Top with cheese.

Tortilla Soup

Joy Mintzer
Newark, DE

Makes 6 servings

4 chicken breast halves
1 garlic clove, minced
2 Tbsp. margarine
2 14½-oz. cans chicken
  broth
2 14½-oz. cans chopped
  stewed tomatoes
1 cup salsa (mild, medium,
  or hot, whichever you
  prefer)
½ cup chopped cilantro
1 Tbsp., *or* more, ground
  cumin
8-oz. Monterey Jack
  cheese, cubed
sour cream
tortilla chips

1. Cook, debone, and
shred chicken.
2. Add minced garlic to
margarine in slow cooker.
Saute.
3. Combine all ingredients
except cheese, sour cream,
and chips.
4. Cover. Cook on Low 8-
10 hours.
5. Divide cubed cheese
among 6 individual soup
bowls. Ladle soup over
cheese. Sprinkle with chips
and top each bowl with a dollop of sour cream.

Tex-Mex Chicken Chowder

Janie Steele
Moore, OK

Makes 8-10 servings

1 cup chopped onions
1 cup thinly sliced celery
2 garlic cloves, minced
1 Tbsp. oil
1½ lbs. boneless, skinless
  chicken breasts, cubed
32-oz. can chicken broth
1 pkg. country gravy mix
2 cups milk
16-oz. jar chunky salsa
32-oz. bag frozen hash
  brown potatoes
4½-oz. can chopped green
  chilies
8 oz. Velveeta cheese,
  cubed

1. Combine onions, celery,
garlic, oil, chicken, and broth
in 5-quart or larger slow
cooker.
2. Cover. Cook on Low 2½
hours, until chicken is no
longer pink.
3. In separate bowl, dis-
solve gravy mix in milk. Stir
into chicken mixture. Add
salsa, potatoes, chilies, and
cheese and combine well.
Cook on Low 2-4 hours, or
until potatoes are fully
cooked.

Chicken and Ham Gumbo

Barbara Tenney
Delta, PA

Makes 4 servings

1½ lbs. boneless, skinless
  chicken thighs
1 Tbsp. oil
10-oz. pkg. frozen okra
½ lb. smoked ham, cut
  into small chunks
1½ cups coarsely chopped
  onions
1½ cups coarsely chopped
  green peppers
2 or 3 10-oz. cans
  cannellini beans,
  drained
6 cups chicken broth
2 10-oz. cans diced
  tomatoes with green
  chilies
2 Tbsp. chopped fresh
  cilantro

1. Cut chicken into bite-
sized pieces. Cook in oil in
skillet until no longer pink.
2. Run hot water over okra
until pieces separate easily.
3. Combine all ingredients
but cilantro in slow cooker.
4. Cover. Cook on Low 6-8
hours. Stir in cilantro before
serving.

Variations:
1. Stir in ½ cup long grain,
dry rice with rest of ingredients.
2. Add ¾ tsp. salt and ¼
tsp. pepper with other ingredients.

Easy Southern Brunswick Stew

Barbara Sparks
Glen Burnie, MD

Makes 10-12 servings

2-3 lbs. pork butt
17-oz. can white corn
14-oz. bottle ketchup
2 cups diced, cooked
  poatotes
10-oz. pkg. frozen peas
2 10¾-oz. cans tomato
  soup
hot sauce to taste
salt to taste
pepper to taste

1. Place pork in slow cooker.
2. Cover. Cook on Low 6-8 hours. Remove meat from bone and shred.
3. Combine all ingredients in slow cooker.
4. Cover. Bring to boil on High. Reduce heat to Low and simmer 30 minutes.

Joy's Brunswick Stew

Joy Sutter
Iowa City, IA

Makes 8 servings

1 lb. skinless, boneless
  chicken breasts, cut into
  bite-sized pieces
2 potatoes, thinly sliced
10¾-oz. can tomato soup
16-oz. can stewed tomatoes
10-oz. pkg. frozen corn
10-oz. pkg. frozen lima
  beans
3 Tbsp. onion flakes
¼ tsp. salt
⅛ tsp. pepper

1. Combine all ingredients in slow cooker.
2. Cover. Cook on High 2 hours. Reduce to Low and cook 2 hours.

Variation:
For more flavor, add 1, or 2, bay leaves during cooking.

Brunswick Soup Mix

Joyce B. Suiter
Garysburg, NC

Makes 14 servings

1 large onion, chopped
4 cups frozen, cubed, hash
  browns, thawed
4 cups chopped cooked
  chicken, *or* 2 20-oz. cans
  canned chicken
14½-oz. can diced
  tomatoes
15-oz. can tomato sauce
15¼-oz. can corn
15¼-oz. can lima beans,
  drained
2 cups chicken broth
½ tsp. salt
½ tsp. pepper
¼ tsp. Worcestershire
  sauce
¼ cup sugar

1. Combine all ingredients in large slow cooker.
2. Cover. Cook on High 7 hours.
3. Cool and freeze in 2-cup portions.
4. To use, empty 1 frozen portion into saucepan with small amount of liquid: tomato juice, V-8 juice, or broth. Cook slowly until soup mixture thaws. Stir frequently, adding more liquid until of desired consistency.

Oriental Turkey Chili
Kimberly Jensen
Bailey, CO

Makes 6 servings

2 cups yellow onions, diced
1 small red bell pepper, diced
1 lb. ground turkey, browned
2 Tbsp. minced gingerroot
3 cloves garlic, minced
1/4 cup dry sherry
1/4 cup hoisin sauce
2 Tbsp. chili powder
1 Tbsp. corn oil
2 Tbsp. soy sauce
1 tsp. sugar
2 cups canned whole tomatoes
16 oz. can dark red kidney beans, undrained

1. Combine all ingredients in slow cooker.
2. Cover. Cook on Low 6 hours.
3. Serve topped with chow mein noodles or over cooked white rice.

Note:
If you serve this chili over rice, this recipe will yield 10-12 servings.

Joyce's Slow-Cooked Chili
Joyce Slaymaker
Strasburg, PA

Makes 10 servings

2 lbs. ground turkey
2 16-oz. cans kidney beans, rinsed and drained
2 14 1/2-oz. cans diced tomatoes, undrained
8-oz. can tomato sauce
2 medium onions, chopped
1 green pepper, chopped
2 cloves garlic, minced
2 Tbsp. chili powder
2 tsp. salt, optional
1 tsp. pepper
shredded cheddar cheese, optional

1. Brown ground turkey in skillet. Drain. Transfer to slow cooker.
2. Stir in remaining ingredients except cheese.
3. Cover. Cook on Low 8-10 hours, or on High 4 hours.
4. Garnish individual servings with cheese.

Turkey Chili
Dawn Day
Westminster, CA

Makes 6-8 servings

1 large chopped onion
2-3 Tbsp. oil
1 lb. ground turkey
1/2 tsp. salt
3 Tbsp. chili powder
6-oz. can tomato paste
3 1-lb. cans small red beans with liquid
1 cup frozen corn

1. Saute onion in oil in skillet until transparent. Add turkey and salt and brown lightly in skillet.
2. Combine all ingredients in slow cooker. Mix well.
3. Cover. Cook on Low 8-9 hours.

Note:
Ground beef can be used in place of turkey.

Variation:
Serve over rice, topped with shredded cheddar cheese and sour cream.

Chili Sans Cholesterol

Dolores S. Kratz
Souderton, PA

Makes 4 servings

1 lb. ground turkey
1/2 cup chopped celery
1/2 cup chopped onions
8-oz. can tomatoes
14-oz. can pinto beans
14 1/2-oz. can diced
    tomatoes
1/2 tsp., *or* more, chili
    powder
1/2 tsp. salt
dash pepper

1. Saute turkey in skillet until browned. Drain.
2. Combine all ingredients in slow cooker.
3. Cover. Cook on Low 6 hours.

Leftover Turkey Soup

Janie Steele
Moore, OK

Makes 8-10 servings

1 small onion, chopped
1 cup chopped celery
1 Tbsp. oil
2-3 cups diced turkey
1 cup cooked rice
leftover gravy, *or*
    combination of leftover
    gravy and chicken broth

1. Saute onion and celery in oil in saucepan until translucent.
2. Combine all ingredients in slow cooker, adding gravy and/or broth until of the consistency you want.
3. Cover. Cook on Low for at least 2-3 hours, or until heated through.

Italian Vegetable Soup

Patti Boston
Newark, OH

Makes 4-6 servings

3 small carrots, sliced
1 small onion, chopped
2 small potatoes, diced
2 Tbsp. chopped parsley
1 garlic clove, minced
3 tsp. beef bouillon
    granules, *or* 3 beef
    bouillon cubes
1 1/4 tsp. dried basil
1/2 tsp. salt
1/4 tsp. pepper
16-oz. can red kidney
    beans, undrained
3 cups water
14 1/2-oz. can stewed
    tomatoes, with juice
1 cup diced, cooked ham

1. Layer carrots, onions, potatoes, parsley, garlic, beef bouillon, basil, salt, pepper, and kidney beans in slow cooker. Do not stir. Add water.
2. Cover. Cook on Low 8-9 hours, or on High 4 1/2-5 1/2 hours, until vegetables are tender.
3. Stir in tomatoes and ham. Cover and cook on High 10-15 minutes.

Chet's Trucker Stew

Janice Muller
Derwood, MD

Makes 8 servings

1 lb. bulk pork sausage,
cooked and drained
1 lb. ground beef, cooked
and drained
31-oz. can pork and beans
16-oz. can light kidney
beans
16-oz. can dark kidney
beans
14 1/2-oz. can waxed beans,
drained
14 1/2-oz. can lima beans,
drained
1 cup ketchup
1 cup brown sugar
1 Tbsp. spicy prepared
mustard

1. Combine all ingredients
in slow cooker.
2. Cover. Simmer on High
2-3 hours.

Spicy Potato Soup

Sharon Kauffman
Harrisonburg, VA

Makes 6-8 servings

1 lb. ground beef, *or* bulk
sausage, browned
4 cups cubed peeled
potatoes
1 small onion, chopped
3 8-oz. cans tomato sauce
2 tsp. salt
1 1/2 tsp. pepper
1/2-1 tsp. hot pepper sauce
water

1. Combine all ingredients
except water in slow cooker.
Add enough water to cover
ingredients.
2. Cover. Cook on Low 8-
10 hours, or High 5 hours,
until potatoes are tender.

Hearty Potato Sauerkraut Soup

Kathy Hertzler
Lancaster, PA

Makes 6-8 servings

4 cups chicken broth
10 3/4-oz. can cream of
mushroom soup
16-oz. can sauerkraut,
rinsed and drained
8 oz. fresh mushrooms,
sliced
1 medium potato, cubed
2 medium carrots, peeled
and sliced
2 ribs celery, chopped
2 lbs. Polish kielbasa
(smoked), cubed
2 1/2 cups chopped cooked
chicken
2 Tbsp. vinegar
2 tsp. dried dillweed
1 1/2 tsp. pepper

1. Combine all ingredients
in large slow cooker.
2. Cover. Cook on Low 10-
12 hours.
3. If necessary, skim fat
before serving.

Sauerkraut Soup

Barbara Tenny
Delta, PA

Makes 8 servings

1 lb. smoked Polish sausage, cut into 1/2-inch pieces
5 medium potatoes, cubed
2 large onions, chopped
2 large carrots, cut into 1/4-inch slices
42-45-oz. can chicken broth
32-oz. can *or* bag sauerkraut, rinsed and drained
6-oz. can tomato paste

1. Combine all ingredients in large slow cooker. Stir to combine.
2. Cover. Cook on High 2 hours, and then on Low 6-8 hours.
3. Serve with rye bread.

Kielbasa Soup

Bernice M. Gnidovec
Streator, IL

Makes 8 servings

16-oz. pkg. frozen mixed vegetables, *or* your choice of vegetables
6-oz. can tomato paste
1 medium onion, chopped
3 medium potatoes, diced
1 1/2 lbs. kielbasa, cut into 1/4-inch pieces
4 qts. water
fresh parsley

1. Combine all ingredients except parsley in large slow cooker.
2. Cover. Cook on Low 12 hours.
3. Garnish individual servings with fresh parsley.

Curried Pork and Pea Soup

Kathy Hertzler
Lancaster, PA

Makes 6-8 servings

1 1/2-lb. boneless pork shoulder roast
1 cup yellow, *or* green, split peas, rinsed and drained
1/2 cup finely chopped carrots
1/2 cup finely chopped celery
1/2 cup finely chopped onions
49 1/2-oz. can (approximately 6 cups) chicken broth
2 tsp. curry powder
1/2 tsp. paprika
1/4 tsp. ground cumin
1/4 tsp. pepper
2 cups torn fresh spinach

1. Trim fat from pork and cut pork into 1/2-inch pieces.
2. Combine split peas, carrots, celery, and onions in slow cooker.
3. Stir in broth, curry powder, paprika, cumin, and pepper. Stir in pork.
4. Cover. Cook on Low 10-12 hours, or on High 4 hours.
5. Stir in spinach. Serve immediately.

Ruth's Split Pea Soup

Ruth Conrad Liechty
Goshen, IN

Makes 6-8 servings

1 lb. bulk sausage, browned and drained
6 cups water
1 bag (2¼ cups) dry split peas
2 medium potatoes, diced
1 onion, chopped
½ tsp. dried marjoram, *or* thyme
½ tsp. pepper

1. Wash and sort dried peas, removing any stones. Then combine all ingredients in slow cooker.
2. Cover. Cook on Low 12 hours.

Kelly's Split Pea Soup

Kelly Evenson
Pittsboro, NC

Makes 8 servings

2 cups dry split peas
2 quarts water
2 onions, chopped
2 carrots, peeled and sliced
4 slices Canadian bacon, chopped
2 Tbsp. chicken bouillon granules, *or* 2 chicken bouillon cubes
1 tsp. salt
¼-½ tsp. pepper

1. Combine all ingredients in slow cooker.
2. Cover. Cook on Low 8-9 hours.

Variation:
For a creamier soup, remove half of soup when done and puree. Stir back into rest of soup.

Karen's Split Pea Soup

Karen Stoltzfus
Alto, MI

Makes 6 servings

2 carrots
2 ribs celery
1 onion
1 parsnip
1 leek (keep 3 inches of green)
1 ripe tomato
1 ham hock
1¾ cups (1 lb.) dried split peas, washed, with stones removed
2 Tbsp. olive oil
1 bay leaf
1 tsp. dried thyme
4 cups chicken broth
4 cups water
1 tsp. salt
¼ tsp. pepper
2 tsp. chopped fresh parsley

1. Cut all vegetables into ¼-inch pieces and place in slow cooker. Add remaining ingredients except salt, pepper, and parsley.
2. Cover. Cook on High 7 hours.
3. Remove ham hock. Shred meat from bone and return meat to pot.
4. Season soup with salt and pepper. Stir in parsley. Serve immediately.

Sally's Split Pea Soup

Sally Holzem
Schofield, WI

Makes 8 servings

1-lb. pkg. split peas
1 ham hock
1 carrot, diced
1 onion, diced
1 rib celery, diced
2 qts. water
1/4 tsp. pepper
1 bay leaf
2 whole allspice
3 potatoes, diced
1 tsp. sugar

1. Wash and sort split peas, removing any stones. Then combine ingredients in slow cooker.
2. Cover. Cook on Low 8-10 hours.
3. Remove ham bone. Cut meat off and dice. Return meat to soup. Stir through.
4. Remove bay leaf before serving.

Dorothy's Split Pea Soup

Dorothy M. Van Deest
Memphis, TN

Makes 6-8 servings

2 Tbsp. butter, *or* margarine
1 cup minced onions
8 cups water
2 cups (1 lb.) green split peas, washed and stones removed
4 whole cloves
1 bay leaf
1/4 tsp. pepper
1 ham hock
1 cup finely minced celery
1 cup diced carrots
1/8 tsp. dried marjoram
1 Tbsp. salt
1/8 tsp. dried savory

1. Combine all ingredients in slow cooker.
2. Cover. Cook on Low 8-10 hours.
3. Remove ham bone and bay leaf before serving. Debone meat, cut into bite-sized pieces, and return to soup. Stir in and serve.

Variation:
For a thick soup, uncover soup after 8-10 hours and turn heat to High. Simmer, stirring occasionally, until the desired consistency is reached.

Rosemarie's Pea Soup

Rosemarie Fitzgerald
Gibsonia, PA
Shirley Sears
Tiskilwa, IL

Makes 4-6 servings

2 cups dried split peas
4 cups water
1 rib celery, chopped
1 cup chopped potatoes
1 large carrot, chopped
1 medium onion, chopped
1/4 tsp. dried thyme, *or* marjoram
1 bay leaf
1/2 tsp. salt
1 garlic clove
1/2 tsp. dried basil

1. Combine all ingredients in slow cooker.
2. Cover. Cook on Low 8-12 hours, or on High 6 hours, until peas are tender.

Variations:
For increased flavor, use chicken broth instead of water. Stir in curry powder, coriander, or red pepper flakes to taste.

55

French Market Soup

Ethel Mumaw
Berlin, OH

Makes 2½ quarts soup

2 cups dry bean mix,
   washed with stones
   removed
2 quarts water
1 ham hock
1 tsp. salt
¼ tsp. pepper
16-oz. can tomatoes
1 large onion, chopped
1 garlic clove, minced
1 chili pepper, chopped, *or*
   1 tsp. chili powder
¼ cup lemon juice

1. Combine all ingredients
in slow cooker.
2. Cover. Cook on Low 8
hours. Turn to High and cook
an additional 2 hours, or until
beans are tender.
3. Debone ham, cut meat
into bite-sized pieces, and stir
back into soup.

Nine Bean Soup with Tomatoes

Violette Harris Denney
Carrollton, GA

Makes 8-10 servings

2 cups dry nine-bean soup
   mix
1 lb. ham, diced
1 large onion, chopped
1 garlic clove, minced
½-¾ tsp. salt
2 qts. water
16-oz. can tomatoes,
   undrained and chopped
10-oz. can tomatoes with
   green chilies, undrained

1. Sort and wash bean
mix. Place in slow cooker.
Cover with water 2 inches
above beans. Let soak
overnight. Drain.
2. Add ham, onion, garlic,
salt, and 2 quarts fresh water.
3. Cover. Cook on Low 7
hours.
4. Add remaining ingredi-
ents and continue cooking on
Low another hour. Stir occasionally.

Note:
   Bean Soup mix is a mix of
barley pearls, black beans,
red beans, pinto beans, navy
beans, Great Northern beans,
lentils, split peas, and black-
eyed peas.

Calico Ham and Bean Soup

Esther Martin
Ephrata, PA

Makes 6-8 servings

1 lb. dry bean mix, rinsed
   and drained, with
   stones removed
6 cups water
2 cups cubed cooked ham
1 cup chopped onions
1 cup chopped carrots
1 tsp. dried basil
1 tsp. dried oregano
¾ tsp. salt
¼ tsp. pepper
2 bay leaves
6 cups water
1 tsp. liquid smoke,
   optional

1. Combine beans and 6
cups water in large saucepan.
Bring to boil, reduce heat,
and simmer uncovered for 10
minutes. Drain, discarding
cooking water, and rinse
beans.
2. Combine all ingredients
in slow cooker.
3. Cover. Cook on Low 8-
10 hours, or High 4-5 hours.
Discard bay leaves before
serving.

Bean and Herb Soup

LaVerne A. Olson
Willow Street, PA

Makes 6-8 servings

1½ cups dry mixed beans
5 cups water
1 ham hock
1 cup chopped onions
1 cup chopped celery
1 cup chopped carrots
2-3 cups water
1 tsp. salt
¼-½ tsp. pepper
1-2 tsp. fresh basil, *or*
  ½ tsp. dried basil
1-2 tsp. fresh oregano, *or*
  ½ tsp. dried oregano
1-2 tsp. fresh thyme, *or*
  ½ tsp. dried thyme
2 cups fresh tomatoes,
  crushed, *or* 14½-oz. can
  crushed tomatoes

1. Combine beans, water, and ham in saucepan. Bring to boil. Turn off heat and let stand 1 hour.
2. Combine onions, celery, and carrots in 2-3 cups water in another saucepan. Cook until soft. Mash slightly.
3. Combine all ingredients in slow cooker.
4. Cover. Cook on High 2 hours, and then on Low 2 hours.

Northern Bean Soup

Patricia Howard
Albuquerque, NM

Makes 6-8 servings

1 lb. dry Northern beans
1 lb. ham
2 medium onions, chopped
half a green pepper, chopped
1 cup chopped celery
16-oz. can diced tomatoes
4 carrots, peeled and chopped
4-oz. can green chili peppers
1 tsp. garlic powder
1-2 qts. water
2-3 tsp. salt

1. Wash beans. Cover with water and soak overnight. Drain. Pour into slow cooker.
2. Dice ham into 1-inch pieces. Add to beans.
3. Stir in remaining ingredients.
4. Cover. Cook on High 2 hours, then on Low 10-12 hours, or until beans are tender.

Easy Lima Bean Soup

Barbara Tenney
Delta, PA

Makes 8-10 servings

1 lb. bag large dry lima beans
1 large onion, chopped
6 ribs celery, chopped
3 large potatoes, cut in ½-inch cubes
2 large carrots, cut in ¼-inch rounds
2 cups ham, sausage, *or* kielbasa
1 Tbsp. salt
1 tsp. pepper
2 bay leaves
3 quarts water, *or* combination water and beef broth

1. Sort beans. Soak overnight. Drain.
2. Combine all ingredients in slow cooker.
3. Cover. Cook on Low 8-10 hours.

Variation:
For extra flavor, add 1 tsp. dried oregano before cooking.

Most slow cookers perform best when more than half full.
Dorothy M. Van Deest
Memphis, TN

Slow Cooked Navy Beans with Ham

Julia Lapp
New Holland, PA

Makes 8-10 servings

1 lb. dry navy beans (2½ cups)
5 cups water
1 garlic clove, minced
1 ham hock
1 tsp. salt

1. Soak beans in water at least 4 hours in slow cooker.
2. Add garlic and ham hock.
3. Cover. Cook on Low 7-8 hours, or High 4 hours. Add salt during last hour of cooking time.
4. Remove ham hock from cooker. Allow to cool. Cut ham from hock and stir back into bean mixture. Correct seasonings and serve in soup bowls with hot corn bread.

Variation:

For added flavor, stir 1 chopped onion, 2-3 chopped celery stalks, 2-3 sliced carrots, and 3-4 cups canned tomatoes into cooker with garlic and ham hock.

Navy Bean Soup

Joyce Bowman
Lady Lake, FL

Makes 8 servings

1 lb. dry navy beans
8 cups water
1 onion, finely chopped
2 bay leaves
½ tsp. ground thyme
½ tsp. nutmeg
2 tsp. salt
½ tsp. lemon pepper
3 garlic cloves, minced
one ham hock, *or* 1-lb. ham pieces

1. Soak beans in water overnight. Strain out stones but reserve liquid.
2. Combine all ingredients in slow cooker.
3. Cover. Cook on Low 8-10 hours. Debone meat and cut into bite-sized pieces. Set ham aside.
4. Puree three-fourths of soup in blender in small batches. When finished blending, stir in meat.

Variation:

Add small chunks of cooked potatoes when stirring in ham pieces after blending.

Overnight Bean Soup

Marie Morucci
Glen Lyon, PA

Makes 6-8 servings

1 lb. dry small white beans
6 cups water
2 cups boiling water
2 large carrots, diced
3 ribs celery, diced
2 tsp. chicken bouillon granules, *or* 2 chicken bouillon cubes
1 bay leaf
½ tsp. dried thyme
½ tsp. salt
¼ tsp. pepper
¼ cup chopped fresh parsley
1 envelope dry onion soup mix
crispy, crumbled bacon, optional

1. Rinse beans. Combine beans and 6 cups water in saucepan. Bring to boil. Reduce heat to low and simmer 2 minutes. Remove from heat. Cover and let stand 1 hour or overnight.
2. Place beans and soaking water in slow cooker. Add 2 cups boiling water, carrots, celery, bouillon, bay leaf, thyme, salt, and pepper.
3. Cover. Cook on High 5-5½ hours, or on Low 10-11 hours, until beans are tender.
4. Stir in parsley and soup mix. Cover. Cook on High 10-15 minutes.

5. Remove bay leaf. Garnish individual servings with bacon.

Old-Fashioned Bean Soup

Gladys M. High
Ephrata, PA

Makes 6 servings

1 lb. dry navy beans, *or* dry green split peas
1-lb. meaty ham bone, *or* 1 lb. ham pieces
1-2 tsp. salt
1/4 tsp. ground pepper
1/2 cup chopped celery leaves
2 qts. water
1 medium onion, chopped
1 bay leaf, optional

1. Soak beans or peas overnight. Drain, discarding soaking water.
2. Combine all ingredients in slow cooker.
3. Cover. Cook on High 8-9 hours.
4. Debone ham bone, cut meat into bite-sized pieces, and stir back into soup.

Caribbean-Style Black Bean Soup

Sheryl Shenk
Harrisonburg, VA

Makes 8-10 servings

1 lb. dried black beans, washed and stones removed
3 onions, chopped
1 green pepper, chopped
4 cloves garlic, minced
1 ham hock, *or* 3/4 cup cubed ham
1 Tbsp. oil
1 Tbsp. ground cumin
2 tsp. dried oregano
1 tsp. dried thyme
1 Tbsp. salt
1/2 tsp. pepper
3 cups water
2 Tbsp. vinegar
sour cream
fresh chopped cilantro

1. Soak beans overnight in 4 quarts water. Drain.
2. Combine beans, onions, green pepper, garlic, ham, oil, cumin, oregano, thyme, salt, pepper, and 3 cups fresh water. Stir well.
3. Cover. Cook on Low 8-10 hours, or on High 4-5 hours.
4. For a thick soup, remove half of cooked bean mixture and puree until smooth in blender or mash with potato masher. Return to cooker. If you like a soup-ier soup, leave as is.
5. Add vinegar and stir well. Debone ham, cut into

bite-sized pieces, and return to soup.
6. Serve in soup bowls with a dollop of sour cream in the middle of each individual serving, topped with fresh cilantro.

Vegetable Bean Soup

Kathi Rogge
Alexandria, IN

Makes 6-8 servings

6 cups cooked beans: navy, pinto, Great Northern, etc.
1 meaty ham bone
1 cup cooked ham, diced
1/4 tsp. garlic powder
1 small bay leaf
1 cup cubed potatoes
1 cup chopped onions
1 cup chopped celery
1 cup chopped carrots
water

1. Combine all ingredients except water in 3 1/2-quart slow cooker. Add water to about 1 inch from top.
2. Cover. Cook on Low 5-8 hours.
3. Remove bay leaf before serving.

Slow-Cooker Black Bean Chili

Mary Seielstad
Sparks, NV

Makes 8 servings

1 lb. pork tenderloin, cut into 1-inch chunks
16-oz. jar thick chunky salsa
3 15-oz. cans black beans, rinsed and drained
1/2 cup chicken broth
1 medium red bell pepper, chopped
1 medium onion, chopped
1 tsp. ground cumin
2-3 tsp. chili powder
1-1 1/2 tsp. dried oregano
1/4 cup sour cream

1. Combine all ingredients except sour cream in slow cooker.
2. Cover. Cook on Low 6-8 hours, or until pork is tender.
3. Garnish individual servings with sour cream.

Note:
This is good served over brown rice.

Katelyn's Black Bean Soup

Katelyn Bailey
Mechanicsburg, PA

Makes 4-6 servings

1/3 cup chopped onions
1 garlic clove, minced
1-2 Tbsp. oil
2 15 1/2-oz. cans black beans, undrained
1 cup water
1 chicken bouillon cube
1/2 cup diced, cooked, smoked ham
1/2 cup diced carrots
1 dash, *or more,* cayenne pepper
1-2 drops, *or more,* Tabasco sauce
sour cream

1. Saute onion and garlic in oil in saucepan.
2. Puree or mash contents of one can of black beans. Add to sauteed ingredients.
3. Combine all ingredients except sour cream in slow cooker.
4. Cover. Cook on Low 6-8 hours.
5. Add dollop of sour cream to each individual bowl before serving.

Baked Bean Soup

Maryann Markano
Wilmington, DE

Makes 5-6 servings

1-lb. 12-oz. can baked beans
6 slices browned bacon, chopped
2 Tbsp. bacon drippings
2 Tbsp. finely chopped onions
14 1/2-oz. can stewed tomatoes
1 Tbsp. brown sugar
1 Tbsp. vinegar
1 tsp. seasoning salt

1. Combine all ingredients in slow cooker.
2. Cover. Cook on Low 4-6 hours.

Mjeodrah or Esau's Lentil Soup

Dianna Milhizer
Springfield, VA

Makes 8 servings

1 cup chopped carrots
1 cup diced celery
2 cups chopped onions
1 Tbsp. olive oil, *or* butter
2 cups brown rice
1 Tbsp. olive oil, *or* butter
6 cups water
1 lb. lentils, washed and
   drained
garden salad
vinaigrette

1. Saute carrots, celery, and onions in 1 Tbsp. oil in skillet. When soft and translucent place in slow cooker.
2. Brown rice in 1 Tbsp. oil until dry. Add to slow cooker.
3. Stir in water and lentils.
4. Cover. Cook on High 6-8 hours.
5. When thoroughly cooked, serve 1 cup each in individual soup bowls. Cover each with a serving of fresh garden salad (lettuce, spinach leaves, chopped tomatoes, minced onions, chopped bell peppers, sliced olives, sliced radishes). Pour favorite vinaigrette over all.

French Onion Soup

Jenny R. Unternahrer
Wayland, IA
Janice Yoskovich
Carmichaels, PA

Makes 10 servings

8-10 large onions, sliced
1/2 cup butter *or* margarine
6 10½-oz. cans condensed
   beef broth
1½ tsp. Worcestershire
   sauce
3 bay leaves
10 slices French bread,
   toasted
grated Parmesan and/or
   shredded mozzarella
   cheese

1. Saute onions in butter until crisp-tender. Transfer to slow cooker.
2. Add broth, Worcestershire sauce, and bay leaves.
3. Cover. Cook on Low 5-7 hours, or until onions are tender. Discard bay leaves.
4. Ladle into bowls. Top each with a slice of bread and some cheese.

Note:
For a more intense beef flavor, add one beef bouillon cube, or use home-cooked beef broth instead of canned broth.

Potato Soup

Jeanne Hertzog, Bethlehem, PA
Marcia S. Myer, Manheim, PA
Rhonda Lee Schmidt
Scranton, PA
Mitzi McGlynchey
Downingtown, PA
Vera Schmucker, Goshen, IN
Kaye Schnell, Falmouth, MA
Elizabeth Yoder
Millersburg, OH

Makes 8-10 servings

6 potatoes, peeled and
   cubed
2 leeks, chopped
2 onions, chopped
1 rib celery, sliced
4 chicken bouillon cubes
1 Tbsp. dried parsley
   flakes
5 cups water
1 Tbsp. salt
pepper to taste
1/3 cup butter
13-oz. can evaporated milk
chopped chives

1. Combine all ingredients except milk and chives in slow cooker.
2. Cover. Cook on Low 10-12 hours, or High 3-4 hours. Stir in milk during last hour.
3. If desired, mash potatoes before serving.
4. Garnish with chives.

Variations:
1. Add one carrot, sliced, to vegetables before cooking.
2. Instead of water and bouillon cubes, use 4-5 cups chicken stock.

No-Fuss Potato Soup

Lucille Amos
Greensboro, NC
Lavina Hochstedler
Grand Blanc, MI
Betty Moore
Plano, IL

Makes 8-10 servings

6 cups diced, peeled
   potatoes
5 cups water
2 cups diced onions
1/2 cup diced celery
1/2 cup chopped carrots
1/4 cup margarine, *or*
   butter
4 tsp. chicken bouillon
   granules
2 tsp. salt
1/4 tsp. pepper
12-oz. can evaporated milk
3 Tbsp. chopped fresh
   parsley
8 oz. cheddar, *or* Colby,
   cheese, shredded

1. Combine all ingredients
except milk, parsley, and
cheese in slow cooker.
2. Cover. Cook on High 7-8
hours, or until vegetables are
tender.
3. Stir in milk and parsley.
Stir in cheese until it melts.
Heat thoroughly.

Variations:
1. For added flavor, stir in
3 slices bacon, browned until
crisp, and crumbled.
2. Top individual servings
with chopped chives.

Baked Potato Soup

Kristina Shull
Timberville, VA

Makes 6-8 servings

4 large baked potatoes
2/3 cup butter
2/3 cup flour
6 cups milk, whole *or* 2%
3/4 tsp. salt
1/2 tsp. pepper
4 green onions, chopped
12 slices bacon, fried and
   crumbled
2 cups shredded cheddar
   cheese
1 cup (8 oz.) sour cream

1. Cut potatoes in half.
Scoop out pulp and put in
small bowl.
2. Melt butter in large kettle. Add flour. Gradually stir
in milk. Continue to stir until
smooth, thickened, and bubbly.
3. Stir in potato pulp, salt,
pepper, and three-quarters of
the onions, bacon, and
cheese. Cook until heated.
Stir in sour cream.
4. Transfer to slow cooker
set on Low. Top with remaining onions, bacon, and
cheese. Take to a potluck, or
serve on a buffet table,
straight from the cooker.

Variation:
Add several slices of
Velveeta cheese to make soup
extra cheesy and creamy.

Sandy's Potato Soup

Sandra D. Thony
Jenks, OK

Makes 8-10 servings

8 large potatoes, cubed
2 medium onions, chopped
3 Tbsp. butter, *or*
   margarine
1/2-1 lb. bacon, cooked
   crisp, drained, and
   crumbled
3 chicken bouillon cubes
2 Tbsp. dried parsley
6 cups water
2 cups milk
1/2 cup flour
1/4 cup water
1 tsp. salt
1/4-1/2 tsp. pepper

1. Combine all ingredients
except flour, 1/4 cup water,
salt, and pepper in large slow
cooker.
2. Cover. Cook on High 6
hours, and then on Low 3
hours.
3. Make paste out of flour
and water. Stir into soup one
hour before serving. Season
with salt and pepper.

Variations:
1. Make Cheesy Potato
Soup by adding 1/4 lb. cubed
Velveeta, or your choice of
cheese, during last hour of
cooking.
2. For added richness, use
1 cup whole milk and 1 cup
evaporated milk.

German Potato Soup

Lee Ann Hazlett
Freeport, IL

Makes 6-8 servings

1 onion, chopped
1 leek, trimmed and diced
2 carrots, diced
1 cup chopped cabbage
1/4 cup chopped fresh
   parsley
4 cups beef broth
1 lb. potatoes, diced
1 bay leaf
1-2 tsp. black pepper
1 tsp. salt, optional
1/2 tsp. caraway seeds,
   optional
1/4 tsp. nutmeg
1 lb. bacon, cooked and
   crumbled
1/2 cup sour cream

1. Combine all ingredients except bacon and sour cream.
2. Cover. Cook on Low 8-10 hours, or High 4-5 hours.
3. Remove bay leaf. Use a slotted spoon to remove potatoes. Mash potatoes and mix with sour cream. Return to slow cooker. Stir in. Add bacon and mix together thoroughly.

Potato Comfort Soup

Charlotte Bull
Cassville, MO

Makes 8 servings

6 cups cubed, peeled
   potatoes
2 cups chopped onions
1/2 cup chopped celery
1 cup chopped carrots
5 cups water
1/4 cup butter, *or*
   margarine
1-2 tsp. salt, optional
1/4-1/2 tsp. pepper
2 cups milk
2 eggs
flour
1-2 Tbsp. dried parsley
butter, *or* margarine

1. Combine vegetables, water, 1/4 cup butter or margarine, salt, and pepper in slow cooker.
2. Cover. Cook on High 7-8 hours, or until vegetables arc tender.
3. Add milk. Stir in.
4. Make "drop noodles" by beating eggs in a small bowl. Add enough flour to make a very soft, almost runny, bat-

ter. Dribble spoonfuls into hot soup in cooker. (You may find it easiest to use two spoons to do this: one spoon to dip up the "noodles"; the other to push them into the cooker. "Noodles" should not be big clumps, yet they need to be big enough to hold together.)
5. Cover. Cook on Low one more hour.
6. When ready to serve, add parsley and a block of butter or margarine to each individual bowl.

Milk products such as cream, milk, and sour cream can curdle and separate when cooked for a long period. Add them during the last 10 minutes if cooking on High, or during the last 20-30 minutes if cooking on Low.

Mrs. J.E. Barthold
Bethlehem, PA
Marilyn Yoder
Archbold, OH

Black-Eye and Vegetable Chili

Julie Weaver
Reinholds, PA

Makes 4-6 servings

1 cup finely chopped onions
1 cup finely chopped carrots
1 cup finely chopped red *or* green pepper, *or* mixture of two
1 garlic clove, minced
4 tsp. chili powder
1 tsp. ground cumin
2 Tbsp. chopped cilantro
14 1/2-oz. can diced tomatoes
3 cups cooked black-eyed beans, *or* 2 15-oz. cans black-eyed beans, drained
4-oz. can chopped green chilies
3/4 cup orange juice
3/4 cup water, *or* broth
1 Tbsp. cornstarch
2 Tbsp. water
1/2 cup shredded cheddar cheese
2 Tbsp. chopped cilantro

1. Combine all ingredients except cornstarch, 2 Tbsp. water, cheese, and cilantro.
2. Cover. Cook on Low 6-8 hours, or High 4 hours.
3. Dissolve cornstarch in water. Stir into soup mixture 30 minutes before serving.
4. Garnish individual servings with cheese and cilantro.

Veggie Chili

Wanda Roth
Napoleon, OH

Makes 6 servings

2 qts. whole *or* diced tomatoes, undrained
6-oz. can tomato paste
1/2 cup chopped onions
1/2 cup chopped celery
1/2 cup chopped green peppers
2 garlic cloves, minced
1 tsp. salt
1 1/2 tsp. ground cumin
1 tsp. dried oregano
1/4 tsp. cayenne pepper
3 Tbsp. brown sugar
15-oz. can garbanzo beans

1. Combine all ingredients except beans in slow cooker.
2. Cook on Low 6-8 hours, or High 3-4 hours. Add beans one hour before serving.

Variation:
If you prefer a less tomatoey taste, substitute 2 vegetable bouillon cubes and 1 cup water for tomato paste.

Beans and Tomato Chili

Becky Harder
Monument, CO

Makes 6-8 servings

15-oz. can black beans, undrained
15-oz. can pinto beans, undrained
16-oz. can kidney beans, undrained
15-oz. can garbanzo beans, undrained
2 14 1/2-oz. cans stewed tomatoes and juice
1 pkg. prepared chili seasoning

1. Pour beans, including their liquid, into slow cooker.
2. Stir in tomatoes and chili seasoning.
3. Cover. Cook on Low 4-8 hours.
4. Serve with crackers, and topped with grated cheddar cheese, sliced green onions, and sour cream, if desired.

Variation:
Add additional cans of white beans or 1 tsp. dried onion.

VEGETARIAN SOUPS

Vegetarian Chili
Connie Johnson
Loudon, NH

Makes 6 servings

3 garlic cloves, minced
2 onions, chopped
1 cup textured vegetable protein (T.V.P.)
1-lb. can beans of your choice, drained
1 green bell pepper, chopped
1 jalapeno pepper, seeds removed, chopped
28-oz. can diced Italian tomatoes
1 bay leaf
1 Tbsp. dried oregano
1/2-1 tsp. salt
1/4 tsp. pepper

1. Combine all ingredients in slow cooker.
2. Cover. Cook on Low 6-8 hours.

Hearty Black Bean Soup
Della Yoder
Kalona, IA

Makes 6-8 servings

3 medium carrots, halved and thinly sliced
2 celery ribs, thinly sliced
1 medium onion, chopped
4 cloves garlic, minced
20-oz. can black beans, drained and rinsed
2 14 1/2-oz. cans chicken broth
15-oz. can crushed tomatoes
1 1/2 tsp. dried basil
1/2 tsp. dried oregano
1/2 tsp. ground cumin
1/2 tsp. chili powder
1/2 tsp. hot pepper sauce

1. Combine all ingredients in slow cooker.
2. Cover. Cook on Low 9-10 hours.

Note:
May be served over cooked rice.

Variation:
If you prefer a thicker soup, use only 1 can chicken broth.

Black Bean and Corn Soup
Joy Sutter
Iowa City, IA

Makes 6-8 servings

2 15-oz. cans black beans, drained and rinsed
14 1/2-oz. can Mexican stewed tomatoes, undrained
14 1/2-oz. can diced tomatoes, undrained
11-oz. can whole kernel corn, drained
4 green onions, sliced
2-3 Tbsp. chili powder
1 tsp. ground cumin
1/2 tsp. dried minced garlic

1. Combine all ingredients in slow cooker.
2. Cover. Cook on High 5-6 hours.

Variations:
1. Use 2 cloves fresh garlic, minced, instead of dried garlic.
2. Add 1 large rib celery, sliced thinly, and 1 small green pepper, chopped.

Tuscan Garlicky Bean Soup

Sara Harter Fredette
Williamsburg, MA

Makes 8-10 servings

1 lb. dry Great Northern, *or* other dry white, beans
1 qt. water
1 qt. beef broth
3 Tbsp. olive oil
2 garlic cloves, minced
4 Tbsp. chopped parsley
olive oil
2 tsp. salt
1/2 tsp. pepper

1. Place beans in large soup pot. Cover with water and bring to boil. Cook 2 minutes. Remove from heat. Cover pot and allow to stand for 1 hour. Drain, discarding water.
2. Combine beans, 1 quart fresh water, and beef broth in slow cooker.
3. Saute garlic and parsley in olive oil in skillet. Stir into slow cooker. Add salt and pepper.
4. Cover. Cook on Low 8-10 hours, or until beans are tender.

Bean Soup

Joyce Cox
Port Angeles, WA

Makes 10-12 servings

1 cup dry Great Northern beans
1 cup dry red beans, *or* pinto beans
4 cups water
28-oz. can diced tomatoes
1 medium onion, chopped
2 Tbsp. vegetable bouillon granules, *or* 4 bouillon cubes
2 garlic cloves, minced
2 tsp. Italian seasoning, crushed
9-oz. pkg. frozen green beans, thawed

1. Soak and rinse dried beans.
2. Combine all ingredients except green beans in slow cooker.
3. Cover. Cook on High 5 1/2-6 1/2 hours, or on Low 11-13 hours.
4. Stir green beans into soup during last 2 hours.

Veggie Stew

Ernestine Schrepfer
Trenton, MO

Makes 10-15 servings

5-6 potatoes, cubed
3 carrots, cubed
1 onion, chopped
1/2 cup chopped celery
2 cups canned diced *or* stewed tomatoes
3 chicken bouillon cubes dissolved in 3 cups water
1 1/2 tsp. dried thyme
1/2 tsp. dried parsley
1/2 cup brown rice, uncooked
1 lb. frozen green beans
1 lb. frozen corn
15-oz. can butter beans
46-oz. can V-8 juice

1. Combine potatoes, carrots, onion, celery, tomatoes, chicken stock, thyme, parsley, and rice in 5-quart cooker, or two medium-sized cookers.
2. Cover. Cook on High 2 hours. Puree one cup of mixture and add back to slow cooker to thicken the soup.
3. Stir in beans, corn, butter beans, and juice.
4. Cover. Cook on High 1 more hour, then reduce to Low and cook 6-8 more hours.

Southwestern Soup

Evelyn L. Ward
Greeley, CO

Makes 4 servings

2 14-oz. cans beef broth
1/2 cup sliced carrots
1/2 cup diced onions
1 cup diced potatoes
1 garlic clove, minced
8-oz. can, *or* 1 cup home-
   canned, crushed
   tomatoes
1 Tbsp. Worcestershire
   sauce
salsa to taste
garnishes:
   grated cheese
   diced avocados
   diced green peppers
   diced cucumbers
   2 1/4-oz. can sliced ripe
      olives
   6-oz. fresh mushrooms,
      sliced and sauteed
      in butter
   6-oz. can cooked and
      peeled tiny shrimp
   1 cup diced cooked ham
   1 cup green onion,
      sliced
   3 hard-cooked eggs,
      chopped
   1 cup diced tomatoes
   sour cream

1. Combine broth, carrots, onions, potatoes, garlic, tomatoes, and Worcestershire sauce in slow cooker. Cook on Low 6-8 hours.
2. Before serving, stir in salsa, sampling as you go to get the right balance of flavors.
3. Serve the soup in bowls, allowing guests to add garnishes of their choice.

Heart Happy Tomato Soup

Anne Townsend
Albuquerque, NM

Makes 6 servings

46-oz. can tomato juice
8-oz. can tomato sauce
1/2 cup water
1 Tbsp. bouillon granules
1 sprig celery leaves,
   chopped
half an onion, thinly sliced
1/2 tsp. dried basil
2 Tbsp. sugar
1 bay leaf
1/2 tsp. whole cloves

1. Combine all ingredients in greased slow cooker. Stir well.
2. Cover. Cook on Low 5-8 hours. Remove bay leaf and cloves before serving.

Note:
   If you prefer a thicker soup, add 1/4 cup instant potato flakes. Stir well and cook 5 minutes longer.

Vegetarian Minestrone Soup

Connie Johnson
Loudon, NH

Makes 6 servings

6 cups vegetable broth
2 carrots, chopped
2 large onions, chopped
3 ribs celery, chopped
2 garlic cloves, minced
1 small zucchini, cubed
1 handful fresh kale,
   chopped
1/2 cup dry barley
1 can chickpeas, *or* white
   kidney beans, drained
1 Tbsp. parsley
1/2 tsp. dried thyme
1 tsp. dried oregano
28-oz. can crushed Italian
   tomatoes
1 tsp. salt
1/4 tsp. pepper
grated cheese

1. Combine all ingredients except cheese in slow cooker.
2. Cover. Cook on Low 6-8 hours, or until vegetables are tender.
3. Sprinkle individual servings with grated cheese.

Joyce's Minestrone

Joyce Shackelford
Green Bay, Wisconsin

Makes 6 servings

3½ cups beef broth
28-oz. can crushed
    tomatoes
2 medium carrots, thinly
    sliced
½ cup chopped onion
½ cup chopped celery
2 medium potatoes, thinly
    sliced
1-2 garlic cloves, minced
16-oz. can red kidney
    beans, drained
2 oz. thin spaghetti,
    broken into 2-inch
    pieces
2 Tbsp. parsley flakes
2-3 tsp. dried basil
1-2 tsp. dried oregano
1 bay leaf

1. Combine all ingredients
in slow cooker.
2. Cover. Cook on Low 10-
16 hours, or on High 4-6
hours.
3. Remove bay leaf. Serve.

Grace's Minestrone Soup

Grace Ketcham
Marietta, GA

Makes 8 servings

¾ cup dry elbow macaroni
2 qts. chicken stock
2 large onions, diced
2 carrots, sliced
half a head of cabbage,
    shredded
½ cup celery, diced
1-lb. can tomatoes
½ tsp. salt
½ tsp. dried oregano
1 Tbsp. minced parsley
¼ cup each frozen corn,
    peas, and lima beans
¼ tsp. pepper
grated Parmesan, *or*
    Romano, cheese

1. Cook macaroni accord-
ing to package directions. Set
aside.
2. Combine all ingredients
except macaroni and cheese
in large slow cooker.
3. Cover. Cook on Low 8
hours. Add macaroni during
last 30 minutes of cooking
time.
4. Garnish individual servings with cheese.

Cabbage Soup

Margaret Jarrett
Anderson, IN

Makes 8 servings

half a head of cabbage,
    sliced thin
2 ribs celery, sliced thin
2-3 carrots, sliced thin
1 onion, chopped
2 chicken bouillon cubes
2 garlic cloves, minced
1 qt. tomato juice
1 tsp. salt
¼ tsp. pepper
water

1. Combine all ingredients
except water in slow cooker.
Add water to within 3 inches
of top of slow cooker.
2. Cover. Cook on High
3½-4 hours, or until vegetables are tender.

Salsa Soup

Sue Hamilton
Minooka, IL

Makes 6 servings

3 cups (26 oz.) corn-black
    bean mild salsa
6 cups beef broth
¼ cup white long grain
    rice, uncooked

1. Combine all ingredients
in slow cooker.

2. Cover. Cook on Low 4-6 hours, or until rice is tender.

Winter Squash and White Bean Stew

Mary E. Herr
Three Rivers, MI

Makes 6 servings

1 cup chopped onions
1 Tbsp. olive oil
1/2 tsp. ground cumin
1/4 tsp. salt
1/4 tsp. cinnamon
1 garlic clove, minced
3 cups peeled, butternut squash, cut into 3/4-inch cubes
1 1/2 cups chicken broth
19-oz. can cannellini beans, drained
14 1/2-oz. can diced tomatoes, undrained
1 Tbsp. chopped fresh cilantro

1. Combine all ingredients in slow cooker.
2. Cover. Cook on High 1 hour. Reduce heat to Low and heat 2-3 hours.

Variations:
1. Beans can be pureed in blender and added during the last hour.
2. Eight ounces dried beans can be soaked overnight, cooked until soft, and used in place of canned beans.

Corn Chowder

Charlotte Fry
St. Charles, MO
Jeanette Oberholtzer
Manheim, PA

Makes 4 servings

6 slices bacon, diced
1/2 cup chopped onions
2 cups diced peeled potatoes
2 10-oz. pkgs. frozen corn
16-oz. can cream-style corn
1 Tbsp. sugar
1 tsp. Worcestershire sauce
1 tsp. seasoned salt
1/4 tsp. pepper
1 cup water

1. In skillet, brown bacon until crisp. Remove bacon, reserving drippings.
2. Add onions and potatoes to skillet and saute for 5 minutes. Drain.
3. Combine all ingredients in slow cooker. Mix well.
4. Cover. Cook on Low 6-7 hours.

Variations:
1. To make Clam Corn Chowder, drain and add 2 cans minced clams during last hour of cooking.
2. Substitute 1 quart home-frozen corn for the store-bought frozen and canned corn.

Cheese and Corn Chowder

Loretta Krahn
Mt. Lake, MN

Makes 8 servings

3/4 cup water
1/2 cup chopped onions
1 1/2 cups sliced carrots
1 1/2 cups chopped celery
1 tsp. salt
1/2 tsp. pepper
15 1/4-oz. can whole kernel corn, drained
15-oz. can cream-style corn
3 cups milk
1 1/2 cup grated cheddar cheese

1. Combine water, onions, carrots, celery, salt, and pepper in slow cooker.
2. Cover. Cook on High 4-6 hours.
3. Add corn, milk, and cheese. Heat on High 1 hour, and then turn to Low until you are ready to eat.

Cream of Broccoli Soup

Barb Yoder
Angola, IN

Makes 6-8 servings

1 small onion, chopped
oil
20-oz. pkg. frozen broccoli
2 10¾-oz. cans cream of
  celery soup
10¾-oz. can cream of
  mushroom soup
1 cup grated American
  cheese
2 soup cans milk

1. Saute onion in oil in skillet until soft.
2. Combine all ingredients in slow cooker.
3. Cover. Cook on Low 3-4 hours.

Broccoli-Cheese Soup

Darla Sathre
Baxter, MN

Makes 8 servings

2 16-oz. pkgs. frozen
  chopped broccoli
2 10¾-oz. cans cheddar
  cheese soup
2 12-oz. cans evaporated
  milk
¼ cup finely chopped onions

½ tsp. seasoned salt
¼ tsp. pepper
sunflower seeds, optional
crumbled bacon, optional

1. Combine all ingredients except sunflower seeds and bacon in slow cooker.
2. Cover. Cook on Low 8-10 hours.
3. Garnish with sunflower seeds and bacon.

Broccoli-Cheese with Noodles Soup

Carol Sherwood
Batavia, NY

Makes 8 servings

2 cups cooked noodles
10-oz. pkg. frozen chopped
  broccoli, thawed
3 Tbsp. chopped onions
2 Tbsp. butter
1 Tbsp. flour
2 cups cubed processed
  cheese
½ tsp. salt
5½ cups milk

1. Cook noodles just until soft in saucepan while combining rest of ingredients in slow cooker. Mix well.
2. Drain cooked noodles and stir into slow cooker.
3. Cover. Cook on Low 4 hours.

Double Cheese Cauliflower Soup

Zona Mae Bontrager
Kokomo, IN

Makes 6 servings

4 cups (1 small head)
  cauliflower pieces
2 cups water
8-oz. pkg. cream cheese,
  cubed
5 oz. American cheese
  spread
¼ lb. dried beef, torn into
  strips *or* shredded
½ cup potato flakes *or*
  buds

1. Combine cauliflower and water in saucepan. Bring to boil. Set aside.
2. Heat slow cooker on Low. Add cream cheese and cheese spread. Pour in cauliflower and water. Stir to be sure the cheese is dissolved and mixed through the cauliflower.
3. Add dried beef and potato flakes. Mix well.
4. Cover. Cook on Low 2-3 hours.

Main Dishes

Beef Stew

Wanda S. Curtin, Bradenton, FL
Paula King, Harrisonburg, VA
Miriam Nolt, New Holland, PA
Jean Shaner, York, PA
Mary W. Stauffer, Ephrata, PA
Alma Z. Weaver, Ephrata, PA

Makes 6 servings

2 lbs. beef chuck, cubed
1 tsp. Worcestershire sauce
1/4-1/2 cup flour
1 1/2 tsp. salt
1/2 tsp. pepper
1 tsp. paprika
1 1/2 cups beef broth
half garlic clove, minced
1 bay leaf
4 carrots, sliced
2 onions, chopped
1 rib celery, sliced
3 potatoes, diced

1. Place meat in slow cooker.
2. Combine flour, salt, pepper, and paprika. Stir into meat until coated thoroughly.
3. Add remaining ingredients. Mix well.
4. Cover. Cook on Low 10-12 hours, or High 4-6 hours. Stir before serving.

Audrey's Beef Stew

Audrey Romonosky
Austin, TX

Makes 4-6 servings

3 carrots, sliced
3 potatoes, cubed
2 lbs. beef chuck, cubed
2 cups water
2 beef bouillon cubes
1 tsp. Worcestershire sauce
1/2 tsp. garlic powder
1 bay leaf
1/4 tsp. salt
1/2 tsp. pepper
1 tsp. paprika
3 onions, chopped
1 rib celery, sliced
1/4 cup flour
1/3 cup cold water

1. Combine all ingredients except flour and 1/3 cup cold water in slow cooker. Mix well.
2. Cover. Cook on Low 8 hours.
3. Dissolve flour in 1/3 cup water. Stir into meat mixture. Cook on High until thickened, about 10 minutes.

Herbed Beef Stew

Carol Findling
Princeton, IL

Makes 6-8 servings

1 lb. beef round, cubed
4 Tbsp. seasoned flour *
1½ cups beef broth
1 tsp. Worcestershire sauce
1 garlic clove
1 bay leaf
4 carrots, sliced
3 potatoes, cubed
2 onions, diced
1 rounded tsp. fresh thyme, *or* ½ tsp. dried thyme
1 rounded tsp. chopped fresh basil, *or* ½ tsp. dried basil
1 Tbsp. fresh parsley, *or* 1 tsp. dried parsley
1 rounded tsp. fresh marjoram, *or* 1 tsp. dried marjoram

1. Put meat in slow cooker. Add seasoned flour. Toss with meat. Stir in remaining ingredients. Mix well.
2. Cover. Cook on High 4-6 hours, or Low 10-12 hours.

* **Seasoned Flour**
1 cup flour
1 tsp. salt
1 tsp. paprika
¼ tsp. pepper

Beef Stew Olé

Andrea O'Neil
Fairfield, CT

Makes 6-8 servings

4 carrots, cubed
4 potatoes, peeled and cubed
1 onion, quartered
1½ lbs. beef stewing meat, cubed
8-oz. can tomato sauce
1 pkg. dry taco seasoning mix
2 cups water, divided
1½ Tbsp. cornstarch
2 tsp. salt
¼ tsp. pepper

1. Layer first four ingredients in slow cooker. Add tomato sauce.
2. Combine taco seasoning with 1½ cups water. Stir cornstarch into remaining ½ cup water until smooth. Stir into rest of water with taco seasoning. Pour over ingredients in slow cooker.
3. Sprinkle with salt and pepper.
4. Cover. Cook on Low 7-8 hours.
5. Serve over rice.

Variation:
If those eating at your table are cautious about spicy food, choose a "mild" taco seasoning mix and add 1 tsp. sugar to the seasonings.

Pot Roast

Carole Whaling
New Tripoli, PA

Makes 8 servings

4 medium potatoes, cubed
4 carrots, sliced
1 onion, sliced
3-4-lb. rump roast, *or* pot roast, cut into serving-size pieces
1 tsp. salt
½ tsp. pepper
1 bouillon cube
½ cup boiling water

1. Put vegetables and meat in slow cooker. Stir in salt and pepper.
2. Dissolve bouillon cube in water, then pour over other ingredients.
3. Cover. Cook on Low 10-12 hours.

Swiss Steak

Marilyn Mowry
Irving, TX

Makes 4-6 servings

3-4 Tbsp. flour
½ tsp. salt
¼ tsp. pepper
1½ tsp. dry mustard
1½-2 lbs. round steak
oil
1 cup sliced onions
1 lb. carrots

14½-oz. can whole
   tomatoes
1 Tbsp. brown sugar
1½ Tbsp. Worcestershire
   sauce

1. Combine flour, salt, pepper, and dry mustard.
2. Cut steak into serving pieces. Dredge in flour mixture. Brown on both sides in oil in saucepan. Place in slow cooker.
3. Add onions and carrots.
4. Combine tomatoes, brown sugar, and Worcestershire sauce. Pour into slow cooker.
5. Cover. Cook on Low 8-10 hours, or High 3-5 hours.

Round Steak Casserole

Gladys High
Ephrata, PA

Makes 6 servings

2 lbs. round steak, cut
   ½-inch thick
1 tsp. salt
¼ tsp. pepper
1 onion, thinly sliced
3-4 potatoes, pared and
   quartered
16-oz. can French-style
   green beans, drained
1 clove garlic, minced
10¾-oz. can tomato soup
14½-oz. can tomatoes

1. Season roast with salt and pepper. Cut into serving pieces and place in slow cooker.

2. Add onion, potatoes, green beans, and garlic. Top with soup and tomatoes.
3. Cover and cook on Low 8-10 hours, or High 4-5 hours. Remove cover during last half hour if too much liquid has collected.

Hearty Beef Stew

Charlotte Shaffer
East Earl, PA

Makes 4-5 servings

2 lbs. stewing beef, cubed
5 carrots, sliced
1 large onion, cut in
   chunks
3 ribs celery, sliced
22-oz. can stewed tomatoes
½ tsp. ground cloves
2 bay leaves
1½ tsp. salt
¼-½ tsp. pepper

1. Combine all ingredients in slow cooker.
2. Cover. Cook on High 5-6 hours.

Variations:
1. Substitute 1 whole clove for the ½ tsp. ground cloves. Remove before serving.
2. Use venison instead of beef.
3. Cut back the salt to 1 tsp. and use 1 tsp. soy sauce.

Betty B. Dennison
Grove City, PA

Judy's Beef Stew

Judy Koczo
Plano, IL

Makes 4-6 servings

2 lbs. stewing meat, cubed
5 carrots, sliced
1 onion, diced
3 ribs celery, diced
5 potatoes, cubed
28-oz. can tomatoes
⅓-½ cup quick-cooking
   tapioca
2 tsp. salt
½ tsp. pepper

1. Combine all ingredients in slow cooker.
2. Cover. Cook on Low 10-12 hours, or High 5-6 hours.

Variation:
Add 1 whole clove and 2 bay leaves to stew before cooking.

L. Jean Moore
Pendleton, IN

Slow-Cooker Stew

Trudy Kutter
Corfu, NY

Makes 6-8 servings

2 lbs. boneless beef, cubed
4-6 celery ribs, sliced
6-8 carrots, sliced
6 potatoes, cubed
2 onions, sliced
28-oz. can tomatoes
1/4 cup minute tapioca
1 tsp. salt
1/4 tsp. pepper
1/2 tsp. dried basil,
  or oregano
1 garlic clove, pressed *or*
  minced

1. Combine all ingredients in slow cooker.
2. Cover. Cook on Low 8-10 hours.

Variation:

Add 2 10 1/2-oz. cans beef gravy and 1/2 cup water in place of the tomatoes. Reduce tapioca to 2 Tbsp.

Italian Stew

Ann Gouinlock
Alexander, NY

Makes 6 servings

1 1/2 lbs. beef cubes
2-3 carrots, cut in 1-inch chunks
3-4 ribs celery, cut in 3/4-1-inch pieces
1-1 1/2 cups coarsely chopped onions
14 1/2-oz. can stewed, *or* diced, tomatoes
1/3 cup minute tapioca
1 1/2 tsp. salt
1/4 tsp. pepper
1/4 tsp. Worcestershire sauce
1/2 tsp. Italian seasoning

1. Combine all ingredients in slow cooker.
2. Cover. Cook on Low 8-10 hours.

Herby Beef Stew

Tracy Supcoe
Barclay, MD

Makes 6 servings

1-2 lbs. stewing meat, cubed
2/3 cup flour
1 1/2 tsp. salt
1/4 tsp. pepper
oil
14 1/2-oz. can diced tomatoes
8-oz. can tomato sauce
14 1/2-oz. can beef broth
2 Tbsp. Worcestershire sauce
1 bay leaf
2 tsp. kitchen bouquet
2 Tbsp. dried parsley
1 tsp. Hungarian sweet paprika
4 celery heart ribs, chopped
5 mushrooms, sliced
3 potatoes, cubed
3 cloves garlic, minced
1 large onion, chopped

1. Combine flour, salt, and pepper in bowl. Dredge meat in seasoned flour, then brown in oil in saucepan. Place meat in slow cooker.
2. Combine remaining ingredients in bowl. Pour over meat and mix well.
3. Cover. Cook on High 5-6 hours, or Low 10-12 hours. Stir before serving.

Liquids don't boil down in a slow cooker. At the end of the cooking time, remove the cover, set dial on High and allow the liquid to evaporate, if the dish is soup-ier than you want.

John D. Allen
Rye, CO

Venison or Beef Stew

Frances B. Musser
Newmanstown, PA

Makes 6 servings

1½ lbs. venison *or* beef cubes
2 Tbsp. oil
1 medium onion, chopped
4 carrots, peeled and cut into 1-inch pieces
1 rib celery, cut into 1-inch pieces
4 medium potatoes, peeled and quartered
12-oz. can whole tomatoes, undrained
10½-oz. can beef broth
1 Tbsp. Worcestershire sauce
1 Tbsp. parsley flakes
1 bay leaf
2½ tsp. salt
¼ tsp. pepper
2 Tbsp. quick-cooking tapioca

1. Brown meat cubes in skillet in oil over medium heat. Transfer to slow cooker.
2. Add remaining ingredients. Mix well.
3. Cover. Cook on Low 8-9 hours.

Variations:
1. Substitute 1½ tsp. garlic salt and 1 tsp. salt for 2½ tsp. salt.
2. For added color and flavor, add 1 cup frozen peas 5 minutes before end of cooking time.

Layered Herby Stew

Elizabeth L. Richards
Rapid City, SD

Makes 8 servings

2½ lbs. lean beef chuck, cubed
1 medium to large onion, cut in 1-inch pieces
8-12 small red potatoes *or* potato chunks
4-6 carrots, cut in 1-inch pieces
2 large ribs celery, cut in 1-inch pieces
2 Tbsp. Worcestershire sauce
¼ cup red wine, *or* water
3 Tbsp. brown sugar
1 tsp. salt
½ tsp. pepper
⅛ tsp. allspice
¼ tsp. dried marjoram
¼ tsp. dried thyme
2 bay leaves
6 Tbsp. minute tapioca (use only 5 Tbsp. if using water instead of red wine)
28-oz. can diced tomatoes
½ cup chopped fresh parsley

1. Layer all ingredients except parsley in slow cooker in order given.
2. Cover. Cook on High 6 hours.
3. Immediately before serving, garnish with parsley.

Waldorf Astoria Stew

Mary V. Warye
West Liberty, OH

Makes 6-8 servings

3 lbs. beef stewing meat, cubed
1 medium onion, chopped
1 cup celery, sliced
2 cups carrots, sliced
4 medium potatoes, cubed
3 Tbsp. minute tapioca
1 Tbsp. sugar
1 Tbsp. salt
½ tsp. pepper
10¾-oz. can tomato soup
⅓ cup water

1. Layer meat, onion, celery, carrots, and potatoes in slow cooker. Sprinkle with seasonings and tapioca. Add soup and water.
2. Cover. Cook on Low 7-9 hours.

Busy Day Beef Stew

Dale Peterson
Rapid City, SC

Makes 6-8 servings

2 lbs. stewing meat, cubed
2 medium onions, diced
1 cup chopped celery
2 cups sliced carrots
4 medium potatoes, diced
2½ Tbsp. quick-cooking
    tapioca
1 Tbsp. sugar
1 tsp. salt
½ tsp. pepper
10¾-oz. can tomato soup
1½ soup cans water

1. Layer meat and vegetables in slow cooker. Sprinkle with tapioca, sugar, salt, and pepper. Combine soup and water and pour into slow cooker. Do not stir.
2. Cover. Cook on Low 6-8 hours.

Pungent Beef Stew

Grace Ketcham
Marietta, GA

Makes 4-6 servings

2 lbs. beef chuck, cubed
1 tsp. Worcestershire sauce
1 garlic clove, minced
1 medium onion, chopped
2 bay leaves
½ tsp. salt
½ tsp. paprika
¼ tsp. pepper
dash of ground cloves, *or*
    allspice
6 carrots, quartered
4 potatoes, quartered
2 ribs celery, chopped
10¾-oz. can tomato soup
½ cup water

1. Combine all ingredients in slow cooker.
2. Cover. Cook on Low 10-12 hours.

Donna's Beef Stew

Donna Treloar
Gaston, IN

Makes 6 servings

2 lbs. beef, cubed
4-5 potatoes, cubed
4-5 carrots, sliced
3 ribs celery, sliced
2 onions, chopped
1 Tbsp. sugar
2 tsp. salt
¼-½ tsp. pepper
2 Tbsp. instant tapioca
3 cups V-8, *or* tomato,
    juice

1. Place meat and vegetables in slow cooker. Sprinkle with sugar, salt, pepper, and tapioca. Toss lightly. Pour juice over the top.
2. Cover. Cook on Low 8-10 hours.

Variation:
Add 10-oz. pkg. frozen succotash or green beans.

When I want to warm rolls to go with a slow-cooker stew, I wrap them in foil and lay them on top of the stew until they're warm.
Donna Barnitz
Jenks, OK

Venison Swiss Steak

Dede Peterson
Rapid City, SD

Makes 6 servings

2 lbs. round venison steak
flour
2 tsp. salt
1/2 tsp. pepper
oil
2 onions, sliced
2 ribs celery, diced
1 cup carrots, diced
2 cups fresh, *or* stewed,
    tomatoes
1 Tbsp. Worcestershire
    sauce

1. Combine flour, salt, and
pepper. Dredge steak in flour
mixture. Brown in oil in skillet. Place in slow cooker.
2. Add remaining ingredi-
ents.
3. Cover. Cook on Low
7 1/2-8 1/2 hours.

Swiss Steak

Wanda S. Curtin
Bradenton, FL
Jeanne Hertzog
Bethlehem, PA

Makes 6 servings

1 1/2 lbs. round steak, about
    3/4" thick
2-4 tsp. flour
1/2-1 tsp. salt
1/4 tsp. pepper
1 medium onion, sliced
1 carrot, chopped
1 rib celery, chopped
14 1/2-oz. can diced
    tomatoes, *or* 15-oz. can
    tomato sauce

1. Cut steak into serving
pieces.
2. Combine flour, salt, and
pepper. Dredge meat in seasoned flour.
3. Place onions in bottom
of slow cooker. Add meat.
Top with carrots and celery
and cover with tomatoes.
4. Cover. Cook on Low 8-
10 hours, or High 3-5 hours.
5. Serve over noodles or
rice.

Jacqueline's Swiss Steak

Jacqueline Stafl
East Bethany, NY

Makes 4 servings

1 1/2 lbs. round steak
2-4 Tbsp. flour
1/2 lb. sliced carrots, *or*
    1 lb. baby carrots
1 pkg. dry onion soup mix
8-oz. can tomato sauce
1/2 cup water

1. Cut steak into serving-
size pieces. Dredge in flour.
2. Place carrots in bottom
of slow cooker. Top with
steak.
3. Combine soup mix,
tomato sauce, and water. Pour
over all.
4. Cover. Cook on Low
8-10 hours.
5. Serve over mashed potatoes.

Margaret's Swiss Steak

Margaret Rich
North Newton, KS

Makes 6 servings

1 cup chopped onions
1/2 cup chopped celery
2-lb. 1/2-inch thick round
  steak
1/4 cup flour
3 Tbsp. oil
1 tsp. salt
1/4 tsp. pepper
16-oz. can diced tomatoes
1/4 cup flour
1/2 cup water

1. Place onions and celery in bottom of slow cooker.
2. Cut steak in serving-size pieces. Dredge in 1/4 cup flour. Brown on both sides in oil in saucepan. Place in slow cooker.
3. Sprinkle with salt and pepper. Pour on tomatoes.
4. Cover. Cook on Low 9 hours. Remove meat from cooker and keep warm.
5. Turn heat to High. Blend together 1/4 cup flour and water. Stir into sauce in slow cooker. Cover and cook 15 minutes. Serve with steak.

Nadine & Hazel's Swiss Steak

Nadine Martinitz, Salina, KS
Hazel L. Propst, Oxford, PA

Makes 6-8 servings

3-lb. round steak
1/3 cup flour
2 tsp. salt
1/2 tsp. pepper
3 Tbsp. shortening
1 large onion, *or* more,
  sliced
1 large pepper, *or* more,
  sliced
14 1/2-oz. can stewed
  tomatoes, *or* 3-4 fresh
  tomatoes, chopped
water

1. Sprinkle meat with flour, salt, and pepper. Pound both sides. Cut into 6 or 8 pieces. Brown meat in shortening over medium heat on top of stove, about 15 minutes. Transfer to slow cooker.
2. Brown onion and pepper. Add tomatoes and bring to boil. Pour over steak. Add water to completely cover steak.
3. Cover. Cook on Low 6-8 hours.

Variation:
  To add some flavor, stir in your favorite dried herbs when beginning to cook the steak, or add fresh herbs in the last hour of cooking.

Beef, Tomatoes, & Noodles

Janice Martins
Fairbank, IA

Makes 8 servings

1 1/2 lbs. stewing beef,
  cubed
1/4 cup flour
2 cups stewed tomatoes (if
  you like tomato chunks),
  or 2 cups crushed
  tomatoes (if you prefer a
  smoother gravy
1 tsp. salt
1/4-1/2 tsp. pepper
1 medium onion, chopped
water
12-oz. bag noodles

1. Combine meat and flour until cubes are coated. Place in slow cooker.
2. Add tomatoes, salt, pepper, and onion. Add water to cover.
3. Cover. Simmer on Low 6-8 hours.
4. Serve over cooked noodles.

Big Beef Stew

Margaret H. Moffitt
Bartlett, TN

Makes 6-8 servings

3-lb. beef roast, cubed
1 large onion, sliced
1 tsp. dried parsley flakes
1 green pepper, sliced
3 ribs celery, sliced
4 carrots, sliced
28-oz. can tomatoes with
　juice, undrained
1 garlic clove, minced
2 cups water

1. Combine all ingredients.
2. Cover. Cook on High 1 hour. Reduce heat to Low and cook 8 hours.
3. Serve on rice or noodles.

Note:

This is a low-salt recipe. For more zest, add 2 tsp. salt and ¾ tsp. black pepper.

Spanish Round Steak

Shari Jensen
Fountain, CO

Makes 4-6 servings

1 small onion, sliced
1 rib celery, chopped
1 green bell pepper, sliced
　in rings
2 lbs. round steak
2 Tbsp. chopped fresh
　parsley, *or* 2 tsp. dried
　parsley
1 Tbsp. Worcestershire
　sauce
1 Tbsp. dry mustard
1 Tbsp. chili powder
2 cups canned tomatoes
2 tsp. dry minced garlic
½ tsp. salt
¼ tsp. pepper

1. Put half of onion, green pepper, and celery in slow cooker.
2. Cut steak into serving-size pieces. Place steak pieces in slow cooker.
3. Put remaining onion, green pepper, and celery over steak.
4. Combine remaining ingredients. Pour over meat.
5. Cover. Cook on Low 8 hours.
6. Serve over noodles or rice.

Slow-Cooked Pepper Steak

Carolyn Baer, Conrath, WI
Ann Driscoll
Albuquerque, NM

Makes 6-8 servings

1½-2 lbs. beef round
　steak, cut in 3" x 1"
　strips
2 Tbsp. oil
¼ cup soy sauce
1 garlic clove, minced
1 cup chopped onions
1 tsp. sugar
½ tsp. salt
¼ tsp. pepper
¼ tsp. ground ginger
2 large green peppers, cut
　in strips
4 tomatoes cut into
　eighths, *or* 16-oz. can
　diced tomatoes
½ cup cold water
1 Tbsp. cornstarch

1. Brown beef in oil in saucepan. Transfer to slow cooker.
2. Combine soy sauce, garlic, onions, sugar, salt, pepper, and ginger. Pour over meat.
3. Cover. Cook on Low 5-6 hours.
4. Add green peppers and tomatoes. Cook 1 hour longer.
5. Combine water and cornstarch to make paste. Stir into slow cooker. Cook on High until thickened, about 10 minutes.
6. Serve over rice or noodles.

Pepper Steak Oriental

Donna Lantgen
Rapid City, SD

Makes 6 servings

1 lb. round steak, sliced thin
3 Tbsp. soy sauce
1/2 tsp. ground ginger
1 garlic clove, minced
1 green pepper, thinly sliced
4-oz. can mushrooms, drained, *or* 1 cup fresh mushrooms
1 onion, thinly sliced
1/2 tsp. crushed red pepper

1. Combine all ingredients in slow cooker.
2. Cover. Cook on Low 6-8 hours.
3. Serve as steak sandwiches topped with provolone cheese, or over rice.

Note:
Round steak is easier to slice into thin strips if it is partially frozen when cut.

Powerhouse Beef Roast with Tomatoes, Onions, and Peppers

Donna Treloar
Gaston, IN

Makes 5-6 servings

3-lb. boneless chuck roast
1 garlic clove, minced
1 Tbsp. oil
2-3 onions, sliced
2-3 sweet green and red peppers, sliced
16-oz. jar salsa
2 14½-oz. cans Mexican-style stewed tomatoes

1. Brown roast and garlic in oil in skillet. Place in slow cooker.
2. Add onions and peppers.
3. Combine salsa and tomatoes and pour over ingredients in slow cooker.
4. Cover. Cook on Low 8-10 hours.
5. Slice meat to serve.

Variation:
Make Beef Burritos with the leftovers. Shred the beef and heat with remaining peppers, onions, and ½ cup of the broth. Add 1 Tbsp. chili powder, 2 tsp. cumin, and salt to taste. Heat thoroughly. Fill warm flour tortillas with mixture and serve with sour cream, salsa, and guacamole.

Steak San Morco

Susan Tjon
Austin, TX

Makes 4-6 servings

2 lbs. stewing meat, cubed
1 envelope dry onion soup mix
29-oz. can peeled, *or* crushed, tomatoes
1 tsp. dried oregano
garlic powder to taste
2 Tbsp. oil
2 Tbsp. wine vinegar

1. Layer meat evenly in bottom of slow cooker.
2. Combine soup mix, tomatoes, spices, oil, and vinegar in bowl. Blend with spoon. Pour over meat.
3. Cover. Cook on High 6 hours, or Low 8-10 hours.

Pat's Meat Stew

Pat Bishop
Bedminster, PA

Makes 4-5 servings

1-2 lbs. beef roast, cubed
2 tsp. salt
1/4 tsp. pepper
2 cups water
2 carrots, sliced
2 small onions, sliced
4-6 small potatoes, cut up in chunks, if desired
1/4 cup quick-cooking tapioca
1 bay leaf
10-oz. pkg. frozen peas, *or* mixed vegetables

1. Brown beef in saucepan. Place in slow cooker.
2. Sprinkle with salt and pepper. Add remaining ingredients except frozen vegetables. Mix well.
3. Cover. Cook on Low 8-10 hours, or on High 4-5 hours. Add vegetables during last 1-2 hours of cooking.

Ernestine's Beef Stew

Ernestine Schrepfer
Trenton, MO

Makes 5-6 servings

1 1/2 lbs. stewing meat, cubed
2 1/4 cups tomato juice
10 1/2-oz. can consomme
1 cup chopped celery
2 cups sliced carrots
4 Tbsp. quick-cooking tapioca
1 medium onion, chopped
3/4 tsp. salt
1/4 tsp. pepper

1. Combine all ingredients in slow cooker.
2. Cover. Cook on Low 7-8 hours. (Do not peek.)

Beef Stew with Vegetables

Joyce B. Suiter
Garysburg, NC

Makes 8 servings

3 lbs. stewing beef, cubed
1 cup water
1 cup red wine
1.2-oz. envelope beef-mushroom soup mix
2 cups diced potatoes
1 cup thinly sliced carrots
10-oz. pkg. frozen peas and onions

1. Layer all ingredients in order in slow cooker.
2. Cover. Cook on Low 8-10 hours.

Note:
You may increase all vegetable quantities with good results!

Becky's Beef Stew

Becky Harder
Monument, CO

Makes 6-8 servings

1 1/2 lbs. beef stewing meat, cubed
2 10-oz. pkgs. frozen vegetables—carrots, corn, peas
4 large potatoes, cubed
1 bay leaf
1 onion, chopped
15-oz. can stewing tomatoes of your choice—Italian, Mexican, *or* regular
8-oz. can tomato sauce
2 Tbsp. Worcestershire sauce
1 tsp. salt
1/4 tsp. pepper

1. Put meat on bottom of slow cooker. Layer frozen vegetables and potatoes over meat.
2. Mix remaining ingredients together in large bowl and pour over other ingredients.
3. Cover. Cook on Low 6-8 hours.

Santa Fe Stew

Jeanne Allen
Rye, CO

Makes 4-6 servings

2 lbs. sirloin, *or* stewing
    meat, cubed
2 Tbsp. oil
1 large onion, diced
2 garlic cloves, minced
1½ cups water
1 Tbsp. dried parsley
    flakes
2 beef bouillon cubes
1 tsp. ground cumin
½ tsp. salt
3 carrots, sliced
14½-oz. can diced
    tomatoes
14½-oz. can green beans,
    drained, *or* 1 lb. frozen
    green beans
14½-oz. can corn, drained,
    or 1 lb. frozen corn
4-oz. can diced green
    chilies
3 zucchini squash, diced,
    optional

1. Brown meat, onion, and
garlic in oil in saucepan until
meat is no longer pink. Place
in slow cooker.
2. Stir in remaining ingredients.
3. Cover. Cook on High 30
minutes. Reduce heat to Low
and cook 4-6 hours.

Gone All-Day Casserole

Beatrice Orgish
Richardson, TX

Makes 12 servings

1 cup uncooked wild rice,
    rinsed and drained
1 cup chopped celery
1 cup chopped carrots
2 4-oz. cans mushrooms,
    stems and pieces,
    drained
1 large onion, chopped
1 clove garlic, minced
½ cup slivered almonds
3 beef bouillon cubes
2½ tsp. seasoned salt
2-lb. boneless round steak,
    cut into 1-inch cubes
3 cups water

1. Please ingredients in
order listed in slow cooker.
2. Cover. Cook on Low 6-8
hours or until rice is tender.
Stir before serving.

Variations:
1. Brown beef in saucepan
in 2 Tbsp. oil before putting
in slow cooker for deeper flavor.
2. Add a bay leaf and 4-6
whole peppercorns to mix-
ture before cooking. Remove
before serving.
3. Substitute chicken legs
and thighs (skin removed) for
beef.

Sweet-Sour Beef and Vegetables

Jo Haberkamp
Fairbank, IA

Makes 6 servings

2 lbs. round steak, cut in
    1-inch cubes
2 Tbsp. oil
2 8-oz. cans tomato sauce
2 tsp. chili powder
2 cups sliced carrots
2 cups small white onions
1 tsp. paprika
¼ cup sugar
1 tsp. salt
⅓ cup vinegar
½ cup light molasses
1 large green pepper, cut in
    1-inch pieces

1. Brown steak in oil in
saucepan.
2. Combine all ingredients
in slow cooker.
3. Cover. Cook on High 4-6
hours.

Irish Beef Stew

Teena Wagner
Waterloo, ON

Makes 4-6 servings

2 lbs. stewing beef, cubed
1 envelope dry onion soup mix
2 10¾-oz. cans tomato soup
1 soup can water
1 tsp. salt
½ tsp. pepper
2 cups diced carrots
2 cups diced potatoes
1-lb. package frozen peas
¼ cup water

1. Place beef, onion soup, tomato soup, soup can of water, salt, pepper, carrots, and potatoes in slow cooker.
2. Cover. Cook on Low 8 hours.
3. Add peas and ¼ cup water. Cover. Cook on Low 1 more hour.

Slow Cooker Stew

Ruth Shank
Gridley, IL

Makes 8-10 servings

3-4-lb. beef round steak, *or* beef roast, cubed
⅓ cup flour
1 tsp. salt
½ tsp. pepper
3 carrots, sliced
1-2 medium onions, cut into wedges
4-6 medium potatoes, cubed
4-oz. can sliced mushrooms, drained
10-oz. pkg. frozen mixed vegetables
10½-oz. can condensed beef broth
½ cup water
2 tsp. brown sugar
14½-oz. can, *or* 1 pint, tomato wedges with juice
¼ cup flour
¼ cup water

1. Toss beef cubes with ⅓ cup flour, salt, and pepper in slow cooker.
2. Combine all vegetables except tomatoes. Add to meat.
3. Combine beef broth, ½ cup water, and brown sugar. Pour over meat and vegetables. Add tomatoes and stir carefully.
4. Cover. Cook on Low 10-14 hours, or on High 4-5½ hours.
5. One hour before serving, mix together ¼ cup flour and ¼ cup water. Stir into slow cooker. Turn to High. Cover and cook remaining time.

Note:
For better color add half of the frozen vegetables (partly thawed) during the last hour.

Full-Flavored Beef Stew

Stacy Petersheim
Mechanicsburg, PA

Makes 6 servings

2-lb. beef roast, cubed
2 cups sliced carrots
2 cups diced potatoes
1 medium onion, sliced
1½ cups peas
2 tsp. quick-cooking tapioca
1 Tbsp. salt
½ tsp. pepper
8-oz. can tomato sauce
1 cup water
1 Tbsp. brown sugar

1. Combine beef and vegetables in slow cooker. Sprinkle with tapioca, salt, and pepper.
2. Combine tomato sauce and water. Pour over ingredients in slow cooker. Sprinkle with brown sugar.
3. Cover. Cook on Low 8 hours.

Variation:
Add peas one hour before cooking time ends to keep their color and flavor.

Lazy Day Stew

Ruth Ann Gingrich
New Holland, PA

Makes 8 servings

2 lbs. stewing beef, cubed
2 cups diced carrots
2 cups diced potatoes
2 medium onions, chopped
1 cup chopped celery
10-oz. pkg. lima beans
2 tsp. quick-cooking
  tapioca
1 tsp. salt
1/2 tsp. pepper
8-oz. can tomato sauce
1 cup water
1 Tbsp. brown sugar

1. Place beef in bottom of slow cooker. Add vegetables.
2. Sprinkle tapioca, salt, and pepper over ingredients.
3. Mix together tomato sauce and water. Pour over top.
4. Sprinkle brown sugar over all.
5. Cover. Cook on Low 8 hours.

Variation:
Instead of lima beans, use 1 1/2 cups green beans.
  Rose M. Hoffman
  Schuylkill Haven, PA

Beef with Mushrooms

Doris Perkins
Mashpee, MA

Makes 4-6 servings

1 1/2 lbs. stewing beef,
  cubed
4-oz. can mushroom
  pieces, drained (save
  liquid)
half a garlic clove, minced
3/4 cup sliced onions
3 Tbsp. shortening
1 beef bouillon cube
1 cup hot water
8-oz. can tomato sauce
2 tsp. sugar
2 tsp. Worcestershire sauce
1 tsp. dried basil
1 tsp. dried oregano
1/2 tsp. salt
1/8 tsp. pepper

1. Brown meat, mushrooms, garlic, and onions in shortening in skillet.
2. Dissolve bouillon cube in hot water. Add to meat mixture.
3. Stir in mushroom liquid and rest of ingredients. Mix well. Pour into slow cooker.
4. Cover. Cook on High 3 hours, or until meat is tender.
5. Serve over cooked noodles, spaghetti, or rice.

Easy Company Beef

Joyce B. Suiter
Garysburg, NC

Makes 8 servings

3 lbs. stewing beef, cubed
10 3/4-oz. can cream of
  mushroom soup
7-oz. jar mushrooms,
  undrained
1/2 cup red wine
1 envelope dry onion soup
  mix

1. Combine all ingredients in slow cooker.
2. Cover. Cook on Low 10 hours.
3. Serve over noodles, rice, or pasta.

To get the best flavor, saute vegetables or brown meat before placing in cooker to cook.
  Connie Johnson
  Loudon, NH

Beef Pot Roast
Alexa Slonin
Harrisonburg, VA

Makes 8-10 servings

12 oz. whole tiny new
potatoes, *or* 2 medium
potatoes, cubed, *or*
2 medium sweet
potatoes, cubed
8 small carrots, cut in
small chunks
2 small onions, cut in
wedges
2 ribs celery, cut up
2½-3 lb. beef chuck, *or* pot
roast
2 Tbsp. cooking oil
¾ cup water, dry wine, *or*
tomato juice
1 Tbsp. Worcestershire
sauce
1 tsp. instant beef bouillon
granules
1 tsp. dried basil

1. Place vegetables in bottom of slow cooker.
2. Brown roast in oil in skillet. Place on top of vegetables.
3. Combine water, Worcestershire sauce, bouillon, and basil. Pour over meat and vegetables.
4. Cover. Cook on Low 10-12 hours.

Easy Pot Roast and Veggies
Tina Houk, Clinton, MO
Arlene Wiens, Newton, KS

Makes 6 servings

3-4-lb. chuck roast
4 medium-sized potatoes,
cubed
4 medium-sized carrots,
sliced, *or* 1 lb. baby
carrots
2 celery ribs, sliced thin,
optional
1 envelope dry onion soup
mix
3 cups water

1. Put roast, potatoes, carrots, and celery in slow cooker.
2. Add onion soup mix and water.
3. Cover. Cook on Low 6-8 hours.

Variations:
1. To add flavor to the broth, stir 1 tsp. kitchen bouquet, ½ tsp. salt, ½ tsp. black pepper, and ½ tsp. garlic powder into water before pouring over meat and vegetables.
Bonita Ensenberger
Albuquerque, NM

2. Before putting roast in cooker, sprinkle it with the dry soup mix, patting it on so it adheres.
Betty Lahman
Elkton, VA

3. Add one bay leaf and 2 cloves minced garlic to Step 2.
Susan Tjon
Austin, TX

Pot Roast
Janet L. Roggie
Linville, NY

Makes 6-8 servings

3 potatoes, thinly sliced
2 large carrots, thinly
sliced
1 onion, thinly sliced
1 tsp. salt
½ tsp. pepper
3-4-lb. pot roast
½ cup water

1. Put vegetables in bottom of slow cooker. Stir in salt and pepper. Add roast. Pour in water.
2. Cover. Cook on Low 10-12 hours.

Variations:
1. Add ½ tsp. dried dill, a bay leaf, and ½ tsp. dried rosemary for more flavor.
2. Brown roast on all sides in saucepan in 2 Tbsp. oil before placing in cooker.
Debbie Zeida
Mashpee, MA

Easy Roast

Lisa Warren
Parkesburg, PA

Makes 6-8 servings

3-4-lb. beef roast
1 envelope dry onion soup
   mix
14 1/2-oz. can stewed
   tomatoes, *or* seasoned
   tomatoes

1. Place roast in slow
cooker. Cover with onion
soup and tomatoes.
2. Cover. Cook on Low 8
hours.

Hearty Beef Stew

Lovina Baer
Conrath, WI

Makes 4-6 servings

2-lb. round steak
4 large potatoes, cubed
2 large carrots, sliced
2 ribs celery, sliced
1 medium onion, chopped
1 qt. tomato juice
1 Tbsp. Worcestershire
   sauce
2 tsp. salt
1/2 tsp. pepper
1/4 cup sugar
1 Tbsp. clear jel

1. Combine meat, pota-
toes, carrots, celery, and
onion in slow cooker.
2. Combine tomato juice,
Worcestershire sauce, salt,
and pepper. Pour into slow
cooker.
3. Mix together sugar and
clear jel. Add to remaining
ingredients, stirring well.
4. Cover. Cook on High 6-7
hours.

Variation:

Instead of clear jel, use 1/4
cup instant tapioca.

Virginia's
Beef Stew

Virginia Bender
Dover, DE

Makes 6 servings

3 lbs. boneless beef
1 envelope dry onion soup
28-oz. can diced tomatoes,
   undrained
1 Tbsp. minute tapioca
4-5 potatoes, cubed
1 onion, chopped
6 carrots, sliced
1 tsp. sugar
1 Tbsp. salt
1/2 tsp. pepper

1. Combine all ingredients
in slow cooker.
2. Cover. Bake on High 5
hours.

Variation:

Add 2 cups frozen peas
during last 10 minutes of
cooking.

Rump Roast and
Vegetables

Kimberlee Greenawalt
Harrisonburg, VA

Makes 6-8 servings

1 1/2 lbs. small potatoes
   (about 10), *or* medium
   potatoes (about 4),
   halved
2 medium carrots, cubed
1 small onion, sliced
10-oz. pkg. frozen lima
   beans
1 bay leaf
2 Tbsp. quick-cooking
   tapioca
2-2 1/2-lb. boneless beef
   round rump, round tip,
   or pot roast
2 Tbsp. oil
10 3/4-oz. can condensed
   vegetable beef soup
1/4 cup water
1/4 tsp. pepper

1. Place potatoes, carrots,
and onion in slow cooker.
Add frozen beans and bay
leaf. Sprinkle with tapioca.
2. Brown roast on all sides
in oil in skillet. Place over
vegetables in slow cooker.
3. Combine soup, water,
and pepper. Pour over roast.
4. Cover. Cook on Low 10-
12 hours, or High 5-6 hours.
5. Discard bay leaf before
serving.

Hearty New England Dinner

Joette Droz
Kalona, IA

Makes 6-8 servings

2 medium carrots, sliced
1 medium onion, sliced
1 celery rib, sliced
3-lb. boneless chuck roast
1/2 tsp. salt
1/4 tsp. pepper
1 envelope dry onion soup mix
2 cups water
1 Tbsp. vinegar
1 bay leaf
half a small head of cabbage, cut in wedges
3 Tbsp. melted margarine, *or* butter
2 Tbsp. flour
1 Tbsp. dried minced onion
2 Tbsp. prepared horseradish
1/2 tsp. salt

1. Place carrots, onion, and celery in slow cooker. Place roast on top. Sprinkle with 1/2 tsp. salt and pepper. Add soup mix, water, vinegar, and bay leaf.
2. Cover. Cook on Low 7-9 hours. Remove beef and keep warm. Just before serving, cut into pieces or thin slices.
3. Discard bay leaf. Add cabbage to juice in slow cooker.
4. Cover. Cook on High 1 hour, or until cabbage is tender.

5. Melt margarine in saucepan. Stir in flour and onion. Add 1 1/2 cups liquid from slow cooker. Stir in horseradish and 1/2 tsp. salt. Bring to boil. Cook over low heat until thick and smooth, about 2 minutes. Return to cooker and blend with remaining sauce in cooker. When blended, serve over or alongside meat and vegetables.

Easy Beef Stew

Connie Johnson
Loudon, NH

Makes 6 servings

1 lb. stewing beef
1 cup cubed turnip
2 medium potatoes, cubed
1 large onion, sliced
1 garlic clove, minced
2 large carrots, sliced
1/2 cup green beans, cut up
1/2 cup peas
1 bay leaf
1/2 tsp. dried thyme
1 tsp. chopped parsley
2 Tbsp. tomato paste
2 Tbsp. celery leaves
1/2 tsp. salt
1/4 tsp. pepper
1 qt., *or* 2 14 1/2-oz. cans, beef broth

1. Place meat, vegetables, and seasonings in slow cooker. Pour broth over all.
2. Cover. Cook on Low 6-8 hours.

Pot Roast

Julie McKenzie
Punxsutawney, PA

Makes 8 servings

3-lb. rump roast
1/2 envelope dry onion soup mix
1 small onion, sliced
4-oz. can mushrooms with liquid
1/3 cup dry red wine
1/3 cup water
1 garlic clove, minced
1 bay leaf
1/2 tsp. dried thyme
2 Tbsp. chopped fresh basil, *or* 1 tsp. dried basil

1. Combine all ingredients in slow cooker.
2. Cover. Cook on Low 10-12 hours.

Variations:
1. Add 1/2 tsp. salt, if desired.
2. Mix 3 Tbsp. cornstarch into 1/2 cup cold water. At the end of the cooking time remove bay leaf and discard. Remove meat to serving platter and keep warm. Stir dissolved cornstarch into hot liquid in slow cooker. Stir until absorbed. Cover and cook on High 10 minutes, until sauce thickens. Serve over top or alongside sliced meat.

Pot Roast with Gravy and Vegetables

Irene Klaeger, Inverness, FL
Jan Pembleton, Arlington, TX

Makes 4-6 servings

3-4-lb. bottom round, rump, *or* arm roast
2-3 tsp. salt
1/2 tsp. pepper
2 Tbsp. flour
1/4 cup cold water
1 tsp. kitchen bouquet, *or* gravy browning seasoning sauce
1 garlic clove, minced
2 medium onions, cut in wedges
4-6 medium potatoes, cubed
2-4 carrots, quartered
1 green pepper, sliced

1. Place roast in slow cooker. Sprinkle with salt and pepper.
2. Make paste of flour and cold water. Stir in kitchen bouquet and spread over roast.
3. Add garlic, onions, potatoes, carrots, and green pepper.
4. Cover. Cook on Low 8-10 hours, or High 4-5 hours.
5. Taste and adjust seasonings before serving.

Round Steak Casserole

Cheryl Bartel, Hillsboro, KS
Barbara Walker, Sturgis, SD

Makes 4-6 servings

2-lb. 1/2"-thick round steak
1/2 tsp. garlic salt
1 tsp. salt
1/4-1/2 tsp. pepper
1 onion, thinly sliced
3-4 potatoes, quartered
3-4 carrots, sliced
14 1/2-oz. can French-style green beans, drained, *or* 1 lb. frozen green beans
10 3/4-oz. can tomato soup
14 1/2-oz. can stewed tomatoes

1. Cut meat into serving-size pieces, place in slow cooker, stir in seasonings, and mix well.
2. Add potatoes, carrots, and green beans. Top with soup and tomatoes.
3. Cover. Cook on High 1 hour. Reduce heat to Low and cook 8 hours, or until done. Remove cover during last half hour if there is too much liquid.

"Smothered" Steak

Susan Yoder Graber
Eureka, IL

Makes 6 servings

1 1/2-lb. chuck, *or* round, steak, cut into strips
1/3 cup flour
1/2 tsp. salt
1/4 tsp. pepper
1 large onion, sliced
1-2 green peppers, sliced
14 1/2-oz. can stewed tomatoes
4-oz. can mushrooms, drained
2 Tbsp. soy sauce
10-oz. pkg. frozen French-style green beans

1. Layer steak in bottom of slow cooker. Sprinkle with flour, salt, and pepper. Stir well to coat steak.
2. Add remaining ingredients. Mix together gently.
3. Cover. Cook on Low 8 hours.
4. Serve over rice.

Variations:
1. Use 8-oz. can tomato sauce instead of stewed tomatoes.
2. Substitute 1 Tbsp. Worcestershire sauce in place of soy sauce.

Mary E. Martin
Goshen, IN

Veal and Peppers

Irma H. Schoen
Windsor, CT

Makes 4 servings

1 1/2 lbs. boneless veal,
cubed
3 green peppers, quartered
2 onions, thinly sliced
1/2 lb. fresh mushrooms,
sliced
1 tsp. salt
1/2 tsp. dried basil
2 cloves garlic, minced
28-oz. can tomatoes

1. Combine all ingredients
in slow cooker.
2. Cover. Cook on Low 7
hours, or on High 4 hours.
3. Serve over rice or noodles.

Variation:

Use boneless, skinless
chicken breast, cut into
chunks, instead of veal.

Beef and Beans

Robin Schrock
Millersburg, OH

Makes 8 servings

1 Tbsp. prepared mustard
1 Tbsp. chili powder
1/2 tsp. salt
1/4 tsp. pepper
1 1/2-lb. boneless round
steak, cut into thin
slices
2 14 1/2-oz. cans diced
tomatoes, undrained
1 medium onion, chopped
1 beef bouillon cube,
crushed
16-oz. can kidney beans,
rinsed and drained

1. Combine mustard, chili
powder, salt, and pepper. Add
beef slices and toss to coat.
Place meat in slow cooker.
2. Add tomatoes, onion,
and bouillon.
3. Cover. Cook on Low 6-8
hours.
4. Stir in beans. Cook 30
minutes longer.
5. Serve over rice.

Roast with Veggies

Arlene Wengerd
Millersburg, OH

Makes 6 servings

2-lb. roast, partially
thawed
1 medium onion, sliced
1 pint tomato juice
1 tsp. salt
1 tsp. black pepper
1 tsp. dried marjoram
4-5 medium potatoes, cut
in thick slices
4-5 carrots, sliced
dash of white vinegar
10 3/4-oz. can golden cream
of mushroom soup

1. Place roast in slow
cooker. Arrange onions on
top.
2. Carefully pour tomato
juice over top. Sprinkle with
spices.
3. Cover. Cook on High 5
hours.
4. Drain juice from roast
into bowl. Pull roast apart
into bite-sized pieces. Return
meat to slow cooker.
5. Partially cook potatoes
and carrots in saucepan in
boiling water with a dash of
white vinegar. (The white
vinegar gives vegetables a
bright color.) Layer veggies on
top of roast.
6. Pour soup over all.
Cover and cook on High
1 more hour.

Fresh vegetables take longer to cook than meats, because,
in a slow cooker, liquid simmers rather than boils.
Remember this if you've adapted range-top recipes to slow
cooking.

Beatrice Orgish
Richardson, TX

89

Round Steak

Janet V. Yocum
Elizabethtown, PA

Makes 4 servings

2-lb. round steak, cut into serving-size chunks
1 onion, chopped
4 ribs celery, chopped
4 carrots, chopped
4 potatoes, cut into bite-sized pieces
2 tsp. salt
1 tsp. seasoning salt
1/2 tsp. pepper
10³/4-oz. can cream of celery, *or* cream of mushroom, soup
water

1. Put steak in bottom of slow cooker.
2. Stir vegetables, seasonings, and soup together in large bowl. Pour over meat.
3. Add water if needed to cover meat and vegetables.
4. Cover. Cook on Low 8 hours.

A slow cooker is perfect for less tender meats such as a round steak. Because the meat is cooked in liquid for hours, it turns out tender and juicy.

Carolyn Baer
Conrath, WI
Barbara Sparks
Glen Burnie, MD

Forget It Pot Roast

Mary Mitchell
Battle Creek, MI

Makes 6 servings

6 potatoes, quartered
6 carrots, sliced
3-3¹/2-lb. chuck roast
1 envelope dry onion soup mix
10³/4-oz. can cream of mushroom soup
2-3 Tbsp. flour
1/4 cup cold water

1. Place potatoes and carrots in slow cooker. Add meat. Top with soups.
2. Cover. Cook on Low 8-9 hours.
3. To make gravy, remove meat and vegetables to serving platter and keep warm. Pour juices into saucepan and bring to boil. Mix 2-3 Tbsp. flour with 1/4 cup cold water until smooth. Stir into juices in pan until thickened. Serve over meat and vegetables, or alongside as a gravy.

Beef Stew Bourguignonne

Jo Haberkamp
Fairbank, IA

Makes 6 servings

2 lbs. stewing beef, cut in 1-inch cubes
2 Tbsp. cooking oil
10³/4-oz. can condensed golden cream of mushroom soup
1 tsp. Worcestershire sauce
1/3 cup dry red wine
1/2 tsp. dried oregano
2 tsp. salt
1/2 tsp. pepper
1/2 cup chopped onions
1/2 cup chopped carrots
4-oz. can mushroom pieces, drained
1/2 cup cold water
1/4 cup flour
noodles, cooked

1. Brown meat in oil in saucepan. Transfer to slow cooker.
2. Mix together soup, Worcestershire sauce, wine, oregano, salt and pepper, onions, carrots, and mushrooms. Pour over meat.
3. Cover. Cook on Low 10-12 hours.
4. Combine water and flour. Stir into beef mixture. Turn cooker to High.
5. Cook and stir until thickened and bubbly.
6. Serve over noodles.

Baked Steak

Shirley Thieszen
Lakin, KS

Makes 6 servings

2 1/2 lbs. round steak, cut
  into 10 pieces
1 Tbsp. salt
1/2 tsp. pepper
oil
1/2 cup chopped onions
1/2 cup chopped green
  peppers
1 cup cream of mushroom
  soup
1/2 cup water

1. Season the steak with
salt and pepper. Brown on
both sides in oil in saucepan.
Place in slow cooker.
2. Stir in onions, green
peppers, mushroom soup,
and water.
3. Cover. Cook on High 1
hour, and then on Low 3-4
hours.

Creamy
Swiss Steak

Jo Ellen Moore
Pendleton, IN

Makes 6 servings

1 1/2-lb. 3/4-inch thick round
  steak
2 Tbsp. flour
1 tsp. salt
1/4 tsp. pepper
1 medium onion, sliced
10 3/4-oz. can cream of
  mushroom soup
1 carrot, chopped
1 small celery rib, chopped

1. Cut steak into serving-
size pieces.
2. Combine flour, salt, and
pepper. Dredge meat in flour.
3. Place onions in bottom
of slow cooker. Add meat.
4. Spread cream of mush-
room soup over meat. Top
with carrots and celery.
5. Cover. Cook on Low 8-
10 hours, or High 3-5 hours.

Saucy Round
Steak Supper

Shirley Sears
Tiskilwa, IL

Makes 6-8 servings

2 lbs. round steak, sliced
  diagonally into 1/8-inch
  strips (reserve meat
  bone)
1/2 cup chopped onions
1/2 cup chopped celery
8-oz. can mushrooms,
  stems and pieces,
  drained (reserve liquid)
1/3 cup French dressing
2 1/2-oz. pkg. sour cream
  sauce mix
1/3 cup water
1 tsp. Worcestershire sauce

1. Place steak and bone in
slow cooker. Add onions, celery, and mushrooms.
2. Combine dressing, sour
cream sauce mix, water,
Worcestershire sauce, and
mushroom liquid. Pour over
mixture in slow cooker.
3. Cover. Cook on Low 8-9
hours.
4. Serve over noodles.

Variation:
Instead of using the sour
cream sauce mix, remove
meat from cooker at end of
cooking time and keep warm.
Stir 1 cup sour cream into
gravy, cover, and cook on
High 10 minutes. Serve over
steak.

Succulent Steak

Betty B. Dennison
Grove City, PA

Makes 4 servings

1½-lb. round steak, cut ½-
¾-inch thick
¼ cup flour
½ tsp. salt
¼ tsp. pepper
¼ tsp. paprika
2 onions, sliced
4-oz. can sliced
mushrooms, drained
½ cup beef broth
2 tsp. Worcestershire sauce
2 Tbsp. flour
3 Tbsp. water

1. Mix together ¼ cup flour, salt, pepper, and paprika.
2. Cut steak into 5-6 pieces. Dredge steak pieces in seasoned flour until lightly coated.
3. Layer half of onions, half of steak, and half of mushrooms into cooker. Repeat.
4. Combine beef broth and Worcestershire sauce. Pour over mixture in slow cooker.
5. Cover. Cook on Low 8-10 hours.
6. Remove steak to serving platter and keep warm. Mix together 2 Tbsp. flour and water. Stir into drippings and cook on High until thickened, about 10 minutes. Pour over steak and serve.

Steak Hi-Hat

Bonita Ensenberger
Albuquerque, NM

Makes 8-10 servings

10¾-oz. can cream of
chicken soup
10¾-oz. can cream of
mushroom soup
1½ Tbsp. Worcestershire
sauce
½ tsp. black pepper
1 tsp. paprika
2 cups onion, chopped
1 garlic clove, minced
1 cup fresh, small button
mushrooms, quartered
2 lbs. round steak, cubed
1 cup sour cream
cooked noodles with
poppy seeds
crisp bacon bits, optional

1. Combine chicken soup, mushroom soup, Worcestershire sauce, pepper, paprika, onion, garlic, and mushrooms in slow cooker.
2. Stir in steak.
3. Cover. Cook on Low 8-9 hours.
4. Stir in sour cream during the last 20-30 minutes.
5. Serve on hot buttered noodles sprinkled with poppy seeds. Garnish with bacon bits.

Variation:
Add 1 tsp. salt with seasonings in Step 1.

Steak Stroganoff

Marie Morucci
Glen Lyon, PA

Makes 6 servings

2 Tbsp. flour
½ tsp. garlic powder
½ tsp. pepper
¼ tsp. paprika
1¾-lb. boneless beef round
steak
10¾-oz. can cream of
mushroom soup
½ cup water
1 envelope dried onion
soup mix
9-oz. jar sliced mushrooms,
drained
½ cup sour cream
1 Tbsp. minced fresh
parsley

1. Combine flour, garlic powder, pepper, and paprika in slow cooker.
2. Cut meat into 1½ x ½-inch strips. Place in flour mixture and toss until meat is well coated.
3. Add mushroom soup, water, and soup mix. Stir until well blended.
4. Cover. Cook on High 3-3½ hours, or Low 6-7 hours.
5. Stir in mushrooms, sour cream, and parsley. Cover and cook on High 10-15 minutes, or until heated through.
6. Serve with rice.

Scrumptious Beef

Julia Lapp
New Holland, PA

Makes 4-8 servings (depending upon amount of beef used)

1-2 lbs. beef, cubed
1/2 lb. mushrooms, sliced
10 1/2-oz. can beef broth, *or*
    1 cup water and
    1 cube beef bouillon
1 onion, chopped
10 3/4-oz. can cream of
    mushroom soup
3 Tbsp. dry onion soup mix

1. Combine all ingredients in slow cooker.
2. Cover. Cook on High 3-4 hours, or on Low 7-8 hours.
3. Serve over hot cooked rice.

Beef Stew with Mushrooms

Dorothy M. Pittman
Pickens, SC

Makes 6 servings

2 lbs. stewing beef, cubed
10 3/4-oz. can cream of
    mushroom soup
4-oz. can mushrooms
1 envelope dry onion soup
    mix
1/2 tsp. salt
1/4 tsp. pepper
half a soup can of water

1. Sprinkle bottom of greased slow cooker with one-fourth of dry soup mix. Layer in meat, mushroom soup, canned mushrooms, and remaining dry onion soup mix. Pour water over.
2. Cover. Cook on Low 8 hours, or High 4 hours.
3. Serve over potatoes, rice, or noodles.

Good 'n Easy Beef 'n Gravy

Janice Crist
Quinter, KS

Makes 8 servings

3-lb. beef roast, cubed
1 envelope dry onion soup
    mix
1/2 cup beef broth
10 3/4-oz. can cream of
    mushroom, *or* cream of
    celery, soup
4-oz. can sliced
    mushrooms, drained

1. Combine all ingredients in slow cooker.
2. Cover. Cook on Low 10-12 hours.

Variation:
Use 1/2 cup sauterne instead of beef broth.
    Joyce Shackelford
    Green Bay, WI

Elaine's Beef Stroganoff

Elaine Unruh
Minneapolis, MN

Makes 4 servings

1-lb. round steak, cubed
1 Tbsp. shortening
1/2 cup chopped onions
1/2 cup chopped celery
10 3/4-oz. can cream of
    celery soup
4-oz. can mushroom
    pieces, drained
1 cup sour cream
1/4 tsp. garlic salt

1. Brown meat in shortening in saucepan. Add onions and celery and saute until just tender.
2. Combine all ingredients in slow cooker.
3. Cover. Cook on Low 6-8 hours.
4. Serve over hot cooked noodles.

Easy Dinner Surprise

Nancy Graves
Manhattan, KS

Makes 4-5 servings

1-1½ lbs. stewing meat, cubed
10¾-oz. can cream of mushroom soup
10¾-oz. can cream of celery soup
1 pkg. dry onion soup mix
4-oz. can mushroom pieces

1. Combine all ingredients in slow cooker.
2. Cover. Cook on Low 8-10 hours.
3. Serve over rice or baked potatoes.

Variation:
Add ¼ cup finely chopped celery for color and texture.

Delicious, Easy Chuck Roast

Mary Jane Musser
Manheim, PA

Makes 4-8 servings

2-4-lb. chuck roast
salt to taste
pepper to taste
1 onion, sliced
10¾-oz. can cream of mushroom soup

1. Season roast with salt and pepper and place in slow cooker.
2. Add onion. Pour soup over all.
3. Cover. Cook on Low 8-10 hours, or on High 6 hours.

Creamy Swiss Steak

Connie B. Weaver
Bethlehem, PA

Makes 4-6 servings

2 lbs. round, *or* Swiss steak, cut ¾-inch thick
salt to taste
pepper to taste
1 large onion, thinly sliced
10¾-oz. can cream of mushroom soup
½ cup water

1. Cut steak into serving-size pieces. Season with salt and pepper. Place in slow cooker. Layer onion over steak.
2. Combine soup and water. Pour into slow cooker.
3. Cover. Cook on Low 8-10 hours.
4. Serve over noodles or rice.

Dale & Shari's Beef Stroganoff

Dale and Shari Mast
Harrisonburg, VA

Makes 4 servings

4 cups beef cubes
10¾-oz. can cream of mushroom soup
1 cup sour cream

1. Place beef in slow cooker. Cover with mushroom soup.
2. Cover. Cook on Low 8 hours, or High 4-5 hours.
3. Before serving stir in sour cream.
4. Serve over cooked rice, pasta, or baked potatoes.

Round Steak

Dorothy Hess, Willow Street, PA
Betty A. Holt, St. Charles, MO
Betty Moore, Plano, IL
Michelle Strite,
Harrisonburg, VA
Barbara Tenney, Delta, PA
Sharon Timpe, Mequon, WI

Makes 4-5 servings

2-lb. boneless round steak
oil
1 envelope dry onion soup
  mix
10³/4-oz. can cream of
  mushroom soup
1/2 cup water

1. Cut steak into serving-size pieces. Brown in oil in saucepan. Place in slow cooker. Sprinkle with soup mix.
2. Combine soup and water. Pour over meat.
3. Cover. Cook on Low 7-8 hours.

Variation:
To make a dish lower in sodium, replace the onion soup mix and mushroom soup with 1 cup diced onions, 1/2 lb. sliced mushrooms, 1 Tbsp. fresh parsley, 1/4 tsp. pepper, 1/2 tsp. dried basil, all stirred gently together. Place on top of meat in cooker. Dissolve 2 Tbsp. flour in 3/4 cup cold water. Pour over vegetables and meat. Mix together. Cover and cook according to directions above.
Della Yoder
Kalona, IA

Pot Roast with Creamy Mushroom Sauce

Colleen Konetzni
Rio Rancho, NM
Janet V. Yocum
Elizabethtown, PA

Makes 6-8 servings

2-2¹/2-lb. boneless beef
  chuck roast
1 envelope dry onion soup
  mix
10³/4-oz. can condensed
  cream of mushroom
  soup

1. Place roast in slow cooker. Sprinkle with dry soup mix. Top with mushroom soup.
2. Cover. Cook on High 1 hour, and then on Low 8 hours, or until meat is tender.
3. Slice. Serve with mashed potatoes or cooked noodles.

Variation:
Add cubed potatoes and sliced carrots to beef. Proceed with directions above.
Marla Folkert
Holland, OH

Slow Cooker Beef

Sara Harter Fredette
Williamsburg, MA

Makes 4-6 servings

1/2 cup flour
2 tsp. salt
1/4 tsp. pepper
2-3 lbs. stewing beef,
  cubed
2 Tbsp. oil
10³/4-oz. can cream of
  mushroom soup
1 envelope dry onion soup
  mix
1/2 cup sour cream

1. Combine flour, salt, and pepper in plastic bag. Add beef in small batches. Shake to coat beef. Saute beef in oil in saucepan. Place browned beef in slow cooker.
2. Stir in mushroom soup and onion soup mix.
3. Cover. Cook on Low 6-8 hours.
4. Stir in sour cream before serving. Heat for a few minutes.
5. Serve with noodles or mashed potatoes.

> For a juicy beef roast to be ready by noon, put a roast in the slow cooker in the evening and let it on all night on Low.
> **Ruth Hershey**
> Paradise, PA

Paul's Beef Bourguignon

Janice Muller
Derwood, MD

Makes 4 servings

3-lb. chuck roast, cubed
2 Tbsp. oil
2 10¾-oz. cans golden cream of mushroom soup
1 envelope dry onion soup mix
1 cup cooking sherry

1. Brown meat in oil in skillet. Drain. Place in slow cooker. Add remaining ingredients and cover.
2. Refrigerate 6-8 hours, or up to 14 hours, to marinate.
3. Remove from refrigerator, cover, and cook on Low 8-10 hours.
4. Serve over cooked egg noodles or rice.

Beef Pot Roast

Julia B. Boyd
Memphis, TN

Makes 6-8 servings

3-4-lb. chuck, *or* English-cut, beef roast
1 envelope dry onion-mushroom soup mix
10¾-oz. can cream of celery soup
1 soup can water
2-3 Tbsp. flour
2-3 beef bouillon cubes
1 medium onion, chopped

1. Combine all ingredients in slow cooker.
2. Cover. Cook on Low 10-12 hours.

Variations:
Use leftover meat to make soup. Add one large can tomatoes and any leftover vegetables you have on hand. Add spices such as minced onion, garlic powder, basil, bay leaf, celery seed. To increase the liquid, use V-8 juice and season with 1-2 tablespoons butter for a richer soup base. Cook on Low 6-12 hours. If you wish, stir in cooked macaroni or rice just before serving.

Chuck Roast

Hazel L. Propst
Oxford, PA

Makes 6-8 servings

4-5-lb. boneless chuck roast
⅓ cup flour
3 Tbsp. oil
1 envelope dry onion soup mix
water
¼ cup flour
⅓ cup cold water

1. Rub roast with flour on both sides. Brown in oil in saucepan. Place in slow cooker (cutting to fit if necessary).
2. Sprinkle dry soup mix over roast. Add water to cover roast.
3. Cover. Cook on Low 8 hours.
4. Stir flour into ⅓ cup cold water until smooth. Remove roast to serving platter and keep warm. Stir paste into hot sauce and stir until dissolved. Cover and cook on High until sauce is thickened.

For more flavorful gravy, first brown the meat in a skillet. Scrape all browned bits from the bottom of the skillet and add to the slow cooker along with the meat.
Carolyn Baer
Conrath, WI

Roast Beef

Judy Buller
Bluffton, OH

Makes 6 servings

2 1/2-3-lb. bottom round
   roast
2 cups water
2 beef bouillon cubes
1/2 tsp. cracked pepper
1/4 cup flour
1/2 tsp. salt
3/4 cup cold water

1. Cut roast into 6-8 pieces and place in slow cooker. Add water and bouillon cubes. Sprinkle with pepper.

2. Cover. Cook on High 2 hours. Reduce heat to Low and cook 4-5 hours, or until meat is tender.

3. Dissolve flour and salt in cold water. Remove roast from cooker and keep warm. Stir flour paste into hot broth in cooker until smooth. Cover and cook on High for 5 minutes. Serve gravy with sliced roast beef.

Roast

Tracey Yohn
Harrisburg, PA

Makes 6 servings

2-3-lb. shoulder roast
1 tsp. salt
1 tsp. pepper
1 tsp. garlic salt
1 small onion, sliced in
   rings
1 cup boiling water
1 beef bouillon cube

1. Place roast in slow cooker. Sprinkle with salt, pepper, and garlic salt. Place onion rings on top.

2. Dissolve bouillon cube in water. Pour over roast.

3. Cover. Cook on Low 10-12 hours, or on High 5-6 hours.

Savory Sweet Roast

Martha Ann Auker
Landisburg, PA

Makes 6-8 servings

3-4-lb. blade, *or* chuck,
   roast
oil
1 onion, chopped
10 3/4-oz. can cream of
   mushroom soup
1/2 cup water
1/4 cup sugar
1/4 cup vinegar
2 tsp. salt
1 tsp. prepared mustard
1 tsp. Worcestershire sauce

1. Brown meat in oil on both sides in saucepan. Put in slow cooker.

2. Blend together remaining ingredients. Pour over meat.

3. Cover. Cook on Low 12-16 hours.

Hungarian Goulash

Kim Stoltzfus
New Holland, PA

Makes 8 servings

2-lb. round steak, cubed
1/2 tsp. onion powder
1/2 tsp. garlic powder
2 Tbsp. flour
1/2 tsp. salt
1/2 tsp. pepper
1 1/2 tsp. paprika
10 3/4-oz. can tomato soup
1/2 soup can water
1 cup sour cream

1. Mix meat, onion powder, garlic powder, and flour together in slow cooker until meat is well coated.
2. Add remaining ingredients, except sour cream. Stir well.
3. Cover. Cook on Low 8-10 hours, or High 4-5 hours.
4. Add sour cream 30 minutes before serving.
5. Serve over hot noodles.

Dilled Pot Roast

C.J. Slagle
Roann, IN

Makes 6 servings

3-3 1/2-lb. beef pot roast
1 tsp. salt
1/4 tsp. pepper
2 tsp. dried dillweed, divided
1/4 cup water
1 Tbsp. vinegar
3 Tbsp. flour
1/2 cup water
1 cup sour cream

1. Sprinkle both sides of meat with salt, pepper, and 1 tsp. dill. Place in slow cooker. Add water and vinegar.
2. Cover. Cook on Low 7-9 hours, or until tender. Remove meat from pot. Turn to High.
3. Dissolve flour in water. Stir into meat drippings. Stir in additional 1 tsp. dill. Cook on High 5 minutes. Stir in sour cream. Cook on High another 5 minutes.
4. Slice meat and serve with sour cream sauce over top.

Herbed Roast with Gravy

Sue Williams
Gulfport, MS

Makes 8-10 servings

4-lb. roast
2 tsp. salt
1/2 tsp. pepper
2 medium onions, sliced
half a can (10 3/4-oz.) condensed cheddar cheese soup
8-oz. can tomato sauce
4-oz. can mushroom pieces and stems, drained
1/4 tsp. dried basil
1/4 tsp. dried oregano

1. Season roast with salt and pepper. Place in slow cooker.
2. Combine remaining ingredients and pour over meat.
3. Cover. Cook on Low 8-10 hours, or on High 4-5 hours.
4. Serve with gravy.

Beef Burgundy

Jacqueline Stefl
East Bethany, NY

Makes 6 servings

5 medium onions, thinly
   sliced
2 lbs. stewing meat, cubed
1½ Tbsp. flour
½ lb. fresh mushrooms,
   sliced
1 tsp. salt
¼ tsp. dried marjoram
¼ tsp. dried thyme
⅛ tsp. pepper
¾ cup beef broth
1½ cups burgundy wine

1. Place onions in slow
cooker.
2. Dredge meat in flour.
Put in slow cooker.
3. Add mushrooms, salt,
marjoram, thyme, and pep-
per.
4. Pour in broth and wine.
5. Cover. Cook 8-10 hours
on Low.
6. Serve over cooked noo-
dles.

Goodtime
Beef Brisket

AmyMarlene Jensen
Fountain, CO

Makes 6-8 servings

3½-4-lb. beef brisket
1 can beer
2 cups tomato sauce
2 tsp. prepared mustard
2 Tbsp. balsamic vinegar
2 Tbsp. Worcestershire
   sauce
1 tsp. garlic powder
½ tsp. ground allspice
2 Tbsp. brown sugar
1 small green, *or* red, bell
   pepper, chopped
1 medium onion, chopped
1 tsp. salt
½ tsp. pepper

1. Place brisket in slow
cooker.
2. Combine remaining
ingredients. Pour over meat.
3. Cover. Cook on Low 8-
10 hours.
4. Remove meat from
sauce. Slice very thin.
5. Serve on rolls or over
couscous.

Pot Roast

Judi Manos
West Islip, NY

Makes 8 servings

4-lb. chuck roast *or* stewing
   meat, cubed
1 Tbsp. oil
¾ can beer
½ cup, plus 1 Tbsp.,
   ketchup
1 onion, sliced
½ cup cold water
1½ Tbsp. flour

1. Brown meat in oil in
saucepan.
2. Combine beer and
ketchup in slow cooker. Stir
in onion and browned meat.
3. Cover. Cook on Low 8
hours.
4. Remove meat and keep
warm. Blend flour into cold
water until dissolved. Stir into
hot gravy until smooth.
5. Serve gravy and meat
together.

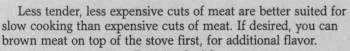

Less tender, less expensive cuts of meat are better suited for
slow cooking than expensive cuts of meat. If desired, you can
brown meat on top of the stove first, for additional flavor.
Beatrice Orgish
Richardson, TX

Italian Beef
Joyce Bowman
Lady Lake, FL

Makes 10-12 servings

**3-4-lb. beef roast
1 pkg. dry Italian dressing
mix
12-oz. can beer**

1. Place roast in slow cooker. Sprinkle with dry Italian dressing mix. Pour beer over roast.
2. Cover. Cook on Low 8-10 hours, or High 3-4 hours.
3. When beef is done, shred and serve with juice on crusty rolls.

Variations:
In place of beef, use pork chops or chicken legs and thighs (skin removed).

Slow-Cooker Roast Beef
Ernestine Schrepfer
Trenton, MO

Makes 6 servings

**3-lb. sirloin tip roast
1/2 cup flour
1 envelope dry onion soup
mix
1 envelope brown gravy
mix
2 cups ginger ale**

1. Coat roast with flour (reserve remaining flour). Place in slow cooker.
2. Combine soup mix, gravy mix, remaining flour, and ginger ale in bowl. Mix well. Pour over roast.
3. Cover. Cook on Low 8-10 hours.

Pepsi Pot Roast
Mrs. Don Martins
Fairbank, IA

Makes 6-8 servings

**3-4-lb. pot roast
10¾-oz. can cream of
mushroom soup
1 envelope dry onion soup
mix
16-oz. bottle Pepsi, *or*
other cola**

1. Place meat in slow cooker.
2. Top with mushroom soup and onion soup mix. Pour in Pepsi.
3. Cover. Cook on High 6 hours.

Cola Roast
Janice Yoskovich
Carmichaels, PA

Makes 8-10 servings

**3-lb. beef roast
1 envelope dry onion soup
mix
2 cans cola**

1. Place roast in slow cooker. Sprinkle with soup mix. Pour soda over all.
2. Cover. Cook on Low 7-8 hours.

Note:
Diet cola does not work with this recipe.

Zippy Beef Tips
Maryann Westerberg
Rosamond, CA

Makes 6-8 servings

**2 lbs. stewing meat, cubed
2 cups sliced fresh
mushrooms
10¾-oz. can cream of
mushroom soup
1 envelope dry onion soup
mix
1 cup 7-Up, *or* other
lemon-lime carbonated
drink**

1. Place meat and mushrooms in slow cooker.

2. Combine mushroom soup, soup mix, and soda. Pour over meat.

3. Cover. Cook on Low 8 hours.

4. Serve over rice.

Hungarian Goulash

Audrey Romonosky
Austin, TX

Makes 5-6 servings

2 lbs. beef chuck, cubed
1 onion, sliced
1/2 tsp. garlic powder
1/2 cup ketchup
2 Tbsp. Worcestershire sauce
1 Tbsp. brown sugar
1/2 tsp. salt
2 tsp. paprika
1/2 tsp. dry mustard
1 cup cold water
1/4 cup flour
1/2 cup water

1. Place meat in slow cooker. Add onion.

2. Combine garlic powder, ketchup, Worcestershire sauce, brown sugar, salt, paprika, mustard, and 1 cup water. Pour over meat.

3. Cover. Cook on Low 8 hours.

4. Dissolve flour in 1/2 cup water. Stir into meat mixture. Cook on High until thickened, about 10 minutes.

5. Serve over noodles.

Horseradish Beef

Barbara Nolan
Pleasant Valley, NY

Makes 6-8 servings

3-4-lb. pot roast
2 Tbsp. oil
1/2 tsp. salt
1/2 tsp. pepper
1 onion, chopped
6-oz. can tomato paste
1/3 cup horseradish sauce

1. Brown roast on all sides in oil in skillet. Place in slow cooker. Add remaining ingredients.

2. Cover. Cook on Low 8-10 hours.

Spicy Pot Roast

Jane Talso
Albuquerque, NM

Makes 6-8 servings

3-4-lb. beef pot roast
salt to taste
pepper to taste
3/4-oz. pkg. brown gravy mix
1/4 cup ketchup
2 tsp. Dijon mustard
1 tsp. Worcestershire sauce
1/8 tsp. garlic powder
1 cup water

1. Sprinkle meat with salt and pepper. Place in slow cooker.

2. Combine remaining ingredients. Pour over meat.

3. Cover. Cook on Low 8-10 hours, or High 4-5 hours.

Chinese Pot Roast

Marsha Sabus
Fallbrook, CA

Makes 6 servings

3-lb. boneless beef pot roast
2 Tbsp. flour
1 Tbsp. oil
2 large onions, chopped
salt to taste
pepper to taste
1/2 cup soy sauce
1 cup water
1/2 tsp. ground ginger

1. Dip roast in flour and brown on both sides in oil in saucepan. Place in slow cooker.

2. Top with onions, salt and pepper.

3. Combine soy sauce, water, and ginger. Pour over meat.

4. Cover. Cook on High 10 minutes. Reduce heat to Low and cook 8-10 hours.

5. Slice and serve with rice.

Peppery Roast

Lovina Baer
Conrath, WI

Makes 8-10 servings

4-lb. beef, *or* venison, roast
1 tsp. garlic salt
1 tsp. onion salt
2 tsp. celery salt
1½ tsp. salt
2 tsp. Worcestershire sauce
2 tsp. pepper
½ cup ketchup
1 Tbsp. liquid smoke
3 Tbsp. brown sugar
1 Tbsp. dry mustard
dash of nutmeg
1 Tbsp. soy sauce
1 Tbsp. lemon juice
3 drops hot pepper sauce

1. Place roast in slow cooker.
2. Combine remaining ingredients and pour over roast.
3. Cover. Cook on High 6-8 hours.

Mexican Pot Roast

Bernice A. Esau
North Newton, KS

Makes 6-8 servings

3 lbs. beef brisket, cubed
2 Tbsp. oil
½ cup slivered almonds
2 cups mild picante sauce,
   or hot, if you prefer
2 Tbsp. vinegar
1 tsp. garlic powder
½ tsp. salt
¼ tsp. cinnamon
¼ tsp. dried thyme
¼ tsp. dried oregano
⅛ tsp. ground cloves
⅛ tsp. pepper
½-¾ cup water, as needed

1. Brown beef in oil in skillet. Place in slow cooker.
2. Combine remaining ingredients. Pour over meat.
3. Cover. Cook on Low 10-12 hours. Add water as needed.
4. Serve with potatoes, noodles, or rice.

Chuck Wagon Beef

Charlotte Bull
Cassville, MO

Makes 8 servings

4-lb. boneless chuck roast
1 tsp. garlic salt
¼ tsp. black pepper
2 Tbsp. oil
6-8 garlic cloves, minced
1 large onion, sliced
1 cup water
1 bouillon cube
2-3 tsp. instant coffee
1 bay leaf, *or* 1 Tbsp.
   mixed Italian herbs
3 Tbsp. cold water
2 Tbsp. cornstarch

1. Sprinkle roast with garlic salt and pepper. Brown on all sides in oil in saucepan. Place in slow cooker.
2. Saute garlic and onion in meat drippings in saucepan. Add water, bouillon cube, and coffee. Cook over low heat for several minutes, stirring until drippings loosen. Pour over meat in cooker.
3. Add bay leaf or herbs.
4. Cover. Cook on Low 8-10 hours, or until very tender. Remove bay leaf and discard. Remove meat to serving platter and keep warm.
5. Mix water and cornstarch together until paste forms. Stir into hot liquid and onions in cooker. Cover. Cook 10 minutes on High, or until thickened.
6. Slice meat and serve with gravy over top or on the side.

French Dip

Barbara Walker
Sturgis, SD

Makes 6-8 servings

3-lb. rump roast
1/2 cup soy sauce
1 beef bouillon cube
1 bay leaf
1 tsp. dried thyme
3-4 peppercorns
1 tsp. garlic powder

1. Combine all ingredients in slow cooker. Add water to almost cover meat.
2. Cover. Cook on Low 10-12 hours.

French Dip Roast

Patti Boston
Newark, OH

Makes 8-10 servings

1 large onion, sliced
3-lb. beef bottom roast
1/2 cup dry white wine, *or* water
1 pkg. dry au jus gravy mix
2 cups beef broth

1. Place onion in slow cooker. Add roast.
2. Combine wine and gravy mix. Pour over roast.
3. Add enough broth to cover roast.

4. Cover. Cook on High 5-6 hours, or Low 10-12 hours.
5. Remove meat from liquid. Let stand 5 minutes before slicing thinly across grain.

Beef Au Jus

Jean Weller
State College, PA

Makes 6-8 servings

3-lb. eye, *or* rump, roast
1 pkg. dry au jus gravy mix
1 tsp. garlic powder
1 tsp. onion powder
1/2 tsp. salt
1/4-1/2 tsp. pepper

1. Place roast in slow cooker.
2. Prepare gravy according to package directions. Pour over roast.
3. Sprinkle with garlic powder, onion powder, salt, and pepper.
4. Cover. Cook on Low 6 hours. After 6 hours, remove meat and trim fat. Shred meat and return to slow cooker, cooking until desired tenderness. Add more water if roast isn't covered with liquid when returning it to cooker.

Dripped Beef

Mitzi McGlynchey
Downingtown, PA

Makes 8 servings

3-4-lb. chuck roast
1 tsp. salt
1 tsp. seasoned salt
1 tsp. white pepper
1 Tbsp. rosemary
1 Tbsp. dried oregano
1 Tbsp. garlic powder
1 cup water

1. Combine all ingredients in slow cooker.
2. Cover. Cook on Low 6-7 hours.
3. Shred meat using two forks. Strain liquid and return liquid and meat to slow cooker. Serve meat and au jus over mashed potatoes, noodles, or rice.

If you use ground herbs and spices, add them during the last hour of cooking.

Darlene Raber
Wellman, IA

Deep Pit Beef

Kristina Shull
Timberville, VA

Makes 6-8 servings

1 tsp. garlic salt, *or* powder
1 tsp. celery salt
1 tsp. lemon pepper
1½ Tbsp. liquid smoke
2 Tbsp. Worcestershire
   sauce
3-4-lb. beef roast

1. Combine seasonings in small bowl. Spread over roast as a marinade. Cover tightly with foil. Refrigerate for at least 8 hours.
2. Place roast in slow cooker. Cover with marinade sauce.
3. Cover. Cook on Low 6-7 hours. Save juice for gravy and serve with roast.

Note:
This is also good served cold, along with picnic foods.

Barbecued Roast Beef

Kim Stoltzfus
New Holland, PA

Makes 10-12 servings

4-lb. chuck roast
1 cup ketchup
1 cup barbecue sauce
2 cups chopped celery
2 cups water
1 cup chopped onions
4 Tbsp. vinegar
2 Tbsp. brown sugar
2 Tbsp. Worcestershire
   sauce
1 tsp. chili powder
1 tsp. garlic powder
1 tsp. salt

1. Combine all ingredients in large bowl. Spoon into 5-quart cooker, or 2 3½-quart cookers.
2. Cover. Cook on Low 6-8 hours, or High 3-4 hours.
3. Slice meat into thin slices and serve in barbecue sauce over mashed potatoes or rice.

Italian Roast Beef

Elsie Russett
Fairbank, IA

Makes 6-8 servings

4-lb. beef rump roast
flour
1 onion
2 garlic cloves
1 large rib celery
2-oz. salt pork, *or* bacon
1 onion, sliced

1. Lightly flour roast.
2. In blender, grind onion, garlic, celery, and salt pork together. Rub ground mixture into roast.
3. Place sliced onion in slow cooker. Place roast on top of onion.
4. Cover. Cook on Low 8-10 hours.

Diane's Gutbuster

Joyce Cox
Port Angeles, WA

Makes 10-15 servings

5-lb. chuck roast
1 large onion, sliced
2 tsp. salt
¾ tsp. pepper
28-oz. can stewed tomatoes
1 Tbsp. brown sugar
1 cup water
half a bottle barbecue sauce
1 Tbsp. Worcestershire sauce

1. Combine all ingredients except barbecue sauce and Worcestershire sauce in slow cooker.

2. Cover. Cook on Low 6-7 hours. Refrigerate for at least 8 hours.

3. Shred meat and place in slow cooker. Add barbecue sauce and Worcestershire sauce.

4. Cover. Cook on Low 4-5 hours.

5. Serve as main dish or in hamburger buns.

Barbecue Brisket

Patricia Howard
Albuquerque, NM

Makes 8-10 servings

4-5-lb. beef brisket
1/8 tsp. celery salt
1/4 tsp. garlic salt
1/4 tsp. onion salt
1/4 tsp. salt
1.5-oz. bottle liquid smoke
1 1/2 cups barbecue sauce

1. Place brisket in slow cooker.

2. Sprinkle with celery salt, garlic salt, onion salt, and salt.

3. Pour liquid smoke over brisket. Cover. Refrigerate for 8 hours.

4. Cook on Low 8-10 hours, or until tender. During last hour pour barbecue sauce over brisket.

Beef Ribs

Maryann Westerberg
Rosamond, CA

Makes 8-10 servings

3-4-lb. boneless beef, *or* short ribs
1 1/2 cups barbecue sauce, divided
1/2 cup apricot, *or* pineapple, jam
1 Tbsp. soy sauce

1. Place ribs in baking pan.

2. Combine 3/4 cup barbecue sauce, jam, and soy sauce. Pour over ribs. Bake at 450° for 30 minutes to brown.

3. Take out of oven. Layer beef and sauce used in oven in slow cooker.

4. Cover. Cook on Low 8 hours.

5. Mix remaining 3/4 cup barbecue sauce with sauce from slow cooker. Pour over ribs and serve.

Reuben Sandwiches

Maryann Markano
Wilmington, DE

Makes 3-4 servings

1-lb. can sauerkraut
1 lb. sliced corned beef brisket
1/4-lb. Swiss cheese, sliced
sliced rye bread
sandwich spread, *or* Thousand Island Dressing

1. Drain sauerkraut in sieve, then on paper towels until very day. Place in bottom of slow cooker.

2. Arrange layer of corned beef slices over sauerkraut. Top with cheese slices.

3. Cover. Cook on Low 3-4 hours.

4. Toast bread. Spread generously with sandwich spread or dressing. Spoon ingredients from slow cooker onto toasted bread, maintaining layers of sauerkraut, meat, and cheese.

If I want to have a hot dish at noon time on Sunday, I bake a casserole on Saturday. Then on Sunday morning I put it into a slow cooker, turn it on High for 30 minutes, then on Low while I'm at church.

Ruth Hershey
Paradise, PA

Smoky Brisket

Angeline Lang
Greeley, CO

Makes 8-10 servings

2 medium onions, sliced
3-4-lb. beef brisket
1 Tbsp. smoke-flavored salt
1 tsp. celery seed
1 Tbsp. mustard seed
1/2 tsp. pepper
12-oz. bottle chili sauce

1. Arrange onions in bottom of slow cooker.
2. Sprinkle both sides of meat with smoke-flavored salt.
3. Combine celery seed, mustard seed, pepper, and chili sauce. Pour over meat.
4. Cover. Cook on Low 10-12 hours.

Easy Barbecued Venison

Tracey B. Stenger
Gretna, LA

Makes 6 servings

2-3-lb. venison, *or* beef, roast, cubed
2 large onions, sliced in rings
1-2 18-oz. bottles barbecue sauce

1. Put layer of meat and layer of onion rings in slow cooker. Drizzle generously with barbecue sauce. Repeat layers until meat and onion rings are all in place.
2. Cover. Cook on Low 8-10 hours.
3. Eat with au gratin potatoes and a vegetable, or slice thin and pile into steak rolls, drizzled with juice.

Note:
To be sure venison cooks tender, marinate overnight in 1 cup vinegar and 2 Tbsp. dried rosemary. In the morning, discard marinade, cut venison into cubes, and proceed with recipe.

Sour Beef

Rosanne Hankins
Stevensville, MD

Makes 6-8 servings

3-4-lb. pot roast
1/3 cup cider vinegar
1 large onion, sliced
3 bay leaves
1/2 tsp. salt
1/4 tsp. ground cloves
1/4 tsp. garlic powder

1. Place roast in slow cooker. Add remaining ingredients.
2. Cover. Cook on Low 8-10 hours.

Old World Sauerbraten

C.J. Slagle
Roann, IN
Angeline Lang
Greeley, CO

Makes 8 servings

31/2-4-lb. beef rump roast
1 cup water
1 cup vinegar
1 lemon, sliced but unpeeled
10 whole cloves
1 large onion, sliced
4 bay leaves
6 whole peppercorns
2 Tbsp. salt
2 Tbsp. sugar
12 gingersnaps, crumbled

1. Place meat in deep ceramic or glass bowl.
2. Combine water, vinegar, lemon, cloves, onion, bay leaves, peppercorns, salt, and sugar. Pour over meat. Cover and refrigerate 24-36 hours. Turn meat several times during marinating.
3. Place beef in slow cooker. Pour 1 cup marinade over meat.
4. Cover. Cook on Low 6-8 hours. Remove meat.
5. Strain meat juices and return to pot. Turn to High. Stir in gingersnaps. Cover and cook on High 10-14 minutes. Slice meat. Pour finished sauce over meat.

Meatloaf Dinner

Esther Lehman
Croghan, NY

Makes 4 servings

6 potatoes, cubed
4 carrots, thinly sliced
1/4 tsp. salt
1 egg, slightly beaten
1 large shredded wheat
   biscuit, crushed
1/4 cup chili sauce
1/4 cup finely chopped
   onion
1/2 tsp. salt
1/4 tsp. dried marjoram
1/8 tsp. pepper
1 lb. ground beef

1. Place potatoes and carrots in slow cooker. Season with salt.
2. Combine egg, shredded wheat, chili sauce, onion, salt, marjoram, and pepper. Add ground beef. Mix well. Shape into loaf, slightly smaller in diameter than the cooker. Place on top of vegetables, not touching sides of cooker.
3. Cover. Cook on Low 9-10 hours.

Variation:
Substitute 1/2 cup bread crumbs or dry oatmeal for crushed shredded wheat biscuit.

Easy, All-Day Meatloaf and Vegetables

Ann Sunday McDowell
Newtown, PA

Makes 6 servings

4 large, *or* 6 medium, potatoes, sliced
6 carrots, sliced
1/4 tsp. salt
1 1/2 lbs. ground beef
2 eggs, beaten
3/4 cup cracker crumbs
1/3 cup ketchup
1/3 cup finely chopped onions
3/4 tsp. salt
1/4 tsp. dried marjoram
1/4 tsp. black pepper

1. Place potatoes and carrots in slow cooker. Sprinkle with 1/4 tsp. salt.
2. Combine remaining ingredients. Mix well and shape into loaf. Place loaf on top of vegetables, making sure that it doesn't touch sides of slow cooker.
3. Cover. Cook on Low 8-10 hours.

Ruth Ann's Meatloaf

Ruth Ann Hoover
New Holland, PA

Makes 4 servings

1 egg
1/4 cup milk
2 slices day-old bread, cubed
1/4 cup chopped onions
2 Tbsp. chopped green peppers
1 tsp. salt
1/4 tsp. pepper
1 1/2 lbs. ground beef
1/4 cup ketchup
8 small red potatoes
4-6 medium carrots, cut in 1-inch chunks

1. Beat together eggs and milk.
2. Stir in bread cubes, onions, green peppers, salt, and pepper. Add beef and mix well.
3. Shape into loaf that is about an inch smaller in circumference than the inside of the slow cooker. Place loaf into slow cooker.
4. Spread top with ketchup.
5. Peel strip around the center of each potato. Place carrots and potatoes around Meatloaf.
6. Cover. Cook on High 1 hour. Reduce heat to Low. Cook 7-8 hours longer.

Don't peek. It takes 15-20 minutes for the cooker to regain lost steam and return to the right temperature.
Janet V. Yocum
Elizabethtown, PA

Betty's Meatloaf

Betty B. Dennison
Grove City, PA

Makes 4-6 servings

2 lbs. ground beef
1/2 cup chopped green
  peppers
1/2 cup chopped onions
1/2 tsp. salt
1 cup cracker crumbs
1 egg
7/8-oz. envelope brown
  gravy mix
1 cup milk
4-6 small potatoes, cut up,
  optional

1. Combine all ingredients
except potatoes in large bowl.
Shape into loaf. Place in slow
cooker.
2. Place potatoes alongside
meatloaf.
3. Cover. Cook on Low 8-
10 hours, or High 4-5 hours.

Tracey's Italian Meatloaf

Tracey Yohn
Harrisburg, PA

Makes 8 servings

2 lbs. ground beef
2 cups soft bread crumbs
1/2 cup spaghetti sauce
1 large egg
2 Tbsp. dried onion
1/4 tsp. pepper
1 1/4 tsp. salt
1 tsp. garlic salt
1/2 tsp. dried Italian herbs
1/4 tsp. garlic powder
2 Tbsp. spaghetti sauce

1. Fold a 30"-long piece of
foil in half lengthwise. Place in
bottom of slow cooker with
both ends hanging over the
edge of cooker. Grease foil.
2. Combine beef, bread
crumbs, 1/2 cup spaghetti
sauce, egg, onion, and seasonings. Shape into loaf. Place on
top of foil in slow cooker.
Spread 2 Tbsp. spaghetti
sauce over top.
3. Cover. Cook on High
2 1/2-3 hours, or Low 5-6
hours.

Mary Ann's Italian Meatloaf

Mary Ann Wasick
West Allis, WI

Makes 8-10 servings

2 lbs. ground beef
2 eggs, beaten
2/3 cup quick-cooking oats
1 envelope dry onion soup
  mix
1/2 cup pasta sauce (your
  favorite)
1 tsp. garlic powder
onion slices

1. Combine ground beef,
eggs, oats, soup mix, pasta
sauce, and garlic powder.
Shape into a loaf. Place in
slow cooker. Garnish top of
loaf with onion slices.
2. Cover. Cook on Low 8
hours.
3. Serve with pasta and
more of the sauce that you
mixed into the meatloaf.

To remove meatloaf or other meats from your cooker,
make foil handles to lift the food out. Use double strips of
heavy foil to make 3 strips, each about 20" x 3". Crisscross
them in the bottom of the pot and bring them up the sides in
a spoke design before putting in the food.
John D. Allen
Rye, CO
Esther Lehman
Croghan, NY

Meatloaf Sensation
Andrea O'Neil
Fairfield, CT

Makes 8 servings

2½ lbs. ground beef
half of an 8-oz. jar salsa
1 pkg. dry taco seasoning,
 divided
1 egg, slightly beaten
1 cup bread crumbs
12-oz. pkg. shredded
 Mexican-mix cheese
2 tsp. salt
½ tsp. pepper

1. Combine all ingredients, except half of taco seasoning. Mix well. Shape into loaf and place in slow cooker. Sprinkle with remaining taco seasoning.

2. Cover. Cook on Low 8-10 hours.

Barbecue Hamburger Steaks
Jeanette Oberholtzer
Manheim, PA

Makes 4 servings

1 lb. ground beef
1 tsp. salt
1 tsp. pepper
½ cup milk
1 cup soft bread crumbs
2 Tbsp. brown sugar
2 Tbsp. vinegar
3 Tbsp. Worcestershire
 sauce
1 cup ketchup

1. Combine beef, salt, pepper, milk, and bread crumbs. Mix well. Form into patties. Brown in saucepan and drain.

2. Combine brown sugar, vinegar, Worcestershire sauce, and ketchup in slow cooker. Add ground beef patties, pushing them down into the sauce, so that each one is well covered.

3. Cover. Cook on Low 4-6 hours.

Nutritious Meatloaf
Elsie Russett
Fairbank, IA

Makes 6 servings

1 lb. ground beef
2 cups finely shredded
 cabbage
1 medium green pepper,
 diced
1 Tbsp. dried onion flakes
½ tsp. caraway seeds
1 tsp. salt

1. Combine all ingredients. Shape into loaf and place on rack in slow cooker.

2. Cover. Cook on High 3-4 hours.

Poor Man's Steak

Elsie Schlabach
Millersburg, OH

Makes 8-10 servings

1 1/2 lbs. ground beef
1 cup milk
1/4 tsp. pepper
1 tsp. salt
1 small onion, finely
    chopped
1 cup cracker crumbs
1 tsp. brown sugar
10 3/4-oz. can cream of
    mushroom soup
1 soup can water

1. Mix together all ingredients except soup and water. Shape into narrow loaf. Refrigerate for at least 8 hours.

2. Slice and fry until brown in skillet.

3. Mix soup and water together until smooth. Spread diluted soup on each piece. Place slices into cooker. Pour any remaining soup over slices in cooker.

4. Cover. Cook on Low 2-3 hours.

Beef Stroganoff

Julette Leaman
Harrisonburg, VA

Makes 6 servings

2 lbs. ground beef
2 medium onions, chopped
2 garlic cloves, minced
6 1/2-oz. can mushrooms
1 1/2 cups sour cream
4 Tbsp. flour
2 1/2 tsp. salt
1/4 tsp. pepper
1 cup bouillon
3 Tbsp. tomato paste

1. In skillet, brown beef, onions, garlic, and mushrooms until meat and onions are brown. Drain. Pour into slow cooker.

2. Combine sour cream and flour. Add to mixture in slow cooker. Stir in remaining ingredients.

3. Cover. Cook on Low 6-8 hours.

4. Serve over hot buttered noodles.

Chili and Cheese on Rice

Dale and Shari Mast
Harrisonburg, VA

Makes 6 servings

1 lb. ground beef
1 onion, diced
1 tsp. dried basil
1 tsp. dried oregano
16-oz. can light red kidney
    beans
15 1/2-oz. can chili beans
1 pint stewed tomatoes,
    drained
cooked rice
grated cheddar cheese

1. Brown ground beef and onion in skillet. Season with basil and oregano.

2. Combine all ingredients except rice and cheese in slow cooker.

3. Cover. Cook on Low 4 hours.

4. Serve over cooked rice. Top with cheese.

Roasting bags work well in the slow cooker. Simply fill with meat and vegetables and cook as directed in slow cooker recipes. Follow manufacturer's directions for filling and sealing bags.

Charlotte Shaffer
East Earl, PA

Loretta's Spanish Rice
Loretta Krahn
Mt. Lake, MN

Makes 8 servings

2 lbs. ground beef,
  browned
2 medium onions, chopped
2 green peppers, chopped
28-oz. can tomatoes
8-oz. can tomato sauce
1½ cups water
2½ tsp. chili powder
2 tsp. salt
2 tsp. Worcestershire sauce
1½ cups rice, uncooked

1. Combine all ingredients
in slow cooker.
2. Cover. Cook on Low 8-
10 hours, or High 6 hours.

Evie's Spanish Rice
Evie Hershey
Atglen, PA

Makes 10-12 servings

2 lbs. lean ground beef
2 onions, chopped
2 green peppers, chopped
1 qt. canned tomatoes
8-oz. can tomato sauce
1 cup water
2½ tsp. chili powder
2 tsp. salt

2 tsp. Worcestershire sauce
1 cup converted rice,
  uncooked

1. Brown beef in skillet.
Drain.
2. Combine all ingredients
in slow cooker. Stir.
3. Cover. Cook on Low 7-9
hours.

A Hearty Western Casserole
Karen Ashworth
Duenweg, MO

Makes 5 servings

1 lb. ground beef, browned
16-oz. can whole corn,
  drained
16-oz. can red kidney
  beans, drained
10¾-oz. can condensed
  tomato soup
1 cup (4 oz.) Colby cheese
¼ cup milk
1 tsp. minced dry onion
  flakes
½ tsp. chili powder

1. Combine beef, corn,
beans, soup, cheese, milk,
onion, and chili powder in
slow cooker.
2. Cover. Cook on Low
1 hour.

Variation:
1 pkg. (of 10) refrigerator
  biscuits
2 Tbsp. margarine
¼ cup yellow cornmeal

Dip biscuits in margarine
and then in cornmeal. Bake
20 minutes or until brown.
Top beef mixture with biscuits before serving.

Green Chili Stew
Jeanne Allen
Rye, CO

Makes 6-8 servings

3 Tbsp. oil
2 garlic cloves, minced
1 large onion, diced
1 lb. ground sirloin
½ lb. ground pork
3 cups chicken broth
2 cups water
2 4-oz. cans diced green
  chilies
4 large potatoes, diced
10-oz. pkg. frozen corn
1 tsp. black pepper
1 tsp. crushed dried
  oregano
½ tsp. ground cumin
1 tsp. salt

1. Brown onion, garlic, sirloin, and pork in oil in skillet.
Cook until meat is no longer
pink.
2. Combine all ingredients
in slow cooker.
3. Cover. Cook on Low 4-6
hours, or until potatoes are
soft.

Note:
Excellent served with
warm tortillas or corn bread.

Cowboy Casserole

Lori Berezovsky
Salina, KS

Makes 4-6 servings

1 onion, chopped
1½ lbs. ground beef,
    browned and drained
6 medium potatoes, sliced
1 clove garlic, minced
16-oz. can kidney beans
15-oz. can diced tomatoes
    mixed with 2 Tbsp.
    flour, *or* 10¾-oz. can
    tomato soup
1 tsp. salt
¼ tsp. pepper

1. Layer onions, ground
beef, potatoes, garlic, and
beans in slow cooker.
2. Spread tomatoes or soup
over all. Sprinkle with salt
and pepper.
3. Cover. Cook on Low 5-6
hours, or until potatoes are
tender.

10-Layer Slow-Cooker Dish

Norma Saltzman
Shickley, NE

Makes 6-8 servings

6 medium potatoes, thinly
    sliced
1 medium onion, thinly
    sliced
salt to taste
pepper to taste
15-oz. can corn
15-oz. can peas
¼ cup water
1½ lbs. ground beef,
    browned
10¾-oz. can cream of
    mushroom soup

1. Layer 1: ¼ of potatoes,
½ of onion, salt, and pepper
2. Layer 2: ½ can of corn
3. Layer 3: ¼ of potatoes
4. Layer 4: ½ can of peas
5. Layer 5: ¼ of potatoes,
½ of onion, salt, and pepper
6. Layer 6: remaining corn
7. Layer 7: remaining potatoes
8. Layer 8: remaining peas
and water
9. Layer 9: ground beef
10. Layer 10: soup
11. Cover. Cook on High 4
hours.

Hamburger Potatoes

Juanita Marner
Shipshewana, IN

Makes 3-4 servings

3 medium potatoes, sliced
3 carrots, sliced
1 small onion, sliced
2 Tbsp. dry rice
1 tsp. salt
½ tsp. pepper
1 lb. ground beef, browned
    and drained
1½-2 cups tomato juice, as
    needed to keep dish
    from getting too dry

1. Combine all ingredients
in slow cooker.
2. Cover. Cook on Low 6-8
hours.

When cooking meats and vegetables together, especially
when cooking on Low, place the vegetables on the bottom
where they will be kept moist.
Roseann Wilson
Albuquerque, NM

Shipwreck
Betty Lahman
Elkton, VA

Makes 8 servings

1 lb. ground beef, browned
4-5 potatoes, cut in French-
   fry-like strips
1-2 onions, chopped
16-oz. can light red kidney
   beans, drained
1/4-lb. Velveeta cheese,
   cubed
10³/4-oz. can tomato soup
1½ tsp. salt
1/4 tsp. pepper
butter

1. Layer in slow cooker in this order: ground beef, potatoes, onions, kidney beans, and cheese. Pour soup over top. Season with salt and pepper. Dot with butter.
2. Cover. Cook on Low 6-8 hours.

Note:
This is particularly good served with Parmesan cheese sprinkled on top at the table.

Beef and Lentils
Esther Porter
Minneapolis, MN

Makes 12 servings

1 medium onion
3 whole cloves
5 cups water
1 lb. lentils
1 tsp. salt
1 bay leaf
1 lb. (or less) ground beef,
   browned and drained
½ cup ketchup
1/4 cup molasses
2 Tbsp. brown sugar
1 tsp. dry mustard
1/4 tsp. Worcestershire
   sauce
1 onion, finely chopped

1. Stick cloves into whole onion. Set aside.
2. In large saucepan, combine water, lentils, salt, bay leaf, and whole onion with cloves. Simmer 30 minutes.
3. Meanwhile, combine all remaining ingredients in slow cooker. Stir in simmered ingredients from saucepan. Add additional water if mixture seems dry.
4. Cover. Cook on Low 6-8 hours (check to see if lentils are tender).

Note:
Freezes well.

Variation:
Top with sour cream and/or salsa when serving.

Judy's Hamburger Stew
Judy Koczo
Plano, IL

Makes 6-8 servings

3 large potatoes, sliced
3 carrots, sliced
1 lb. frozen peas
1 onion, diced
2 ribs celery, sliced thin
salt to taste
pepper to taste
1½ lbs. ground beef,
   browned and drained
10³/4-oz. can tomato soup
1 soup can water

1. Put vegetables in slow cooker in layers as listed. Season each layer with salt and pepper.
2. Layer beef on top of celery. Mix together soup and water. Pour over ground beef.
3. Cover. Cook on Low 6-8 hours, or High 2-4 hours, stirring occasionally.

Variation:
Substitute 28-oz. can whole or diced tomatoes in place of tomato soup and water.

   Ann Bender
   Fort Defiance, VA

Taters n' Beef
Maryland Massey
Millington, MD

Makes 6-8 servings

2 lbs. ground beef,
  browned
1 tsp. salt
1/2 tsp. pepper
1/4 cup chopped onions
1 cup canned tomato soup
6 potatoes, sliced
1 cup milk

1. Combined beef, salt, pepper, onions, and soup.
2. Place a layer of potatoes in bottom of slow cooker. Cover with a portion of the meat mixture. Repeat layers until ingredients are used.
3. Cover. Cook on Low 4-6 hours. Add milk and cook on High 15-20 minutes.

Variations:
1. Use home-canned spaghetti sauce instead of tomato soup.
2. Add a layer of chopped raw cabbage after each layer of sliced potatoes to add to the flavor, texture, and nutritional value of the meal.

Jeanne's Hamburger Stew
Jeanne Heyerly
Chenoa, IL

Makes 8 servings

2 lbs. ground beef
1 medium onion, chopped
1 garlic clove, minced
2 cups tomato juice
2-3 carrots, sliced
2-3 ribs celery, sliced
half a green pepper,
  chopped
2 cups green beans
2 medium potatoes, cubed
2 cups water
1 Tbsp. Worcestershire
  sauce
1/4 tsp. dried oregano
1/4 tsp. dried basil
1/4 tsp. dried thyme
dash of hot pepper sauce
2 Tbsp. dry onion soup
  mix, *or* 1 beef bouillon
  cube
1 tsp. salt
1/4 tsp. pepper

1. Brown meat and onion in saucepan. Drain. Stir in garlic and tomato juice. Heat to boiling.
2. Combine all ingredients in slow cooker.
3. Cover. Cook on Low 8-10 hours.

Variation:
Use 1 cup barley in place of potatoes.

Supper-in-a-Dish
Martha Hershey
Ronks, PA

Makes 8 servings

1 lb. ground beef, browned
  and drained
1 1/2 cups sliced raw
  potatoes
1 cup sliced carrots
1 cup peas
1/2 cup chopped onions
1/2 cup chopped celery
1/4 cup chopped green
  peppers
1 tsp. salt
1/4 tsp. pepper
10 3/4 -oz. can cream of
  chicken, *or* mushroom,
  soup
1/4 cup milk
2/3 cup grated sharp cheese

1. Layer ground beef, potatoes, carrots, peas, onions, celery, green peppers, salt, and pepper in slow cooker.
2. Combine soup and milk. Pour over layered ingredients. Sprinkle with cheese.
3. Cover. Cook on High 4 hours.

Working-Woman Favorite

Martha Ann Auker
Landisburg, PA

Makes 6-8 servings

2 lbs. ground beef, browned and drained
4 ribs celery, chopped
1 small green pepper, chopped
1 onion, chopped
2 tsp. sugar
1/2 tsp. salt
dash of pepper
10 3/4-oz. can cream of mushroom soup

1. Combine all ingredients in slow cooker.
2. Cover. Cook on Low 8-10 hours.
3. Serve over warm biscuits.

Note:
Sprinkle individual servings with shredded cheddar cheese.

Ground Beef Casserole

Lois J. Cassidy
Willow Street, PA

Makes 6-8 servings

1 1/2 lbs. ground beef
6-8 potatoes, sliced
1 medium onion, sliced
14 1/2-oz. can cut green beans with juice
1/2 tsp. salt
dash of pepper
10 3/4-oz. can cream of mushroom soup

1. Crumble uncooked ground beef in bottom of slow cooker. Add potatoes, onion, salt, and pepper. Pour beans over all. Spread can of mushroom soup over beans.
2. Cover. Cook on Low 6-8 hours.

Variation:
Brown the beef before putting in the slow cooker. Mix half a soup can of water with the mushroom soup before placing over beans.

Chinese Hamburger

Esther J. Yoder
Hartville, OH

Makes 8 servings

1 lb. ground beef, browned and drained
1 onion, diced
2 ribs celery, diced
10 3/4-oz. can chicken noodle soup
10 3/4-oz. can cream of mushroom soup
12-oz. can Chinese vegetables
salt to taste, about 1/4-1/2 tsp.
pepper to taste, about 1/4 tsp.
1 green pepper, diced
1 tsp. soy sauce

1. Combine all ingredients in slow cooker.
2. Cover. Cook on High 3-4 hours.
3. Serve over rice.

You may want to revise herb amounts when using a slow cooker. Whole herbs and spices increase their flavoring power, while ground spices tend to lose some flavor. It's a good idea to season to taste before serving.
Irma H. Schoen
Windsor, CT

Tater Tot Casserole

Shirley Hinh
Wayland, IA

Makes 6-8 servings

32-oz. bag frozen tater tots
1 lb. ground beef, browned
1/2 tsp. salt
1/4 tsp. pepper
2 14 1/2-oz. cans green
  beans, drained
10 3/4-oz. can cream of
  mushroom soup
1 Tbsp. dried onions
1/4 cup milk

1. Line slow cooker with
frozen tater tots.
2. Combine remaining
ingredients. Pour over potatoes.
3. Cover. Cook on High 3
hours.

Note:
Sprinkle individual serv-
ings with your choice of
grated cheese.

Bean Tator Tot Casserole

Marjora Miller
Archbold, OH

Makes 6 servings

1 lb. ground beef
1/2 tsp. salt
1/4 tsp. pepper
1 onion, chopped
1-lb. bag frozen string
  beans
10 3/4-oz. can cream of
  mushroom soup
1 cup shredded cheese
21-oz. bag. frozen tator tots

1. Crumble raw ground
beef in bottom of slow
cooker. Sprinkle with salt and
pepper.
2. Layer remaining ingredients on beef in order listed.
3. Cover. Cook on High 1
hour. Reduce heat to Low
and cook 3 hours.

Variation:
In order to reduce the
calorie content of this dish,
use raw shredded potatoes
instead of tater tots.

Meal-in-One-Casserole

Elizabeth Yoder
Millersburg, OH
Marcella Stalter
Flanagan, IL

Makes 4-6 servings

1 lb. ground beef
1 medium onion, chopped
1 medium green pepper,
  chopped
15 1/4-oz. can whole kernel
  corn, drained
4-oz. can mushrooms,
  drained
1 tsp. salt
1/4 tsp. pepper
11-oz. jar salsa
5 cups uncooked medium
  egg noodles
28-oz. can diced tomatoes,
  undrained
1 cup shredded cheddar
  cheese

1. Cook beef and onion in
saucepan over medium heat
until meat is no longer pink.
Drain. Transfer to slow
cooker.
2. Top with green pepper,
corn, and mushrooms.
Sprinkle with salt and pepper.
Pour salsa over mushrooms.
Cover and cook on Low 3
hours.
3. Cook noodles according
to package in separate pan.
Drain and add to slow cooker
after mixture in cooker has
cooked for 3 hours. Top with
tomatoes. Sprinkle with
cheese.

4. Cover. Cook on Low 1 more hour.

Variation:

Add uncooked noodles after salsa. Pour tomatoes and 1 cup water over all. Sprinkle with cheese. Cover and cook on Low 4 hours, or until noodles are tender.

Nadine Martinitz
Salina, KS

Noodle Hamburger Dish

Esther J. Yoder
Hartville, OH

Makes 10 servings

1 1/2 lbs. ground beef, browned and drained
1 green pepper, diced
1 qt. whole tomatoes
10 3/4-oz. can cream of mushroom soup
1 large onion, diced
1 1/2 Tbsp. Worcestershire sauce
8-oz. pkg. noodles, uncooked
1 tsp. salt
1/4 tsp. pepper
1 cup shredded cheese

1. Combine all ingredients except cheese in slow cooker.
2. Cover. Cook on High 3-4 hours.
3. Sprinkle with cheese before serving.

Yum-e-setti

Elsie Schlabach
Millersburg, OH

Makes 6-8 servings

1 1/2 lbs. ground beef, browned and drained
10 3/4-oz. can tomato soup
8-oz. pkg. wide noodles, cooked
10 3/4-oz. can cream of chicken soup
1 cup chopped celery, cooked tender
2 tsp. salt
1 lb. frozen mixed vegetables
1/2 lb. Velveeta cheese, cubed

1. Combine ground beef and tomato soup.
2. Combine chicken soup, noodles, and celery.
3. Layer beef mixture, chicken mixture, and vegetables. Sprinkle with salt. Lay cheese over top.
4. Cover. Cook on Low 2-3 hours.

Variation:

For more "bite," use shredded cheddar cheese instead of cubed Velveeta.

Shell Casserole

Jean Butzer
Batavia, NY

Makes 4-5 servings

1 lb. ground beef
1 small onion, chopped
3/4 tsp. salt
1/4 tsp. garlic powder
1 tsp. Worcestershire sauce
1/4 cup flour
1 1/4 cups hot water
2 tsp. beef bouillon granules
2 Tbsp. red wine
6 oz. medium-sized shell pasta, uncooked
4-oz. can sliced mushrooms, drained
1 cup sour cream

1. Brown ground beef and onion in saucepan. Drain. Place in slow cooker.
2. Stir in salt, garlic powder, Worcestershire sauce, and flour.
3. Add water, bouillon, and wine. Mix well.
4. Cover. Cook on Low 2-3 hours.
5. Cook pasta in separate pan according to package directions. Stir cooked pasta, mushrooms, and sour cream into slow cooker. Cover. Cook on High 10-15 minutes.

117

Family Favorite Casserole

Lizzie Weaver
Ephrata, PA

Makes 6-8 servings

1 1/2 lbs. ground beef
1 onion, chopped
1 1/2 cups diced potatoes
1 1/2 cups sliced carrots
1 1/2 cups peas
1 1/2 cups macaroni, cooked
10 3/4-oz. can cream of celery soup
1/2 lb. cheddar cheese, grated
2 cups milk
1 1/2 tsp. salt

1. Fry beef and onion in saucepan until brown. Drain.
2. Cook vegetables just until soft.
3. Combine all ingredients in slow cooker.
4. Cover. Cook on High 2 hours, or Low 4-5 hours.

Variation:

Skip pre-cooking the vegetables; add them raw to the slow cooker. Increase cooking time to 4 hours on High, or 8-10 hours on Low. Add the cooked macaroni and the milk during the last 15 minutes if cooking on High, or during the last 30 minutes if cooking on Low.

Tastes-Like-Turkey

Lizzie Weaver
Ephrata, PA

Makes 6 servings

2 lbs. hamburger, browned
1 tsp. salt
1/2 tsp. pepper
2 10 3/4-oz. cans cream of chicken soup
10 3/4-oz. can cream of celery soup
4 scant cups milk
1 large pkg. bread stuffing, *or* large loaf of bread, torn in pieces

1. Combine all ingredients in large buttered slow cooker.
2. Cover. Cook on High 3 hours, or Low 6-8 hours.

Meatball Stew

Nanci Keatley, Salem, OR
Ada Miller, Sugarcreek, OH

Makes 8 servings

2 lbs. ground beef
1/2 tsp. salt
1/2 tsp. pepper
6 medium potatoes, cubed
1 large onion, sliced
6 medium carrots, sliced
1 cup ketchup
1 cup water
1 1/2 tsp. balsamic vinegar
1 tsp. dried basil
1 tsp. dried oregano
1/2 tsp. salt
1/2 tsp. pepper

1. Combine beef, 1/2 tsp. salt, and 1/2 tsp. pepper. Mix well. Shape into 1-inch balls. Brown meatballs in saucepan over medium heat. Drain.
2. Place potatoes, onion, and carrots in slow cooker. Top with meatballs.
3. Combine ketchup, water, vinegar, basil, oregano, 1/2 tsp. salt, and 1/2 tsp. pepper. Pour over meatballs.
4. Cover. Cook on High 4-5 hours, or until vegetables are tender.

Here's a real time-saver from our house: Brown large quantities (10 lbs.) of ground beef, seasoned with onion, basil, and oregano to taste. Drain and cool. Freeze in pint freezer containers. The meat is readily available with no prep time or cleanup need when preparing a slow cooker recipe or casserole that calls for browned ground beef.
Dale and Shari Mast
Harrisonburg, VA

Sweet and Sour Meatballs

Barbara Katrine Rose
Woodbridge, VA

Makes 4-6 servings

4 tsp. Worcestershire sauce
2 tsp. vinegar
1 tsp. dried Italian
  seasoning
1/4 tsp. garlic powder
1/4 tsp. cinnamon
1/4 tsp. pepper
2 4-oz. cans sliced
  mushrooms, undrained
2 cups sliced carrots
3 cups tomato juice
4 tsp. instant minced
  onion
4 Tbsp. minced green
  peppers
1 recipe Meatballs (see
  next recipe)

1. Combine all ingredients
in slow cooker.
2. Cover. Cook on High 3-4
hours.
3. Serve over rice.

Meatballs

Makes 24 small meatballs

1 lb. ground beef
1 cup drained,
  unsweetened crushed
  pineapple
2 slices crumbled whole
  wheat bread
2 tsp. instant minced
  onion
2 tsp. Worcestershire sauce
1/4 tsp. garlic powder
1/4 tsp. dry mustard
1/4 tsp. pepper

1. Combine all ingredients.
Shape into meatballs, using 1
heaping tablespoon mixture
for each. Place on rack in
baking pan.
2. Bake at 350° for 30 minutes, or until done.

BBQ Meatballs

Kathryn Yoder
Minot, ND

*Makes 12-15 main-dish servings,
or 20-25 appetizer servings*

Meatballs:
3 lbs. ground beef
5-oz. can evaporated milk
1 cup dry oatmeal (rolled
  or instant)
1 cup cracker crumbs
2 eggs

1/2 cup chopped onions
1/2 tsp. garlic powder
2 tsp. salt
1/2 tsp. pepper
2 tsp. chili powder

Sauce:
2 cups ketchup
1 cup brown sugar
1 1/2 tsp. liquid smoke
1/2 tsp. garlic powder
1/4 cup chopped onions

1. Combine all meatball
ingredients. Shape into wal-
nut-sized balls. Place on
waxed paper-lined cookie
sheets. Freeze. When fully
frozen, place in plastic bag
and store in freezer until
needed.
2. When ready to use,
place frozen meatballs in
slow cooker. Cover. Cook on
High as you mix up sauce.
3. Pour combined sauce
ingredients over meatballs.
Stir.
4. Cover. Continue cooking
on High 1 hour. Stir. Turn to
Low and cook 6-9 hours.

Variation:
Instead of using barbecue
sauce, cook meatballs with
spaghetti sauce or cream of
mushroom soup.

Mary Ellen's Barbecued Meatballs

Mary Ellen Wilcox
Scatia, NY

Makes about 60 small meatballs

Meatballs:
3/4-lb. ground beef
3/4 cup bread crumbs
1 1/2 Tbsp. minced onion
1/2 tsp. horseradish
3 drops Tabasco sauce
2 eggs, beaten
3/4 tsp. salt
1/2 tsp. pepper
butter

Sauce:
3/4 cup ketchup
1/2 cup water
1/4 cup cider vinegar
2 Tbsp. brown sugar
1 Tbsp. minced onion
2 tsp. horseradish
1 tsp. salt
1 tsp. dry mustard
3 drops Tabasco
dash pepper

1. Combine all meatball ingredients except butter. Shape into 3/4-inch balls. Brown in butter in skillet. Place in slow cooker.
2. Combine all sauce ingredients. Pour over meatballs.
3. Cover. Cook on Low 5 hours.

Cocktail Meatballs

Irene Klaeger
Inverness, FL

Makes 6 main-dish servings, or 12 appetizer servings

2 lbs. ground beef
1/3 cup ketchup
3 tsp. dry bread crumbs
1 egg, beaten
2 tsp. onion flakes
3/4 tsp. garlic salt
1/2 tsp. pepper
1 cup ketchup
1 cup packed brown sugar
6-oz. can tomato paste
1/4 cup soy sauce
1/4 cup cider vinegar
1-1 1/2 tsp. hot pepper sauce

1. Combine ground beef, 1/3 cup ketchup, bread crumbs, egg, onion flakes, garlic salt, and pepper. Mix well. Shape into 1-inch meatballs. Place on jelly roll pan. Bake at 350° for 18 minutes, or until brown. Place in slow cooker.
2. Combine 1 cup ketchup, brown sugar, tomato paste, soy sauce, vinegar, and hot pepper sauce. Pour over meatballs.
3. Cover. Cook on Low 4 hours.

Sweet and Sour Meatballs

Elaine Unruh
Minneapolis, MN

Makes 6-8 main-dish servings, or 20-30 appetizer servings

Meatballs:
2 lbs. ground beef
1 1/4 cups bread crumbs
1 1/2 tsp. salt
1 tsp. pepper
2-3 Tbsp. Worcestershire sauce
1 egg
1/2 tsp. garlic salt
1/4 cup finely chopped onions

Sauce:
1 can pineapple chunks, juice reserved
3 Tbsp. cornstarch
1/4 cup cold water
1-1 1/4 cups ketchup
1/4 cup Worcestershire sauce
1/4 tsp. salt
1/4 tsp. pepper
1/4 tsp. garlic salt
1/2 cup chopped green peppers

1. Combine all meatball ingredients. Shape into 60-80 meatballs. Brown in skillet, rolling so all sides are browned. Place meatballs in slow cooker.
2. Pour juice from pineapples into skillet. Stir into drippings.
3. Combine cornstarch and cold water. Add to skillet and

stir until thickened.

4. Stir in ketchup and Worcestershire sauce. Season with salt, pepper, and garlic salt. Add green peppers and pineapples. Pour over meatballs.

5. Cover. Cook on Low 6 hours.

Festive Cocktail Meatballs

Sharon Timpe
Mequon, WI

Makes about 4 dozen meatballs

Sauce:
2 cups ketchup
1 cup brown sugar
2 Tbsp. Worcestershire
    sauce

Meatballs:
2 lbs. ground beef
1 envelope dry onion soup
    mix
1/2 cup milk

1. Mix together ketchup, brown sugar, and Worcestershire sauce in slow cooker. Turn on High while mixing up meatballs.

2. Combine ground beef, soup mix, and milk. Mix well. Shape into 1-inch balls. Bake at 325° for 20 minutes. Drain. Add to slow cooker.

3. Cover. Cook on Low 2-2 1/2 hours, stirring gently, twice throughout the cooking time.

Barbecued Meatballs

Esther Becker
Gordonville, Pa
Ruth Shank, Gridley, IL

Makes 30 small meatballs

1 1/2 cups chili sauce
1 cup grape, *or* apple, jelly
3 tsp. brown spicy
    mustard
1 lb. ground beef
1 egg
3 Tbsp. dry bread crumbs
1/2 tsp. salt

1. Combine chili sauce, jelly, and mustard in slow cooker. Mix well.

2. Cover. Cook on High while preparing meatballs.

3. Mix together remaining ingredients. Shape into 30 balls. Place in baking pan and bake at 400° for 15-20 minutes. Drain well. Spoon into slow cooker. Stir gently to coat well.

4. Cover. Cook on Low 6-10 hours.

Variations:
1. To increase flavor, add 1/4 tsp. pepper, 1/4 tsp. Italian spice, and a dash of garlic powder to the meatball mixture.

Sandra Thom
Jenks, OK

2. Use Italian or seasoned bread crumbs in meatball mixture. Add 1 tsp. Worcestershire sauce and 1 1/2 Tbsp.

fresh parsley to meatball mixture.

Barbara Sparks
Glen Burnie, MD

3. Make meatballs larger and serve with rice or noodles.

Great Meatballs

Judy Denney
Lawrenceville, GA

Makes 12-16 main dish-size servings, or 24 appetizer-size servings

4 lbs. ground beef
2 eggs
4 slices fresh bread, torn
    into bread crumbs
1 1/2 tsp. salt
1/2 tsp. pepper
1 cup tomato juice
2 10-oz. jars chili sauce
2 cans whole cranberry
    sauce

1. Mix together beef, eggs, bread crumbs, seasonings, and tomato juice. Form into small meatballs. Place in slow cooker.

2. Pour chili sauce and cranberry sauce on top of meatballs. Stir lightly.

3. Cover. Cook on High 2 hours. Reduce heat to Low and cook 3 more hours.

Nancy's Meatballs

Betty Richards
Rapid City, SD

Makes 8 main-dish servings

3-4-lb. bag prepared
   meatballs (or make your
   own, using recipe for
   meatballs with BBQ
   Meatballs, page 119)
3 10¾-oz. cans cream of
   mushroom, *or* cream of
   celery, soup
4-oz. can button mushrooms
16-oz. jar Cheese Whiz
1 medium onion, diced

  1. Combine all ingredients
in slow cooker.
  2. Cover. Cook on Low 6-8
hours.
  3. Use as an appetizer, or
as a main dish served over
noodles or rice.

Party Meatballs

Marie Miller
Scotia, NY

Makes 8-10 main-dish servings

16-oz. jar salsa
16-oz. can jellied cranberry
   sauce
2 lbs. frozen meatballs (see
   recipe for making BBQ
   Meatballs on page 119)

  1. Melt cranberry sauce in
saucepan. Stir in salsa and
meatballs. Bring to boil. Stir.
Pour into slow cooker.
  2. Cover. Cook on Low 2-4
hours.

Swedish Cabbage Rolls

Jean Butzer, Batavia, NY
Pam Hochstedler, Kalona, IA

Makes 6 servings

12 large cabbage leaves
1 egg, beaten
¼ cup milk
¼ cup finely chopped onions
1 tsp. salt
¼ tsp. pepper
1 lb. ground beef, browned
   and drained
1 cup cooked rice
8-oz. can tomato sauce
1 Tbsp. brown sugar
1 Tbsp. lemon juice
1 tsp. Worcestershire sauce

  1. Immerse cabbage leaves
in boiling water for about 3
minutes or until limp. Drain.
  2. Combine egg, milk,
onions, salt, pepper, beef, and
rice. Place about ¼ cup meat
mixture in center of each leaf.
Fold in sides and roll ends over
meat. Place in slow cooker.
  3. Combine tomato sauce,
brown sugar, lemon juice,
and Worcestershire sauce.
Pour over cabbage rolls.
  4. Cover. Cook on Low 7-9
hours.

Cabbage Dinner

Kathi Rogge
Alexandria, IN

Makes 6-8 servings

medium head of cabbage
6-8 medium-sized potatoes
2 lbs. smoked sausage, *or*
   turkey sausage
salt to taste
1 qt. water

  1. Cut cabbage into 1-2
inch-wide wedges. Place in
slow cooker.
  2. Wash and quarter potatoes. Do not peel. Add to cabbage in slow cooker.
  3. Cut sausage into bite-
sized pieces. Add to slow
cooker. Add salt and mix
well.
  4. Pour water into slow
cooker.
  5. Cover. Cook on High
2 hours, and then on Low 6-8
hours, or until vegetables are
tender.

Stuffed Cabbage

Barbara Nolan
Pleasant Valley, NY

Makes 6 servings

4 cups water
12 large cabbage leaves
1 lb. ground beef, lamb, *or* turkey
1/2 cup cooked rice
1/2 tsp. salt
1/8 tsp. pepper
1/4 tsp. dried thyme
1/4 tsp. nutmeg
1/4 tsp. cinnamon
6-oz. can tomato paste
3/4 cup water

1. Boil 4 cups water in deep kettle. Remove kettle from heat. Soak cabbage leaves in hot water 5 minutes, or just until softened. Remove. Drain. Cool.
2. Combine ground beef, rice, salt, pepper, thyme, nutmeg, and cinnamon. Place 2 Tbsp. of mixture on each leaf. Roll up firmly. Stack stuffed leaves in slow cooker.
3. Combine tomato paste and 3/4 cup water until smooth. Pour over cabbage rolls.
4. Cover. Cook on Low 6-8 hours.

Stuffed Green Peppers

Lois Stoltzfus
Honey Brook, PA

Makes 6 servings

6 large green peppers
1 lb. ground beef, browned
2 Tbsp. minced onion
1 tsp. salt
1/8 tsp. garlic powder
2 cups cooked rice
15-oz. can tomato sauce
3/4 cup shredded mozzarella cheese

1. Cut peppers in half and remove seeds.
2. Combine all ingredients except peppers and cheese.
3. Stuff peppers with ground beef mixture. Place in slow cooker.
4. Cover. Cook on Low 6-8 hours, or High 3-4 hours. Sprinkle with cheese during last 30 minutes.

Stuffed Bell Peppers

Mary Puterbaugh
Elwood, IN

Makes 8 servings

8 large bell peppers
2 lbs. ground beef, lightly browned
1 large onion, chopped
1 cup cooked rice
2 eggs, beaten
1/2 cup milk
1/2 cup ketchup
dash hot pepper sauce
2 tsp. salt
1/2 tsp. pepper

1. Combine all ingredients except peppers. Gently pack mixture into peppers which have been capped and seeded. Place in greased slow cooker.
2. Cover. Cook on Low 9-11 hours, or High 5-6 hours.

I often start the slow cooker on High until I'm ready for work, then switch it to Low as I go out the door. It may only be 45 minutes to 1 hour on High, but I feel it starts the cooking process faster, thus preserving flavor.
Evie Hershey
Atglen, PA

Stuffed Peppers

Eleanor J. Ferreira
N. Chelmsford, MA

Makes 6-8 servings

6-8 green peppers
1-2 lbs. ground beef
1 onion, chopped
1/4 tsp. salt
1/4 tsp. pepper
1 egg
1 slice white bread
28-oz. can whole, *or*
stewed, tomatoes

1. Cut peppers in half and remove seeds.
2. Combine ground beef, onion, salt, pepper, and egg. Tear bread into small pieces. Add to ground beef mixture. Stuff into peppers.
3. Form remaining meat into oblong shape. Place meatloaf and peppers into slow cooker. Pour in tomatoes.
4. Cover. Cook on Low 6-12 hours, or High 4-5 hours.

Helen's Lasagna

Helen King, Fairbank, IA
Clarice Williams,
Fairbank, IA
Nancy Zimmerman
Loysville, PA

Makes 6-8 servings

1 lb. ground beef
1 medium onion, chopped
2 cloves garlic, minced
29-oz. can tomato sauce
1 cup water
6-oz. can tomato paste
1 tsp. salt
1 tsp. dried oregano
8-oz. pkg. lasagna noodles, uncooked
4 cups (16 oz.) shredded mozzarella cheese
1 1/2 cups (12 oz.) small-curd cottage cheese
1/2 cup grated Parmesan cheese

1. Cook beef, onion, and garlic together in saucepan until browned. Drain.
2. Stir in tomato sauce, water, tomato paste, salt, and oregano. Mix well.
3. Spread one-fourth of meat sauce in ungreased slow cooker. Arrange one third of noodles over sauce.
4. Combine the cheeses. Spoon one-third of mixture over noodles. Repeat layers twice. Top with remaining meat sauce.
5. Cover. Cook on Low 4-5 hours.

Variation:
For a fuller flavor, use 24-oz. can tomato sauce instead of 6-oz. can tomato paste and water. Add 1/2 tsp. garlic powder, 1 tsp. dried basil, and 1/4 tsp. pepper.
Dolores S. Kratz
Souderton, PA

Spicy Lasagna

Kathy Hertzler, Lancaster, PA
L. Jean Moore, Pendleton, IN
Mary Ellen Musser
Reinholds, PA

Makes 6 servings

10-oz. pkg. lasagna noodles, broken into bite-sized pieces, cooked
1 lb. ground beef, browned
1/2 lb. Italian sausage, sliced and browned
1 onion, chopped
1 clove garlic, minced
12 oz. mozzarella cheese, shredded
12 oz. cottage, *or* ricotta, cheese
16-oz. can tomato sauce
1 tsp. dried basil
1/2 tsp. dried oregano
1 1/2 Tbsp. dried parsley flakes
1/2 tsp. pepper
1 1/2 tsp. salt

1. Combine all ingredients in greased slow cooker.
2. Cover. Cook on Low 7-9 hours, or High 3-5 hours.

Variation:
Replace mix of ground beef and sausage with 1½ lbs. ground beef.

Violette's Lasagna
Violette Harris Denney
Carrollton, GA

Makes 8 servings

8 lasagna noodles, uncooked
1 lb. ground beef
1 tsp. Italian seasoning
28-oz. jar spaghetti sauce
⅓ cup water
4-oz. can sliced mushrooms
15 oz. ricotta cheese
2 cups shredded mozzarella cheese

1. Break noodles. Placc half in bottom of greased slow cooker.
2. Brown ground beef in saucepan. Drain. Stir in Italian seasoning. Spread half over noodles in slow cooker.
3. Layer half of sauce and water, half of mushrooms, half of ricotta cheese, and half of mozzarella cheese over beef. Repeat layers.
4. Cover. Cook on Low 5 hours.

Rigatoni
Susan Alexander
Baltimore, MD

Makes 10 servings

28-oz. jar spaghetti sauce
12 oz. rigatoni, cooked
1-1½ lbs. ground beef, browned
3 cups shredded mozzarella cheese
½ lb. pepperoni slices
sliced mushrooms, optional
sliced onions, optional

1. In 4-quart slow cooker, layer half of each ingredient in order listed. Repeat.
2. Cover. Cook on Low 4-5 hours.

Variation:
Use 1 lb. ground beef and 1 lb. sausage.

Beef Enchiladas
Jane Talso
Albuquerque, NM

Makes 12-16 servings

4-lb. boneless chuck roast
2 Tbsp. oil
4 cups sliced onions
2 tsp. salt
2 tsp. black pepper
2 tsp. cumin seeds
2 4½-oz. cans peeled, diced green chilies
14½-oz. can peeled, diced tomatoes
8 large tortillas (10-12 inch size)
1 lb. cheddar cheese, shredded
4 cups green, *or* red, enchilada sauce

1. Brown roast on all sides in oil in saucepan. Place roast in slow cooker.
2. Add remaining ingredients except tortillas, cheese, and sauce.
3. Cover. Cook on High 4-5 hours.
4. Shred meat with fork and return to slow cooker.
5. Warm tortillas in oven. Heat enchilada sauce. Fill each tortilla with ¾ cup beef mixture and ½ cup cheese. Roll up and serve with sauce.

Variation:
Use 2 lbs. ground beef instead of chuck roast. Brown without oil in saucepan, along with chopped onions.

Slow Cooker Enchiladas

Lori Berezovsky, Salina, KS
Tracy Clark,
Mt. Crawford, VA
Mary E. Herr and Michelle Reineck, Three Rivers, MI
Marcia S. Myer, Manheim, PA
Renee Shirk, Mt. Joy, PA
Janice Showalter, Flint, MI

Makes 4 servings

1 lb. ground beef
1 cup chopped onions
½ cup chopped green peppers
16-oz. can red kidney beans, rinsed and drained
15-oz. can black beans, rinsed and drained
10-oz. can diced tomatoes with green chilies, undrained
⅓ cup water
1½ tsp. chili powder
½ tsp. ground cumin
½ tsp. salt
¼ tsp. pepper
1 cup (4 ozs.) shredded sharp cheddar cheese
1 cup (4 ozs.) shredded Monterey Jack, *or* pepper Monterey Jack, cheese
6 flour tortillas (6-7 inches in diameter)

1. Cook beef, onions, and green peppers in skillet until beef is browned and vegetables are tender. Drain.
2. Add next 8 ingredients and bring to boil. Reduce heat. Cover and simmer 10 minutes.
3. Combine cheeses.
4. In slow cooker, layer about ¾ cup beef mixture, one tortilla, and about ⅓ cup cheese. Repeat layers.
5. Cover. Cook on Low 5-7 hours or until heated through.
6. To serve, reach to bottom with each spoonful to get all the layers, or carefully invert onto large platter and cut into wedges. Serve with sour cream and/or guacamole.

Shredded Beef for Tacos

Dawn Day
Westminster, CA

Makes 6-8 servings

2-3-lb. round roast, cut into large chunks
1 large onion, chopped
3 Tbsp. oil
2 serrano chilies, chopped
3 garlic cloves, minced
1 tsp. salt
1 cup water

1. Brown meat and onion in oil. Transfer to slow cooker.
2. Add chilies, garlic, salt, and water.

3. Cover. Cook on High 6-8 hours.
4. Pull meat apart with two forks until shredded.
5. Serve with fresh tortillas, lettuce, tomatoes, cheese, and guacamole.

Southwestern Flair

Phyllis Attig
Reynolds, IL

Makes 8-12 servings

3-4-lb. chuck roast, *or* flank steak
1 envelope dry taco seasoning
1 cup chopped onions
1 Tbsp. white vinegar
1¼ cup green chilies
flour tortillas
grated cheese
refried beans
shredded lettuce
chopped tomatoes
salsa
sour cream
guacamole

1. Combine meat, taco seasoning, onions, vinegar, and chilies in slow cooker.
2. Cover. Cook on Low 9 hours.
3. Shred meat with fork.
4. Serve with tortillas and your choice of the remaining ingredients.

Tostadas
Elizabeth L. Richards
Rapid City, SD

Makes 6-10 servings

1 lb. ground beef, browned
2 cans refried beans
1 envelope dry taco
    seasoning mix
8-oz. can tomato sauce
1/2 cup water
10 tostada shells
1 1/2 cups shredded lettuce
2 tomatoes, diced
1/2 lb. shredded cheddar
    cheese
1 can sliced black olives
1 pint sour cream
guacamole
salsa

1. Combine ground beef, refried beans, taco seasoning mix, tomato sauce, and water in slow cooker.
2. Cover. Cook on Low 6 hours.
3. Crisp tostada shells.
4. Spread hot mixture on tostada shells. Top with remaining ingredients.

Pecos River Red Frito Pie
Donna Barnitz
Jerks, OK

Makes 6 servings

1 large onion, chopped
    coarsely
3 lbs. coarsely ground
    hamburger
2 garlic cloves, minced
3 Tbsp. ground hot red
    chili peppers
2 Tbsp. ground mild red
    chili peppers
1 1/2 cups water
corn chips
shredded Monterey Jack
    cheese
shredded cheddar cheese

1. Combine onion, hamburger, garlic, chilies, and water in slow cooker.
2. Cover. Cook on Low 8-10 hours. Drain.
3. Serve over corn chips. Top with mixture of Monterey Jack and cheddar cheeses.

Nachos
Arlene Miller
Hutchinson, KS

Makes 8 servings

1 lb. ground beef
1/4 cup diced onions
1/4 cup diced green peppers
1 pint taco sauce
1 can refried beans
10 3/4-oz. can cream of
    mushroom soup
1 envelope dry taco
    seasoning
salt to taste
2 cups Velveeta, *or*
    cheddar, cheese
tortilla chips
lettuce
chopped tomatoes
sour cream

1. Brown ground beef, onions, and green peppers in saucepan. Drain.
2. Combine all ingredients except tortilla chips, lettuce, tomatoes, and sour cream in slow cooker.
3. Cover. Cook on High 1 hour, stirring occasionally until cheese is fully melted.
4. Pour into serving bowl and serve immediately with chips, lettuce, tomatoes, and sour cream, or turn to Low to keep warm and serve from cooker.

If a recipe calls for cooked noodles, macaroni, etc., cook them before adding to the cooker. Don't overcook; instead, cook just till slightly tender.

If cooked rice is called for, stir in raw rice with the other ingredients. Add 1 cup extra liquid per cup of raw rice. Use long grain converted rice for best results in all-day cooking.
Mrs. Don Martins
Fairbank, IA

Mexican Corn Bread

Jeanne Heyerly
Chenoa, IL

Makes 6 servings

16-oz. can cream-style corn
1 cup cornmeal
1/2 tsp. baking soda
1 tsp. salt
1/4 cup oil
1 cup milk
2 eggs, beaten
1/2 cup taco sauce
2 cups shredded cheddar
    cheese
1 medium onion, chopped
1 garlic clove, minced
4-oz. can diced green
    chilies
1 lb. ground beef, lightly
    cooked and drained

1. Combine corn, corn-
meal, baking soda, salt, oil,
milk, eggs, and taco sauce.
Pour half of mixture into slow
cooker.
2. Layer cheese, onion,
garlic, green chilies, and
ground beef on top of cornmeal mixture. Cover with
remaining cornmeal mixture.
3. Cover. Cook on High
1 hour and on Low 31/2-4
hours, or only on Low 6
hours.

Tamale Pie

Jeannine Janzen
Elbing, KS

Makes 8 servings

3/4 cup cornmeal
11/2 cups milk
1 egg, beaten
1 lb. ground beef, browned
    and drained
1 envelope dry chili
    seasoning mix
16-oz. can diced tomatoes
16-oz. can corn, drained
1 cup grated cheddar
    cheese

1. Combine cornmeal,
milk, and egg.
2. Stir in meat, chili seasoning mix, tomatoes, and
corn until well blended. Pour
into slow cooker.
3. Cover. Cook on High 1
hour, then on Low 3 hours.
4. Sprinkle with cheese.
Cook another 5 minutes until
cheese is melted.

Piquant French Dip

Marcella Stalter
Flanagan, IL

Makes 8 servings

3-lb. chuck roast
2 cups water
1/2 cup soy sauce
1 tsp. dried rosemary
1 tsp. dried thyme
1 tsp. garlic powder
1 bay leaf
3-4 whole peppercorns
8 French rolls

1. Place roast in slow
cooker. Add water, soy sauce,
and seasonings.
2. Cover. Cook on High 5-6
hours, or until beef is tender.
3. Remove beef from
broth. Shred with fork. Keep
warm.
4. Strain broth. Skim fat.
Pour broth into small cups for
dipping. Serve beef on rolls.

Note:
    If you have leftover broth,
freeze it to use later for gravy
or as a soup base.

Carol's Italian Beef

Carol Findling
Princeton, IL

Makes 6-8 servings

3-4-lb. lean rump roast
2 tsp. salt, divided
4 garlic cloves
2 tsp. Romano, *or*
  Parmesan, cheese,
  divided
12-oz. can beef broth
1 tsp. dried oregano

1. Place roast in slow cooker. Cut 4 slits in top of roast. Fill each slit with 1/2 tsp. salt, 1 garlic clove, and 1/2 tsp. cheese.
2. Pour broth over meat. Sprinkle with oregano.
3. Cover. Cook on Low 10-12 hours, or High 4-6 hours.
4. Remove meat and slice or shred. Serve on buns with meat juices on the side.

Lauren's Italian Beef

Lauren Eberhard
Seneca, IL

Makes 16 servings

4-5-lb. boneless roast,
  cubed
1 medium onion, chopped
1-2 garlic cloves, minced
2-3 pkgs. dry Good Seasons
  Italian dressing mix
1/2 cup water
16 steak rolls
mozzarella cheese,
  shredded

1. Combine first five ingredients in slow cooker.
2. Cover. Cook on Low 10 hours. Stir occasionally.
3. Slice meat into thin slices. Pile on rolls, top with cheese, and serve immediately.

Tangy Barbecue Sandwiches

Lavina Hochstedler
Grand Blanc, MI
Lois M. Martin, Lititz, PA

Makes 14-18 sandwiches

3 cups chopped celery
1 cup chopped onions
1 cup ketchup
1 cup barbecue sauce
1 cup water
2 Tbsp. vinegar
2 Tbsp. Worcestershire
  sauce
2 Tbsp. brown sugar
1 tsp. chili powder
1 tsp. salt
1/2 tsp. pepper
1/2 tsp. garlic powder
3-4-lb. boneless chuck
  roast
14-18 hamburger buns

1. Combine all ingredients except roast and buns in slow cooker. When well mixed, add roast.
2. Cover. Cook on High 6-7 hours.
3. Remove roast. Cool and shred meat. Return to sauce. Heat well.
4. Serve on buns.

Always defrost meat or poultry before putting it into the slow cooker, or cook recipes containing frozen meats an additional 4-6 hours on Low, or 2 hours on High.
Rachel Kauffman
Alto, MI

Mile-High Shredded Beef Sandwiches

Miriam Christophel
Battle Creek, MI
Mary Seielstad, Sparks, NV

Makes 8 servings

3-lb. chuck roast, *or* round
   steak
2 Tbsp. oil
1 cup chopped onions
1/2 cup sliced celery
2 cups beef broth, *or*
   bouillon
1 garlic clove
1 tsp. salt
3/4 cup ketchup
4 Tbsp. brown sugar
2 Tbsp. vinegar
1 tsp. dry mustard
1/2 tsp. chili powder
3 drops Tabasco sauce
1 bay leaf
1/4 tsp. paprika
1/4 tsp. garlic powder
1 tsp. Worcestershire sauce

1. In skillet brown both sides of meat in oil. Add onions and celery and saute briefly. Transfer to slow cooker. Add broth or bouillon.

2. Cover. Cook on Low 6-8 hours, or until tender. Remove meat from cooker and cool. Shred beef.

3. Remove vegetables from cooler and drain, reserving 1 1/2 cups broth. Combine vegetables and meat.

4. Return shredded meat and vegetables to cooker. Add broth and remaining ingredients and combine well.

5. Cover. Cook on High 1 hour. Remove bay leaf.

6. Pile into 8 sandwich rolls and serve.

Slow-Cooker Beef Sandwiches

Elaine Unruh
Minneapolis, MN
Winifred Ewy, Newton, KS

Makes 6-8 servings

2-3-lb. chuck roast, cubed
1 pkg. dry onion soup mix
12-oz. can cola

1. Place meat in slow cooker.

2. Sprinkle soup mix over meat. Pour cola over all.

3. Cover. Cook on Low 8-10 hours.

4. Serve as roast or shred the beef, mix with sauce, and serve on buns.

Variation:

Layer 4 medium potatoes, sliced, and 4 carrots, sliced, in bottom of pot. Place meat and rest of ingredients on top, and follow recipe for cooking.

Barbecue Beef

Elizabeth Yoder
Millersburg, OH

Makes 12 servings

3-lb. boneless chuck roast
1 cup barbecue sauce
1/2 cup apricot preserves
1/3 cup chopped green
   peppers
1 small onion, chopped
1 Tbsp. Dijon mustard
2 tsp. brown sugar
12 sandwich rolls

1. Cut roast into quarters. Place in greased slow cooker.

2. Combine barbecue sauce, preserves, green peppers, onion, mustard, and brown sugar. Pour over roast.

3. Cover. Cook on Low 6-8 hours. Remove roast and slice thinly. Return to slow cooker. Stir gently.

4. Cover. Cook 20-30 minutes.

5. Serve beef and sauce on rolls.

Fill the cooker no more than 2/3 full and no less than half-full.

Rachel Kauffman
Alto, MI

Barbecue Beef Sandwiches

Eleanor Larson
Glen Lyon, PA

Makes 18-20 sandwiches

3 1/2-4-lb. beef round steak,
   cubed
1 cup finely chopped
   onions
1/2 cup firmly packed
   brown sugar
1 Tbsp. chili powder
1/2 cup ketchup
1/3 cup cider vinegar
12-oz. can beer
6-oz. can tomato paste
buns

1. Combine all ingredients except buns in slow cooker.
2. Cover. Cook on Low 10-12 hours.
3. Remove beef from sauce with slotted spoon. Place in large bowl. Shred with 2 forks.
4. Add 2 cups sauce from slow cooker to shredded beef. Mix well.
5. Pile into buns and serve immediately.
6. Reserve any remaining sauce for serving over pasta, rice, or potatoes.

Hearty Italian Sandwiches

Rhonda Lee Schmidt
Scranton, PA
Robin Schrock
Millersburg, OH

Makes 8 servings

1 1/2 lbs. ground beef
1 1/2 lbs. bulk Italian
   sausage
2 large onions, chopped
2 large green peppers,
   chopped
2 large sweet red peppers,
   chopped
1 tsp. salt
1 tsp. pepper
shredded Monterey Jack
   cheese
8 sandwich rolls

1. In skillet brown beef and sausage. Drain.
2. Place one-third onions and peppers in slow cooker. Top with half of meat mixture. Repeat layers. Sprinkle with salt and pepper.
3. Cover. Cook on Low 6 hours, or until vegetables are tender.
4. With a slotted spoon, serve about 1 cup mixture on each roll. Top with cheese.

Note:
   For some extra flavor, add a spoonful of salsa to each roll before topping with cheese.

Barbecued Spoonburgers

Mrs. Paul Gray
Beatrice, NE

Makes 8-10 servings

2 Tbsp. oil
1 1/2 lbs. ground beef
1/2 cup chopped onions
1/2 cup diced celery
half a green pepper,
   chopped
1 Tbsp. Worcestershire
   sauce
1/2 cup ketchup
1 garlic clove, minced
1 tsp. salt
3/4 cup water
1/8 tsp. pepper
1/2 tsp. paprika
6-oz. can tomato paste
2 Tbsp. vinegar
2 tsp. brown sugar
1 tsp. dry mustard

1. Brown beef in oil in saucepan. Drain.
2. Combine all ingredients in slow cooker.
3. Cover. Cook on Low 6-8 hours, or High 3-4 hours.
4. Serve on buns or over mashed potatoes, pasta, or rice.

Jean & Tammy's Sloppy Joes

Jean Shaner, York, PA
Tammy Smoker
Cochranville, PA

Makes 12 servings

3 lbs. ground beef,
  browned and drained
1 onion, finely chopped
1 green pepper, chopped
2 8-oz. cans tomato sauce
¾ cup ketchup
1 Tbsp. Worcestershire
  sauce
1 tsp. chili powder
¼ tsp. pepper
¼ tsp. garlic powder
sandwich rolls

1. Combine all ingredients
except rolls in slow cooker.
2. Cover. Cook on Low 8-
10 hours, or High 3-4 hours.
3. Serve in sandwich rolls.

Penny's Sloppy Joes

Penny Blosser
Beavercreek, OH

Makes 6 servings

1 lb. ground beef, browned
  and drained
10¾-oz. can cream of
  mushroom soup
¼ cup ketchup
1 small onion, diced

1. Combine all ingredients
in slow cooker.
2. Cover. Cook on Low 1-2
hours.
3. Serve on rolls or over
baked potatoes.

Nan's Sloppy Joes

Nan Decker
Albuquerque, NM

Makes 4-6 servings

1 lb. ground beef
1 onion, chopped
¾ cup ketchup
2 Tbsp. chili sauce
1 Tbsp. Worcestershire
  sauce
1 Tbsp. prepared mustard
1 Tbsp. vinegar
1 Tbsp. sugar
whole wheat buns

1. Brown beef and onion
in saucepan. Drain.

2. Combine all ingredients
in slow cooker.
3. Cover. Cook on Low 4-5
hours.
4. Serve on buns.

Corned Beef

Margaret Jarrett
Anderson, IN

Makes 6-7 servings

2-3-lb. cut of marinated
  corned beef
2-3 garlic cloves, minced
10-12 peppercorns

1. Place meat in bottom of
cooker. Top with garlic and
peppercorns. Cover with
water.
2. Cover. Cook on High 4-5
hours, or until tender.
3. Cool meat, slice thin,
and use to make Reuben
sandwiches along with sliced
Swiss cheese, sauerkraut, and
Thousand Island dressing on
toasted pumpernickel bread.

Corned Beef and Cabbage

Rhoda Burgoon
Collingswood, NJ
Jo Ellen Moore, Pendleton, IN

Makes 6-8 servings

3 carrots, cut in 3" pieces
3-4-lb. corned beef brisket
2-3 medium onions,
quartered
3/4-1 1/4 cups water
half a small head of
cabbage, cut in wedges

1. Layer all ingredients except cabbage in slow cooker.
2. Cover. Cook on Low 8-10 hours, or High 5-6 hours.
3. Add cabbage wedges to liquid, pushing down to moisten. Turn to High and cook an additional 2-3 hours.

Note:
To cook more cabbage than slow cooker will hold, cook separately in skillet. Remove 1 cup broth from slow cooker during last hour of cooking. Pour over cabbage wedges in skillet. Cover and cook slowly for 20-30 minutes.

Variations:
1. Add 4 medium potatoes, halved, with the onions.
2. Top individual servings with mixture of sour cream and horseradish.
Kathi Rogge
Alexandria, IN

Eleanor's Corned Beef and Cabbage

Eleanor J. Ferreira
N. Chelmsford, MA

Makes 6 servings

2 medium onions, sliced
2 1/2-3-lb. corned beef
brisket
1 cup apple juice
1/4 cup brown sugar,
packed
2 tsp. finely shredded
orange peel
6 whole cloves
2 tsp. prepared mustard
6 cabbage wedges

1. Place onions in slow cooker. Place beef on top of onions.
2. Combine apple juice, brown sugar, orange peel, cloves, and mustard. Pour over meat.
3. Place cabbage on top.
4. Cover. Cook on Low 10-12 hours, or High 5-6 hours.

Cranberry Pork Roast

Barbara Aston
Ashdown, AR

Makes 6-8 servings

3-4-lb. pork roast
salt to taste
pepper to taste
1 cup ground, *or* finely
chopped, cranberries
1/4 cup honey
1 tsp. grated orange peel
1/8 tsp. ground cloves
1/8 tsp. ground nutmeg

1. Sprinkle roast with salt and pepper. Place in slow cooker.
2. Combine remaining ingredients. Pour over roast.
3. Cover. Cook on Low 8-10 hours.

Use your slow cooker to cook a hen, turkey, or roast beef for use in salads or casseroles. The meat can even be frozen when you put it in the slow cooker. Set the cooker on Low, and let the meat cook all night while you sleep.
Julia B. Boyd
Memphis, TN

Cranberry Pork Roast

Phyllis Attig, Reynolds, IL
Mrs. J.E. Barthold
Bethlehem, PA
Kelly Bailey
Mechanicsburg, PA
Joyce Kaut, Rochester, NY

Makes 4-6 servings

2½-3-lb. boneless rolled
  pork loin roast
16-oz. can jellied cranberry
  sauce
½ cup sugar
½ cup cranberry juice
1 tsp. dry mustard
¼ tsp. ground cloves
2 Tbsp. cornstarch
2 Tbsp. cold water
1 tsp. salt

1. Place roast in slow cooker.
2. Combine cranberry sauce, sugar, cranberry juice, mustard, and cloves. Pour over roast.
3. Cover. Cook on Low 6-8 hours, or until meat is tender.
4. Remove roast and keep warm.
5. Skim fat from juices. Measure 2 cups, adding water if necessary. Pour into saucepan. Bring to boil over medium heat. Combine the cornstarch and cold water to make a paste. Stir into gravy. Cook and stir until thickened. Season with salt.
6. Serve with sliced pork.

Savory Pork Roast

Betty A. Holt
St. Charles, MO

Makes 8-10 servings

4-5-lb. pork loin roast
large onion, sliced
1 bay leaf
2 Tbsp. soy sauce
1 Tbsp. garlic powder

1. Place roast and onion in slow cooker. Add bay leaf, soy sauce, and garlic powder.
2. Cover. Cook on High 1 hour and then on Low 6 hours.
3. Slice and serve.

Teriyaki Pork Roast

Janice Yoskovich
Carmichaels, PA

Makes 8 servings

¾ cup unsweetened apple
  juice
2 Tbsp. sugar
2 Tbsp. soy sauce
1 Tbsp. vinegar
1 tsp. ground ginger
¼ tsp. garlic powder
⅛ tsp. pepper
3-lb. boneless pork loin
  roast, halved
2½ Tbsp. cornstarch
3 Tbsp. cold water

1. Combine apple juice, sugar, soy sauce, vinegar, ginger, garlic powder, and pepper in greased slow cooker.
2. Add roast. Turn to coat.
3. Cover. Cook on Low 7-8 hours. Remove roast and keep warm.
4. In saucepan, combine cornstarch and cold water until smooth. Stir in juices from roast. Bring to boil. Cook and stir for 2 minutes, or until thickened. Serve with roast.

> Since I work full-time, I often put my dinner into the slow cooker to cook until I get home. My three teenagers and umpire/referee husband can all get a hot nutritious meal no matter what time they get home.
> **Rhonda Burgoon**
> Collingswood, NJ

Pork Roast with Potatoes and Onions

Trudy Kutter
Corfu, NY

Makes 6-8 servings

2½-3-lb. boneless pork
   loin roast
1 large garlic clove, slivered
5-6 potatoes, cubed
1 large onion, sliced
¾ cup broth, tomato juice,
   or water
1½ Tbsp. soy sauce
1 Tbsp. cornstarch
1 Tbsp. cold water

1. Make slits in roast and insert slivers of garlic. Put under broiler to brown.
2. Put potatoes in slow cooker. Add half of onions. Place roast on onions and potatoes. Cover with remaining onions.
3. Combine broth and soy sauce. Pour over roast.
4. Cover. Cook on Low 8 hours. Remove roast and vegetables from liquid.
5. Combine cornstarch and water. Add to liquid in slow cooker. Turn to High until thickened. Serve over sliced meat and vegetables.

Variation:
   Use sweet potatoes instead of white potatoes.

Chalupa

Jeannine Janzen
Elbing, KS

Makes 12-16 servings

3-lb. pork roast
1 lb. dry pinto beans
2 garlic cloves, minced
1 Tbsp. ground cumin
1 Tbsp. dried oregano
2 Tbsp. chili powder
1 Tbsp. salt
4-oz. can chopped green
   chilies
water

1. Cover beans with water and soak overnight in slow cooker.
2. In the morning, remove beans (reserve soaking water), and put roast in bottom of cooker. Add remaining ingredients (including the beans and their soaking water) and more water if needed to cover all the ingredients.
3. Cook on High 1 hour, and then on Low 6 hours. Remove meat and shred with two forks. Return meat to slow cooker.
4. Cook on High 1 more hour.
5. Serve over a bed of lettuce. Top with grated cheese and chopped onions and tomatoes.

Tangy Pork Chops

Tracy Clark, Mt. Crawford, VA
Lois M. Martin, Lititz, PA
Becky Oswald, Broadway, PA

Makes 4 servings

4 ½-inch thick pork chops
½ tsp. salt
⅛ tsp. pepper
2 medium onions, chopped
2 celery ribs, chopped
1 large green pepper, sliced
14½-oz. can stewed
   tomatoes
½ cup ketchup
2 Tbsp. cider vinegar
2 Tbsp. brown sugar
2 Tbsp. Worcestershire sauce
1 Tbsp. lemon juice
1 beef bouillon cube
2 Tbsp. cornstarch
2 Tbsp. water

1. Place chops in slow cooker. Sprinkle with salt and pepper.
2. Add onions, celery, pepper, and tomatoes.
3. Combine ketchup, vinegar, brown sugar, Worcestershire sauce, lemon juice, and bouillon. Pour over vegetables.
4. Cover. Cook on Low 5-6 hours.
5. Combine cornstarch and water until smooth. Stir into slow cooker.
6. Cover. Cook on High 30 minutes, or until thickened.
7. Serve over rice.

Variation:
   Use chunks of beef or chicken legs and thighs instead of pork.

Spicy Pork Chops

Mary Puskar
Forest Hill, MD

Makes 5 servings

5-6 center-cut loin pork
  chops
3 Tbsp. oil
1 onion, sliced
1 green pepper, cut in
  strips
8-oz. can tomato sauce
3-4 Tbsp. brown sugar
1 Tbsp. vinegar
1½ tsp. salt
1-2 tsp. Worcestershire
  sauce

1. Brown chops in oil in
skillet. Transfer to slow
cooker.
2. Add remaining ingredi-
ents to cooker.
3. Cover. Cook on Low 6-8
hours.
4. Serve over rice.

Saucy Pork Chops

Bonita Ensenberger
Albuquerque, NM

Makes 4 servings

4 pork chops
salt to taste
pepper to taste
1 tsp. garlic powder
1 Tbsp. oil
2-2½ cups ketchup
½ cup brown sugar
1 Tbsp. hickory-flavored
  liquid smoke
1 cup onions, chopped

1. Season chops with salt,
pepper, and garlic powder.
Brown on both sides in oil in
skillet. Drain.
2. Combine ketchup,
brown sugar, and liquid
smoke in bowl.
3. Place onions in slow
cooker. Dip browned pork
chops in sauce mixture and
place on onions. Pour remaining sauce over chops.
4. Cover. Cook on Low 7-9
hours, or High 4-5 hours.
5. Makes a great meal
served with cole slaw and
oven-roasted, cut-up root vegetables.

Barbecue Pork Chops

Annabelle Unternahrer
Shipshewana, IN
Evelyn L. Ward
Greeley, CO

Makes 8 servings

8 pork chops
1 cup (or more) barbecue,
  or sweet-sour, sauce

1. Brush each pork chop
generously with sauce, then
place in slow cooker.
2. Cover. Cook on Low 7-8
hours.

Trim as much visible fat from meat as possible before
placing it in the slow cooker in order to avoid greasy gravy.
Carolyn Baer
Conrath, WI

Pork Chops in Bean Sauce

Shirley Sears
Tiskilwa, IL

Makes 6 servings

6 pork chops
1/3 cup chopped onions
1/2 tsp. salt
1/3 tsp. garlic salt
1/8 tsp. pepper
28-oz. can vegetarian, *or* baked, beans
1/4 tsp. hot pepper sauce
13 1/2-oz. can crushed pineapple, undrained
1/3 cup chili sauce

1. Brown pork chops in skillet five minutes per side. Place in slow cooker.
2. Saute onion in skillet in meat juices. Spread over pork chops.
3. Sprinkle with salt, garlic salt, and pepper.
4. Combine beans and hot sauce. Pour over chops.
5. Combine pineapple and chili sauce. Spread evenly over beans.
6. Cover. Cook on Low 7-8 hours.

Chops and Beans

Mary L. Casey
Scranton, PA

Makes 4-6 servings

2 1-lb. cans pork and beans
1/2 cup ketchup
2 slices bacon, browned and crumbled
1/2 cup chopped onions, sauteed
1 Tbsp. Worcestershire sauce
1/4 cup firmly packed brown sugar
4-6 pork chops
2 tsp. prepared mustard
1 Tbsp. brown sugar
1/4 cup ketchup
one lemon

1. Combine beans, 1/2 cup ketchup, bacon, onions, Worcestershire sauce, and 1/4 cup brown sugar in slow cooker.
2. Brown chops in skillet. In separate bowl, mix together 2 tsp. mustard, 1 Tbsp. brown sugar, and 1/4 cup ketchup. Brush each chop with sauce, then carefully stack into cooker, placing a slice of lemon on each chop. Submerge in bean/bacon mixture.
3. Cover. Cook on Low 4-6 hours.

Italian Chops

Jan Moore
Wellsville, KS

Makes 2-4 servings

16-oz. bottle Italian salad dressing (use less if cooking only 2 chops)
2-4 pork chops

1. Place pork chops in slow cooker. Pour salad dressing over chops.
2. Cover. Cook on High 6-8 hours.

Variation:
Add cubed potatoes and thinly sliced carrots and onions to meat before pouring dressing over top.

Cooker Chops

Lucille Metzler
Wellsboro, PA

Makes 4 servings

4 pork chops
10³/4-oz. can cream of
    mushroom soup
¹/4 cup ketchup
2 tsp. Worcestershire sauce

1. Put chops in slow
cooker.
2. Combine remaining
ingredients. Pour over chops.
3. Cover. Cook on High 3-4
hours, or Low 8-10 hours.

Variation:
    Add one sliced onion to
mixture.
      Maryland Massey
      Mellington, MD

Easy Sweet and Sour Pork Chops

Jeanne Hertzog
Bethlehem, PA

Makes 6 servings

16-oz. bag frozen Oriental
    vegetables
6 pork chops
12-oz. bottle sweet and
    sour sauce
¹/2 cup water
1 cup frozen pea pods

1. Place partially thawed
Oriental vegetables in slow
cooker. Arrange chops on top.
2. Combine sauce and
water. Pour over chops
3. Cover. Cook on Low 7-8
hours.
4. Turn to High and add
pea pods.
5. Cover. Cook on High 5
minutes.

Chicken-Fried Pork Chops

Martha Ann Auker
Landisburg, PA

Makes 6 servings

¹/2 cup flour
³/4 tsp. salt
1¹/2 tsp. dry mustard
³/4 tsp. garlic powder
6 pork chops
2 Tbsp. oil
10³/4-oz. can cream of
    chicken soup
1 soup can water

1. Combine flour, salt, dry
mustard, and garlic powder.
Dredge pork chops in flour
mixture. Brown in oil in skillet. Place in slow cooker.
2. Combine soup and
water. Pour over meat.
3. Cover. Cook on High 6-8
hours.

Golden Glow Pork Chops

Pam Hochstedler
Kalona, IA

Makes 5-6 servings

5-6 pork chops
salt to taste
pepper to taste
29-oz. can cling peach
    halves, drained (reserve
    juice)
¹/4 cup brown sugar
¹/2 tsp. ground cinnamon
¹/4 tsp. ground cloves
8-oz. can tomato sauce
¹/4 cup vinegar

1. Lightly brown pork
chops on both sides in
saucepan. Drain. Arrange in
slow cooker. Sprinkle with
salt and pepper.
2. Place drained peach
halves on top of pork chops.
3. Combine brown sugar,
cinnamon, cloves, tomato
sauce, ¹/4 cup peach syrup,
and vinegar. Pour over
peaches and pork chops.
4. Cover. Cook on Low 3-4
hours.

Perfect Pork Chops

Brenda Pope
Dundee, OH

Makes 2 servings

2 small onions
2 ¾-inch thick, boneless,
    center loin pork chops,
    frozen
fresh ground pepper to
    taste
1 chicken bouillon cube
¼ cup hot water
2 Tbsp. prepared mustard
    with white wine
fresh parsley sprigs, *or*
    lemon slices, optional

1. Cut off ends of onions and peel. Cut onions in half crosswise to make 4 thick "wheels." Place in bottom of slow cooker.
2. Sear both sides of frozen chops in heavy skillet. Place in cooker on top of onions. Sprinkle with pepper.
3. Dissolve bouillon cube in hot water. Stir in mustard. Pour into slow cooker.
4. Cover. Cook on High 3-4 hours.
5. Serve topped with fresh parsley sprigs or lemon slices, if desired.

Pork Chops and Gravy

Sharon Wantland
Menomonee Falls, WI

Makes 8 servings

8 pork chops
salt to taste
pepper to taste
2 Tbsp. oil
2 10¾-oz. cans cream of
    mushroom soup
1 large onion, sliced
12-oz. can evaporated milk

1. Season pork chops with salt and pepper. Brown in oil. Drain. Transfer to slow cooker.
2. In separate bowl, whisk together mushroom soup, onion, and evaporated milk until smooth. Pour over chops.
3. Cook on High 3-4 hours, or Low 6-8 hours.

Variations:
To increase flavor, stir ½-1 cup sour cream, or ¼ cup sherry, into mixture during last 30 minutes of cooking time.

Pork Chops and Mushrooms

Michele Ruvola
Selden, NY

Makes 4 servings

4 boneless pork chops,
    ½-inch thick
2 medium onions, sliced
4-oz. can sliced
    mushrooms, drained
1 envelope dry onion soup
    mix
¼ cup water
10¾-oz. can golden cream
    of mushroom soup

1. Place pork chops in greased slow cooker. Top with onions and mushrooms.
2. Combine soup mix, water, and mushroom soup. Pour over mushrooms.
3. Cover. Cook on Low 6-8 hours.

Lightly grease your slow cooker before adding casserole ingredients.

Sara Wilson
Blainstown, MO

Pork Chops with Mushroom Sauce

Jennifer J. Gehman
Harrisburg, PA

Makes 4-6 servings

4-6 boneless thin or thick
  pork chops
10¾-oz. can cream of
  mushroom soup
¾ cup white wine
4-oz. can sliced
  mushrooms
2 Tbsp. quick cooking
  tapioca
2 tsp. Worcestershire sauce
1 tsp. beef bouillon
  granules, *or* 1 beef
  bouillon cube
¼ tsp. minced garlic
¾ tsp. dried thyme,
  optional

1. Place pork chops in
slow cooker.
2. Combine remaining
ingredients and pour over
pork chops.
3. Cook on Low 8-10
hours, or on High 4½-5
hours.
4. Serve over rice.

Pork Chops and Gravy

Barbara J. Fabel
Wausau, WI

Makes 3-4 servings

3 large onions, quartered
  or sliced
3 ribs of celery, chunked *or*
  sliced
3-4 pork chops
10¾-oz. can cream of
  mushroom, *or* cream of
  celery, soup

1. Place onions and celery
in slow cooker. Wash pork
chops and place on top of
onions and celery. Pour soup
over all.
2. Cover. Cook on High 1
hour. Reduce heat to Low
and cook 3-4 hours, or until
chops are tender.

Pork Chop Surprise

Jan Moore
Wellsville, KS

Makes 4 servings

4 pork chops
6 potatoes, sliced
10¾-oz. can cream of
  mushroom soup
water

1. Brown pork chops on
both sides in skillet. Transfer
to slow cooker.
2. Add potatoes. Pour soup
over top. Add enough water
to cover all ingredients.
3. Cover. Cook on High 6-8
hours.

Variation:
  Combine 1 envelope dry
onion soup mix with mush-
room soup before pouring
over chops and potatoes.
  Trudy Kutter
  Corfu, NY

Pork Chop Casserole

Doris Bachman
Putnam, IL

Makes 4-6 servings

4-6 pork chops
3 cups water
1 cup rice, uncooked
10¾-oz. can cream of
  mushroom soup
1 tsp. salt
1 tsp. dried parsley
¼ tsp. pepper

1. Saute pork chops in skillet until brown. Transfer to
slow cooker.
2. Mix remaining ingredi-
ents and pour over chops in
cooker.
3. Cover. Cook on Low 6-8
hours, or High 3-4 hours.

Jean's Pork Chops

Jean Weller
State College, PA

Makes 6 servings

1/2 cup flour
1 Tbsp. salt
1 1/2 tsp. dry mustard
1/2 tsp. garlic powder
6-8 1-inch thick pork
  chops
2 Tbsp. oil
15 1/2-oz. can chicken and
  rice soup

1. Combine flour, salt, dry mustard, and garlic powder. Dredge pork chops in flour mixture. Brown in oil in skillet. Transfer to slow cooker. Add soup.
2. Cover. Cook on Low 6-8 hours, or on High 3 1/2 hours.

Variation:

For increased flavor, step up the dry mustard to 1 Tbsp. and add 1 tsp. pepper.
Mary Puskar
Forest Hill, MD

Tender
Pork Chops

Dawn M. Propst
Levittown, PA
Kim McEuen
Lincoln University, PA

Makes 6 servings

6 pork chops
1/2 cup flour
1 tsp. salt
1/2 tsp. garlic powder
1 1/2 tsp dry mustard
2 Tbsp. oil
15-oz. can chicken gumbo
  soup

1. Coat chops with a combination of flour, salt, garlic powder, and mustard. Brown chops in skillet. Place in slow cooker. Drain drippings from skillet.
2. Add soup to skillet. Stir to loosen brown bits from pan. Pour over pork chops.
3. Cover. Cook on Low 6-8 hours.

Pork and Cabbage
Dinner

Mrs. Paul Gray
Beatrice, NE

Makes 8 servings

2 lbs. pork steaks, *or*
  chops, *or* shoulder
3/4 cup chopped onions
1/4 cup chopped fresh
  parsley, *or* 2 Tbsp. dried
  parsley
4 cups shredded cabbage
1 tsp. salt
1/8 tsp. pepper
1/2 tsp. caraway seeds
1/8 tsp. allspice
1/2 cup beef broth
2 cooking apples, cored
  and sliced 1/4-inch thick

1. Place pork in slow cooker. Layer onions, parsley, and cabbage over pork.
2. Combine salt, pepper, caraway seeds, and allspice. Sprinkle over cabbage. Pour broth over cabbage.
3. Cover. Cook on Low 5-6 hours.
4. Add apple slices 30 minutes before serving.

Put your cooker meal together the night before you want to cook it. The following morning put the mixture in the slow cooker, cover, and cook.
Sara Wilson
Blairstown, MO

Ham and Cabbage Supper

Louise Stackhouse
Benten, PA

Makes 4 servings

1 medium-size cabbage
  head, cut into quarters
4-lb. smoked picnic ham
1/4 cup water

1. Place cabbage quarters
in bottom of slow cooker.
Place ham on top. Pour in
water.
2. Cover. Cook on Low 8-
10 hours.

Variation:
  To cabbage quarters, add
2 sliced carrots, 1 sliced
onion, 2 potatoes cut into
cubes, and 2 bay leaves for
additional flavor and nutri-
tion.

Ham and Scalloped Potatoes

Penny Blosser
Beavercreek, OH
Jo Haberkamp, Fairbank, IA
Ruth Hofstetter
Versailles, Missouri
Rachel Kauffman, Alto, MI
Mary E. Martin, Goshen, IN
Brenda Pope, Dundee, OH
Joyce Slaymaker
Strasburg, PA

Makes 6-8 servings

6-8 slices ham
8-10 medium potatoes,
  thinly sliced
2 onions, thinly sliced
salt to taste
pepper to taste
1 cup grated cheddar, *or*
  American, cheese
10 3/4-oz. can cream of
  celery, *or* mushroom,
  soup
paprika

1. Put half of ham, pota-
toes, and onions in slow
cooker. Sprinkle with salt, pepper, and cheese. Repeat layers.
2. Spoon soup over top.
Sprinkle with paprika.
3. Cover. Cook on Low 8-
10 hours, or High 4 hours.

Variation:
  If you like a lot of creamy
sauce with your ham and
potatoes, stir 3/4 soup can of
milk into the soup before
pouring it over the layers.
  Alma Z. Weaver
  Ephrata, PA

Miriam's Scalloped Potatoes with Ham

Miriam Christophel
Battle Creek, MI

Makes 6 servings

6 cups raw potatoes, cut
  into small cubes
1 medium onion, minced
1 tsp. salt
1/2 lb. cooked ham, cubed
4 Tbsp. butter
4 Tbsp. flour
1 tsp. salt
2 cups milk
1 1/2 cups shredded cheddar
  cheese

1. Layer potatoes, onion,
1 tsp. salt, and ham into slow
cooker.
2. Melt butter in saucepan.
Stir in flour and 1 tsp. salt.
Cook until bubbly. Gradually
add milk. Cook until smooth
and thickened. Add cheese
and stir until melted. Pour
over potato-ham mixture, stirring lightly.
3. Cover. Cook on Low 6-7
hours, or High 3-4 hours.

Michelle's Scalloped Potatoes and Ham

Michelle Strite
Harrisonburg, VA

Makes 6-8 servings

6 cups cooked, shredded
  potatoes
4 cups diced ham
dash pepper, if desired
10¾-oz. can cream of
  mushroom soup
10¾-oz. can cream of
  celery soup
1 cup milk

1. Combine all ingredients
in slow cooker.
2. Cover. Cook on Low 3-4
hours.

Potatoes and Ham

Janice Martins
Fairbank, IA

Makes 8 serving

5 potatoes, sliced
½ lb. ham, diced
¼-lb. Velveeta cheese,
  cubed
half a small onion, diced
10¾-oz. can cream of
  chicken soup

1. Layer potatoes, ham,
cheese, and onion in slow
cooker. Top with soup.
2. Cover. Cook on Low 6
hours.

Barbara's Scalloped Potatoes with Ham

Barbara Katrine Rose
Woodbridge, VA

Makes 10-12 servings

4-lb. potatoes, sliced
1½ lbs. cooked ham, cut
  into ¼-inch strips
3 Tbsp. minced dried
  onions
1 cup water
2 11-oz. cans condensed
  cheddar cheese soup

1. Layer potatoes, ham,
and onions in very large slow
cooker.
2. Combine soup and
water. Pour over layers in pot.
3. Cover. Cook on Low 6-8
hours.

Country Scalloped Potatoes and Ham

Deb Unternahrer
Wayland, IA

Makes 10 servings

8 potatoes, thinly sliced
1 onion, chopped
1 lb. fully-cooked ham,
  cubed
1-oz. pkg. dry country-style
  gravy mix
10¾-oz. can cream of
  mushroom soup
2 cups water
2 cups shredded cheddar
  cheese

1. Combine potatoes,
onion, and ham in lightly
greased slow cooker.
2. Combine gravy mix,
mushroom soup, and water.
Whisk until combined. Pour
over potaotes.
3. Cover. Cook on Low 7-9
hours, or High 3-4 hours.
4. Top with cheese during
last 30 minutes of cooking.

Variation:
  Put half the potatoes,
onion, and ham in cooker.
Top with half the grated
cheese. Repeat layers. Spoon
undiluted soup over top.
Cover and cook on Low 7-9
hours, or High 3-4 hours.
Sprinkle individual servings
with paprika.
Doris Bachman
Putnam, IL

Au Gratin Potatoes and Ham

Donna Lantgen
Rapid City, SD

Makes 6-8 servings

10 potatoes, thinly sliced
1 onion, chopped
2 Tbsp. flour
1/4 tsp. pepper, optional
1/2 lb. Velveeta cheese, cubed
1/2 cup milk
1/2-1 cup fully cooked ham, *or* sliced hot dogs

1. Combine all ingredients in slow cooker.
2. Cover. Cook on Low 7-8 hours.

Ham and Potatoes

Ruth Shank
Gridley, IL

Makes 6-8 servings

6-8 medium red, *or* russet, potatoes, cut into chunks
2-3-lb. boneless ham
1/2 cup brown sugar
1 tsp. dry mustard

1. Prick potato pieces with fork. Place in slow cooker.
2. Place ham on top of potatoes. Crumble brown sugar over ham. Sprinkle with dry mustard.
3. Cover. Cook on Low 10 or more hours, until potatoes are tender.
4. Pour juices over ham and potatoes to serve.

Ham 'n Cola

Carol Peachey
Lancaster, PA

Makes 8-10 servings

1/2 cup brown sugar
1 tsp. dry mustard
1 tsp. prepared horseradish
1/4 cup cola-flavored soda
3-4-lb. precooked ham

1. Combine brown sugar, mustard, and horseradish. Moisten with just enough

cola to make a smooth paste. Reserve remaining cola.
2. Rub entire ham with mixture. Place ham in slow cooker and add remaining cola.
3. Cover. Cook on Low 6-10 hours, or High 2-3 hours.

Ham in Cider

Dorothy M. Van Deest
Memphis, TN

Makes 6-8 servings

3-lb. ham (or larger; whatever fits your slow cooker)
4 cups sweet cider, *or* apple juice
1 cup brown sugar
2 tsp. dry mustard
1 tsp. ground cloves
2 cups white seedless raisins

1. Place ham and cider in slow cooker.
2. Cover. Cook on Low 8-10 hours.
3. Remove ham from cider and place in baking pan.
4. Make a paste of sugar, mustard, cloves, and a little hot cider. Brush over ham. Pour a cup of juice from slow cooker into baking pan. Stir in raisins.
5. Bake at 375° for 30 minutes, until the paste has turned into a glaze.

Sweet-Sour Pork

Mary W. Stauffer
Ephrata, PA

Makes 4-6 servings

2 lbs. pork shoulder, cut in strips
1 green pepper, cut in strips
half a medium onion, thinly sliced
3/4 cup shredded carrots
2 Tbsp. coarsely chopped sweet pickles
1/4 cup brown sugar, packed
2 Tbsp. cornstarch
1/4 cup water
1 cup pineapple syrup (reserved from pineapple chunks)
1/4 cup cider vinegar
1 Tbsp. soy sauce
2 cups pineapple chunks

1. Place pork strips in slow cooker.
2. Add green pepper, onion, carrots, and pickles.
3. In bowl, mix together brown sugar and cornstarch. Add water, pineapple syrup, vinegar, and soy sauce. Stir until smooth.
4. Pour over ingredients in slow cooker.
5. Cover. Cook on Low 5-7 hours. One hour before serving, add pineapple chunks. Stir.
6. Serve over buttered noodles with an additional dash of vinegar or garlic to taste.

Barbecued Spareribs

Mrs. Paul Gray
Beatrice, NE

Makes 4 servings

4-lb. country-style spareribs, cut into serving-size pieces
10 3/4-oz. can tomato soup
1/2 cup cider vinegar
1/2 cup brown sugar
1 Tbsp. soy sauce
1 tsp. celery seed
1 tsp. salt
1 tsp. chili powder
dash cayenne pepper

1. Place ribs in slow cooker.
2. Combine remaining ingredients and pour over ribs.
3. Cover. Cook on Low 6-8 hours.
4. Skim fat from juices before serving.

Tender and Tangy Ribs

Betty Moore, Plano, IL
Renee Shirk, Mount Joy, PA

Makes 2-3 servings

3/4-1 cup vinegar
1/2 cup ketchup
2 Tbsp. sugar
2 Tbsp. Worcestershire sauce
1 garlic clove, minced
1 tsp. dry mustard
1 tsp. paprika
1/2 tsp. salt
1/8 tsp. pepper
2 lbs. pork spareribs
1 Tbsp. oil

1. Combine all ingredients except spareribs and oil in slow cooker.
2. Brown ribs in oil in skillet. Transfer to slow cooker.
3. Cover. Cook on Low 4-6 hours.

"High" on most slow cookers is approximately 300°F. "Low" is approximately 200°F.
Annabelle Unternahrer
Shipshewana, IN

Michele's Barbecued Ribs

Michele Ruvola
Selden, NY

Makes 8 servings

3 lbs. pork loin back ribs,
  cut into serving-size
  pieces
2 Tbsp. instant minced
  onion
1 tsp. crushed red pepper
1/2 tsp. ground cinnamon
1/2 tsp. garlic powder
1 medium onion, sliced
1/2 cup water
1 1/2 cups barbecue sauce

1. Combine onion, red
pepper, cinnamon, and garlic
powder. Rub mixture into
ribs. Layer ribs and onion in
slow cooker. Pour water
around ribs.
2. Cover. Cook on Low 8-9
hours.
3. Remove ribs from slow
cooker. Drain and discard liquid. Pour barbecue sauce in
bowl and dip ribs in sauce.
Return ribs to slow cooker.
Pour remaining sauce over
ribs.
4. Cover. Cook on Low 1
hour.

Sharon's Barbecued Ribs

Sharon Easter
Yuba City, CA

Makes 4-6 servings

3-4-lb. boneless pork ribs,
  cut into serving-size
  pieces
1 cup barbecue sauce
1 cup Catalina salad
  dressing

1. Place ribs in slow
cooker.
2. Combine barbecue
sauce and salad dressing.
Pour over ribs.
3. Cover. Cook on Low 8
hours.

Variation:
Add 1 garlic clove sliced
thin to top of sauce before
cooking.

Awfully Easy Barbecued Ribs

Sara Harter Fredette,
Williamsburg, MA
Colleen Konetzni,
Rio Rancho, NM
Mary Mitchell,
Battle Creek, MI
Audrey Romonosky
Austin, TX
Iva Schmidt, Fergus Falls, MN
Susan Tjon
Austin, TX

Makes 4-6 servings

3-4-lb. baby back, *or*
  country-style, spareribs
1/2 tsp. salt, optional
1/2 tsp. pepper, optional
2 onions, sliced
16-24-oz. bottle barbecue
  sauce (depending upon
  how saucy you like your
  chops)

1. Brown ribs under
broiler. Slice into serving-size
pieces, season, and place in
slow cooker.
2. Add onions and barbe-
cue sauce.
3. Cover. Cook on Low 6
hours. These are good served
with baked beans and corn
on the cob.

Variation:
Instead of broiling the ribs,
place them in slow cooker
with other ingredients and
cook on High 1 hour. Turn to
Low and cook 8 more hours.

Barbecued Pork Ribs

Julia B. Boyd
Memphis, TN

Makes 4 servings

3 lbs. spareribs, cut into
   serving-size pieces
water
1/4 tsp. salt
1/4 tsp. pepper
1 large onion, diced
1 garlic clove, minced
2 cups barbecue sauce

1. Place ribs in slow
cooker. Cover with water.
2. Cover. Cook on Low 3-4
hours. Drain water, reserving
it to make Dumplings (see
below), if desired.
3. Add remaining ingredi-
ents to slow cooker.
4. Cover. Cook on Low 3-5
hours.

Dumplings:
2 Tbsp. butter, *or*
   margarine
1/2 cup boiling broth (from
   parboiling spareribs,
   above)
flour
remaining broth
salt to taste
pepper to taste

1. Pour 1/2 cup broth over
butter to melt. Add flour to
make dough. Roll out on
floured board until pastry-
thin.
2. Pour remaining reserved
broth into soup pot and add

salt and pepper to taste. Bring
to boil.
3. Slice dough into 1 1/2"
strips and drop into boiling
broth in soup pot. Cover, but
watch carefully that the broth
does not boil over. The
dumplings will rise to the
surface and be done within 5-
10 minutes. Serve with barbecued ribs.

Just Peachy Ribs

Amymarlene Jensen
Fountain, CO

Makes 4-6 servings

4-lb. boneless pork
   spareribs
1/2 cup brown sugar
1/4 cup ketchup
1/4 cup white vinegar
1 garlic clove, minced
1 tsp. salt
1 tsp. pepper
2 Tbsp. soy sauce
15-oz. can spiced cling
   peaches, cubed, with
   juice

1. Cut ribs in serving-size
pieces and brown in broiler
or in saucepan in oil. Drain.
Place in slow cooker.
2. Combine remaining
ingredients. Pour over ribs.
3. Cover. Cook on Low 8-
10 hours.

Sesame Pork Ribs

Joette Droz
Kalona, IA

Makes 6 servings

1 medium onion, sliced
3/4 cup packed brown
   sugar
1/4 cup soy sauce
1/2 cup ketchup
1/4 cup honey
2 Tbsp. cider, *or* white
   vinegar
3 garlic cloves, minced
1 tsp. ground ginger
1/4-1/2 tsp. crushed red
   pepper flakes
5 lbs. country-style pork
   ribs
2 Tbsp. sesame seeds,
   toasted
2 Tbsp. chopped green
   onions

1. Place onions in bottom
of slow cooker.
2. Combine brown sugar,
soy sauce, ketchup, honey,
vinegar, garlic, ginger, and
red pepper flakes in large
bowl. Add ribs and turn to
coat. Place on top of onions
in slow cooker. Pour sauce
over meat.
3. Cover. Cook on Low 5-6
hours.
4. Place ribs on serving
platter. Sprinkle with sesame
seeds and green onions. Serve
sauce on the side.

147

Barbecued Pork

Grace Ketcham, Marietta, GA
Mary Seielstad, Sparks, NV

Makes 6 servings

3 lbs. pork, cubed
2 cups chopped onions
3 green peppers, chopped
1/2 cup brown sugar
1/4 cup vinegar
6-oz. can tomato paste
1 1/2 Tbsp. chili powder
1 tsp. dry mustard
2 tsp. Worcestershire sauce
2 tsp. salt

1. Combine all ingredients in slow cooker.
2. Cover. Cook on High 8 hours.
3. Shred meat with fork. Mix into sauce and heat through.
4. Serve on hamburger buns with grated cheese and cole slaw on top.

Variation:
Substitute cubed chuck roast or stewing beef for the pork, or use half beef, half pork.

Barbecued Pork in the Slow Cooker

Dawn Day
Westminster, CA

Makes 6-8 servings

2-3-lb. boneless pork roast, cubed
2 onions, chopped
12-oz. bottle barbecue sauce
1/4 cup honey
sandwich rolls

1. Place meat in slow cooker. Add onions, barbecue sauce, and honey.
2. Cover. Cook on Low 6-8 hours.
3. Use 2 forks to shred meat.
4. Serve on rolls with sauce.

Pork Barbecue

Mary Sommerfeld
Lancaster, PA

Makes 8-12 sandwiches

2 onions, sliced
4-5-lb. pork roast, *or* fresh picnic ham
5-6 whole cloves
2 cups water

Sauce:
1 large onion, chopped
16-oz. bottle barbecue sauce

1. Put half of sliced onions in bottom of slow cooker. Add meat, cloves, and water. Cover with remaining sliced onions.
2. Cover. Cook on Low 8-12 hours.
3. Remove bone from meat. Cut up meat. Drain liquid.
4. Return meat to slow cooker. Add chopped onion and barbecue sauce.
5. Cover. Cook on High 1-3 hours, or Low 4-8 hours, stirring two or three times.
6. Serve on buns.

Note:
This freezes well.

A word of caution—it is a common mistake to add too much liquid.

Mrs. J.E. Barthold
Bethlehem, PA

148

Shredded Pork

Sharon Easter
Yuba City, CA

Makes 4-6 servings

2-3-lb. pork butt roast, *or*
boneless country-style
spareribs
1/2-1 cup water
1 pkg. dry taco seasoning
mix

1. Place meat in slow
cooker. Add water and seasoning mix.
2. Cover. Cook on Low 24
hours. Shred meat with two
forks.
3. Use in tacos or in rolls,
or use the sauce as gravy and
serve over rice.

Melt-in-Your-Mouth Sausages

Ruth Ann Gingrich,
New Holland, PA
Ruth Hershey, Paradise, PA
Carol Sherwood, Batavia, NY
Nancy Zimmerman
Loysville, PA

Makes 6-8 servings

2 lbs. sweet Italian
sausage, cut into 5-inch
lengths
48-oz. jar spaghetti sauce
6-oz. can tomato paste
1 large green pepper,
thinly sliced
1 large onion, thinly sliced
1 Tbsp. grated Parmesan
cheese
1 tsp. dried parsley, *or*
1 Tbsp. chopped fresh
parsley
1 cup water

1. Place sausage in skillet.
Cover with water. Simmer 10
minutes. Drain.
2. Combine remaining
ingredients in slow cooker.
Add sausage.
3. Cover. Cook on Low 6
hours.
4. Serve in buns, or cut
sausage into bite-sized pieces
and serve over cooked
spaghetti. Sprinkle with more
Parmesan cheese.

Sauerkraut & Trail Bologna

Carol Sommers
Millersburg, OH

Makes 10 servings

32-oz. bag sauerkraut,
rinsed
1/4-1/2 cup brown sugar
1 ring Trail Bologna

1. Combine sauerkraut
and brown sugar in slow
cooker.
2. Remove casing from
bologna and cut into 1/4-inch
slices. Add to sauerkraut. Stir.
3. Cover. Cook on Low 6-8
hours.

Note:
If you don't have access to
Holmes County, Ohio's spe-
cialty Trail Bologna, use 1
large ring bologna.

Kraut and Sausage

Kathi Rogge
Alexandria, IN

Makes 4 servings

2 16-oz. cans sauerkraut,
drained and rinsed
2 Tbsp. dark brown sugar
1 large onion, chopped
2 strips bacon, diced
1 lb. fully-cooked sausage,
sliced

1. Combine sauerkraut
and brown sugar. Place in
slow cooker. Add layers of
onion, bacon, and sausage.
Add enough water to cover
half of sausage.
2. Cover. Cook on Low 5-6
hours, or on High 3 hours.

Sauerkraut and Kielbasa

Mary Ellen Wilcox
Scotia, NY

Makes 4-6 servings

64-oz. can sauerkraut
1 medium onion, chopped
1 large bay leaf
1 lb. kielbasa, cut into
serving-sized pieces

1. Combine all ingredients
in slow cooker. Add enough
water to cover all ingredients.

2. Cover. Cook on High 30
minutes, and then on Low 6
hours. Remove bay leaf
before serving.

Polish Kraut 'n Apples

Lori Berezovsky, Salina, KS
Marie Morucci,
Glen Lyon, PA

Makes 4 servings

1 lb. fresh, *or* canned,
sauerkraut
1 lb. lean smoked Polish
sausage
3 tart cooking apples,
thinly sliced
1/2 cup packed brown
sugar
3/4 tsp. salt
1/8 tsp. pepper
1/2 tsp. caraway seeds,
optional
3/4 cup apple juice, *or* cider

1. Rinse sauerkraut and
squeeze dry. Place half in
slow cooker.
2. Cut sausage into 2-inch
lengths and add to cooker.
3. Continue to layer
remaining ingredients in slow
cooker in order given. Top
with remaining sauerkraut.
Do not stir.
4. Cover. Cook on High
3-3 1/2 hours, or Low 6-7
hours. Stir before serving.

Old World Sauerkraut Supper

Josie Bollman, Maumee, OH
Joyce Bowman, Lady Lake, FL
Vera Schmucker, Goshen, IN

Makes 8 servings

3 strips bacon, cut into
small pieces
2 Tbsp. flour
2 15-oz. cans sauerkraut
2 small potatoes, cubed
2 small apples, cubed
3 Tbsp. brown sugar
1 1/2 tsp. caraway seeds
3 lbs. Polish sausage, cut
into 3-inch pieces
1/2 cup water

1. Fry bacon until crisp.
Drain, reserving drippings.
2. Add flour to bacon drippings. Blend well. Stir in
sauerkraut and bacon.
Transfer to slow cooker.
3. Add remaining ingredients.
4. Cover. Cook on Low 6-8
hours, or High 3-4 hours.

Polish Sausage Stew

Jeanne Heyerly, Chenoa, IL
Joyce Kaut, Rochester, NY
Joyce B. Suiter,
Garysburg, NC

Makes 6-8 servings

10¾-oz. can cream of
  celery soup
⅓ cup packed brown
  sugar
27-oz. can sauerkraut,
  drained
1½ lbs. Polish sausage, cut
  into 2-inch pieces and
  browned
4 medium potatoes, cubed
1 cup chopped onions
1 cup (4 oz.) shredded
  Monterey Jack cheese

1. Combine soup, sugar,
and sauerkraut. Stir in
sausage, potatoes, and onions.
2. Cover. Cook on Low 8
hours, or on High 4 hours.
3. Stir in cheese and serve.

Sausage Sauerkraut Supper

Ruth Ann Hoover,
New Holland, PA
Robin Schrock,
Millersburg, OH

Makes 10-12 servings

4 cups cubed carrots
4 cups cubed red potatoes
2 14-oz. cans sauerkraut,
  rinsed and drained
2½ lbs. fresh Polish
  sausage, cut into 3-inch
  pieces
1 medium onion, thinly
  sliced
3 garlic cloves, minced
1½ cups dry white wine,
  or chicken broth
½ tsp. pepper
1 tsp. caraway seeds

1. Layer carrots, potatoes,
and sauerkraut in slow
cooker.
2. Brown sausage in skil-
let. Transfer to slow cooker.
Reserve 1 Tbsp. drippings in
skillet.
3. Sautc onion and garlic
in drippings until tender. Stir
in wine. Bring to boil. Stir to
loosen brown bits. Stir in pepper and caraway seeds. Pour
over sausage.
4. Cover. Cook on Low 8-9
hours.

Kielbasa and Cabbage

Barbara McGinnis
Jupiter, FL

Makes 6 servings

1½ lb.-head green cabbage,
  shredded
2 medium onions, chopped
3 medium red potatoes,
  peeled and cubed
1 red bell pepper, chopped
2 garlic cloves, minced
⅔ cup dry white wine
1½ lbs. Polish kielbasa,
  cut into 3-inch long
  links
28-oz. can cut-up tomatoes
  with juice
1 Tbsp. Dijon mustard
¾ tsp. caraway seeds
½ tsp. pepper
¾ tsp. salt

1. Combine all ingredients
in slow cooker.
2. Cover. Cook on Low 7-8
hours, or until cabbage is tender.

Aunt Lavina's Sauerkraut

Pat Unternahrer
Wayland, IA

Makes 8-12 servings

2-3 lbs. smoked sausage, cut into 1-inch pieces
2 Tbsp. water, *or* oil
2 bell peppers, chopped
2 onions, sliced
1/2 lb. fresh mushrooms, sliced
1 qt. sauerkraut, drained
2 14 1/2-oz. cans diced tomatoes with green peppers
1 tsp. salt
1/2 tsp. pepper
2 Tbsp. brown sugar

1. Place sausage in slow cooker. Heat on Low while you prepare other ingredients.
2. Saute peppers, onions, and mushrooms in small amount of water or oil in saucepan.
3. Combine all ingredients in slow cooker.
4. Cover. Cook on Low 5-6 hours, or High 3-4 hours.
5. Serve with mashed potatoes.

Pork and Kraut

Joyce B. Suiter
Garysburg, NC

Makes 6 servings

4-lb. pork loin
29-oz. can sauerkraut
1/4 cup water
1 onion, sliced
1 large white potato, sliced
10 3/4-oz. can cheddar cheese soup
1 Tbsp. caraway seeds
1 large Granny Smith apple, peeled and sliced
salt to taste
pepper to taste

1. Brown roast on all sides in skillet. Place in slow cooker.
2. Rinse sauerkraut and drain well. Combine sauerkraut, water, onion, potato, soup, caraway seeds, and apple. Pour over roast.
3. Cover. Cook on Low 10 hours.
4. Season with salt and pepper before serving.

Note:
Apple and potato disappear into the cheese soup as they cook, making a good sauce.

Pork Roast with Sauerkraut

Gail Bush
Landenberg, PA

Makes 8 servings

2 3-lb. pork shoulder roasts
1 large can sweet Bavarian sauerkraut with caraway seeds
1/4 cup brown sugar
1 envelope dry onion soup mix
1/2 cup water

1. Place roasts in slow cooker.
2. Rinse and drain sauerkraut. Combine sauerkraut, brown sugar, and onion soup mix. Layer over roasts. Pour water over all.
3. Cover. Cook on Low 7 hours.

Note:
If you can't find Bavarian sauerkraut with caraway seeds, substitute with a 27-oz. can regular sauerkraut and 1/2 tsp. caraway seeds.

Browning the meat, onions, and vegetables before putting them in the cooker improves their flavor, but this extra step can be skipped in most recipes. The flavor will still be good.
Dorothy M. Van Deest
Memphis, TN

Pork and Sauerkraut

Carole Whaling
New Tripoli, PA

Makes 6 servings

4 large potatoes, cubed
32-oz. bag sauerkraut, drained
1 large onion, chopped
1 large tart apple, chopped
2 Tbsp. packed brown sugar
1 tsp. caraway seeds
1 tsp. minced garlic
1/2 tsp. pepper
2 1/2-lb. boneless pork loin roast

1. Put potatoes in slow cooker.
2. Combine remaining ingredients, except pork, in slow cooker. Place half of the sauerkraut mixture on top of the potatoes. Add roast. Top with remaining sauerkraut mixture.
3. Cover. Cook on High 3-4 hours.

Country Ribs and Sauerkraut

Andrea O'Neil
Fairfield, CT

Makes 4-6 servings

2 27-oz. cans sauerkraut, drained and rinsed
2-3 lbs. country-style pork ribs, cut into serving-size pieces
6 slices bacon, browned
3-4 Tbsp. caraway seeds
2 cups water

1. Place alternating layers of sauerkraut and ribs in slow cooker, starting and ending with sauerkraut.
2. Crumble bacon and mix gently into top layer of sauerkraut. Sprinkle with caraway seeds. Pour water over all.
3. Cover. Cook on Low 7-8 hours.

Sauerkraut and Ribs

Margaret H. Moffitt
Bartlett, TN

Makes 6 servings

27-oz. can sauerkraut with juice
1 small onion, chopped
2 lbs. pork, *or* beef, ribs, cut into serving-size pieces
1 tsp. salt
1/4 tsp. pepper
half a sauerkraut can of water

1. Pour sauerkraut and juice into slow cooker. Add onion.
2. Season ribs with salt and pepper. Place on top of kraut. Add water.
3. Cover. Cook on High until mixture boils. Reduce heat to Low and cook 4 hours.
4. Serve with mashed potatoes.

Pork Spareribs with Sauerkraut

Char Hagner
Montague, MI

Makes 4-6 servings

2 small cooking apples, sliced in rings
1½-2 lbs. spareribs, cut into serving-size pieces and browned
1 qt. sauerkraut
½ cup apple cider, *or* juice
½ tsp. caraway seeds, optional

1. Layer apples, ribs, and sauerkraut into slow cooker. Pour on juice. Sprinkle with caraway seeds.
2. Cover. Cook on Low 8 hours, or High 4 hours.

Pork Rib and Kraut Dinner

Betty A. Holt
St. Charles, MO

Makes 6-8 servings

3-4 lbs. country-style ribs
4 Tbsp. brown rice
1 Tbsp. caraway seeds
28-oz. can sauerkraut, rinsed
12-oz. can V-8 juice

1. Place ingredients in slow cooker in order listed.
2. Cover. Cook on Low 6-8 hours, or High 3-4 hours.

Variation:
To take the edge off the sour flavor of sauerkraut, stir in 3 Tbsp. mild molasses or honey before cooking.

Ham Hock and Sauerkraut

Bernice M. Gnidovec
Streator, IL

Makes 2 servings

2 small ham hocks, *or* pork chops
14-oz. can sauerkraut, rinsed
1 large potato, cubed
1 Tbsp. butter
half a small onion, diced
1 Tbsp. flour
2 Tbsp. cold water

1. Place ham hocks or chops in slow cooker. Top with sauerkraut. Add enough water to cover meat and sauerkraut.
2. Cover. Cook on High 4 hours, or Low 6-8 hours.
3. Saute onions in butter in saucepan until transparent. Stir in flour and brown. Add 2 Tbsp. cold water, stirring until thickened. Pour over ingredients in slow cooker. Cover and cook on High 5-10 minutes.

In recipes calling for rice, don't use minute or quick-cooking rice.

Mary Puskar
Forest Hill, MD

154

Simply Pork and Sauerkraut

Gladys Longacre
Susquehanna, PA

Makes 2-4 servings

2-4 pork chops
14-oz. can sauerkraut, *or* **more if you like sauerkraut**

1. Place pork chops in slow cooker. Cover with sauerkraut.
2. Cover. Cook on Low 7-8 hours.

Variations:
1. Brown pork chops before placing in slow cooker.
2. Substitute spareribs for pork chops.

Chops and Kraut

Willard E. Roth
Elkhart, IN

Makes 6 servings

1-lb. bag fresh sauerkraut
2 large Vidalia onions, sliced
6 pork chops

1. Make 3 layers in well-greased cooker: kraut, onions, and chops.
2. Cover. Cook on Low 6 hours.
3. Serve with mashed potatoes and applesauce or cranberry sauce.

Sauerkraut and Pork

Ethel Mumaw
Berlin, OH

Makes 6-8 servings

2 lbs. pork cutlets
2 14-oz. cans sauerkraut
2 apples, chopped
2 Tbsp. brown sugar

1. Cut pork into serving-size pieces. Brown under broiler or in 2 Tbsp. oil in skillet. Place in slow cooker.
2. Add remaining ingredients.
3. Cover. Cook on Low 7-8 hours.

Smothered Lentils

Tracey B. Stenger
Gretna, LA

Makes 6 servings

2 cups dry lentils, rinsed and sorted
1 medium onion, chopped
1/2 cup chopped celery
2 garlic cloves, minced
1 cup ham, cooked and chopped
1/2 cup chopped carrots
1 cup diced tomatoes
1 tsp. dried marjoram
1 tsp. ground coriander
salt to taste
pepper to taste
3 cups water

1. Combine all ingredients in slow cooker.
2. Cover. Cook on Low 8 hours. (Check lentils after 5 hours of cooking. If they've absorbed all the water, stir in 1 more cup water.)

Green Beans and Sausage

Alma Weaver
Ephrata, PA

Makes 4-6 servings

1 qt. green beans, cut into
  2-inch pieces
1 carrot, chopped
1 small green pepper,
  chopped
8-oz. can tomato sauce
1/4 tsp. dried thyme
1/2 tsp. salt
1 lb. bulk pork sausage, *or*
  link sausage cut into 1-
  inch pieces

1. Combine all ingredients
except sausage in slow
cooker.
2. Cover. Cook on High 3-4
hours. Add sausage and cook
another 2 hours on Low.

Sausage Supreme

Jan Moore
Wellsville, KS

Makes 4 servings

1 lb. fresh sausage, cut into
  1-inch pieces and
  browned
2 10³/4-oz. cans cream of
  mushroom soup
1 onion, chopped
4 potatoes, cubed

1. Combine all ingredients
in slow cooker.
2. Cover. Cook on Low 8
hours. If mixture becomes too
dry, stir in half a soup can or
more of water.

Variation:
  Substitute 1 can cheese
soup for 1 can cream of
mushroom soup.

Sausage and Apples

Evelyn L. Ward
Greeley, CO

Makes 4 servings

20-oz. can apple pie filling
1/4 cup water
ground nutmeg
10-oz. pkg. fully cooked
  and browned sausage
  patties

1. Spoon pie filling into
slow cooker. Stir in water.
Sprinkle with nutmeg. Top
with sausage.
2. Cover. Cook on Low 4-6
hours.

Kielbasa and Cheese Casserole

Dolores S. Kratz
Souderton, PA

Makes 4-5 servings

3 cups uncooked noodles
oil
2 beef bouillon cubes
1 cup boiling water
1/4 cup flour
2 Tbsp. butter, melted
4 oz. cheese, shredded
1 lb. kielbasa, sliced
1 small onion, chopped
2 ribs celery, diced
2 carrots, grated
2-oz. jar pimentos

1. Cook noodles until
barely tender. Drain. Toss
with small amount of oil.
2. Dissolve bouillon in
boiling water.
3. Combine all ingredients
in slow cooker.
4. Cover. Cook on Low 8
hours.

Variation:
  Instead of noodles, use
gnocchi.

Supreme Sausage Dish

Shirley Thieszen
Lakin, KS

Makes 6 servings

1 lb. smoky wieners, cut in 1-inch pieces
2 cups cooked macaroni
1 cup frozen peas, *or* corn
1/2 cup chopped onions
1 tsp. dry parsley
1 small jar chopped pimentos (about 3 Tbsp.)
3/4 cup shredded American, *or* Velvecta, cheese
3 Tbsp. flour
3/4 tsp. salt
1/4 tsp. pepper
1 cup milk
1 cup water
1/2 Tbsp. vinegar

1. Combine wieners, macaroni, peas, onions, parsley, and pimentos in greased slow cooker.
2. In saucepan, combine cheese, flour, salt, pepper, milk, water, and vinegar. Cook until smooth and thickened. Pour into slow cooker. Mix well.
3. Cover. Cook on High 1 hour, and then on Low 3-4 hours.

Variation:
Use smoked sausage instead of smoky wieners.

Barbecued Sausage Pieces

Elizabeth Yutzy
Wauseon, OH

Makes 4-5 main-dish servings, or 8-10 snack-sized servings

1 lb. smoked sausage
1 cup hickory-flavored barbecue sauce
1/4 cup honey
2 Tbsp. brown sugar

1. Cut sausage in 1/2-inch pieces. Brown in skillet. Place in slow cooker.
2. Combine remaining ingredients. Pour over sausage.
3. Cover. Cook on Low 2 hours.
4. Serve over rice or noodles as a main dish or with toothpicks as a party snack.

Perfection Hot Dogs

Audrey L. Kneer
Williamsfield, IL

Makes 12 servings

12 hot dogs, bratwurst, *or* Polish sausage links

1. Place hot dogs or sausages in slow cooker.
2. Cover. Cook on High 1-2 hours.

Beer Brats

Mary Ann Wasick
West Allis, WI

Makes 6 servings

6 fresh bratwurst
2 garlic cloves, minced
2 Tbsp. olive oil
12-oz. can beer

1. Brown sausages and garlic in olive oil in skillet. Pierce sausage casings and cook 5 more minutes. Transfer to slow cooker.
2. Pour beer into cooker to cover sausages.
3. Cover. Cook on Low 6-7 hours.

Spiced Hot Dogs

Tracey Yohn
Harrisburg, PA

Makes 3-4 servings

1 lb. hot dogs, cut in pieces
2 Tbsp. brown sugar
3 Tbsp. vinegar
1/2 cup ketchup
2 tsp. prepared mustard
1/2 cup water
1/2 cup chopped onions

1. Place hot dogs in slow cooker.
2. Combine all ingredients except hot dogs in saucepan. Simmer. Pour over hot dogs.
3. Cover. Cook on Low 2 hours.

Barbecued Hot Dogs

Jeanette Oberholtzer
Manheim, PA

Makes 8 servings

1 cup apricot preserves
4 oz. tomato sauce
1/3 cup vinegar
2 Tbsp. soy sauce
2 Tbsp. honey
1 Tbsp. oil
1 tsp. salt
1/4 tsp. ground ginger
2 lbs. hot dogs, cut into
  1-inch pieces

1. Combine all ingredients except hot dogs in slow cooker.
2. Cover. Cook on High 30 minutes. Add hot dog pieces. Cook on Low 4 hours.
3. Serve over rice as a main dish, or as an appetizer.

Bits and Bites

Betty Richards
Rapid City, SD

Makes 12 servings

12-oz. can beer
1 cup ketchup
1 cup light brown sugar
1/2-1 cup barbecue sauce
1 lb. all-beef hot dogs,
  sliced 1 1/2-inches thick
2 lbs. cocktail sausages

1. Combine beer, ketchup, brown sugar, and barbecue sauce. Pour into slow cooker.
2. Add hot dogs and sausages. Mix well.
3. Cover. Cook on Low 3-4 hours.

Barbecued Mini-Franks

Zona Mae Bontrager
Kokomo, IN

*Makes 8-10 full-sized servings, or
16-20 appetizer-sized servings*

1 cup finely chopped
  onions
1 cup ketchup
1/3 cup Worcestershire
  sauce
1/4 cup sugar
1/4 cup vinegar
4 tsp. prepared mustard
1 tsp. pepper
4-lbs. miniature hot dogs

1. Combine all ingredients except hot dogs in slow cooker.
2. Cover. Heat on High 1 1/2 hours, or until hot. Add hot dogs.
3. Reduce heat to Low and simmer 4 hours.

Variations:
1. Add 1 Tbsp. finely chopped green pepper and 2 garlic cloves, pressed.
2. Use miniature smoked sausages instead of mini-hot dogs.

Spicy Franks

Char Hagner
Montague, MI

*Makes 4-6 full-sized servings, or
32 appetizer-sized servings*

2 1-lb. pkgs. cocktail
  wieners
1 cup chili sauce
1 cup bottled barbecue
  sauce
8-oz. can jellied cranberry
  sauce

1. Place wieners in slow
cooker.
2. In separate bowl, com-
bine chili sauce, barbecue
sauce, and cranberry sauce.
Pour over wieners.
3. Cover. Cook on Low 3-4
hours, or High 1½-2 hours.

Little Smokies

Sharon Kauffman
Harrisonburg, VA

*Makes 6-8 full-sized servings, or
12-15 appetizer-sized servings*

2 pkgs. Li'l Smokies
1 bottle chili sauce
1 small jar grape jelly

1. Combine all ingredients
in slow cooker.
2. Cover. Cook on Low 1-2
hours, or until heated
through.

Sweet and Sour Vienna Sausages

Judy Denney
Lawrenceville, GA

*Makes 10 full-sized servings, or
20 appetizer-sized servings*

8 cans Vienna sausages,
  drained
2 cups grape jelly
2 cups ketchup

1. Put sausages in slow
cooker.
2. Combine jelly and
ketchup. Pour over sausages.
Stir lightly. (Add more jelly
and ketchup if sausages are
not covered.)
3. Cover. Cook on High 1
hour, then turn to Low for 5
hours.

Variations:
Instead of Vienna
sausages, use smoky links.
Add 1 can pineapple chunks
and juice to jelly and
ketchup.

Barbecued Ham Sandwiches

Jane Steiner
Orrville, OH

Makes 4-6 full-sized servings

1 lb. turkey ham chipped,
  or chipped honey-glazed
  ham
1 small onion, finely diced
½ cup ketchup
1 Tbsp. vinegar
3 Tbsp. brown sugar
buns

1. Place half of meat in
greased slow cooker.
2. Combine other ingredi-
ents. Pour half of mixture
over meat. Repeat layers.
3. Cover. Cook on Low 5
hours.
4. Fill buns and serve.

A slow cooker set on Low does not burn food and will not
spoil a meal if cooked beyond the designated time.
Eleanor J. Ferreira
North Chelmsford, MA

Ham Barbecue

Janet V. Yocum
Elizabethtown, PA

Makes 6-8 servings

1 lb. boiled ham, cut into cubes
1 cup cola-flavored soda
1 cup ketchup

1. Place ham in slow cooker. Pour cola and ketchup over ham.
2. Cover. Cook on Low 8 hours.
3. Serve in hamburger rolls.

Spaghetti Sauce

Doris Perkins
Mashpee, MA

Makes 18-24 servings

1/4-lb. bacon, diced
1 1/4-lb. ground beef
1/2 lb. ground pork
1 cup chopped onions
1/2 cup chopped green peppers
3 garlic cloves, minced
2 2-lb., 3-oz. cans Italian tomaoes
2 6-oz. cans tomao paste
1 cup dry red wine, *or* water
2 1/2 tsp. dried oregano
2 1/2 tsp. dried basil
1 bay leaf, crumbled
3/4 cup water
1/4 cup chopped fresh parsley
1 tsp. dried thyme
1 Tbsp. salt
1/4 tsp. pepper
1/4 cup dry red wine, *or* water

1. Brown bacon in skillet until crisp. Remove. Add ground beef and pork. Crumble and cook until brown. Stir in onions, green peppers, and garlic. Cook 10 minutes.
2. Pour tomatoes into slow cooker and crush with back of spoon.
3. Add all other ingredients, except 1/4 cup wine, in slow cooker.
4. Cover. Bring to boil on High. Reduce heat to Low for 3-4 hours.

5. During last 30 minutes, stir in 1/4 cup red wine *or* water.

Italian Spaghetti Sauce

Michele Ruvola
Selden, NY

Makes 8-10 servings

2 lbs. sausage, *or* ground beef
3 medium onions, chopped (about 2 1/4 cups)
2 cups sliced mushrooms
6 garlic cloves, minced
2 14 1/2-oz. cans diced tomatoes, undrained
29-oz. can tomato sauce
12-oz. can tomato paste
2 Tbsp. dried basil
1 Tbsp. dried oregano
1 Tbsp. sugar
1 tsp. salt
1/2 tsp. crushed red pepper flakes

1. Cook sausage, onions, mushrooms, and garlic in skillet over medium heat for 10 minutes. Drain. Transfer to slow cooker
2. Stir in remaining ingredients.
3. Cover. Cook on Low 8-9 hours.

Note:
This is also a good sauce to use in lasagna.

Chunky Spaghetti Sauce

Patti Boston
Newark, OH

Makes 6 cups

1 lb. ground beef, browned and drained
1/2 lb. bulk sausage, browned and drained
14 1/2-oz. can Italian tomatoes with basil
15-oz. can Italian tomato sauce
1 medium onion, chopped
1 green pepper, chopped
8-oz. can sliced mushrooms
1/2 cup dry red wine
2 tsp. sugar
1 tsp. minced garlic

1. Combine all ingredients in slow cooker.
2. Cover. Cook on High 3 1/2-4 hours, or Low 7-8 hours.

Variations:
1. For added texture and zest, add 3 fresh, medium-sized tomatoes, chopped, and 4 large fresh basil leaves, torn. Stir in 1 tsp. salt and 1/2 tsp. pepper.
2. To any leftover sauce, add chickpeas or kidney beans and serve chili!

Sausage-Beef Spaghetti Sauce

Jeannine Janzen
Elbing, KS

Makes 16-20 servings

1 lb. ground beef
1 lb. Italian sausage, sliced
2 28-oz. cans crushed tomatoes
3/4 can (28-oz. tomato can) water
2 tsp. garlic powder
1 tsp. pepper
2 Tbsp. or more parsley
2 Tbsp. dried oregano
2 12-oz. cans tomato paste
2 12-oz. cans tomato puree

1. Brown ground beef and sausage in skillet. Drain. Transfer to large slow cooker.
2. Add crushed tomatoes, water, garlic powder, pepper, parsley, and oregano.
3. Cover. Cook on High 30 minutes. Add tomato paste and tomato puree. Cook on Low 6 hours.

Note:
Leftovers freeze well.

Italian Sausage Spaghetti

Eleanor Larson
Glen Lyon, PA

Makes 12 servings

6 Italian turkey sausage links (1 1/2 lbs.), cut into 1 1/2-inch pieces
1 cup diced onions
3 Tbsp. sugar
1 tsp. dried oregano
1/2 tsp. salt
2 garlic cloves, minced
28-oz. can crushed tomatoes, undrained
15-oz. can tomato sauce
12-oz. can tomato paste
1 1/2 lbs. dry spaghetti

1. Combine all ingredients except spaghetti in slow cooker.
2. Cover. Cook on Low 8-10 hours.
3. Cook spaghetti in large soup pot. Drain and top with sauce.

> Cooked pasta and rice should be added during the last 1-1 1/2 hours of cooking time to prevent them from disintegrating.
> **John D. Allen**
> Rye, CO

Easy-Does-It Spaghetti

Rachel Kauffman, Alto, MI
Lois Stoltzfus, Honey Brook, PA
Deb Unternahrer, Wayland, IA

Makes 8 servings

2 lbs. ground chuck,
  browned and drained
1 cup chopped onions
2 cloves garlic, minced
2 15-oz. cans tomato sauce
2-3 tsp. Italian seasoning
1½ tsp. salt
¼ tsp. pepper
2 4-oz. cans sliced
  mushrooms, drained
6 cups tomato juice
16-oz. dry spaghetti,
  broken into 4-5-inch
  pieces
grated Parmesan cheese

1. Combine all ingredients
except spaghetti and cheese
in 4-quart (or larger) slow
cooker.
2. Cover. Cook on Low 6-8
hours, or High 3-5 hours.
Turn to High during last 30
minutes and stir in dry
spaghetti. (If spaghetti is not
fully cooked, continue cooking another 10 minutes,
checking to make sure it is
not becoming over-cooked.)
3. Sprinkle individual servings with Parmesan cheese.

Variation:
   Add 1 tsp. dry mustard
and ½ tsp. allspice in Step 1.
   Kathy Hertzler
   Lancaster, PA

Mom's Spaghetti and Meatballs

Mary C. Casey
Scranton, PA

Makes 8-10 servings

Sauce:
2 Tbsp. oil
¼-½ cup chopped onions
3 garlic cloves, minced
29-oz. can tomato puree
29-oz. can water
12-oz. can tomato paste
12-oz. can water
1 tsp. salt
1 Tbsp. sugar
2 tsp. dried oregano
¼ tsp. Italian seasoning
½ tsp. dried basil
⅛ tsp. pepper
¼ cup diced green peppers

Meatballs:
1 lb. ground beef
1 egg
2 Tbsp. water
¾ cup Italian bread
  crumbs
⅛ tsp. black pepper
½ tsp. salt
2 Tbsp. oil

1. Saute onions and garlic
in oil in saucepan.
2. Combine all sauce ingredients in slow cooker.
3. Cover. Cook on Low.
4. Mix together all meat-
ball ingredients except oil.
Form into small meatballs,
then brown on all sides in oil
in saucepan. Drain on paper
towels. Add to sauce.
5. Cover. Cook on Low 4-5
hours.

Spaghetti with Meat Sauce

Esther Lehman
Croghan, NY

Makes 8-10 servings

1 lb. ground beef, browned
2 28-oz. cans tomatoes
2 medium onions, quartered
2 medium carrots, cut into
  chunks
2 garlic cloves, minced
6-oz. can tomato paste
2 Tbsp. chopped fresh
  parsley
1 bay leaf
1 Tbsp. sugar
1 tsp. dried basil
¾ tsp. salt
½ tsp. dried oregano
dash pepper
2 Tbsp. cold water
2 Tbsp. cornstarch
hot cooked spaghetti
grated Parmesan cheese

1. Place meat in slow
cooker.
2. In blender, combine 1
can tomatoes, onions, carrots,
and garlic. Cover and blend
until finely chopped. Stir into
meat.
3. Cut up the remaining can
of tomatoes. Stir into meat mixture. Add tomato paste, parsley,
bay leaf, sugar, basil, salt,
oregano, and pepper. Mix well.
4. Cover. Cook on Low 8-10
hours.
5. To serve, turn to High.
Remove bay leaf. Cover and
heat until bubbly, about 10
minutes.

6. Combine water and cornstarch. Stir into tomato mixture. Cook 10 minutes longer.

7. Serve with spaghetti and cheese.

Slow Cooker Spaghetti Sauce

Lucille Amos, Greensboro, NC
Julia Lapp, New Holland, PA

Makes 6-8 servings

1 lb. ground beef
1 medium onion, chopped
2 14-oz. cans diced tomatoes, with juice
6-oz. can tomato paste
8-oz. can tomato sauce
1 bay leaf
4 garlic cloves, minced
2 tsp. dried oregano
1 tsp. salt
2 tsp. dried basil
1 Tbsp. brown sugar
1/2-1 tsp. dried thyme

1. Brown meat and onion in saucepan. Drain well. Transfer to slow cooker.

2. Add remaining ingredients.

3. Cover. Cook on Low 7 hours. If the sauce seems too runny, remove lid during last hour of cooking.

Nancy's Spaghetti Sauce

Nancy Graves
Manhattan, KS

Makes 4-6 servings

1/4 cup minced onion
garlic powder to taste
3 cups chopped fresh tomatoes, *or* 1-lb., 12-oz. can diced tomatoes with juice
6-oz. can tomato paste
3 1/2 tsp. salt
dash of pepper
1 basil leaf
1 chopped green pepper
1 lb. ground beef, browned and drained
4-oz. can sliced mushrooms

1. Combine all ingredients in slow cooker.

2. Cover. Cook on Low 3 hours.

Pasta Sauce with Meat and Veggies

Marla Folkerts
Holland, OH

Makes 6 servings

1/2 lb. ground turkey
1/2 lb. ground beef
1 rib celery, chopped
2 medium carrots, chopped
1 garlic clove, minced
1 medium onion, chopped
28-oz. can diced tomatoes with juice
1/2 tsp. salt
1/4 tsp. dried thyme
6-oz. can tomato paste
1/8 tsp. pepper

1. Combine turkey, beef, celery, carrots, garlic, and onion in slow cooker.

2. Add remaining ingredients. Mix well.

3. Cover. Cook on Low 7-8 hours.

4. Serve over pasta or rice.

Katelyn's Spaghetti Sauce

Katelyn Bailey
Mechanicsburg, PA

Makes 10-12 servings

1 lb. ground beef, browned and drained
3/4 cup chopped onions
1 garlic clove, minced
3 Tbsp. oil
2 6-oz. cans tomato paste
1 Tbsp. sugar
1 1/2 tsp. salt
1-1 1/2 tsp. dried oregano
1/2 tsp. pepper
1 bay leaf
2 qts. tomatoes, *or* tomato sauce

1. Combine all ingredients in slow cooker.
2. Cover. Cook on Low 8-10 hours. Remove bay leaf before serving.

Note:
This sauce freezes well.

Char's Spaghetti Sauce

Char Hagner
Montague, MI

Makes 16-20 servings

4 lbs. ground beef
2 large onions, chopped
1/4-lb. bacon, cut into small squares
5 garlic cloves, minced
1 Tbsp. salt
1/4 tsp. celery salt
4 10 3/4-oz. cans tomato soup
2 6-oz. cans tomato paste
8-oz. can mushrooms
3 green peppers, chopped

1. Brown ground beef, onions, bacon, and garlic in saucepan. Drain.
2. Combine all ingredients in large slow cooker.
3. Cover. Cook on Low 6 hours.

So-Easy Spaghetti

Ruth Ann Swartzendruber
Hydro, OK

Makes 4-6 servings

1 lb. ground beef
1/2 cup diced onions
1 pkg. dry spaghetti sauce mix
8-oz. can tomato sauce
3 cups tomato juice
4 oz. dry spaghetti, broken into 4-inch pieces

1. Brown meat and onions in skillet. Drain. Transfer to greased slow cooker.
2. Add remaining ingredients, except spaghetti.
3. Cover. Cook on Low 6-8 hours, or High 3 1/2 hours.
4. During last hour, turn to High and add spaghetti. Stir frequently to keep spaghetti from clumping together.

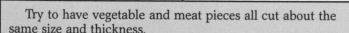

Try to have vegetable and meat pieces all cut about the same size and thickness.

Mary Puskar
Forest Hill, MD

Creamy Spaghetti
Dale Peterson
Rapid City, SD

Makes 6 servings

1 cup chopped onions
1 cup chopped green
  peppers
1 Tbsp. butter, *or*
  margarine
28-oz. can tomatoes with
  juice
4-oz. can mushrooms,
  chopped and drained
2¼-oz. can sliced ripe
  olives, drained
2 tsp. dried oregano
1 lb. ground beef, browned
  and drained
12 oz. spaghetti, cooked
  and drained
10¾-oz. can cream of
  mushroom soup
½ cup water
2 cups (8 oz.) shredded
  cheddar cheese
¼ cup grated Parmesan
  cheese

1. Saute onions and green
peppers in butter in skillet
until tender. Add tomatoes,
mushrooms, olives, oregano,
and beef. Simmer for 10 minutes. Transfer to slow cooker.
2. Add spaghetti. Mix well.
3. Combine soup and
water. Pour over casserole.
Sprinkle with cheeses.
4. Cover. Cook on Low 4-6
hours.

Tomato Spaghetti Sauce
Jean Butzer
Batavia, NY

Makes 6 servings

1 cup finely chopped
  onions
2 garlic cloves, minced
2 lbs. fresh tomatoes,
  peeled and chopped, *or*
  28-oz. can tomatoes, cut
  up, with juice
6-oz. can tomato paste
1 Tbsp. sugar
2 tsp. instant beef bouillon
  granules
1 tsp. dried oregano
½ tsp. dried basil
1 large bay leaf
salt to taste
pepper to taste
4-oz. can sliced
  mushrooms
2 Tbsp. cornstarch
2 Tbsp. cold water

1. Combine all ingredients
except mushrooms, corn-
starch, and water in slow
cooker.
2. Cover. Cook on Low 10-
12 hours.
3. Remove bay leaf. Stir in
mushrooms.
4. Combine cornstarch and
water. Stir into sauce.
5. Cover. Cook on High
until thickened and bubbly,
about 25 minutes.

Italian Vegetable Pasta Sauce
Sherril Bieberly
Salina, KS

Makes 2½ quarts sauce

3 Tbsp. olive oil
1 cup packed chopped
  fresh parsley
3 ribs celery, chopped
1 medium onion, chopped
2 garlic cloves, minced
2-inch sprig fresh
  rosemary, *or* ½ tsp.
  dried rosemary
2 small fresh sage leaves,
  or ½ tsp. dried sage
32-oz. can tomato sauce
32-oz. can chopped
  tomatoes
1 small dried hot chili
  pepper
¼ lb. fresh mushrooms,
  sliced, *or* 8-oz. can sliced
  mushrooms, drained
1½ tsp. salt

1. Heat oil in skillet. Add
parsley, celery, onion, garlic,
rosemary, and sage. Saute
until vegetables are tender.
Place in slow cooker.
2. Add tomatoes, chili pepper, mushrooms, and salt.
3. Cover. Cook on Low 12-
18 hours, or on High 5-6
hours.

Variation:
Add 2 lbs. browned
ground beef to olive oil and
sauted vegetables. Continue
with recipe.

Louise's Vegetable Spaghetti Sauce

Louise Stackhouse
Benton, PA

Makes 4-6 servings

6-7 fresh tomatoes, peeled
  and crushed
1 medium onion, chopped
2 green peppers, chopped
2 cloves garlic, minced
1/2 tsp. dried basil
1/2 tsp. dried oregano
1/4 tsp. salt
1/4 cup sugar
6-oz. can tomato paste,
  optional

1. Combine all ingredients
in slow cooker.
2. Cover. Cook on Low 8-
10 hours. If the sauce is too
watery for your liking, stir in
a 6-oz. can of tomato paste
during the last hour of cooking.
3. Serve over cooked
spaghetti or other pasta.

Pizza in a Pot

Marianne J. Troyer
Millersburg, OH

Makes 6-8 servings

1 lb. bulk Italian sausage,
  browned and drained
28-oz. can crushed
  tomatoes
15 1/2-oz. can chili beans
2 1/4-oz. can sliced black
  olives, drained
1 medium onion, chopped
1 small green pepper,
  chopped
2 garlic cloves, minced
1/4 cup grated Parmesan
  cheese
1 Tbsp. quick-cooking
  tapioca
1 Tbsp. dried basil
1 bay leaf
1 tsp. salt
hot cooked pasta
shredded mozzarella
  cheese

1. Combine all ingredients
in slow cooker except pasta
and mozzarella cheese.
2. Cover. Cook on Low 8-9
hours.
3. Discard bay leaf. Stir
well.
4. Serve over pasta. Top
with mozzarella cheese.

Slow-Cooker Pizza

Marla Folkerts, Holland, OH
Ruth Ann Swartzendruber
Hydro, OK
Arlene Wiens, Newton, KS

Makes 6-8 servings

1 1/2 lbs. ground beef, *or*
  bulk Italian sausage
1 medium onion, chopped
1 green pepper, chopped
half a box rigatoni, cooked
7-oz. jar sliced mushrooms,
  drained
3 oz. sliced pepperoni
16-oz. jar pizza sauce
10 oz. mozzarella cheese,
  shredded
10 oz. cheddar cheese,
  shredded

1. Brown ground beef and
onions in saucepan. Drain.
2. Layer half of each of the
following, in the order given,
in slow cooker: ground beef
and onions, green pepper,
noodles, mushrooms, pepperoni, pizza sauce, cheddar
cheese, and mozzarella
cheese. Repeat layers.
3. Cover. Cook on Low 3-4
hours.

Note:
Keep rigatoni covered with
sauce so they don't become
dry and crunchy.

Variation:
Add a 10 3/4-oz. can cream
of mushroom soup to the
mix, putting half of it in as a
layer after the first time the
noodles appear, and the other

half after the second layer of noodles.

Dorothy Horst
Tiskilwa, IL

Pizza Rice

Sue Hamilton
Minooka, IL

Makes 6 servings

2 cups rice, uncooked
3 cups chunky pizza sauce
2½ cups water
7-oz. can mushrooms, undrained
4 oz. pepperoni, sliced
1 cup grated cheese

1. Combine rice, sauce, water, mushrooms, and pepperoni. Stir.
2. Cover. Cook on Low 10 hours, or on High 6 hours. Sprinkle with cheese before serving.

Wild Rice Hot Dish

Barbara Tenney
Delta, PA

Makes 8-10 servings

2 cups wild rice, uncooked
½ cup slivered almonds
½ cup chopped onions
½ cup chopped celery
8-12-oz. can mushrooms, drained
2 cups cut-up chicken
6 cups chicken broth
¼-½ tsp. salt
¼ tsp. pepper
¼ tsp. garlic powder
1 Tbsp. parsley

1. Wash and drain rice.
2. Combine all ingredients in slow cooker. Mix well.
3. Cover. Cook on Low 4-6 hours, or until rice is finished. Do not remove lid before rice has cooked 4 hours.

Frances' Roast Chicken

Frances Schrag
Newton, KS

Makes 6 servings

3-4-lb. whole frying chicken
half an onion, chopped
1 rib celery, chopped
salt to taste
pepper to taste
½ tsp. poultry seasoning
¼ tsp. dried basil

1. Sprinkle chicken cavity with salt, pepper, and poultry seasoning. Put onion and celery inside cavity. Put chicken in slow cooker. Sprinkle with basil.
2. Cover. Cook on Low 8-10 hours, or High 4-6 hours.

When adapting range-top recipes to slow cooking, reduce the amount of onion you normally use because the onion flavor gets stronger during slow cooking.
Beatrice Orgish
Richardson, TX

Donna's Cooked Chicken

Donna Treloar
Gaston, IN

Makes 1 chicken

chicken (boneless, skinless
  breasts are the easiest,
  but any chicken pieces
  will do)
1 onion, sliced
seasoned salt
pepper
minced garlic, *or* garlic
  powder

1. Layer onion in bottom
of slow cooker. Add chicken
and sprinke with seasoned
salt, pepper, minced garlic, or
garlic powder.
2. Cook on Low 4 hours or
until done but not dry. (Time
will vary according to
amount of chicken and size of
pieces.)
3. Use in stir-frys, chicken
salads, or casseroles, slice for
sandwiches, shred for enchiladas, or cut up and freeze for
later use.

Variation:
  Splash chicken with
2 Tbsp. soy sauce before
cooking.

Valerie's & Stacy's Roast Chicken

Valerie Hertzler
Weyers Cave, VA
Stacy Petersheim
Mechanicsburg, PA

Makes 4-6 servings

3-4-lb. chicken
salt to taste
pepper to taste
butter
basil to taste

1. Wash chicken thor-
oughly. Pat dry. Sprinkle cavity
with salt and pepper. Place in
slow cooker. Dot with butter.
Sprinkle with basil.
2. Cover. Cook on High
1 hour, and then on Low 8-10
hours.

Chicken-at-the-Ready

Mary Mitchell
Battle Creek, MI

Makes 2-3 pints cooked chicken

1 large whole chicken,
  skinned
1 cup water

1. Place chicken in greased
slow cooker. Add water.
2. Cover. Cook on Low 6-8
hours.

3. Remove meat from
bones, pack cooked meat into
plastic boxes, and store in
freezer to use in recipes that
call for cooked chicken.

Note:
  I frequently put this on
late at night so that it is done
when I wake up in the morning.

Chicken in a Pot

Carolyn Baer, Conrath, WI
Evie Hershey, Atglen, PA
Judy Koczo, Plano, IL
Mary Puskar, Forest Hill, MD
Mary Wheatley, Mashpee, MA

Makes 6 servings

2 carrots, sliced
2 onions, sliced
2 celery ribs, cut in 1-inch
  pieces
3 lb. chicken, whole *or*
  cut up
2 tsp. salt
1/2 tsp. dried coarse black
  pepper
1 tsp. dried basil
1/2 cup water, chicken
  broth, *or* white cooking
  wine

1. Place vegetables in bottom of slow cooker. Place
chicken on top of vegetables.
Add seasonings and water.
2. Cover. Cook on Low 8-
10 hours, or High 3½-5 hours
(use 1 cup liquid if cooking
on High).
3. This is a great founda-

tion for soups—chicken vegetable, chicken noodle . . .

Note:
To make this a full meal, add 2 medium-sized potatoes, quartered, to vegetables before cooking.

Another Chicken in a Pot

Jennifer J. Gehman
Harrisburg, PA

Makes 4-6 servings

1-lb. bag baby carrots
1 small onion, diced
14½-oz. can green beans
3-lb. whole chicken, cut into serving-size pieces
2 tsp. salt
½ tsp. black pepper
½ cup chicken broth
¼ cup white wine
½-1 tsp. dried basil

1. Put carrots, onion, and beans on bottom of slow cooker. Add chicken. Top with salt, pepper, broth, and wine. Sprinkle with basil.
2. Cover. Cook on Low 8-10 hours, or High 3½-5 hours.

Savory Slow-Cooker Chicken

Sara Harter Fredette
Williamsburg, MA

Makes 4 servings

2½ lbs. chicken pieces, skinned
1 lb. fresh tomatoes, chopped, *or* 15-oz. can stewed tomatoes
2 Tbsp. white wine
1 bay leaf
¼ tsp. pepper
2 garlic cloves, minced
1 onion, chopped
½ cup chicken broth
1 tsp. dried thyme
1½ tsp. salt
2 cups broccoli, cut into bite-sized pieces

1. Combine all ingredients except broccoli in slow cooker.
2. Cover. Cook on Low 8-10 hours.
3. Add broccoli 30 minutes before serving.

Chicken and Vegetables

Rosanne Hankins
Stevensville, MD

Makes 6 servings

1 chicken, cut up
salt to taste
pepper to taste
1 bay leaf
2 tsp. lemon juice
¼ cup diced onions
¼ cup diced celery
1 lb. frozen mixed vegetables

1. Sprinkle salt and pepper over chicken and place chicken in slow cooker. Add bay leaf and lemon juice.
2. Cover. Cook on Low 6-8 hours, or High 3-5 hours. Remove chicken from bones. Reserve liquid, skimming fat if desired.
3. Cook ½ cup liquid, celery and onions in microwave on High for 2 minutes. Add frozen vegetables and microwave until cooked through.
4. Return all ingredients to slow cooker and cook on High 30 minutes.
5. Serve over cooked rice.

Baked Chicken Breasts

Janice Crist, Quinter, KS
Tracy Supcoe, Barclay, MD

Makes 4-6 servings

2-3 whole chicken breasts, halved
2 Tbsp. butter, *or* margarine
10¾-oz. can cream of chicken soup
½ cup dry sherry
1 tsp. dried tarragon, *or* rosemary, *or* both
1 tsp. Worcestershire sauce
¼ tsp. garlic powder
4-oz. can sliced mushrooms, drained

1. Place chicken breasts in slow cooker.
2. In saucepan, combine remaining ingredients. Heat until smooth and hot. Pour over chicken.
3. Cover. Cook on Low 8-10 hours.

Chicken Delicious

Janice Crist
Quinter, KS

Makes 8-12 servings

4-6 whole skinless chicken breasts, boned and halved
lemon juice
salt to taste
pepper to taste
celery salt to taste
paprika to taste
10¾-oz. can cream of mushroom soup
10¾-oz. can cream of celery soup
⅓ cup dry sherry, *or* white wine
grated Parmesan cheese

1. Season chicken with lemon juice, salt, pepper, celery salt, and paprika. Place in slow cooker.
2. Combine soups with sherry. Pour over chicken. Sprinkle with cheese.
3. Cover. Cook on Low 8-10 hours.
4. Serve with rice.

Chicken in Wine

Mary Seielstad
Sparks, NV

Makes 4-6 servings

2-3 lbs. chicken breasts, *or* pieces
10¾-oz. can cream of mushroom soup
10¾-oz. can French onion soup
1 cup dry white wine, *or* chicken broth

1. Put chicken in slow cooker.
2. Combine soups and wine. Pour over chicken.
3. Cover. Cook on Low 6-8 hours.
4. Serve over rice, pasta, or potatoes.

In place of ground meat in a recipe, use vegetarian burgers. Cut them up, and you won't need to brown the meat.
Sue Hamilton
Minooka, IL

Chicken in Mushroom Gravy

Rosemarie Fitzgerald
Gibsonia, PA
Audrey L. Kneer
Williamsfield, IL

Makes 6 servings

6 boneless, skinless
chicken-breast halves
salt to taste
pepper to taste
1/4 cup dry white wine, *or*
chicken broth
10 3/4-oz. can cream of
mushroom soup
4-oz. can sliced
mushrooms, drained

1. Place chicken in slow
cooker. Season with salt and
pepper.
2. Combine wine and
soup. Pour over chicken. Top
with mushrooms.
3. Cover. Cook on Low 7-9
hours.

Ruth's Slow-Cooker Chicken

Sara Harter Fredette
Williamsburg, MA

Makes 6 servings

6 boneless chicken-breast
halves
10 3/4-oz. can cream of
mushroom soup
1 pkg. dry mushroom soup
mix
1/4-1/2 cup sour cream
4-oz. can mushrooms,
drained

1. Combine chicken and
soups in slow cooker.
2. Cover. Cook on Low 6-8
hours.
3. Just before serving, stir
in sour cream and mush-
rooms. Reheat briefly.
4. Serve on noodles.

Note:
Leftover sauce makes a flavorful topping for grilled
hamburgers.

Creamy Cooker Chicken

Violette Harris Denney
Carrollton, GA

Makes 6 servings

1 envelope dry onion soup
mix
2 cups sour cream
10 3/4-oz. can cream of
mushroom soup
6 boneless, skinless
chicken-breast halves

1. Combine soup mix, sour
cream, and cream of mush-
room soup in slow cooker.
Add chicken, pushing it down
so it is submerged in the
sauce.
2. Cover. Cook on Low 8
hours.
3. Serve over rice or noodles.

Mushroom Chicken

Brenda Pope
Dundee, OH

Makes 4 servings

1 lb. boneless, skinless
  chicken breast
1 pkg. dry chicken gravy
  mix
10¾-oz. can cream of
  mushroom, *or* chicken,
  soup
1 cup white wine
8-oz. pkg. cream cheese,
  softened

1. Put chicken in slow
cooker. Sprinkle gravy mix on
top. In separate bowl, combine soup and wine and pour
over gravy mix.
2. Cover. Cook on Low 8
hours.
3. During last 30 minutes
of cooking time, stir in cream
cheese. Before serving,
remove chicken (keeping it
warm) and whisk the sauce
until smooth.
4. Serve chicken and sauce
over noodles or rice.

Creamy Mushroom Chicken

Patricia Howard
Albuquerque, NM

Makes 4-5 servings

2-3 lbs. chicken parts,
  skinned
4-oz. can mushrooms
2 10¾-oz. cans cream of
  chicken soup
1 envelope dry onion soup
  mix
½-1 cup chicken broth

1. Place chicken in slow
cooker.
2. Combine remaining ingredients and pour over chicken.
3. Cover. Cook on Low 5-6
hours.

So You Forgot to Defrost!

Mary Seielstad
Sparks, NV

Makes 6 servings

6 boneless, skinless frozen
  chicken-breast halves
2 10¾-oz. cans cream of
  chicken soup
4-oz. can sliced
  mushrooms, *or* ½ cup
  sliced fresh mushrooms
¾ tsp. salt
¼ tsp. pepper

1. Place frozen chicken in
slow cooker.
2. Mix together soup,
mushrooms, salt, and pepper
and pour over chicken.
3. Cover. Cook on Low 10-
12 hours.
4. Serve over rice.

Continental Chicken

Jennifer J. Gehman,
Harrisburg, PA
Gladys M. High, Ephrata, PA
L. Jean Moore, Pendleton, IN

Makes 4-6 servings

2¼-oz. pkg. dried beef
3-4 whole chicken breasts,
  halved, skinned, and
  boned
6-8 slices bacon
10¾-oz. can cream of
  mushroom soup,
  undiluted
¼ cup sour cream
¼ cup flour

1. Arrange dried beef in
bottom of slow cooker.
2. Wrap each piece of
chicken with a strip of bacon.
Place on top of dried beef.
3. Combine soup, sour
cream, and flour. Pour over
chicken.
4. Cover. Cook on Low 7-9
hours, or High 3-4 hours.
5. Serve over hot buttered
noodles.

Wanda's Chicken and Rice Casserole

Wanda Roth
Napoleon, OH

Makes 6-8 servings

1 cup long-grain rice, uncooked
3 cups water
2 tsp. chicken bouillon granules
10¾-oz can cream of chicken soup
16-oz. bag frozen broccoli
2 cups chopped, cooked chicken
¼ tsp. garlic powder
1 tsp. onion salt
1 cup grated cheddar cheese

1. Combine all ingredients in slow cooker.
2. Cook on High 3-4 hours.

Note:
If casserole is too runny, remove lid from slow cooker for 15 minutes while continuing to cook on High.

Chicken Rice Dish

Esther Porter
Minneapolis, MN

Makes 4 servings

1 cup cooked rice
10¾-oz. can cream of chicken soup
1 cup chicken broth
4 chicken thighs, partially cooked
10-oz. pkg. broccoli, frozen

1. Combine rice, soup, chicken broth, and chicken thighs. Place mixture in slow cooker.
2. Cover. Cook on Low 4 hours.
3. During last hour of cooking time, stir in broccoli.

Sharon's Chicken and Rice Casserole

Sharon Anders
Alburtis, PA

Makes 2 servings

10¾-oz. can cream of celery soup
2-oz. can sliced mushrooms, undrained
½ cup raw long grain rice
2 chicken-breast halves, skinned and boned
1 Tbsp. dry onion soup mix

1. Combine soup, mushrooms, and rice in greased slow cooker. Mix well.
2. Layer chicken breasts on top of mixture. Sprinkle with onion soup mix.
3. Cover. Cook on Low 4-6 hours.

Barbara's Chicken Rice Casserole

Barbara A. Yoder
Goshen, IN

Makes 6-8 servings

2 chicken bouillon cubes
2 cups hot water
½ cup margarine, melted
6-oz. box Uncle Ben's Long Grain and Wild Rice (Original Recipe), uncooked
4½-oz. jar sliced mushrooms
10-oz. can cooked chicken

1. Dissolve bouillon in hot water.
2. Combine all ingredients, including rice seasoning packet, in slow cooker.
3. Cover. Cook on High 2 hours, or until rice is tender.

Note:
To reduce salt in recipe, use 2 cups low- or no-sodium chicken broth instead of 2 chicken bouillon cubes and water.

Scalloped Potatoes and Chicken

Carol Sommers
Millersburg, OH

Makes 6-8 servings

1/4 cup chopped green
  peppers
1/2 cup chopped onions
1 1/2 cups diced Velveeta
  cheese
7-8 medium potatoes,
  sliced
salt to taste
10 3/4-oz. can cream of
  celery soup
1 soup can milk
3-4 whole boneless,
  skinless chicken breasts
salt to taste

1. Place layers of green peppers, onions, cheese, and potatoes and a sprinkling of salt in slow cooker.
2. Sprinkle salt over chicken breasts and lay on top of potatoes.
3. Combine soup and milk and pour into slow cooker, pushing meat down into liquid.
4. Cover. Cook on High 1 1/2 hours. Reduce temperature to Low and cook 3-4 hours. Test that potatoes are soft. If not, continue cooking on Low another hour and test again, continuing to cook until potatoes are finished.

Scalloped Chicken

Carolyn W. Carmichael
Berkeley Heights, NJ

Makes 4 servings

5-oz. pkg. scalloped
  potatoes
scalloped potatoes dry
  seasoning pack
4 chicken-breast halves, *or*
  8 legs
10-oz. pkg. frozen peas
2 cups water

1. Put potatoes, seasoning pack, chicken, and peas in slow cooker. Pour water over all.
2. Cover. Cook on Low 8-10 hours, or High 4 hours.

Chicken-Vegetable Dish

Cheri Jantzen
Houston, TX

Makes 4 servings

4 skinless chicken-breast
  halves, with bone in
15-oz. can crushed
  tomatoes
10-oz. pkg. frozen green
  beans
2 cups water, *or* chicken
  broth
1 cup brown rice,
  uncooked
1 cup sliced mushrooms

2 carrots, chopped
1 onion, chopped
1/2 tsp. minced garlic
1/2 tsp. herb-blend
  seasoning
1/4 tsp. dried tarragon

1. Combine all ingredients in slow cooker.
2. Cover. Cook on High 2 hours, and then on Low 3-5 hours.

Chicken and Vegetables

Jeanne Heyerly
Chenoa, IL

Makes 2 servings

2 medium potatoes,
  quartered
2-3 carrots, sliced
2 frozen chicken breasts, *or*
  2 frozen drumstick/thigh
  pieces
salt to taste
pepper to taste
1 medium onion, chopped
2 garlic cloves, minced
1-2 cups shredded cabbage
16-oz. can chicken broth

1. Place potatoes and carrots in slow cooker. Layer chicken on top. Sprinkle with salt, pepper, onion, and garlic. Top with cabbage. Carefully pour chicken broth around edges.
2. Cover. Cook on Low 8-9 hours.

California Chicken

Shirley Sears
Tiskilwa, IL

Makes 4-6 servings

3-lb. chicken, quartered
1 cup orange juice
1/3 cup chili sauce
2 Tbsp. soy sauce
1 Tbsp. molasses
1 tsp. dry mustard
1 tsp. garlic salt
2 Tbsp. chopped green
  peppers
3 medium oranges, peeled
  and separated into
  slices, *or* 13 1/2-oz. can
  mandarin oranges

1. Arrange chicken in slow cooker.
2. In separate bowl, combine juice, chili sauce, soy sauce, molasses, dry mustard, and garlic salt. Pour over chicken.
3. Cover. Cook on Low 8-9 hours.
4. Stir in green peppers and oranges. Heat 30 minutes longer.

Variation:
Stir 1 tsp. curry powder in with sauces and seasonings. Stir 1 small can pineapple chunks and juice in with green peppers and oranges.

Orange Chicken Leg Quarters

Kimberly Jensen
Bailey, CO

Makes 4-5 servings

4 chicken drumsticks
4 chicken thighs
1 cup strips of green and
  red bell peppers
1/2 cup canned chicken
  broth
1/2 cup prepared orange
  juice
1/2 cup ketchup
2 Tbsp. soy sauce
1 Tbsp. light molasses
1 Tbsp. prepared mustard
1/2 tsp. garlic salt
11-oz. can mandarin
  oranges
2 tsp. cornstarch
1 cup frozen peas
2 green onions, sliced

1. Place chicken in slow cooker. Top with pepper strips.
2. Combine broth, juice, ketchup, soy sauce, molasses, mustard, and garlic salt. Pour over chicken.
3. Cover. Cook on Low 6-7 hours.
4. Remove chicken and vegetables from slow cooker. Keep warm.
5. Measure out 1 cup of cooking sauce. Put in saucepan and bring to boil.
6. Drain oranges, reserving 1 Tbsp. juice. Stir cornstarch into reserved juice. Add to boiling sauce in pan.
7. Add peas to sauce and cook, stirring for 2-3 minutes until sauce thickens and peas are warm. Stir in oranges.
8. Arrange chicken pieces on platter of cooked white rice, fried cellophane noodles, or lo mein noodles. Pour orange sauce over chicken and rice or noodles. Top with sliced green onions.

Cranberry Chicken

Teena Wagner
Waterloo, ON

Makes 6-8 servings

3-4-lb. chicken pieces
1/2 tsp. salt
1/4 tsp. pepper
1/2 cup diced celery
1/2 cup diced onions
16-oz. can whole berry
  cranberry sauce
1 cup barbecue sauce

1. Combine all ingredients in slow cooker.
2. Cover. Bake on High for 4 hours, or on Low 6-8 hours.

Chicken Sweet and Sour

Willard E. Roth
Elkhart, IN

Makes 8 servings

4 medium potatoes, sliced
8 boneless, skinless
   chicken-breast halves
2 Tbsp. cider vinegar
1/4 tsp. ground nutmeg
1 tsp. dry basil, *or* 1 Tbsp.
   chopped fresh basil
2 Tbsp. brown sugar
1 cup orange juice
dried parsley flakes
17-oz. can waterpack
   sliced peaches, drained
fresh parsley
fresh orange slices

1. Place potatoes in greased slow cooker. Arrange chicken on top.
2. In separate bowl, combine vinegar, nutmeg, basil, brown sugar, and orange juice. Pour over chicken. Sprinkle with parsley.
3. Cover. Cook on Low 6 hours.
4. Remove chicken and potatoes from sauce and arrange on warm platter.
5. Turn cooker to High. Add peaches. When warm, spoon peaches and sauce over chicken and potatoes. Garnish with fresh parsley and orange slices.

Chicken with Tropical Barbecue Sauce

Lois Stoltzfus
Honey Brook, PA

Makes 6 servings

1/4 cup molasses
2 Tbsp. cider vinegar
2 Tbsp. Worcestershire
   sauce
2 tsp. prepared mustard
1/8-1/4 tsp. hot pepper sauce
2 Tbsp. orange juice
3 whole chicken breasts,
   halved

1. Combine molasses, vinegar, Worcestershire sauce, mustard, hot pepper sauce, and orange juice. Brush over chicken.
2. Place chicken in slow cooker.
3. Cover. Cook on Low 7-9 hours, or High 3-4 hours.

Fruited Barbecue Chicken

Barbara Katrine Rose
Woodbridge, VA

Makes 4-6 servings

29-oz. can tomato sauce
20-oz. can unsweetened
   crushed pineapple,
   undrained
2 Tbsp. brown sugar
3 Tbsp. vinegar
1 Tbsp. instant minced
   onion
1 tsp. paprika
2 tsp. Worcestershire sauce
1/4 tsp. garlic powder
1/8 tsp. pepper
3 lbs. chicken, skinned and
   cubed
11-oz. can mandarin
   oranges, drained

1. Combine all ingredients except chicken and oranges. Add chicken pieces.
2. Cover. Cook on High 4 hours.
3. Just before serving, stir in oranges. Serve over hot rice.

When I use mushrooms or green peppers in the slow cooker, I usually stir them in during the last hour so they don't get too mushy.
Trudy Kutter
Corfu, NY

Orange Chicken and Sweet Potatoes

Kimberlee Greenawalt
Harrisonburg, VA

Makes 6 servings

2-3 sweet potatoes, peeled
  and sliced
3 whole chicken breasts,
  halved
2/3 cup flour
1 tsp. salt
1 tsp. nutmeg
1/2 tsp. cinnamon
dash pepper
dash garlic powder
10 3/4-oz. can cream of
  celery, *or* cream of
  chicken, soup
4-oz. can sliced
  mushrooms, drained
1/2 cup orange juice
1/2 tsp. grated orange rind
2 tsp. brown sugar
3 Tbsp. flour

1. Place sweet potatoes in bottom of slow cooker.
2. Rinse chicken breasts and pat dry. Combine flour, salt, nutmeg, cinnamon, pepper, and garlic powder. Thoroughly coat chicken in flour mixture. Place on top of sweet potatoes.
3. Combine soup with remaining ingredients. Stir well. Pour over chicken breasts.
4. Cover. Cook on Low 8-10 hours, or High 3-4 hours.
5. Serve over rice.

Orange-Glazed Chicken Breasts

Leona Miller
Millersburg, OH

Makes 6 servings

6-oz. can frozen orange
  juice concentrate,
  thawed
1/2 tsp. dried marjoram
6 boneless, skinless
  chicken-breast halves
1/4 cup cold water
2 Tbsp. cornstarch

1. Combine orange juice and marjoram in shallow dish. Dip each breast in orange-juice mixture and place in slow cooker. Pour remaining sauce over breasts.
2. Cover. Cook on Low 7-9 hours, or High 3 1/2-4 hours.
3. Remove chicken from slow cooker. Turn cooker to High and cover.
4. Combine water and cornstarch. Stir into liquid in slow cooker. Place cover slightly ajar on slow cooker. Cook until sauce is thick and bubbly, about 15-20 minutes. Serve over chicken.

Variation:
To increase "spice" in dish, add 1/2-1 tsp. Worcestershire sauce to orange juice-marjoram glaze.

Sweet and Sour Chicken

Bernice A. Esau
North Newton, KS

Makes 6 servings

1 1/2 cups sliced carrots
1 large green pepper,
  chopped
1 medium onion, chopped
2 Tbsp. quick-cooking
  tapioca
2 1/2-3 lb. chicken, cut into
  serving-size pieces
8-oz. can pineapple chunks
  in juice
1/3 cup brown sugar
1/3 cup vinegar
1 Tbsp. soy sauce
1/2 tsp. instant chicken
  bouillon
1/4 tsp. garlic powder
1/4 tsp. ground ginger,
  or 1/2 tsp. freshly grated
  ginger
1 tsp. salt

1. Place vegetables in bottom of slow cooker. Sprinkle with tapioca. Add chicken.
2. In separate bowl, combine pineapple, brown sugar, vinegar, soy sauce, bouillon, garlic powder, ginger, and salt. Pour over chicken.
3. Cover. Cook on Low 8-10 hours.
4. Serve over cooked rice.

Easy Teriyaki Chicken

Barbara Shie
Colorado Springs, CO

Makes 5-6 servings

2-3 lbs. skinless chicken pieces
20-oz. can pineapple chunks
dash of ground ginger
1 cup teriyaki sauce

1. Place chicken in slow cooker. Pour remaining ingredients over chicken.
2. Cover. Cook on Low 6-8 hours, or High 4-6 hours.

Creamy Chicken Italiano

Sharon Easter, Yuba City, CA
Rebecca Meyerkorth, Wamego, KS
Bonnie Milller, Cochranville, PA

Makes 4 servings

4 boneless, skinless chicken-breast halves
1 envelope dry Italian salad dressing mix
1/4 cup water
8-oz. pkg. cream cheese, softened
10 3/4-oz. can cream of chicken soup
4-oz. can mushroom stems and pieces, drained

1. Place chicken in slow cooker.
2. Combine salad dressing mix and water. Pour over chicken.
3. Cover. Cook on Low 3 hours.
4. Combine cheese and soup until blended. Stir in mushrooms. Pour over chicken.
5. Cover. Cook on Low 1 hour, or until chicken juices run clear.
6. Serve over noodles or rice.

Creamy Mushroom Chicken

Barbara Shie
Colorado Springs, CO

Makes 4-6 servings

4-6 boneless, skinless chicken-breast halves
12-oz. jar mushroom gravy
1 cup milk
8-oz. pkg. cream cheese, cubed
4 1/2-oz. can chopped green chilies
1 pkg. dry Italian salad dressing

1. Combine all ingredients in slow cooker.
2. Cover. Cook on Low 6 hours.
3. Serve over noodles or rice.

Super Easy Chicken

Mary Seielstad
Sparks, NV

Makes 4 servings

4 frozen chicken-breast halves
1 pkg. dry Italian dressing mix
1 cup warm water, *or* chicken stock

1. Place chicken in slow cooker. Sprinkle with dressing mix. Pour water over chicken.
2. Cover. Cook on Low 8-10 hours.

Ann's Chicken Cacciatore

Ann Driscoll
Albuquerque, NM

Makes 6-8 servings

1 large onion, thinly sliced
2 1/2-3 lb. chicken, cut up
2 6-oz. cans tomato paste
4-oz. can sliced mushrooms, drained
1 tsp. salt
1/4 cup dry white wine
1/4 tsp. pepper
1-2 garlic cloves, minced
1-2 tsp. dried oregano
1/2 tsp. dried basil

½ tsp. celery seed,
  optional
1 bay leaf

1. Place onion in slow
cooker. Add chicken.
2. Combine remaining
ingredients. Pour over
chicken.
3. Cover. Cook on Low 7-9
hours, or High 3-4 hours.
4. Serve over spaghetti.

Darla's Chicken Cacciatore

Darla Sathre
Baxter, MN

Makes 6 servings

2 onions, thinly sliced
4 boneless chicken breasts,
  cubed
3 garlic cloves, minced
¼ tsp. pepper
2 tsp. dried oregano
1 tsp. dried basil
1 bay leaf
2 15-oz. cans diced
  tomatoes
8-oz. can tomato sauce
4-oz. can sliced
  mushrooms

1. Place onions in bottom
of slow cooker. Add remaining ingredients.
2. Cover. Cook on Low 8
hours.
3. Serve over hot spaghetti.

Dorothea's Chicken Cacciatore

Dorothea K. Ladd
Ballston Lake, NY

Makes 4-6 servings

1 frying chicken, cut into
  serving-size pieces
¼ cup flour
2 Tbsp. oil
1 garlic clove, minced
46-oz. can tomato juice, *or*
  V-8 juice
12-oz. can tomato paste
2 Tbsp. dried parsley
2 Tbsp. sugar
2 tsp. salt
1 Tbsp. dried oregano
½ tsp. dried thyme
1 bay leaf

1. Put flour and chicken
pieces in bag and shake to
coat. Brown chicken and garlic in oil in skillet. Transfer
chicken pieces and garlic to
slow cooker.
2. Mix together tomato
juice, tomato paste, parsley,
sugar, salt, oregano, thyme,
and bay leaf. Pour over
chicken and garlic.
3. Cover. Cook on Low 8-
10 hours.
4. Serve over spaghetti or
rice.

Dale & Shari's Chicken Cacciatore

Dale and Shari Mast
Harrisonburg, VA

Makes 4 servings

4 chicken quarters, *or*
  4 boneless, skinless
  chicken-breast halves
15-oz. can tomato, *or*
  spaghetti, sauce
4-oz. can sliced
  mushrooms, drained
½ cup water
1 tsp. dry chicken broth
  granules
½ tsp. Italian seasoning

1. Place chicken in slow
cooker. Pour on sauce, mushrooms, and water. Sprinkle
with granules and seasoning.
2. Cover. Cook on High 3-4
hours, or Low 6-8 hours.
3. Serve over rice.

Chicken Parmigiana

Brenda Pope
Dundee, OH

Makes 6 servings

1 egg
1 tsp. salt
1/4 tsp. pepper
6 boneless, skinless
   chicken-breast halves
1 cup Italian bread crumbs
2-4 Tbsp. butter
14-oz. jar pizza sauce
6 slices mozzarella cheese
grated Parmesan cheese

1. Beat egg, salt, and pepper together. Dip chicken into egg and coat with bread crumbs. Saute chicken in butter in skillet. Arrange chicken in slow cooker.
2. Pour pizza sauce over chicken.
3. Cover. Cook on Low 6-8 hours.
4. Layer mozzarella cheese over top and sprinkle with Parmesan cheese. Cook an additional 15 minutes.

Easy Chicken A la King

Jenny R. Unternahrer
Wayland, IA

Makes 4 servings

1 1/2 lbs. boneless, skinless
   chicken breasts
10 3/4-oz. can cream of
   chicken soup
3 Tbsp. flour
1/4 tsp. pepper
9-oz. pkg. frozen peas and
   onions, thawed and
   drained
2 Tbsp. chopped pimentos
1/2 tsp. paprika

1. Cut chicken into bite-sized pieces and place in slow cooker.
2. Combine soup, flour, and pepper. Pour over chicken. Do not stir.
3. Cover. Cook on High 2 1/2 hours, or Low 5-5 1/2 hours.
4. Stir in peas and onions, pimentos, and paprika.
5. Cover. Cook on High 20-30 minutes.

Variation:
   Add 1/4-1/2 cup chopped green peppers to Step 2.
   Sharon Brubaker
   Myerstown, PA

Coq au Vin

Kimberlee Greenawalt
Harrisonburg, VA

Makes 6 servings

2 cups frozen pearl onions,
   thawed
4 thick slices bacon, fried
   and crumbled
1 cup sliced button
   mushrooms
1 garlic clove, minced
1 tsp. dried thyme leaves
1/8 tsp. black pepper
6 boneless, skinless
   chicken-breast halves
1/2 cup dry red wine
3/4 cup chicken broth
1/4 cup tomato paste
3 Tbsp. flour

1. Layer ingredients in slow cooker in the following order: onions, bacon, mushrooms, garlic, thyme, pepper, chicken, wine, broth.
2. Cover. Cook on Low 6-8 hours.
3. Remove chicken and vegetables. Cover and keep warm.
4. Ladle 1/2 cup cooking liquid into small bowl. Cool slightly. Turn slow cooker to High. Cover. Mix reserved liquid, tomato paste, and flour until smooth. Return mixture to slow cooker, cover, and cook 15 minutes, or until thickened.
5. Serve chicken, vegetables, and sauce over noodles.

When using raw meat, begin by cooking it for 1-2 hours on High to avoid cooking it too slowly.
Joy Sutter
Iowa City, IA

Lemon Garlic Chicken

Cindy Krestynick
Glen Lyon, PA

Makes 4 servings

1 tsp. dried oregano
1/2 tsp. seasoned salt
1/4 tsp. pepper
2 lbs. chicken-breast
  halves, skinned and
  rinsed
2 Tbsp. butter, *or*
  margarine
1/4 cup water
3 Tbsp. lemon juice
2 garlic cloves, minced
1 tsp. chicken bouillon
  granules
1 tsp. minced fresh parsley

1. Combine oregano, salt, and pepper. Rub all of mixture into chicken. Brown chicken in butter or margarine in skillet. Transfer to slow cooker.
2. Place water, lemon juice, garlic, and bouillon cubes in skillet. Bring to boil, loosening browned bits from skillet. Pour over chicken.
3. Cover. Cook on High 2-2½ hours, or Low 4-5 hours.
4. Add parsley and baste chicken. Cover. Cook on High 15-30 minutes, until chicken is tender.

Lemon Honey Chicken

Carolyn W. Carmichael
Berkeley Heights, NJ

Makes 4-6 servings

1 lemon
1 whole roasting chicken,
  rinsed
1/2 cup orange juice
1/2 cup honey

1. Pierce lemon with fork. Place in chicken cavity. Place chicken in slow cooker.
2. Combine orange juice and honey. Pour over chicken.
3. Cover. Cook on Low 8 hours. Remove lemon and squeeze over chicken.
4. Carve chicken and serve.

Melanie's Chicken Cordon Bleu

Melanie Thrower
McPherson, KS

Makes 6 servings

3 whole chicken breasts,
  split and deboned
6 pieces thinly sliced ham
6 slices Swiss cheese
salt to taste
pepper to taste
6 slices bacon
1/4 cup water
1 tsp. chicken bouillon
  granules
1/2 cup white cooking wine
1 tsp. cornstarch
1/4 cup cold water

1. Flatten chicken to 1/8-1/4-inch thickness. Place a slice of ham and a slice of cheese on top of each flattened breast. Sprinkle with salt and pepper. Roll up and wrap with strip of bacon. Secure with toothpick. Place in slow cooker.
2. Combine 1/4 cup water, granules, and wine. Pour into slow cooker.
3. Cover. Cook on High 4 hours.
4. Combine cornstarch and 1/4 cup cold water. Add to slow cooker. Cook until sauce thickens.

181

Chicken Cordon Bleu

Barbara Nolan
Pleasant Valley, NY
Jenny R. Unternahrer,
Wayland, IA

Makes 6 servings

3 whole boneless, skinless
  chicken breasts
3 large Swiss cheese slices,
  halved
3 large, thin ham slices,
  halved
2 Tbsp. margarine
10¾-oz. can cream of
  mushroom soup, *or*
  cream of chicken soup
3 Tbsp. milk
3 Tbsp. sherry, optional
¼ tsp. pepper

1. Cut whole breasts in
half. Flatten each half with
wooden mallet. Cover each
half breast with half slice of
cheese and ham. Roll up and
secure with toothpicks.
Brown each chicken roll in
margarine in skillet. Transfer
to slow cooker.

2. Combine remaining
ingredients. Pour over
chicken, making sure chicken
pieces are fully covered.

3. Cover. Cook on Low 4-5
hours.

Stuffed Chicken Rolls

Lois M. Martin, Lititz, PA
Renee Shirk, Mount Joy, PA

Makes 6 servings

6 large boneless, skinless
  chicken-breast halves
6 slices fully cooked ham
6 slices Swiss cheese
¼ cup flour
¼ cup grated Parmesan
  cheese
½ tsp. rubbed sage
¼ tsp. paprika
¼ tsp. pepper
¼ cup oil
10¾-oz. can cream of
  chicken soup
½ cup chicken broth
chopped fresh parsley,
  optional

1. Flatten chicken to ⅛-
inch thickness. Place ham
and cheese slices on each
breast. Roll up and tuck in
ends. Secure with toothpick.

2. Combine flour,
Parmesan cheese, sage,
paprika, and pepper. Coat
chicken on all sides. Cover
and refrigerate for 1 hour.

3. Brown chicken in oil in
skillet. Transfer to slow
cooker.

4. Combine soup and
broth. Pour over chicken.

5. Cover. Cook on Low 4-5
hours.

6. Remove toothpicks.
Garnish with parsley.

Ham and Swiss Chicken

Nanci Keatley, Salem, OR
Janice Yoskovich
Carmichaels, PA

Makes 6 servings

2 eggs, beaten
1½ cups milk
2 Tbsp. butter, melted
½ cup chopped celery
¼ cup diced onion
10 slices bread, cubed
12 thin slices deli ham,
  rolled up
2 cups grated Swiss cheese
2½ cups cubed cooked
  chicken
10¾-oz. can cream of
  chicken soup
½ cup milk

1. Combine eggs and milk.
Add butter, celery, and onion.
Stir in bread cubes. Place half
of mixture in greased slow
cooker. Top with half the
ham, cheese, and chicken.

2. Combine soup and milk.
Pour half over chicken.
Repeat layers.

3. Cover. Cook on Low 4-5
hours.

Dawn's Barbecued Chicken

Dawn M. Propst
Levittown, PA

Makes 6 servings

3 whole boneless, skinless chicken breasts, cut in half
1/4 cup flour
1/4 cup oil
1 medium onion, sliced
1 green, *or* yellow, pepper, sliced
1/2 cup chopped celery
2 Tbsp. Worcestershire sauce
1 cup ketchup
2 cups water
1/4 tsp. salt
1/4 tsp. paprika

1. Roll chicken breasts in flour. Brown in oil in skillet. Transfer chicken to slow cooker.

2. Saute onion, peppers, and celery in skillet, also, cooking until tender. Add remaining ingredients and bring to boil. Pour over chicken.

3. Cover. Cook on Low 8 hours.

4. Serve over noodles or rice.

Marcy's Barbecued Chicken

Marcy Engle
Harrisonburg, VA

Makes 6 servings

2 lbs. chicken pieces
1/4 cup flour
1 cup ketchup
2 cups water
1/3 cup Worcestershire sauce
1 tsp. chili powder
1/2 tsp. salt
1/2 tsp. pepper
2 drops Tabasco sauce
1/4 tsp. garlic salt
1/4 tsp. onion salt

1. Dust chicken with flour. Transfer to slow cooker.

2. Combine remaining ingredients. Pour over chicken.

3. Cover. Cook on Low 5 hours.

Oriental Chicken

Marcia S. Myer
Manheim, PA

Makes 6 servings

2 2 1/2-3 lb. broiler/fryer chickens, cut up
1/4 cup flour
1 1/2 tsp. salt
2 Tbsp. oil
6-oz. can lemonade concentrate, thawed
2 Tbsp. brown sugar
3 Tbsp. ketchup
1 Tbsp. vinegar
2 Tbsp. cold water
2 Tbsp. cornstarch

1. Combine flour with salt. Coat chicken. Brown chicken in oil in skillet. Transfer to slow cooker.

2. Combine lemonade concentrate, brown sugar, ketchup, and vinegar. Pour over chicken.

3. Cover. Cook on High 3-4 hours.

4. Remove chicken. Pour liquid into saucepan. Return chicken to cooker and cover to keep warm. Skim fat from liquid.

5. Combine water and cornstarch. Stir into hot liquid. Cook and stir until thick and bubbly.

6. Serve chicken and sauce over rice.

Awfully Easy Chicken

Martha Hershey
Ronks, PA

Makes 8 servings

1/2 cup water
4-lb. chicken legs and thighs
14-oz. bottle barbecue sauce

1. Place water in bottom of slow cooker. Add chicken. Pour barbecue sauce over top.
2. Cover. Cook on Low 8 hours.

Note:
Serve any additional sauce over mashed potatoes.
Judy Denney
Lawrenceville, GA

Variation:
Place 3 large onions, quartered or sliced, in bottom of slow cooker. Then add chicken and sauce.
Barbara J. Fabel
Wausau, WI

Tracy's Barbecued Chicken Wings

Tracy Supcoe
Barclay, MD

Makes 8 full-sized servings

4-lb. chicken wings
2 large onions, chopped
2 6-oz. cans tomato paste
2 large garlic cloves, minced
1/4 cup Worcestershire sauce
1/4 cup cider vinegar
1/2 cup brown sugar
1/2 cup sweet pickle relish
1/2 cup red, *or* white, wine
2 tsp. salt
2 tsp. dry mustard

1. Cut off wing tips. Cut wings at joint. Place in slow cooker.
2. Combine remaining ingredients. Add to slow cooker. Stir.
3. Cover. Cook on Low 5-6 hours.

Mary's Chicken Wings

Mary Casey
Scranton, PA

Makes 8-12 full-sized servings

3-6 lbs. chicken wings
1-3 Tbsp. oil
3/4-1 cup vinegar
1/2 cup ketchup
2 Tbsp. sugar
2 Tbsp. Worcestershire sauce
3 garlic cloves, minced
1 Tbsp. dry mustard
1 tsp. paprika
1/2-1 tsp. salt
1/8 tsp. pepper

1. Brown wings in oil in skillet, or brush wings with oil and broil, watching carefully so they do not burn.
2. Combine remaining ingredients in 5-61/2-quart slow cooker. Add wings. Stir gently so that they are all well covered with sauce.
3. Cover. Cook on Low 4-6 hours, or until tender.

Don't have enough time? A lot of dishes can be made in less time by increasing the temperature to High and cooking the dish for about half the time as is necessary on Low.
Jenny R. Unternahrer
Wayland, IA

Rosemarie's Barbecued Chicken Wings

Rosemarie Fitzgerald
Gibsonia, PA

Makes 10 full-sized servings

5 lbs. chicken wings, tips cut off
12-oz. bottle chili sauce
1/3 cup lemon juice
1 Tbsp. Worcestershire sauce
2 Tbsp. molasses
1 tsp. salt
2 tsp. chili powder
1/4 tsp. hot pepper sauce
dash garlic powder

1. Place wings in cooker.
2. Combine remaining ingredients and pour over chicken.
3. Cover. Cook on Low 6-8 hours, or High 2-3 hours.

Note:
These wings are also a great appetizer, yielding about 15 appetizer-size servings.
Take any leftover chicken off the bone and combine with leftover sauce. Serve over cooked pasta for a second meal.

Donna's Chicken Wings

Donna Conto
Saylorsburg, PA

Makes 10 full-sized servings

5 lbs. chicken wings
28-oz. jar spaghetti sauce
1 Tbsp. Worcestershire sauce
1 Tbsp. molasses
1 Tbsp. prepared mustard
1 tsp. salt
1/2 tsp. pepper

1. Place wings in slow cooker.
2. Combine remaining ingredients. Pour over wings and stir them gently, making sure all are covered with sauce.
3. Cover. Cook on High 3-4 hours.

Sweet Aromatic Chicken

Anne Townsend
Albuquerque, NM

Makes 4 servings

1/2 cup coconut milk
1/2 cup water
8 chicken thighs, skinned
1/2 cup brown sugar
2 Tbsp. soy sauce
1/8 tsp. ground cloves
2 garlic cloves, minced

1. Combine coconut milk and water. Pour into greased slow cooker.
2. Add remaining ingredients in order listed.
3. Cover. Cook on Low 5-6 hours.

Note:
What to do with leftover coconut milk?
1. Two or three spoonfuls over vanilla ice cream, topped with a cherry, makes a flavorful, quick dessert.
2. Family Pina Coladas are good. Pour the coconut milk into a pitcher and add one large can pineapple juice, along with some ice cubes. Decorate with pineapple chunks and cherries.

Chicken Casablanca

Joyce Kaut
Rochester, NY

Makes 6-8 servings

2 Tbsp. oil
2 large onions, sliced
1 tsp. ground ginger
3 garlic cloves, minced
3 large carrots, diced
2 large potatoes, diced
3 lbs. skinless chicken
　　pieces
1/2 tsp. ground cumin
1/2 tsp. salt
1/2 tsp. pepper
1/4 tsp. cinnamon
2 Tbsp. raisins
14 1/2-oz. can chopped
　　tomatoes
3 small zucchini, sliced
15-oz. can garbanzo beans,
　　drained
2 Tbsp. chopped parsley

1. Saute onions, ginger, and garlic in oil in skillet. (Reserve oil.) Transfer to slow cooker. Add carrots and potatoes.

2. Brown chicken over medium heat in reserved oil. Transfer to slow cooker. Mix gently with vegetables.

3. Combine seasonings in separate bowl. Sprinkle over chicken and vegetables. Add raisins and tomatoes.

4. Cover. Cook on High 4-6 hours.

5. Add sliced zucchini, beans, and parsley 30 minutes before serving.

6. Serve over cooked rice or couscous.

Variation:
　　Add 1/2 tsp. turmeric and 1/4 tsp. cayenne pepper to Step 3.

Michelle Mann
Mt. Joy, PA

Chicken Kapaman

Judy Govotsus
Monrovia, MD

Makes 4-6 servings

4-6 potatoes, quartered
4-6 carrots, sliced
2-3-lbs. chicken pieces
2 onions, chopped
1 whole garlic bulb,
　　minced
2 Tbsp. tomato paste
1 1/2 cups water
1 cinnamon stick
1/2 tsp. salt
1/4 tsp. pepper

1. Layer potatoes and carrots in slow cooker. Add chicken.

2. In separate bowl, mix remaining ingredients together and pour over vegetables and chicken in cooker.

3. Cover. Cook on High 4 hours. Remove lid and cook on Low an additional 1-1 1/2 hours.

Greek Chicken

Judy Govotsus
Monrovia, MD

Makes 4-6 servings

4-6 potatoes, quartered
2-3 lbs. chicken pieces
2 large onions, quartered
1 whole bulb garlic,
　　minced
3 tsp. dried oregano
1 tsp. salt
1/2 tsp. pepper
1 Tbsp. olive oil

1. Place potatoes in bottom of slow cooker. Add chicken, onions, and garlic. Sprinkle with seasonings. Top with oil.

2. Cover. Cook on High 5-6 hours, or on Low 9-10 hours.

Cathy's Chicken Creole

Cathy Boshart
Lebanon, PA

Makes 6 servings

2 Tbsp. butter
half a medium green
    pepper, chopped
2 medium onions, chopped
1/2 cup chopped celery
1 lb. 4 oz.-can tomatoes
1/2 tsp. pepper, *or* your
    choice of dried herbs
1 1/2 tsp. salt, *or* your
    choice of dried herbs
1/8 tsp. red pepper
1 cup water
2 Tbsp. cornstarch
1 tsp. sugar
1 1/2 Tbsp. cold water
2 cups cooked and cubed
    chicken
6 green, *or* black, olives,
    sliced
1/2 cup sliced mushrooms

1. Melt butter in slow
cooker. Add green pepper,
onions, and celery. Heat.
2. Add tomatoes, pepper,
salt and 1 cup water.
3. Cover. Cook on High
while preparing remaining
ingredients.
4. Combine cornstarch and
sugar. Add 1 1/2 Tbsp. cold
water and make a smooth
paste. Stir into mixture in
slow cooker. Add chicken,
olives, and mushrooms.
5. Cover. Cook on Low 2-3
hours.

Barbara's Creole Chicken

Barbara McGinnis
Jupiter, FL

Makes 4 servings

2 (.9-oz.) pkgs. dry
    bearnaise sauce mix
1/2 cup dry white wine
1 lb. boneless, skinless
    chicken breasts, cut into
    bite-sized cubes
9-oz. pkg. frozen mixed
    vegetables
1 lb. cooked ham, cubed
1 lb. red potatoes, cubed
1 red bell pepper, chopped
1 green bell pepper,
    chopped
3 shallots, minced
1/2 tsp. garlic powder
1/2 tsp. turmeric powder
1/2 tsp. dried tarragon

1. Combine all ingredients
in slow cooker.
2. Cover. Cook on Low 6
hours.

Chicken Curry

Maricarol Magill
Freehold, NJ

Makes 4 servings

4 boneless, skinless
    chicken-breast halves
1 small onion, chopped
2 sweet potatoes (about
    1 1/2 lbs.), cubed
2/3 cup orange juice
1 garlic clove, minced
1 tsp. chicken bouillon
    granules
1 tsp. salt
1/4 tsp. pepper
4 tsp. curry powder
2 Tbsp. cornstarch
2 Tbsp. cold water
rice

Toppings:
sliced green onions
shredded coconut
peanuts
raisins

1. Place chicken in slow
cooker. Cover with onions
and sweet potatoes.
2. Combine orange juice,
garlic, chicken bouillon granules, salt, pepper, and curry
powder. Pour over vegetables.
3. Cover. Cook on Low 5-6
hours.
4. Remove chicken and
vegetables and keep warm.
5. Turn slow cooker to
High. Dissolve cornstarch in
cold water. Stir into sauce in
slow cooker. Cover. Cook on
High 15-20 minutes.
6. Serve chicken and sauce
over rice. Sprinkle with your
choice of toppings.

Groundnut Stew

Cathy Boshart
Lebanon, PA

Makes 8 servings

2 green peppers, cut into
   rings
1 medium onion, cut into
   rings
2 Tbsp. shortening
6-oz. can tomato paste
3/4 cup peanut butter
3 cups chicken broth
1 1/2 tsp. salt
1 tsp. chili powder
1 tsp. sugar
1/2 tsp. ground nutmeg
4 cups cubed, cooked
   chicken
6 cups hot cooked rice

Toppings:
coconut
peanuts
raisins
hard-boiled eggs, chopped
bananas, chopped
oranges, cut up
eggplant, chopped
apples, chopped
tomatoes, chopped
carrots, shredded
green pepper, chopped
onion, chopped
pineapple, crushed

1. Cook and stir green pepper and onion rings in shortening in hot slow cooker.
2. Combine tomato paste
and peanut butter. Stir into
slow cooker.
3. Add broth and season-
ings. Stir in chicken.
4. Cover. Cook on Low
3 hours.

5. Serve over hot rice with
your choice of toppings.

Mulligan Stew

Carol Ambrose
Ripon, CA

Makes 8-10 servings

3-lb. stewing hen, cut up,
   or 4 lbs. chicken legs
   and thighs
1 1/2 tsp. salt
1/4-lb. salt pork, *or* bacon,
   cut in 1-inch squares
4 cups tomatoes, peeled
   and sliced
2 cups fresh corn, *or* 1-lb.
   pkg. frozen corn
1 cup coarsely chopped
   potatoes
10-oz. pkg. lima beans,
   frozen
1/2 cup chopped onions
1 tsp. salt
1/4 tsp. pepper
dash of cayenne pepper

1. Place chicken in very
large slow cooker. Add water
to cover. Add 1 1/2 tsp. salt.
2. Cover. Cook on Low
2 hours. Add more water if
needed.
3. Add remaining ingredi-
ents. (If you don't have a
large cooker, divide the stew
between 2 average-sized
ones.) Simmer on Low 5
hours longer.

Notes:
1. Flavor improves if stew
is refrigerated and reheated

the next day. May also be
made in advance and frozen.
2. You can debone the
chicken after the first cooking
for 2 hours. Stir chicken
pieces back into cooker with
other ingredients and continue with directions above.

African
Chicken Treat

Anne Townsend
Albuquerque, NM

Makes 4 servings

1 1/2 cups water
2 tsp. chicken bouillon
   granules
2 ribs celery, thinly sliced
2 onions, thinly sliced
1 red bell pepper, sliced
1 green bell pepper, sliced
8 chicken thighs, skinned
1/2 cup extra crunchy
   peanut butter
crushed chili pepper of
   your choice

1. Combine water, chicken
bouillon granules, celery,
onions, and peppers in slow
cooker.
2. Spread peanut butter
over both sides of chicken
pieces. Sprinkle with chili
pepper. Place on top of ingredients in slow cooker.
3. Cover. Cook on Low
5-6 hours.

Gran's Big Potluck

Carol Ambrose
Ripon, CA

Makes 10-15 servings

2½-3 lb. stewing hen, cut
 into pieces
½ lb. stewing beef, cubed
½-lb. veal shoulder, *or* roast,
 cubed
1½ qts. water
½ lb. small red potatoes,
 cubed
½ lb. small onions, cut in
 half
1 cup sliced carrots
1 cup chopped celery
1 green pepper, chopped
1-lb. pkg. frozen lima beans
1 cup okra, whole *or* diced,
 fresh *or* frozen
1 cup whole kernel corn
8-oz. can whole tomatoes
 with juice
15-oz. can tomato puree
1 tsp. salt
¼-½ tsp. pepper
1 tsp. dry mustard
½ tsp. chili powder
¼ cup chopped fresh
 parsley

1. Combine all ingredients
except last 5 seasonings in one
very large slow cooker, or
divide between two medium-
sized ones.

2. Cover. Cook on Low 10-
12 hours. Add seasonings during last hour of cooking.

Note:
 You may want to debone the
chicken and mix it back into
the cooker before serving the
meal.

Marsha's Chicken Enchilada Casserole

Marsha Sabus
Fallbrook, CA

Makes 4-6 servings

1 onion, chopped
1 garlic clove, minced
1 Tbsp. oil
10-oz. can enchilada sauce
8-oz. can tomato sauce
salt to taste
pepper to taste
8 corn tortillas
3 boneless chicken-breast
 halves, cooked and cubed
15-oz. can ranch-style beans,
 drained
11-oz. can Mexicorn, drained
¾-lb. cheddar cheese, grated
2¼-oz. can sliced black
 olives, drained

1. Saute onion and garlic in
oil in saucepan. Stir in enchilada sauce and tomato sauce.
Season with salt and pepper.

2. Place two tortillas in bottom of slow cooker. Layer one-
third chicken on top. Top with
one-third sauce mixture, one-
third beans, one-third corn,
one-third cheese, and one-third
black olives. Repeat layers 2
more times. Top with 2 tortillas.

3. Cover. Cook on Low 6-8
hours.

Variation:
 Substitute 1 lb. cooked and
drained hamburger for the
chicken.

Chicken Olé

Barb Yoder
Angola, IN

Makes 8 servings

10¾-oz. can cream of
 mushroom soup
10¾-oz. can cream of
 chicken soup
1 cup sour cream
2 Tbsp. grated onion
1½ cups grated cheddar
 cheese
12 flour tortillas, each torn
 into 6-8 pieces
3-4 cups cubed, cooked
 chicken
7-oz. jar salsa
½ cup grated cheddar
 cheese

1. In separate bowl, com-
bine soups, sour cream,
onion, and 1½ cups cheese.

2. Place one-third of each
of the following in layers in
slow cooker: torn tortillas,
soup mixture, chicken, and
salsa. Repeat layers 2 more
times.

3. Cover. Cook on Low 4-5
hours. (This recipe does not
respond well to cooking on
High.)

4. Gently stir. Sprinkle
with remaining ½ cup
cheese. Cover. Cook on Low
another 15-30 minutes.

5. Serve with tortilla chips
and lettuce.

Chicken Enchilada Casserole

Jane Talso
Albuquerque, NM

Makes 6-8 servings

3-4-lb. chicken
1 medium onion, finely chopped
1 Tbsp. oil
10¾-oz. can cream of mushroom soup
10¾-oz. can cream of chicken soup
1 cup sour cream
10-oz. can green enchilada sauce
4.5-oz. can peeled, diced green chilies
20 corn tortillas
3 cups shredded cheddar cheese

1. Boil chicken. Shred meat and discard bones and skin.
2. Saute onion in oil in saucepan until translucent. Stir in soups, sour cream, green enchilada sauce, and chilies. Heat until warm.
3. Tear tortillas into bite-sized pieces.
4. Layer half of sauce, chicken, tortillas, and cheese in slow cooker, alternating layers. Repeat, ending with cheese and sauce.
5. Cover. Cook on Low 5-6 hours, or High 2-3 hours.

Chicken Tortillas

Julette Leaman
Harrisonburg, VA

Makes 4 servings

1 fryer chicken, cooked and cubed
10¾-oz. can cream of chicken soup
½ cup (can) tomatoes with chilies
2 Tbsp. quick-cooking tapioca
6-8 tortillas, torn into pieces
1 medium onion, chopped
2 cups grated cheddar cheese

1. Combine chicken, soup, tomatoes with chilies, and tapioca.
2. Line bottom of slow cooker with one-third tortilla pieces. Add one-third chicken mixture. Sprinkle with one-third onion and cheese. Repeat layers.
3. Cover. Cook on Low 6-8 hours. (This recipe does not respond well to being cooked on High.)

Note:
Serve, if you wish, with shredded lettuce, chopped fresh tomatoes, diced raw onions, sour cream, and salsa.

Chicken at a Whim

Colleen Heatwole
Burton, MI

Makes 6-8 servings

6 medium-sized, boneless, skinless chicken-breast halves
1 small onion, sliced
1 cup dry white wine, chicken broth, *or* water
15-oz. can chicken broth
2 cups water
6-oz. can sliced black olives, with juice
1 small can artichoke hearts, with juice
5 garlic cloves, minced
1 cup dry elbow macaroni, *or* small shells
1 envelope dry savory garlic soup

1. Place chicken in slow cooker. Spread onion over chicken.
2. Combine remaining ingredients, except dry soup mix, and pour over chicken. Sprinkle with dry soup.
3. Cover. Cook on Low 4½ hours.

Browning meat in another pan means an extra step, but it adds a lot to a recipe's appearance and flavor.

Mary Puskar
Forest Hill, MD

Joyce's Chicken Tetrazzini

Joyce Slaymaker
Strasburg, PA

Makes 4 servings

2-3 cups diced cooked chicken
2 cups chicken broth
1 small onion, chopped
1/4 cup sauterne, white wine, *or* milk
1/2 cup slivered almonds
2 4-oz. cans sliced mushrooms, drained
10 3/4-oz. can cream of mushroom soup
1 lb. cooked spaghetti
grated Parmesan cheese

1. Combine all ingredients except spaghetti and cheese in slow cooker.
2. Cover. Cook on Low 6-8 hours.
3. Serve over buttered spaghetti. Sprinkle with Parmesan cheese.

Variations:
1. Place spaghetti in large baking dish. Pour sauce in center. Sprinkle with Parmesan cheese. Broil until lightly browned.
2. Add 10-oz. pkg. frozen peas to Step 1.
Darlene Raber
Wellman, IA

Dorothy's Chicken Tetrazzini

Dorothy Shank
Sterling, IL

Makes 6 servings

3-4 cups diced, cooked chicken
2 cups chicken broth
10 3/4-oz. can cream of mushroom soup
1/2 lb. fresh mushrooms, sliced
1 cup half-and-half
1 lb. cooked spaghetti

1. Combine chicken, broth, and soup in slow cooker.
2. Cover. Cook on Low 4-6 hours.
3. During last hour of cooking, stir in half-and-half.
4. Serve chicken and sauce over cooked spaghetti.

Chickenetti

Miriam Nolt, New Holland, PA
Ruth Hershey, Paradise, PA

Makes 10 servings

1 cup chicken broth
16-oz. pkg. spaghetti, cooked
4-6 cups cubed and cooked chicken, *or* turkey, breast
10 3/4-oz. can cream of mushroom soup, *or* cream of celery soup
1 cup water
1/4 cup green peppers, chopped
1/2 cup diced celery
1/2 tsp. pepper
1 medium onion, grated
1/2 lb. white, *or* yellow, American cheese, cubed

1. Put cup of chicken broth into very large slow cooker. Add spaghetti and meat.
2. In large bowl, combine soup and water until smooth. Stir in remaining ingredients, then pour into slow cooker.
3. Cover. Cook on Low 2-3 hours.

Variations:
1. For a creamier dish, add a 10 3/4-oz. can cream of chicken soup to Step 2.
Arlene Miller
Hutchinson, KS

2. Add 4 1/2-oz. can chopped green chilies to Step 2, for more zest.

191

Golden Chicken and Noodles

Sue Pennington
Bridgewater, VA

Makes 6 servings

6 boneless, skinless
chicken-breast halves
2 10¾-oz. cans broccoli
cheese soup
2 cups milk
1 small onion, chopped
½-1 tsp. salt
½-1 tsp. dried basil
⅛ tsp. pepper

1. Place chicken pieces in
slow cooker.
2. Combine remaining
ingredients. Pour over
chicken.
3. Cover. Cook on High 1
hour. Reduce heat to Low.
Cook 5-6 hours.
4. Serve over noodles.

Easy Casserole

Ruth Conrad Liechty
Goshen, IN

Makes 6-8 servings

2 10¾-oz. cans chicken
gumbo soup
2 10¾-oz. cans cream of
mushroom soup
1-2 cups cut up chicken, *or*
turkey
1 cup milk
6-oz. can chow mein
noodles
1 pint frozen green beans,
or corn, cooked

1. Combine all ingredients
in slow cooker.
2. Cover. Cook on Low 7-8
hours, or High 3-4 hours.

Chicken and Stuffing

Janice Yoskovich
Carmichaels, PA
Jo Ellen Moore, Pendleton, IN

Makes 14-16 servings

2½ cups chicken broth
1 cup butter, *or* margarine,
melted
½ cup chopped onions
½ cup chopped celery
4-oz. can mushrooms, stems
and pieces, drained
¼ cup dried parsley flakes
1½ tsp. rubbed sage
1 tsp. poultry seasoning
1 tsp. salt
½ tsp. pepper
12 cups day-old bread
cubes (½-inch pieces)
2 eggs
10¾-oz. can cream of
chicken soup
5-6 cups cubed cooked
chicken

1. Combine all ingredients
except bread, eggs, soup, and
chicken in saucepan. Simmer
for 10 minutes.
2. Place bread cubes in
large bowl.
3. Combine eggs and soup.
Stir into broth mixture until
smooth. Pour over bread and
toss well.
4. Layer half of stuffing and
then half of chicken into very
large slow cooker (or two
medium-sized cookers). Repeat
layers.
5. Cover. Cook on Low 4½-
5 hours.

When using fresh herbs you may want to experiment with
the amounts to use, because the strength is enhanced in the
slow cooker, rather than becoming weaker.
Annabelle Unternahrer
Shipshewana, IN

Chicken Dressing
Mary V. Warye
West Liberty, OH

Makes 25-30 servings

12-13 cups bread cubes
1 tsp. poultry seasoning
1½ tsp. salt
1 tsp. dried thyme
½ tsp. pepper
½ tsp. dried marjoram
¾ cup margarine, *or*
   butter
2 cups chopped onions
2 cups chopped celery
¼ cup chopped fresh
   parsley
8-oz. can mushrooms,
   drained
3½-4½ cups chicken broth
4 cups diced, cooked
   chicken
2 eggs, beaten
1 tsp. baking powder

1. Put bread cubes in large bowl. Add all seasonings and mix well.
2. Melt margarine in skillet. Saute onions, celery, parsley, and mushrooms. Add to bread cubes.
3. Heat broth and pour into bread cubes, stirring until well moistened. Fold in chicken.
4. Add eggs. Toss well. Add baking powder. Toss well.
5. Pack lightly into very large slow cooker, or two medium-sized cookers.
6. Cover. Cook on Low 5-6 hours.

One-Dish Chicken Supper
Louise Stackhouse
Benton, PA

Makes 4 servings

4 boneless, skinless
   chicken-breast halves
10¾-oz. can cream of
   chicken, *or* celery, *or*
   mushroom, soup
⅓ cup milk
1 pkg. Stove Top stuffing
   mix and seasoning
   packet
1⅔ cups water

1. Place chicken in slow cooker.
2. Combine soup and milk. Pour over chicken.
3. Combine stuffing mix, seasoning packet, and water. Spoon over chicken.
4. Cover. Cook on Low 6-8 hours.

Chicken and Dumplings
Elva Ever
North English, IA

Makes 8-10 servings

4 whole chicken breasts, *or*
   1 small chicken
¾ cup sliced carrots
¼ cup chopped onions
¼ cup chopped celery
1½ cups peas
4-6 Tbsp. flour
1 cup water
salt to taste
pepper to taste
buttermilk baking mix
   dumplings
paprika to taste

1. Cook chicken in water in soup pot. Cool, skin, and debone chicken. Return broth to boiling in soup pot.
2. Cook vegetables in microwave on High for 5 minutes.
3. Meanwhile, combine flour and water until smooth. Add to boiling chicken broth. Add enough extra water to make 4 cups broth, making sure gravy is fairly thick. Season with salt and pepper.
4. Combine chicken, vegetables, and gravy in slow cooker.
5. Mix dumplings as directed on baking mix box. Place dumplings on top of chicken in slow cooker. Sprinkle with paprika.
6. Cover. Cook on High 3 hours.

Sloppy Chicken

Marjora Miller
Archbold, OH

Makes 4-6 servings

28-oz. can boneless
chicken
10¾-oz. can cream of
chicken soup
1 stack butter crackers,
crushed
15-oz. can chicken broth
10¾-oz. can cream of
mushroom soup

1. Combine all ingredients
in slow cooker.
2. Cover. Cook on Low 5-6
hours, stirring occasionally.

Elizabeth's Hot Chicken Sandwiches

Elizabeth Yutzy
Wauseon, OH

Makes 8 servings

3 cups cubed cooked
chicken
2 cups chicken broth
1 cup crushed soda
crackers
¼-½ tsp. salt
dash pepper
8 sandwich buns

1. Combine chicken,
broth, crackers, and seasoning in slow cooker.
2. Cover. Cook on Low 2-3
hours, until mixture thickens
and can be spread.
3. Fill sandwich buns and
serve while warm.

Loretta's Hot Chicken Sandwiches

Loretta Krahn
Mt. Lake, MN

Makes 12 servings

8 cups cubed cooked
chicken, *or* turkey
1 medium onion, chopped
1 cup chopped celery
2 cups mayonnaise
1 cup cubed American
cheese
buns

1. Combine all ingredients
except buns in slow cooker.
2. Cover. Cook on High 2
hours.
3. Serve on buns.

Barbecue Chicken for Buns

Linda Sluiter
Schererville, IN

Makes 16-20 servings

6 cups diced cooked
chicken
2 cups chopped celery
1 cup chopped onions
1 cup chopped green
peppers
4 Tbsp. butter
2 cups ketchup
2 cups water
2 Tbsp. brown sugar
4 Tbsp. vinegar
2 tsp. dry mustard
1 tsp. pepper
1 tsp. salt

1. Combine all ingredients
in slow cooker.
2. Cover. Cook on Low 8
hours.
3. Stir chicken until it
shreds.
4. Pile into steak rolls and
serve.

Chicken Reuben Bake

Gail Bush
Landenberg, PA

Makes 4 servings

4 boneless, skinless
chicken-breast halves
2-lb. bag sauerkraut,
drained and rinsed
4-5 slices Swiss cheese
1¼ cups Thousand Island
salad dressing
2 Tbsp. chopped fresh
parsley

1. Place chicken in slow
cooker. Layer sauerkraut over
chicken. Add cheese. Top
with salad dressing. Sprinkle
with parsley.
2. Cover. Cook on Low 6-8
hours.

No-Fuss Turkey Breast

Dorothy Miller
Gulfport, MI

Makes 3-4 pints cooked meat

1 turkey breast
olive oil
1-2 Tbsp. water

1. Rub turkey breast with
oil. Place in slow cooker. Add
water.

2. Cover. Cook on High 1
hour, or Low 4-5 hours.
3. Cool. Debone and cut
into bite-sized pieces and
store in pint-size plastic boxes
in freezer. Use when cooked
turkey or chicken is called
for.

Turkey in a Pot

Dorothy M. Pittman
Pickens, SC

Makes 10-12 servings

4-5 lb. turkey breast (if
frozen, it doesn't have to
be thawed)
1 medium onion, chopped
1 rib celery, chopped
¼ cup melted margarine
salt to taste
lemon-pepper seasoning to
taste
1½ cups chicken broth

1. Wash turkey breast. Pat
dry. Place in greased slow
cooker. Put onion and celery
in cavity.
2. Pour margarine over
turkey. Sprinkle with seasonings. Pour broth around
turkey.
3. Cover. Cook on High 6
hours. Let stand 10 minutes
before carving.

Turkey Breast

Barbara Katrine Rose
Woodbridge, VA

Makes 6-8 servings

1 large boneless turkey
breast
¼ cup apple cider, *or* juice
1 tsp. salt
¼ tsp. pepper

1. Put turkey breast in
slow cooker. Drizzle apple
cider over turkey. Sprinkle on
both sides with salt and pepper.
2. Cover. Cook on High 3-4
hours.
3. Remove turkey breast.
Let stand for 15 minutes
before slicing.

Onion Turkey Breast

Mary Ann Wasick
West Allis, WI

Makes 6-8 servings

4-6-lb. boneless, skinless
   turkey breast
1 tsp. garlic powder
1 envelope dry onion soup
   mix

1. Place turkey in slow
cooker. Sprinkle garlic powder and onion soup mix over
breast.
2. Cover. Cook on Low 8-
10 hours.

Note:
Use au jus over rice or
pasta.

Easy and Delicious Turkey Breast

Gail Bush
Landenberg, PA

Makes 4-6 servings

1 turkey breast
15-oz. can whole berry
   cranberry sauce
1 envelope dry onion soup
   mix
1/2 cup orange juice
1/2 tsp. salt
1/4 tsp. pepper

1. Place turkey in slow
cooker.
2. Combine remaining
ingredients. Pour over turkey.
3. Cover. Cook on Low 6-8
hours.

Turkey Stew

Ruth S. Weaver
Reinholds, PA

Makes 8 servings

2 lbs. skinless turkey
   thighs
1 lb., *or* 5 large, carrots,
   sliced
2 medium onions, chopped
8 medium potatoes, cubed
4 ribs celery, chopped
3 garlic cloves, minced
1 tsp. salt
1/4 tsp. pepper
2 Tbsp. Worcestershire
   sauce
15-oz. can tomato sauce
2 bay leaves

1. Place turkey in large
slow cooker.
2. In separate bowl, mix
together carrots, onions, potatoes, celery, garlic, salt, pepper, Worcestershire sauce,
tomato sauce, and bay.
3. Pour over turkey. Cover.
Cook on Low 8-12 hours, or
High 6-8 hours. Remove bay
leaves before serving.

Pheasant a la Elizabeth

Elizabeth L. Richards
Rapid City, SD

Makes 4 servings

6 pheasant breasts,
   deboned and cubed
3/4 cup teriyaki sauce
1/3-1/2 cup flour
1 1/2 tsp. garlic salt
pepper to taste
1/3 cup olive oil
1 large onion, sliced
12-oz. can beer
3/4 cup fresh mushrooms,
   sliced

1. Marinate pheasant in
teriyaki sauce for 2-4 hours.
2. Combine flour, garlic
salt, and pepper. Dredge
pheasant in flour. Brown in
olive oil in skillet. Add onion
and saute for 3 minutes, stirring frequently. Transfer to
slow cooker.
3. Add beer and mush-
rooms.
4. Cover. Cook on Low 6-8
hours.

Variation:
Instead of pheasant, use
chicken.

Pot-Roasted Rabbit

Donna Treloar
Gaston, IN

Makes 4 servings

2 onions, sliced
4-5-lb. roasting rabbit
salt to taste
pepper to taste
1 garlic clove, sliced
2 bay leaves
1 whole clove
1 cup hot water
2 Tbsp. soy sauce
2 Tbsp. flour
1/2 cup cold water

1. Place onion in bottom of slow cooker.
2. Rub rabbit with salt and pepper. Insert garlic in cavity. Place rabbit in slow cooker.
3. Add bay leaves, clove, hot water, and soy sauce.
4. Cover. Cook on Low 10-12 hours.
5. Remove rabbit and thicken gravy by stirring 2 Tbsp. flour blended into 1/2 cup water into simmering juices in cooker. Continue stirring until gravy thickens. Cut rabbit into serving-size pieces and serve with gravy.

Baked Lamb Shanks

Irma H. Schoen
Windsor, CT

Makes 4-6 servings

1 medium onion, thinly sliced
2 small carrots, cut in thin strips
1 rib celery, chopped
3 lamb shanks, cracked
1-2 cloves garlic, split
1 1/2 tsp. salt
1/4 tsp. pepper
1 tsp. dried oregano
1 tsp. dried thyme
2 bay leaves, crumbled
1/2 cup dry white wine
8-oz. can tomato sauce

1. Place onions, carrots, and celery in slow cooker.
2. Rub lamb with garlic and season with salt and pepper. Add to slow cooker.
3. Mix remaining ingredients together in separate bowl and add to meat and vegetables.
4. Cover. Cook on Low 8-10 hours, or High 4-6 hours.

Herb Potato-Fish Bake

Barbara Sparks
Glen Burnie, MD

Makes 4 servings

10 3/4-oz. can cream of celery soup
1/2 cup water
1-lb. perch fillet, fresh *or* thawed
2 cups cooked, diced potatoes, drained
1/4 cup grated Parmesan cheese
1 Tbsp. chopped parsley
1/2 tsp. salt
1/2 tsp. dried basil
1/4 tsp. dried oregano

1. Combine soup and water. Pour half in slow cooker. Spread fillet on top. Place potatoes on fillet. Pour remaining soup mix over top.
2. Combine cheese and herbs. Sprinkle over ingredients in slow cooker.
3. Cover. Cook on High 1-2 hours, being careful not to overcook fish.

If you have them available, use whole or leaf herbs and spices rather than crushed or ground ones.
Barbara Sparks
Glen Burnie, MD

Shrimp Jambalaya

Karen Ashworth
Duenweg, MO

Makes 6-8 servings

2 Tbsp. margarine
2 medium onions, chopped
2 green bell peppers,
  chopped
3 ribs celery, chopped
1 cup chopped cooked
  ham
2 garlic cloves, chopped
1 1/2 cups minute rice
1 1/2 cups beef broth
28-oz. can chopped
  tomatoes
2 Tbsp. chopped parsley
1 tsp. dried basil
1/2 tsp. dried thyme
1/4 tsp. pepper
1/8 tsp. cayenne pepper
1 lb. shelled, deveined,
  medium-size shrimp
1 Tbsp. chopped parsley
  for garnish

1. Melt margarine in slow cooker set on High. Add onions, peppers, celery, ham, and garlic. Cook 30 minutes.
2. Add rice. Cover and cook 15 minutes.
3. Add broth, tomatoes, 2 Tbsp. parsley, and remaining seasonings. Cover and cook on High 1 hour.
4. Add shrimp. Cook on High 30 minutes, or until liquid is absorbed.
5. Garnish with 1 Tbsp. parsley.

Jambalaya

Doris M. Coyle-Zipp
South Ozone Park, NY

Makes 5-6 servings

3 1/2-4-lb. roasting chicken,
  cut up
3 onions, diced
1 carrot, sliced
3-4 garlic cloves, minced
1 tsp. dried oregano
1 tsp. dried basil
1 tsp. salt
1/8 tsp. white pepper
14-oz. can crushed
  tomatoes
1 lb. shelled raw shrimp
2 cups cooked rice

1. Combine all ingredients except shrimp and rice in slow cooker.
2. Cover. Cook on Low 2-3 1/2 hours, or until chicken is tender.
3. Add shrimp and rice.
4. Cover. Cook on High 15-20 minutes, or until shrimp are done.

Shrimp Creole

Carol Findling
Princeton, IL

Makes 8-10 servings

1/2 cup butter
1/3 cup flour
1 3/4 cups sliced onions
1 cup diced green peppers
1 cup diced celery
1 1/2 large carrots, shredded
2 3/4-lb. can tomatoes
3/4 cup water
1/2 tsp. dried thyme
1 garlic clove, minced
pinch of rosemary
1 Tbsp. sugar
3 bay leaves
1 Tbsp. Worcestershire
  sauce
1 Tbsp. salt
1/8 tsp. dried oregano
2 lbs. shelled shrimp,
  deveined

1. Melt butter in skillet. Add flour and brown, stirring constantly. Add onions, green peppers, celery, and carrots. Cook 5-10 minutes. Transfer to slow cooker.
2. Add remaining ingredients, except shrimp, and stir well.
3. Cover. Cook on Low 6-8 hours.
4. Add shrimp during last hour.
5. Serve over rice.

Seafood Gumbo

Barbara Katrine Rose
Woodbridge, VA

Makes 10 servings

1 lb. okra, sliced
2 Tbsp. butter, melted
1/4 cup butter, melted
1/4 cup flour
1 bunch green onions,
    sliced
1/2 cup chopped celery
2 garlic cloves, minced
16-oz. can tomatoes and
    juice
1 bay leaf
1 Tbsp. chopped fresh
    parsley
1 fresh thyme sprig
1 1/2 tsp. salt
1/2-1 tsp. red pepper
3-5 cups water, depending
    upon the consistency
    you like
1 lb. peeled and deveined
    fresh shrimp
1/2 lb. fresh crabmeat

1. Saute okra in 2 Tbsp. butter until okra is lightly browned. Transfer to slow cooker.
2. Combine remaining butter and flour in skillet. Cook over medium heat, stirring constantly until roux is the color of chocolate, 20-25 minutes. Stir in green onions, celery, and garlic. Cook until vegetables are tender. Add to slow cooker. Gently stir in remaining ingredients.
3. Cover. Cook on High 3-4 hours.
4. Serve over rice.

Seafood Medley

Susan Alexander
Baltimore, MD

Makes 10-12 servings

1 lb. shrimp, peeled and
    deveined
1 lb. crabmeat
1 lb. bay scallops
2 10 3/4-oz. cans cream of
    celery soup
2 soup cans milk
2 Tbsp. butter, melted
1 tsp. Old Bay seasoning
1/4-1/2 tsp. salt
1/4 tsp. pepper

1. Layer shrimp, crab, and scallops in slow cooker.
2. Combine soup and milk. Pour over seafood.
3. Mix together butter and spices and pour over top.
4. Cover. Cook on Low 3-4 hours.
5. Serve over rice or noodles.

Salmon Cheese Casserole

Wanda S. Curtin
Bradenton, FL

Makes 6 servings

14 3/4-oz. can salmon with
    liquid
4-oz. can mushrooms,
    drained
1 1/2 cups bread crumbs
2 eggs, beaten
1 cup grated cheese
1 Tbsp. lemon juice
1 Tbsp. minced onion

1. Flake fish in bowl, removing bones. Stir in remaining ingredients. Pour into lightly greased slow cooker.
2. Cover. Cook on Low 3-4 hours.

Tuna Barbecue

Esther Martin
Ephrata, PA

Makes 4 servings

12-oz. can tuna, drained
2 cups tomato juice
1 medium green pepper,
  finely chopped
2 Tbsp. onion flakes
2 Tbsp. Worcestershire
  sauce
3 Tbsp. vinegar
2 Tbsp. sugar
1 Tbsp. prepared mustard
1 rib celery, chopped
dash chili powder
1/2 tsp. cinnamon
dash of hot sauce, optional

1. Combine all ingredients
in slow cooker.
2. Cover. Cook on Low 8-
10 hours, or High 4-5 hours.
If mixture becomes too dry
while cooking, add 1/2 cup
tomato juice.
3. Serve on buns.

Tuna Salad Casserole

Charlotte Fry, St. Charles, MO
Esther Becker, Gordonville, PA

Makes 4 servings

2 7-oz. cans tuna
10 3/4-oz. can cream of
  celery soup
3 hard-boiled eggs,
  chopped
1/2 to 1 1/2 cups diced celery
1/2 cup diced onions
1/2 cup mayonnaise
1/4 tsp. ground pepper
1 1/2 cups crushed potato
  chips

1. Combine all ingredients
except 1/4 cup potato chips in
slow cooker. Top with
remaining chips.
2. Cover. Cook on Low 5-8
hours.

Tuna Noodle Casserole

Leona Miller
Millersburg, OH

Makes 6 servings

2 6 1/2-oz. cans water-
  packed tuna, drained
2 10 1/2-oz. cans cream of
  mushroom soup
1 cup milk
2 Tbsp. dried parsley
10-oz. pkg. frozen mixed
  vegetables, thawed
10-oz. pkg. noodles, cooked
  and drained
1/2 cup toasted sliced
  almonds

1. Combine tuna, soup,
milk, parsley, and vegetables.
Fold in noodles. Pour into
greased slow cooker. Top with
almonds.
2. Cover. Cook on Low 7-9
hours, or High 3-4 hours.

If your recipe turns out to have too much liquid, remove
the cover and use the High setting for about 45 minutes.
Esther Porter
Minneapolis, MN

Tempeh-Stuffed Peppers

Sara Harter Fredette
Williamsburg, MA

Makes 4 servings

4 oz. tempeh, cubed
1 garlic clove, minced
28-oz. can crushed
  tomatoes
2 tsp. soy sauce
1/4 cup chopped onions
1 1/2 cups cooked rice
1 1/2 cups shredded cheese
Tabasco sauce, optional
4 green, red, *or* yellow, bell
  peppers, tops removed
  and seeded
1/4 cup shredded cheese

1. Steam tempeh 10 minutes in saucepan. Mash in bowl with the garlic, half the tomatoes, and soy sauce.
2. Stir in onions, rice, 1 1/2 cups cheese, and Tabasco sauce. Stuff into peppers.
3. Place peppers in slow cooker, 3 on the bottom and one on top. Pour remaining half of tomatoes over peppers.
4. Cover. Cook on Low 6-8 hours, or High 3-4 hours. Top with remaining cheese in last 30 minutes.

Tastes-Like-Chili-Rellenos

Roseann Wilson
Albuquerque, NM

Makes 6 servings

2 tsp. butter
2 4-oz. cans whole green
  chilies
1/2 lb. grated cheddar
  cheese
1/2 lb. grated Monterey Jack
  cheese
14 1/2-oz. can stewed
  tomatoes
4 eggs
2 Tbsp. flour
3/4 cup evaporated milk

1. Grease sides and bottom of slow cooker with butter.
2. Cut chilies into strips. Layer chilies and cheeses in slow cooker. Pour in stewed tomatoes.
3. Combine eggs, flour, and milk. Pour into slow cooker.
4. Cover. Cook on High 2-3 hours.

Barbecued Lentils

Sue Hamilton
Minooka, IL

Makes 8 servings

2 cups barbecue sauce
3 1/2 cups water
1 lb. dry lentils
1 pkg. vegetarian hot dogs,
  sliced

1. Combine all ingredients in slow cooker.
2. Cover. Cook on Low 6-8 hours.

Cheryl's Macaroni and Cheese

Cheryl Bartel
Hillsboro, KS

Makes 6 servings

8 oz. dry elbow macaroni,
  cooked
3-4 cups (about 3/4-lb.)
  shredded sharp cheddar
  cheese, divided
13-oz. can evaporated milk
1½ cups milk
2 eggs
1 tsp. salt
¼ tsp. black pepper
chopped onion to taste

1. Combine all ingredients,
except 1 cup cheese, in
greased slow cooker. Sprinkle
reserved cup of cheese over
top.

2. Cover. Cook on Low 3-4
hours. Do not remove the lid
or stir until the mixture has
finished cooking.

Variation:

For some extra zest, add ½
tsp. dry mustard when combining all ingredients. Add
thin slices of cheese to top of
cooker mixture.

Dorothy M. Pittman
Pickens, SC

Macaroni and Cheese

Martha Hershey, Ronks, PA
Marcia S. Myer, Manheim, PA
LeAnne Nolt, Leola, PA
Ellen Ranck, Gap, PA
Mary Sommerfeld, Lancaster, PA
Kathryn Yoder, Minot, ND

Makes 6 servings

8-oz. pkg. dry macaroni,
  cooked
2 Tbsp. oil
13-oz. can evaporated milk
  (fat-free will work)
1½ cups milk
1 tsp. salt
3 cups (about ½ lb.)
  shredded cheese:
  cheddar, American,
  Velveeta, *or a*
  combination
2-4 Tbsp. melted butter
2 Tbsp. onion, chopped fine
4 hot dogs, sliced, optional

1. In slow cooker, toss macaroni in oil. Stir in remaining
ingredients except hot dogs.

2. Cover. Cook on Low 2-3
hours. Add hot dogs, if
desired, and cook 1 hour
longer.

Variations:

1. Use 3 cups evaporated
milk, instead of 13-oz. evaporated milk and 1½ cups milk.

2. Add more onion, up to
¼ cup total.

3. Add ½ tsp. pepper
Stacy Petersheim
Mechanicsburg, PA
Sara Wilson, Blairstown, MO

When cooking on High, stir occasionally for more even
cooking and improved flavor.
Roseann Wilson
Albuquerque, NM

Bean Main Dishes

From-Scratch Baked Beans

Wanda Roth
Napoleon, OH

Makes 6 servings

2½ cups Great Northern
    dried beans
4 cups water
1½ cups tomato sauce
½ cup brown sugar
2 tsp. salt
1 small onion, chopped
½ tsp. chili powder

1. Wash and drain dry
beans. Combine beans and
water in slow cooker. Cook
on Low 8 hours, or overnight.
2. Stir in remaining ingredients. Cook on Low 6 hours.

New England Baked Beans

Mary Wheatley
Mashpee, MA
Jean Butzer
Batavia, NY

Makes 8 servings

1 lb. dried beans—Great
    Northern, pea beans, *or*
    navy beans
¼ lb. salt pork, sliced *or*
    diced
1 qt. water
1 tsp. salt
1-4 Tbsp. brown sugar,
    according to your
    preference
½ cup molasses
½-1 tsp. dry mustard,
    according to your
    preference
½ tsp. baking soda
1 onion, coarsely chopped
5 cups water

1. Wash beans and remove
any stones or shriveled beans.
2. Meanwhile, simmer salt
pork in 1 quart water in
saucepan for 10 minutes.
Drain. Do not reserve liquid.
3. Combine all ingredients
in slow cooker.
4. Cook on High until contents come to boil. Turn to
Low. Cook 14-16 hours, or
until beans are tender.

Variations:
1. Add ½ tsp. pepper to
Step 3.
    Rachel Kauffman
    Alton, MI

2. Add ¼ cup ketchup to
Step 3.
    Cheri Jantzen
    Houston, TX

Mom's New England Baked Beans

Debbie Zeida
Mashpee, MA

Makes 6-8 servings

3 cups dried navy beans
9 cups water
1 medium onion, chopped
1 cup ketchup
1 cup brown sugar
1 cup water
2 tsp. dry mustard
2 Tbsp. dark molasses
1 Tbsp. salt
1/4 lb. salt pork, ground *or* diced

1. Cook beans in water in soup pot until softened, or bring to boil, cover, and let stand for 1 1/2 hours. Drain. Pour beans into slow cooker.
2. Stir in remaining ingredients. Mix well.
3. Cover. Cook on Low 8 hours, or High 4 hours, stirring occasionally.

Variation:
Use 1 lb. dried Great Northern beans instead of 3 cups navy beans.
Dorothy Miller
Gulfport, MI

Home-Baked Beans

Carolyn Baer
Conrath, WI

Makes 15-25 servings

2 lbs. (4 cups) dried navy, *or* pea, beans
1 lb. salt pork, *or* bacon, chopped
1 lb. (2 1/2 cups), *or* less, brown sugar
1-lb. 3-oz. can tomatoes
2 medium onions, chopped
2 Tbsp. prepared mustard
1/2 tsp. salt
1/2 tsp. pepper

1. Wash and pick over beans. Cover generously with water and soak overnight. Simmer in salted water until tender. Drain. Save liquid.
2. Place pork or bacon in bottom of slow cooker.
3. Mix together brown sugar, tomatoes, onions, mustard, salt, and pepper. Alternately layer sauce mixture and beans over pork.
4. Add enough reserved water to cover beans.
5. Cover. Cook on Low 8-10 hours, stirring occasionally.

Note:
These beans freeze well.

Barbecued Lima Beans

Hazel L. Propst
Oxford, PA

Makes 10 servings

1 1/2 lbs. dried lima beans
6 cups water
2 1/4 cups chopped onions
1 1/4 cups brown sugar
1 1/2 cups ketchup
13 drops Tabasco sauce
1 cup dark corn syrup
1 Tbsp. salt
1/2 lb. bacon, diced

1. Soak washed beans in water overnight. Do not drain.
2. Add onion. Bring to boil. Simmer 30-60 minutes, or until beans are tender. Drain beans, reserving liquid.
3. Combine all ingredients except bean liquid in slow cooker. Mix well. Pour in enough liquid so that beans are barely covered.
4. Cover. Cook on Low 10 hours, or High 4-6 hours. Stir occasionally.

Refried Beans with Bacon

Arlene Wengerd
Millersburg, OH

Makes 8 servings

2 cups dried red, *or* pinto,
    beans
6 cups water
2 garlic cloves, minced
1 large tomato, peeled,
    seeded, and chopped, *or*
    1 pint tomato juice
1 tsp. salt
1/2 lb. bacon
shredded cheese

1. Combine beans, water, garlic, tomato, and salt in slow cooker.

2. Cover. Cook on High 5 hours, stirring occasionally. When the beans become soft, drain off some liquid.

3. While the beans cook, brown bacon in skillet. Drain, reserving drippings. Crumble bacon. Add half of bacon and 3 Tbsp. drippings to beans. Stir.

4. Mash or puree beans with a food processor. Fry the mashed bean mixture in the remaining bacon drippings. Add more salt to taste.

5. To serve, sprinkle the remaining bacon and shredded cheese on top of beans.

Variations:

1. Instead of draining off liquid, add 1/3 cup dry minute rice and continue cooking about 20 minutes. Add a dash of hot sauce and a dollop of sour cream to individual servings.

2. Instead of frying the mashed bean mixture, place several spoonfuls on flour tortillas, roll up, and serve.
    Susan McClure
    Dayton, VA

Red Beans and Rice

Margaret A. Moffitt
Bartlett, TN

Makes 8-10 servings

1-lb. pkg. dried red beans
water
salt pork, ham hocks, *or*
    sausage, cut into small
    chunks
2 tsp. salt
1 tsp. pepper
3-4 cups water
6-oz. can tomato paste
8-oz. can tomato sauce
4 garlic cloves, minced

1. Soak beans for 8 hours. Drain. Discard soaking water.

2. Mix together all ingredients in slow cooker.

3. Cover. Cook on Low 10-12 hours, or until beans are soft. Serve over rice.

Variation:
    Use canned red kidney beans. Cook 1 hour on High and then 3 hours on Low.

Note:
    These beans freeze well.

New Mexico Pinto Beans

John D. Allen
Rye, CO

Makes 8-10 servings

2 1/2 cups dried pinto beans
3 qts. water
1/2 cup ham, *or* salt pork,
    diced, *or* a small ham
    shank
2 garlic cloves, crushed
1 tsp. crushed red chili
    peppers, optional
salt to taste
pepper to taste

1. Sort beans. Discard pebbles, shriveled beans, and floaters. Wash beans under running water. Place in saucepan, cover with 3 quarts water, and soak overnight.

2. Drain beans and discard soaking water. Pour beans into slow cooker. Cover with fresh water.

3. Add meat, garlic, chili, salt, and pepper. Cook on Low 6-10 hours, or until beans are soft.

Scandinavian Beans

Virginia Bender
Dover, DE

Makes 8 servings

1 lb. dried pinto beans
6 cups water
12 ozs. bacon, *or* 1 ham hock
1 onion, chopped
2-3 garlic cloves, minced
1/4 tsp. pepper
1 tsp. salt
1/4 cup molasses
1 cup ketchup
Tabasco to taste
1 tsp. Worcestershire sauce
3/4 cup brown sugar
1/2 cup cider vinegar
1/4 tsp. dry mustard

1. Soak beans in water in soup pot for 8 hours. Bring beans to boil and cook 1 1/2-2 hours, or until soft. Drain, reserving liquid.

2. Combine all ingredients in slow cooker, using just enough bean liquid to cover everything. Cook on Low 5-6 hours. If using ham hock, debone, cut ham into bite-sized pieces, and mix into beans.

New Orleans Red Beans

Cheri Jantzen
Houston, TX

Makes 6 servings

2 cups dried kidney beans
5 cups water
2 Tbsp. bacon drippings
1/2 lb. hot sausage, cut in small pieces
2 onions, chopped
2 cloves garlic, minced
1 tsp. salt

1. Wash and sort beans. In saucepan, combine beans and water. Boil 2 minutes. Remove from heat. Soak 1 hour.

2. Heat bacon drippings in skillet. Add sausage and brown slowly. Add onions and garlic and saute until tender.

3. Combine all ingredients, including the bean water, in slow cooker.

4. Cover. Cook on Low 8-10 hours. During last 20 minutes of cooking, stir frequently and mash lightly with spoon.

5. Serve over hot cooked white rice.

No Meat Baked Beans

Esther Becker
Gordonville, PA

Makes 8-10 servings

1 lb. dried navy beans
6 cups water
1 small onion, chopped
3/4 cup ketchup
3/4 cup brown sugar
3/4 cup water
1 tsp. dry mustard
2 Tbsp. dark molasses
1 tsp. salt

1. Soak beans in water overnight in large soup kettle. Cook beans in water until soft, about 1 1/2 hours. Drain, discarding bean water.

2. Mix together all ingredients in slow cooker. Mix well.

3. Cover. Cook on Low 10-12 hours.

Hot Bean Dish Without Meat

Jeannine Janzen
Elbing, KS

Makes 8-10 servings

16-oz. can kidney beans,
  drained
15-oz. can lima beans,
  drained
1/4 cup vinegar
2 Tbsp. molasses
2 heaping Tbsp. brown
  sugar
2 Tbsp. minced onion
mustard to taste
Tabasco sauce to taste

1. Place beans in slow
cooker.
2. Combine remaining
ingredients. Pour over beans.
3. Cover. Cook on Low 3-4
hours.

Variation:
Add 1 lb. browned ground
beef to make this a meaty
main dish.

Barbecued Beans

Jane Steiner
Orrville, OH

Makes 12-15 servings

4 11-oz. cans pork and
  beans
3/4 cup brown sugar
1 tsp. dry mustard
1/2 cup ketchup
6 slices bacon, diced

1. Pour 2 cans pork and
beans into slow cooker.
2. Combine brown sugar
and mustard. Sprinkle half of
mixture over beans.
3. Cover with remaining
cans of pork and beans.
Sprinkle with rest of brown
sugar and mustard.
4. Layer bacon over top.
Spread ketchup over all.
5. Cut through bean mix-
ture a bit before heating.
6. Cover. Cook on Low 4
hours.

Frances' Slow-Cooker Beans

Frances B. Musser
Newmanstown, PA

Makes 6-8 servings

1/2 cup ketchup
1 Tbsp. prepared mustard
1/2 cup brown sugar
1 small onion, chopped
1 tsp. salt
1/4 tsp. ground ginger
1/2 cup molasses
1 lb. turkey bacon,
  browned and crumbled
2-lb., 8-oz. can Great
  Northern beans, drained

1. Combine all ingredients
in slow cooker.
2. Cover. Cook on Low 4
hours.

If there is too much liquid in your cooker, stick a toothpick under the edge of the lid to tilt it slightly and to allow
the steam to escape.

Carol Sherwood
Batavia, NY

Kelly's Baked Beans

Kelly Bailey
Mechanicsburg, PA

Makes 6 servings

40-oz. can Great Northern
  beans, juice reserved
15½-oz. can Great
  Northern beans, juice
  reserved
¾ cup brown sugar
¼ cup white corn syrup
½ cup ketchup
½ tsp. salt
half a medium-sized
  onion, chopped
8-9 slices bacon, browned
  and crumbled, optional

1. Drain beans overnight
in colander. Save ¼ cup liquid.
2. Mix together brown
sugar, corn syrup, and
ketchup. Mix well. Add salt
and onion.
3. Stir in beans and pour
into greased slow cooker. If
beans appear dry while cooking, add some of the ¼ cup
reserved bean juice.
4. Cover. Cook on Low 6-8
hours.

Four Beans and Sausage

Mary Seielstad
Sparks, NV

Makes 8 servings

15-oz. can Great Northern
  beans, drained
15½-oz. can black beans,
  rinsed and drained
16-oz. can red kidney
  beans, drained
15-oz. can butter beans,
  drained
1½ cups ketchup
½ cup chopped onions
1 green pepper, chopped
1 lb. smoked sausage,
  cooked and cut into
  ½-inch slices
¼ cup brown sugar
2 garlic cloves, minced
1 tsp. Worcestershire sauce
½ tsp. dry mustard
½ tsp. Tabasco sauce

1. Combine all ingredients
in slow cooker.
2. Cover. Cook on Low 9-
10 hours, or High 4-5 hours.

Mary Ellen's Three-Bean Dish

Mary Ellen Musser
Reinholds, PA

Makes 10-20 servings

10-oz. pkg. frozen lima
  beans, cooked
3 16-oz. cans baked beans
40-oz. can kidney beans,
  drained
1 lb. sausage links,
  browned and cut into
  pieces
½ lb. cooked ham, cubed
1 medium onion, chopped
8-oz. can tomato sauce
½ cup ketchup
¼ cup packed brown sugar
1 tsp. salt
½ tsp. pepper
½ tsp. prepared mustard

1. Combine lima beans,
baked beans, kidney beans,
sausage, and ham in 3½-4-
quart slow cooker.
2. In separate bowl, com-
bine onion, tomato sauce,
ketchup, brown sugar, salt,
pepper, and mustard and
pour into slow cooker. Mix
gently.
3. Cover. Cook on Low 4-6
hours.

Sausage Bean Casserole

Juanita Marner
Shipshewana, IN

Makes 8 servings

1 lb. ground pork sausage
½ cup chopped onions
½ cup chopped green
   peppers
1 lb. cooked speckled
   butter beans
2 cups diced canned
   tomatoes
½ cup tomato sauce
¼ tsp. salt
⅛ tsp. pepper

1. Brown sausage, onions, and green peppers in saucepan.
2. Combine all ingredients in slow cooker.
3. Cover. Cook on High 2 hours, or Low 4 hours.

Cajun Sausage and Beans

Melanie Thrower
McPherson, KS

Makes 4-6 servings

1 lb. smoked sausage,
   sliced into ¼-inch pieces
16-oz. can red beans
16-oz. can crushed
   tomatoes with green
   chilies
1 cup chopped celery
half an onion, chopped
2 Tbsp. Italian seasoning
Tabasco sauce to taste

1. Combine all ingredients in slow cooker.
2. Cover. Cook on Low 8 hours.
3. Serve over rice or as a thick zesty soup.

Sausage Bean Quickie

Ellen Ranck
Gap, PA

Makes 4 servings

4-6 cooked brown 'n serve
   sausage links, cut into 1-
   inch pieces
2 tsp. cider vinegar
2 16-oz. cans red kidney *or*
   baked, beans, drained
7-oz. can pineapple
   chunks, undrained
2 tsp. brown sugar
3 Tbsp. flour

1. Combine sausage, vinegar, beans, and pineapple in slow cooker.
2. Combine brown sugar with flour. Add to slow cooker. Stir well.
3. Cover. Cook on Low 5-10 hours, or High 1-2 hours.

Beans with Rice

Miriam Christophel
Battle Creek, MI

Makes 8 servings

3 cups dried small red
   beans
8 cups water
3 garlic cloves, minced
1 large onion, chopped
8 cups fresh water
1-2 ham hocks
1/2- 3/4 cup ketchup
2 tsp. salt
pinch of pepper
1 1/2-2 tsp. ground cumin
1 Tbsp. parsley
1-2 bay leaves

1. Soak beans overnight in
8 cups water. Drain. Place
soaked beans in slow cooker
with garlic, onion, 8 cups
fresh water, and ham hocks.
2. Cover. Cook on High 12-
14 hours.
3. Take ham hocks out of
cooker and allow to cool.
Remove meat from bones.
Cut up and return to slow
cooker. Add remaining ingredients.
4. Cover. Cook on High 2-3
hours.
5. Serve over rice with dollop of sour cream.

Nan's Barbecued Beans

Nan Decker
Albuquerque, NM

Makes 10-12 servings

1 lb. ground beef
1 onion, chopped
5 cups canned baked
   beans
2 Tbsp. cider vinegar
1 Tbsp. Worcestershire
   sauce
2 Tbsp. brown sugar
1/2 cup ketchup

1. Brown ground beef and
onion in skillet. Drain.
2. Combine all ingredients
in slow cooker.
3. Cover. Cook on Low 4-6
hours.

Betty's Calico Beans

Betty Lahman
Elkton, VA

Makes 6-8 servings

1 lb. ground beef, browned
   and drained
14 3/4-oz. can lima beans
15 1/2-oz. can pinto beans
15 1/4-oz. can corn
1/4 cup brown sugar
1 cup ketchup
1 Tbsp. vinegar
2 tsp. prepared mustard
1 medium onion, chopped

1. Combine all ingredients
in slow cooker.
2. Cover. Cook on High 3-4
hours.

Three-Bean Barbecue

Ruth Hofstetter
Versailles, MO
Kathryn Yoder
Minot, ND

Makes 6-8 servings

1 1/2-2 lbs. ground beef
3/4 lb. bacon
1 cup chopped onions
2 31-oz. cans pork and
   beans
1-lb. can kidney beans,
   drained
1-lb. can lima beans,
   drained
1 cup ketchup
1/4 cup brown sugar
1 Tbsp. liquid smoke
3 Tbsp. white vinegar
1 tsp. salt
dash of pepper

1. Brown beef in
saucepan. Drain.
2. Fry bacon and onions in
saucepan. Drain.
3. Combine all ingredients
in slow cooker.
4. Cover. Cook on Low 4-6
hours.

Note:
   This is good served with
baked potatoes.

Baked Beans in Slow Cooker

Ruth Hershey
Paradise, PA

Makes 12 servings

1½ lbs. ground beef
½-1 cup chopped onions, according to your preference
3 lbs. pork and beans
1-lb. can kidney beans, drained
1 cup ketchup
¼ cup brown sugar, packed
3 Tbsp. cider vinegar

1. Brown ground beef and onion in skillet. Drain.
2. Combine all ingredients in slow cooker. Mix well.
3. Cover. Cook on Low 4-6 hours. Stir occasionally.

Roseann's Baked Beans

Roseann Wilson
Albuquerque, NM

Makes 12 servings

2 42-oz. cans baked beans, drained
1 lb. ground beef, cooked and drained
½ cup barbecue sauce
¼ cup ketchup

1 Tbsp. prepared mustard
3 strips bacon, diced
¼ cup brown sugar
2 Tbsp. minced onion
3 strips bacon, cut in half

1. Combine all ingredients except half strips of bacon in slow cooker. Place 6 half-strips of bacon over top.
2. Cover. Cook on Low 3 hours.

Carla's Baked Beans

Carla Koslowsky
Hillsboro, KS

Makes 8-10 servings

½ lb. ground beef
½ lb. bacon, chopped
1 medium onion, minced
1 tsp. salt
½ tsp. pepper
16-oz. can red kidney beans, drained
16-oz. can pork and beans, drained
15-oz. can butter, or green lima, beans
⅓ cup brown sugar
¼ cup sugar
¼ cup barbecue sauce
¼ cup ketchup
1 Tbsp. prepared mustard
2 Tbsp. molasses

1. Brown meats and onion in skillet. Drain.
2. Add salt, pepper, and beans. Stir in remaining ingredients. Mix well. Pour into slow cooker.

3. Cover. Cook on High 4-5 hours.

Five-Bean Hot Dish

Dede Peterson
Rapid City, SD

Makes 10 servings

1 lb. ground beef
1 tsp. prepared mustard
2 tsp. vinegar
½ lb. bacon, finely diced
¾ cup brown sugar
15-oz. can lima beans, drained
1 tsp. salt
15-oz. can butter beans, drained
1 cup ketchup
16-oz. can kidney beans, drained
32-oz. can pork & beans, undrained
15-oz. can red beans, drained

1. Brown ground beef in deep saucepan. Drain.
2. Stir in mustard, vinegar, and bacon.
3. Add remaining ingredients. Mix well. Pour into large cooker.
4. Cover. Cook on Low 3-5 hours.

Note:
These beans freeze well.

Char's Calico Beans

Char Hagner
Montague, MI

Makes 10-12 servings

1/4 lb. bacon
1 onion, chopped
1 lb. ground beef
1/2 cup brown sugar
1/2 cup ketchup
1 Tbsp. prepared mustard
1 tsp. salt
2 15-oz. cans lima beans, drained
28-oz. can Boston baked beans
2 16-oz. cans kidney beans, drained

1. Cut bacon in pieces. Brown in skillet and drain. Brown onion with beef in skillet. Drain.

2. Combine all ingredients in slow cooker.

3. Cover. Cook on Low 6 hours.

Casey's Beans

Cheryl Bartel
Hillsboro, KS

Makes 10-12 servings

1/2 lb. ground beef
10 slices bacon, diced
1/2 cup chopped onions
1/3 cup brown sugar
1/3 cup sugar, optional
1/4 cup ketchup
1/4 cup barbecue sauce
2 Tbsp. prepared mustard
2 Tbsp. molasses
1/2 tsp. salt
1/2 tsp. chili powder
1/2 tsp. pepper
1-lb. can kidney beans, drained
1-lb. can butter beans, drained
1-lb. can black beans, drained
1-lb. can pork and beans

1. Brown ground beef, bacon, and onion in deep saucepan. Drain.

2. Stir in remaining ingredients, except beans. Mix well. Stir in beans. Pour into slow cooker.

3. Cover. Cook on Low 5-6 hours.

Hearty Slow-Cooker Beans

Kim McEuen
Lincoln University, PA

Makes 10 servings

1 lb. ground beef
1/2 lb. bacon, diced
1 onion, chopped
16-oz. can red kidney beans, drained
15-oz. can butter beans, drained
15-oz. can pork and beans
15-oz. can hot chili beans
1/2 cup brown sugar
1/2 cup sugar
1 Tbsp. prepared mustard
1 Tbsp. cider vinegar
1/2 cup ketchup

1. Brown beef, bacon, and onion in skillet. Drain.

2. Combine all ingredients in slow cooker. Mix well.

3. Cover. Cook on High 3 hours, or Low 5-6 hours.

Allen's Beans

John D. Allen
Rye, CO

Makes 10-12 servings

1 large onion, chopped
1 lb. ground beef, browned
15-oz. can pork and beans
15-oz. can ranch-style
  beans, drained
16-oz. can kidney beans,
  drained
1 cup ketchup
1 tsp. salt
1 Tbsp. prepared mustard
2 Tbsp. brown sugar
2 Tbsp. hickory-flavored
  barbecue sauce
1/2-1 lb. small smoky link
  sausages, optional

1. Brown ground beef and onion in skillet. Drain. Transfer to slow cooker set on High.
2. Add remaining ingredients. Mix well.
3. Reduce heat to Low and cook 4-6 hours. Use a paper towel to absorb oil that's risen to the top before stirring and serving.

Six-Bean Barbecued Beans

Gladys Longacre
Susquehanna, PA

Makes 15-18 servings

1-lb. can kidney beans,
  drained
1-lb. can pinto beans,
  drained
1-lb. can Great Northern
  beans, drained
1-lb. can butter beans,
  drained
1-lb. can navy beans,
  drained
1-lb. can pork and beans
1/4 cup barbecue sauce
1/4 cup prepared mustard
1/3 cup ketchup
1 small onion, chopped
1 small pepper, chopped
1/4 cup molasses, *or*
  sorghum molasses
1 cup brown sugar

1. Mix together all ingredients in slow cooker.
2. Cook on Low 4-6 hours.

Four-Bean Medley

Sharon Brubaker
Myerstown, PA

Makes 8 servings

8 bacon slices, diced and
  browned until crisp
2 medium onions, chopped
3/4 cup brown sugar
1/2 cup vinegar
1 tsp. salt
1 tsp. dry mustard
1/2 tsp. garlic powder
16-oz. can baked beans,
  undrained
16-oz. can kidney beans,
  drained
15 1/2-oz. can butter beans,
  drained
14 1/2-oz. can green beans,
  drained
2 Tbsp. ketchup

1. Mix together all ingredients. Pour into slow cooker.
2. Cover. Cook on Low 6-8 hours.

Variation:

Make this a main dish by adding 1 lb. hamburger to the bacon, browning it along with the bacon and chopped onions in skillet, then adding that mixture to the rest of the ingredients before pouring into slow cooker.

I generally spray the inside of my slow cooker with non-stick cooking spray prior to putting my ingredients in. It helps with cleanup.

Barb Yoder
Angola, IN

Lauren's Calico Beans

Lauren Eberhard
Seneca, IL

Makes 12-16 servings

8 slices bacon
1 cup chopped onions
1/2 cup brown sugar
1/2 cup ketchup
2 Tbsp. vinegar
1 tsp. dry mustard
14 1/2-oz. can green beans, drained
16-oz. can kidney beans, drained
15 1/2-oz. can butter beans, drained
15 1/2-oz. can pork and beans

1. Brown bacon in saucepan, reserving drippings. Crumble bacon. Cook onions in bacon drippings. Drain.
2. Combine all ingredients in slow cooker.
3. Cover. Cook on Low 6-8 hours.

Sweet and Sour Beans

Julette Leaman
Harrisonburg, VA

Makes 6-8 servings

10 slices bacon
4 medium onions, cut in rings
1/2-1 cup brown sugar, according to your preference
1 tsp. dry mustard
1 tsp. salt
1/4 cup cider vinegar
1-lb. can green beans, drained
2 1-lb. cans butter beans, drained
1-lb., 11-oz. can pork and beans

1. Brown bacon in skillet and crumble. Drain all but 2 Tbsp. bacon drippings. Stir in onions, brown sugar, mustard, salt, and vinegar. Simmer 20 minutes.
2. Combine all ingredients in slow cooker.
3. Cover. Cook on Low 3 hours.

Mixed Slow-Cooker Beans

Carol Peachey
Lancaster, PA

Makes 6 servings

16-oz. can kidney beans, drained
15 1/2-oz. can baked beans
1 pint home-frozen, *or* 1-lb. pkg. frozen, lima beans
1 pint home-frozen green beans, *or* 1-lb. pkg. frozen green beans
4 slices bacon, browned and crumbled
1/2 cup ketchup
1/2 cup sugar
1/2 cup brown sugar
2 Tbsp. vinegar
salt to taste

1. Combine beans and bacon in slow cooker.
2. Stir together remaining ingredients. Add to beans and mix well.
3. Cover. Cook on Low 8-10 hours.

Lizzie's California Beans

Lizzie Weaver
Ephrata, PA

Makes 12 servings

2 medium onions, cut in rings
1 cup brown sugar
1 tsp. dry mustard
1 tsp. salt
1/4 cup vinegar
1/3 cup ketchup
1 lb. bacon, browned and crumbled
16-oz. can green beans, drained
40-oz. can butter beans, drained
2 16-oz. cans baked beans

1. In saucepan, mix together onions, brown sugar, dry mustard, salt, vinegar, and ketchup. Simmer in covered pan for 20 minutes. Add bacon and beans.
2. Pour into slow cooker. Cover. Cook on High 2 hours.

Marcia's California Beans

Marcia S. Myer
Manheim, PA

Makes 10-12 servings

16-oz. can barbecue beans, *or* pork and beans
16-oz. can baked beans
16-oz. can kidney beans
14 1/2-oz. can green beans
15-oz. can lima beans
15 1/2-oz. can Great Northern beans
1 onion, chopped
1 tsp. prepared mustard
1 cup brown sugar
1 tsp. salt
1/4 cup vinegar
1/2 lb. bacon, browned until crisp and crumbled

1. Drain juice from beans. Combine beans in slow cooker.
2. In saucepan, combine onion, mustard, brown sugar, salt, vinegar, and bacon. Simmer for 10 minutes. Pour sauce over beans.
3. Cover. Cook on Low 3 hours.

LeAnne's Calico Beans

LeAnne Nolt
Leola, PA

Makes 10 servings

1/4-1/2 lb. bacon
1 lb. ground beef
1 medium onion, chopped
2-lb. can pork and beans
1-lb. can Great Northern beans, drained
14 1/2-oz. can French-style green beans, drained
1/2 cup brown sugar
1/2 cup ketchup
1/2 tsp. salt
2 Tbsp. cider vinegar
1 Tbsp. prepared mustard

1. Brown bacon, ground beef, and onion in skillet until soft. Drain.
2. Combine all ingredients in slow cooker.
3. Cover. Cook on Low 5-6 hours, or on High 2-3 hours.

Mixed Bean Casserole

Margaret Rich
North Newton, KS

Makes 8 servings

3 slices bacon, cut up
2 Tbsp. grated onion
31-oz. can pork and beans
  in tomato sauce
16-oz. can kidney beans,
  drained
15-oz. can lima beans, *or*
  butter beans, drained
3 Tbsp. brown sugar,
  packed
1/2 tsp. dry mustard
3 Tbsp. ketchup

1. Combine all ingredients in slow cooker.
2. Cover. Cook on Low 7-8 hours.

LaVerne's Baked Beans

LaVerne Olson
Willow Street, PA

Makes 16 servings

1/2 lb. bacon
1 medium onion, chopped
1/2 cup molasses
1/2 cup brown sugar
1/2 tsp. dry mustard
40-oz. can butter beans,
  drained

2 16-oz. cans kidney beans,
  drained
40-oz. can Great Northern
  beans, drained

1. Brown bacon and onion in skillet until bacon is crisp and crumbly. Drain.
2. Combine all ingredients in slow cooker.
3. Cover. Cook on Low 1-3 hours.

Joan's Calico Beans

Joan Becker
Dodge City, KS

Makes 10-12 servings

1/4-1/3 lb. bacon, diced
1/2 cup chopped onions
2 16-oz. cans pork and
  beans
15-oz. can butter beans,
  drained
16-oz. can kidney beans,
  drained
1/2 cup packed brown sugar
1/2 cup ketchup
1/2 tsp. salt
1 tsp. dry mustard

1. Brown bacon in skillet until crisp. Drain, reserving 2 Tbsp. drippings. Cook onion in drippings until tender. Add bacon and onion to slow cooker.
2. Stir in beans, brown sugar, ketchup, salt, and mustard. Mix well.
3. Cover. Cook on Low

4 1/2-5 1/2 hours, or on High 3-3 1/2 hours.

Pat's Calico Baked Beans

Pat Bishop
Bedminster, PA

Makes 10-12 servings

2 cups green lima beans
2 cups limas, cooked
2 cups kidney beans
2 cups baked beans
6 slices bacon
1 1/2 cups onion, diced
3/4 cup brown sugar
2 tsp. salt
1 tsp. dry mustard
1 clove garlic, minced
1/2 cup vinegar
1/2 cup ketchup

1. Combine beans in slow cooker.
2. Brown bacon in skillet and crumble. Add to beans. Stir in onion.
3. Mix together brown sugar, salt, mustard, garlic, vinegar, and ketchup. Pour over beans. Mix well.
4. Cover. Cook on High 4 hours, or Low 6 hours.

Variation:
Add a chopped green pepper to the mixture in Step 2.
Barbara Tenney
Delta, PA

Barbara's Calico Beans

Barbara Kuhns
Millersburg, OH

Makes 12 servings

1 lb. bacon, diced
1 onion, chopped
1/2 cup ketchup
1/3-1/2 cup brown sugar, according to taste
3 Tbsp. cider vinegar
28-oz. can pork and beans, drained
16-oz. can kidney beans, drained
16-oz. can butter beans, drained

1. Brown bacon in skillet. Drain, reserving 2 Tbsp. drippings. Saute onion in bacon drippings.
2. Mix together ketchup, sugar, and vinegar.
3. Combine all ingredients in slow cooker.
4. Cover Cook on Low 3-4 hours.

Doris' Sweet-Sour Bean Trio

Doris Bachman
Putnam, IL

Makes 6-8 large servings

4 slices bacon
1 onion, chopped
1/4 cup brown sugar
1 tsp. crushed garlic
1 tsp. salt
3 Tbsp. cider vinegar
1 tsp. dry mustard
1-lb. can lima beans, drained
1-lb. can baked beans, drained
1-lb. can kidney beans, drained

1. Cook bacon in skillet. Reserve 2 Tbsp. bacon drippings. Crumble bacon.
2. In slow cooker, combine bacon, bacon drippings, onion, brown sugar, garlic, salt, and vinegar. Add beans. Mix well.
3. Cover. Cook on Low 6-8 hours.

Carol's Calico Beans

Carol Sommers
Millersburg, OH

Makes 10-12 servings

1/2 lb. bacon, *or* ground beef
32-oz. can pork and beans
1-lb. can green limas, drained
16-oz. can kidney beans, drained
1-lb. can whole kernel corn, drained
1 tsp. prepared mustard
2 medium onions, chopped
3/4 cup brown sugar
1 cup ketchup

1. Brown bacon or ground beef in skillet. Drain and crumble.
2. Combine beans and meat in slow cooker.
3. Combine mustard, onions, brown sugar, and ketchup. Pour over beans. Mix well.
4. Cover. Cook on Low 4-6 hours.

Ethel's Calico Beans

Ethel Mumaw
Berlin, OH

Makes 6-8 servings

1/2 lb. ground beef
1 onion, chopped
1/2 lb. bacon, diced
1/2 cup ketchup
2 Tbsp. cider vinegar
1/2 cup brown sugar, packed
16-oz. can red kidney beans, drained
14 1/2-oz. can pork and beans, undrained
15-oz. can butter beans, drained

1. Brown ground beef, onion, and bacon in skillet. Drain.
2. Combine all ingredients in slow cooker.
3. Cover. Cook on Low 8 hours.

Mary Ellen's and Nancy's Calico Beans

Mary Ellen Wilcox
Scotia, NY
Nancy W. Huber
Green Park, PA

Makes 12-15 servings

1/2 lb. bacon
1 lb. ground beef
2 15 1/2-oz. cans pork and beans
2 15 1/2-oz. cans butter beans, drained
2 16-oz. cans kidney beans, drained
1/2 cup sugar
1/2 cup brown sugar
1/4 cup ketchup
1 tsp. prepared mustard
1 tsp. garlic, finely chopped

1. Brown bacon in skillet and then crumble. Drain drippings. Add ground beef and brown. Drain.
2. Combine all ingredients in slow cooker.
3. Cover. Cook on Low 4-6 hours.

Variation:
Add 1 Tbsp. liquid smoke in Step 2.
Jan Pembleton
Arlington, TX

Sara's Bean Casserole

Sara Harter Fredette
Williamsburg, MA

Makes 6 servings

16-oz. can kidney beans, drained
2 1-lb. cans pork and beans
1 cup ketchup
1 Tbsp. Worcestershire sauce
1 tsp. salt
2 cups chopped onions
1 Tbsp. prepared mustard
1 tsp. cider vinegar

1. Combine all ingredients in slow cooker.
2. Cover. Cook on High 2 hours, or Low 4 hours.

Main Dish Baked Beans

Sue Pennington
Bridgewater, VA

Makes 6-8 main-dish servings, or 12-16 side-dish servings

1 lb. ground beef
28-oz. can baked beans
8-oz. can pineapple tidbits, drained
4½-oz. can sliced mushrooms, drained
1 large onion, chopped
1 large green pepper, chopped
½ cup barbecue sauce
2 Tbsp. soy sauce
1 clove garlic, minced
½ tsp. salt
¼ tsp. pepper

1. Brown ground beef in skillet. Drain. Place in slow cooker.
2. Stir in remaining ingredients. Mix well.
3. Cover. Cook on Low 4-8 hours, or until bubbly. Serve in soup bowls.

Fruity Baked Bean Casserole

Elaine Unruh
Minneapolis, MN

Makes 6-8 servings

½ lb. bacon
3 medium onions, chopped
16-oz. can lima beans, drained
16-oz. can kidney beans, drained
2 16-oz. cans baked beans
15½-oz. can pineapple chunks
¼ cup brown sugar
¼ cup cider vinegar
¼ cup molasses
½ cup ketchup
2 Tbsp. prepared mustard
½ tsp. garlic salt
1 green pepper, chopped

1. Cook bacon in skillet. Crumble. Reserve 2 Tbsp. drippings in skillet. Place bacon in slow cooker.
2. Add onions to drippings and saute until soft. Drain. Add to bacon in slow cooker.
3. Add beans and pineapple to cooker. Mix well.
4. Combine brown sugar, vinegar, molasses, ketchup, mustard, garlic salt, and green pepper. Mix well. Stir into mixture in slow cooker.
5. Cover. Cook on High 2-3 hours.

Apple Bean Bake

Barbara A. Yoder
Goshen, IN

Makes 10-12 servings

4 Tbsp. butter
2 large Granny Smith apples, cubed
½ cup brown sugar
¼ cup sugar
½ cup ketchup
1 tsp. cinnamon
1 Tbsp. molasses
1 tsp. salt
24-oz. can Great Northern beans, undrained
24-oz. can pinto beans, undrained
ham chunks, optional

1. Melt butter in skillet. Add apples and cook until tender.
2. Stir in brown sugar and sugar. Cook until they melt. Stir in ketchup, cinnamon, molasses, and salt.
3. Add beans and ham chunks. Mix well. Pour into slow cooker.
4. Cover. Cook on High 2-4 hours.

Apple-Bean Pot

Charlotte Bull
Cassville, MO

Makes 12 servings

53-oz. can baked beans,
well drained
1 large onion, chopped
3 tart apples, peeled and
chopped
½ cup ketchup, *or*
barbecue sauce
½ cup firmly packed
brown sugar
1 pkg. smoky cocktail
sausages, *or* chopped
hot dogs, *or* chopped
ham chunks, optional

1. Place beans in slow
cooker.
2. Add onions and apples.
Mix well.
3. Stir in ketchup or barbecue sauce, brown sugar, and
meat. Mix.
4. Cover. Heat on Low 3-4
hours, and then on High 30
minutes.

Linda's Baked Beans

Linda Sluiter
Schererville, IN

Makes 12 servings

16-oz. can red kidney
beans, drained
15½-oz. can butter beans,
drained
18-oz. jar B&M beans
¼ lb. Velveeta cheese,
cubed
½ lb. bacon, diced
½ cup brown sugar
⅓ cup sugar
2 dashes Worcestershire
sauce

1. Combine all ingredients
in slow cooker.
2. Cover. Cook on Low 6
hours. Do not stir until nearly
finished cooking.

Ann's Boston Baked Beans

Ann Driscoll
Albuquerque, MN

Makes 20 servings

1 cup raisins
2 small onions, diced
2 tart apples, diced
1 cup chili sauce
1 cup chopped ham, *or*
crumbled bacon
2 1-lb., 15-oz. cans baked
beans
3 tsp. dry mustard
½ cup sweet pickle relish

1. Mix together all ingredients.
2. Cover. Cook on Low 6-8
hours.

Vegetables

Very Special Spinach

Jeanette Oberholtzer
Manheim, PA

Makes 8 servings

3 10-oz. boxes frozen
  spinach, thawed and
  drained
2 cups cottage cheese
1½ cups grated cheddar
  cheese
3 eggs
¼ cup flour
1 tsp. salt
½ cup butter, *or*
  margarine, melted

1. Mix together all ingredients.
2. Pour into slow cooker.
3. Cook on High 1 hour.
Reduce heat to Low and cook
4 more hours.

Spinach Casserole

Ann Bender
Ft. Defiance, VA

Makes 6 servings

2 10-oz. pkgs. frozen
  spinach, thawed and
  drained
2 cups white sauce, *or*
  cottage cheese
¼ cup butter, cubed
1¼ cups American cheese,
  cut into squares
2 eggs, beaten
¼ cup flour
1 tsp. salt
1 clove garlic, *or* ¼ tsp.
  garlic power

1. Combine all ingredients.
Mix well. Pour into greased
slow cooker.
2. Cover. Cook on High 1
hour. Reduce heat to Low
and cook 4-5 hours.

Caramelized Onions

Mrs. J.E. Barthold
Bethlehem, PA

Makes 6-8 servings

6-8 large Vidalia *or* other
  sweet onions
4 Tbsp. butter, *or*
  margarine
10-oz. can chicken, *or*
  vegetable, broth

1. Peel onions. Remove
stems and root ends. Place in
slow cooker.
2. Pour butter and broth
over.
3. Cook on Low 12 hours.

Note:
  Serve as a side dish, or use
onions and liquid to flavor
soups or stews, or as topping
for pizza.

Barbecued Green Beans

Arlene Wengerd
Millersburg, OH

Makes 4-6 servings

1 lb. bacon
1/4 cup chopped onions
3/4 cup ketchup
1/2 cup brown sugar
3 tsp. Worcestershire sauce
3/4 tsp. salt
4 cups green beans

1. Brown bacon in skillet until crisp and then break into pieces. Reserve 2 Tbsp. bacon drippings.
2. Saute onions in bacon drippings.
3. Combine ketchup, brown sugar, Worcestershire sauce, and salt. Stir into bacon and onions.
4. Pour mixture over green beans and mix lightly.
5. Pour into slow cooker and cook on High 3-4 hours, or on Low 6-8 hours.

Dutch Green Beans

Edwina Stoltzfus
Narvon, PA

Makes 4-6 servings

1/2 lb. bacon, *or* ham chunks
4 medium onions, sliced
2 qts. fresh, frozen, *or* canned, green beans
4 cups canned stewed tomatoes, *or* diced fresh tomatoes
1/2 -3/4 tsp. salt
1/4 tsp. pepper

1. Brown bacon until crisp in skillet. Drain, reserving 2 Tbsp. drippings. Crumble bacon into small pieces.
2. Saute onions in bacon drippings.
3. Combine all ingredients in slow cooker.
4. Cover. Cook on Low 4 1/2 hours.

Orange Glazed Carrots

Cyndie Marrara
Port Matilda, PA

Makes 6 servings

32-oz. (2 lbs.) pkg. baby carrots
1/2 cup packed brown sugar
1/2 cup orange juice
3 Tbsp. butter, *or* margarine
3/4 tsp. cinnamon
1/4 tsp. nutmeg
2 Tbsp. cornstarch
1/4 cup water

1. Combine all ingredients except cornstarch and water in slow cooker.
2. Cover. Cook on Low 3-4 hours until carrots are tender crisp.
3. Put carrots in serving dish and keep warm, reserving cooking juices. Put reserved juices in small saucepan. Bring to boil.
4. Mix cornstarch and water in small bowl until blended. Add to juices. Boil one minute or until thickened, stirring constantly.
5. Pour over carrots and serve.

Vegetables do not overcook as they do when boiled on your range. Therefore, everything can go into the cooker at one time, with the exception of milk, sour cream, and cream, which should be added during the last hour.
Darlene Raber
Wellman, IA

Glazed Root Vegetable Medley

Teena Wagner
Waterloo, ON

Makes 6 servings

2 medium parsnips
4 medium carrots
1 turnip, about 4½ inches around
½ cup water
1 tsp. salt
½ cup sugar
3 Tbsp. butter
½ tsp. salt

1. Clean and peel vegetables. Cut in 1-inch pieces.
2. Dissolve salt in water in saucepan. Add vegetables and boil for 10 minutes. Drain, reserving ½ cup liquid.
3. Place vegetables in slow cooker. Add liquid.
4. Stir in sugar, butter, and salt.
5. Cover. Cook on Low 3 hours.

Acorn Squash

Valerie Hertzler
Weyers Cave, VA

Makes 2 servings

1 acorn squash
salt
cinnamon
butter

1. Place whole, rinsed squash in slow cooker.
2. Cover. Cook on Low 8-10 hours.
3. Split and remove seeds. Sprinkle each half with salt and cinnamon, dot with butter, and serve.

Zucchini Special

Louise Stackhouse
Benten, PA

Makes 4 servings

1 medium to large zucchini, peeled and sliced
1 medium onion, sliced
1 qt. stewed tomatoes with juice, *or* 2 14½-oz. cans stewed tomatoes with juice
¼ tsp. salt
1 tsp. dried basil
8 oz. mozzarella cheese, shredded

1. Layer zucchini, onion, and tomatoes in slow cooker.
2. Sprinkle with salt, basil, and cheese.
3. Cover. Cook on Low 6-8 hours.

Squash Casserole

Sharon Anders
Alburtis, PA

Makes 4-6 servings

2 lbs. yellow summer squash, *or* zucchini, thinly sliced (about 6 cups)
half a medium onion, chopped
1 cup peeled, shredded carrot
10¾-oz. can condensed cream of chicken soup
1 cup sour cream
¼ cup flour
8-oz. pkg. seasoned stuffing crumbs
½ cup butter, *or* margarine, melted

1. Combine squash, onion, carrots, and soup.
2. Mix together sour cream and flour. Stir into vegetables.
3. Toss stuffing mix with butter. Spread half in bottom of slow cooker. Add vegetable mixture. Top with remaining crumbs.
4. Cover. Cook on Low 7-9 hours.

Doris' Broccoli and Cauliflower with Cheese

Doris G. Herr
Manheim, PA

Makes 8 servings

1 lb. frozen cauliflower
2 10-oz. pkgs. frozen broccoli
½ cup water
2 cups shredded cheddar cheese

1. Place cauliflower and broccoli in slow cooker.
2. Add water. Top with cheese.
3. Cook on Low 1½-3 hours, depending upon how crunchy or soft you want the vegetables.

Julia's Broccoli and Cauliflower with Cheese

Julia Lapp
New Holland, PA

Makes 6 servings

5 cups raw broccoli and cauliflower
¼ cup water
2 Tbsp. butter, *or* margarine
2 Tbsp. flour
½ tsp. salt
1 cup milk

1 cup shredded cheddar cheese

1. Cook broccoli and cauliflower in saucepan in water, until just crispy tender. Set aside.
2. Make white sauce by melting the butter in another pan over low heat. Blend in flour and salt. Add milk all at once. Cook quickly, stirring constantly until mixture thickens and bubbles. Add cheese. Stir until melted and smooth.
3. Combine vegetables and sauce in slow cooker. Mix well.
4. Cook on Low 1½ hours.

Variation:
Substitute green beans and carrots or other vegetables for broccoli and cauliflower.

Golden Cauliflower

Carol Peachey
Lancaster, PA

Makes 4-6 servings

2 10-oz. pkgs. frozen cauliflower, thawed
8-oz. jar cheese sauce
4 slices bacon, crisply browned and crumbled

1. Place cauliflower in slow cooker
2. Pour cheese over top. Top with bacon.
3. Cover. Cook on High 1½ hours and then reduce to Low for an additional 2 hours. Or cook only on Low 4-5 hours.

Broccoli Cheese Casserole

Janie Steele
Moore, OK

Makes 8-10 servings

10-oz. pkg. frozen chopped broccoli, thawed
1 cup cooked rice
¼ cup chopped celery
10¾-oz. can cream of chicken soup
4-oz. jar cheese sauce
4-oz. can mushrooms, optional
⅛ tsp. garlic powder
⅛ tsp. pepper
¼-½ tsp. salt

1. Mix together all ingredients in slow cooker.
2. Cook on Low 1½ hours, or until heated through.

Sweet-Sour Cabbage

Irma H. Schoen
Windsor, CT

Makes 6 servings

1 medium-sized head red, *or* green, cabbage, shredded
2 onions, chopped
4 tart apples, pared, quartered
½ cup raisins
¼ cup lemon juice

¼ cup cider, *or* apple juice
3 Tbsp. honey
1 Tbsp. caraway seeds
⅛ tsp. allspice
½ tsp. salt

1. Combine all ingredients in slow cooker.
2. Cook on High 3-5 hours, depending upon how crunchy or soft you want the cabbage and onions.

Bavarian Cabbage
Joyce Shackelford
Green Bay, WI

Makes 4-8 servings, depending upon the size of the cabbage head

1 small head red cabbage, sliced
1 medium onion, chopped
3 tart apples, cored and quartered
2 tsp. salt
1 cup hot water
2 Tbsp. sugar
⅓ cup vinegar
3 Tbsp. bacon drippings

1. Place all ingredients in slow cooker in order listed.
2. Cover. Cook on Low 8 hours, or High 3 hours. Stir well before serving.

Variation:
Add 6 slices bacon, browned until crisp and crumbled.
Jean M. Butzer
Batavia, NY

Cabbage Casserole
Edwina Stoltzfus
Narvon, PA

Makes 6 servings

1 large head cabbage, chopped
2 cups water
1 Tbsp. salt
⅓ cup butter
¼ cup flour
½-1 tsp. salt
¼ tsp. pepper
1⅓ cups milk
1⅓ cups shredded cheddar cheese

1. Cook cabbage in saucepan in boiling water and salt for 5 minutes. Drain. Place in slow cooker.
2. In saucepan, melt butter. Stir in flour, salt, and pepper. Add milk, stirring constantly on low heat for 5 minutes. Remove from heat. Stir in cheese. Pour over cabbage.
3. Cover. Cook on Low 4-5 hours.

Variation:
Replace cabbage with cauliflower.

Vegetable Curry
Sheryl Shenk
Harrisonburg, VA

Makes 8-10 servings

16-oz. pkg. baby carrots
3 medium potatoes, cubed
1 lb. fresh, *or* frozen, green beans, cut in 2-inch pieces
1 green pepper, chopped
1 onion, chopped
1-2 cloves garlic, minced
15-oz. can garbanzo beans, drained
28-oz. can crushed tomatoes
3 Tbsp. minute tapioca
3 tsp. curry powder
2 tsp. salt
1¾ cups boiling water
2 tsp. chicken bouillon granules, *or* 2 chicken bouillon cubes

1. Combine carrots, potatoes, green beans, pepper, onion, garlic, garbanzo beans, and crushed tomatoes in large bowl.
2. Stir in tapioca, curry powder, and salt.
3. Dissolve bouillon in boiling water. Pour over vegetables. Mix well. Spoon into large cooker, or two medium-sized ones.
4. Cover. Cook on Low 8-10 hours, or High 3-4 hours. Serve with cooked rice.

Variation:
Substitute canned green beans for fresh beans but add toward the end of the cooking time.

Wild Mushrooms Italian

Connie Johnson
Loudon, NH

Makes 4-5 servings

2 large onions, chopped
3 large red bell peppers, chopped
3 large green bell peppers, chopped
2-3 Tbsp. oil
12-oz. pkg. oyster mushrooms, cleaned and chopped
4 garlic cloves, minced
3 fresh bay leaves
10 fresh basil leaves, chopped
1 Tbsp. salt
1½ tsp. pepper
28-oz. can Italian plum tomatoes, crushed *or* chopped

1. Saute onions and peppers in oil in skillet until soft. Stir in mushrooms and garlic. Saute just until mushrooms begin to turn brown. Pour into slow cooker.
2. Add remaining ingredients. Stir well.
3. Cover. Cook on Low 6-8 hours.

Note:

Good as an appetizer or on pita bread, or serve over rice or pasta for main dish.

Corn Pudding

Barbara A. Yoder
Goshen, IN

Makes 10 plus servings

2 10-oz. cans whole kernel corn with juice
2 1-lb. cans creamed corn
2 boxes corn muffin mix
1 stick (¼ lb.) margarine
8-oz. box sour cream

1. Combine all ingredients in slow cooker.
2. Cover. Heat on Low 2-3 hours until thickened and set.

Corn on the Cob

Donna Conto
Saylorsburg, PA

Makes 3-4 servings

6-8 ears of corn (in husk)
½ cup water

1. Remove silk from corn, as much as possible, but leave husks on.
2. Cut off ends of corn so ears can stand in the cooker.

3. Add water.
4. Cover. Cook on Low 2-3 hours.

Cheesy Corn

Tina Snyder
Manheim, PA
Jeannine Janzen
Elbing, KS
Nadine Martinitz
Salina, KS

Makes 10 servings

3 16-oz. pkgs. frozen corn
8-oz. pkg. cream cheese, cubed
¼ cup butter, cubed
3 Tbsp. water
3 Tbsp. milk
2 Tbsp. sugar
6 slices American cheese, cut into squares

1. Combine all ingredients in slow cooker. Mix well.
2. Cover. Cook on Low 4 hours, or until heated through and the cheese is melted.

Be careful about adding liquids to food in a slow cooker. Foods have natural juices in them, and unlike oven cooking which is dry, food juices remain in the slow cooker as the food cooks.

Ann Sunday McDowell
Newtown, PA

Slow-Cooker Rice

Dorothy Horst
Tiskilwa, IL

Makes 10 servings

1 Tbsp. butter
4 cups converted long
   grain rice, uncooked
10 cups water
4 tsp. salt

1. Pour rice, water, and salt into greased slow cooker.
2. Cover. Cook on High 2-3 hours, or until rice is tender, but not overcooked. Stir occasionally.

Risi Bisi
(Peas and Rice)

Cyndie Marrara
Port Matilda, PA

Makes 6 servings

1 1/2 cups converted long
   grain white rice,
   uncooked
3/4 cup chopped onions
2 garlic cloves, minced
2 14 1/2-oz. cans reduced-
   sodium chicken broth
1/3 cup water
3/4 tsp. Italian seasoning
1/2 tsp. dried basil leaves
1/2 cup frozen baby peas,
   thawed
1/4 cup grated Parmesan
   cheese

1. Combine rice, onions, and garlic in slow cooker.
2. In saucepan, mix together chicken broth and water. Bring to boil. Add Italian seasoning and basil leaves. Stir into rice mixture.
3. Cover. Cook on Low 2-3 hours, or until liquid is absorbed.
4. Stir in peas. Cover. Cook 30 minutes. Stir in cheese.

Green Rice
Casserole

Ruth Hofstetter
Versailles, Missouri

Makes 6 servings

1 1/3 cups evaporated milk
2 Tbsp. vegetable oil
3 eggs
one-fourth of a small
   onion, minced
half a small carrot,
   minced, optional
2 cups minced fresh
   parsley, *or* 10-oz. pkg.
   frozen chopped spinach,
   thawed and drained
2 tsp. salt
1/4 tsp. pepper
1 cup shredded sharp
   cheese
3 cups cooked long grain
   rice

1. Beat together milk, oil, and eggs until well combined.
2. Stir in remaining ingredients. Mix well. Pour into greased slow cooker.

3. Cover. Cook on High 1 hour. Stir. Reduce heat to Low and cook 4-6 hours.

Wild Rice

Ruth S. Weaver
Reinholds, PA

Makes 4-5 servings

1 cup wild rice, *or* wild
   rice mixture, uncooked
1/2 cup sliced mushrooms
1/2 cup diced onions
1/2 cup diced green, *or* red,
   peppers
1 Tbsp. oil
1/2 tsp. salt
1/4 tsp. pepper
2 1/2 cups chicken broth

1. Layer rice and vegetables in slow cooker. Pour oil, salt, and pepper over vegetables. Stir.
2. Heat chicken broth. Pour over ingredients in slow cooker.
3. Cover. Cook on High 2 1/2-3 hours, or until rice is soft and liquid is absorbed.

Baked Potatoes

Lucille Metzler, Wellsboro, PA
Elizabeth Yutzy, Wauseon, OH
Glenda S. Weaver, Manheim, PA
Mary Jane Musser, Manheim, PA
Esther Becker, Gordonville, PA

Makes 6 servings

**6 medium baking potatoes
butter, *or* margarine**

1. Prick potatoes with fork. Rub each with either butter or margarine. Place in slow cooker.
2. Cover. Cook on High 3-5 hours, or Low 6-10 hours.

Baked Potatoes

Valerie Hertzler
Weyers Cave, VA
Carol Peachey, Lancaster, PA
Janet L. Roggie, Lowville, NY

Potatoes

1. Prick potatoes with fork and wrap in foil.
2. Cover. Do not add water. Cook on High 2½-4 hours, or Low 8-10 hours.

Pizza Potatoes

Margaret Wenger Johnson
Keezletown, VA

Makes 4-6 servings

**6 medium potatoes, sliced
1 large onion, thinly sliced
2 Tbsp. olive oil
2 cups grated mozzarella cheese
2 oz. sliced pepperoni
1 tsp. salt
8-oz. can pizza sauce**

1. Saute potato and onion slices in oil in skillet until onions appear transparent. Drain well.
2. In slow cooker, combine potatoes, onions, cheese, pepperoni, and salt.
3. Pour pizza sauce over top.
4. Cover. Cook on Low 6-10 hours, or until potatoes are soft.

Mustard Potatoes

Frances B. Musser
Newmanstown, PA
Nancy Zimmerman
Loysville, PA

Makes 6 servings

**6 medium potatoes, peeled, cooked, cooled, and grated
½ cup chopped onions
¼ cup butter
1½ tsp. prepared mustard
1 tsp. salt
¼ tsp. pepper
½ cup milk
¼ lb. American, *or* cheddar, cheese**

1. Put potatoes in greased slow cooker.
2. Saute onion in butter in skillet. Add mustard, salt, pepper, milk, and cheese. Pour over potatoes.
3. Cover. Cook on Low 3 hours. Stir or toss lightly when ready to serve.

Cut up vegetables for your slow-cooker dish the night before and place them in ziplock bags in the refrigerator. This cuts down on preparation time in the morning.
Tracy Supcoe
Barclay, MD

Potatoes O'Brien

Rebecca Meyerkorth
Wamego, KS

Makes 6 servings

32-oz. pkg. shredded
  potatoes
1/4 cup chopped onions
1/4 cup chopped green
  peppers
2 Tbsp. chopped pimento,
  optional
1 cup chopped ham,
  optional
3/4 tsp. salt
1/4 tsp. pepper
3 Tbsp. butter
3 Tbsp. flour
1/2 cup milk
10³/4-oz. can cream of
  mushroom soup
1 cup shredded cheddar
  cheese, divided

1. Place potatoes, onions,
green peppers, pimento, and
ham in slow cooker. Sprinkle
with salt and pepper.
2. Melt butter in sauce-
pan. Stir in flour; then add
half of milk. Stir rapidly to
remove all lumps. Stir in
remaining milk. Stir in mushroom soup and 1/2 cup cheese.
Pour over potatoes.
3. Cover. Cook on Low 4-5
hours. Sprinkle remaining
cheese on top about 1/2 hour
before serving.

Potluck Potatoes

Lovina Baer
Conrath, WI

Makes 6-8 servings

4 cups potatoes, cooked,
  peeled, diced
10³/4-oz. can cream of
  chicken soup
1 cup sour cream
1 cup shredded cheddar
  cheese
1/3 cup butter, *or*
  margarine, melted
1/4 cup chopped onions
1/2 tsp. garlic salt
1/2 tsp. salt
1/2 tsp. pepper

1. Combine all ingredients
in slow cooker. Mix well.
2. Cover. Cook on Low 3-4
hours.

Variations:
1. If you prefer soft
onions, saute in skillet in butter or margarine before combining with other ingredients.
  Tracey Yohn
  Harrisburg, PA

2. Add chopped ham or
dried beef.

German Potato Salad

Lauren Eberhard
Seneca, IL

Makes 8 servings

6 slices bacon
3/4 cup chopped onions
10³/4-oz. can cream of
  chicken soup
1/4 cup water
2 Tbsp. cider vinegar
1/2 tsp. sugar
pepper to taste
4 cups parboiled, cubed
  potatoes
parsley

1. Brown bacon in skillet
and then crumble. Reserve
2 Tbsp. bacon drippings.
Saute onions in drippings.
2. Blend together soup,
water, vinegar, sugar, and
pepper. Add bacon and
onions. Mix well.
3. Add potatoes and pars-
ley. Mix well. Pour into slow
cooker.
4. Cover. Cook on Low 4
hours.
5. Serve warm or at room
temperature.

Slow-Cooker Scalloped Potatoes

Ruth S. Weaver
Reinholds, PA

Makes 10 servings

1/2 tsp. cream of tartar
1 cup water
8-10 medium potatoes, thinly sliced
half an onion, chopped
salt to taste
pepper to taste
1 cup grated American, *or* cheddar, cheese
10 3/4-oz. can cream of celery, *or* mushroom, *or* chicken, soup
1 tsp. paprika

1. Dissolve cream of tartar in water. Add potatoes and toss together. Drain.
2. Place half of potatoes in slow cooker. Sprinkle with onions, salt, pepper, and half of cheese.
3. Repeat with remaining potatoes and cheese.
4. Spoon soup over the top. Sprinkle with paprika.
5. Cover. Cook on Low 8-10 hours, or High 4 hours.

Variations:
1. For thicker scalloped potatoes, sprinkle each layer of potatoes with 2 Tbsp. flour.
Ruth Hershey
Paradise, PA

2. Instead of sprinkling the layers of potatoes with grated cheese, place 1/4 lb. Velveeta,
or American cheese slices over top during last 30 minutes of cooking.
Pat Bishop
Bedminster, PA
Mary Ellen Musser
Reinholds, PA
Annabelle Unternahrer
Shipshewana, IN

Saucy Scalloped Potatoes

Sue Pennington
Bridgewater, VA

Makes 4-6 servings

4 cups peeled, thinly sliced potatoes
10 3/4-oz. can cream of celery, *or* mushroom, soup
12-oz. can evaporated milk
1 large onion, sliced
2 Tbsp. butter, *or* margarine
1/2 tsp. salt
1/4 tsp. pepper
1 1/2 cups chopped, fully cooked ham

1. Combine potatoes, soup, evaporated milk, onion, butter, salt, and pepper in slow cooker. Mix well.
2. Cover. Cook on High 1 hour. Stir in ham. Reduce to
Low. Cook 6-8 hours, or until potatoes are tender.

Creamy Red Potatoes

Mrs. J.E. Barthold
Bethlehem, PA

Makes 4-6 servings

2 lbs. small red potatoes, quartered
8-oz. pkg. cream cheese, softened
10 3/4-oz. can cream of potato soup
1 envelope dry Ranch salad dressing mix

1. Place potatoes in slow cooker.
2. Beat together cream cheese, soup, and salad dressing mix. Stir into potatoes.
3. Cover. Cook on Low 8 hours, or until potatoes are tender.

Be sure vegetables are thinly sliced or chopped because they cook slowly in a slow cooker.
Marilyn Yoder
Archbold, OH

Extra Good Mashed Potatoes

Zona Mae Bontrager
Kokomo, IN
Mary Jane Musser, Manheim, PA
Elsie Schlabach, Millersburg, OH
Carol Sommers, Millersburg, OH
Edwina Stoltzfus, Narvon, PA

Makes 12 servings

5 lbs. potatoes, peeled,
 cooked, and mashed
8-oz. pkg. cream cheese,
 softened
1½ cups sour cream
3 tsp. onion, *or garlic*, salt
1½ tsp. salt
¼-½ tsp. pepper
2 Tbsp. butter, melted

1. Combine all ingredients.
Pour into slow cooker.
2. Cover. Cook on Low 5-6
hours.

Note:
These potatoes may be
prepared 3-4 days in advance
of serving and kept in the
refrigerator until ready to
use.

Variations:
1. Add 1½ cups shredded
cheddar cheese to Step 1.
Maricarol Magill
Freehold, NJ

2. Sprinkle with paprika
before cooking.
Pat Unternahrer
Wayland, IA

Potato Cheese Puff

Mary Sommerfeld
Lancaster, PA

Makes 10 servings

12 medium potatoes,
 boiled and mashed
1 cup milk
6 Tbsp. butter
¾ tsp. salt
2¼ cups Velveeta cheese,
 cubed
2 eggs, beaten

1. Combine all ingredients.
Pour into slow cooker.
2. Cover. Cook on High
2½ hours, or Low 3-4 hours.

Creamy Hash Browns

Judy Buller, Bluffton, OH
Elaine Patton
West Middletown, PA
Melissa Raber, Millersburg, OH

Makes 14 servings

2-lb. pkg. frozen, cubed
 hash brown potatoes
2 cups cubed *or* shredded
 American cheese
1 pint (2 cups) sour cream
10¾-oz. can cream of
 celery soup
10¾-oz. can cream of
 chicken soup
½ lb. sliced bacon, cooked
 and crumbled

1 medium onion, chopped
¼ cup margarine, melted
¼ tsp. pepper

1. Place potatoes in slow
cooker. Combine remaining
ingredients and pour over
potatoes. Mix well.
2. Cover. Cook on Low 4-5
hours, or until potatoes are
tender.

Cheese and Potato Bake

Ann Gouinlock
Alexander, NY

Makes 8 servings

2-lb. bag frozen hash
 browns
10¾-oz. can cheddar
 cheese soup
10¾-oz. can cream of
 chicken soup
1 cup milk
2.8-oz. can French-fried
 onion rings
½ cup grated cheddar
 cheese

1. Combine hash browns,
soups, and milk in slow
cooker. Mix well.
2. Top with half can of
onion rings.
3. Cover. Cook on Low 6-8
hours. Sprinkle with cheddar
cheese and remaining onion
rings about 1 hour before
serving.

Cheesy Hash Brown Potatoes

Clarice Williams
Fairbank, IA

Makes 6-8 servings

2 10³/4-oz. cans cheddar
cheese soup
1¹/3 cups buttermilk
2 Tbsp. butter, *or*
margarine, melted
¹/2 tsp. seasoned salt
¹/4 tsp. garlic powder
¹/4 tsp. pepper
2-lb. pkg. frozen, cubed
hash brown potatoes
¹/4 cup grated Parmesan
cheese
1 tsp. paprika

1. Combine soup, butter-
milk, butter, seasoned salt,
garlic powder, and pepper in
slow cooker. Mix well.
2. Stir in hash browns.
Sprinkle with Parmesan
cheese and paprika.
3. Cover. Cook on Low 4-
4¹/2 hours, or until potatoes
are tender.

Slow-Cooker Cheese Potatoes

Bernice M. Wagner
Dodge City, KS
Marilyn Yoder
Archbold, OH

Makes 6 servings

2-lb. pkg. frozen hash
browns
10³/4-oz. can cream of
potato soup
10³/4-oz. can cream of
mushroom soup
8 oz. (2 cups) shredded
cheddar cheese
1 cup grated Parmesan
cheese
1 pint sour cream

1. Mix together all ingredients in slow cooker.
2. Cover. Cook on Low 7
hours.

Scalloped Taters

Sara Wilson
Blairstown, MD

Makes 6-8 servings

¹/2 cup melted margarine
¹/4 cup dried onions
16-oz. pkg. frozen hash
brown potatoes
10³/4-oz. can cream of
chicken soup
1¹/2 cups milk
1 cup shredded cheddar
cheese
¹/8 tsp. black pepper
1 cup crushed cornflakes,
divided

1. Stir together margarine,
onions, potatoes, soup, milk,
cheese, pepper, and ¹/2 cup
cornflakes. Pour into greased
slow cooker. Top with
remaining cornflakes.
2. Cover. Cook on High 3-4
hours.

To prevent potatoes from darkening, slice them, then stir
a mixture of 1 cup water and ¹/2 tsp. cream of tartar into
them. Drain, then place potatoes in cooker and proceed with
the recipe.

Dale Peterson
Rapid City, SD

Slow-Cooker Cottage Potatoes

Marjora Miller
Archbold, OH

Makes 10-12 servings

2 lbs. frozen hash brown
   potatoes
1 pint sour cream
10¾-oz. can cream of
   chicken soup
dash of pepper
2 cups Velveeta cheese,
   cubed
½ cup chopped onions
¾ tsp. salt
¼ tsp. pepper

1. Combine all ingredients
except potatoes in large bowl.
Then fold in potatoes. Spoon
into slow cooker.
2. Cover. Cook on High
1½ hours, and then on Low
2½ hours.

Cheesy Potatoes

Darla Sathre
Baxter, MN

Makes 6 servings

2-lb. pkg. frozen hash
   browns, partly thawed
2 10¾-oz.cans cheddar
   cheese soup
12-oz. can evaporated milk
2.8-oz. can French-fried
   onion rings
salt to taste
pepper to taste

1. Combine all ingredients.
Pour into greased slow
cooker.
2. Cover. Cook on Low 6-8
hours, or on High 3-4 hours.

Slow-Cooker Potatoes

Arlene Wiens
Newton, KS

Makes 8 servings

32-oz. pkg. frozen hash
   brown potatoes
2 10¾-oz. cans cheddar
   cheese soup
2.8-oz. can French-fried
   onion rings

1. Combine all ingredients
in greased slow cooker.
2. Cover. Cook on Low 7-8
hours.

Au Gratin Hash Brown Potatoes

Penny Blosser
Beavercreek, OH

Makes 12 servings

2 lb.-pkg. frozen hash
   brown potatoes, thawed
1 small onion, diced
1 stick butter, melted
16-oz. container French
   onion dip
16-oz. jar Cheez Whiz,
   heated

1. Place hash browns in
slow cooker.
2. Combine onion, butter,
dip, and Cheez Whiz. Pour
over hash browns. Mix well.
3. Cover. Cook on Low 4-6
hours, or High 2-3 hours.
(Use the greater number of
hours if potatoes are frozen.)

Candied Sweet Potatoes

Julie Weaver
Reinholds, PA

Makes 8 servings

6-8 medium sweet potatoes
1/2 tsp. salt
1/4 cup butter, *or*
  margarine, melted
20-oz. can crushed
  pineapples, undrained
1/4 cup brown sugar
1 tsp. nutmeg
1 tsp. cinnamon

1. Cook sweet potatoes until soft. Peel. Slice and place in slow cooker.
2. Combine remaining ingredients. Pour over sweet potatoes.
3. Cover. Cook on High 4 hours.

Potato Filling

Miriam Nolt
New Holland, PA

Makes 16-20 servings

1 cup celery, chopped fine
1 medium onion, minced
1 cup butter
2 15-oz. pkgs. bread cubes
6 eggs, beaten
1 qt. milk
1 qt. mashed potatoes
3 tsp. salt
2 pinches saffron
1 cup boiling water
1 tsp. pepper

1. Saute celery and onion in butter in skillet for about 15 minutes.
2. Combine sauted mixture with bread cubes. Stir in remaining ingredients. Add more milk if mixture isn't very moist.
3. Pour into large, or several medium-sized, slow cookers. Cook on High 3 hours, stirring up from bottom every hour or so to make sure the filling isn't sticking.

Mild Dressing

Jane Steiner
Orrville, OH

Makes 6 servings

16-oz. loaf homemade
  white bread
2 eggs, beaten
1/2 cup celery
1/4 cup diced onions
3/4 tsp. salt
1/2 tsp. pepper
giblets, cooked and cut up
  fine
milk

1. Set bread slices out to dry the day before using. Cut into small cubes.
2. Combine all ingredients except milk.
3. Moisten mixture with enough milk to make bread cubes soft but not soggy.
4. Pour into greased slow cooker. Cook on Low 3 1/2 hours, stirring every hour. When stirring, add a small amount of milk to sides of cooker—if needed—to keep dressing moist and to prevent sticking.

It's quite convenient to use a slow cooker to cook potatoes for salads or for fried potatoes or as baked potatoes. Just fill the slow cooker with cleaned potatoes and cook all day until done.

Darla Sathre
Baxter, MN

Slow Cooker Stuffing with Poultry

Pat Unternahrer
Wayland, IA

Makes 18 servings

1 large loaf dried bread, cubed
1 1/2-2 cups chopped cooked turkey, *or* chicken, meat & giblets
1 large onion, chopped
3 ribs celery with leaves, chopped
1/2 cup butter, melted
4 cups chicken broth
1 Tbsp. poultry seasoning
1 tsp. salt
4 eggs, beaten
1/2 tsp. pepper

1. Mix together all ingredients. Pour into slow cooker.
2. Cover and cook on High 1 hour, then reduce to Low 6-8 hours.

Moist Poultry Dressing

Virginia Bender, Dover, DE
Josie Bollman, Maumee, OH
Sharon Brubaker, Myerstown, PA
Joette Droz, Kalona, IA
Jacqueline Stefl, E. Bethany, NY

Makes 14 servings

2 4 1/2-oz. cans sliced mushrooms, drained
4 celery ribs, chopped (about 2 cups)
2 medium onions, chopped
1/4 cup minced fresh parsley
1/4-3/4 cup margarine (enough to flavor bread)
13 cups cubed day-old bread
1 1/2 tsp. salt
1 1/2 tsp. sage
1 tsp. poultry seasoning
1 tsp. dried thyme
1/2 tsp. pepper
2 eggs
1 *or* 2 14 1/2-oz. cans chicken broth (enough to moisten bread)

1. In large skillet, saute mushrooms, celery, onions, and parsley in margarine until vegetables are tender.
2. Toss together bread cubes, salt, sage, poultry seasoning, thyme, and pepper. Add mushroom mixture.
3. Combine eggs and broth and add to bread mixture. Mix well.

4. Pour into greased slow cooker. Cook on Low 5 hours, or until meat thermometer reaches 160°.

Note:
This is a good way to free up the oven when you're making a turkey.

Variations:
1. Use 2 bags bread cubes for stuffing. Make one mixed bread (white and wheat) and the other corn bread cubes.
2. Add 1/2 tsp. dried marjoram to Step 2.

Arlene Miller
Hutchinson, KS

235

Fresh Herb Stuffing

Barbara J. Fabel
Wausau, WI

Makes 6-8 servings

½ cup butter
2 onions, chopped
3 celery ribs, chopped
½ cup chopped fresh
 parsley
1 Tbsp. chopped fresh
 rosemary
1 Tbsp. chopped fresh
 thyme
1 Tbsp. chopped fresh
 marjoram
1 Tbsp. chopped fresh sage
1 tsp. salt
½ tsp. freshly ground
 pepper
1 loaf stale sourdough
 bread, cut in 1-inch
 cubes
1½-2 cups chicken broth

1. Saute onions and celery
in butter in skillet for 10 minutes. Remove from heat and
stir in fresh herbs and seasonings.
2. Place bread cubes in
large bowl. Add onion/herb
mixture. Add enough broth to
moisten. Mix well. Turn into
greased slow cooker.
3. Cover. Cook on High 1
hour. Reduce heat to Low
and continue cooking 3-4
hours.

Slow-Cooker Dressing

Helen King
Fairbank, IA

Makes 10-12 servings

14-15 cups bread cubes
3 cups chopped celery
1½ cups chopped onions
1½ tsp. sage
1 tsp. salt
½ tsp. pepper
1½ cups *or more* chicken
 broth (enough to
 moisten the bread)
¼-1 cup melted butter, *or*
 margarine (enough to
 flavor the bread)

1. Combine all ingredients
but butter. Mix well. Toss
with butter.
2. Spoon into slow cooker.
Cook on Low 4-5 hours.

Slow Cooker Stuffing

Dede Peterson
Rapid City, SD

Makes 10 servings

12 cups toasted bread
 crumbs, *or* dressing mix
1 lb. bulk sausage,
 browned and drained
¼-1 cup butter, *or*
 margarine (enough to
 flavor bread)

1 cup *or more* finely
 chopped onions
1 cup *or more* finely
 chopped celery
8-oz. can sliced
 mushrooms, with liquid
¼ cup chopped fresh
 parsley
2 tsp. poultry seasoning
 (omit if using dressing
 mix)
dash of pepper
½ tsp. salt
2 eggs, beaten
4 cups chicken stock

1. Combine bread crumbs
and sausage.
2. Melt butter in skillet.
Add onions and celery and
saute until tender. Stir in
mushrooms and parsley. Add
seasonings. Pour over bread
crumbs and mix well.
3. Stir in eggs and chicken
stock.
4. Pour into slow cooker
and bake on High 1 hour, and
on Low an additional 3 hours.

Variations:
1. For a drier stuffing,
reduce the chicken stock to
1½ cups (or 14½-oz. can
chicken broth) and eliminate
the sausage.
2. For a less spicy stuffing,
reduce the poultry seasoning
to ½ tsp.
Dolores Metzler
Mechanicsburg, PA

3. Substitute 3½-4½ cups
cooked and diced giblets in
place of sausage. Add another
can mushrooms and 2 tsp.
sage in Step 2.
Mrs. Don Martins
Fairbank, IA

Desserts

Bread Pudding

Winifred Ewy, Newton, KS
Helen King, Fairbank, IA
Elaine Patton
West Middletown, PA

Makes 6 servings

**8 slices bread (raisin bread
   is especially good),
   cubed
4 eggs
2 cups milk
1/4 cup sugar
1/4 cup melted butter,** *or*
**   margarine
1/2 cup raisins (use only
   1/4 cup if using raisin
   bread)
1/2 tsp. cinnamon**

**Sauce:
2 Tbsp. butter,** *or*
**   margarine
2 Tbsp. flour
1 cup water
3/4 cup sugar
1 tsp. vanilla**

1. Place bread cubes in greased slow cooker.
2. Beat together eggs and milk. Stir in sugar, butter, raisins, and cinnamon. Pour over bread and stir.
3. Cover and cook on High 1 hour. Reduce heat to Low and cook 3-4 hours, or until thermometer reaches 160°.
4. Make sauce just before pudding is done baking. Begin by melting butter in saucepan. Stir in flour until smooth. Gradually add water, sugar, and vanilla. Bring to boil. Cook, stirring constantly for 2 minutes, or until thickened.
5. Serve sauce over warm bread pudding.

Variations:

1. Use dried cherries instead of raisins. Use cherry flavoring in sauce instead of vanilla.

Char Hagnes
Montague, MI

2. Use 1/4 tsp. ground cinnamon and 1/4 tsp. ground nutmeg, instead of 1/2 tsp. ground cinnamon in pudding.
3. Use 8 cups day-old unfrosted cinnamon rolls instead of the bread.

Beatrice Orgist
Richardson, TX

4. Use 1/2 tsp. vanilla and 1/4 tsp. ground nutmeg instead of 1/2 tsp. cinnamon.

Nanci Keatley
Salem, OR

To achieve the best volume in baked goods, always use large fresh eggs.

Sara Wilson
Blairstown, MO

Old-Fashioned Rice Pudding

Ann Bender, Fort Defiance, VA
Gladys M. High, Ephrata, PA
Mrs. Don Martins, Fairbank, IA

Makes 6 servings

2½ cups cooked rice
1½ cups evaporated milk
   (or scalded milk)
⅔ cup brown, *or* white,
   sugar
3 Tbsp. soft butter
2 tsp. vanilla
½-1 tsp. nutmeg
3 eggs, beaten
½-1 cup raisins

1. Mix together all ingredients. Pour into lightly greased slow cooker.
2. Cover and cook on High 2 hours, or on Low 4-6 hours. Stir after first hour.
3. Serve warm or cold.

Mama's Rice Pudding

Donna Barnitz, Jenks, OK
Shari Jensen, Fountain, CO

Makes 4-6 servings

½ cup white rice,
   uncooked
½ cup sugar
1 tsp. vanilla
1 tsp. lemon extract
1 cup plus 2 Tbsp. milk
1 tsp. butter
2 eggs, beaten
1 tsp. cinnamon
½ cup raisins
1 cup whipping cream,
   whipped
nutmeg

1. Combine all ingredients except whipped cream and nutmeg in slow cooker. Stir well.
2. Cover pot. Cook on Low 6-7 hours, until rice is tender and milk absorbed. Be sure to stir once every 2 hours during cooking.
3. Pour into bowl. Cover with plastic wrap and chill.
4. Before serving, fold in whipped cream and sprinkle with nutmeg.

Ann's Rice Pudding

Ann Sunday McDowell
Newtown, PA

Makes 6-8 servings

1 cup uncooked, long grain
   white rice
3 cups milk
3 Tbsp. butter
½ tsp. salt
¾ cup sugar
3 eggs, beaten
½ tsp. freshly ground
   nutmeg
1 tsp. vanilla

1. Cook rice according to package directions.
2. Mix together all ingredients in greased 1½-qt. casserole dish. Cover with greased foil and set inside slow cooker. Add 1 cup water to slow cooker (around the outside of the casserole).
3. Cover and cook on High 2 hours.

Chopping dried fruit can be difficult. Make it easier by spraying your kitchen scissors with nonstick cooking spray before chopping. Fruits won't stick to the blade.
Cyndie Marrara
Port Matilda, PA

Dolores' Rice Pudding

Dolores Metzler
Mechanicsburg, PA

Makes 8-10 servings

1 cup white uncooked rice
1 cup sugar
8 cups milk
3 eggs
1½ cups milk
2 tsp. vanilla
¼ tsp. salt
nutmeg, *or* cinnamon

1. In slow cooker, mix together rice, sugar, and 8 cups milk.
2. Cook on High 3 hours.
3. Beat together, eggs, 1½ cups milk, vanilla, and salt. Add to slow cooker. Stir.
4. Cook on High 25-30 minutes.
5. Sprinkle with nutmeg *or* cinnamon. Serve warm.

Custard Rice Pudding

Iva Schmidt
Fergus Falls, MN

Makes 4-6 servings

¼ cup rice, uncooked
2 eggs
⅓ cup sugar
¼ tsp. salt

½ tsp. vanilla
1½ cups milk
⅓ cup raisins
nutmeg, *or* cinnamon
2 cups water

1. Cook rice according to package directions.
2. Beat together eggs, sugar, salt, vanilla, and milk. Stir in rice and raisins.
3. Put in 1-quart baking dish that will fit into your slow cooker. Sprinkle with nutmeg or cinnamon.
4. Cover with foil and set on metal trivet or a canning jar ring in bottom of slow cooker. Pour water around casserole.
5. Cover cooker. Cook on High 2-2½ hours, or until set.
6. Serve warm or cold.

Slow-Cooker Tapioca

Nancy W. Huber
Green Park, PA

Makes 10-12 servings

2 quarts milk
1 cup small pearl tapioca
1 to 1½ cups sugar
4 eggs, beaten
1 tsp. vanilla
whipped cream, *or* fruit of choice, optional

1. Combine milk, tapioca, and sugar in slow cooker. Cook on High 3 hours.
2. Mix together eggs, vanilla, and a little hot milk from slow cooker. Add to slow cooker. Cook on High 20 more minutes. Chill.
3. Serve with whipped cream or fruit.

Tapioca Salad

Karen Ashworth
Duenweg, MO

Makes 10-12 servings

10 Tbsp. large pearl tapioca
½ cup sugar to taste
dash salt
4 cups water
1 cup grapes, cut in half
1 cup crushed pineapple
1 cup whipped cream

1. Mix together tapioca, sugar, salt, and water in slow cooker.
2. Cook on High 3 hours, or until tapioca pearls are almost translucent.
3. Cool thoroughly in refrigerator.
4. Stir in remaining ingredients. Serve cold.

Variation:
Add 1 small can mandarin oranges, drained, when adding rest of fruit.

239

Blushing Apple Tapioca

Julie Weaver
Reinholds, PA

Makes 8-10 servings

8-10 tart apples
½ cup sugar
4 Tbsp. minute tapioca
4 Tbsp. red cinnamon
    candy
½ cup water
whipped topping, optional

1. Pare and core apples. Cut into eighths lengthwise and place in slow cooker.
2. Mix together sugar, tapioca, candy, and water. Pour over apples.
3. Cook on High 3- 4 hours.
4. Serve hot or cold. Top with whipped cream.

Baked Apples with Raisins

Vera Schmucker
Goshen, IN
Connie B. Weaver
Bethlehem, PA

Makes 6-8 servings

6-8 medium-sized baking
    apples, cored
2 Tbsp. raisins
¼ cup sugar
1 tsp. cinnamon
1 Tbsp. butter
½ cup water

1. Remove top inch of peel from each apple.
2. Mix together raisins and sugar. Spoon into center of apples.
3. Sprinkle with additional sugar and dot with butter.
4. Place apples in slow cooker. Add water. Cover and cook on Low 7-9 hours, or on High 2½-3½ hours.

Raisin Nut-Stuffed Apples

Margaret Rich
North Newton, KS

Makes 6 servings

6 baking apples, cored
2 Tbsp. butter, *or*
    margarine, melted
¼ cup packed brown sugar
¾ cup raisins
3 Tbsp. chopped walnuts
½ cup water

1. Peel a strip around apple about one-third of the way below the stem end to prevent splitting.
2. Mix together butter and brown sugar. Stir in raisins and walnuts. Stuff into apple cavities.
3. Place apples in slow cooker. Add water.
4. Cover and cook on Low 6-8 hours.

"Bake" cakes in a cake pan set directly on the bottom of your slow cooker. Cover the top with 4-5 layers of paper towels to help absorb the moisture from the top of the cake. Leave the cooker lid open slightly to let extra moisture escape.

Eleanor J. Ferreira
North Chelmsford, MA

Fruit/Nut Baked Apples

Cyndie Marrara
Port Matilda, PA

Makes 4 servings

4 large firm baking apples
1 Tbsp. lemon juice
1/3 cup chopped dried apricots
1/3 cup chopped walnuts, *or* pecans
3 Tbsp. packed brown sugar
1/2 tsp. cinnamon
2 Tbsp. melted butter
1/2 cup water, *or* apple juice
4 pecan halves, optional

1. Scoop out center of apples creating a cavity 1½ inches wide and stopping ½ inch from the bottom of each. Peel top of each apple down about 1 inch. Brush edges with lemon juice.

2. Mix together apricots, nuts, brown sugar, and cinnamon. Stir in butter. Spoon mixture evenly into apples.

3. Put ½ cup water or juice in bottom of slow cooker. Put 2 apples in bottom, and 2 apples above, but not squarely on top of other apples. Cover and cook on Low 1½-3 hours, or until tender.

4. Serve warm or at room temperature. Top each apple with a pecan half, if desired.

Nut-Filled Baked Apples

Joyce Cox
Port Angeles, WA

Makes 8 servings

1 cup nuts of your choice, ground
1/4 cup (packed) brown sugar
1/2 tsp. cinnamon
1 egg, beaten
8 medium baking apples, kept whole, but cored
1 cup sugar
1/3 cup water
2 Tbsp. butter
1/2 cup water

1. Mix together nuts, brown sugar, cinnamon, and egg. Place apples on rack in large, rectangular slow cooker. Spoon nut-sugar mixture into apples until they are two-thirds full.

2. In saucepan, combine sugar, 1/3 cup water, and butter. Stir over medium heat until sugar dissolves. Pour syrup over the filling in the apples until their cavities are filled.

3. Add ½ cup water to slow cooker around apples.

4. Cover and cook on Low 8-10 hours, or on High 3-4 hours. Serve warm. Top with whipped cream, whipped topping, ice cream, or frozen yogurt, if you wish.

Caramel Apples

Elaine Patton
West Middletown, PA
Rhonda Lee Schmidt
Scranton, PA
Renee Shirk
Mount Joy, PA

Makes 4 servings

4 very large tart apples, cored
1/2 cup apple juice
8 Tbsp. brown sugar
12 hot cinnamon candies
4 Tbsp. butter, *or* margarine
8 caramel candies
1/4 tsp. ground cinnamon
whipped cream

1. Remove ½-inch-wide strip of peel off the top of each apple and place apples in slow cooker.

2. Pour apple juice over apples.

3. Fill the center of each apple with 2 Tbsp. brown sugar, 3 hot cinnamon candies, 1 Tbsp. butter, or margarine, and 2 caramel candies. Sprinkle with cinnamon.

4. Cover and cook on Low 4-6 hours, or until tender.

5. Serve hot with whipped cream.

Golden Fruit Compote

Cindy Krestynick
Glen Lyon, PA
Judi Manos
West Islip, NY

Makes 6-8 servings

1-lb. 13-oz. can peach, *or* pear, slices, undrained
1/2 cup dried apricots
1/4 cup golden raisins
1/8 tsp. cinnamon
1/8 tsp. nutmeg
3/4 cup orange juice

1. Combine undrained peach or pear slices, apricots, raisins, cinnamon, and nutmeg in slow cooker. Stir in orange juice. Completely immerse fruit in liquid.
2. Cover and cook on Low 6-8 hours.
3. Serve cold with angel food or pound cake, or ice cream. Serve warm as a side dish in the main meal.

Variation:
If you prefer a thicker compote, mix together 2 Tbsp. cornstarch and 1/4 cup cold water until smooth. Stir into hot fruit 15 minutes before end of cooking time. Stir until absorbed in juice.

Fruit Compote Dessert

Beatrice Orgish
Richardson, TX

Makes 8 servings

2 medium tart apples, peeled
2 medium fresh peaches, peeled and cubed
2 cups unsweetened pineapple chunks
1 1/4 cups unsweetened pineapple juice
1/4 cup honey
2 1/4-inch thick lemon slices
3 1/2-inch cinnamon stick
1 medium firm banana, thinly sliced
whipped cream, optional
sliced almonds, optional
maraschino cherries, optional

1. Cut apples into 1/4-inch slices and then in half horizontally. Place in slow cooker.
2. Add peaches, pineapple, pineapple juice, honey, lemon, and cinnamon. Cover and cook on Low 3-4 hours.
3. Stir in banana slices just before serving. Garnish with whipped cream, sliced almonds, and cherries, if you wish.

Hot Curried Fruit Compote

Cathy Boshart
Lebanon, PA

Makes 12 servings

1-lb. can peach halves
1-lb. can pear halves
1-lb. can apricot halves
1-lb. can pineapple chunks
4 medium bananas, sliced
15 maraschino cherries
1/3 cup walnut halves
1/3 cup margarine
2/3 cup brown sugar
1/2 tsp. curry powder (or to taste)

1. Drain fruit. Pour canned fruit into slow cooker. Add bananas.
2. Scatter cherries and walnuts on top.
3. In skillet, melt margarine. Mix in sugar and curry powder. Pour over fruit.
4. Cook on Low 2 hours.
5. Serve hot as a side dish to beef, pork, or poultry; serve warm as a dessert; or serve cold as a topping for ice cream.

Scandinavian Fruit Soup

Willard E. Roth
Elkhart, IN

Makes 12 servings

1 cup dried apricots
1 cup dried sliced apples
1 cup dried pitted prunes
1 cup canned pitted red cherries
1/2 cup quick-cooking tapioca
1 cup grape juice, *or* red wine
3 cups water, *or* more
1/2 cup orange juice
1/4 cup lemon juice
1 Tbsp. grated orange peel
1/2 cup brown sugar

1. Combine apricots, apples, prunes, cherries, tapioca, and grape juice in slow cooker. Cover with water.
2. Cook on Low for at least 8 hours.
3. Before serving, stir in remaining ingredients.
4. Serve warm or cold, as a soup or dessert. Delicious served chilled over vanilla ice cream or frozen yogurt.

Hot Fruit Compote

Sue Williams
Gulfport, MS

Makes 4-6 servings

1 lb. dried prunes
1 1/3 cups dried apricots
13 1/2-oz. can pineapple chunks, undrained
1-lb. can pitted dark sweet cherries, undrained
1/4 cup dry white wine
2 cups water
1 cup sugar

1. Mix together all ingredients in slow cooker.
2. Cover and cook on Low 7-8 hours, or High 3-4 hours.
3. Serve warm.

Fruit Medley

Angeline Lang
Greeley, CO

Makes 6-8 servings

1 1/2 lbs. mixed dried fruit
2 1/2 cups water
1 cup sugar
1 Tbsp. honey
peel of half a lemon, cut into thin strips
1/8 tsp. nutmeg
1 cinnamon stick
3 Tbsp. cornstarch
1/4 cup cold water
1/4 cup Cointreau

1. Place dried fruit in slow cooker. Pour in water.
2. Stir in sugar, honey, lemon peel, nutmeg, and cinnamon.
3. Cover and cook on Low 2-3 hours. Turn cooker to High.
4. Mix cornstarch into water until smooth. Stir into fruit mixture. Cook on High 10 minutes, or until thickened.
5. Stir in Cointreau.
6. Serve warm or chilled. Serve as a side dish with the main course, as a dessert on its own, or as a topping for ice cream.

Rhubarb Sauce

Esther Porter
Minneapolis, MN

Makes 4-6 servings

1 1/2 lbs. rhubarb
1/8 tsp. salt
1/2 cup water
1/2-2/3 cup sugar

1. Cut rhubarb into 1/2-inch slices.
2. Combine all ingredients in slow cooker. Cook on Low 4-5 hours.
3. Serve chilled.

Variation:
Add 1 pint sliced strawberries about 30 minutes before removing from heat.

Strawberry Rhubarb Sauce

Tina Snyder
Manheim, PA

Makes 6-8 servings

6 cups chopped rhubarb
1 cup sugar
1 cinnamon stick
1/2 cup white grape juice
2 cups sliced strawberries

1. Place rhubarb in slow cooker. Pour sugar over rhubarb. Add cinnamon stick and grape juice. Stir well.
2. Cover and cook on Low 5-6 hours, or until rhubarb is tender.
3. Stir in strawberries. Cook 1 hour longer.
4. Remove cinnamon stick. Chill.
5. Serve over cake or ice cream.

Old-Fashioned Rice Pudding

Ann Bender
Fort Defiance, VA

Makes 6 servings

2 1/2 cups cooked rice
1 1/2 cups whole milk
2/3 cup brown sugar
3 eggs, beaten
3 Tbsp. butter, melted
2 tsp. vanilla
1/2 tsp. ground nutmeg
1/2 tsp. ground cinnamon
1/2 cup raisins

1. Mix together all ingredients. Pour into a lightly greased slow cooker.
2. Cover and cook on High 1-2 hours, or on Low 4-6 hours. Stir once during last 30 minutes.
3. Serve warm or cold.

Spiced Applesauce

Judi Manos
West Islip, NY

Makes 6 cups

12 cups pared, cored, thinly sliced, cooking apples
1/2 cup sugar
1/2 tsp. cinnamon
1 cup water
1 Tbsp. lemon juice
freshly grated nutmeg, optional

1. Place apples in slow cooker.
2. Combine sugar and cinnamon. Mix with apples. Stir in water and lemon juice, and nutmeg, if desired.
3. Cover. Cook on Low 5-7 hours, or High 2 1/2-3 1/2 hours.
4. Stir for a chunky sauce. Serve hot or cold.

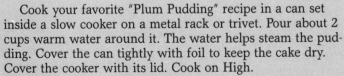

Cook your favorite "Plum Pudding" recipe in a can set inside a slow cooker on a metal rack or trivet. Pour about 2 cups warm water around it. The water helps steam the pudding. Cover the can tightly with foil to keep the cake dry. Cover the cooker with its lid. Cook on High.
Eleanor J. Ferreira
North Chelmsford, MA

Chunky Applesauce

Joan Becker
Dodge City, KS
Rosanne Hankins
Stevensville, MD

Makes 8-10 servings

8 apples, peeled, cored, and cut into chunks *or* slices (6 cups)
1 tsp. cinnamon
1/2 cup water
1/2-1 cup sugar, *or* cinnamon red hot candies

1. Combine all ingredients in slow cooker.
2. Cook on Low 8-10 hours, or High 3-4 hours.

Applesauce

Charmaine Caesar
Lancaster, PA

Makes 4 cups

10 medium Winesap, *or* Golden Delicious, cooking apples
1/2 cup water
3/4 cup sugar
cinnamon, optional

1. Core, peel, and thinly slice apples.
2. Combine all ingredients in slow cooker.

3. Cover. Cook on Low 5 hours.
4. Stir until well blended. If you want a smooth sauce, put through blender or mix with a hand mixer. Cool and serve.

Quick Yummy Peaches

Willard E. Roth
Elkhart, IN

Makes 6 servings

1/3 cup buttermilk baking mix
2/3 cup dry quick oats
1/2 cup brown sugar
1 tsp. cinnamon
4 cups sliced peaches (canned *or* fresh)
1/2 cup peach juice, *or* water

1. Mix together baking mix, oats, brown sugar, and cinnamon in greased slow cooker.
2. Stir in peaches and peach juice.
3. Cook on Low for at least 5 hours. (If you like a drier cobbler, remove lid for last 15-30 minutes of cooking.)
4. Serve with frozen yogurt or ice cream.

Scalloped Pineapples

Shirley Hinh
Wayland, IA

Makes 8 servings

2 cups sugar
3 eggs
3/4 cup butter, melted
3/4 cup milk
1 large can crushed pineapple, drained
8 slices bread (crusts removed), cubed

1. Mix together all ingredients in slow cooker.
2. Cook on High 2 hours. Reduce heat to Low and cook 1 more hour.
3. Delicious served as a side dish to ham or poultry, or as a dessert served warm or cold. Eat hot or chilled with vanilla ice cream or frozen yogurt.

Black and Blue Cobbler

Renee Shirk
Mount Joy, PA

Makes 6 servings

1 cup flour
3/4 cup sugar
1 tsp. baking powder
1/4 tsp. salt
1/4 tsp. ground cinnamon
1/4 tsp. ground nutmeg
2 eggs, beaten
2 Tbsp. milk
2 Tbsp. vegetable oil
2 cups fresh, *or* frozen, blueberries
2 cups fresh, *or* frozen, blackberries
3/4 cup water
1 tsp. grated orange peel
3/4 cup sugar
whipped topping, *or* ice cream, optional

1. Combine flour, 3/4 cup sugar, baking powder, salt, cinnamon, and nutmeg.
2. Combine eggs, milk, and oil. Stir into dry ingredients until moistened.
3. Spread the batter evenly over bottom of greased 5-quart slow cooker.
4. In saucepan, combine berries, water, orange peel, and 3/4 cup sugar. Bring to boil. Remove from heat and pour over batter. Cover.
5. Cook on High 2-2 1/2 hours, or until toothpick inserted into batter comes out clean. Turn off cooker.
6. Uncover and let stand 30 minutes before serving. Spoon from cooker and serve with whipped topping or ice cream, if desired.

Cranberry Pudding

Margaret Wheeler
North Bend, OR

Makes 8-10 servings

Pudding:
1 1/3 cups flour
1/2 tsp. salt
2 tsp. baking soda
1/3 cup boiling water
1/2 cup dark molasses
2 cups whole cranberries
1/2 cup chopped nuts

1/2 cup water

Butter Sauce:
1 cup confectioners sugar
1/2 cup heavy cream, *or* evaporated milk
1/2 cup butter
1 tsp. vanilla

1. Mix together flour and salt.
2. Dissolve soda in boiling water. Add to flour and salt.
3. Stir in molasses. Blend well.
4. Fold in cranberries and nuts.
5. Pour into well greased and floured bread or cake pan that will sit in your cooker. Cover with greased tin foil.
6. Pour 1/2 cup water into cooker. Place foil-covered pan in cooker. Cover with cooker lid and steam on High 3 to 4 hours, or until pudding tests done with a wooden pick.
7. Remove pan and uncover. Let stand 5 minutes, then unmold.
8. To make butter sauce, mix together all ingredients in saucepan. Cook, stirring over medium heat until sugar dissolves.
9. Serve warm butter sauce over warm cranberry pudding.

Slow Cooker Pumpkin Pie Pudding

Joette Droz
Kalona, IA

Makes 4-6 servings

15-oz. can solid pack pumpkin
12-oz. can evaporated milk
3/4 cup sugar
1/2 cup buttermilk baking mix
2 eggs, beaten
2 Tbsp. melted butter, *or* margarine
1 Tbsp. pumpkin pie spice
2 tsp. vanilla
whipped cream

1. Mix together all ingredients except whipped cream. Pour into greased slow cooker.
2. Cover and cook on Low 6-7 hours, or until thermometer reads 160°.
3. Serve in bowls topped with whipped cream.

Lemon Pudding Cake

Jean Butzer
Batavia, NY

Makes 5-6 servings

3 eggs, separated
1 tsp. grated lemon peel
1/4 cup lemon juice
3 Tbsp. melted butter
1 1/2 cups milk
3/4 cup sugar
1/4 cup flour
1/8 tsp. salt

1. Beat eggs whites until stiff peaks form. Set aside.
2. Beat eggs yolks. Blend in lemon peel, lemon juice, butter, and milk.
3. In separate bowl, combine sugar, flour, and salt. Add to egg-lemon mixture, beating until smooth.
4. Fold into beaten egg whites.
5. Spoon into slow cooker.
6. Cover and cook on High 2-3 hours.
7. Serve with spoon from cooker.

Apple Cake

Esther Becker
Gordonville, PA
Wanda S. Curtin
Bradenton, FL

Makes 8-10 servings

2 cups sugar
1 cup oil
2 eggs
1 tsp. vanilla
2 cups chopped apples
2 cups flour
1 tsp. salt
1 tsp. baking soda
1 tsp. nutmeg
1 cup chopped walnuts, *or* pecans

1. Beat together sugar, oil, and eggs. Add vanilla.
2. Add apples. Mix well.
3. Sift together flour, salt, baking soda, and nutmeg. Add dry ingredients and nuts to apple mixture. Stir well.
4. Pour batter into greased and floured bread or cake pan that fits into your slow cooker. Cover with pan's lid, or greased tin foil. Place pan in slow cooker. Cover cooker.
5. Bake on High 3 1/2-4 hours. Let cake stand in pan for 5 minutes after removing from slow cooker.
6. Remove cake from pan, slice, and serve.

Variation:

Instead of a bread or cake pan, pour batter into greased and floured 2-lb. coffee can. Cover top of can with 6 to 8 paper towels. Place can in slow cooker. Cover cooker, tilting lid slightly to allow release of extra moisture. Continue with Step 5 above.

Apple Peanut Crumble

Phyllis Attig, Reynolds, IL
Joan Becker, Dodge City, KS
Pam Hochstedler, Kalona, IA

Makes 4-5 servings

4-5 cooking apples, peeled and sliced
2/3 cup packed brown sugar
1/2 cup flour
1/2 cup quick-cooking dry oats
1/2 tsp. cinnamon
1/4-1/2 tsp. nutmeg
1/3 cup butter, softened
2 Tbsp. peanut butter
ice cream, *or* whipped cream

1. Place apple slices in slow cooker.
2. Combine brown sugar, flour, oats, cinnamon, and nutmeg.
3. Cut in butter and peanut butter. Sprinkle over apples.
4. Cover cooker and cook on Low 5-6 hours.
5. Serve warm or cold, plain or with ice cream or whipped cream.

Harvey Wallbanger Cake

Roseann Wilson
Albuquerque, NM

Makes 8 servings

Cake:
16-oz. pkg. pound cake mix
1/3 cup vanilla instant pudding (reserve rest of pudding from 3-oz. pkg. for glaze)
1/4 cup salad oil
3 eggs
2 Tbsp. Galliano liqueur
2/3 cup orange juice

Glaze:
remaining pudding mix
2/3 cup orange juice
1 Tbsp. Galliano liqueur

1. Mix together all ingredients for cake. Beat for 3 minutes. Pour batter into greased and floured bread or cake pan that will fit into your slow cooker. Cover pan.
2. Bake in covered slow cooker on High 2½-3½ hours.
3. Invert cake onto serving platter.
4. Mix together glaze ingredients. Spoon over cake.

Cherry Delight

Anna Musser
Manheim, PA
Marianne J. Troyer
Millersburg, OH

Makes 10-12 servings

21-oz. can cherry pie filling
1 pkg. yellow cake mix
1/2 cup butter, melted
1/3 cup walnuts, optional

1. Place pie filling in greased slow cooker.
2. Combine dry cake mix and butter (mixture will be crumbly). Sprinkle over filling. Sprinkle with walnuts.
3. Cover and cook on Low 4 hours, or on High 2 hours.
4. Allow to cool, then serve in bowls with dips of ice cream.

Note:
For a less rich, less sweet dessert, use only half the cake mix and only 1/4 cup butter, melted.

Chocolate Fondue

Eleanor J. Ferriera
North Chelmsford, MA

Makes 6 servings

1 pkg. (8 squares) semisweet chocolate
4-oz. pkg. sweet cooking chocolate
3/4 cup sweetened condensed milk
1/4 cup sugar
2 Tbsp. kirsch
fresh cherries with stems
squares of sponge cake

1. Break both chocolates into pieces and place in cooker. Set cooker to High and stir chocolate constantly until it melts.
2. Turn cooker to Low and stir in milk and sugar. Stir until thoroughly blended.
3. Stir in kirsch. Cover and cook on Low until fondue comes to a very gentle simmer.
4. Bring fondue to table, along with cherries and sponge cake squares to dip into it.

You can use a 2-lb. coffee can, 2 1-lb. coffee cans, 3 16-oz. vegetable cans, a 6-7 cup mold, or a 1½-2-quart baking dish for "baking" cakes in a slow cooker. Leave the cooker lid slightly open to let extra moisture escape.
Eleanor J. Ferreira
North Chelmsford, MA

Hot Fudge Cake

Maricarol Magill
Freehold, NJ

Makes 6-8 servings

1 cup packed brown sugar
1 cup flour
3 Tbsp. unsweetened cocoa
   powder
2 tsp. baking powder
1/2 tsp. salt
1/2 cup milk
2 Tbsp. melted butter
1/2 tsp. vanilla
3/4 cup packed brown sugar
1/4 cup unsweetened cocoa
   powder
1 3/4 cups boiling water
vanilla ice cream

1. Mix together 1 cup brown sugar, flour, 3 Tbsp. cocoa, baking powder, and salt.
2. Stir in milk, butter, and vanilla. Spread over the bottom of slow cooker.
3. Mix together 3/4 cup brown sugar and 1/4 cup cocoa. Sprinkle over mixture in slow cooker.
4. Pour in boiling water. Do not stir.
5. Cover and cook on High 2-3 hours, or until a toothpick inserted comes out clean.
6. Serve warm with vanilla ice cream.

Self-Frosting Fudge Cake

Mary Puterbaugh
Elwood, IN

Makes 8-10 servings

2 1/2 cups of 18 1/2-oz. pkg. chocolate fudge pudding cake mix
2 eggs
3/4 cup water
3 Tbsp. oil
1/3 cup pecan halves
1/4 cup chocolate syrup
1/4 cup warm water
3 Tbsp. sugar

1. Combine cake mix, eggs, 3/4 cup water, and oil in electric mixer bowl. Beat 2 minutes.
2. Pour into greased and floured bread or cake pan that will fit into your slow cooker.
3. Sprinkle nuts over mixture.
4. Blend together chocolate syrup, 1/4 cup water, and sugar. Spoon over batter.
5. Cover. Bake on High 2-3 hours.
6. Serve warm from slow cooker.

Chocolate Pudding Cake

Lee Ann Hazlett
Freeport, IL
Della Yoder
Kalona, IA

Makes 10-12 servings

18 1/2-oz. pkg. chocolate cake mix
3.9-oz. pkg. instant chocolate pudding mix
2 cups (16 oz.) sour cream
4 eggs
1 cup water
3/4 cup oil
1 cup (6 oz.) semisweet chocolate chips
whipped cream, *or* ice cream, optional

1. Combine cake mix, pudding mix, sour cream, eggs, water, and oil in electric mixer bowl. Beat on medium speed for 2 minutes. Stir in chocolate chips.
2. Pour into greased slow cooker. Cover and cook on Low 6-7 hours, or on High 3-4 hours, or until toothpick inserted near center comes out with moist crumbs.
3. Serve with whipped cream or ice cream.

249

Peanut Butter and Hot Fudge Pudding Cake

Sara Wilson
Blairstown, MO

Makes 6 servings

1/2 cup flour
1/4 cup sugar
3/4 tsp. baking powder
1/3 cup milk
1 Tbsp. oil
1/2 tsp. vanilla
1/4 cup peanut butter
1/2 cup sugar
3 Tbsp. unsweetened cocoa powder
1 cup boiling water
vanilla ice cream

1. Combine flour, 1/4 cup sugar, and baking powder. Add milk, oil, and vanilla. Mix until smooth. Stir in peanut butter. Pour into slow cooker.

2. Mix together 1/2 cup sugar and cocoa powder. Gradually stir in boiling water. Pour mixture over batter in slow cooker. Do not stir.

3. Cover and cook on High 2-3 hours, or until toothpick inserted comes out clean.

4. Serve warm with ice cream.

Seven Layer Bars

Mary W. Stauffer
Ephrata, PA

Makes 6-8 servings

1/4 cup melted butter
1/2 cup graham cracker crumbs
1/2 cup chocolate chips
1/2 cup butterscotch chips
1/2 cup flaked coconut
1/2 cup chopped nuts
1/2 cup sweetened condensed milk

1. Layer ingredients in a bread or cake pan that fits in your slow cooker, in the order listed. Do not stir.

2. Cover and bake on High 2-3 hours, or until firm. Remove pan and uncover. Let stand 5 minutes.

3. Unmold carefully on plate and cool.

Easy Chocolate Clusters

Marcella Stalter
Flanagan, IL

Makes 3 1/2 dozen clusters

2 lbs. white coating chocolate, broken into small pieces
2 cups (12 oz.) semisweet chocolate chips
4-oz. pkg. sweet German chocolate
24-oz. jar roasted peanuts

1. Combine coating chocolate, chocolate chips, and German chocolate. Cover and cook on High 1 hour. Reduce heat to Low and cook 1 hour longer, or until chocolate is melted, stirring every 15 minutes.

2. Stir in peanuts. Mix well.

3. Drop by teaspoonfuls onto waxed paper. Let stand until set. Store at room temperature.

Beverages

Apple-Honey Tea

Jeanne Allen
Rye, CO

Makes 6 1-cup servings

12-oz. can frozen apple
    juice/cider concentrate
2 Tbsp. instant tea powder
1 Tbsp. honey
½ tsp. ground cinnamon

1. Reconstitute the apple
juice/cider concentrate
according to package directions. Pour into slow cooker.
2. Add tea powder, honey,
and cinnamon. Stir to blend.
3. Heat on Low 1-2 hours.
Stir well before serving since
cinnamon tends to settle on
bottom.

Hot Mulled Cider

Phyllis Attig, Reynolds, IL
Jean Butzer, Batavia, NY
Doris G. Herr, Manheim, PA
Mary E. Martin, Goshen, IN
Leona Miller, Millersburg, OH
Marjora Miller, Archbold, OH
Janet L. Roggie, Lowville, NY
Shirley Sears, Tiskilwa, IL
Charlotte Shaffer, East Earl, PA
Berenice M. Wagner
Dodge City, KS
Connie B. Weaver
Bethlehem, PA
Maryann Westerberg
Rosamond, CA
Carole Whaling, New Tripoli, PA

Makes 8 1-cup servings

¼-½ cup brown sugar
2 quarts apple cider
1 tsp. whole allspice
1½ tsp. whole cloves
2 cinnamon sticks
2 oranges sliced, with peels
    on

1. Combine brown sugar
and cider in slow cooker.
2. Put spices in tea strainer
or tie in cheesecloth. Add to
slow cooker. Stir in orange
slices.
3. Cover and simmer on
Low 2-8 hours.

Variation:
Add a dash of ground nut-
meg and salt.
    Marsha Sabus
    Fallbrook, CA

Autumn Sipper

Shari Jensen
Fountain, CO

Makes 8 1-cup servings

1 Tbsp. whole allspice
3 3-inch cinnamon sticks
2 whole cloves
1 piece each lemon and
    orange peel, each about
    the size of a half dollar
1 piece crystallized ginger,
    about the size of a
    quarter
3 cups apricot nectar
5 cups apple juice
cinnamon sticks and
    orange slices, optional

1. Place spices, citrus peels, and ginger in a cheese-cloth or coffee filter. Tie securely. Place in bottom of slow cooker.
2. Pour in apple juice and nectar. Cover.
3. Cook on High 1 hour, then on Low 3 hours.
4. Garnish filled glasses with cinnamon sticks and orange slices.

Hot Mulled Apple Tea

Barbara Tenney
Delta, PA

Makes 16 1-cup servings

1/2 gallon apple cider
1/2 gallon strong tea
1 sliced lemon
1 sliced orange
3 3-inch cinnamon sticks
1 Tbsp. whole cloves
1 Tbsp. allspice
brown sugar to taste

1. Combine all in slow cooker.
2. Heat on Low 2 hours.

Spiced Apple Cider

Janice Muller
Derwood, MD

Makes 18-20 servings

2 sticks cinnamon
1 cup orange juice
1 tsp. cinnamon
1 tsp. ground cloves
1/4 cup lemon juice
2 tsp. whole cloves
1 gallon apple cider
2 tsp. ground nutmeg
1/2 cup pineapple juice
1 tsp. ginger
1 tsp. lemon peel
1 cup sugar

1. Mix all ingredients in 6-quart slow cooker.
2. Simmer on Low 4-6 hours.

Yummy Hot Cider

Char Hagner
Montague, MI

Makes 10-11 1-cup servings

3 3-inch sticks cinnamon
2 tsp. whole cloves
1 tsp. whole nutmeg, *or*
    1/2 tsp. ground nutmeg
1/2 gallon apple cider
1 cup sugar
2 cups orange juice
1/2 cup lemon juice

1. Tie spices in cheesecloth or tea strainer and place in slow cooker.
2. Add apple cider and sugar, stirring well.
3. Cover. Simmer on Low 1 hour. Remove spices and stir in orange juice and lemon juice. Continue heating 1 more hour. Serve cider from cooker, set on Low.

Great Mulled Cider

Charlotte Shaffer
East Earl, PA
Barbara Sparks
Glen Burnie, MD

Makes 8-10 1-cup servings

2 qts. apple cider
½ cup frozen orange juice concentrate
½ cup brown sugar
½ tsp. ground allspice, *or* 1 tsp. whole allspice
1½ tsp. whole cloves
2 cinnamon sticks
orange slices

1. Tie all whole spices in cheesecloth bag, then combine all ingredients in slow cooker.
2. Cover and simmer on Low 3 hours.

Hot Spiced Cider

Elva Evers
North English, IA

Makes 6 1-cup servings

12-oz. can frozen apple juice
3 3-inch cinnamon sticks
6 whole cloves

1. Combine all ingredients in slow cooker.
2. Cover and simmer on Low 4 hours.
3. Remove cinnamon and cloves before serving.

Variation:
Omit the cinnamon and cloves. Use ¼ cup fresh or dried mint tea leaves instead.

Spiced Cider

Mary Puterbaugh
Elwood, IN

Makes 12 1-cup servings

12 whole cloves
½ gallon apple cider
⅔ cup red hot candies
¼ cup dry orange drink mix
1 qt. water

1. Place cloves in cheesecloth bag or tea ball.
2. Combine all ingredients in slow cooker.

3. Cover. Cook on Low 3-4 hours.
4. Serve hot from cooker during fall, or on Halloween.

Hot Wassail Drink

Dale Peterson
Rapid City, SC

Makes 24-27 1-cup servings

12-oz. can frozen orange juice
12-oz. can frozen lemonade
2 qts. apple juice
2 cups sugar, *or* less
3 Tbsp. whole cloves
2 tbsp. ground ginger
4 tsp. ground cinnamon
10 cups hot water
6 cups strong tea

1. Mix juices, sugar, and spices in slow cooker.
2. Add hot water and tea.
3. Heat on High until Hot (1-2 hours), then on Low while serving.

Holiday Wassail

Dolores S. Kratz
Souderton, PA

Makes 8 1-cup servings

16-oz. can apricot halves, undrained
4 cups unsweetened pineapple juice
2 cups apple cider
1 cup orange juice
18 whole cloves
6 3½-inch cinnamon sticks, broken

1. In blender or food processor, blend apricots and liquid until smooth.
2. Place cloves and cinnamon sticks in cheesecloth bag.
3. Put all ingredients in slow cooker. Cook on Low 3-4 hours. Serve hot.

Hot Cider

Ilene Bontrager
Arlington, KS

Makes 18-20 1-cup servings

1 gallon cider
1 qt. cranberry juice
5-6 cinnamon sticks
2 tsp. whole cloves
½ tsp. ginger
1 whole orange, sliced

1. Combine cider and cranberry juice in slow cooker.
2. Place cinnamon sticks and cloves in cheesecloth bag and add to slow cooker. Stir in ginger.
3. Heat on High 5-6 hours.
4. Float orange slices on top before serving.

Wassail

John D. Allen, Rye, CO
Susan Yoder Graber
Eureka, IL
Jan Pembleton, Arlington, TX

Makes 12 1-cup servings

2 qts. cider
1 pint cranberry juice
⅓-⅔ cup sugar
1 tsp. aromatic bitters
2 sticks cinnamon
1 tsp. whole allspice
1 small orange, studded with whole coves
1 cup rum, optional

1. Put all ingredients into cooker. Cover and cook on High 1 hour, then on Low 4-8 hours.
2. Serve warm from cooker.

Note:
If the wassail turns out to be too sweet for you, add more cranberry juice until you find the flavor balance to be more pleasing.

Holiday Spice Punch

Maryland Massey
Millington, MD

Makes 10 1-cup servings

2 qts. apple cider
2 cups cranberry juice
2 Tbsp. mixed whole spices — allspice, cloves, coriander, and ginger
2 3-inch cinnamon sticks, broken
lemon, *or* orange, slices studded with whole cloves

1. Pour cider and juice into slow cooker. Place mixed spices in muslin bag or tea ball. Add to juice.
2. Cover and simmer on Low 2 hours.
3. Float cinnamon sticks and fruit slices in individual mugs as you serve.

Hot Cranberry-Apple Punch

Barbara Sparks
Glen Burnie, MD
Shirley Thieszen
Larkin, KS

Makes 10-11 1-cup servings

4½ cups cranberry juice
6 cups apple juice
¼ cup + 1 Tbsp. brown
  sugar
¼ tsp. salt
3 cinnamon sticks
1 tsp. whole cloves

1. Pour juices into slow cooker. Mix in brown sugar and salt. Stir until sugar is dissolved.
2. Tie cinnamon sticks and cloves in cheesecloth and drop into liquid.
3. Cover. Simmer on High 2 hours. Remove spice bag. Keep warm on Low.

Hot Cranberry Tea

Sherrill Bieberly
Salina, KS

Makes 14 1-cup servings

1 cup sugar
2 qts. water
3 cinnamon sticks
1 qt. cranberry juice
6-oz. can frozen orange
  juice

1¼ cups water
3 Tbsp. lemon juice
fresh lemon and/or orange
  slices

1. In saucepan, mix together sugar, 2 quarts water, and cinnamon sticks. Bring to boil.
2. Pour into slow cooker along with remaining ingredients. Cover and cook on High 1 hour. Turn to Low. Serve warm.

Josie's Hot Cranberry Punch

Josie Bollman
Maumee, OH

Makes 6 1-cup servings

32-oz. bottle cranberry
  juice
2 sticks cinnamon
6-oz. can frozen lemonade
12-oz. can frozen orange
  juice

1. Mix together all ingredients in slow cooker.
2. Cook on High 3-4 hours.

Spiced Wassail

Dorothy Horst
Tiskilwa, IL

Makes 10-11 1-cup servings

2 32-oz. jars cranberry
  juice
2 cups water
6-oz. can frozen orange
  juice concentrate
3 3-inch cinnamon sticks
3 whole cloves

1. Combine all ingredients in 5-quart slow cooker.
2. Cover and cook on Low 2-8 hours.

Variation:
Use small candy canes as stir sticks in individual cups during the holiday season.

Note:
This is a refreshing cold drink to serve over ice on a hot day.

Hot Cranberry Punch

Marianne Troyer
Millersburg, OH

Makes 13-14 1-cup servings

2 qts. hot water
1½ cups sugar
1 qt. cranberry juice
¾ cup orange juice
¼ cup lemon juice
12 whole cloves, optional
½ cup red hot candies

1. Combine water, sugar, and juices. Stir until sugar is dissolved.
2. Place cloves in double thickness of cheesecloth and tie with string. Add to slow cooker.
3. Add cinnamon candies.
4. Cover and Cook on Low 2-3 hours, or until heated thoroughly.
5. Remove spice bag before serving.

Hot Spicy Lemonade Punch

Mary E. Herr
The Hermitage
Three Rivers, MI

Makes 9-10 1-cup servings

4 cups cranberry juice
⅓-⅔ cup sugar
12-oz. can lemonade concentrate, thawed
4 cups water
1-2 Tbsp. honey
6 whole cloves
2 cinnamon sticks, broken
1 lemon, sliced

1. Combine juice, sugar, lemonade, water, and honey in slow cooker.
2. Tie cloves and cinnamon in small cheesecloth square. Add spice bag and lemon slices to slow cooker.
3. Cover and cook on Low 3-4 hours. Remove spice bag. Keep hot in slow cooker until ready to serve.

Hot Fruit Punch

Karen Stoltzfus
Alto, MI

Makes 10 1-cup servings

1 qt. cranberry juice
3 cups water
6-oz. can frozen orange juice concentrate, thawed
10-oz. pkg. frozen red raspberries, thawed
2 oranges, sliced
6 sticks cinnamon
12 whole allspice

1. Combine all ingredients in slow cooker.
2. Heat on High 1 hour, or until hot. Turn to Low while serving.

Punch

Kathy Hertzler
Lancaster, PA

Makes 12 1-cup servings

1 tsp. whole cloves
5 cups pineapple juice
5 cups cranberry juice
2 1/4 cups water
1/2 cup brown sugar
2 cinnamon sticks
1/4 tsp. salt

1. Place cloves in small cheesecloth bag or tea ball.
2. Mix together all ingredients in slow cooker.
3. Cook on Low 6 hours. Remove cloves. Serve hot.

Wine-Cranberry Punch

C. J. Slagle
Roann, IN

Makes 8 1-cup servings

1 pint cranberry juice cocktail
1 cup water
3/4 cup sugar
2 sticks cinnamon
6 whole cloves
4/5 qt. burgundy wine
1 lemon, sliced thin

1. Combine ingredients in slow cooker.

2. Heat on Low 1-2 hours. Strain and serve hot.
3. Keep hot and serve from slow cooker set on lowest setting.

Hot Cranberry Punch

Barbara Aston
Ashdown, AR

Makes 10 1-cup servings

2 16-oz. cans jellied cranberry sauce
2 qts. water
2 cups frozen orange juice concentrate
1 qt. pineapple juice, optional
half a stick of butter
3/4 cup firmly packed brown sugar
1/2 tsp. ground cinnamon
1/2 tsp. ground allspice
1/4 tsp. ground cloves
1/4 tsp. ground nutmeg
1/4 tsp. salt

1. Mix together all ingredients.
2. Heat on High until boiling, then reduce to Low for 4 hours. Serve hot.

Kate's Mulled Cider / Wine

Mitzi McGlynchey
Downingtown, PA

Makes 8-10 1-cup servings

1/2 tsp. whole cloves
1/2 tsp. whole allspice
1/2 gallon apple cider, *or* red burgundy wine
2 3-inch cinnamon sticks
1 tsp. ground nutmeg
orange slices, optional
cinnamon sticks, optional

1. Place cloves and allspice in cheesecloth bag or tea ball.
2. Combine spices, apple cider or wine, 2 cinnamon sticks, and nutmeg in slow cooker.
3. Cook on High 1 hour. Reduce heat, and simmer 2-3 hours.
4. Garnish individual servings with orange slices or cinnamon sticks.

Mulled Wine

Julie McKenzie
Punxsutawney, PA

Makes 8 1-cup servings

½ cup sugar
1½ cups boiling water
half a lemon, sliced thin
3 cinnamon sticks
3 whole cloves
1 bottle red dinner wine
(burgundy *or* claret)

1. Dissolve sugar in boiling water in saucepan.
2. Add remaining ingredients.
3. Pour into slow cooker. Heat on Low for at least 1 hour, until wine is hot. Do not boil.
4. Serve from cooker into mugs.

Almond Tea

Frances Schrag
Newton, KS

Makes 12 1-cup servings

10 cups boiling water
1 Tbsp. instant tea
⅔ cup lemon juice
1 cup sugar
1 tsp. vanilla
1 tsp. almond extract

1. Mix together all ingredients in slow cooker.

2. Turn to High and heat thoroughly (about 1 hour). Turn to Low while serving.

Carolers Hot Chocolate

Pat Unternahrer
Wayland, IA

Makes 12-14 1-cup servings

10 cups milk
¾ cup sugar
¾ cup cocoa, *or* hot chocolate mix
½ tsp. salt
2 cups hot water
marshmallows

1. Measure milk into slow cooker. Turn on High.
2. Mix together sugar, salt, and cocoa in heavy pan. Add hot water. Stir and boil 3 minutes, stirring often.
3. Pour into milk. Cook on High 2-2½ hours.

Home-Style Tomato Juice

Jean Butzer
Batavia, NY

Makes 4-5 1-cup servings

10-12 large tomatoes
1 tsp. salt
1 tsp. seasoned salt
¼ tsp. pepper
1 Tbsp. sugar

1. Wash and drain tomatoes. Remove cores and blossom ends. Place in slow cooker.
2. Cover and cook on Low 4-6 hours, or until tomatoes are soft.
3. Press through sieve or food mill.
4. Stir in seasonings. Chill.

Index

Index

About the Authors

Dawn J. Ranck has been a convinced slow-cooker user for years. She, along with her many friends, have been lining up their various-sized cookers on their kitchen counters before they set off each morning—and coming home to richly flavored full dinners.

Ranck , who lives in Harrisonburg, Virginia, is the co-author of *A Quilter's Christmas Cookbook* and *Favorite Recipes with Herbs*.

Phyllis Pellman Good has been part of many cookbook projects, authoring *The Best of Amish Cooking* and *The Festival Cookbook*, and co-authoring *Recipes from Central Market, Favorite Recipes with Herbs, The Best of Mennonite Fellowship Meals,* and *From Amish and Mennonite Kitchens.*

Good and her husband, Merle, live in Lancaster, Pennsylvania, and are co-directors of The People's Place, a heritage interpretation center in the Lancaster County village of Intercourse, Pennsylvania.

Fix-It and Forget-It™ Recipes for Entertaining

Fix-It and Forget-It™ Recipes for Entertaining

Slow Cooker Favorites for All the Year Round

Phyllis Pellman Good
& Dawn J. Ranck

Good Books

Intercourse, PA 17534
800/762-7171
www.goodbks.com

Cover design and illustrations by Cheryl Benner
Design by Dawn J. Ranck

FIX-IT AND FORGET-IT RECIPES FOR ENTERTAINING
Copyright © 2002 by Good Books, Intercourse, PA 17534
International Standard Book Number: 1-56148-491-1 (special edition)
International Standard Book Number: 1-56148-377-X (paperback edition)
International Standard Book Number: 1-56148-378-8 (comb-bound paperback edition)
International Standard Book Number: 1-56148-379-6 (hardcover gift edition)
Library of Congress Catalog Card Number: 2002073876

Library of Congress Cataloging-in-Publication Data
Good, Phyllis Pellman
   Fix-it and forget-it recipes for entertaining : slow cooker favorites for all the year round / Phyllis Pellman Good & Dawn J. Ranck.
      p. cm.
   Includes index.
   ISBN 1-56148-379-6 -- ISBN 1-56148-377-X (pbk.) -- ISBN 1-56148-378-8 (plastic comb.)
   1. Electric cookery, Slow. 2. Entertaining. I. Ranck, Dawn J. II. Title.
TX827.G66 2002
641.5′884-dc21   2002073876

Table of Contents

About
Fix-It and Forget-It
Recipes for Entertaining

Can you lead a busy life and still have guests for dinner?

Can you have people over without spending hours in the kitchen?

Would you love to try some new recipes in your slow cooker—maybe just for your own household?

Fix-It and Forget-It Recipes for Entertaining answers "yes" to all those questions.

This cookbook—in the ***Fix-It and Forget-It*** tradition—has more than 580 irresistible recipes (and no duplicates with the original *Fix-it and Forget-It Cookbook*).

Use these wonderful recipes to share dinner with your neighbors, with your summer weekend visitors, with friends after a chilly soccer game, with family for a birthday party.

All the dishes in this bountiful collection share two qualities—little fuss and lots of flavor.

Most of the recipes in this collection will fit in a 4-qt. or a 5-qt. slow cooker. We indicate those that require a larger cooker; with those we suggest that you use a 6-qt. cooker, or two smaller ones.

Many stove-top or oven recipes can be adapted for a slow cooker. If you want to experiment, use these conversion factors:

- Low (in a slow cooker) = 200°, approximately (in an oven)
- High (in a slow cooker) = 300°, approximately (in an oven)
- In a slow-cooker, 2 hours on Low = 1 hour, approximately, on High

And don't forget, every time you lift the lid and peek, you need to add 15 minutes to the cooking time.

So, relieve the pressures of hosting. Get rid of the last-minute stress of putting food on the table.

Visit with your guests until it's time to eat—then lift the lids of your steaming slow cookers—and offer them Fruited Pork Chops, Garlic Lime Chicken, Navy Bean Soup, Oriental Shrimp Dish, Hot Cranberry Punch—and more.

Fix-It and Forget-It Recipes for Entertaining is bursting with absolutely delicious recipes, as well as Tips for Hosting, Menus for Meals with Friends, and Ideas for Go-Alongs that complement slow cooker dishes.

You'll love cooking, hosting, and eating from this treasure of good food.

— Phyllis Pellman Good and Dawn J. Ranck

Beef Main Dishes

Beef and Gravy

Arlene Groff
Lewistown, PA

Makes 8 servings

1 onion, chopped
1 Tbsp. butter
3-4-lb. beef roast, cubed
1 tsp. salt
1/4 tsp. pepper
2 cups water
3 beef bouillon cubes
1/2 cup flour

1. Saute onion in skillet in butter until brown. Place onion in slow cooker, but reserve drippings.
2. Brown roast in skillet in drippings. Add meat to slow cooker, again reserving drippings.
3. Combine salt, pepper, water, bouillon, and flour. Add to meat drippings. Cook until thickened. Pour over meat.
4. Cover. Cook on low 6-8 hours.
5. Serve over noodles.

Hickory Smoked Brisket

Janet Roggie
Lowville, NY

Makes 12-14 servings

3-4-lb. beef brisket
1/4 cup liquid smoke
1/2 tsp. celery salt
1/2 tsp. garlic salt
1/2 tsp. onion powder

1. Place beef on piece of foil.
2. Sprinkle with remaining ingredients. Wrap foil securely around beef. Place in slow cooker.
3. Cover. Cook on low 8-12 hours.
4. Serve warm with juice ladled over each slice.

Can-It-Really-Be-So-Easy? Roast Beef

Laverne Stoner
Scottdale, PA

Makes 8 servings

4-lb. beef roast
10³/4-oz. can cream of mushroom soup
1 pkg. dry onion soup mix
1 cup water

1. Place beef roast on double layer of aluminum foil.
2. Combine soup and dry soup mix. Spread on all sides of roast. Wrap foil around roast. Place in slow cooker. Pour water around roast.
3. Cover. Cook on low 6-8 hours.

Rich and Tasty Beef Roast

Reita F. Yoder
Carlsbad, NM

Makes 6-8 servings

10³/4-oz. can cream of mushroom soup
3-5-lb. beef roast
oil
1 pkg. dry onion soup mix

1. Spread mushroom soup in bottom of slow cooker.
2. Sear roast on all sides in oil in hot skillet. Add to slow cooker.
3. Sprinkle meat with dry onion soup mix.
4. Cook on high 5-6 hours.

Easy Stroganoff

Vicki Dinkel
Sharon Springs, KS

Makes 6-8 servings

10³/4-oz. can cream of mushroom soup
14¹/2-oz. can beef broth
1 lb. beef stewing meat or round steak, cut in 1″ pieces
1 cup sour cream
2 cups cooked noodles

1. Combine soup and broth in slow cooker. Add meat.
2. Cover. Cook on high 3-4 hours. Reduce heat to low and cook 3-4 hours.
3. Stir in sour cream.
4. Stir in noodles.
5. Cook on high 20 minutes.

Since I'm in school part-time and work two part-time jobs, this nearly complete meal is great to come home to. It smells wonderful when you open the door. A vegetable or salad and some crispy French bread are good additions.

Garlic Beef Stroganoff

Sharon Miller
Holmesville, OH

Makes 6-8 servings

2 tsp. beef bouillon granules
2 4½-oz. jars sliced mushrooms, drained
   with juice reserved
1 cup mushroom juice, with boiling water
   added to make a full cup
10¾-oz. can cream of mushroom soup
1 large onion, chopped
3 garlic cloves, minced
1 Tbsp. Worcestershire sauce
1½-2-lb. boneless round steak, cut into
   thin strips
2 Tbsp. oil
8-oz. pkg. cream cheese, cubed and
   softened

1. Dissolve bouillon in mushroom juice and water in slow cooker.
2. Add soup, mushrooms, onion, garlic, and Worcestershire sauce.
3. Saute beef in oil in skillet. Transfer to slow cooker and stir into sauce.
4. Cover. Cook on low 7-8 hours. Turn off heat.
5. Stir in cream cheese until smooth.
6. Serve over noodles.

Home-Style Beef Cubes

Dorothy Horst
Tiskilwa, IL

Makes 8-10 servings

½ cup flour
1 tsp. salt
⅛ tsp. pepper
4 lbs. beef cubes
½ cup chopped shallots or green onions
2 4-oz. cans sliced mushrooms, drained,
   or ½ lb. fresh mushrooms, sliced
14½-oz. can beef both
1 tsp. Worcestershire sauce
2 tsp. ketchup
¼ cup water
3 Tbsp. flour

1. Combine ½ cup flour, salt, and pepper. Toss beef in flour mixture to coat. Place in slow cooker.
2. Cover with onions and mushrooms.
3. Combine broth and Worcestershire sauce. Pour into slow cooker. Mix well.
4. Cover. Cook on low 7-12 hours.
5. One hour before serving, make a smooth paste of water and 3 Tbsp. flour. Stir into slow cooker. Cover and cook until broth thickens.
6. Serve over hot buttered noodles.

Menu Idea

Home-Style Beef Cubes
Hot Buttered Noodles
Tossed Salad with Oil and Vinegar
   Dressing
   To make Dressing combine:
      ½ cup red wine vinegar
      ½ cup olive oil
      1 tsp. salt
      1 cup sugar

Machaca Beef

Jeanne Allen
Rye, CO

Makes 10-12 servings

1½-lb. beef roast
1 large onion, sliced
4-oz. can chopped green chilies
2 beef bouillon cubes
1½ tsp. dry mustard
½ tsp. garlic powder
1 tsp. seasoning salt
½ tsp. pepper
1 cup salsa

1. Combine all ingredients except salsa in slow cooker. Add just enough water to cover.
2. Cover cooker and cook on low 10-12 hours, or until beef is tender. Drain and reserve liquid.
3. Shred beef using two forks to pull it apart.
4. Combine beef, salsa, and enough of the reserved liquid to make of desired consistency.
5. Use this filling for burritos, chalupas, quesadillas, or tacos.

After living in New Mexico for the past 30 years, I get homesick for New Mexican cuisine now that I live in Colorado. I keep memories of New Mexico alive by cooking foods that remind me of home.

Menu Idea

Machaca Beef
Refried Beans or Mexican Rice
Guacamole with Greens or Chips

Salsa Chuck Roast

Hazel L. Propst
Oxford, PA

Makes 6 servings

3-4-lb. chuck or round roast
1 Tbsp. oil
1 pkg. dry onion soup mix
2 cups water
1 cup salsa

1. Brown meat in skillet in oil on both sides. Place in slow cooker.
2. Add remaining ingredients to drippings in pan. Simmer 2-3 minutes. Add to slow cooker.
3. Cover. Cook on low 7-8 hours.
4. Serve with broth over noodles or rice.

Salsa Beef

Sarah Niessen
Akron, PA

Makes 5-6 servings

2-2½ lbs. beef, cut up in bite-sized cubes
1 Tbsp. oil
16-oz. jar salsa
8-oz. can tomato sauce
2 garlic cloves, minced
2 Tbsp. brown sugar
1 Tbsp. soy sauce
1 cup canned tomatoes

1. Brown beef in skillet in oil. Place in slow cooker.
2. Add remaining ingredients.
3. Cover. Cook on low 6-8 hours.
4. Serve over rice.

Variation: For added flavor, use Italian tomato sauce.

DietWatch

Veggies, grains, beans help lower cholesterol

Not all low-fat diets are equal.

A study has found that low-fat diets drive down cholesterol more effectively if they include lots of plant foods.

One-hundred-and-twenty adults with moderately high cholesterol were assigned to either a typical low-fat diet or one heavy on whole grains, veggies and beans.

The diets contained identical amounts of fats, protein, carbohydrates and cholesterol. Meals, snacks and beverages were provided, and calories were adjusted so participants' weight would not change.

After four weeks, total cholesterol had dropped about 18 points for people who ate more foods from plants, compared with a nine-point drop for those on the conventional low-fat diet.

The message is that people with high cholesterol can help themselves by including more vegetables, whole grains and beans in their diet.

The study appeared in the May 3 issue of the Annals of Internal Medicine, abstract available online at www.annals.org.

IS BENNINGHOFF, (574) 235-6345, CBENNINGHOFF@

Melt-in-Your-Mouth Mexican Meat Dish

Marlene Bogard
Newton, KS

Makes 6 servings

4-lb. chuck roast
1 tsp. salt
1 tsp. pepper
2 Tbsp. oil
1 onion, chopped
1 tsp. chili powder
1 tsp. garlic powder
1¼ cups diced green chili peppers
¾ cup hot pepper sauce
water

1. Season roast with salt and pepper. Sear on all sides in oil in skillet. Place in slow cooker.
2. Mix together remaining ingredients, except water, and spoon over meat. Pour in water down along the side of the cooker (so as not to wash off the topping) until roast is one-third covered.
3. Cover. Cook on high 6 hours. Reduce to low 2-4 hours, until meat falls apart.
4. Thicken sauce with flour if you like.
5. This highly seasoned meat is perfect for shredded beef Mexican tacos, burritos, etc.

Hosting Idea

Get two slow cookers going—one with this beef dish and one with the same recipe, but using chicken as the meat. Host a Mexican fiesta and let guests build their own combinations. Prepare bowls of olives, cheese (either shredded or cubed), chopped tomatoes, shredded lettuce, a variety of beans, and guacamole as go-alongs.

Green Chili Roast

Anna Kenagy
Carlsbad, NM

Makes 8-10 servings

3-4-lb. beef roast
1 tsp. seasoned meat tenderizer
oil, optional
1 tsp. salt
3-4 green chili peppers, or 4-oz. can green chilies, undrained
1 Tbsp. Worchestershire sauce
½ tsp. black pepper

1. Sprinkle roast with meat tenderizer. Brown under broiler or in skillet in oil. Place in slow cooker.
2. Pour in water until roast is half covered.
3. Add remaining ingredients over top.
4. Cover. Cook on low 8 hours.
5. Serve with mashed potatoes and green beans.

Apple and Onion Beef Pot Roast

Betty K. Drescher
Quakertown, PA

Makes 8-10 servings

3-lb. boneless beef roast, cut in half
oil
1 cup water
1 tsp. seasoning salt
1/2 tsp. soy sauce
1/2 tsp. Worcestershire sauce
1/4 tsp. garlic powder
1 large tart apple, quartered
1 large onion, sliced
2 Tbsp. cornstarch
2 Tbsp. water

1. Brown roast on all sides in oil in skillet. Transfer to slow cooker.
2. Add water to skillet to loosen browned bits. Pour over roast.
3. Sprinkle with seasoning salt, soy sauce, Worcestershire sauce, and garlic powder.
4. Top with apple and onion.
5. Cover. Cook on low 5-6 hours.
6. Remove roast and onion. Discard apple. Let stand 15 minutes.
7. To make gravy, pour juices from roast into saucepan and simmer until reduced to 2 cups. Combine cornstarch and water until smooth in small bowl. Stir into beef broth. Bring to boil. Cook and stir for 2 minutes until thickened.
8. Slice pot roast and serve with gravy.

Menu Idea

Apple and Onion Beef Pot Roast with Gravy
Mashed Potato Filling (page 214)
Peas or Green Beans

Fruited Beef Tagine

Naomi E. Fast
Hesston, KS

Makes 6-8 servings

1 Tbsp. oil
2 lbs. beef, cut into 2" cubes
4 cups sliced onions
2 tsp. ground coriander
1 1/2 tsp. ground cinnamon
3/4 tsp. ground ginger
14 1/2-oz. can beef broth, plus enough
    water to equal 2 cups
16 ozs. pitted prunes
salt to taste
fresh ground pepper to taste
juice of one lemon

1. Brown beef cubes in oil in skillet. Place beef in slow cooker. Reserve drippings.
2. Saute onions in drippings until lightly browned, adding more oil if needed. Add to slow cooker.
3. Add remaining ingredients, except lemon juice.
4. Simmer on low 5-6 hours, adding lemon juice during the last 10 minutes.
5. This recipe, accompanied with a tossed green salad and rolls, makes a complete meal.

Variations:
1. Mix in a few very thin slices of lemon rind to add flavor and eye appeal.

2. You can substitute lamb cubes for the beef.

There's-No-Easier Roast Beef

Sue Pennington
Bridgewater, VA

Makes 6-8 servings

12-oz. bottle barbecue sauce
3-4-lb. beef roast

1. Pour half of barbecue sauce into bottom of slow cooker.
2. Add roast. Top with remaining barbecue sauce.
3. Cover. Cook on low 6-8 hours.
4. Slice roast and serve with sauce.

Variation: *Use an 18-oz. bottle of barbecue sauce if you prefer a juicier outcome.*

Barbecue Roast Beef

Vicki Dinkel
Sharon Springs, KS

Makes 6-8 servings

1½-2-lb. beef roast, cooked

Sauce:
1 cup ketchup
½ cup minced onions
2 tsp. Worcestershire sauce
1 cup water
1 Tbsp. brown sugar

1. Cut roast into cubes and place in slow cooker.
2. Combine sauce ingredients and pour over meat.

3. Cover. Cook on high 2 hours, then on low for 4. Return to high 30 minutes before serving.

8-Hour Tangy Beef

Mary Martins
Fairbank, IA

Makes 6-8 servings

3½-4-lb. beef roast
12-oz. can ginger ale
1½ cups ketchup

1. Put beef in slow cooker.
2. Pour ginger ale and ketchup over roast.
3. Cover. Cook on low 8-9 hours.
4. Shred with 2 forks and serve on buns. Or break up into chunks and serve over rice, potatoes, or pasta.

Variations:
1. This recipe produces a lot of juice. You can add chopped onions, potatoes, and green beans in Step 2, if you want. Or stir in sliced mushrooms and/or peas 30 minutes before the end of the cooking time.

2. For a tangier finished dish, add chili powder or cumin, along with black pepper, in Step 2.

Beef Roast in Beer

Evelyn Page
Riverton, WY

Makes 5-6 servings

2-3-lb. beef roast
1 can beer
1 onion, sliced

1. Place roast in slow cooker. Poke all over surface with fork.
2. Pour beer over roast. Cover. Refrigerate for 8 hours.
3. Add sliced onion to slow cooker.
4. Cover. Cook on low 6-8 hours.

Variations:

1. Brown roast in oil in skillet on top and bottom before placing in cooker.

2. Mix together 1 cup cider vinegar and 2 Tbsp. Worcestershire sauce. Marinate roast in mixture in refrigerator for 2-4 hours. Either discard marinade when placing roast in cooker, or add it to the cooker.

To thicken broth, mix together 1/4 cup flour and 1 cup water until smooth. Twenty minutes before end of cooking time, remove roast from cooker. Stir flour paste into beef broth until smooth. Return roast to cooker and continue cooking. When finished, cut roast into chunks and serve with gravy.

Italian Beef Au Jus

Carol Sherwood
Batavia, NY

Makes 8 servings

3-5-lb. boneless beef roast
10-oz. pkg. au jus mix
1 pkg. Italian salad dressing mix
14 1/2-oz. can beef both
half a soup can water

1. Place beef in slow cooker.
2. Combine remaining ingredients. Pour over roast.
3. Cover. Cook on low 8 hours.
4. Slice meat and spoon onto hard rolls with straining spoon to make sandwiches. Or shred with 2 forks and serve over noodles or rice in broth thickened with flour.

Note: To thicken broth, mix 3 Tbsp. cornstarch into 1/4 cup cold water. Stir until smooth. Remove 1/2 cup beef broth from cooker and blend into cornstarch-water. Stir back into broth in cooker, stirring until smooth. Cook 10-15 minutes on high until broth becomes of gravy consistency.

Saucy Italian Roast

Sharon Miller
Holmesville, OH

Makes 8-10 servings

3-3½-lb. boneless rump roast
½ tsp. salt
½ tsp. garlic powder
¼ tsp. pepper
4½-oz. jar mushroom pieces, drained
1 medium onion, diced
14-oz. jar spaghetti sauce
¼-½ cup beef broth
hot cooked pasta

1. Cut roast in half.
2. Combine salt, garlic powder, and pepper. Rub over both halves of the roast. Place in slow cooker.
3. Top with mushrooms and onions.
4. Combine spaghetti sauce and broth. Pour over roast.
5. Cover. Cook on low 8-9 hours.
6. Slice roast. Serve in sauce over pasta.

Simply Super Supper

Anne Townsend
Albuquerque, NM

Makes 4 servings

2 ribs celery, sliced
3 carrots, cut in strips
2 potatoes, cubed
2 onions, coarsely chopped
2-lb. beef roast
1 pkg. dry onion soup mix
1 Tbsp. liquid smoke
1½ cups water

1. Place vegetables in slow cooker.
2. Place roast on top of vegetables.
3. Sprinkle with dry soup mix.
4. Combine liquid smoke and water. Pour over roast.
5. Cover. Cook on low 7-8 hours, or until vegetables are tender.
6. Slice meat and serve with cole slaw and French bread. Lemon pie makes a nice finish.

This is a welcoming dinner to come home to because the house smells so yummy as you walk in. And the wonderful aroma lingers.

Tomato-y Beef Stew

Janie Steele
Moore, OK

Makes 6-8 servings

5 lbs. stewing meat, cubed
2 onions, chopped
14½-oz. can chopped tomatoes
10¾-oz. can tomato soup
5-6 carrots, sliced
5-6 potatoes, peeled and cubed
1 cup sliced celery
1 bell pepper, sliced
2 tsp. salt
½ tsp. pepper
2 cloves minced garlic

1. Combine all ingredients in slow cooker.
2. Cover. Cook on low 8 hours.
3. Serve with warm bread or cornbread.

Note: This recipe is very adaptable. You can reduce the amount of meat and increase the vegetables as you wish.

After-Work Stew

Vera M. Kuhns
Harrisonburg, VA

Makes 5 servings

3 medium-sized potatoes,
   pared and cubed
4 medium-sized carrots, quartered
2 celery ribs, sliced
2 medium-sized onions, sliced
1½ lbs. beef, cut into 1½" cubes, browned
2 tsp. salt
½ tsp. dried basil
½ tsp. pepper
10¾-oz. can tomato soup
half a soup can water

   1. Layer potatoes, carrots, celery, and onions in slow cooker.
   2. Mix beef with salt, basil, and pepper in bowl and place on top of vegetables.
   3. Combine soup and water. Pour into slow cooker.
   4. Cover. Bake on low 8-9 hours, or until vegetables and meat are tender.

Best Ever Beef Stew

Barbara Walker
Sturgis, SD

Makes 6 servings

2 cups water
1 pkg. beef stew mix
2 lbs. stewing meat, cubed
3 15-oz. cans whole new potatoes,
   or 3 lbs. fresh new potatoes
1 cup sliced celery
10-12 small white onions, peeled
1-1½ cups sliced carrots
8 ozs. fresh mushrooms

   1. Combine water and beef stew mix in slow cooker.
   2. Layer meat in slow cooker.
   3. Add remaining ingredients.
   4. Cover. Cook on high 6-7 hours.

Favorite Sunday Pot Roast

Amber Swarey
Donalds, SC

Makes 6 servings

4-lb. chuck roast
meat tenderizer
1 pkg. dry onion soup mix
fresh mushrooms, sliced
carrots, sliced
potatoes, chunked
1 cup boiling water

   1. Place roast in slow cooker. Sprinkle with meat tenderizer and onion soup mix.
   2. Layer mushrooms over roast.
   3. Add carrots and potatoes around roast.

4. Pour water over vegetables.

5. Cover. Cook on high 4-5 hours.

6. Add a fresh salad and your meal is ready.

This is a recipe I grew up with at home. When Sunday came around, we looked forward to roast, potatoes, and carrots.

New Mexico Stew

Helen Kenagy
Carlsbad, NM

Makes 8 servings

2 lbs. stewing meat or steak, cubed
salt to taste
pepper to taste
1 Tbsp. oil
5-6 potatoes, cubed
6-8 carrots, diced
other vegetables — diced
1-2 4.25-oz. cans chopped green chilies
1½ lbs. raw pork sausage, crumbled

1. Salt and pepper stewing meat. Brown in oil in skillet.

2. Place half the stewing meat in bottom of slow cooker.

3. Layer half the vegetables and chilies over the beef. Crumble half the sausage over top. Sprinkle each layer with salt and pepper.

4. Continue layering until all ingredients are used.

5. Cover. Cook on high until ingredients begin to boil. Then turn cooker to low for 8-10 hours. Do not lift lid and do not stir during cooking.

6. Serve with a green salad and fresh bread.

Beef Stew with Shiitake Mushrooms

Kathy Hertzler
Lancaster, PA

Makes 4-6 servings

12 new potatoes, cut into quarters
½ cup chopped onions
8-oz. pkg. baby carrots
3.4-oz. pkg. fresh shiitake mushrooms, sliced, or 2 cups regular white mushrooms, sliced
16-oz. can whole tomatoes
14½-oz. can beef broth
½ cup flour
1 Tbsp. Worcestershire sauce
1 tsp. salt.
1 tsp. sugar
1 tsp. dried marjoram leaves
¼ tsp. pepper
1 lb. beef stewing meat, cubed

1. Combine all ingredients except beef in slow cooker. Add beef.

2. Cover. Cook on low 8-9 hours. Stir well before serving.

Menu Idea

Beef Stew with Shiitake Mushrooms
Tossed Salad of Mesclun Greens,
    sauteed almonds, mandarin oranges
    and a Caesar dressing
Homemade Multigrain Bread
Fresh Fruit

Sunday Roast Beef

Beverly Flatt-Getz
Warriors Mark, PA

Makes 8 servings

4 potatoes, peeled and quartered
1/2 cup peeled small onions
1 cup carrot chunks
4-lb. beef chuck roast
1 Tbsp. olive oil
1 pkg. G. Washington Seasoning
1/2 tsp. onion salt
1/2 tsp. minced garlic
1/2 tsp. garlic salt
1 cup water
few drops Worcestershire sauce
1/2 cup cold water
1 Tbsp. cornstarch

1. Place potatoes, onions, and carrots in bottom of slow cooker.
2. Sear beef in olive oil in skillet. Add to vegetables in slow cooker.
3. Sprinkle with seasonings.
4. Pour water around roast.
5. Cover. Cook on low 8-10 hours.
6. Remove meat and vegetables from juice. Season juice with Worcestershire sauce.
7. Dissolve cornstarch in cold water. Add to slow cooker. Cook on high until thick and bubbly.

When I was growing up we often had this for Sunday lunch after church. Mom put it in the oven very early. I adapted the recipe for making it in a slow cooker.

Menu Idea

Sunday Roast Beef
Creamed Onions, or Creamed Peas and Onions
Dinner Rolls with Butter
Hot Apple Pie with Vanilla Ice Cream and Cinnamon Sauce

Slow Cooker Stew

Arlene Groff
Lewistown, PA

Makes 10 servings

1 qt. canned stewing beef, or 2 lbs. stewing beef, cut into 1" pieces
1 qt. tomato soup
1 cup diced carrots
1/2 cup diced celery
1/2 cup chopped onions
2-3 cups diced potatoes
1 cup diced cabbage
1 qt. canned green beans, or 2 1-lb. pkgs. frozen green beans
1 tsp. salt
1/2 tsp. pepper
1/2 tsp. Italian seasoning
2 cups water or tomato juice

1. Combine all ingredients in slow cooker.
2. Cover. Cook on low 7-8 hours.

Easy Beef Stew

Janie Steele
Moore, OK

Makes 14-18 servings

2-3 lbs. beef, cubed
16-oz. pkg. frozen green beans
   or mixed vegetables
16-oz. pkg. frozen corn
16-oz. pkg. frozen peas
2 lbs. carrots, chopped
1 large onion, chopped
4 medium potatoes, peeled and chopped
$10\frac{3}{4}$-oz. can tomato soup
$10\frac{3}{4}$-oz. can celery soup
$10\frac{3}{4}$-oz. can mushroom soup
bell pepper chopped, optional

  1. Combine all ingredients in 2 4-qt. slow cookers (this is a very large recipe).
  2. Cover. Cook on low 10-11 hours.

Bavarian Beef

Naomi E. Fast
Hesston, KS

Makes 6 servings

$3-3\frac{1}{2}$-lb. boneless beef chuck roast
oil
3 cups sliced carrots
3 cups sliced onions
2 large kosher dill pickles, chopped
1 cup sliced celery
$\frac{1}{2}$ cup dry red wine or beef broth
$\frac{1}{3}$ cup German-style mustard
2 tsp. coarsely ground black pepper
2 bay leaves
$\frac{1}{4}$ tsp. ground cloves
1 cup water
$\frac{1}{3}$ cup flour

  1. Brown roast on both sides in oil in skillet. Transfer to slow cooker.
  2. Add remaining ingredients.
  3. Cover. Cook on low 6-7 hours.
  4. Remove meat and vegetables to large platter. Cover to keep warm.
  5. Mix flour with 1 cup of broth until smooth. Return to cooker. Turn on high and stir, cooking until broth is smooth and thickened.
  6. Serve over noodles or spaetzle.

Menu Idea

Bavarian Beef
Buttered Noodles or Spaetzle
Gingerbread with Custard Sauce

Italian Beef Stew

Kathy Hertzler
Lancaster, PA

Makes 4-6 servings

2 Tbsp. flour
2 tsp. chopped fresh thyme
1 tsp. salt
1/4-1/2 tsp. freshly ground pepper
2 1/4 lbs. beef stewing meat, cubed
3 Tbsp. olive oil
1 onion, chopped
1 cup tomato sauce
1 cup beef stock
1 cup red wine
3 garlic cloves, minced
2 Tbsp. tomato paste
2 cups frozen peas, thawed but not cooked
1 tsp. sugar

1. Spoon flour into small dish. Season with thyme, salt, and pepper. Add beef cubes and coat evenly.
2. Heat oil in slow cooker on high. Add floured beef and brown on all sides.
3. Stir in remaining ingredients except peas and sugar.
4. Cover. Cook on low 6 hours.
5. Add peas and sugar. Cook an additional 30 minutes, or until beef is tender and peas are warm.

Dawn's Mushroom Beef Stew

Dawn Day
Westminster, CA

Makes 8-10 servings

1 lb. sirloin, cubed
2 Tbsp. flour
oil
1 large onion, chopped
2 garlic cloves, minced
1/2 lb. button mushrooms, sliced
2 ribs celery, sliced
2 carrots, sliced
3-4 large potatoes, cubed
2 tsp. seasoning salt
14 1/2-oz. can beef stock, or 2 bouillon cubes dissolved in 1 2/3 cups water
1/2-1 cup good red wine

1. Dredge sirloin in flour and brown in skillet. Reserve drippings. Place meat in slow cooker.
2. Saute onion, garlic, and mushrooms in drippings just until soft. Add to meat.
3. Add all remaining ingredients.
4. Cover. Cook on low 6 hours. Test to see if vegetables are tender. If not, continue cooking on low for another 1-1 1/2 hours.
5. Serve with crusty bread.

Beef Mushroom Casserole

Susan Stephani Smith
Monument, CO

Makes 12 servings

4 lbs. lean beef sirloin, cut into 1" cubes
2 10¾-oz. cans cream of mushroom soup
2 pkgs. dry onion soup mix
¼-1 tsp. pepper, according to your taste
    preference
½ tsp. salt
1-2 cups red Burgundy wine, optional
1½ lbs. fresh mushrooms, quartered
¼ cup sour cream, optional

1. Combine all ingredients except wine, mushrooms, and sour cream in slow cooker.
2. Cover. Cook on low 4-5 hours, stirring occasionally.
3. Add mushrooms and wine. Cook 30 minutes longer.
4. Ten minutes before end of cooking time, stir in sour cream, if you wish.
5. Serve over egg noodles.

Beef Burgundy

Joyce Kaut
Rochester, NY

Makes 6 servings

2 slices bacon, cut in squares
2 lbs. sirloin tip or round steak, cubed
¼ cup flour
1 tsp. salt
½ tsp. seasoning salt
¼ tsp. dried marjoram
¼ tsp. dried thyme
¼ tsp. pepper
1 garlic clove, minced
1 beef bouillon cube, crushed
1 cup burgundy wine
¼ lb. fresh mushrooms, sliccd
2 Tbsp. cornstarch
2 Tbsp. cold water

1. Cook bacon in skillet until browned. Remove bacon, reserving drippings.
2. Coat beef with flour and brown on all sides in bacon drippings.
3. Combine steak, bacon drippings, bacon, seasonings, garlic, bouillon, and wine in slow cooker.
4. Cover. Cook on low 6-8 hours.
5. Add mushrooms.
6. Dissolve cornstarch in water. Add to slow cooker.
7. Cover. Cook on high 15 minutes.
8. Serve over noodles.

Beef Stew with Wine

Andrea O'Neil
Fairfield, CT

Makes 8-10 servings

1 lb. stewing meat, cubed
oil
2 onions, quartered
4 carrots, sliced
4-5 potatoes, cubed
28-oz. can crushed tomatoes
½ cup wine
1 pkg. dry onion soup mix
1 cup water
2 tsp. salt
¾ tsp. pepper
3 Tbsp. cornstarch
¼ cup water

1. Brown beef cubes in skillet in oil.
2. Place in slow cooker. Add other ingredients and stir to combine.
3. Cover. Cook on low 9-10 hours.
4. Ten minutes before serving, stir cornstarch into water until smooth. Stir into hot stew.

Variation: For added zest, add ½ tsp. Old Bay Seasoning and 1 rib celery, diced, in Step 2.

Tempting Beef Stew

Patricia Howard
Albuquerque, NM

Makes 10-12 servings

2-3 lbs. beef stewing meat
3 carrots, sliced thin
1-lb. pkg. frozen green peas with onions
1-lb. pkg. frozen green beans
16-oz. can whole or stewed tomatoes
½ cup beef broth
½ cup white wine
½ cup brown sugar
4 Tbsp. tapioca
½ cup bread crumbs
2 tsp. salt
1 bay leaf
pepper to taste

1. Combine all ingredients in slow cooker.
2. Cover. Cook on low 10-12 hours.
3. Serve over noodles, rice, couscous, or biscuits.

Variation: In place of the tapioca, thicken stew with ¼ cup flour dissolved in ⅓-½ cup water. Mix in and turn cooker to high. Cover and cook for 15-20 minutes.

Prepare this Tempting Beef Stew before your guests arrive. Give yourself time to relax instead of panicking in a last-minute rush.

Beef Pot Roast

Nancy Wagner Graves
Manhattan, KS

Makes 6-8 servings

4-5-lb. beef chuck roast
1 garlic clove, cut in half
salt to taste
pepper to taste
1 carrot, chopped
1 rib celery, chopped
1 small onion, sliced
3/4 cup sour cream
3 Tbsp. flour
1/2 cup dry white wine

1. Rub roast with garlic. Season with salt and pepper. Place in slow cooker.
2. Add carrots, celery, and onion.
3. Combine sour cream, flour, and wine. Pour into slow cooker.
4. Cover. Cook on low 6-7 hours.

Pot-Roast Complete

Naomi E. Fast
Hesston, KS

Makes 6-8 servings

3-3 1/2-lb. arm roast, boneless
2 large onions, sliced
1/2 cup brown sugar
1/3 cup soy sauce
1/3 cup cider vinegar
2 bay leaves
2-3 garlic cloves, minced
1 tsp. grated fresh ginger
1 cup julienned carrots, matchstick size
2 cups sliced button mushrooms
2-3 cups fresh spinach leaves,
    or 2 10-oz. pkgs. frozen spinach, drained
2 Tbsp. cornstarch

1. Place meat, topped with onions, in slow cooker.
2. Combine brown sugar, soy sauce, and vinegar. Pour over beef.
3. Add bay leaves, garlic, and ginger.
4. Cover. Cook on high 6-7 hours.
5. Spread carrots, mushrooms, and spinach over beef.
6. Cover. Cook on high 20 minutes.
7. Mix cornstarch with 1/2 cup broth from slow cooker. Return to slow cooker.
8. Cover. Cook 10 minutes more.
9. Serve over rice.

I can't count how many times I have used this recipe over the last 15-20 years as a guest meal.

Hungarian Barley Stew

Naomi E. Fast
Hesston, KS

Makes 8 servings

2 Tbsp. oil
1½ lbs. beef cubes
2 large onions, diced
1 medium-sized green pepper, chopped
28-oz. can whole tomatoes
½ cup ketchup
⅔ cup dry small pearl barley
1 tsp. salt
½ tsp. pepper
1 Tbsp. paprika
10-oz. pkg. frozen baby lima beans
3 cups water
1 cup sour cream

1. Brown beef cubes in oil in skillet. Add onions and green peppers. Saute. Pour into slow cooker.
2. Add remaining ingredients except sour cream.
3. Cover. Cook on high 5 hours.
4. Stir in sour cream before serving.
5. Serve with your favorite cabbage slaw.

Hungarian Beef Stew

Esther Becker
Gordonville, PA

Makes 6 servings

2 lbs. beef cubes
1 onion, chopped
2 medium potatoes, peeled and cubed
2 carrots, sliced
10-oz. pkg. frozen lima beans
2 tsp. parsley
½ cup beef broth
2 tsp. paprika
1 tsp. salt
16-oz. can diced tomatoes

1. Combine beef, onion, potatoes, carrots, lima beans, and parsley in slow cooker.
2. Combine remaining ingredients and pour into slow cooker.
3. Cover. Cook on low 10-12 hours.
4. Serve with Seven Layer Salad and Homemade Rolls.

Crockery Cooking

Betty Sue Good
Broadway, VA

Makes 8 servings

2 lbs. beef cubes
oil
1 large onion, chopped
2 potatoes, cubed
2 carrots, sliced
1 pt. frozen lima beans, thawed
1 qt. stewed tomatoes
1-1½ tsp. salt, according to your taste
 preference
¼-½ tsp. pepper, according to your taste
 preference

1. Brown beef on all sides in oil in skillet. Place in slow cooker.
2. Layer onions, potatoes, carrots, and lima beans over beef.
3. Mix tomatoes and seasonings together in bowl. Pour over meat and vegetables.
4. Cover. Cook on low 8-10 hours.
5. Serve over rice with warm rolls, pickles, pecan pie, and vanilla ice cream.

Wash-Day Stew

Naomi E. Fast
Hesston, KS

Makes 8-10 servings

1½-2 lbs. lean lamb or beef, cubed
2 15-oz. cans garbanzo beans, drained
2 15-oz. cans white beans, drained
2 medium onions, peeled and quartered
1 qt. water
1 tsp. salt
1 tomato, peeled and quartered
1 tsp. turmeric
3 Tbsp. fresh lemon juice
8-10 pita bread pockets

1. Combine ingredients in slow cooker.
2. Cover. Cook on high 6-7 hours.
3. Lift stew from cooker with a strainer spoon and stuff in pita bread pockets.

I learned to prepare this nutritious meal from a student from Iran, who was attending graduate school at the University of Nebraska. Fatimeh explained to me that her family prepared this dish every wash day. Very early in the morning, they made a fire in a large rock-lined pit outside. Then they placed a large covered kettle, filled with the above ingredients, over the coals to cook slowly all day. At the end of a day of doing laundry, the food was ready with a minimum of preparation. Of course, they started with dry beans and dry garbanzos, presoaked the night before. They served this Wash-Day Stew spooned into pita bread and ate it with their hands.

Menu Idea

Wash-Day Stew
Cucumber/Onion Salad with sour
 cream, salt, and mint

Pepper Beef Goulash

Anna Stoltzfus
Honey Brook, PA

Makes 4-6 servings

1/2 cup water
6-oz. can tomato paste
2 Tbsp. vinegar
1 pkg. dry sloppy Joe seasoning
2-2 1/4 lbs. beef stewing meat, cubed
1 rib celery, sliced
1 medium green pepper,
  cut into 1/2" pieces

1. Combine water, tomato paste, vinegar, and seasoning mix in slow cooker.
2. Stir in beef, celery, and green peppers.
3. Cover. Cook on high 4-5 hours.
4. Serve over noodles.

Tender Texas-Style Steaks

Janice Muller
Derwood, MD

Makes 4-6 servings

steaks or chops
1 cup brown sugar
1 cup ketchup
salt to taste
pepper to taste
few dashes of Worcestershire sauce

1. Lay steaks in bottom of slow cooker.
2. Combine sugar and ketchup. Pour over steaks
3. Sprinkle with salt and pepper and a few dashes of Worcestershire sauce.

4. Cover. Cook on high 3 hours and low 3 hours.
5. Serve with wide egg noodles, green beans, and applesauce. Use some of the juice from the cooker over the noodles. Thicken the juice if you like with a little flour.

Swiss Steak

Judi Manos
West Islip, NY

Makes 6 servings

1 1/2 lbs. boneless beef round steak
1 tsp. peppered seasoning salt
6-8 potatoes, cubed
1 1/2 cups baby carrots
1 medium onion, sliced
14 1/2-oz. can diced tomatoes with basil,
  garlic, oregano
12-oz. jar home-style beef gravy
chopped fresh parsley

1. Cut beef into 6 pieces. Sprinkle with seasoning salt. Brown in skillet for about 8 minutes.
2. Layer potatoes, carrots, onions, and beef in slow cooker.
3. Combine tomatoes and gravy. Pour over beef and vegetables.
4. Cover. Cook on low 7-9 hours.
5. Sprinkle with parsley.

Variation: For more flavor add 1/2 tsp. dried basil, 1/2 tsp. dried oregano, and 2 minced garlic cloves to the tomatoes and gravy in Step 3.

Swiss Steak

Marie Shank
Harrisonburg, VA

Makes 6-8 servings

2-lb. round steak, cut into serving pieces
1 tsp. salt
½ tsp. pepper
1 large onion, sliced, or 1 pkg. dry onion
    soup mix
16-oz. can tomatoes

1. Combine ingredients in slow cooker.
2. Cover. Cook on low 6-10 hours or high 3-4 hours.

Note: You may want to omit the salt if you use the onion soup mix.

Slow Cooker Pepper Steak

Esther Hartzler
Carlsbad, NM

Makes 6-8 servings

1½-2 lbs. round beef steak
2 Tbsp. oil
¼ cup soy sauce
1 cup chopped onions
1 garlic clove, minced
1 tsp. sugar
½ tsp. salt
¼ tsp. pepper
¼ tsp. ground ginger
4 tomatoes, cut in eighths,
    or 16-oz. can tomatoes
2 large green peppers, cut in strips
½ cup cold water
1 Tbsp. cornstarch

1. Cut beef into 3″ x 1″ strips. Brown in oil in skillet. Drain. Transfer to slow cooker.
2. In separate bowl, combine soy sauce, onions, garlic, sugar, salt, pepper, and ginger. Pour over beef.
3. Cover. Cook on low 5-6 hours.
4. Add tomatoes and green peppers. Cook 1 hour longer.
5. Combine cold water and cornstarch to make paste. Stir into slow cooker. Cook on high until thickened.
6. Serve over noodles or rice.

Savory Pepper Steak

Grace W. Yoder
Harrisonburg, VA

Makes 6 servings

1½-lb. beef round steak, cut ½" thick
¼ cup flour
½ tsp. salt
⅛ tsp. pepper
1 medium onion, chopped or sliced
1 garlic clove, minced
2 large green peppers, sliced in ½" strips
29-oz. can whole tomatoes
1 Tbsp. beef flavor base, or 1 beef
   bouillon cube
1 Tbsp. soy sauce
2 tsp. Worcestershire sauce
3 Tbsp. flour
3 Tbsp. water

1. Cut beef into strips.
2. Combine ¼ cup flour, salt, and pepper. Toss with beef until well coated. Place in slow cooker.
3. Add onions, garlic, and half the green pepper slices. Mix well.
4. Combine tomatoes, beef base, soy sauce, and Worcestershire sauce. Pour into slow cooker.
5. Cover. Cook on low 8-10 hours.
6. One hour before serving, turn to high and stir in remaining green pepper.
7. Combine 3 Tbsp. flour and water to make smooth paste. Stir into slow cooker. Cover. Cook until thickened.
8. Serve over rice.

Slow Cooker Beef with Mushrooms

Grace W. Yoder
Harrisonburg, VA

Makes 6 servings

2 medium onions, thinly sliced
½ lb. mushrooms, sliced, or 2 4-oz. cans
   sliced mushrooms, drained
2½-lb. beef flank or round steak
salt to taste
pepper to taste
1 Tbsp. Worcestershire sauce
1 Tbsp. oil
paprika to taste

1. Place sliced onions and mushrooms in slow cooker.
2. Score top of meat about ½" deep in diamond pattern.
3. Season with salt and pepper. Rub in Worcestershire sauce and oil. Sprinkle top with paprika.
4. Place meat on top of onions.
5. Cover. Cook on low 7-8 hours.
6. To serve, cut beef across grain in thin slices. Top with mushrooms and onions.

Barbecued Chuck Steak

Rhonda Burgoon
Collingswood, NJ

Makes 4 servings

1 ½-lb. boneless chuck steak, 1 ½" thick
1 clove garlic, minced
¼ cup wine vinegar
1 Tbsp. brown sugar
1 tsp. paprika
2 Tbsp. Worcestershire sauce
½ cup ketchup
1 tsp. salt
1 tsp. prepared mustard
¼ tsp. black pepper

1. Cut beef on diagonal across the grain into 1"-thick slices. Place in slow cooker.
2. Combine remaining ingredients. Pour over meat. Stir to mix.
3. Cover. Cook on low 3-5 hours.

Fruited Flank Steak

Ruth A. Feister
Narvon, PA

Makes 6 servings

1 flank steak
salt to taste
pepper to taste
14 ½-oz. can mixed fruit,
   or your choice of canned fruit
1 Tbsp. salad oil
1 Tbsp. lemon juice
¼ cup teriyaki sauce
1 tsp. vinegar
1 garlic clove, minced

1. Sprinkle steak with salt and pepper. Place in slow cooker.
2. Drain fruit, saving ¼ cup syrup. Combine ¼ cup syrup with remaining ingredients. Pour over steak.
3. Cover. Cook on low 6-8 hours. Add drained fruit during the last 15 minutes of cooking.
4. Lift from cooker onto platter. Using sharp knife slice across the grain making thin slices. Spoon fruit over meat.
5. Serve with baked rice.

Pigs in Blankets

Linda Sluiter
Schererville, IN

Makes 4-6 servings

2-3-lb. round steak, cut about 1" thick
1 lb. bacon
1 cup ketchup
¾ cup brown sugar
1 cup water
half a yellow onion, chopped

1. Cut steak into strips 1" thick x 3" long.
2. Lay a bacon strip down, then a strip of beef on top of the bacon slice. Roll up and secure with toothpick. Place in slow cooker.
3. Combine remaining ingredients. Pour over meat roll-ups.
4. Cover. Cook on high 8 hours.

Apple and Brown Sugar Corned Beef

Mary Seielstad
Sparks, NV

Makes 8-10 servings

2½-3-lb. corned beef brisket
8 small red potatoes
3 medium carrots, peeled and sliced
1 large onion, cut in 6-8 pieces
1 small head cabbage, cut in chunks
1 qt. apple juice
1 cup brown sugar
1 Tbsp. prepared mustard

1. Place meat, potatoes, carrots, onion, and cabbage in 6-qt. slow cooker, or divide between 2 4- or 5-qt. cookers.
2. Combine apple juice, brown sugar, and mustard. Pour into slow cooker(s).
3. Cover. Cook on high 6-6½ hours or low 10-12 hours, or until vegetables and meat are tender.
4. Remove meat and vegetables from slow cooker. Thinly slice meat across the grain. Serve topped with vegetables.
5. Delicious eaten with cornbread.

Note: If potatoes are not small, quarter them.

Corned Beef

Elaine Vigoda
Rochester, NY

Makes 8 servings

3 large carrots, cut into chunks
1 cup chopped celery
1 tsp. salt
½ tsp. pepper
1 cup water
3-4-lb. corned beef
1 large onion, cut into pieces
half a small head of cabbage, cut in
    wedges
4 potatoes, peeled and chunked

1. Place carrots, celery, seasonings, and water in slow cooker.
2. Add beef. Cover with onions.
3. Cover. Cook on low 8-10 hours, or on high 5-6 hours.
4. Lift corned beef out of cooker and add cabbage and potatoes, pushing them to bottom of slow cooker. Return beef to cooker.
5. Cover. Cook on high 2 hours.
6. Remove corned beef. Cool and slice on the diagonal. Serve surrounded by vegetables.

Corned Beef and Cabbage with Potatoes and Carrots

Rosaria Strachan
Fairfield, CT

Makes 6-7 servings

3-4 carrots, sliced
3-4 potatoes, cubed
1 onion, sliced
2½-3½-lb. corned beef brisket
10-12 peppercorns
4-6 cabbage wedges

1. Place carrots, potatoes, and onions in bottom of slow cooker.
2. Place beef over vegetables.
3. Cover with water.
4. Add peppercorns.
5. Cover. Cook on low 8-10 hours or on high 5-6 hours.
6. Add cabbage. Cook on high 2-3 hours more.
7. Cut up meat and serve on large platter with mustard or horseradish as condiments. Pass vegetables with meat or in their own serving dish.

Corned Beef Dinner

Shirley Sears
Tiskilwa, IL

Makes 6 servings

2 onions, sliced
2 garlic cloves, minced
3 potatoes, pared and quartered
3 carrots, sliced
2 bay leaves
1 small head cabbage, cut into 4 wedges
3-4-lb. corned beef brisket
1 cup water
½ cup brown sugar
1 Tbsp. prepared mustard
dash of ground cloves

1. Layer onions, garlic, potatoes, carrots, bay leaves, and cabbage in slow cooker.
2. Place brisket on top.
3. Add water.
4. Cover. Cook on low 10-11 hours.
5. During last hour of cooking, combine brown sugar, mustard, and cloves. Spread over beef.
6. Discard bay leaves. Slice meat and arrange on platter of vegetables.

Slow-Cooked Short Ribs

Jean A. Shaner
York, PA
Barbara L. McGinnis
Jupiter, FL

Makes 12 servings

²⁄₃ cup flour
2 tsp. salt
¹⁄₂ tsp. pepper
4-4¹⁄₂ lbs. boneless beef short ribs,
    or 6-7 lbs. bone-in beef short ribs
oil, or ¹⁄₃ cup butter
1 large onion, chopped
1¹⁄₂ cups beef broth
³⁄₄ cup wine or cider vinegar
¹⁄₂-³⁄₄ cup packed brown sugar,
    according to your taste preference
¹⁄₂ cup chili sauce
¹⁄₃ cup ketchup
¹⁄₃ cup Worcestershire sauce
5 garlic cloves, minced
1¹⁄₂ tsp. chili powder

1. Combine flour, salt, and pepper in plastic bag. Add ribs and shake to coat.
2. Brown meat in small amount of oil, or in butter, in batches in skillet. Transfer to slow cooker.
3. Combine remaining ingredients in saucepan. Cook, stirring up browned drippings, until mixture comes to boil. Pour over ribs.
4. Cover. Cook on low 9-10 hours.
5. Debone and serve.
6. It is ideal to cook these ribs one day in advance of serving. Refrigerate for several hours or overnight. Remove layer of congealed fat before serving over rice or noodles.

Beef Ribs with Sauerkraut

Rosaria Strachan
Fairfield, CT

Makes 8-10 servings

3-4 lbs. beef short ribs
32-oz. bag, or 27-oz. can, sauerkraut,
    drained
2 Tbsp. caraway seeds
¹⁄₄ cup water

1. Put ribs in 6-qt. slow cooker.
2. Place sauerkraut and caraway seeds on top of ribs.
3. Pour in water.
4. Cover. Cook on high 3-4 hours or on low 7-8 hours.
5. Serve with mashed potatoes.

Variation: *If you really enjoy sauerkraut, double the amount of sauerkraut, and divide the recipe between 2 4- or 5-qt. cookers.*

Ribs and Limas

Miriam Friesen
Staunton, VA

Makes 6 servings

3 lbs. beef short ribs
2 Tbsp. oil
1 onion, chopped
4 carrots, sliced
1/4 cup packed brown sugar
2 Tbsp. flour
2 tsp. dry mustard
1 1/2 tsp. salt
1/4 tsp. pepper
1 1/4 cups water
1/4 cup cider vinegar
1 large bay leaf, broken in half
10-oz. pkg. frozen lima beans or peas,
  cooked

1. Cut ribs into serving-size pieces. Brown ribs in skillet in oil.
2. Place onions and carrots in slow cooker. Add ribs.
3. Combine brown sugar, flour, mustard, salt, and pepper. Stir in water and vinegar until smooth. Pour over ribs. Push bay leaves into liquid.
4. Cover. Cook on high 5-6 hours or on low 10-12 hours.
5. Stir in lima beans.
6. Cover. Cook on high 20-30 minutes.
7. Remove bay leaf before serving.
8. Serve with a citrus salad and crusty rolls.

Potluck Beef Barbecue Sandwiches

Carol Sommers
Millersburg, OH

Makes 16 servings

4-lb. beef chuck roast
1 cup brewed coffee or water
1 Tbsp. cider or red-wine vinegar
1 tsp. salt
1/2 tsp. pepper
14-oz. bottle ketchup
15-oz. can tomato sauce
1 cup sweet pickle relish
2 Tbsp. Worcestershire sauce
1/4 cup brown sugar

1. Place roast, coffee, vinegar, salt, and pepper in slow cooker.
2. Cover. Cook on high 6-8 hours, or until meat is very tender.
3. Pour off cooking liquid. Shred meat with two forks.
4. Add remaining ingredients. Stir well.
5. Cover. Cook on high 30-45 minutes. Reduce heat to low for serving.

Barbara Jean's Junior Beef

Barbara Jean Fabel
Wausau, WI

Makes 8 servings

3 1/2-5 lb. beef roast
1/2 tsp. salt
1/2 tsp. cayenne pepper
1/2 tsp. black pepper
1 tsp. seasoned salt
1 medium onion, chopped
1 qt. dill pickle juice
4 dill pickles, chopped
8 hamburger rolls
1/2 lb. fresh mushrooms,
   sliced and sauteed
2 cups grated cheddar or Swiss cheese

1. Combine all ingredients except rolls, mushrooms, and cheese in slow cooker.
2. Cover. Cook on high 4-5 hours.
3. Shred meat using two forks. Reduce heat to low and cook 1 hour, or until meat is very tender.
4. Serve on hamburger buns with sauteed, sliced, fresh mushrooms and grated cheddar or Swiss cheese.

Beef Barbecue Sandwiches

Melba Eshleman
Manheim, PA

Makes 12-16 servings

3-4 lb. beef roast (bottom round or rump
   is best)
1/2 cup water
1/2 cup ketchup
1 tsp. chili powder
1 1/2 Tbsp. Worcestershire sauce
2 Tbsp. vinegar
1 tsp. salt
1 Tbsp. sugar
1 tsp. dry mustard
1 medium onion, finely chopped
1/2 cup water
10-12 kaiser rolls

1. The night before serving, place roast in slow cooker with 1/2 cup water.
2. Cover. Cook on low 10-12 hours.
3. Also the night before serving, combine remaining ingredients and refrigerate 8-10 hours.
4. In the morning, shred roast with fork and return to cooker. Pour remaining ingredients over top. Mix together.
5. Heat on low until mealtime.
6. Serve on kaiser rolls.

Ranch Hand Beef

Sharon Timpe
Mequon, WI

Makes 10-12 servings

3-3½-lb. boneless beef chuck roast
1 cup thinly sliced onions
10¾-oz. can cream of celery soup
4-oz. can sliced mushrooms
12-oz. can beer
½ cup ketchup
1 large bay leaf
½ tsp. salt
¼ tsp. lemon pepper
2 Tbsp. chopped fresh parsley,
  or 1½ tsp. dried parsley

1. Place roast in slow cooker.
2. Combine remaining ingredients. Pour over roast.
3. Cover. Cook on low 7-9 hours or on medium setting 4-6 hours, until meat is tender.
4. Remove bay leaf.
5. Shred roast with two forks. Mix meat through sauce.
6. Serve on buns for sandwiches or over cooked noodles as a main dish.

Variation: If you prefer a thicker sauce, stir 2 Tbsp. cornstarch into ¼ cup water. When smooth, sitr into hot sauce, 15 minutes before serving.

Note: To give this dish a Mexican theme, serve the beef over tortilla chips or fritos and have bowls of shredded lettuce, diced avocado, sliced green onions, sliced ripe olives, sour cream, diced tomatoes, and shredded cheese for garnishing the meat.

Menu Idea

For a Mexican theme:
  Ranch Hand Beef
  Sliced Tomatoes marinated in oil,
    vinegar, and herb dressing
  Cornbread
  Fresh Fruit with Yogurt Dip
  Buffalo Chip Cookies
  Mexican Fruitcake

Easy Roast Beef Barbecue

Rose Hankins
Stevensville, MD

Makes 12-16 servings

3-4-lb. beef roast
12-oz. bottle barbecue sauce
½ cup water
½ cup ketchup
½ cup chopped onions
½ cup chopped green pepper
12-16 sandwich rolls

1. Combine ingredients in slow cooker.
2. Cover. Cook on low 12 hours.
3. Shred meat using 2 forks. Mix thoroughly through sauce.
4. Serve on rolls with cole slaw.

Hot Beef Sandwiches

Evelyn L. Ward
Greeley, CO

Makes 10 servings

3 lbs. beef chuck roast
1 large onion, chopped
1/4 cup vinegar
1 clove garlic, minced
1-1 1/2 tsp. salt
1/4-1/2 tsp. pepper

1. Place meat in slow cooker. Top with onions.
2. Combine vinegar, garlic, salt, and pepper. Pour over meat.
3. Cover. Cook on low 8-10 hours.
4. Drain broth but save for dipping.
5. Shred meat.
6. Serve on hamburger buns with broth on side.

I volunteer with Habitat for Humanity. I don't do construction, but I provide lunch sometimes for work crews. This sandwich is a favorite. I make the most colorful tossed salad that I can and serve fresh fruit that is in season and pie.

Herby Beef Sandwiches

Jean A. Shaner
York, PA

Makes 10-12 servings

3-4-lb. boneless beef chuck roast
3 Tbsp. fresh basil, or 1 Tbsp. dried basil
3 Tbsp. fresh oregano,
    or 1 Tbsp. dried oregano
1 1/2 cups water
1 pkg. dry onion soup mix
10-12 Italian rolls

1. Place roast in slow cooker.
2. Combine basil, oregano, and water. Pour over roast.
3. Sprinkle with onion soup mix.
4. Cover. Cook on low 7-8 hours. Shred meat with fork.
5. Serve on Italian rolls.

Middle Eastern Sandwiches (for a crowd)

Esther Mast
East Petersburg, PA

Makes 10-16 sandwiches

4 lbs. boneless beef or venison, cut in
    1/2" cubes
4 Tbsp. cooking oil
2 cups chopped onions
2 garlic cloves, minced
1 cup dry red wine
6-oz. can tomato paste
1 tsp. dried oregano
1 tsp. dried basil
1/2 tsp. dried rosemary
2 tsp. salt

dash of pepper
¼ cup cold water
¼ cup cornstarch
pita pocket breads
2 cups shredded lettuce
1 large tomato, seeded and diced
1 large cucumber, seeded and diced
8-oz. carton plain yogurt

1. Brown meat, 1 lb. at a time, in skillet in 1 Tbsp. oil. Reserve drippings and transfer meat to slow cooker.

2. Saute onion and garlic in drippings until tender. Add to meat.

3. Add wine, tomato paste, oregano, basil, rosemary, salt, and pepper.

4. Cover. Cook on low 6-8 hours.

5. Turn cooker to high. Combine cornstarch and water in small bowl until smooth. Stir into meat mixture. Cook until bubbly and thickened, stirring occasionally.

6. Split pita breads to make pockets. Fill each with meat mixture, lettuce, tomato, cucumber, and yogurt.

7. Serve with jello salad or applesauce.

Meat Loaf

Colleen Heatwole
Burton, MI

Makes 8 servings

2 lbs. ground beef
2 eggs
⅔ cup quick oats
1 pkg. dry onion soup mix
½-1 tsp. liquid smoke
1 tsp. ground mustard
½ cup ketchup, divided

1. Combine ground beef, eggs, dry oats, dry soup mix, liquid smoke, ground mustard, and all but 2 Tbsp. ketchup. Shape into loaf and place in slow cooker.

2. Top with remaining ketchup.

3. Cover. Cook on low 8-10 hours or on high 4-6 hours.

Hosting Idea

I like to invite guests for Sunday evening supper and suggest they come by 3:30-4:00. That gives me time to prepare the place, so that when they arrive we have time to relax and visit before the meal. After the meal we have time for games and the evening doesn't get late.

—Esther Mast

Comfort Meat Loaf

Trudy Kutter
Corfu, NY

Makes 6 servings

2 eggs, beaten
1/2 cup milk
2/3 cup bread crumbs
2 Tbsp. grated or finely chopped onion
1 tsp. salt
1/2 tsp. sage
1 1/2 lbs. ground beef
2-3 Tbsp. tomato sauce or ketchup

1. Combine everything but tomato sauce. Shape into 6" round loaf and place in cooker.
2. Cover. Cook on low 6 hours.
3. Spoon tomato sauce over meat loaf.
4. Cover. Cook on high 30 minutes.

Savory Meat Loaf

Betty B. Dennison
Grove City, PA

Makes 6-8 servings

2 lbs. ground beef or turkey
1 cup dry rolled oats
tomato juice (just enough to moisten meat if needed)
2 eggs
1 onion, diced
1 Tbsp. prepared mustard
1 tsp. garlic salt
2 Tbsp. ketchup
1 Tbsp. Worcestershire sauce
1 tsp. salt

Sauce:
26-oz. can, or 2 10 3/4-oz. cans, mushroom soup
6-10 fresh mushrooms, diced
1 Tbsp. onion flakes
half soup can water
1/4 tsp. salt
1/8 tsp. pepper

1. Combine all meat loaf ingredients. Shape into either a round or an oval loaf, to fit the shape of your slow cooker, and place in greased cooker.
2. Cover. Cook on high 1 hour.
3. Combine sauce ingredients. Pour over meat loaf.
4. Cover. Cook on low 6 hours.

Note: Be careful when you remove the lid, not to let the moisture that has gathered on the lid drop back into the sauce, thereby thinning it.

Magic Meat Loaf

Carolyn Baer
Conrath, WI

Makes 6 servings

1 egg, beaten
1/4 cup milk
1 1/2 tsp. salt
2 sliccs bread, crumbled
1 1/2 lbs. ground beef
half a small onion, chopped
2 Tbsp. chopped green peppers
2 Tbsp. chopped celery
ketchup
green pepper rings
4-6 potatoes, cubed
3 Tbsp. butter, melted

1. Combine egg, milk, salt, and bread crumbs in large bowl. Allow bread crumbs to soften.
2. Add meat, onions, green peppers, and celery. Shape into loaf and place off to the side in slow cooker.
3. Top with ketchup and green pepper rings.
4. Toss potatoes with melted butter. Spoon into cooker alongside meat loaf.
5. Cover. Cook on high 1 hour, then on low 8-10 hours.

Gourmet Meat Loaf

Anne Townsend
Albuquerque, NM

Makes 8 servings

2 medium potatoes, cut in strips

Meat loaf:
2 lbs. ground beef
1/2 lb. bulk sausage
1 onion, finely chopped
2-3 cloves garlic, minced, according to your taste preference
1/2 cup ketchup
3/4 cup crushed saltines
2 eggs
2 tsp. Worcestershire sauce
2 tsp. seasoning salt
1/4 tsp. pepper

Sauce:
1/2 cup ketchup
1/4 cup brown sugar
1 1/2 tsp. dry mustard
1/2 tsp. ground nutmeg

1. Place potatoes in bottom of slow cooker.
2. Combine meat loaf ingredients. Form into loaf and place on top of potatoes.
3. Combine sauce ingredients. Spoon over meat loaf.
4. Cover. Cook on low 8-12 hours.

Note: The potatoes take longer to cook than the meat so make sure you allow enough time.

My husband has this at the top of his list of favorite meat loaf recipes.

Menu Idea

Gourmet Meat Loaf
Spinach Salad
Grilled Tomatoes

Cheese Meat Loaf

Mary Sommerfeld
Lancaster, PA

Makes 8 servings

2 lbs. ground chuck or ground beef
2 cups shredded sharp cheddar or
    American cheese
1 tsp. salt
1 tsp. dry mustard
1/4 tsp. pepper
1/2 cup chili sauce
2 cups crushed cornflakes
2 eggs
1/2 cup milk

1. Combine all ingredients. Shape into loaf. Place in greased slow cooker.
2. Cover. Cook on low 6-8 hours.
3. Slice and serve with your favorite tomato sauce or ketchup.

Variation: Before baking, surround meat loaf with quartered potatoes, tossed lightly in oil.

Festive Meatballs

Jean Butzer
Batavia, NY

Makes 5-7 servings

1 1/2 lbs. ground beef
4 1/2-oz. can deviled ham
2/3 cup evaporated milk
2 eggs, beaten slightly
1 Tbsp. grated onion
2 cups soft bread crumbs
1 tsp. salt
1/4 tsp. allspice
1/4 tsp. pepper
1/4 cup flour
1/4 cup water
1 Tbsp. ketchup
2 tsp. dill weed
1 cup sour cream

1. Combine beef, ham, milk, eggs, onion, bread crumbs, salt, allspice, and pepper. Shape into 2" meatballs. Arrange in slow cooker.
2. Cover. Cook on low 2 1/2-3 1/2 hours. Turn control to high.
3. Dissolve flour in water until smooth. Stir in ketchup and dill weed. Add to meatballs, stirring gently.
4. Cook on high 15-20 minutes, or until slightly thickened.
5. Turn off heat. Stir in sour cream.
6. Serve over rice or pasta.

Easy Meatballs

Carlene Horne
Bedford, NH

Makes 10-12 servings

2 10¾-oz. cans cream of mushroom soup
2 8-oz. pkgs. cream cheese, softened
4-oz. can sliced mushrooms, undrained
1 cup milk
2-3 lbs. frozen meatballs

1. Combine soup, cream cheese, mushrooms, and milk in slow cooker.
2. Add meatballs. Stir.
3. Cover. Cook on low 4-5 hours.
4. Serve over noodles.

Swedish Meat Balls

Zona Mae Bontrager
Kokomo, IN

Makes 6-8 servings

1 lb. ground beef
½ lb. ground pork
½ cup minced onions
¾ cup fine dry bread crumbs
1 Tbsp. minced parsley
1 tsp. salt
⅛ tsp. pepper
½ tsp. garlic powder
1 Tbsp. Worcestershire sauce
1 egg
½ cup milk
¼ cup oil

Gravy:
¼ cup flour
¼ tsp. salt
¼ tsp. garlic powder
⅛ tsp. pepper
1 tsp. paprika
2 cups boiling water
¾ cup sour cream

1. Combine meats, onions, bread crumbs, parsley, salt, pepper, garlic powder, Worcestershire sauce, egg, and milk.
2. Shape into balls the size of a walnut. Brown in oil in skillet. Reserve drippings, and place meatballs in slow cooker.
3. Cover. Cook on high 10-15 minutes.
4. Stir flour, salt, garlic powder, pepper, and paprika into hot drippings in skillet. Stir in water and sour cream. Pour over meatballs.
5. Cover. Reduce heat to low. Cook 4-5 hours.
6. Serve over rice or noodles.

Italian Meatball Subs

Bonnie Miller
Louisville, OH

Makes 6-7 servings

2 eggs, beaten
1/4 cup milk
1/2 cup dry bread crumbs
2 Tbsp. grated Parmesan cheese
1 tsp. salt
1/4 tsp. pepper
1/8 tsp. garlic powder
1 lb. ground beef
1/2 lb. bulk pork sausage

Sauce
15-oz. can tomato sauce
6-oz. can tomato paste
1 small onion, chopped
1/2 cup chopped green bell pepper
1/2 cup red wine, or beef broth
1/3 cup water
2 garlic cloves, minced
1 tsp. dried oregano
1 tsp. salt
1/2 tsp. pepper
1/2 tsp. sugar

1. Make meatballs by combining eggs and milk. Add bread crumbs, cheese and seasonings. Add meats. Mix well. Shape into 1" balls. Broil or saute until brown. Put in slow cooker.
2. Combine sauce ingredients. Pour over meatballs.
3. Cover. Cook on low 4-6 hours.
4. Serve on rolls with creamy red potatoes, salad, and dessert.

Arlene's BBQ Meatballs

Arlene Groff
Lewistown, PA

Makes 12 servings

2 lbs. ground beef
2 eggs
1 small onion, chopped
1/4 cup milk
1 1/2 cup crushed crackers (equal to one packaged column of saltines)
1 tsp. prepared mustard
1 tsp. salt
1/2 tsp. pepper
oil
1 1/2 cups tomato juice
1/3 cup vinegar
1 Tbsp. soy sauce
1 Tbsp. Worcestershire sauce
3/4 cup brown sugar
2 Tbsp. cornstarch
1 tsp. prepared mustard

1. Combine beef, eggs, onion, milk, crackers, 1 tsp. mustard, salt, and pepper. Form into small balls. Brown in oil in skillet. Place in slow cooker.
2. Combine remaining ingredients. Pour over meatballs.
3. Cover. Cook on high 2 hours. Stir well. Cook an additional 2 hours.

Menu Idea

Arlene's BBQ Meatballs
Macaroni and Cheese (page 145)
Vegetable of your choice

Cocktail Meatballs
Kathy Purcell
Dublin, OH

Makes 10-12 servings

3 lbs. ground beef
1 pkg. dry onion soup mix
14-oz. can sweetened condensed milk

Sauce:
18-oz. bottle ketchup
1/2 cup brown sugar
1/4 cup Worcestershire sauce

1. Combine beef, soup mix, and condensed milk. Form into about 3 dozen meatballs, each about 1 1/2" around.
2. Place meatballs on baking sheet. Brown in 350° oven for 30 minutes. Remove from oven and drain. Place meatballs in slow cooker.
3. Combine sauce ingredients. Pour over meatballs.
4. Cover. Cook on low 3-4 hours.

I have made these meatballs for many different parties and events and they are always a big hit. Everyone asks for the recipe.

Easy Meatballs for a Group
Penny Blosser
Beavercreek, OH

Makes 10-12 main-dish servings

80-100 frozen small meatballs
16-oz. jar barbecue sauce
16-oz. jar apricot jam

1. Fill slow cooker with meatballs.
2. Combine sauce and jam. Pour over meatballs.
3. Cover. Cook on low 4 hours, stirring occasionally.
4. This works well as an appetizer, or as a main dish over rice.

Sweet 'n Tangy Meatballs
Donna Lantgen
Rapid City, SD

Makes 8 servings

1 1/2 lbs. ground beef
1/4 cup plain dry bread crumbs
3 Tbsp. prepared mustard
1 tsp. Italian seasoning
3/4 cup water
1/4 cup ketchup
2 Tbsp. honey
1 Tbsp. red-hot cayenne pepper sauce
3/4-oz. pkg. brown gravy mix

1. Combine ground beef, bread crumbs, mustard, and Italian seasoning. Shape into 1" balls. Bake or microwave until cooked. Drain. Place meatballs in slow cooker.
2. Cover. Cook on low 3 hours.
3. Combine remaining ingredients in saucepan. Cook for 5 minutes. Pour over meatballs.
4. Cover. Cook on low 2 hours.

Variation: For a fuller flavor, use orange juice instead of water in sauce.

Meat Balls and Spaghetti Sauce

Carol Sommers
Millersburg, OH

Makes 6-8 servings

Meatballs:
1½ lbs. ground beef
2 eggs
1 cup bread crumbs
oil

Sauce:
28-oz. can tomato puree
6-oz. can tomato paste
10¾-oz. can tomato soup
¼-½ cup grated Romano or Parmesan
    cheese
1 tsp. oil
1 garlic clove, minced

sliced mushrooms (either canned or fresh),
    optional

1. Combine ground beef, eggs, and bread crumbs. Form into 16 meatballs. Brown in oil in skillet.
2. Combine sauce ingredients in slow cooker. Add meatballs. Stir together gently.
3. Cover. Cook on low 6-8 hours. Add mushrooms 1-2 hours before sauce is finished.
4. Serve over cooked spaghetti.

Mexican Meatballs

Anna Kenagy
Carlsbad, NM

Makes 4-5 servings

1 lb. ground beef
4 slices bread, torn into small pieces
1 onion, chopped
⅓ cup milk
1 egg yolk, beaten (reserve white)
1 tsp. salt
dash of pepper
1 egg white, beaten
1 cup cornflakes, crushed
oil
10¾-oz. can tomato soup
1 small green bell pepper, chopped
½ cup water

1. Combine ground beef, bread, onion, milk, egg yolk, salt, and pepper. Form into balls.
2. Roll balls in egg white and then in crumbs. Brown in hot oil in skillet and then place in slow cooker.
3. Combine soup, pepper, and water. Pour over meatballs.
4. Cover. Cook on low 8 hours or high 3-4 hours.

Snappy Meatballs

Clara Newswanger
Gordonville, PA

*Makes 6-8 main-dish servings,
or 25 appetizer servings*

Meatballs:
2 lbs. ground beef
1/2 cup chopped onions
1 cup bread crumbs
2 eggs
1 tsp. salt

Sauce:
3 1/2 cups tomato juice
1 cup brown sugar
1/4 cup vinegar
1 tsp. grated onion
12 gingersnap cookies, crushed

1. Combine meatball ingredients. Shape into balls. Brown in skillet. Drain well. Spoon into slow cooker.
2. Combine sauce ingredients in slow cooker. Pour over meatballs. Mix gently.
3. Cover. Cook on low 4 hours.

Our son married a woman from the West Coast. He brought his new bride "home" on their honeymoon. We held an informal reception for friends who could not attend their wedding. Served with a light lunch, this recipe brought raves! Now we think of our children 3000 miles away whenever we make these meatballs.

Sweet and Sour Meatballs

Alice Miller
Stuarts Draft, VA

Makes 4 servings

1 lb. ground beef
1/2 cup dry bread crumbs
1/4 cup milk
1 tsp. salt
1 egg, beaten
2 Tbsp. finely chopped onions
1/2 tsp. Worcestershire sauce

Sauce:
1/2 cup packed brown sugar
2 Tbsp. cornstarch
13 1/4-oz. can pineapple chunks, undrained
1/3 cup vinegar
1 Tbsp. soy sauce
1 green pepper, chopped

1. Combine meatball ingredients. Shape into 1 1/2" balls. Brown in skillet. Drain. Place in slow cooker.
2. Add brown sugar and cornstarch to skillet. Stir in remaining ingredients. Heat to boiling, stirring constantly. Pour over meatballs.
3. Cover. Cook on low 3-4 hours.

Note: If you like pineapples, use a 20-oz. can of chunks, instead of the 13 1/4-oz. can.

Chinese Meatballs
Evelyn L. Ward
Greeley, CO

Makes 6 servings

1 lb. ground beef
1 egg
5 Tbsp. cornstarch, divided
1/2 tsp. salt
2 Tbsp. minced onions
2 cups pineapple juice
2 Tbsp. soy sauce
1/2 cup wine vinegar
3/4 cup water
1/2 cup sugar
1 green pepper, cut in strips
1 can water chestnuts, drained
canned chow mein noodles
6 slices pineapple, cut into halves

1. Combine beef, egg, 1 Tbsp. cornstarch, salt, and onions. Mix well. Shape into 1" meatballs. Brown on all sides under broiler.
2. Mix remaining cornstarch with pineapple juice. When smooth, mix in soy sauce, vinegar, water, and sugar. Bring to boil. Simmer, stirring until thickened.
3. Combine meatballs and sauce in slow cooker.
4. Cover. Cook on low 2 hours.
5. Add green peppers and water chestnuts.
6. Cover. Cook 1 hour.
7. Serve over chow mein noodles and garnish with pineapple slices.

Applesauce Meatballs
Mary E. Wheatley
Mashpee, MA

Makes 6 servings

3/4 lb. ground beef
1/4 lb. ground pork
1 egg
3/4 cup soft bread crumbs
1/2 cup unsweetened applesauce
3/4 tsp. salt
1/4 tsp. pepper
oil
1/4 cup ketchup
1/4 cup water

1. Combine beef, pork, egg, bread crumbs, applesauce, salt, and pepper. Form into 1 1/2" balls.
2. Brown in oil in batches in skillet. Transfer meat to slow cooker, reserving drippings.
3. Combine ketchup and water and pour into skillet. Stir up browned drippings and mix well. Spoon over meatballs.
4. Cover. Cook on low 4-6 hours.
5. Serve with steamed rice and green salad.

Holiday Meat Balls

Jean Robinson
Cinnaminson, NJ

Makes 20 servings

2 15-oz. bottles hot ketchup
2 cups blackberry wine
2 12-oz. jars apple jelly
2 lbs. frozen, precooked meatballs, or your
own favorite meatballs, cooked

1. Heat ketchup, wine, and jelly in slow cooker on high.
2. Add frozen meatballs.
3. Cover. Cook on high 4-6 hours. (If the meatballs are not frozen, cook on high 3-4 hours.)

Variations:

1. For those who like it hotter and spicier, put a bottle of XXXtra hot sauce on the table for them to add to their individual servings.

2. If you prefer a less wine-y flavor, use 1 cup water and only 1 cup wine.

Swedish Meatballs

Arlene Leaman Kliewer
Lakewood, Co

Makes 8-10 servings, or 60 very small meatballs

2 lbs. ground beef
2 eggs, slightly beaten
1 cup bread crumbs
2 tsp. salt
1/4 tsp. pepper

Sauce:
12-oz. bottle chili sauce
10-oz. jar grape jelly
1/2 cup ketchup
1 tsp. Worcestershire sauce

1. Combine ground beef, eggs, bread crumbs, salt, and pepper. Form into 60 small balls. Place on baking sheet.
2. Bake at 400° for 15-17 minutes. Place in slow cooker.
3. Combine sauce ingredients in saucepan. Heat. Pour over meatballs.
4. Heat on low until ready to serve.

We often make this recipe for our family's Christmas evening snack.

Variations:
1. Liven up the meatballs by adding 2/3 cup chopped onions, 2 Tbsp. snipped fresh parsley, and 1 tsp. Worcestershire sauce in Step 1.
    —Joan Rosenberger, Stephens City, VA

2. Add juice of half a lemon to the Sauce in Step 3.
    —Linda Sluiter, Schererville, IN

3. Use 1/2 cup crushed cornflakes in place of the 1 cup bread crumbs in the meatball mixture. Add 1 Tbsp. bottled lemon juice to the Sauce in Step 3.
    —Alice Miller, Stuarts Draft, VA

Meatball-Barley Casserole

Marjorie Y. Guengerich
Harrisonburg, VA

Makes 6 servings

2/3 cup pearl barley
1 lb. ground beef
1/2 cup soft bread crumbs
1 small onion, chopped
1/4 cup milk
1/4 tsp. pepper
1 tsp. salt
oil
1/2 cup thinly sliced celery
1/2 cup finely chopped sweet peppers
10 3/4-oz. can cream of celery soup
1/3 cup water
paprika

1. Cook barley as directed on package. Set aside.
2. Combine beef, bread crumbs, onion, milk, pepper, and salt. Shape into 20 balls. Brown on all sides in oil in skillet. Drain and place in slow cooker.
3. Add barley, celery, and peppers.
4. Combine soup and water. Pour into slow cooker. Mix all together gently.
5. Sprinkle with paprika.
6. Cover. Cook on low 6-8 hours or on high 4 hours.

Barbecue Sauce and Hamburgers

Dolores Kratz
Souderton, PA

Makes 6 servings

14 3/4-oz. can beef gravy
1/2 cup ketchup
1/2 cup chili sauce
1 Tbsp. Worcestershire sauce
1 Tbsp. prepared mustard
6 grilled hamburger patties
6 slices cheese, optional

1. Combine all ingredients except hamburger patties and cheese slices in slow cooker.
2. Add hamburger patties.
3. Cover. Cook on low 5-6 hours.
4. Serve in buns, each topped with a slice of cheese if you like.

Notes:
1. Freeze leftover sauce for future use.

2. This is both a practical and a tasty recipe for serving a crowd (picnics, potlucks, etc). You can grill the patties early in the day, rather than at the last minute when your guests are arriving.

1. Brown ground beef and onion in skillet. Drain.

2. Add remaining ingredients. Mix well. Pour into slow cooker.

3. Cover. Cook on low 1-2 hours.

4. Serve on hamburger buns.

No-More-Bottled Barbecue Sauce

Lauren Eberhard
Seneca, IL

Makes 2-2½ cups sauce

1 cup finely chopped onions
¼ cup oil
6-oz. can tomato paste
½ cup water
¼ cup brown sugar
¼ cup lemon juice (freshly squeezed juice is best)
3 Tbsp. Worcestershire sauce
2 Tbsp. prepared mustard
2 tsp. salt
¼ tsp. pepper

1. Combine ingredients in slow cooker.

2. Cover. Cook on low 3 hours.

3. Use on hamburgers, sausage, pork chops, ribs, steaks, chicken, turkey, or fish.

Note: Sauce will keep in refrigerator for up to 2 weeks.

New Mexico Cheeseburgers

Colleen Konetzni
Rio Rancho, NM

Makes 8 servings

1 lb. ground beef, browned
6 potatoes, peeled and sliced
½ cup chopped green chilies
1 onion, chopped
10¾-oz. can cream of mushroom soup
2 cups cubed Velveeta cheese

1. Layer beef, potatoes, green chilies, and onions in slow cooker.

2. Spread soup over top.

3. Top with cheese.

4. Cover. Cook on high 1 hour. Reduce heat to low and cook 6-8 hours.

Pizzaburgers

Deborah Swartz
Grottoes, VA

Makes 4-6 servings

1 lb. ground beef
½ cup chopped onions
¼ tsp. salt
⅛ tsp. pepper
8 ozs. pizza sauce
10¾-oz. can cream of mushroom soup
2 cups shredded cheddar cheese

Menu Idea

New Mexico Cheeseburgers
Favorite Green Salad
Fresh Rolls

Yum-Yums

Evelyn L. Ward
Greeley, CO

Makes 12 servings

3 lbs. ground beef
2 onions, chopped
10³/4-oz. can cream of chicken soup
1¹/2 cups tomato juice
1 tsp. prepared mustard
1 tsp. Worcestershire sauce
1 tsp. salt
¹/4 tsp. pepper

1. Brown beef and onions in skillet. Drain.
2. Add remaining ingredients. Pour into slow cooker.
3. Cover. Cook on low 4-6 hours.
4. Serve on hamburger buns.

This is a great recipe for serving a crowd. A club I am a part of serves it when we do fund raisers. Our menu is Yum-yums, marinated bean salad, and strawberry short cake. We make the food in our homes and carry it to the meeting site.

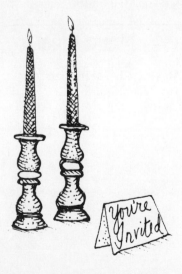

Dianna's Barbecue

Lauren Eberhard
Seneca, IL

Makes 12 servings

4 lbs. ground beef, browned
24-oz. bottle ketchup
4 Tbsp. prepared mustard
2 Tbsp. vinegar
4 Tbsp. sugar
³/4 cup water
1 tsp. pepper
1 Tbsp. paprika
1 cup chopped celery
1 cup chopped onion
sandwich rolls

1. Combine all ingredients except rolls in slow cooker.
2. Cover. Cook on high 1-2 hours or on low 4 hours.
3. Serve in sandwich rolls.

Chili Spaghetti

Clara Newswanger
Gordonville, PA

Makes 8-10 servings

¹/2 cup diced onions
2 cups tomato juice
2 tsp. chili powder
1 tsp. salt
³/4 cup grated mild cheese
1¹/2 lbs. ground beef, browned
12-oz. dry spaghetti, cooked

1. Combine all ingredients in slow cooker.

2. Cover. Cook on low 4 hours. Check mixture about halfway through the cooking time. If it's becoming dry, stir in an additional cup of tomato juice.

Variations:

1. Add 8-oz. can sliced mushrooms to Step 1.

2. Use 2 Tbsp. chili powder instead of 2 tsp. chili powder for added flavor.

Dawn's Spaghetti and Meat Sauce

Dawn Day
Westminster, CA

Makes 6-8 servings

1 lb. ground beef
1 Tbsp. oil, if needed
1/2 lb. mushrooms, sliced
1 medium onion, chopped
3 garlic cloves, minced
1/2 tsp. dried oregano
1/2 tsp. salt
1/4 cup grated Parmesan or Romano cheese
6-oz. can tomato paste
2 15-oz. cans tomato sauce
15-oz. can chopped or crushed tomatoes

1. Brown ground beef in skillet, in oil if needed. Reserve drippings and transfer meat to slow cooker.

2. Saute mushrooms, onion, and garlic until onions are transparent. Add to slow cooker.

3. Add remaining ingredients to cooker. Mix well.

4. Cover. Cook on low 6 hours.

5. Serve with pasta and garlic bread.

Note: This recipe freezes well.

Quick and Easy Spaghetti

Beverly Getz
Warriors Mark, PA

Makes 8 servings

1 1/2 lbs. ground beef
2 onions, chopped
26-oz. jar spaghetti sauce with mushrooms
10 3/4-oz. can tomato soup
1 or 2 14.5-oz. cans stewed tomatoes
1 can mushrooms
1/2 tsp. garlic powder
1/2 tsp. garlic salt
1/2 tsp. minced dried garlic
1/2 tsp. onion salt
1/2 tsp. Italian seasoning
1 lb. spaghetti, cooked

1. Brown beef and onion in skillet. Pour into slow cooker.

2. Add remaining ingredients to cooker except spaghetti.

3. Cover. Cook on low 4 hours.

4. Serve over spaghetti.

Spaghetti Sauce for a Crowd

Sue Pennington
Bridgewater, VA

Makes 18 cups

1 lb. ground beef
1 lb. ground turkey
1 Tbsp. oil
5 15-oz. cans tomato sauce
3 6-oz. cans tomato paste
1 cup water
½ cup minced fresh parsley, or 3 Tbsp. dried parsley
½ cup minced fresh oregano, or 3 Tbsp. dried oregano
4 tsp. salt

1. Brown meat in oil in skillet. Place in 6-qt. slow cooker. (A 5-qt. cooker will work, but it will be brimful.)
2. Add remaining ingredients. Mix together thoroughly.
3. Cover. Cook on low 4-6 hours.

Notes:
1. Add 1 medium onion, chopped, and/or 3 cloves garlic, minced, to Step 1, browning along with the meat.

2. Add 1 can crushed tomatoes, or 2 cups cut-up fresh tomatoes, to Step 2 to add a fresh-tomato taste. (This will make your cooker even fuller, so you may want to switch to two 4- or 5-qt. cookers.)

3. Make the sauce without meat if you prefer.

4. Use as a pizza sauce, especially if you make it meatless.

5. Sauce can be refrigerated for a week or frozen up to 3 months.

Beef and Sausage Spaghetti Sauce

Sherri Grindle
Goshen, IN

Makes 10-12 servings

1 lb. ground beef
1 lb. Italian sausage, bulk, or cut in thin slices
1 large onion, chopped
3 Tbsp. oil, if needed
5 lbs. tomato puree, or 3 28-oz. cans
6 cloves garlic, minced
2 Tbsp. parsley
1 Tbsp. salt
¼ rounded tsp. pepper
3 bay leaves
1 Tbsp. dried oregano
crushed red pepper, optional

1. Brown meat and onion in skillet in oil, unless they produce enough of their own drippings.
2. Combine all ingredients in slow cooker.
3. Cover. Cook on low 8 hours.
4. Serve over pasta.

Variation: Add 1 box spaghetti noodles 1 hour before serving and cook on high for last hour.

Hosting Idea

Keep the meal simple and do as much ahead as possible. People usually don't care so much what is served. They are just happy for a chance to sit and visit with each other.
—Sherri Grindle

Spaghetti Sauce with a Kick

Andrea O'Neil
Fairfield, CT

Makes 4-6 servings

1 lb. ground beef
1 onion, chopped
2 28-oz. cans crushed tomatoes
16-oz. can tomato sauce
1-lb. Italian sausage, cut in chunks
3 cloves garlic, crushed
1 Tbsp. Italian seasoning
2 tsp. dried basil
red pepper flakes to taste

1. Brown beef and onions in skillet. Drain and transfer to slow cooker.
2. Add remaining ingredients.
3. Cover. Cook on low 4-6 hours.
4. Serve over your favorite pasta.

Variation: Add 1-2 tsp. salt and 1-2 Tbsp. brown sugar or honey, if desired.

Slow Cooker Lasagna

Crystal Brunk
Singers Glen, VA

Makes 6-8 servings

1 lb. ground beef, browned
4-5 cups spaghetti sauce, depending upon how firm or how juicy you want the finished lasagna
24-oz. container cottage cheese
1 egg
8-10 lasagna noodles, uncooked
2-3 cups mozzarella cheese

1. Combine ground beef and spaghetti sauce.
2. Combine egg and cottage cheese.
3. Layer half of the ground beef mixture, the dry noodles, the cottage cheese mixture, and the mozzarella cheese in the slow cooker. Repeat layers.
4. Cover. Cook on high 4-5 hours or on low 6-8 hours.

Menu Idea

Slow Cooker Lasagna
Peas or Corn
Garlic Bread

Lazy Lasagna

Deborah Santiago
Lancaster, PA

Makes 6 servings

1 lb. ground beef, browned
32-oz. jar spaghetti sauce
8-oz. bag curly-edged noodles, cooked, or lasagna noodles cut up, cooked
16-oz. carton cottage cheese
8 ozs. shredded mozzarella cheese
Parmesan cheese to taste

1. Combine beef and spaghetti sauce.
2. Combine noodles, cottage cheese, and mozzarella cheese.
3. Layer one-third of the beef mixture, followed by half the noodle mixture in slow cooker. Repeat layers, ending with beef mixture. Sprinkle with Parmesan cheese.
4. Cover. Cook on low 3-4 hours.
5. Serve with salad and French bread.

Slow Cooker Almost Lasagna

Jeanette Oberholtzer
Manheim, PA

Makes 8-10 servings

1 box rotini or ziti, cooked
2 Tbsp. olive oil
2 28-oz. jars pasta sauce with tomato
   chunks
2 cups tomato juice
1/2 lb. ground beef
1/2 lb. bulk sausage, crumbled, or links cut
   into 1/4" slices
1 cup Parmesan cheese
1/2 cup Italian bread crumbs
1 egg
2 cups mozzarella cheese, divided
2 cups ricotta cheese
2 eggs
1 cup Parmesan cheese
1 1/2 tsp. parsley flakes
3/4 tsp. salt
1/4 tsp. pepper

1. In large bowl, toss pasta with olive oil. Add pasta sauce and tomato juice and mix well.
2. Brown beef and sausage together in skillet. Drain.
3. Add 1 cup Parmesan cheese, bread crumbs, 1 egg, and 1 cup mozarella cheese to meat.
4. In separate bowl, beat together ricotta cheese, 2 eggs, 1 cup Parmesan cheese, parsley, salt, and pepper.
5. Pour half of pasta-sauce mixture into slow cooker. Spread entire ricotta mixture over pasta. Cover with remaining pasta-sauce mixture. Sprinkle with remaining 1 cup mozzarella cheese.
6. Cover. Cook on low 4-6 hours.

Egg Noodle Lasagna

Anna Stoltzfus
Honey Brook, PA

Makes 12-16 servings

6 1/2 cups wide egg noodles, cooked
3 Tbsp. butter or margarine
2 1/4 cups spaghetti sauce
1 1/2 lbs. ground beef, browned
6 ozs. Velveeta cheese, cubed
3 cups shredded mozzarella cheese

1. Toss butter with hot noodles.
2. Spread one-fourth of spaghetti sauce in slow cooker. Layer with one-third of noodles, beef, and cheeses. Repeat layers 2 more times.
3. Cover. Cook on low 4 hours, or until cheese is melted.

Meat Loaf Burgers

Lafaye M. Musser
Denver, PA

Makes 6 servings

1 large onion, sliced
1 rib celery, chopped
2 lbs. ground beef
1 tsp. salt
1 1/4 tsp. pepper
2 cups tomato juice
4 garlic cloves, minced
1 Tbsp. ketchup
1 tsp. Italian seasoning
1/2 tsp. salt
6 hamburger buns

1. Place onion and celery in slow cooker.
2. Combine beef, salt, and pepper. Shape into 6 patties. Place in slow cooker.

3. Combine tomato juice, garlic, ketchup, Italian seasoning, and salt. Pour over patties.

4. Cover. Cook on low 7-9 hours.

5. Serve on hamburger buns.

Barbecued Hamburgers

Martha Hershey
Ronks, PA

Makes 4 serving

1 lb. ground beef
1/4 cup chopped onions
3 Tbsp. ketchup
1 tsp. salt
1 egg, beaten
1/4 cup seasoned bread crumbs
18-oz. bottle of your favorite barbecue
   sauce

1. Combine beef, onions, ketchup, salt, egg, and bread crumbs. Form into 4 patties. Brown both sides lightly in skillet. Place in slow cooker.

2. Cover with barbecue sauce.

3. Cover. Bake on high 3 hours or low 6 hours.

We first had Barbecued Hamburgers at a 4-H picnic, and they have been a family favorite ever since.

Note: Mix the hamburger patties, brown them, and freeze them in advance, and you'll have little to do at the last minute.

Menu Idea

Barbecued Hamburgers
Baked Beans (pages 133-140)
Fresh Fruit, cut-up
Iced Tea

Hamburger-Potato Slow Cooker Dinner

Lafaye M. Musser
Denver, PA

Makes 6-8 servings

1 lb. ground beef
1 cup water
1/2 tsp. cream of tartar
6 medium potatoes, thinly sliced
1 onion, chopped
1/4 cup flour
1/2 tsp. salt
1/4 tsp. pepper
1 cup grated cheddar cheese, divided
2 Tbsp. butter or margarine
10 3/4-oz. can cream of mushroom soup

1. Brown ground beef in skillet, using oil if necessary.

2. In separate bowl, combine water and cream of tartar. Toss potatoes in water. Drain.

3. In another bowl, mix together onion, flour, salt, pepper, and half of cheese.

4. Place browned beef in bottom of cooker. Top with a layer of sliced potatoes. Add onion-cheese mixture.

5. Dot top with butter.

6. Pour soup over all.

7. Cover. Cook on low 7-9 hours or high 3-4 hours.

8. Sprinkle remaining cheese over top, 30 minutes before serving.

Variations:
1. Use cream of celery soup instead of cream of mushroom soup.
   —Mary Sommerfeld, Lancaster, PA

2. Use cream of chicken soup instead of cream of mushroom soup.
   —Yvonne Boettger, Harrisonburg, VA

1-2-3-4 Casserole

Betty K. Drescher
Quakertown, PA

Makes 8 servings

1 lb. ground beef
2 onions, sliced
3 carrots, thinly sliced
4 potatoes, thinly sliced
1/2 tsp. salt
1/8 tsp. pepper
1 cup cold water
1/2 tsp. cream of tartar
10 3/4-oz. can cream of mushroom soup
1/4 cup milk
1/2 tsp. salt
1/8 tsp. pepper

1. Layer in greased slow cooker: ground beef, onions, carrots, 1/2 tsp. salt, and 1/8 tsp. pepper.
2. Dissolve cream of tartar in water in bowl. Toss sliced potatoes with water. Drain.
3. Combine soup and milk. Toss with potatoes. Add remaining salt and pepper. Arrange potatoes in slow cooker.
4. Cover. Cook on low 7-9 hours.

Variations:

1. Substitute sour cream for the milk.

2. Top potatoes with 1/2 cup shredded cheese.

Cooker Casserole

Carol Eberly
Harrisonburg, VA

Makes 6-8 servings

2 cups grated carrots
1 medium-sized onion, sliced
4 cups grated raw potatoes
1 lb. ground beef, browned
1 tsp. salt
1/4 tsp. pepper
1 Tbsp. Worcestershire sauce
10 3/4-oz. can cream of mushroom soup

1. Layer carrots, onions, potatoes, and ground beef in slow cooker.
2. Combine salt, pepper, Worcestershire sauce, and soup in bowl. Pour over ground beef.
3. Cover. Cook on low 8-10 hours.

Hamburger Potato Casserole

Sue Pennington
Bridgewater, VA

Makes 6-10 servings

1 lb. ground beef
1 Tbsp. oil
6-8 potatoes, peeled and sliced
4-6 carrots, sliced
2 medium onions, sliced
1 cup peas
1 cup grated cheddar cheese
1 tsp. salt
1/4 tsp. pepper
10-oz. can cream of chicken soup

1. Brown ground beef in oil in skillet.
2. Layer half of beef, potatoes, carrots, onions, peas and cheese in cooker. Sprinkle with salt and pepper. Repeat layers.
3. Pour cream of chicken soup over top.
4. Cover. Cook on low 8-10 hours.

My husband came up with this recipe. Our family loves it and often requests it when I ask them what they want to eat.

Hamburger Casserole

Kelly Evenson
Pittsboro, NC

Makes 6-8 servings

2 large potatoes, sliced
2-3 medium carrots, sliced
1 cup frozen peas, thawed and drained
3 medium onions, sliced
2 celery ribs, sliced
garlic salt to taste
pepper to taste
salt to taste
1 lb. ground beef, browned and drained
10³/4-oz. can tomato soup
1 soup can of water

1. Layer vegetables in order given into slow cooker.
2. Sprinkle each layer with garlic salt, pepper, and salt.
3. Place meat on top of celery.
4. Combine soup and water. Pour over all.
5. Cover. Cook on low 8 hours.
6. Serve with applesauce.

Wholesome Hamburger Dinner

Reba Rhodes
Bridgewater, VA

Makes 6-8 servings

1 lb. ground beef
1 tsp. salt
1/4 tsp. pepper
1 cup sliced carrots
1 cup coarsely chopped celery
1 medium onion, sliced
1 cup green beans
2 tsp. sugar
2-3 cups tomato juice
1/2 lb. grated cheese

1. Brown ground beef in skillet. Place in bottom of slow cooker.
2. Layer remaining ingredients, except cheese, over ground beef in order given.
3. Cover. Cook on high 3-4 hours or low 5-6 hours.
4. Thirty minutes before the end of the cooking time, layer cheese on top. Cover and resume cooking.
5. Serve with cornbread.

Note: You can double all the vegetable amounts, if you wish. Increase cooking time to 5-6 hours on high or 9-11 hours on low, or until vegetables are as tender as you like.

Hosting Idea

If you wait until you have all your work done, you will never have company. They don't usually care about what's undone anyway.
—Reba Rhodes

Stuffed Baked Topping

Fannie Miller
Hutchinson, KS

Makes 12 servings

3 lbs. ground beef
1 cup chopped green peppers
1/2 cup chopped onions
6 Tbsp. butter
1/4 cup flour
3 cups milk
1/2 cup pimento, or chopped sweet red
   peppers
3/4 lb. cheddar cheese
3/4 lb. your favorite mild cheese
1/2 tsp. hot pepper sauce
1/4 tsp. dry mustard
salt to taste
12 baked potatoes

1. Brown ground beef, green peppers, and onions in butter. Transfer mixture to slow cooker, reserving drippings.
2. Stir flour into drippings. Slowly add milk. Cook until thickened.
3. Add pimento, cheeses, and seasonings. Pour over ingredients in slow cooker.
4. Cover. Heat on low.
5. Serve over baked potatoes, each one split open on an individual dinner plate.

Hosting Idea

When we have a large family gathering of 25 to 30 people, I like to butter our slow cooker, then mash the potatoes, and place them in the slow cooker on low. That saves me last-minute scurrying to mash them, and it keeps the potatoes warm until all are served.

—Mary Martins

Ground Beef Stew

Ruth Ann Hoover
New Holland, PA
Kim Stoltzfus
New Holland, PA

Makes 8-10 servings

1 lb. ground beef, browned
6 medium potatoes, peeled and cubed
16-oz. pkg. baby carrots
3 cups water
3 Tbsp. dry onion soup mix
1 garlic clove, minced
1 1/2 tsp. Italian seasoning
1-1 1/2 tsp. salt
1/2 tsp. garlic powder
1/4 tsp. pepper
10 3/4-oz. can tomato soup
6-oz. can Italian tomato paste

1. Combine all ingredients except tomato soup and paste in slow cooker.
2. Cover. Cook on high 3 1/2-4 hours.
3. Stir in soup and tomato paste.
4. Cover. Cook on high 1 hour more.

Variation: If you'd like to add color and more vegetables to the stew, stir in 1 1/2 cups frozen peas in Step 3.

1. Combine beef, onions, salt, pepper, bread crumbs, egg, and tomato juice. Place one-third of mixture in slow cooker.

2. Spread with one-third of mashed potatoes and 3 slices cheese. Repeat 2 times.

3. Cover. Cook on low 3 hours.

Prompt
Mary Martins
Fairbank, IA

Makes 6-8 servings

4-6 medium-sized potatoes, sliced
1/2-3/4 cup minute rice
1 onion, sliced
1 1/2 lbs. ground beef
1 diced green pepper, optional
1 qt. tomatoes with juice
salt to taste
pepper to taste

1. Layer ingredients in order given in greased slow cooker. Salt and pepper each layer to taste.

2. Cover. Cook on high for 1 1/2-2 hours.

Variation: You may substitute 1 qt. V-8 juice for the quart of tomatoes with juice.

Hamburger/Green Bean Dish
Hazel L. Propst
Oxford, PA

Makes 4-5 servings

1 lb. ground beef
1 onion, chopped
1 qt. string beans
10 3/4-oz. can tomato soup
3/4 tsp. salt
1/4 tsp. pepper
6-7 cups mashed potatoes
1 egg, beaten

1. Brown meat and onion in skillet. Stir in beans, soup, and seasonings. Pour into slow cooker.

2. Combine mashed potatoes with egg. Spread over meat mixture in slow cooker.

3. Cover. Cook on low 5-6 hours, or until beans are tender.

Cheeseburger Casserole
Erma Kauffman
Cochranville, PA

Makes 6 servings

1 lb. ground beef
1 small onion, chopped
1 tsp. salt
dash of pepper
1/2 cup bread crumbs
1 egg
tomato juice to moisten
4 1/2 cups mashed potatoes
   (leftover mashed potatoes work well)
9 slices American cheese

Meal-in-One

Melanie L. Thrower
McPherson, KS

Makes 6-8 servings

2 lbs. ground beef
1 onion, diced
1 green bell pepper, diced
1 tsp. salt
1/4 tsp. pepper
1 large bag frozen hash brown potatoes
16-oz. container sour cream
24-oz. container cottage cheese
1 cup Monterey Jack cheese, shredded

1. Brown ground beef, onion, and green pepper in skillet. Drain. Season with salt and pepper.
2. In slow cooker, layer one-third of the potatoes, meat, sour cream, and cottage cheese. Repeat twice.
3. Cover. Cook on low 4 hours, sprinkling Monterey Jack cheese over top during last hour.
4. Serve with red or green salsa.

Variation: For a cheesier dish, prepare another cup of shredded cheese and sprinkle 1/2 cup over the first layer of potatoes, meat, sour cream, and cottage cheese, and another 1/2 cup over the second layer of those ingredients.

Cedric's Casserole

Kathy Purcell
Dublin, OH

Makes 4-6 servings

1 medium onion, chopped
3 Tbsp. butter or margarine
1 lb. ground beef
1/2-3/4 tsp. salt
1/4 tsp. pepper
3 cups shredded cabbage
10 3/4-oz. can tomato soup

1. Saute onion in skillet in butter.
2. Add ground beef and brown. Season with salt and pepper.
3. Layer half of cabbage in slow cooker, followed by half of meat mixture. Repeat layers.
4. Pour soup over top.
5. Cover. Cook on low 3-4 hours.
6. Serve with garlic bread and canned fruit.

I grew up with this recipe and remember my mother serving it often. It makes a wonderful potluck take-a-long.

Beef and Macaroni

Esther J. Yoder
Hartville, OH

Makes 4-5 servings

1 lb. ground beef
1 small onion, chopped
half a green pepper, chopped
1 cup cooked macaroni
1/2 tsp. dried basil
1/2 tsp. dried thyme
1 tsp. Worcestershire sauce
1 tsp. salt
10³/4-oz. can cheddar cheese soup

1. Brown beef, onions, and green pepper in skillet. Pour off drippings and place meat and vegetables in slow cooker.
2. Combine all ingredients in cooker.
3. Cover. Cook on high 2-2½ hours, stirring once or twice.
4. Serve with broccoli and applesauce.

Plenty More in the Kitchen

Jean Robinson
Cinnaminson, NJ

Makes 12-16 servings

3 lbs. ground beef
1 cup chopped onions
1 Tbsp. oil
26-oz. jar tomato sauce or spaghetti sauce
1 tsp. salt
2 tsp. chili powder
1 tsp. pepper
2 Tbsp. dark brown sugar
16-oz. can whole-kernel corn
2 14½-oz. cans beef broth
8-oz. pkg. dry elbow macaroni
1 cup grated sharp cheese

1. Brown beef and onion in oil.
2. Combine all ingredients except cheese. Pour into slow cooker.
3. Cover. Cook on high 1 hour. Turn to low and cook 4 more hours.
4. Sprinkle with cheese and cook 10 minutes more.

Variation: You can change the balance of ingredients by using only 1-1½ lbs. ground beef and adding another 1/2-1 cup dry macaroni.

This is a tried and true recipe adapted from an old 1984 Pennsylvania Grange Cookbook. *An easy meal to carry outside to the picnic table or a Little League game.*

Menu Idea

Plenty More in the Kitchen
Garlic Bread
A Big Salad

Cheese and Pasta in a Pot

Cathy Boshart
Lebanon, PA

Makes 8 servings

2 lbs. ground beef
1 Tbsp. oil
2 medium onions, chopped
1 garlic clove, minced
14-oz. jar spaghetti sauce
16-oz. can stewed tomatoes
4-oz. can sliced mushrooms
8 ozs. dry shell macaroni, cooked al dente
1½ pints sour cream
½ lb. provolone cheese, sliced
½ lb. mozzarella cheese, sliced thin or
  shredded

1. Brown ground beef in oil in skillet. Drain off all but 2 Tbsp. drippings.
2. Add onions, garlic, spaghetti sauce, stewed tomatoes, and undrained mushrooms to drippings. Mix well. Simmer 20 minutes, or until onions are soft.
3. Pour half of macaroni into slow cooker. Cover with half the tomato/meat sauce. Spread half the sour cream over sauce. Top with provolone cheese. Repeat, ending with mozzarella cheese.
4. Cover. Cook on high 2 hours or low 3 hours.

Menu Idea

Cheese and Pasta in a Pot
Italian Bread with Garlic and Butter
  Spread
Tossed Salad
Angel Food Cake with Fruit Sauce

Hearty Rice Casserole

Dale Peterson
Rapid City, SD

Makes 12-16 servings

10¾-oz. can cream of mushroom soup
10¾-oz. can creamy onion soup
10¾-oz. can cream of chicken soup
1 cup water
1 lb. ground beef, browned
1 lb. pork sausage, browned
1 large onion, chopped
1 large green pepper, chopped
1½ cups long grain rice
shredded cheese, optional

1. Combine all ingredients except cheese in slow cooker. Mix well.
2. Cover. Cook on low 6-7 hours, sprinkling with cheese during last hour, if you wish.

Hamburger Rice Casserole

Shari Mast
Harrisonburg, VA

Makes 6-8 servings

1/2 lb. ground beef
1 onion, chopped
1 cup diced celery
1 tsp. dried basil
1 tsp. dried oregano
10 3/4-oz. can cream of mushroom soup
1 soup can water
4 cups cooked rice
4-oz. can mushroom pieces, drained
Velveeta cheese slices

1. Brown ground beef, onion, and celery in skillet. Season with basil and oregano.
2. Combine soup and water in bowl.
3. In well greased slow cooker, layer half of rice, half of mushrooms, half of ground-beef mixture, and half of soup. Repeat layers.
4. Cover. Cook on high 4 hours.
5. Top with cheese 30 minutes before serving.
6. This casserole, served with cornbread and applesauce, makes a well-rounded meal that is quick and easy to prepare and well-received by children and adults.

Beef and Pepper Rice

Liz Ann Yoder
Hartville, OH

Makes 4-6 servings

1 lb. ground beef
2 green peppers, or 1 green and 1 red pepper, coarsely chopped
1 cup chopped onions
1 cup brown rice, uncooked
2 beef bouillon cubes, crushed
3 cups water
1 Tbsp. soy sauce

1. Brown beef in skillet. Drain.
2. Combine all ingredients in slow cooker. Mix well.
3. Cover. Cook on low 5-6 hours or on high 3 hours, or until liquid is absorbed.

Menu Idea

Beef and Pepper Rice
Applesauce
Lima Beans

Stuffed Green Peppers

Patricia Howard
Albuquerque, NM

Makes 6 servings

6 green peppers
1 lb. ground beef
1/4 cup chopped onions
1 tsp. salt
1/4 tsp. pepper
1 1/4 cups cooked rice
1 Tbsp. Worcestershire sauce
8-oz. can tomato sauce
1/4 cup beef broth

1. Cut stem ends from peppers. Carefully remove seeds and membrane without breaking pepper apart. Parboil in water for 5 minutes. Drain. Set aside.
2. Brown ground beef and onions in skillet. Drain off drippings. Place meat and onions in mixing bowl.
3. Add seasonings, rice, and Worcestershire sauce to meat and combine well. Stuff green peppers with mixture. Stand stuffed peppers upright in large slow cooker.
4. Mix together tomato sauce and beef broth. Pour over peppers.
5. Cover. Cook on low 5-7 hours.

Stuffed Peppers with Cheese

Rosaria Strachan
Fairfield, CT

Makes 6-8 servings

6-8 medium-sized green peppers
1-2 lbs. ground beef
1 onion, chopped and sauteed
salt to taste
pepper to taste
1 egg
1 1/2 cups cooked rice
15-oz. can tomato sauce, divided
1/2-3/4 cup shredded cheddar cheese

1. Remove caps and seeds from peppers, but keep them whole.
2. Combine ground beef, onion, salt, pepper, egg, rice, 1/3 can tomato sauce, and cheddar cheese. Stuff into peppers. Stand in large slow cooker, or two smaller cookers.
3. Cover with remaining tomato sauce.
4. Cover. Cook on low 8-10 hours.

Spanish Stuffed Peppers

Katrine Rose
Woodbridge, VA

Makes 4 servings

1 lb. ground beef
7-oz. pkg. Spanish rice mix
1 egg
¼ cup chopped onions
4 medium-sized green bell peppers,
    halved lengthwise, cored, and seeded
28-oz. can tomatoes
10¾-oz. can tomato soup
1 cup water
shredded cheese, optional

1. Combine beef, rice mix (reserving seasoning packet), egg, and onions. Divide meat mixture among pepper halves.
2. Pour tomatoes into slow cooker. Arrange pepper halves over tomatoes.
3. Combine tomato soup, rice-mix seasoning packet, and water. Pour over peppers.
4. Cover. Cook on low 8-10 hours.
5. Twenty minutes before the end of the cooking time, top stuffed peppers with cheese.

Haystacks

Judy Buller
Bluffton, OH

Makes 10-12 servings

2 lbs. ground beef, browned
1 small onion, chopped
2 8-oz. cans tomato sauce
2 15-oz. cans chili beans with chili gravy,
    or red beans

2 10-oz. cans mild enchilada sauce,
    or mild salsa
½ tsp. chili powder
1 tsp. garlic salt
pepper to taste

Condiments:
raisins
chopped apples
shredded lettuce
chopped tomatoes
shredded cheese
corn chips
rice or baked potatoes

1. Combine beef, onion, tomato sauce, chili beans, enchilada sauce, chili powder, garlic salt, and pepper. Pour into slow cooker.
2. Cover. Bake on low 2-3 hours or high 1 hour.
3. Serve over baked potatoes or rice and add condiment of your choice on top.

Because this recipe offers such a wide choice of toppings, all diners are sure to find something they like. Haystacks are easy to serve buffet-style. The wide array of condiments sparks conversation— and becomes an adventure in eating. Members of my family like a little of each topping over the chili. Guests are often surprised to see how large their haystacks are when they're finished serving themselves. They frequently fill their entire plates! The atmosphere can be comfortable when everything is prepared ahead. And with this recipe, the serving time can vary.

Do the rice or baked potatoes in a second slow cooker.

Menu Idea

Haystacks
Rice or Baked Potatoes
Cut-Up Fresh Fruit
Light Dessert

Mexican Goulash

Sheila Plock
Boalsburg, PA

Makes 8-10 servings

1½-2 lbs. ground beef
2 onions, chopped
1 green pepper, chopped
½ cup celery, chopped
1 garlic clove, minced
28-oz. can whole tomatoes, cut up
6-oz. can tomato paste
4.25-oz. can sliced black olives, drained
14½-oz. can green beans, drained
15.25-oz. can Mexicorn, drained
15-oz. can dark red kidney beans
diced jalapeno peppers to taste
1 tsp. salt
¼ tsp. pepper
1 Tbsp. chili powder
3 dashes Tabasco sauce
grated cheddar cheese

1. Brown ground beef. Reserve drippings and transfer beef to slow cooker.
2. Saute onions, pepper, celery, and garlic in drippings in skillet. Transfer to slow cooker.
3. Add remaining ingredients. Mix well.
4. Cover. Cook on high 3-4 hours.
5. Sprinkle individual servings with grated cheese. Serve with tortilla chips.

Tortilla Bake

Kelly Evenson
Pittsboro, NC

Makes 6-8 servings

10¾-oz. can cheddar cheese soup
1½-oz. pkg. dry taco seasoning mix
8 corn tortillas
1½ lbs. ground beef, browned and drained
3 medium tomatoes, coarsely chopped
toppings: sour cream, grated cheese, thinly
    sliced green onions, cut-up bell peppers,
    diced avocado, shredded lettuce

1. Combine soup and taco seasoning.
2. Cut each tortilla into 6 wedges. Spoon one-quarter of ground beef into slow cooker. Top with one-quarter of all tortilla wedges. Spoon one-quarter of soup mixture on tortillas. Top with one-quarter of tomatoes. Repeat layers 3 times.
3. Cover. Cook on low 6-8 hours.
4. To serve, spoon onto plates and offer toppings as condiments.

Menu Idea

Tortilla Bake
Yellow Rice
Tortilla Chips and Salsa
Sherbet

Three-Bean Burrito Bake

Darla Sathre
Baxter, MN

Makes 6 servings

1 Tbsp. oil
1 onion, chopped
1 green bell pepper, chopped
2 garlic cloves, minced
16-oz. can pinto beans, drained
16-oz. can kidney beans, drained
15-oz. can black beans, drained
4-oz. can sliced black olives, drained
4-oz. can green chilies
2 15-oz. cans diced tomatoes
1 tsp. chili powder
1 tsp. ground cumin
6-8 6" flour tortillas
2 cups shredded Co-Jack cheese
sour cream

1. Saute onions, green peppers, and garlic in large skillet in oil.
2. Add beans, olives, chilies, tomatoes, chili powder, and cumin.
3. In greased slow cooker, layer ¾ cup vegetables, a tortilla, ⅓ cup cheese. Repeat layers until all those ingredients are used, ending with sauce.
4. Cover. Cook on low 8-10 hours.
5. Serve with dollops of sour cream on individual servings.

Taco Casserole

Marcia S. Myer
Manheim, PA

Makes 6 servings

1½ lbs. ground beef, browned
14½-oz. can diced tomatoes with chilies
10¾-oz. can cream of onion soup
1 pkg. dry taco seasoning mix
¼ cup water
6 corn tortillas cut in ½" strips
½ cup sour cream
1 cup shredded cheddar cheese
2 green onions, sliced, optional

1. Combine beef, tomatoes, soup, seasoning mix, and water in slow cooker.
2. Stir in tortilla strips.
3. Cover. Cook on low 7-8 hours.
4. Spread sour cream over casserole. Sprinkle with cheese.
5. Cover. Let stand 5 minutes until cheese melts.
6. Remove cover. Garnish with green onions. Allow to stand for 15 more minutes before serving.

Casserole Verde

Julia Fisher
New Carlisle, OH

Makes 6 servings

1 lb. ground beef
1 small onion, chopped
1/8 tsp. garlic powder
8-oz. can tomato sauce
1/3 cup chopped black olives
4-oz. can sliced mushrooms
8-oz. container sour cream
8-oz. container cottage cheese
4.25-oz. can chopped green chilies
12-oz. pkg. tortilla chips
8 ozs. Monterey Jack cheese, grated

1. Brown ground beef, onions, and garlic in skillet. Drain. Add tomato sauce, olives, and mushrooms.
2. In a separate bowl, combine sour cream, cottage cheese, and green chilies.
3. In slow cooker, layer a third of the chips, and half the ground beef mixture, half the sour cream mixture, and half the shredded cheese. Repeat all layers, except reserve last third of the chips to add just before serving.
4. Cover. Cook on low 4 hours.
5. Ten minutes before serving time, scatter reserved chips over top and continue cooking, uncovered.

Tiajuana Tacos

Helen Kenagy
Carlsbad, NM

Makes 6 servings

3 cups cooked chopped beef
1-lb. can refried beans
1/2 cup chopped onions
1/2 cup chopped green peppers
1/2 cup chopped ripe olives
8-oz. can tomato sauce
3 tsp. chili powder
1 Tbsp. Worcestershire sauce
1/2 tsp. garlic powder
1/4 tsp. pepper
1/4 tsp. paprika
1/8 tsp. celery salt
1/8 tsp. ground nutmeg
3/4 cup water
1 tsp. salt
1 cup crushed corn chips
6 taco shells
shredded lettuce
chopped tomatoes
grated cheddar cheese

1. Combine first 15 ingredients in slow cooker.
2. Cover. Cook on high 2 hours.
3. Just before serving, fold in corn chips.
4. Spoon mixture into taco shells. Top with lettuce, tomatoes, and cheese.

Pork
Main Dishes

Barbecued Ribs

Virginia Bender
Dover, DE

Makes 6 servings

4 lbs. pork ribs
1/2 cup brown sugar
12-oz. jar chili sauce
1/4 cup balsamic vinegar
2 Tbsp. Worcestershire sauce
2 Tbsp. Dijon mustard
1 tsp. hot sauce

1. Place ribs in slow cooker.
2. Combine remaining ingredients. Pour half of sauce over ribs.
3. Cover. Cook on low 8-10 hours.
4. Serve with remaining sauce.

Sweet and Sour Ribs

Cassandra Ly
Carlisle, PA

Makes 8-10 servings

3-4 lbs. boneless country-style pork ribs
20-oz. can pineapple tidbits
2 8-oz. cans tomato sauce
1/2 cup thinly sliced onions
1/2 cup thinly sliced green peppers
1/2 cup packed brown sugar
1/4 cup cider vinegar
1/4 cup tomato paste
2 Tbsp. Worcestershire sauce
1 garlic clove, minced
1 tsp. salt
1/2 tsp. pepper

1. Place ribs in slow cooker.
2. Combine remaining ingredients. Pour over ribs.
3. Cover. Cook on low 8-10 hours.
4. Serve over rice.

Country-Style Ribs and Sauerkraut

Rhonda Burgoon
Collingswood, NJ

Makes 4-6 servings

16-oz. bag sauerkraut, rinsed and drained
1 onion, diced
1 red-skinned apple, chopped
2-3 lbs. country-style pork ribs
1 cup beer

1. Combine sauerkraut, onion, and apple in bottom of slow cooker.
2. Layer ribs over sauerkraut.
3. Pour beer over ribs just before turning on cooker.
4. Cover. Cook on low 8-10 hours.
5. Serve with homemade cornbread and mashed potatoes, or serve deboned on a kaiser roll as a sandwich.

1-2-3 Barbecued Country Ribs

Barbara Walker
Sturgis, SD

Makes 4 servings

4 lbs. spareribs, or 3 lbs. country-style
   ribs, cut in serving-size pieces
18-oz. bottle prepared barbecue sauce

1. Pour a little sauce into bottom of slow cooker. Put in a layer of ribs, meaty side up. Cover with barbecue sauce.

2. Continue layering until all ribs are in the pot. Submerge them as much as possible in the sauce.
3. Cover. Cook on low 8-10 hours.

Note: No need to precook the ribs if they're lean. If they're fattier than you like, parboil in water in stockpot before placing in cooker, to cook off some of the grease.

Tender 'N Tangy Ribs

Sherri Grindle
Goshen, IN

Makes 2-3 servings

3/4-1 cup vinegar
1/2 cup ketchup
2 Tbsp. sugar
2 Tbsp. Worcestershire sauce
1 clove garlic, minced
1 tsp. ground mustard
1 tsp. paprika
1/2-1 tsp. salt
1/8 tsp. pepper
2 lbs. pork spareribs or country-style ribs
1 Tbsp. oil

1. Combine first nine ingredients in slow cooker.
2. Cut ribs into serving-size pieces. Brown in oil in skillet. Transfer to slow cooker.
3. Cover. Cook on low 4-6 hours.
4. Serve with baked potatoes and rice.

I often use this recipe if I am having company for Sunday lunch.

Barbara Jean's Whole Pork Tenderloin

Barbara Jean Fabel
Wausau, WI

Makes 6-8 servings

1/2 cup sliced celery
1/4 lb. fresh mushrooms, quartered
1 medium onion, sliced
1/4 cup melted butter
2 1 1/4-lb. pork tenderloins
1 Tbsp. butter
2 tsp. salt
1/4 tsp. pepper
1 Tbsp. butter
1/2 cup beef broth
1 Tbsp. flour

1. Placed celery, mushrooms, onion, and 1/4 cup melted butter in slow cooker.
2. Brown tenderloins in skillet in 1 Tbsp. butter. Layer over vegetables in slow cooker.
3. Sprinkle with salt and pepper.
4. Combine bouillon and flour until smooth. Pour over tenderloins.
5. Cover. Cook on high 3 hours or low 4-5 hours.

Autumn Harvest Pork Loin

Stacy Schmucker Stoltzfus
Enola, PA

Makes 4-6 servings

1 cup cider or apple juice
1 1/2-2-lb. pork loin
salt
pepper
2 large Granny Smith apples, peeled and sliced
1 1/2 whole butternut squashes, peeled and cubed
1/2 cup brown sugar
1/4 tsp. cinnamon
1/4 tsp. dried thyme
1/4 tsp. dried sage

1. Heat cider in hot skillet. Sear pork loin on all sides in cider.
2. Sprinkle meat with salt and pepper on all sides. Place in slow cooker, along with juices.
3. Combine apples and squash. Sprinkle with sugar and herbs. Stir. Place around pork loin.
4. Cover. Cook on low 5-6 hours.
5. Remove pork from cooker. Let stand 10-15 minutes. Slice into 1/2"-thick slices.
6. Serve topped with apples and squash.

Pork Roast

Lucille Amos
Greensboro, NC

Makes 6-8 servings

1 Boston butt roast
1 cup Worcestershire sauce
1 cup brown sugar

1. Place roast in greased slow cooker.
2. Pour Worcestershire sauce over roast.
3. Pat brown sugar on roast.
4. Cover. Cook on high 1 hour. Reduce heat to low for 8-10 hours.
5. Slice and serve topped with broth and drippings from cooker.

Pork Roast with Sauerkraut

Betty K. Drescher
Quakertown, PA

Makes 8-10 servings

3-4-lb. pork roast
32-oz. bag sauerkraut
2 apples, peeled and sliced
1 medium onion, sliced thin
14½-oz. can Italian tomatoes, drained and smashed

1. Place roast in slow cooker.
2. Add sauerkraut.
3. Layer apples and onion over roast.
4. Top with tomatoes.
5. Cover. Cook on low 7-9 hours, or until meat is tender.

Variation: If you like a brothy dish, add 1 cup water along with sauerkraut in Step 2.

No Fuss Sauerkraut

Vera M. Kuhns
Harrisonburg, VA

Makes 12 servings

3-lb. pork roast
3 2-lb. pkgs. sauerkraut (drain off juice from 1 pkg.)
2 apples, peeled and sliced
½ cup brown sugar
1 cup apple juice

1. Place meat in large slow cooker.
2. Place sauerkraut on top of meat.
3. Add apples and brown sugar. Add juice.
4. Cover. Cook on high 4-5 hours.
5. Serve with mashed potatoes.

Note: If your slow cooker isn't large enough to hold all the ingredients, cook one package of sauerkraut and half the apples, brown sugar, and apple juice in another cooker. Mix the ingredients of both cookers together before serving.

Flautas with Pork Filling

Donna Lantgen
Rapid City, SD

Makes 6-8 servings

1 lb. pork roast or chops, cubed
¼ cup chopped onions
4-oz. can diced green chilies
7-oz. can green chile salsa or chile salsa
1 tsp. cocoa powder
16-oz. can chili

1. Brown cubed pork in skillet. Drain. Place in slow cooker.
2. Add remaining ingredients except chili.
3. Cover. Cook on low 2-3 hours.
4. Add chili. Cook 2-3 hours longer.
5. Serve on flour tortillas with guacamole dip.

Note: This is especially good on spinach-herb tortillas.

Pork Chops

Linda Sluiter
Schererville, IN

Makes 4 servings

4 boneless pork chops, 1″ thick
½ tsp. dry mustard
¼ cup flour
½ tsp. sugar
1 tsp. vinegar
½ cup water
½ cup ketchup
½ tsp. salt

1. Place pork chops in slow cooker.
2. Combine remaining ingredients and pour over pork chops.
3. Cover. Cook on high 2-3 hours, and then low 3-4 hours, or cook on low 8 hours.

Pork Chops Hong Kong

Marjorie Y. Guengerich
Harrisonburg, VA

Makes 6-8 servings

10-oz. bottle soy sauce
6-8 Tbsp. sugar
6-8 pork chops
10¾-oz. can cream of mushroom soup

1. Combine soy sauce and sugar. Pour over pork chops. Marinate for 60 minutes.
2. Transfer pork chops to slow cooker.
3. Add soup.
4. Cover. Cook on low 6 hours or high 3 hours.

Barbecued Pork Chops

LaVerne A. Olson
Lititz, PA

Makes 6-8 servings

6-8 pork chops, lightly browned in skillet
1/2 cup ketchup
1 tsp. salt
1 tsp. celery seed
1/2 tsp. ground nutmeg
1/3 cup vinegar
1/2 cup water
1 bay leaf

1. Place pork chops in slow cooker.
2. Combine remaining ingredients. Pour over chops.
3. Cover. Cook on low 2-3 hours, or until chops are tender.
4. Remove bay leaf before serving.

Pork Chop Casserole

Nancy Wagner Graves
Manhattan, KS

Makes 4-6 servings

6-8 pork chops
salt to taste
pepper to taste
oil
2 medium potatoes, peeled and sliced
1 large onion, sliced
1 large green pepper, sliced
1/2 tsp. dried oregano
16-oz. can tomatoes

1. Season pork chops with salt and pepper. Brown in oil in skillet. Transfer to slow cooker.
2. Add remaining ingredients in order listed.
3. Cover. Cook on low 8-10 hours or on high 3-4 hours.

Pork Chop
Slow Cooker Casserole

Janice Crist
Quinter, KS

Makes 5 servings

5 pork chops
4-5 medium potatoes, quartered or sliced
10¾-oz. can cream of chicken soup
10¾-oz. can cream of celery soup
15-oz. can green beans, drained

1. Layer ingredients in slow cooker in order listed.
2. Cover. Cook on low 5-6 hours or on high 4 hours.

Pork Chops with Vegetables

LaVerne A. Olson
Lititz, PA

Makes 6 servings

6 boneless pork chops
2 Tbsp. butter or margarine
1 1/2 cups sliced mushrooms
1 tsp. crushed rosemary
10 3/4-oz. can cream of mushroom soup
2 Tbsp. water
1/2-1 lb. green beans, cut in 2" pieces

1. Brown pork chops in skillet in 1 Tbsp. butter. Transfer to slow cooker.
2. Cook mushrooms and rosemary in 1 Tbsp. butter until just wilted. Add to chops.
3. Combine soup, rosemary, mushrooms, water, and beans. Pour over chops.
4. Cover. Cook on low 6-8 hours or on high 4 hours.
5. Serve over hot noodles.

Pork Chops on Rice

Hannah D. Burkholder
Bridgewater, VA

Makes 4 servings

1/2 cup brown rice
2/3 cup converted white rice
1/4 cup butter or margarine
1/2 cup chopped onions
4-oz. can sliced mushrooms, drained
1/2 tsp. dried thyme
1/2 tsp. sage
1/2 tsp. salt
1/4 tsp. black pepper
4 boneless pork chops, 3/4"-1" thick
10 1/2-oz. can beef consomme
2 Tbsp. Worcestershire sauce
1/2 tsp. dried thyme
1/2 tsp. paprika
1/4 tsp. ground nutmeg

1. Saute white and brown rice in butter in skillet until rice is golden brown.
2. Remove from heat and stir in onions, mushrooms, thyme, sage, salt, and pepper. Pour into greased slow cooker.
3. Arrange chops over rice.
4. Combine consomme and Worcestershire sauce. Pour over chops.
5. Combine thyme, paprika, and nutmeg. Sprinkle over chops.
6. Cover. Cook on low 7-9 hours or on high 4-5 hours.

Baked Beans and Chops

John D. Allen
Rye, CO

Makes 6 servings

2 16½-oz. cans baked beans
6 rib pork chops, ½" thick
1½ tsp. prepared mustard
1½ Tbsp. brown sugar
1½ Tbsp. ketchup
6 onion slices, ¼" thick

1. Pour baked beans into bottom of greased slow cooker.
2. Layer pork chops over beans.
3. Spread mustard over pork chops. Sprinkle with brown sugar and drizzle with ketchup.
4. Top with onion slices.
5. Cover. Cook on high 4-6 hours.

Oxford Canal Chops Deluxe

Willard E. Roth
Elkhart, IN

Makes 6 servings

6 6-oz. boneless pork chops
¼ cup flour
1 tsp. powdered garlic
1 tsp. sea salt
1 tsp. black pepper
1 tsp. dried basil and/or dried oregano
2 Tbsp. oil
2 medium onions, sliced
1 cup burgundy wine
14½-oz. can beef broth
1 soup can water
6-oz. can tomato sauce
8 ozs. dried apricots
½ lb. fresh mushroom caps

1. Shake chops in bag with flour and seasonings.
2. Glaze onions in oil in medium hot skillet. Add chops and brown.
3. Pour extra flour over chops in skillet. In large bowl mix together wine, broth, water, and tomato sauce, then pour over meat. Bring to boil.
4. Remove chops from skillet and place in cooker. Layer in apricots and mushrooms. Pour broth over top.
5. Cover. Cook on high 4 hours or low 6 hours.
6. Serve with the Celtic speciality Bubble and Squeak—Irish potatoes mashed with green cabbage or brussels sprouts.

This was a hit when prepared in the tiny kitchen of a houseboat on the Oxford Canal and then shared by six friends.

Fruited Pork Chops

Jean Butzer
Batavia, NY

Makes 4 servings

4 pork chops
½ tsp. salt
dash of pepper
1 Tbsp. prepared mustard
2 Tbsp. wine vinegar
⅛ tsp. dried dill weed
17-oz. can fruit cocktail
2 Tbsp. cornstarch
2 Tbsp. water

1. Sprinkle chops with salt and pepper. Place in slow cooker.
2. Combine mustard, vinegar, and dill.
3. Drain fruit cocktail, reserving ½ cup syrup. Add ½ cup syrup to mustard mixture. Pour over chops.
4. Cover. Cook on low 4-6 hours, or until meat is tender.
5. Remove chops. Turn to high.
6. Dissolve cornstarch in water. Stir into slow cooker. Add fruit cocktail.
7. Cover. Cook on high 10-15 minutes. Spoon fruit sauce over chops.

Cherry Pork Chops

Jo Haberkamp
Fairbank, IA

Makes 6 servings

6 pork chops, each cut ¾" thick
1 Tbsp. oil
salt
pepper
1 cup cherry pie filling
2 tsp. lemon juice
½ tsp. instant chicken bouillon granules
⅛ tsp. ground mace

1. Brown pork chops in oil in skillet. Sprinkle each chop with salt and pepper.
2. Combine remaining ingredients in slow cooker. Mix well.
3. Place browned pork chops on top of cherry mixture.
4. Cover. Cook on low 4-5 hours.
5. Place chops on platter. Spoon some of the cherry sauce on top. Pass remaining sauce and serve with rice or baked potatoes.

Pork Chops in Orange Sauce

Kelly Evenson
Pittsboro, NC

Makes 4 servings

4 thick, center-cut pork chops
salt to taste
pepper to taste
1 Tbsp. oil
1 orange
1/4 cup ketchup
3/4 cup orange juice
1 Tbsp. orange marmalade
1 Tbsp. cornstarch
1/4 cup water

1. Season pork chops on both sides with salt and pepper.
2. Brown chops lightly on both sides in skillet in oil. Transfer to slow cooker. Reserve 2 Tbsp. drippings and discard the rest.
3. Grate 1/2 tsp. orange zest from top or bottom of orange. Combine zest with ketchup, orange juice, and marmalade. Pour into skillet. Simmer 1 minute, stirring constantly. Pour over chops.
4. Cover. Cook on low 5-6 hours. Remove chops and keep warm.
5. Dissolve cornstarch in water. Stir into slow cooker until smooth. Cook on high 15 minutes, or until thickened.
6. Serve with orange sauce on top, along with slices of fresh orange.
7. Serve over noodles or rice with a green salad.

Apples, Sauerkraut, and Chops

Carol Sherwood
Batavia, NY

Makes 4 servings

4 pork chops, 1/2" thick, browned
1 onion, sliced and separated into rings
1/8 tsp. garlic flakes or powder
3 cups sauerkraut, drained
1 cup unpeeled apple slices
1 1/2 tsp. caraway seeds
1/4 tsp. salt
1/4 tsp. dried thyme
1/4 tsp. pepper
3/4 cup apple juice

1. Place half of onions, garlic flakes, sauerkraut, apple slices, and caraway seeds in slow cooker. Season with half the salt, thyme, and pepper.
2. Add pork chops.
3. Layer remaining ingredients in order given.
4. Pour apple juice over all.
5. Cover. Cook on low 6-8 hours or high 4 hours.

Pork Chops with Stuffing

Erma Kauffman
Cochranville, PA

Makes 2 servings

4 slices bread, cubed
1 egg
¼ cup grated, or finely chopped, celery
¼-½ tsp. salt
⅛ tsp. pepper
2 thickly cut pork chops
1 cup water

1. Combine bread cubes, eggs, celery, salt, and pepper.
2. Cut pork chops part way through, creating a pocket. Fill with stuffing.
3. Pour water into slow cooker. Add chops.
4. Cover. Cook on low 4-5 hours.

Pork Chops and Stuffing with Curry

Mary Martins
Fairbank, IA

Makes 3-4 servings

1 box stuffing mix
1 cup water
10¾-oz. can cream of mushroom soup
1 tsp., or more, curry powder,
   according to your taste preference
3-4 pork chops

1. Combine stuffing mix and water. Place half in bottom of slow cooker.

2. Combine soup and curry powder. Pour half over stuffing. Place pork chops on top.
3. Spread remaining stuffing over pork chops. Pour rest of soup on top.
4. Cover. Cook on low 6-7 hours.
5. Serve with a tossed salad and a cooked vegetable.

Autumn Pork Chops

Leesa Lesenski
Whately, MA

Makes 4-6 servings

4-6 boneless pork chops
2 cups apple juice
½ tsp. ground cinnamon

1. Place pork chops in slow cooker.
2. Cover with apple juice.
3. Sprinkle with cinnamon.
4. Cover. Cook on low 10 hours.

Menu Idea

Autumn Pork Chops
Rice or Potatoes
Applesauce

Italian Sausage

Lauren Eberhard
Seneca, IL

Makes 15 servings

5 lbs. Italian sausage in casing
4 large green peppers, sliced
3 large onions, sliced
1 or 2 garlic cloves, minced
28-oz. can tomato puree
14-oz. can tomato sauce
12-oz. can tomato paste
1 Tbsp. dried oregano
1 Tbsp. dried basil
½ tsp. garlic powder
1½ tsp. salt
2 tsp. sugar

1. Cut sausage into 4" or 5" pieces and brown on all sides in batches in skillet.

2. Saute peppers, onions, and garlic in drippings.

3. Combine tomato puree, sauce, and paste in bowl. Add seasonings and sugar.

4. Layer half of sausage, onions, and peppers in 6-qt. slow cooker, or in 2 4-qt. cookers. Cover with half the tomato mixture. Repeat layers.

5. Cover. Cook on high 1 hour and low 5-6 hours.

6. Serve over pasta, or dip mixture with a straining spoon onto Italian sandwich rolls.

Dawn's Sausage and Peppers

Dawn Day
Westminster, CA

Makes 8-10 servings

3 medium onions, sliced
1 sweet red pepper, sliced
1 sweet green pepper, sliced
1 sweet yellow pepper, sliced
4 garlic cloves, minced
1 Tbsp. oil
28 oz.-can chopped tomatoes
1 tsp. salt
½ tsp. red crushed pepper
2-3 lbs. sweet Italian sausage,
    cut into 3" pieces

1. Saute onions, peppers, and garlic in oil in skillet. When just softened, place in slow cooker.

2. Add tomatoes, salt, and crushed red pepper. Mix well.

3. Add sausage links.

4. Cover. Cook on low 6 hours.

5. Serve on rolls, or over pasta or baked potatoes.

Variation: For a thicker sauce, stir in 3 Tbsp. ClearJell during the last 15 minutes of the cooking time.

Savory Sausage Sandwiches

Mary Jane Musser
Manheim, PA

Makes 8 servings

2 lbs. fresh sausage, cut into bun-length
  pieces
2 pkgs. dry spaghetti sauce mix
12-oz. can tomato paste
3 cups water
½ cup brown sugar
¼ cup vinegar
8 Italian or hot dog rolls
grated cheese

1. Cook sausage in skillet in water for 10
minutes. Drain. Place in slow cooker.
2. Combine remaining ingredients. Simmer
5 minutes in saucepan. Pour over sausage.
3. Cover. Cook on high 3 hours or low 6
hours.
4. Serve in rolls topped with grated cheese.

*Variation: Use 1 qt. spaghetti sauce, either
homemade or bought, instead of sauce mix,
tomato paste, and water.*

Sausage and Sauerkraut

Eileen Lehman
Kidron, OH

Makes 12 servings

2-3 lbs. fresh sausage, cut in 3"-lengths, or
  removed from casings
3 32-oz. cans sauerkraut

1. Brown sausage in skillet.
2. Combine sausage and sauerkraut in slow
cooker.
3. Cover. Cook on low 4-8 hours.
4. Serve with mashed potatoes, a jello salad,
and pumpkin pie.

*It is traditional to serve sauerkraut on New
Year's Day in Kidron.*

Brats and Spuds

Kathi Rogge
Alexandria, IN

Makes 6 servings

5-6 bratwurst links, cut into 1" pieces
5 medium-sized potatoes, peeled and
  cubed
27-oz. can sauerkraut, rinsed and drained
1 medium tart apple, chopped
1 small onion, chopped
¼ cup packed brown sugar
½ tsp. salt

1. Brown bratwurst on all sides in skillet.
2. Combine remaining ingredients in slow
cooker. Stir in bratwurst and pan drippings.
3. Cover. Cook on high 4-6 hours, or until
potatoes and apples are tender.

*Variation: Add a small amount of caraway seeds
or crisp bacon pieces, just before serving.*

Sausage-Potato Slow Cooker Dinner

Deborah Swartz
Grottoes, VA

Makes 6-8 servings

1 cup water
1/2 tsp. cream of tartar
6 medium potatoes, thinly sliced
3/4 lb. sausage, casings removed and browned
1 onion, chopped
1/4 cup flour
salt to taste
pepper to taste
1 1/2 cups grated cheddar cheese, divided
2 Tbsp. butter or margarine
10 3/4-oz. can cream of mushroom soup

1. Combine water and cream of tartar. Toss sliced potatoes in water. Drain.

2. Layer potatoes, sausage, onion, flour, a sprinkling of salt and pepper, and half of cheddar cheese in slow cooker. Repeat layers until ingredients are used.

3. Dot butter over top. Pour soup over all.

4. Cover. Cook on low 7-9 hours or on high 3-4 hours.

5. Sprinkle reserved cheese over top just before serving.

Sausage and Scalloped Potatoes

Carolyn Baer
Conrath, WI

Makes 5 servings

2 1/2 lbs. potatoes, sliced 1/4" thick
1 lb. fully cooked smoked sausage links, sliced 1/2" thick
2 medium onions, chopped
10 3/4-oz. can cheddar cheese soup
10 3/4-oz. can cream of celery soup

1. Layer one-third of potatoes, one-third of sausage, one-third of onions, one-third of cheddar cheese soup, and one-third of celery soup into slow cooker. Repeat 2 times.

2. Cover. Cook on low 10 hours or high 5 hours.

I like to prepare this delicious dish when I will be gone for the day, but know I will have guests for the evening meal. When I get home, the meat and potatoes are already cooked. I simply have to heat the peas, fix a salad, and slice the dessert.

Sausage and Sweet Potatoes

Ruth Hershey
Paradise, PA

Makes 4-6 servings

1 lb. bulk sausage, browned in skillet
2 sweet potatoes, peeled and sliced
3 apples, peeled and sliced
2 Tbsp. brown sugar
1 Tbsp. flour
1/4 tsp. ground cinnamon
1/4 tsp. salt
1/4 cup water

1. Layer sausage, sweet potatoes, and apples in slow cooker.
2. Combine remaining ingredients and pour over ingredients in slow cooker.
3. Cover. Cook on low 8-10 hours or high 4 hours.

Golden Autumn Stew

Naomi E. Fast
Hesston, KS

Makes 8-10 servings

2 cups cubed Yukon gold potatoes
2 cups cubed, peeled sweet potatoes
2 cups cubed, peeled butternut squash
1 cup cubed, peeled rutabaga
1 cup diced carrots
1 cup sliced celery
1 lb. smoked sausage
2 cups apple juice or cider
1 tart apple, thinly sliced
salt to taste
pepper to taste
1 Tbsp. sugar or honey

1. Combine vegetables in slow cooker.
2. Place ring of sausage on top.
3. Add apple juice and apple slices.
4. Cover. Cook on high 2 hours and on low 4 hours, or until vegetables are tender. Do not stir.
5. To serve, remove sausage ring. Season with salt, pepper, and sugar as desired. Place vegetables in bowl. Slice meat into rings and place on top.
6. Serve with hot baking-powder biscuits and honey, and a green salad or cole slaw.

Don't omit the rutabaga! Get acquainted with its rich uniqueness. It will surprise and please your taste buds.

Harvest Kielbasa

Christ Kaczynski
Schenectady, NY

Makes 6 servings

2 lbs. smoked kielbasa
3 cups unsweetened applesauce
1/2 cup brown sugar
3 medium onions, sliced

1. Slice kielbasa into 1/4" slices. Brown in skillet. Drain.
2. Combine applesauce and brown sugar.
3. Layer kielbasa, onions, and applesauce mixture in slow cooker.
4. Cover. Cook on low 4-8 hours.

The longer it cooks, the better the flavor.

Keilbasa Stew

Fannie Miller
Hutchinson, KS

Makes 6-8 servings

6 strips of bacon
1 onion, chopped
1-1½ lbs. smoked, fully cooked kielbasa, thinly sliced
2 15½-oz. cans Great Northern beans
2 8-oz. cans tomato sauce
4-oz. can chopped green chilies
2 medium carrots, thinly sliced
1 medium green pepper, chopped
½ tsp. Italian seasoning
½ tsp. dried thyme
½ tsp. black pepper

1. Fry bacon in skillet until crisp. Crumble bacon and place in large slow cooker. Add onions and sausage to drippings in skillet. Cook until onions are soft.
2. Transfer onions and sausage to slow cooker.
3. Add all remaining ingredients to cooker and stir together well.
4. Cover. Cook on low 8-10 hours, or until vegetables are tender.

Rice and Beans— and Sausage

Marcia S. Myer
Manheim, PA

Makes 8 servings

3 celery ribs, chopped
1 onion, chopped
2 garlic cloves, minced
1¾ cups tomato juice
2 16-oz. cans kidney beans, drained
¾ tsp. dried oregano
¾ tsp. dried thyme
¼ tsp. red pepper flakes
¼ tsp. pepper
½ lb. (or more) fully cooked smoked turkey sausage, or kielbasa, cut into ¼" slices
4 cups cooked rice
shredded cheese, optional

1. Combine all ingredients except rice and shredded cheese in slow cooker.
2. Cover. Cook on low 4-6 hours.
3. Serve over rice. Garnish with shredded cheese, if you wish.

Hosting Idea

My mother always had a small centerpiece, usually flowers, on the table. I learned how important that is.

Two other tips from Mother. If you don't have a lot of food, serve it in a pretty dish. If all you have for tea is peanut butter sandwiches, cut them in fancy geometric shapes.

—Sharon Miller

Election Lunch

Alix Nancy Botsford
Seminole, OK

Makes 6-12 servings

2-3 Tbsp. olive oil
1 large onion, chopped
1 lb. sausage, cut into thin slices, or
    casings removed and crumbled
1 rib celery, sliced
1 Tbsp. Worcestershire sauce
1½ tsp. dry mustard
¼ cup honey
10-oz. can tomatoes with green chili
    peppers
1-lb. can lima or butter beans, drained,
    with liquid reserved
1-lb. can red kidney beans, drained, with
    liquid reserved
1-lb. can garbanzo beans, drained, with
    liquid reserved

   1. Brown onion and sausage in oil.
   2. Combine ingredients in 6-qt. slow cooker, or divide between 2 4-qt. cookers and stir to combine. Add reserved juice from lima, kidney, and garbanzo beans if there's enough room in the cookers.
   3. Cover. Cook on low 2-4 hours.

I mixed up this hearty stew the night before Election Day and took it to the voting site the next morning. I plugged it in, and all day long we could smell the stew cooking. I work at a very sparsely populated, country poling place and ended up giving out the recipe and little water-cup samples to many voters!

I have four different sizes of slow cookers. One is very tiny, with only an on and off switch, for keeping cheese sauce hot. One I use for heating gravy. Another I often use to keep mashed potatoes warm.

Menu Idea

Election Lunch
Toast Fingers
(Toast all the slices in a loaf of
    whole-grain bread. Let cool.
    Butter and toast a second time.
    Cut twice-toasted bread into strips.)
Your Favorite Salad

Chili Casserole

Sharon Miller
Holmesville, OH

Makes 6 servings

1 lb. bulk pork sausage, browned
2 cups water
15½-oz. can chili beans
14½-oz. can diced tomatoes
¾ cup brown rice
¼ cup chopped onions
1 Tbsp. chili powder
1 tsp. Worcestershire sauce
1 tsp. prepared mustard
¾ tsp. salt
⅛ tsp. garlic powder
1 cup shredded cheddar cheese

   1. Combine all ingredients except cheese in slow cooker.
   2. Cover. Cook on low 7 hours.
   3. Stir in cheese during last 10 minutes of cooking time.

Sausage Pasta Stew
Betty K. Drescher
Quakertown, PA 18951

Makes 8 servings

1 lb. Italian sausage, casings removed
4 cups water
26-oz. jar meatless spaghetti sauce
16-oz. can kidney beans, rinsed and
    drained
1 medium yellow summer squash, cut in
    1" pieces
2 medium carrots, cut in 1/4" slices
1 medium red or green sweet pepper,
    diced
1/3 cup chopped onions
1 1/2 cups uncooked spiral pasta
1 cup frozen peas
1 tsp. sugar
1/2 tsp. salt
1/4 tsp. pepper

1. Saute sausage in skillet until no longer
pink. Drain and place in slow cooker.
2. Add water, spaghetti sauce, kidney beans,
squash, carrots, pepper, and onions. Mix well.
3. Cover. Cook on low 7-9 hours, or until
vegetables are tender.
4. Add remaining ingredients. Mix well.
5. Cover. Cook on high 15-20 minutes until
pasta is tender.

*Note: Add 1 Tbsp. tapioca in Step 5 if you like a
thicker stew.*

Pizza Rigatoni
Tina Snyder
Manheim, PA

Makes 6-8 servings

1 1/2 lbs. bulk sausage
3 cups rigatoni, lightly cooked
4 cups shredded mozzarella cheese
10 3/4-oz. can cream of mushroom soup
1 small onion, sliced
15-oz. can pizza sauce
8-oz. can pizza sauce
3 1/2-oz. pkg. sliced pepperoni
6-oz. can sliced ripe olives

1. Cook and drain sausage. Place half in
4-qt., or larger, slow cooker.
2. Layer half of pasta, cheese, soup, onion,
pizza sauce, pepperoni, and olives over
sausage. Repeat layers.
3. Cover. Cook on low 4 hours.

*Note: If your store doesn't carry 8-oz. cans pizza
sauce, substitute an 8-oz. can tomato sauce with
basil, garlic, and oregano.*

Crockpot Pizza

Sharon Miller
Holmesville, OH

Makes 6 servings

1½ lbs. bulk sausage
1 small onion, chopped
1-lb. pkg. pasta or noodles, uncooked
28-oz. jar spaghetti sauce
16-oz. can tomato sauce
¾ cup water
4-oz. can mushrooms, drained
16-oz. pkg. shredded mozzarella cheese
8-oz. pkg. pepperoni, chopped

1. Brown sausage and onion in skillet. Drain. Place one-third of mixture in cooker.
2. Layer in one-third of uncooked pasta.
3. Combine spaghetti sauce, tomato sauce, water, and mushrooms in bowl. Ladle one-third of that mixture over noodles.
4. Repeat the above layers 2 more times.
5. Top with pepperoni. Top that with shredded cheese.
6. Cover. Cook on low 6-8 hours.

Ham in Foil

Jeanette Oberholtzer
Manheim, PA
Vicki Dinkel
Sharon Springs, KS
Janet Roggie
Lowville, NY

Makes 8 servings

½ cup water
3-4-lb. precooked ham
liquid smoke

1. Pour water into slow cooker.
2. Sprinkle ham with liquid smoke. Wrap in foil. Place in slow cooker.
3. Cover. Cook on high 1 hour, then on low 6 hours.
4. Cut into thick chunks or ½" slices and serve.

Glazed Ham in a Bag

Eleanor J. Ferreira
North Chelmsford, MA

Makes 12 servings

5-lb. cooked ham
3 Tbsp. orange juice
1 Tbsp. Dijon mustard

1. Rinse meat. Place in cooking bag.
2. Combine orange juice and mustard. Spread over ham.
3. Seal bag with twist tie. Poke 4 holes in top of bag. Place in slow cooker.
4. Cover. Cook on low 6-8 hours.
5. To serve, remove ham from bag, reserving juices. Slice ham and spoon juices over. Serve additional juice alongside in small bowl.

Cheesy Potatoes and Ham

Beth Maurer
Harrisonburg, VA

Makes 4-6 servings

6 cups sliced, peeled potatoes
2½ cups cooked ham, cubed
1½ cups shredded cheddar cheese
10¾-oz. can cream of mushroom soup
½ cup milk

1. In slow cooker, layer one-third of potatoes, of ham, and of cheese. Repeat two more times.
2. Combine soup and milk. Pour over ingredients in slow cooker.
3. Cover. Cook on high 1 hour. Reduce to low for 6-8 hours, or just until potatoes are soft.

Ham, Bean, and Potato Dish

Hazel L. Propst
Oxford, PA

Makes 6-8 servings

8-10 small potatoes
3-4 cans string beans, undrained
ham hock or leftover ham
salt to taste
pepper to taste

1. Place potatoes in bottom of slow cooker.
2. Alternate layers of beans and ham over potatoes. Sprinkle with salt and pepper.
3. Cover. Cook on low 8 hours if using ham hock; 6 hours if using leftover ham.

Creamy Ham Topping (for baked potatoes)

Judy Buller
Bluffton, OH

Makes 6 servings

¼ cup butter or margarine
¼ cup flour
2 cups milk
¼ cup half-and-half
1 Tbsp. chopped parsley
1 Tbsp. chicken bouillon granules
½ tsp. Italian seasoning
2 cups diced cooked ham
¼ cup Romano cheese, grated
1 cup sliced mushrooms
baked potatoes
shredded cheese
sour cream

1. Melt butter in saucepan. Stir in flour. Add milk and half-and-half.
2. Stir in remaining ingredients (except baked potatoes, shredded cheese, and sour cream). Pour into slow cooker.
3. Cover. Cook on low 1-2 hours.
4. Serve over baked potatoes. Top with shredded cheese and sour cream.

Ham and Lima Beans

Charlotte Shaffer
East Earl, PA

Makes 6 servings

1 lb. dry lima beans
1 onion, chopped
1 bell pepper, chopped
1 tsp. dry mustard
1 tsp. salt
1 tsp. pepper
½ lb. ham, finely cubed
1 cup water
10¾-oz. can tomato soup

1. Cover beans with water. Soak 8 hours. Drain.
2. Combine ingredients in slow cooker.
3. Cover. Cook on low 7 hours or high 4 hours.
4. If mixture begins to dry out, add ½ cup water or more and stir well.
5. This is delicious served with hot cornbread.

Ham and Hash Browns

Evelyn Page
Riverton, WY
Anna Stoltzfus
Honey Brook, PA

Makes 6-8 servings

28-oz. pkg. frozen hash brown potatoes
2½ cups cubed cooked ham
2-oz. jar pimentos, drained and chopped
10¾-oz. can cheddar cheese soup
¾ cup half-and-half, or milk
dash of pepper
salt to taste

1. Combine potatoes, ham, and pimentos in slow cooker.
2. Combine soup, half-and-half, and seasonings. Pour over potatoes.
3. Cover. Cook on low 6-8 hours. (If you turn the cooker on when you go to bed, you'll have a wonderfully tasty breakfast in the morning.)

Variation: Add a 4-oz. can of mushrooms, drained, or ¼ lb. sliced fresh mushrooms, to Step 1.

Black Beans with Ham

Colleen Heatwole
Burton, MI

Makes 8-10 servings

4 cups dry black beans
1-2 cups diced ham
1 tsp. salt, optional
1 tsp. cumin
½-1 cup minced onion
2 garlic cloves, minced
3 bay leaves
1 qt. diced tomatoes
1 Tbsp. brown sugar

1. Cover black beans with water and soak for 8 hours, or over night. Drain and pour beans into slow cooker.
2. Add all remaining ingredients and stir well. Cover with water.
3. Cover cooker. Cook on low 10-12 hours.
4. Serve over rice.

This is our favorite black bean recipe. We make it frequently in the winter.

Ham 'n Cabbage Stew

Dede Peterson
Rapid City, SD

Makes 4-5 servings

1/2 lb. cooked ham, cubed
1/2 cup diced onions
1 garlic clove, minced
4-oz. can sliced mushrooms
4 cups shredded cabbage
2 cups sliced carrots
1/4 tsp. pepper
1/4 tsp. caraway seeds
2/3 cup beef broth
1 Tbsp. cornstarch
2 Tbsp. water

1. Combine all ingredients except cornstarch and water in slow cooker.
2. Cover. Cook on low 4-6 hours.
3. Mix cornstarch into water until smooth. Stir into slow cooker during last hour to thicken slightly.

Hosting Idea

Get your guests to help. Plan in advance where each dish of food should be placed on the serving table. Write the name of each food, including any special notations such as "sugar-free," "low-fat," etc., on a small piece of stiff paper that can be folded and stood, tent-fashion, where that food should be placed. Stand those signs in their positions on the serving table. Now anyone can help carry food to the table. When the dish is put in its spot, its sign should stand in front of it, so guests will know what they are choosing.

— Dolores Kratz

Ham and Corn Slow Cooker Casserole

Vicki Dinkel
Sharon Springs, KS

Makes 8 servings

1/2 cup butter or margarine
1 small green pepper, chopped
1 medium onion, chopped
1/2 cup flour
1/2 tsp. paprika
1/2 tsp. salt
1/2 tsp. pepper
1/4 tsp. dried thyme
1 tsp. dry mustard
4 cups milk
8-oz. can cream-style corn
2 cups diced, slightly cooked potatoes
4 cups diced cooked ham
1 cup shredded cheddar cheese

1. Saute green pepper and onion in butter in skillet.
2. Stir in flour and seasonings.
3. Gradually stir in milk and cook until thickened. Pour into slow cooker.
4. Stir in remaining ingredients.
5. Cover. Cook on low 8 hours or high 4 hours.

Cheesy Ham and Broccoli

Dolores Kratz
Souderton, PA

Makes 6 servings

1 bunch fresh broccoli
1½ cups chopped ham
¾ cup uncooked rice
4-oz. can mushrooms, drained
1 small onion, chopped
10¾-oz. can cheddar cheese soup
¾ cup water
¼ cup half-and-half, or milk
dash of pepper
½-1 can chow mein noodles

1. Cut broccoli into pieces and steam for 4 minutes in microwave. Place in slow cooker.
2. Add remaining ingredients except noodles. Mix well.
3. Sprinkle with noodles.
4. Cover. Cook on low 6-7 hours.
5. Serve with tossed salad or applesauce.

Broccoli Casserole

Rebecca Meyerkorth
Wamego, KS

Makes 4 servings

16-oz. pkg. frozen broccoli cuts, thawed and drained
2-3 cups cubed, cooked ham
10¾-oz. can cream of mushroom soup
4 ozs. of your favorite mild cheese, cubed
1 cup milk
1 cup instant rice, uncooked
1 rib celery, chopped
1 small onion, chopped

1. Combine broccoli and ham in slow cooker.
2. Combine soup, cheese, milk, rice, celery, and onion. Stir into broccoli.
3. Cover. Cook on low 4-5 hours.

Casserole in the Cooker

Ruth Ann Hoover
New Holland, PA

Makes 4 servings

16-oz. pkg. frozen broccoli, thawed and drained
3 cups cubed fully cooked ham
10¾-oz. can cream of mushroom soup
8-oz. jar processed cheese sauce
1 cup milk
1 cup instant rice
1 celery rib, chopped
1 small onion, chopped

1. Combine broccoli and ham in slow cooker.
2. Combine remaining ingredients. Stir into broccoli/ham mixture.
3. Cover. Cook on low 4-5 hours.

Ham and Broccoli

Dede Peterson
Rapid City, SD

Makes 6-8 servings

¾ lb. fresh broccoli, chopped,
   or 10-oz. pkg. frozen chopped broccoli
10¾-oz. can cream of mushroom soup
8-oz. jar processed cheese sauce
2½ cups milk
1¼ cups long-grain rice, uncooked
1 rib celery, sliced
⅛ tsp. pepper
3 cups cooked and cubed ham
8-oz. can water chestnuts, drained and
   sliced
½ tsp. paprika

1. Combine all ingredients except ham, water chestnuts, and paprika in slow cooker.
2. Cover. Cook on high 3-4 hours.
3. Stir in ham and water chestnuts. Cook 15-20 minutes, until heated through. Let stand 10 minutes before serving.
4. Sprinkle with paprika before serving.

Schnitz und Knepp

Jean Robinson
Cinnaminson, NJ

Makes 6 servings

Snitz:
1 qt. dried sweet apples
3 lbs. ham slices, cut into 2" cubes
2 Tbsp. brown sugar
1 cinnamon stick

Knepp (Dumplings):
2 cups flour
4 tsp. baking powder
1 egg, well beaten
3 Tbsp. melted butter
scant ½ cup milk
1 tsp. salt
¼ tsp. pepper

1. Cover apples with water in large bowl and let soak for a few hours.
2. Place ham in slow cooker. Cover with water.
3. Cover cooker. Cook on high 2 hours.
4. Add apples and water in which they have been soaking.
5. Add brown sugar and cinnamon stick. Mix until dissolved.
6. Cover. Cook on low 3 hours.
7. Combine dumpling ingredients in bowl. Drop into hot liquid in cooker by tablespoonfuls. Turn to high. Cover. Do not lift lid for 15 minutes.
8. Serve piping hot on a large platter. A celery-carrot jello salad rounds out the meal well.

This was my grandmother's recipe and she had no slow cooker. Schnitz und Knepp cooked on the back of the woodstove till the quilting was done. I was allowed to drop in the dumplings.

Ham with Sweet Potatoes and Oranges

Esther Becker
Gordonville, PA

Makes 4 servings

2-3 sweet potatoes, peeled and sliced
   1/4" thick
1 large ham slice
3 seedless oranges, peeled and sliced
3 Tbsp. orange juice concentrate
3 Tbsp. honey
1/2 cup brown sugar
2 Tbsp. cornstarch

1. Place sweet potatoes in slow cooker.
2. Arrange ham and orange slices on top.
3. Combine remaining ingredients. Drizzle over ham and oranges.
4. Cover. Cook on low 7-8 hours.
5. Delicious served with lime jello salad.

Southwest Hominy

Rcita F. Yoder
Carlsbad, NM

Makes 12-14 servings

4 20-oz. cans hominy, drained
10³/4-oz. can cream of mushroom soup
10³/4-oz. can cream of chicken soup
1 cup diced green chilies
1/2 lb. Velveeta cheese, cubed
1 lb. hot dogs or ham, diced

1. Combine all ingredients in slow cooker.
2. Cover. Cook on low 2-4 hours. Stir before serving.

Underground Ham and Cheese

Carol Sommers
Millersburg, OH

Makes 12-16 servings

4 cups cooked ham, cut into chunks
4 Tbsp. butter or margarine
1/2 cup chopped onions
1 Tbsp. Worcestershire sauce
2 10³/4-oz. cans cream of mushroom soup
1 cup milk
2 cups Velveeta cheese, cubed
4 qts. mashed potatoes
1 pt. sour cream
browned and crumbled bacon

1. Combine ham, butter, onions, and Worcestershire sauce in saucepan. Cook until onions are tender. Place in large slow cooker, or divide between 2 4- or 5-qt. cookers.
2. In saucepan, heat together soup, milk, and cheese until cheese melts. Pour into cooker(s).
3. Combine potatoes and sour cream. Spread over mixture in slow cooker(s).
4. Sprinkle with bacon.
5. Cover. Cook on low 3-4 hours, or until cheese mixture comes to top when done (hence, the name "underground").

Verenike Casserole

Jennifer Yoder Sommers
Harrisonburg, VA 22802

Makes 8-10 servings

24 ozs. cottage cheese
3 eggs
1 tsp. salt
1/2 tsp. pepper
1 cup sour cream
2 cups evaporated milk
2 cups cubed cooked ham
7-9 dry lasagna noodles

1. Combine all ingredients except noodles.
2. Place half of creamy ham mixture in bottom of cooker. Add uncooked noodles. Cover with remaining half of creamy ham sauce. Be sure noodles are fully submerged in sauce.
3. Cover. Cook on low 5-6 hours.
4. Serve with green salad, peas, and zwiebach or bread.

This is an easy way to make the traditional Russian Mennonite dish—verenike, or cheese pockets. Its great taste makes up for its appearance!

Shepherd's Pie

Melanie Thrower
McPherson, KS

Makes 3-4 servings

1 lb. ground pork
1 Tbsp. vinegar
1 tsp. salt
1/4 tsp. hot pepper
1 tsp. paprika
1/4 tsp. dried oregano
1/4 tsp. black pepper
1 tsp. chili powder
1 small onion, chopped
15-oz. can corn, drained
3 large potatoes
1/4 cup milk
1 tsp. butter
1/4 tsp. salt
dash of pepper
shredded cheese

1. Combine pork, vinegar, and spices. Cook in skillet until brown. Add onion and cook until onions begin to glaze. Spread in bottom of slow cooker.
2. Spread corn over meat.
3. Boil potatoes until soft. Mash with milk, butter, 1/4 tsp. salt, and dash of pepper. Spread over meat and corn.
4. Cover. Cook on low 3 hours. Sprinkle top with cheese a few minutes before serving.

Variation: You can substitute ground beef for the pork.

This is my 9-year-old son's favorite dish.

Ham Balls

Jo Haberkamp
Fairbank, IA

Makes 12-16 servings

Ham Balls:
3 eggs
3 cups crushed graham crackers
2 cups milk
1 tsp. salt
1 tsp. onion salt
1/4 tsp. pepper
2 lbs. ground ham
1 1/2 lbs. ground beef
1 1/2 lbs. ground pork

Topping:
1/2 cup ketchup
1/4 cup water
1 cup brown sugar
1/4 cup plus 2 Tbsp. vinegar
1/2 tsp. dry mustard

1. Beat eggs slightly in large bowl. Add graham crackers, milk, salt, onion salt, pepper, and ground meats. Mix well.
2. Form into 24 balls, using 1/2 cup measuring cup for each ball.
3. Combine topping ingredients.
4. Layer meat balls and topping in greased slow cooker.
5. Cover. Cook on high 1 hour. Reduce heat to low and cook 3-4 hours more.

Ham Balls

Deborah Swartz
Grottoes, VA

Makes 24 large meatballs or 8 servings

Ham Balls:
1 1/2 lbs. ground pork
1 1/2 lbs. ground ham
1 1/4 cups cracker crumbs
1/4 tsp. salt
1/8 tsp. pepper
1 cup milk
2 eggs, beaten

Syrup:
1 1/2 cups brown sugar
1/2 cup vinegar
1/2 cup water
1 Tbsp. prepared mustard

1. Combine ham ball ingredients. Shape into 24 meatballs. Place in 9" x 13" pan.
2. Combine syrup ingredients. Pour over meatballs.
3. Bake at 350° for 10 minutes. Remove from oven. Place meatballs in slow cooker. Pour syrup over top.
4. Cover. Cook on high 3 1/4 hours.

Ham Loaf or Balls

Michelle Strite
Goshen, IN

Makes 8-10 servings

Ham Loaf or Balls:
1 lb. ground ham
1 lb. ground pork or ground beef
1 cup soft bread crumbs
2 eggs, slightly beaten
1 cup milk
2 Tbsp. minced onions
1 1/4 tsp. salt
1/8 tsp. pepper

Glaze:
3/4 cup brown sugar
1 tsp. dry mustard
1 Tbsp. cornstarch
1/4 cup vinegar
1/2 cup water

1. Combine ham loaf or balls ingredients. Form into loaf or balls and place in slow cooker.
2. Combine dry ingredients for glaze in bowl. Mix in vinegar and water until smooth. Pour into saucepan. Cook until slightly thickened. Pour over meat.
3. Cover. Cook on high 4-6 hours.

Variations:
1. For a firmer loaf, or balls, use dry bread crumbs instead of soft. Use only 3/4 cup milk instead of 1 cup.

2. Form meat mixture into 1" balls. Brown lightly by baking on cookie sheet in 400° for 5-10 minutes. Place balls in slow cooker. Pour cooked glaze over balls, cover, and cook on high 2-4 hours.

—Julia A. Fisher, New Carlisle, OH

Menu Idea

Ham Loaf
Garlic Mashed Potatoes (page 204), or Hash Brown Potato Casserole (page 211)
Apple Crisp

Barbecue Sandwiches

Sherry L. Lapp
Lancaster, PA

Makes 6-8 sandwiches

1 1/2 lbs. cubed pork
1 lb. stewing beef, cubed
6-oz. can tomato paste
1/4 cup vinegar
1/2 cup brown sugar
1 tsp. salt
1 Tbsp. chili powder
1 large onion, chopped
1 green pepper, chopped

1. Combine ingredients in slow cooker.
2. Cover. Cook on low 8 hours.
3. Shred meat with fork before serving on rolls.
4. Bring to the table with creamy cole slaw.

Pork Barbecue

Barbara L. McGinnis
Jupiter, FL

Makes 6 servings

3-4-lb. pork loin
salt to taste
pepper to taste
2 cups cider vinegar
2 tsp. sugar
1/2 cup ketchup
crushed red pepper to taste
Tabasco sauce to taste
sandwich rolls

1. Sprinkle pork with salt and pepper. Place in slow cooker.
2. Pour vinegar over meat. Sprinkle sugar on top.
3. Cover. Cook on low 8 hours.
4. Remove pork from cooker and shred meat.
5. In bowl mix together ketchup, red pepper, Tabasco sauce, and 1/2 cup vinegar-sugar drippings. Stir in shredded meat.
6. Serve on sandwich rolls with cole slaw.

Variation: To increase the tang, add 1 tsp. dry mustard in Step 5. Use 1/4 cup ketchup and 1/4 cup orange juice, instead of 1/2 cup ketchup.

Frankwiches

Esther Mast
East Petersburg, PA

Makes 16-18 servings

2 10³/4-oz. cans cheddar cheese soup
1/2 cup finely chopped onions
1/2 cup sweet pickle relish
4 tsp. prepared mustard
2 lbs. hot dogs, thinly sliced
8-oz. container sour cream

1. Combine soup, onions, relish, and mustard. Stir in sliced hot dogs.
2. Cover. Cook on low 4 hours.
3. Stir in sour cream.
4. Cover. Cook on high 10-15 minutes, stirring occasionally.
5. Serve over toasted English muffin halves or squares of hot cornbread.

Notes: Instead of using this as sandwich filling you can serve it over rice as a main dish. Add a green vegetable and a jello salad and you have a easy, refreshing, quick meal!

This will also bring smiles to the faces of your grandchildren! Add a relish tray and some chips, and you have a quick summer meal on the patio. Top it off with frozen popsicles.

Zesty Wieners

Lisa F. Good
Harrisonburg, VA

Makes 6-8 servings

1 dozen hot dogs
1/2 cup chopped onions
1 tsp. butter
1 tsp. pepper
2 Tbsp. sugar
2 tsp. prepared mustard
1 cup ketchup
3 Tbsp. Worcestershire sauce

1. Place hot dogs in slow cooker.
2. Saute onions in butter in skillet until almost tender.
3. Add remaining ingredients. Pour over hot dogs in slow cooker.
4. Cover. Cook on low 4 hours.

Menu Idea

Zesty Wieners
Macaroni and Cheese (pages 145-146)
Creamed Lima Beans

Bandito Chili Dogs

Sue Graber
Eureka, IL

Makes 10 servings

1 lb. hot dogs
2 15-oz. cans chili, with or without beans
10 3/4-oz. can condensed cheddar cheese soup
4-oz. can chopped green chilies
10 hot dog buns
1 medium onion, chopped
1-2 cups corn chips, coarsely crushed
1 cup shredded cheddar cheese

1. Place hot dogs in slow cooker.
2. Combine chili, soup, and green chilies. Pour over hot dogs.
3. Cover. Cook on low 3-3 1/2 hours.
4. Serve hot dogs in buns. Top with chili mixture, onion, corn chips, and cheese.

This is a fun recipe for after a football game or outside activity. The main part of your meal is ready when you get home.

Menu Idea

Bandito Chili Dogs
Applesauce
Carrot and Celery Sticks, Cauliflower and Broccoli Crudites
Cookies

Hot Dogs and Noodles

Dolores Kratz
Souderton, PA

Makes 6 servings

8-oz. pkg. medium egg noodles, cooked
  and drained
1¼ cups grated Parmesan cheese
1 cup milk
¼ cup butter or margarine, melted
1 Tbsp. flour
¼ tsp. salt
1-lb. pkg. hot dogs, sliced
¼ cup packed brown sugar
¼ cup mayonnaise
2 Tbsp. prepared mustard

1. Place noodles, cheese, milk, butter, flour, and salt in slow cooker. Mix well.

2. Combine hot dogs with remaining ingredients. Spoon evenly over noodles.

3. Cover. Cook on low 5-6 hours.

Super-Bowl Little Smokies

Mary Sommerfeld
Lancaster, PA
Alicia Denlinger
Lancaster, PA

*Makes 9-10 main-dish servings,
or 15-20 appetizer servings*

3 1-lb. pkgs. Little Smokies
8-oz. bottle Catalina dressing
splash of liquid smoke

1. Combine all ingredients in slow cooker.
2. Cover. Cook on low 2 hours.
3. Use toothpicks to serve.

These are always a hit at parties, whether it's Christmas, New Year's, or the Super Bowl. They are good any time that you'd like to serve food beyond dessert, but you don't want to have a sit-down meal.

Menu Idea

**Super-Bowl Little Smokies
Raw Veggies and Dip
Fruit Tray
Cheese Cubes and Crackers
Brownies and Ice Cream**

Cranberry Franks

Loretta Krahn
Mountain Lake, MN

Makes 15-20 servings

2 pkgs. cocktail wieners or little smoked
   sausages
16-oz. can jellied cranberry sauce
1 cup ketchup
3 Tbsp. brown sugar
1 Tbsp. lemon juice

1. Combine all ingredients in slow cooker.
2. Cover. Cook on high 1-2 hours.

Great picnic, potluck, or buffet food.

Crockpot Smokies

Dede Peterson
Rapid City, SD

Makes 8-10 servings

2 lbs. Little Smokies
18-oz. bottle barbecue sauce (your choice
   of flavors)

1. Put Little Smokies in slow cooker.
2. Cover with barbecue sauce.
3. Cover. Cook on low 3-4 hours.

Hosting Idea

When you're going to host a party,
plan to spread your counter or long
table with lots of slow cookers. Borrow
them ahead of time from your
neighbors and friends.

Early in the day of your get-together,
line up as many slow cookers as needed
and get the foods started—the corn,
sweet potatoes, baked pineapple,
mashed potatoes, meats, appetizer,
soup. When your guests arrive, you
have no last-minute fixin's to do.

Remove the slow cookers' lids, add
long-handled utensils, and invite your
guests to help themselves.
—Dolores Kratz

Chicken Main Dishes

Sunday Roast Chicken

Ruth A. Feister
Narvon, PA

Makes 4-5 servings

Seasoning Mix:
1 Tbsp. salt
2 tsp. paprika
1½ tsp. onion powder
1½ tsp. garlic powder
1½ tsp. dried basil
1 tsp. dry mustard
1 tsp. cumin
2 tsp. pepper
½ tsp. dried thyme
½ tsp. savory

2 Tbsp. butter
2 cups chopped onions
1 cup chopped green pepper
1 roasting chicken
¼ cup flour
1-2 cups chicken stock

1. Combine seasoning mix ingredients in small bowl.
2. Melt butter over high heat in skillet. When butter starts to sizzle, add chopped onions and peppers, and 3 Tbsp. seasoning mix. Cook until onions are golden brown. Cool.
3. Stuff cavity of chicken with cooled vegetables.
4. Sprinkle outside of chicken with 1 Tbsp. seasoning mix. Rub in well.
5. Place chicken in large slow cooker.
6. Cover. Cook on low 6 hours.
7. Empty vegetable stuffing and juices into saucepan. Whisk in flour and 1 cup stock. Cook over high heat until thickened. Add more stock if you prefer a thinner gravy.

The first time I served this dish was when we had family visiting us from Mississippi. We had a wonderful time sitting around a large table sharing many laughs and catching up on the years since our last visit.

Menu Idea

Sunday Roast Chicken
Mashed Potatoes (pages 204-206)
Green Beans Almondine

Old-Fashioned Stewed Chicken

Bonnie Goering
Bridgewater, VA

Makes 6-8 servings

3-4-lb. chicken, cut up
1 small onion, cut into wedges
1 rib celery, sliced
1 carrot, sliced
1 Tbsp. chopped fresh parsley
   (1 tsp. dried)
1 Tbsp. chopped fresh thyme (1 tsp. dried)
1 Tbsp. chopped fresh rosemary
   (1 tsp. dried)
3 tsp. salt
1/4 tsp. pepper
3-4 cups hot water

1. Place chicken in slow cooker. Add remaining ingredients.
2. Cover. Cook on low 8 hours.
3. Use broth as a base to make gravy. Debone chicken and set aside. Thicken broth with flour-water paste. When bubbly and thickened, stir chicken pieces into gravy.
4. Serve with mashed potatoes or noodles and creamed peas.

I cook every Thursday afternoon for a 93-year-old woman who lives by herself. She taught me how to cook with fresh herbs from her garden. I've found they make food taste so much better that I've started an herb garden. And I dry some herbs to use during the winter.

One-Pot Easy Chicken

Jean Robinson
Cinnaminson, NJ

Makes 6 servings

6-8 potatoes, quartered
1-2 large onions, sliced
3-5 carrots, cubed
5-lbs. chicken, skin removed (quarters or legs and thighs work well)
1 small onion, chopped
1 tsp. black pepper
1 Tbsp. whole cloves
1 Tbsp. garlic salt
1 Tbsp. chopped fresh oregano
1 tsp. dried rosemary
1/2 cup lemon juice or chicken broth

1. Layer potatoes, sliced onions, and carrots in bottom of slow cooker.
2. Rinse and pat chicken dry. In bowl mix together chopped onions, pepper, cloves, and garlic salt. Dredge chicken in seasonings. Place in cooker over vegetables. Spoon any remaining seasonings over chicken.
3. Sprinkle with oregano and rosemary. Pour lemon juice over chicken.
4. Cover. Cook on low 6 hours.

This is a lifesaver when the grandchildren come for a weekend. I get to play with them, and dinner is timed and ready when we are.

Menu Idea

One-Pot Easy Chicken
Celery and Carrot Sticks
Green Beans
Jello Salad

Chicken Cacciatore with Spaghetti

Phyllis Pellman Good
Lancaster, PA

Makes 4-5 servings

2 onions, sliced
2½-3 lbs. chicken legs
2 garlic cloves, minced
16-oz. can stewed tomatoes
8-oz. can tomato sauce
1 tsp. salt
¼ tsp. pepper
1-2 tsp. dried oregano
½ tsp. dried basil
1 bay leaf
¼ cup white wine

1. Place onions in bottom of slow cooker.
2. Lay chicken legs over onions.
3. Combine remeaining ingredients. Pour over chicken.
4. Cover. Cook on low 6-6½ hours.
5. Remove bay leaf. Serve over hot buttered spaghetti, linguini, or fettucini.

Chicken Cacciatore

Eleanor J. Ferreira
North Chelmsford, MA

Makes 8 servings

2 chickens, cut into pieces
1 cup flour
2 tsp. salt
½ tsp. pepper
olive oil
2 4-oz. cans sliced mushrooms
3 medium onions, sliced
2 celery ribs, chopped
4 large green peppers, cut into 1" strips
28-oz. can tomatoes
28-oz. can tomato puree
½ tsp. dried basil
½ tsp. dried oregano
½ tsp. salt
¼ tsp. pepper
½ tsp. dried parsley

1. Shake chicken pieces, one at a time, in bag with flour, salt, and pepper. When well coated, brown chicken pieces on both sides in skillet in oil. Place chicken in large slow cooker or two medium-sized cookers, reserving drippings.
2. Saute mushrooms, onions, celery, and peppers in drippings from chicken. Spread over chicken.
3. Mix remaining ingredients together in bowl and pour over chicken and vegetables.
4. Cover. Cook on low 7-8 hours.
5. Serve over hot spaghetti.

Chicken and Sausage Cacciatore

Joyce Kaut
Rochester, NY

Makes 4-6 servings

1 large green pepper, sliced in 1″ strips
1 cup sliced mushrooms
1 medium onion, sliced in rings
1 lb. skinless, boneless chicken breasts, browned
1 lb. Italian sausage, browned
1/2 tsp. dried oregano
1/2 tsp. dried basil
1 1/2 cups Italian-style tomato sauce

1. Layer vegetables in slow cooker.
2. Top with meat.
3. Sprinkle with oregano and basil.
4. Top with tomato sauce.
5. Cover. Cook on low 8 hours.
6. Remove cover during last 30 minutes of cooking time to allow sauce to cook-off and thicken.
7. Serve over cooked spiral pasta.

Menu Idea

Chicken and Sausage Cacciatore
Spiral Pasta
Stewed Tomatoes
Crusty Bread

Con Pollo

Dorothy Van Deest
Memphis, TN

Makes 4-6 servings

3-4-lb. whole chicken
salt to taste
pepper to taste
paprika to taste
garlic salt to taste
6-oz. can tomato paste
1/2 cup beer
3-oz. jar stuffed olives with liquid

1. Wash chicken. Sprinkle all over with salt, pepper, paprika, and garlic salt. Place in slow cooker.
2. Combine tomato paste and beer. Pour over chicken. Add olives.
3. Cover. Cook on low 8-10 hours or high 3-4 hours.
4. Serve over rice or noodles, along with salad and cornbread, and sherbet for dessert.

This is chicken with a Spanish flair. This easy supper is quick, too, by slow-cooker standards, if you use the high temperature. Let your slow cooker be the chef.

Basil Chicken

Sarah Niessen
Akron, PA

Makes 4-6 servings

1 lb. baby carrots
2 medium onions, sliced
1-2 cups celery slices and leaves
3-lb. chicken

½ cup chicken broth,
   or white cooking wine
2 tsp. salt
½ tsp. black pepper
1 tsp. dried basil

1. Place carrots, onions, and celery in bottom of slow cooker.

2. Add chicken.

3. Pour broth over chicken.

4. Sprinkle with salt, pepper, and basil.

5. Cover. Cook on low 7-10 hours, or until chicken and vegetables are tender.

Curry

Dawn Ranch
Harrisonburg, VA

Makes 6-8 servings

28-oz. can tomatoes
4 whole chicken breasts, cut in half
1 onion, chopped
half a green pepper, chopped
2 carrots, chopped
2 ribs celery, chopped
1-2 Tbsp. curry
1 tsp. turmeric
½ tsp. salt
¼ tsp. pepper
1 Tbsp. sugar
1 chicken bouillon cube dissolved in
   ¼ cup hot water

1. Combine all ingredients in slow cooker.

2. Cover. Cook on high 2-3 hours or on low 5-6 hours.

Dad's Spicy Chicken Curry

Tom & Sue Ruth
Lancaster, PA

Makes 8 servings

4 lbs. chicken pieces, with bones
water
2 onions, diced
10-oz. pkg. frozen chopped spinach,
   thawed and squeezed dry
1 cup plain yogurt
2-3 diced red potatoes
3 tsp. salt
1 tsp. garlic powder
1 tsp. ground ginger
1 tsp. ground cumin
1 tsp. ground coriander
1 tsp. pepper
1 tsp. ground cloves
1 tsp. ground cardamom
1 tsp. ground cinnamon
½ tsp. chili powder
1 tsp. red pepper flakes
3 tsp. turmeric

1. Place chicken in large slow cooker. Cover with water.

2. Cover. Cook on high 2 hours, or until tender.

3. Drain chicken. Remove from slow cooker. Cool briefly and cut/shred into small pieces. Return to slow cooker.

4. Add remaining ingredients.

5. Cover. Cook on low 4-6 hours, or until potatoes are tender.

6. Serve on rice. Accompany with fresh mango slices or mango chutney.

Variation: Substitute 5 tsp. curry powder for the garlic, ginger, cumin, coriander, and pepper.

Delicious Chicken with Curried Cream Sauce

Jennifer J. Gehman
Harrisburg, PA

Makes 4-6 servings

4-6 boneless, skinless, chicken breasts or
    legs and thighs
oil
salt to taste
pepper to taste
10¾-oz. can cream of chicken soup
½ cup mayonnaise
1-2 Tbsp. curry powder
½ tsp. salt
⅛ tsp. pepper
1 lb. fresh, or 15-oz. can, asparagus spears
½-1 cup shredded cheddar cheese

1. Brown chicken on all sides in skillet in oil. Season with salt and pepper. Place in slow cooker.
2. Combine soup, mayonnaise, curry powder, salt, and pepper. Pour over chicken.
3. Cover. Cook on high 3 hours or on low 5 hours.
4. If using fresh asparagus, steam lightly until just-tender. If using canned asparagus, heat. Drain asparagus and place in bottom of serving dish.
5. Cover asparagus with chicken. Sprinkle with cheese.
6. Serve with egg noodles or white rice. Add another cooked vegetable, along with fruit salad, applesauce, or mandarin oranges, as side dishes.

Curried Chicken

Marlene Bogard
Newton, KS

Makes 5 servings

2½-3½-lb. fryer chicken, cut up
salt to taste
pepper to taste
1 Tbsp. curry powder
1 garlic clove, crushed or minced
1 Tbsp. melted butter
½ cup chicken broth, or 1 chicken
    bouillon cube dissolved in ½ cup water
2 Tbsp. onion, chopped fine
29-oz. can cling peaches
½ cup pitted prunes
3 Tbsp. cornstarch
3 Tbsp. cold water

1. Sprinkle chicken with salt and pepper. Place in slow cooker.
2. Combine curry, garlic, butter, broth, and onions in bowl.
3. Drain peaches, reserving syrup. Add ½ cup syrup to curry mixture. Pour over chicken.
4. Cover. Cook on low 4-6 hours. Remove chicken from pot. Turn on high.
5. Stir in prunes.
6. Dissolve cornstarch in cold water. Stir into pot.
7. Cover. Cook on high 10 minutes, or until thickened. Add peaches. Add cooked chicken.
8. Serve over rice. Offer peanuts, shredded coconut, and fresh pineapple chunks as condiments.

Garlic Lime Chicken
Loretta Krahn
Mountain Lake, MN

Makes 5 servings

5 chicken breast halves
1/2 cup soy sauce
1/4-1/3 cup lime juice, according to your
    taste preference
1 Tbsp. Worcestershire sauce
2 garlic cloves, minced,
    or 1 tsp. garlic powder
1/2 tsp. dry mustard
1/2 tsp. ground pepper

1. Place chicken in slow cooker.
2. Combine remaining ingredients and pour over chicken.
3. Cover. Cook on high 4-6 hours or on low 6-8 hours.

Herbed Chicken
LaVerne A. Olson
Lititz, PA

Makes 8 serving

4 whole chicken breasts, halved
10 3/4-oz. can cream of mushroom or
    chicken soup
1/4 cup soy sauce
1/4 cup oil
1/4 cup wine vinegar
3/4 cup water
1/2 tsp. minced garlic
1 tsp. ground ginger
1/2 tsp. dried oregano
1 Tbsp. brown sugar

1. Place chicken in slow cooker.
2. Combine remaining ingredients. Pour over chicken.
3. Cover. Cook on low 2-2 1/2 hours. Uncover and cook 15 minutes more.
Serve with rice.

A favorite with the whole family, even grandchildren. The gravy is delicious.

Teriyaki Chicken
Colleen Konetzni
Rio Rancho, NM

Makes 6 servings

6-8 skinless chicken thighs
1/2 cup soy sauce
2 Tbsp. brown sugar
2 Tbsp. grated fresh ginger
2 garlic cloves, minced

1. Wash and dry chicken. Place in slow cooker.
2. Combine remaining ingredients. Pour over chicken.
3. Cover. Cook on high 1 hour. Reduce heat to low and cook 6-7 hours.
4. Serve over rice with a fresh salad.

Easy Chicken

Ruth Liebelt
Rapid City, SD

Makes 6-8 servings

8-10 chicken wings or legs and thighs
1/2 cup soy sauce
1/2 cup sugar
1/2 tsp. Tabasco sauce
pinch of ground ginger

1. Place chicken in greased slow cooker.
2. Combine remaining ingredients and pour over chicken.
3. Cover. Cook on low 8 hours.
4. Serve with cooked rice, rolls, and salad.

Barbecued Chicken

Gladys Longacre
Susquehanna, PA

Makes 4-6 servings

3-4 lbs. boneless, skinless, chicken breasts
oil
1 onion, chopped
1/4 cup chopped green pepper
1 cup ketchup
1-2 Tbsp. hickory-smoked barbecue sauce
1 Tbsp. prepared mustard
1 Tbsp. Worcestershire sauce
1 Tbsp. lemon juice
2 Tbsp. vinegar
3 Tbsp. brown sugar
1/4 cup water
1/2 tsp. salt
1/8 tsp. pepper

1. Lightly brown chicken in oil in skillet. Place in slow cooker.
2. Layer onions and green pepper over chicken.
3. Combine remaining ingredients and pour over chicken.
4. Cover. Cook on low 6 hours or high 3 1/2-4 hours.
5. Serve chicken and sauce over cooked rice.

Barbecued Chicken

Joanne Kennedy
Plattsburgh, NY

Makes 4 servings

2 whole boneless, skinless chicken breasts, cubed
1 medium onion, sliced
1 green pepper, sliced
1 cup chopped celery
2 Tbsp. Worcestershire sauce
2 Tbsp. brown sugar
1 1/2 cups ketchup
1 1/2 cups water
1/2 tsp. pepper

1. Combine all ingredients in slow cooker.
2. Cover. Cook on low 8 hours or high 4 hours.
3. Serve over rice with a tossed salad.

Chicken Stew with Peppers and Pineapples

Judi Manos
West Islip, NY

Makes 4 servings

1 lb. boneless, skinless chicken breasts, cut
   in 1½" cubes
4 medium carrots, sliced into 1" pieces
½ cup chicken broth
2 Tbsp. gingerroot, chopped
1 Tbsp. brown sugar
2 Tbsp. soy sauce
½ tsp. ground allspice
½ tsp. red pepper sauce
8-oz. can pineapple chunks, drained
   (reserve juice)
1 Tbsp. cornstarch
1 medium sweet green pepper,
   cut in 1" pieces

1. Combine chicken, carrots, chicken broth,
gingerroot, sugar, soy sauce, allspice, and red
pepper sauce in slow cooker.
2. Cover. Cook on low 7-8 hours or on high
3-4 hours.
3. Combine pineapple juice and cornstarch
until smooth. Stir into chicken mixture. Add
pineapple and green pepper.
4. Cover. Cook on high 15 minutes, or until
slightly thickened.
5. Serve over cooked rice.

*Variation: Add 1 cut-up fresh tomato 30 minutes
before end of cooking time.*

Maui Chicken

John D. Allen
Rye, CO

Makes 6 servings

6 boneless chicken breast halves
2 Tbsp. oil
14½-oz. can chicken broth
20-oz. can pineapple chunks
¼ cup vinegar
2 Tbsp. brown sugar
2 tsp. soy sauce
1 garlic clove, minced
1 medium green bell pepper, chopped
3 Tbsp. cornstarch
¼ cup water

1. Brown chicken in oil. Transfer chicken to
slow cooker.
2. Combine remaining ingredients. Pour
over chicken.
3. Cover. Cook on high 4-6 hours.
4. Serve over rice.

Chicken in a Hurry
Yvonne Boettger
Harrisonburg, VA

Makes 4-5 servings

2½-3 lbs. skinless chicken drumsticks
½ cup ketchup
¼ cup water
¼ cup brown sugar
1 pkg. dry onion soup mix

1. Arrange chicken in slow cooker.
2. Combine remaining ingredients. Pour over chicken.
3. Cover. Cook on high 4-5 hours or low 7-8 hours.

Tender Barbecued Chicken
Betty Stoltzfus
Honeybrook, PA

Makes 4-6 servings

3-4 lb. broiler chicken
1 medium onion, thinly sliced
1 medium lemon, thinly sliced
18-oz. bottle barbecue sauce
¾ cup cola-flavored soda

1. Place chicken in slow cooker.
2. Top with onion and lemon.
3. Combine barbecue sauce and cola. Pour into slow cooker.
4. Cover. Cook on low 8-10 hours, or until chicken juices run clear.
5. Cut into serving-sized pieces and serve with barbecue sauce. Slice any leftovers and use in sandwiches.

Spicy Sweet Chicken
Carolyn Baer
Conrath, WI

Makes 4 servings

2½-3 lbs. chicken breasts, thighs, and/or legs, skinned
1 Tbsp. oil
16-oz. can whole cranberry sauce
¼ cup spicy-sweet Catalina salad dressing
2 Tbsp. dry onion soup mix
1 Tbsp. cornstarch

1. Rinse chicken. Pat dry. Brown in hot oil in skillet. Place in slow cooker.
2. Combine half of cranberry sauce, and all of salad dressing and soup mix. Pour over chicken.
3. Cover. Cook on low 6 hours or high 3 hours.
4. Stir cornstarch into remaining cranberry sauce. Stir into chicken mixture.
5. Turn slow cooker to high. Cover and cook 30-45 minutes more, or until thickened and bubbly.
6. Serve over cooked noodles or rice.

Aloha Chicken Cosmopolitan

Dianna Milhizer
Brighton, MI

Makes 12 servings

**5 lbs. boneless, skinless chicken breasts,
cut into strips or cubed
dash of salt
1 cup frozen orange juice
1 cup coconut milk
1 cup soy sauce
1/4 cup sesame oil**

1. Lightly salt chicken and then refrigerate for 30 minutes.
2. Drain chicken of any juices that have gathered and combine with other ingredients in large slow cooker.
3. Cover. Cook on low 6 hours.
4. Serve with white rice.

Blue Ribbon
Cranberry Chicken

Marjorie Y. Guengerich
Harrisonburg, VA

Makes 4-6 servings

**2 1/2-3-lb. chicken, cut up
16-oz. can whole cranberry sauce
8-oz. bottle Russian salad dressing
1 pkg. dry onion soup mix**

1. Rinse chicken. Pat dry with paper towel. Place in slow cooker.
2. Combine cranberry sauce, salad dressing, and soup mix. Pour over chicken.
3. Cover and chill 1-8 hours, or overnight.

4. Cover. Cook on high 4 hours or on low 6-8 hours.
5. Serve over rice or noodles.

Chicken with Applesauce

Kelly Evenson
Pittsboro, NC

Makes 4 servings

**4 boneless, skinless chicken breast halves
salt to taste
pepper to taste
4-5 Tbsp. oil
2 cups applesauce
1/4 cup barbecue sauce
1/2 tsp. poultry seasoning
2 tsp. honey
1/2 tsp. lemon juice**

1. Season chicken with salt and pepper. Brown in oil for 5 minutes per side.
2. Cut up chicken into 1" chunks and transfer to slow cooker.
3. Combine remaining ingredients. Pour over chicken and mix together well.
4. Cover. Cook on high 2-3 hours, or until chicken is tender.
5. Serve over rice or noodles.

Saucy Apricot Chicken

Anna Stoltzfus
Honey Brook, PA

Makes 6 servings

6 boneless, skinless chicken breast halves
2 12-oz. jars apricot preserves
1 pkg. dry onion soup mix

1. Place chicken in slow cooker.
2. Combine preserves and onion soup mix in separate bowl. Spoon over chicken.
3. Cover. Cook on low 4-5 hours.
4. Serve over rice.

Chicken ala Orange

Carlene Horne
Bedford, NH

Makes 8 servings

8 boneless, skinless chicken breast halves
1/2 cup chopped onion
12-oz. jar orange marmalade
1/2 cup Russian dressing
1 Tbsp. dried parsley, or to taste

1. Place chicken and onion in slow cooker.
2. Combine marmalade and dressing. Pour over chicken.
3. Sprinkle with parsley.
4. Cover. Cook on low 4-6 hours.
5. Serve with rice.

Scrumptious Chicken

Kathi Rogge
Alexandria, IN

Makes 8 servings

8 skinned chicken breast halves
10¾-oz. can cream of mushroom, or cream of chicken soup
16 ozs. sour cream
1 pkg. dry onion soup mix
fresh basil or oregano, chopped

1. Place chicken in slow cooker.
2. Combine all remaining ingredients except fresh herbs. Pour over chicken.
3. Cover. Cook on low 6 hours. (If convenient for you, stir after 3 hours of cooking.)
4. Sprinkle with fresh herbs just before serving.
5. Serve with brown and wild rice, mixed, or couscous.

Variations:
1. Cut up 4 lightly cooked chicken breast halves. Place in slow cooker.

2. Add 8 ozs. sour cream, 1 pkg. dry onion soup mix, and a 10¾-oz. can cream of mushroom soup. Mix together well.

3. Cover and cook on low 3-4 hours.

4. Serve over rice or noodles.
—Sherry Conyers, McPherson, KS

Menu Idea

Scrumptious Chicken
Brown and Wild Rice, mixed
Mexican Corn or Seasoned Green Beans
Chilled Fruit Salad

Creamy Chicken Breasts
Judy Buller
Bluffton, OH

Makes 6-8 servings

6-8 chicken breast halves
salt to taste
pepper to taste
paprika to taste
10¾-oz. can cream of mushroom soup
½ cup sour cream

1. Season chicken breasts with salt, pepper, and paprika. Place in slow cooker.
2. Combine mushroom soup and sour cream. Pour over chicken.
3. Cover. Cook on low 6 hours.
4. Serve with rice, noodles, or mashed potatoes.

Miriam's Chicken
Arlene Leaman Kliewer
Lakewood, CO

Makes 6 servings

4 chicken breast halves, cut up into
    1" chunks and uncooked
8-oz. pkg. cream cheese, cubed
2 10¾-oz. cans cream soup (your
    favorite—or a combination of your
    favorites)
6 croissants
paprika
fresh parsley, minced

1. Place chicken in slow cooker.
2. Combine cream cheese and soups. Pour over chicken. Stir.

3. Cover. Cook on low 8 hours.
4. Serve over croissants split in half. Sprinkle with paprika and parsley.

Elegant Chicken with Gravy
Leesa Lesenski
South Deerfield, MA

Makes 6 serving

6 boneless chicken breast halves
10¾-oz. can cream of broccoli, or broccoli
    cheese, soup
10¾-oz. can cream of chicken soup
½ cup white wine
4-oz. can sliced mushrooms, undrained,
    optional

1. Place chicken breasts in slow cooker.
2. In bowl mix together soups, wine, and mushroom slices. Pour over chicken.
3. Cover. Cook on high 3 hours or on low 6 hours, or until chicken is tender but not dry.
4. Serve over rice or noodles.

Janie's Chicken a La King

Lafaye M. Musser
Denver, PA

Makes 4 servings

10¾-oz. can cream of chicken soup
3 Tbsp. flour
½ tsp. salt
¼ tsp. pepper
dash cayenne pepper
1 lb. boneless chicken, uncooked and cut
   in pieces
1 rib celery, chopped
½ cup chopped green pepper
¼ cup chopped onions
9-oz. bag frozen peas, thawed

1. Combine soup, flour, salt, pepper, and cayenne pepper in slow cooker.
2. Stir in chicken, celery, green pepper, and onion.
3. Cover. Cook on low 7-8 hours.
4. Stir in peas.
5. Cover. Cook 30 minutes longer.
6. Serve in pastry cups or over rice, waffles, or toast.

Savory Chicken

Shari Mast
Harrisonburg, VA

Makes 8-10 servings

4 boneless, skinless chicken breast halves
4 skinless chicken quarters
10¾-oz. can cream of chicken soup
1 Tbsp. water
¼ cup chopped sweet red peppers
1 Tbsp. chopped fresh parsley,
   or 1 tsp. dried parsley
1 Tbsp. lemon juice
½ tsp. paprika

1. Layer chicken in slow cooker.
2. Combine remaining ingredients and pour over chicken.
3. Cover. Cook on high 4-5 hours.

Savory Chicken, Meal #2

leftover chicken and broth from first
   Savory Chicken Meal
2 carrots
1 rib celery
2 medium-sized onions
2 Tbsp. flour or cornstarch
¼ cup cold water

1. For a second Savory Chicken Meal, pick leftover chicken off bone. Set aside.
2. Return remaining broth to slow cooker and stir in thinly sliced carrots and celery and onions cut up in chunks. Cook 3-4 hours on high.
3. In separate bowl, mix flour or cornstarch with cold water. When smooth, stir into hot broth.
4. Stir in cut-up chicken. Heat 15-20 minutes, or until broth thickens and chicken is hot.
5. Serve over rice or pasta.

Creamy Chicken and Vegetables

Dawn M. Propst
Levittown, PA

Makes 4 servings

10³/4-oz. can cream of mushroom soup, divided
4 boneless, skinless chicken breast halves
16-oz. pkg. frozen vegetable medley (broccoli, cauliflower, and carrots), thawed and drained
¹/2 tsp. salt
¹/8-¹/4 tsp. pepper
1 cup shredded cheddar cheese, divided

1. Pour small amount of soup in bottom of slow cooker.
2. Add chicken breasts, vegetables, and seasonings.
3. Mix in ¹/2 cup cheddar cheese. Cover with remaining soup.
4. Cover. Cook on low 5-6 hours, or until vegetables are cooked and chicken is no longer pink.
5. Sprinkle with remaining cheese 10-15 minutes before serving.

Szechwan-Style Chicken and Broccoli

Jane Meiser
Harrisonburg, VA

Makes 4 servings

2 whole boneless, skinless chicken or turkey breasts
oil
¹/2 cup picante sauce
2 Tbsp. soy sauce
¹/2 tsp. sugar
¹/2 Tbsp. quick-cooking tapioca
1 medium onion, chopped
2 garlic cloves, minced
¹/2 tsp. ground ginger
2 cups broccoli florets
1 medium red pepper, cut into pieces

1. Cut chicken into 1" cubes and brown lightly in oil in skillet. Place in slow cooker.
2. Stir in remaining ingredients.
3. Cover. Cook on high 1-1¹/2 hours or on low 2-3 hours.

113

Creamy Chicken and Noodles

Rhonda Burgoon
Collingswood, NJ

Makes 4-6 servings

2 cups sliced carrots
1½ cups chopped onions
1 cup sliced celery
2 Tbsp. snipped fresh parsley
bay leaf
3 medium-sized chicken legs and thighs
  (about 2 lbs.)
2 10¾-oz. cans cream of chicken soup
½ cup water
1 tsp. dried thyme
1 tsp. salt
¼ tsp. pepper
1 cup peas
10 ozs. wide noodles, cooked

1. Place carrots, onions, celery, parsley, and bay leaf in bottom of slow cooker.
2. Place chicken on top of vegetables.
3. Combine soup, water, thyme, salt, and pepper. Pour over chicken and vegetables.
4. Cover. Cook on low 8-9 hours or high 4-4½ hours.
5. Remove chicken from slow cooker. Cool slightly. Remove from bones, cut into bite-sized pieces and return to slow cooker.
6. Remove and discard bay leaf.
7. Stir peas into mixture in slow cooker. Allow to cook for 5-10 more minutes.
8. Pour over cooked noodles. Toss gently to combine.
9. Serve with crusty bread and a salad.

Chicken Alfredo

Dawn M. Propst
Levittown, PA

Makes 4-6 servings

16-oz. jar Alfredo sauce
4-6 boneless, skinless chicken breast
  halves
8 ozs. dry noodles, cooked
4-oz. can mushroom pieces and stems,
  drained
1 cup shredded mozzarella cheese,
  or ½ cup grated Parmesan cheese

1. Pour about one-third of Alfredo sauce in bottom of slow cooker.
2. Add chicken and cover with remaining sauce.
3. Cover. Cook on low 8 hours.
4. Fifteen minutes before serving, add noodles and mushrooms, mixing well. Sprinkle top with cheese. Dish is ready to serve when cheese is melted.
5. Serve with green salad and Italian bread.

Gourmet Chicken Breasts

Sharon Swartz Lambert
Dayton, VA
Deborah Santiago
Lancaster, PA

Makes 4-6 servings

6-8 slices dried beef
4-6 boneless, skinless chicken breast
  halves
2-3 slices bacon, cut in half lengthwise
10³/4-oz. cream of mushroom soup
8-oz. carton sour cream
1/2 cup flour

1. Line bottom of slow cooker with dried beef.
2. Roll up each chicken breast half and wrap with a half-slice of bacon. Place in slow cooker.
3. Combine remaining ingredients in bowl. Pour over breasts.
4. Cover. Cook on low 6-8 hours.
5. Serve with cooked noodles, rice, or mashed potatoes.

Creamy Nutmeg Chicken

Amber Swarey
Donalds, SC

Makes 6 servings

6 boneless chicken breast halves
oil
1/4 cup chopped onions
1/4 cup minced parsley
2 10³/4-oz. cans cream of mushroom soup
1/2 cup sour cream
1/2 cup milk

1 Tbsp. ground nutmeg
1/4 tsp. sage
1/4 tsp. dried thyme
1/4 tsp. crushed rosemary

1. Brown chicken in skillet in oil. Reserve drippings and place chicken in slow cooker.
2. Saute onions and parsley in drippings until onions are tender.
3. Stir in remaining ingredients. Mix well. Pour over chicken.
4. Cover. Cook on low 3 hours, or until juices run clear.
5. Serve over mashed or fried potatoes, or rice.

Slow Cooker
Creamy Chicken Italian

Sherri Grindle
Goshen, IN

Makes 6 servings

8 boneless, skinless chicken breast halves
1 pkg. dry Italian salad dressing mix
1/4 cup water
8-oz. pkg. cream cheese, softened
10³/4-oz. can cream of chicken soup
4-oz. can mushrooms, drained

1. Place chicken in greased slow cooker.
2. Combine salad dressing and water. Pour over chicken.
3. Cover. Cook on low 4-5 hours.
4. In saucepan, combine cream cheese and soup. Heat slightly to melt cream cheese. Stir in mushrooms. Pour over chicken.
5. Cover. Cook 1 additional hour on low.
6. Serve over noodles or rice.

Variation: Add frozen vegetables along with the mushrooms.

Mushroom Chicken in Sour Cream Sauce

Lavina Hochstedler
Grand Blanc, MI
Joyce Shackelford
Green Bay, WI

Makes 6 servings

1½ tsp. salt
¼ tsp. pepper
½ tsp. paprika
¼ tsp. lemon pepper
1 tsp. garlic powder
6 skinless, bone-in chicken breast halves
10¾-oz. can cream of mushroom soup
8-oz. container sour cream
½ cup dry white wine or chicken broth
½ lb. fresh mushrooms, sliced

1. Combine salt, pepper, paprika, lemon pepper, and garlic powder. Rub over chicken. Place in slow cooker.
2. Combine soup, sour cream, and wine or broth. Stir in mushrooms. Pour over chicken.
3. Cover. Cook on low 6-8 hours or high 5 hours.
4. Serve over potatoes, rice, or couscous. Delicious accompanied with broccoli-cauliflower salad and applesauce.

Oriental Chicken Cashew Dish

Dorothy Horst
Tiskilwa, IL

Makes 6 servings

14-oz. can bean sprouts, drained
3 Tbsp. butter or margarine, melted
4 green onions, chopped
4-oz. can mushroom pieces
10¾-oz. can cream of mushroom soup
1 cup sliced celery
12½-oz. can chunk chicken breast, or 1 cup cooked chicken cubed
1 Tbsp. soy sauce
1 cup cashew nuts

1. Combine all ingredients except nuts in slow cooker.
2. Cover. Cook on low 4-9 hours or on high 2-3 hours.
3. Stir in cashew nuts before serving.
4. Serve over rice.

Menu Idea

Oriental Chicken Cashew Dish
Rice
Egg Rolls, accompanied by Fish Sauce
Hot Jasmine or Lotus Tea

I teach English as a Second Language to Vietnamese women. Occasionally they invite us to join them for dinner on Vietnamese New Year. We enjoy the fellowship and Vietnamese traditions immensely. They always have a "Lucky Tree," a tree with yellow flowers which blooms in Vietnam on New Year's. They decorate the tree by hanging red envelopes in it. Each contains a money gift; one is given to each unmarried person present, including the babies.

Chicken Azteca

Katrine Rose
Woodbridge, VA

Makes 10-12 servings

2 15-oz. cans black beans, drained
4 cups frozen corn kernels
2 garlic cloves, minced
3/4 tsp. ground cumin
2 cups chunky salsa, divided
10 skinless, boneless chicken breast halves
2 8-oz. pkgs. cream cheese, cubed
cooked rice
shredded cheddar cheese

1. Combine beans, corn, garlic, cumin, and half of salsa in slow cooker.
2. Arrange chicken breasts over top. Pour remaining salsa over top.
3. Cover. Cook on high 2-3 hours or on low 4-6 hours.
4. Remove chicken and cut into bite-sized pieces. Return to cooker.
5. Stir in cream cheese. Cook on high until cream cheese melts.
6. Spoon chicken and sauce over cooked rice. Top with shredded cheese.

Tamale Chicken

Jeanne Allen
Rye, CO

Makes 6 servings

1 medium onion, chopped
4-oz. can chopped green chilies
2 Tbsp. oil
10 3/4-oz. can cream of chicken soup
2 cups sour cream
1 cup sliced ripe olives
1 cup chopped stewed tomatoes
2 cups shredded cheddar cheese
8 chicken breast halves, cooked and chopped
16-oz. can beef tamales, chopped
1 tsp. chili powder
1 tsp. garlic powder
1 tsp. pepper
1/2 cup shredded cheddar cheese

1. Saute onion and chilies in oil in skillet.
2. Combine all ingredients except 1/2 cup shredded cheese. Pour into slow cooker.
3. Top with remaining cheese.
4. Cover. Cook on high 3-4 hours.
5. Pass chopped fresh tomatoes, shredded lettuce, sour cream, salsa, and or guacamole so guests can top their Tamale Chicken with these condiments.

Tex-Mex Chicken and Rice

Kelly Evenson
Pittsboro, NC

Makes 8 servings

1 cup converted uncooked white rice
28-oz. can diced peeled tomatoes
6-oz. can tomato paste
3 cups hot water
1 pkg. dry taco seasoning mix
4 whole boneless, skinless chicken breasts, uncooked and cut into 1/2" cubes
2 medium onions, chopped
1 green pepper, chopped
4-oz. can diced green chilies
1 tsp. garlic powder
1/2 tsp. pepper

1. Combine all ingredients except chilies and seasonings in large slow cooker.
2. Cover. Cook on low 4-4 1/2 hours, or until rice is tender and chicken is cooked.
3. Stir in green chilies and seasonings and serve.
4. Serve with mixed green leafy salad and refried beans.

Red Pepper Chicken

Sue Graber
Eureka, IL

Makes 4 servings

4 boneless, skinless chicken breast halves
15-oz. can black beans, drained
12-oz. jar roasted red peppers, undrained
14 1/2-oz. can Mexican stewed tomatoes, undrained
1 large onion, chopped
1/2 tsp. salt
pepper to taste
hot cooked rice

1. Place chicken in slow cooker.
2. Combine beans, red peppers, stewed tomatoes, onion, salt, and pepper. Pour over chicken.
3. Cover. Cook on low 4-6 hours, or until chicken is no longer pink.
4. Serve over rice.

Chicken Gumbo

Virginia Bender
Dover, DE

Makes 6-8 servings

1 large onion, chopped
3-4 garlic cloves, minced
1 green pepper, diced
2 cups okra, sliced
2 cups tomatoes, chopped
4 cups chicken broth
1 lb. chicken breast, cut into 1" pieces
2 tsp. Old Bay Seasoning

1. Combine all ingredients in slow cooker.

2. Cover. Cook on low 8-10 hours or high 3-4 hours.

3. Serve over rice.

Chicken and Seafood Gumbo

Dianna Milhizer
Brighton, MI

Makes 12 servings

1 cup chopped celery
1 cup chopped onions
½ cup chopped green peppers
¼ cup olive oil
¼ cup, plus 1 Tbsp., flour
6 cups chicken stock
2 lbs. chicken, cut up
3 bay leaves
1½ cups sliced okra
12-oz. can diced tomatoes
1 tsp. Tabasco sauce
salt to taste
pepper to taste
1 lb. ready-to-eat shrimp
½ cup snipped fresh parsley

1. Saute celery, onions, and peppers in oil. Blend in flour and chicken stock until smooth. Cook 5 minutes. Pour into slow cooker.

2. Add remaining ingredients except seafood and parsley.

3. Cover. Cook on low 10-12 hours.

4. One hour before serving add shrimp and parsley.

5. Remove bay leaves before serving.

6. Serve with white rice.

Chicken Rice Special

Jeanne Allen
Rye, CO

Makes 6-8 servings

6 chicken breast halves, cooked and
  chopped (save 4 cups broth)
1 lb. pork or turkey sausage, browned
half a large sweet green pepper, chopped
1 medium onion, chopped
4 ribs celery, chopped
1 cup rice, uncooked
2-oz. pkg. dry noodle-soup mix
½ cup sliced almonds
1-2 oz. jar pimentos, chopped

1. Combine all ingredients except almonds and pimentos in slow cooker.

2. Top with almonds and pimentos.

3. Cover. Cook on high 4-6 hours, or until rice is done and liquid has been absorbed.

4. Stir up 1 hour before serving.

119

Company Casserole

Vera Schmucker
Goshen, IN

Makes 4-6 servings

1¼ cups uncooked rice
½ cup (1 stick) butter, melted
3 cups chicken broth
3-4 cups cut-up cooked chicken breast
2 4-oz. cans sliced mushrooms, drained
⅓ cup soy sauce
12-oz. pkg. shelled frozen shrimp
8 green onions, chopped, 2 Tbsp. reserved
⅔ cup slivered almonds

1. Combine rice and butter in slow cooker. Stir to coat rice well.
2. Add remaining ingredients except almonds and 2 Tbsp. green onions.
3. Cover. Cook on low 6-8 hours or on high 3-4 hours, until rice is tender.
4. Sprinkle almonds and green onions over top before serving.
5. Serve with green beans, tossed salad, and fruit salad.

Chicken Broccoli Rice Casserole

Gloria Julien
Gladstone, MI

Makes 4-6 servings

1 onion, chopped
3 Tbsp. oil
2-3 cups uncooked chicken, cut in 1" pieces
10¾-oz. can cream of chicken soup
12-oz. can evaporated milk
2 cups cubed Velveeta cheese
3 cups cooked rice
2 cups frozen broccoli cuts, thawed
¼ tsp. pepper
4-oz. can mushrooms, drained

1. Saute onion in oil in skillet.
2. Add chicken and saute until no longer pink.
3. Combine all ingredients in slow cooker.
4. Cover. Cook on low 2-3 hours.

Notes:
1. This is an ideal dish for people who are not big meat-eaters.

2. This is good carry-in for potluck or fellowship meals. I put the ingredients together the night before.

Menu Idea

Chicken Broccoli Rice Casserole
Baked Beans (pages 133-140)
Salad of your choice
Homemade Bread

Baked Chicken and Rice

Fannie Miller
Hutchinson, KS

Makes 10-12 servings

2 cups dry instant rice
10¾-oz. can cream of chicken soup
10¾-oz. can cream of mushroom soup
10¾-oz. can cream of celery soup
½ cup butter or margarine
1 soup can water
10 skinless chicken breast halves,
 or 1 chicken, cut into 10-12 pieces
1 pkg. dry onion soup mix

1. Place rice in large slow cooker.
2. Combine soups, butter, and water. Pour half over rice.
3. Lay chicken over rice. Pour remaining soup mixture over chicken.
4. Sprinkle with dry onion soup mix.
5. Cover. Cook on low 4-6 hours, or until chicken is done but not dry, and rice is tender but not mushy.

Chicken Pasta

Evelyn L. Ward
Greeley, CO

Makes 4 servings

1½-lb. boneless chicken breast
1 large zucchini, diced
1 pkg. chicken gravy mix
2 Tbsp. water
2 Tbsp. evaporated milk or cream
1 large tomato, chopped
4 cups cooked macaroni
8 ozs. smoked Gouda cheese, grated

1. Cut chicken into 1" cubes. Place in slow cooker.
2. Add zucchini, gravy mix, and water, and stir together.
3. Cover. Cook on low 6 hours.
4. Add milk and tomato. Cook an additional 20 minutes.
5. Stir in pasta. Top with cheese. Serve immediately.

Comforting Chicken Stuffing

Ruth Liebelt
Rapid City, SD
Esther J. Yoder
Hartville, OH

Makes 4-6 servings

2 6-oz. boxes stuffing mix
1-2 cups cooked, diced chicken
10¾-oz. can cream of chicken soup
⅓ cup water or milk
½ tsp. salt, optional
⅛-¼ tsp. pepper, optional
4 Tbsp. (¼ cup) butter or margarine,
 melted, optional

1. Prepare stuffing mix per package instructions. Spread in bottom of greased slow cooker.
2. Combine chicken, soup, water, and seasonings, if desired. Spread over stuffing. Top with melted butter, if you want.
3. Cover. Cook on low 4-6 hours or on high 2½-3 hours. Loosen edges once or twice, or at least just before serving.
4. Delicious served with cole slaw and mixed fruit.

Chicken Dressing

Lydia A. Yoder
London, ON

Makes 20 servings

3/4 cup butter or margarine
1 cup chopped onions
2 cups chopped celery
2 Tbsp. parsley flakes
1 1/2 tsp. salt
1/2 tsp. pepper
3 1/2-4 cups chicken broth
12-14 cups dried bread cubes
4 cups cut-up chicken
2 eggs, beaten
1 tsp. baking powder

1. Saute onion and celery in butter in skillet.
2. Combine seasonings and broth. Mix with bread cubes in large bowl.
3. Fold in chicken and sauteed onions and celery.
4. Add eggs and baking powder.
5. Lightly pack into large slow cooker.
6. Cover. Cook on low 3-4 hours.
7. Serve with turkey or chicken, mashed potatoes, a vegetable, and lettuce salad.

Note: The longer the dressing cooks, the drier it will become. Keep that in mind if you do not care for moist stuffing.

Chicken and Stuffing Dinner

Trudy Kutter
Corfu, NY

Makes 4-6 servings

4-6 skinless chicken breast halves
10 3/4-oz. can cream of chicken or celery soup
4-6 potatoes, peeled and sliced
6-oz. pkg. stuffing mix
1 1/4 cups water
2 Tbsp. melted butter
1-1 1/2 cups frozen green beans, thawed

1. Place chicken in slow cooker.
2. Spoon soup over chicken.
3. Top with potatoes.
4. Combine stuffing mix, water, and butter. Spoon over potatoes.
5. Cover. Cook on low 6 hours.
6. Sprinkle green beans over stuffing.
7. Cover. Cook on low 45-60 minutes, or until beans are just tender.
8. Serve with a salad.

Chicken and Dumplings

Bonnie Miller
Louisville, OH

Makes 4 servings

2 lbs. boneless, skinless chicken breasts
1 3/4 cups chicken broth
2 chicken bouillon cubes
2 tsp. salt
1 tsp. pepper
1 tsp. poultry seasoning
2 celery ribs, cut into 1" pieces
6 small carrots, cut into 1" chunks

Biscuits:
2 cups buttermilk biscuit mix
½ cup, plus 1 Tbsp., milk
1 tsp. parsley

1. Place chicken in slow cooker.
2. Dissolve bouillon in both. Add to chicken.
3. Add salt, pepper, and poultry seasoning.
4. Spread celery and carrots over top.
5. Cover. Cook on low 6-8 hours or high 3 - 3½ hours.
6. Combine biscuit ingredients until just moistened. Drop by spoonfuls over steaming chicken.
7. Cover. Cook on high 35 minutes. Do not remove cover while dumplings are cooking. Serve immediately.

Menu Idea

Chicken and Dumplings
Cole Slaw
Baked Apples (page 221)
Cookies

Scalloped Chicken
Brenda Joy Sonnie
Newton, PA

Makes 4-6 servings

4 cups cooked chicken
1 box stuffing mix for chicken
2 eggs
1 cup water
1½ cups milk
1 cup frozen peas

1. Combine chicken and dry stuffing mix. Place in slow cooker.
2. Beat together eggs, water, and milk. Pour over chicken and stuffing.

---

3. Cover. Cook on high 2-3 hours. Add frozen peas during last hour of cooking.

Variation: For more flavor use chicken broth instead of water.

Hot Chicken Sandwiches
Glenna Fay Bergey
Lebanon, OR

Makes 6-8 servings

1 large chicken
1 cup water

1. Place chicken in slow cooker. Add water.
2. Cover. Cook on low 6-7 hours.
3. Debone chicken. Mix cut-up chicken with broth.
4. Spoon into dinner rolls with straining spoon to make small hot sandwiches. Top with your favorite condiments.

Note: This is also a great way to prepare a chicken for soups or casseroles. Save the broth if you're making soup.

Menu Idea

Hot Chicken Sandwiches
Carrot and Celery Sticks
Pickles and Olives
Chips

Chicken Wings Colorado

Nancy Rexrode Clark
Woodstock, MD

Makes 6-8 servings

1 1/2 cups sugar
1/4 tsp. salt
1 chicken bouillon cube
1 cup cider vinegar
1/2 cup ketchup
2 Tbsp. soy sauce
12-16 chicken wings
1/4 cup cornstarch
1/2 cup cold water
red hot sauce to taste, optional

1. Combine sugar, salt, bouillon cube, vinegar, ketchup, and soy sauce and bring to boil in slow cooker.
2. Add chicken wings, pushing them down into the sauce.
3. Cover. Cook on low 6-7 hours.
4. Combine cornstarch and cold water. Add to slow cooker.
5. Cover. Cook on high until liquid thickens, about 30 minutes.
6. Season with red hot sauce, or let each diner add to his or her own serving.

Levi's Sesame Chicken Wings

Shirley Unternahrer Hinh
Wayland, IA

*Makes 16 appetizer servings,
or 6-8 main-dish servings*

3 lbs. chicken wings
salt to taste
pepper to taste
1 3/4 cups honey
1 cup soy sauce
1/2 cup ketchup
2 Tbsp. canola oil
2 Tbsp. sesame oil
2 garlic cloves, minced
toasted sesame seeds

1. Rinse wings. Cut at joint. Sprinkle with salt and pepper. Place on broiler pan.
2. Broil 5 inches from top, 10 minutes on each side. Place chicken in slow cooker.
3. Combine remaining ingredients except sesame seeds. Pour over chicken.
4. Cover. Cook on low 5 hours or high 2 1/2 hours.
5. Sprinkle sesame seeds over top just before serving.
6. Serve as appetizer, or with white or brown rice and shredded lettuce to turn this appetizer into a meal.

My husband and his co-workers have a "pot-luck-lunch" at work. I think this is a nice way to break the monotony of the week or month. And it gives them a chance to share. What better way to keep it ready than a slow cooker!

Turkey Main Dishes

Slow Cooker Turkey Breast

Liz Ann Yoder
Hartville, OH

Makes 8-10 servings

6-lb. turkey breast
2 tsp. oil
salt to taste
pepper to taste
1 medium onion, quartered
4 garlic cloves, peeled
¹/₂ cup water

1. Rinse turkey and pat dry with paper towels.

2. Rub oil over turkey. Sprinkle with salt and pepper. Place, meaty side up, in large slow cooker.

3. Place onion and garlic around sides of cooker.

4. Cover. Cook on low 9-10 hours, or until meat thermometer stuck in meaty part of breast registers 170°.

5. Remove from slow cooker and let stand 10 minutes before slicing.

6. Serve with mashed potatoes, cranberry salad, and corn or green beans.

Variations:

1. Add carrot chunks and chopped celery to Step 3 to add more flavor to the turkey broth.

2. Reserve broth for soups, or thicken with flour-water paste and serve as gravy over sliced turkey.

3. Freeze broth in pint-sized containers for future use.

4. Debone turkey and freeze in pint-sized containers for future use. Or freeze any leftover turkey after serving the meal described above.

Turkey Breast with Orange Sauce

Jean Butzer
Batavia, NY

Makes 4-6 servings

1 large onion, chopped
3 garlic cloves, minced
1 tsp. dried rosemary
1/2 tsp. pepper
2-3-lb. boneless, skinless turkey breast
1 1/2 cups orange juice

1. Place onions in slow cooker.
2. Combine garlic, rosemary, and pepper.
3. Make gashes in turkey, about 3/4 of the way through at 2" intervals. Stuff with herb mixture. Place turkey in slow cooker.
4. Pour juice over turkey.
5. Cover. Cook on low 7-8 hours, or until turkey is no longer pink in center.

This very easy, impressive-looking and -tasting recipe is perfect for company.

Turkey Crockpot

Arlene Leaman Kliewer
Lakewood, CO

Makes 8 servings

5-lb. turkey breast
1 pkg. dry onion soup mix
16-oz. can whole cranberry sauce

1. Place turkey in slow cooker.
2. Combine soup mix and cranberry sauce. Spread over turkey.
3. Cover. Cook on low 8 hours.

Easy Turkey Breast

Susan Stephani Smith
Monument, CO

Makes 12 servings

1 Jenny O'Turkey Breast — with bone in and with gravy packet
salt

1. Wash frozen breast and sprinkle with salt.
2. Place turkey, gravy packet up, in slow cooker that's large enough to be covered when the turkey breast is in it.
3. Cover. Cook turkey on low 6-7 hours, or until tender, removing gravy packet when the turkey is partially thawed.(Keep packet in refrigerator.)
4. Make gravy according to directions on packet. Warm before serving.

Stuffed Turkey Breast

Jean Butzer
Batavia, NY

Makes 8 servings

1/4 cup butter, melted
1 small onion, finely chopped
1/2 cup finely chopped celery
21/2-oz. pkg. croutons with real bacon bits
1 cup chicken broth
2 Tbsp. fresh minced parsley
1/2 tsp. poultry seasoning
1 whole uncooked turkey breast,
    or 2 halves (about 5 lbs.)
salt to taste
pepper to taste
24" x 26" piece of cheesecloth for each
    breast half
dry white wine

1. Combine butter, onion, celery, croutons, broth, parsley, and poultry seasoning.
2. Cut turkey breast in thick slices from breastbone to rib cage, leaving slices attached to bone (crosswise across breast).
3. Sprinkle turkey with salt and pepper.
4. Soak cheesecloth in wine. Place turkey on cheesecloth. Stuff bread mixture into slits between turkey slices. Fold one end of cheesecloth over the other to cover meat. Place on metal rack or trivet in 5- or 6-qt. slow cooker.
5. Cover. Cook on low 7-9 hours or until tender. Pour additional wine over turkey during cooking.
6. Remove from pot and remove cheesecloth immediately. If browner breast is preferred, remove from pot and brown in 400° oven for 15-20 minutes. Let stand 10 minutes before slicing through and serving.
7. Thicken the drippings, if you wish, for gravy. Mix together 3 Tbsp. cornstarch and 1/4 cup cold water. When smooth, stir into broth (with turkey removed from cooker).

Turn cooker to high and stir until cornstarch paste is dissolved. Allow to cook for about 10 minutes, until broth is thickened and smooth.

Slow Cooker Turkey and Dressing

Carol Sherwood
Batavia, NY

Makes 4-6 servings

8-oz. pkg., or 2 6-oz. pkgs., stuffing mix
1/2 cup hot water
2 Tbsp. butter, softened
1 onion, chopped
1/2 cup chopped celery
1/4 cup sweetened, dried cranberries
3-lb. boneless turkey breast
1/4 tsp. dried basil
1/2 tsp. salt
1/2 tsp. pepper

1. Spread dry stuffing mix in greased slow cooker.
2. Add water, butter, onion, celery, and cranberries. Mix well.
3. Sprinkle turkey breast with basil, salt, and pepper. Place over stuffing mixture.
4. Cover. Cook on low 5-6 hours, or until turkey is done but not dry.
5. Remove turkey. Slice and set aside.
6. Gently stir stuffing and allow to sit for 5 minutes before serving.
7. Place stuffing on platter, topped with sliced turkey.

Zucchini and Turkey Dish

Dolores Kratz
Souderton, PA

Makes 6 servings

3 cups zucchini, sliced
1 small onion, chopped
1/4 tsp. salt
1 cup cubed cooked turkey
2 fresh tomatoes, sliced,
    or 14 1/2-oz. can diced tomatoes
1/2 tsp. dried oregano
1 tsp. dried basil
1/4 cup grated Parmesan cheese
1/2 cup shredded provolone cheese
3/4 cup Pepperidge Farms stuffing

1. Combine zucchini, onion, salt, turkey, tomatoes, oregano, and basil in slow cooker. Mix well.
2. Top with cheeses and stuffing.
3. Cover. Cook on low 8-9 hours.

Slow-Cooked Turkey Dinner

Miriam Nolt
New Holland, PA

Makes 4-6 servings

1 onion, diced
6 small red potatoes, quartered
2 cups sliced carrots
1 1/2-2 lbs. boneless, skinless turkey thighs
1/4 cup flour
2 Tbsp. dry onion soup mix
10 3/4-oz. can cream of mushroom soup
2/3 cup chicken broth or water

1. Place vegetables in bottom of slow cooker.
2. Place turkey thighs over vegetables.
3. Combine remaining ingredients. Pour over turkey.
4. Cover. Cook on high 30 minutes. Reduce heat to low and cook 7 hours.

Barbecued Turkey Legs

Barbara Walker
Sturgis, SC

Makes 4-6 servings

4 turkey drumsticks
1-2 tsp. salt
1/4-1/2 tsp. pepper
1/3 cup molasses
1/4 cup vinegar
1/2 cup ketchup
3 Tbsp. Worcestershire sauce
3/4 tsp. hickory smoke
2 Tbsp. instant minced onion

1. Sprinkle turkey with salt and pepper. Place in slow cooker.
2. Combine remaining ingredients. Pour over turkey.
3. Cover. Cook on low 5-7 hours.

Barbecued Turkey Cutlets

Maricarol Magill
Freehold, NJ

Makes 6-8 servings

6-8 (1 1/2-2 lbs.) turkey cutlets
1/4 cup molasses
1/4 cup cider vinegar
1/4 cup ketchup
3 Tbsp. Worcestershire sauce
1 tsp. garlic salt
3 Tbsp. chopped onion
2 Tbsp. brown sugar
1/4 tsp. pepper

1. Place turkey cutlets in slow cooker.
2. Combine remaining ingredients. Pour over turkey.
3. Cover. Cook on low 4 hours.
4. Serve over white or brown rice.

Turkey and Sweet Potato Casserole

Michele Ruvola
Selden, NY

Makes 4 servings

3 medium sweet potatoes, peeled and cut into 2" pieces
10-oz. pkg. frozen cut green beans
2 lbs. turkey cutlets
12-oz. jar home-style turkey gravy
2 Tbsp. flour
1 tsp. parsley flakes
1/4-1/2 tsp. dried rosemary leaves, crumbled
1/8 tsp. pepper

1. Layer sweet potatoes, green beans, and turkey in slow cooker.
2. Combine remaining ingredients until smooth. Pour over mixture in slow cooker.
3. Cover. Cook on low 8-10 hours.
4. Remove turkey and vegetables and keep warm. Stir sauce. Serve with sauce over meat and vegetables, or with sauce in a gravy boat.
5. Serve with biscuits and cranberry sauce.

Turkey Barbecue

Marcia S. Myer
Manheim, PA

Makes 8 servings

2 lbs. chopped cooked turkey
1¼ cups ketchup
1 tsp. dry mustard
4 tsp. vinegar
4 tsp. Worcestershire sauce
2 Tbsp. sugar
1 tsp. onion salt
8 hamburger buns

1. Combine all ingredients in slow cooker.
2. Cover. Cook on low 3-4 hours.
3. Serve on hamburger buns.

Note: You can make the turkey by putting 2 lbs. uncooked turkey tenderloins in slow cooker, adding ½ cup water, and cooking the meat on low for 6 hours, or until juices run clear.

Turkey Sloppy Joes

Marla Folkerts
Holland, OH

Makes 6 servings

1 red onion, chopped
1 sweet pepper, chopped
1½ lbs. boneless turkey, finely chopped
1 cup chili sauce or ketchup
¼ tsp. salt
1 garlic clove, minced
1 tsp. Dijon-style mustard
⅛ tsp. pepper
thickly sliced homemade bread,
    or 6 sandwich rolls

1. Place onion, sweet pepper, and turkey in slow cooker.
2. Combine chili sauce, salt, garlic, mustard, and pepper. Pour over turkey mixture. Mix well.
3. Cover. Cook on low 4½-6 hours.
4. Serve on homemade bread or sandwich rolls.

Turkey Loaf and Potatoes
Lizzie Weaver
Ephrata, PA

Makes 6-7 servings

2 lbs. ground turkey
1½ cups soft bread crumbs, or oatmeal
2 eggs, slightly beaten
1 small onion, chopped
1 tsp. salt
1 tsp. dry mustard
¼ cup ketchup
¼ cup evaporated milk
6 medium-sized potatoes, quartered

1. Combine all ingredients except potatoes. Form into loaf to fit in slow cooker.
2. Tear 4 strips of aluminum foil, each 18" x 2". Position them in the slow cooker, spoke-fashion, with the ends sticking out over the edges of the cooker to act as handles. Place loaf down in the cooker, centered over the foil strips.
3. Place potatoes around meat.
4. Cover. Cook on high 4-5 hours, or until potatoes are soft.
5. Serve with gravy, green vegetable, and cole slaw.

Savory Turkey Meatballs in Italian Sauce
Marla Folkerts
Holland, OH

Makes 8 servings

28-oz. can crushed tomatoes
1 Tbsp. red wine vinegar
1 medium onion, finely chopped
2 garlic cloves, minced
¼ tsp. Italian herb seasoning
1 tsp. dried basil
1 lb. ground turkey
⅛ tsp. garlic powder
⅛ tsp. black pepper
⅓ cup dried parsley
2 egg whites
¼ tsp. dried minced onion
⅓ cup quick oats
¼ cup grated Parmesan cheese
¼ cup flour
oil

1. Combine tomatoes, vinegar, onions, garlic, Italian seasonings, and basil in slow cooker. Turn to low.
2. Combine remaining ingredients, except flour and oil. Form into 1" balls. Dredge each ball in flour. Brown in oil in skillet over medium heat. Transfer to slow cooker. Stir into sauce.
3. Cover. Cook on low 6-8 hours.
4. Serve over pasta or rice.

Note: The meatballs and sauce freeze well.

Tricia's Cranberry Turkey Meatballs

Shirley Unternahrer Hinh
Wayland, IA

Makes 12 servings

16-oz. can jelled cranberry sauce
1/2 cup ketchup or barbecue sauce
1 egg
1 lb. ground turkey
half a small onion, chopped
1 tsp. salt
1/4 tsp. black pepper
1-2 tsp. grated orange peel, optional

1. Combine cranberry sauce and ketchup in slow cooker.
2. Cover. Cook on high until sauce is mixed.
3. Combine remaining ingredients. Shape into 24 balls.
4. Cook over medium heat in skillet for 8-10 minutes, or just until browned. Add to sauce in slow cooker.
5. Cover. Cook on low 3 hours.
6. Serve with rice and a steamed vegetable.

Turkey Meatballs and Gravy

Betty Sue Good
Broadway, VA

Makes 8 servings

2 eggs, beaten
3/4 cup bread crumbs
1/2 cup finely chopped onions
1/2 cup finely chopped celery
2 Tbsp. chopped fresh parsley
1/4 tsp. pepper
1/8 tsp. garlic powder
1 tsp. salt
2 lbs. ground raw turkey
1 1/2 Tbsp. cooking oil
10 3/4-oz. can cream of mushroom soup
1 cup water
7/8-oz. pkg. turkey gravy mix
1/2 tsp. dried thyme
2 bay leaves

1. Combine eggs, bread crumbs, onions, celery, parsley, pepper, garlic powder, salt, and meat. Shape into 1 1/2" balls.
2. Brown meat balls in oil in skillet. Drain meatballs and transfer to slow cooker.
3. Combine soup, water, dry gravy mix, thyme, and bay leaves. Pour over meatballs.
4. Cover. Cook on low 6-8 hours or high 3-4 hours. Discard bay leaves before serving.
5. Serve over mashed potatoes or buttered noodles.

Meat and Bean Main Dishes

"Famous" Baked Beans

Katrine Rose
Woodbridge, VA

Makes 10 servings

1 lb. ground beef
1/4 cup minced onions
1 cup ketchup
4 15-oz. cans pork and beans
1 cup brown sugar
2 Tbsp. liquid smoke
1 Tbsp. Worcestershire sauce

1. Brown beef and onions in skillet. Drain. Spoon meat and onions into slow cooker.
2. Add remaining ingredients and stir well.
3. Cover. Cook on high 3 hours or on low 5-6 hours.

There are many worthy baked bean recipes, but these are both easy and absolutely delicious. The secret to this recipe is the liquid smoke. I get many requests for this recipe, and some friends have added the word "famous" to its name.

Esther's Barbecued Beans

Esther J. Yoder
Hartville, OH

Makes 10 servings

1 lb. ground beef
1/2 cup chopped onions
1/2 tsp. salt
1/4 tsp. pepper
28-oz. can pork and beans (your favorite variety)
1/2 cup ketchup
1 Tbsp. Worcestershire sauce
1 Tbsp. vinegar
1/4 tsp. Tabasco sauce

1. Brown beef and onions together in skillet. Drain.
2. Combine all ingredients in slow cooker.
3. Cover. Cook on high 2-3 hours, stirring once or twice.
4. Serve with fresh raw vegetables and canned peaches.

Note: These beans' flavor gets better on the second and third days.

Dollywood Cowboy Beans
Reba Rhodes
Bridgewater, VA

Makes 8 servings

1 lb. ground beef
1 large onion, finely chopped
1 small green bell pepper, finely chopped
28-oz. can pork and beans
1½ cups ketchup
1 tsp. vinegar
3 Tbsp. brown sugar
2 tsp. prepared mustard
2 tsp. salt
1 tsp. pepper

1. Brown ground beef, onion, and bell pepper in skillet. Transfer to slow cooker.
2. Combine all ingredients in slow cooker. Mix well.
3. Cover. Cook on low 1-2 hours.

This travels well to a potluck or a picnic.

Hamburger Beans
Joanne Kennedy
Plattsburgh, NY

Makes 6 servings

1 lb. ground beef
1 onion, chopped
2 15-oz. cans pork and beans
15-oz. can butter beans, drained
15-oz. can kidney beans, drained
½ tsp. garlic powder
1 cup ketchup
¾ cup molasses
½ cup brown sugar

1. Brown ground beef and onion in skillet. Drain and transfer beef and onion into slow cooker.
2. Add remaining ingredients. Mix well.
3. Cover. Cook on low 6-7 hours.

One-Pot Dinner
Vicki Dinkel
Sharon Springs, KS

Makes 4 servings

½-1 lb. ground beef, according to your preference
½ lb. bacon, cut in pieces
1 cup chopped onions
2 31-oz. cans pork and beans
16-oz. can kidney beans, drained
1 cup ketchup
16-oz. can butter beans, drained
¼ cup brown sugar
1 Tbsp. liquid smoke
3 Tbsp. white vinegar
1 tsp. salt
dash of pepper

1. Brown ground beef in skillet. Drain off drippings. Place beef in slow cooker.
2. Brown bacon and onions in skillet. Drain off drippings. Add bacon and onions to slow cooker.
3. Stir remaining ingredients into cooker.
4. Cover. Cook on low 5-9 hours or high 3 hours.

Calico Beans
Mary Rogers
Waseca, MN

Makes 12-15 servings

1 lb. bacon
1 lb. ground beef
1/2 cup chopped onions
1/2 cup chopped celery
1/2 cup ketchup
1 Tbsp. prepared mustard
16-oz. can kidney beans, undrained
16-oz. can Great Northern beans,
   undrained
1/2 cup brown sugar
1 Tbsp. vinegar
16-oz. can butter beans, undrained
28-oz. can Bush's Baked Beans

1. Cut bacon in small pieces. Brown in skillet. Drain.
2. Brown ground beef in skillet and drain, reserving drippings.
3. Saute onions and celery in drippings until soft.
4. Combine all ingredients in slow cooker.
5. Cover. Simmer on low 3-4 hours.

This is a favorite dish that we serve at neighborhood and family gatherings any time of the year. Our children especially enjoy it.

Calico Beans
Alice Miller
Stuarts Draft, VA

Makes 10-12 servings

1/2 lb. ground beef
1/2 lb. bacon, chopped
1/2 cup chopped onions
1/2 cup ketchup
3/4 cup brown sugar
1/4 cup sugar
2 Tbsp. vinegar
1 tsp. dry mustard
1 tsp. salt
16-oz. can pork and beans, undrained
16-oz. can red kidney beans, undrained
16-oz. can yellow limas, undrained
16-oz. can navy beans, undrained

1. Brown ground beef, bacon, and onions together in skillet. Drain off all but 2 Tbsp. drippings. Spoon meat and onions into slow cooker.
2. Stir ketchup, brown sugar, sugar, vinegar, mustard, and salt into drippings. Mix together well. Add to slow cooker.
3. Pour beans into slow cooker and combine all ingredients thoroughly.
4. Cover. Cook on high 3-4 hours.
5. Serve over rice, or take to a picnic as is.

Cowboy Beans

Sharon Timpe
Mequon, WI

Makes 10-12 servings

6 slices bacon, cut in pieces
1/2 cup onions, chopped
1 garlic clove, minced
16-oz. can baked beans
16-oz. can kidney beans, drained
15-oz. can butter beans or pinto beans, drained
2 Tbsp. dill pickle relish or chopped dill pickles
1/3 cup chili sauce or ketchup
2 tsp. Worcestershire sauce
1/2 cup brown sugar
1/8 tsp. hot pepper sauce, optional

1. Lightly brown bacon, onions, and garlic in skillet. Drain.
2. Combine all ingredients in slow cooker. Mix well.
3. Cover. Cook on low 5-7 hours or high 3-4 hours.

Trio Bean Casserole

Stacy Schmucker Stoltzfus
Enola, PA

Makes 4-6 servings

16-oz. can kidney beans, drained
16-oz. can green beans, drained
16-oz. can pork and beans with tomato sauce
1/2 cup chopped onions
1/2 cup brown sugar
1/2 cup ketchup

1 Tbsp. vinegar
1 tsp. prepared mustard
1 lb. bacon, fried and crumbled, or 1 lb. cooked ham, cubed
1 Tbsp. barbecue sauce

1. Combine all ingredients in slow cooker. Stir well.
2. Cover. Cook on high 2 hours or low 3-4 hours.

Menu Idea

Trio Bean Casserole
White Rice
Cornbread
Raw Veggies with Dip

Deb's Baked Beans

Deborah Swartz
Grottoes, VA

Makes 4-6 servings

4 slices bacon, fried and drained
2 Tbsp. reserved drippings
1/2 cup chopped onions
2 15-oz. cans pork and beans
1/2 tsp. salt, optional
2 Tbsp. brown sugar
1 Tbsp. Worcestershire sauce
1 tsp. prepared mustard

1. Fry bacon in skillet until crisp. Reserve 2 Tbsp. drippings. Crumble bacon.
2. Cook onions in bacon drippings.
3. Combine all ingredients in slow cooker.
4. Cover. Cook on high 1 1/2-2 hours.

Lotsa-Beans Pot

Dorothy Van Deest
Memphis, TN

Makes 15-20 servings

8 bacon strips, diced
2 onions, thinly sliced
1 cup packed brown sugar
1/2 cup cider vinegar
1 tsp. salt
1 tsp. ground mustard
1/2 tsp. garlic powder
28-oz. can baked beans
16-oz. can kidney beans, rinsed and drained
15 1/2-oz. can pinto beans, rinsed and drained
15-oz. can lima beans, rinsed and drained
15 1/2-oz. can black-eyed peas, rinsed and rained

1. Cook bacon in skillet until crisp. Remove to paper towels.
2. Drain, reserving 2 Tbsp. drippings.
3. Saute onions in drippings until tender.
4. Add brown sugar, vinegar, salt, mustard, and garlic powder to skillet. Bring to boil.
5. Combine beans and peas in slow cooker. Add onion mixture and bacon. Mix well.
6. Cover. Cook on high 3-4 hours.

This hearty bean concoction tastes especially yummy when the gang comes in from a Saturday afternoon of raking leaves. Keep it warm to hot and serve it from the pot.

Menu Idea

Lotsa-Beans Pot
Herby Garlic Bread
Cheese Cubes
Pickles and Celery

Auntie Ginny's Baked Beans

Becky Harder
Monument, CO

Makes 8 servings

4 slices bacon, diced
28-oz. can pork and beans
1 tsp. dark molasses
1 Tbsp. brown sugar
1 cup dates, cut up
1 medium onion, chopped

1. Partially fry bacon. Drain.
2. Combine ingredients in slow cooker.
3. Cover. Cook on low 4-5 hours.

Note: There are many varieties of canned baked beans available. Choose a flavor that fits your guests—from vegetarian (you'll want to leave out the bacon above if this is important to your diners) to country-style to onion.

Written down at the bottom of this recipe was this note: "Harder picnic—1974." Notations such as that one help us remember special family get-togethers or reunions. This recipe was shared almost 20 years ago as we gathered cousins and aunts together in our hometown. Today no one from our family lives in the hometown and we cousins are scattered over six states, but one way to enjoy fond memories is to record dates or events on recipes we share with each other.

Menu Idea

Grilled Chicken
Aunt Ginny's Baked Beans
Chips
Fresh Vegetables, cut-up
Fresh Fruit, cut-up
S'mores

Creole Black Beans

Joyce Kaut
Rochester, NY

Makes 6-8 servings

1½-2 lbs. smoked sausage,
  sliced in ½" pieces, browned
3 15-oz. cans black beans, drained
1½ cups chopped onions
1½ cups chopped green peppers
1½ cups chopped celery
4 garlic cloves, minced
2 tsp. dried thyme
1½ tsp. dried oregano
1½ tsp. pepper
1 chicken bouillon cube
3 bay leaves
8-oz. can tomato sauce
1 cup water

1. Combine all ingredients in slow cooker.
2. Cover. Cook on low 8 hours or on high 4 hours.
3. Remove bay leaves.
4. Serve over rice, with a salad and fresh fruit for dessert.

Variation: You may substitute a 14.5-oz. can of stewed tomatoes for the tomato sauce.

Pizza Beans

Kelly Evenson
Pittsboro, NC

Makes 6 servings

16-oz. can pinto beans, drained
16-oz. can kidney beans, drained
2.25-oz. can ripe olives sliced, drained
28-oz. can stewed or whole tomatoes
¾ lb. bulk Italian sausage
1 Tbsp. oil
1 green pepper, chopped
1 medium onion, chopped
1 garlic clove, minced
1 tsp. salt
1 tsp. dried oregano
1 tsp. dried basil
Parmesan cheese

1. Combine beans, olives, and tomatoes in slow cooker.
2. Brown sausage in oil in skillet. Drain, reserving drippings. Transfer sausage to slow cooker.
3. Saute green pepper in drippings 1 minute, stirring constantly. Add onions and continue stirring until onions start to become translucent. Add garlic and cook 1 more minute. Transfer to slow cooker.
4. Stir in seasonings.
5. Cover. Cook on low 7-9 hours.
6. To serve, sprinkle with Parmesan cheese.

Variation: For a thicker soup, 20 minutes before serving remove ¼ cup liquid from cooker and add 1 Tbsp. cornstarch. Stir until dissolved. Return to soup. Cook on high for 15 minutes, or until thickened.

Pioneer Beans
Kay Magruder
Seminole, OK

Makes 4-6 servings

1 lb. dry lima beans
1 bunch green onions, chopped
3 beef bouillon cubes
6 cups water
1 lb. smoked sausage
1/2 tsp. garlic powder
3/4 tsp. Tabasco sauce

1. Combine all ingredients in slow cooker. Mix well.
2. Cover. Cook on high 8-9 hours, or until beans are soft but not mushy.
3. Serve with home-baked bread and butter.

Dawn's Special Beans
Dawn Day
Westminster, CA

Makes 8-10 servings

16-oz. can kidney beans
16-oz. can small white beans
16-oz. can butter beans
16-oz. can small red beans
1 cup chopped onions
2 tsp. dry mustard
1/2 tsp. hickory-smoke flavoring
1/2 cup dark brown sugar
1/2 cup honey
1 cup barbecue sauce
2 Tbsp. apple cider vinegar

1. Combine all ingredients in slow cooker.
2. Cover. Cook on low 6 hours.

3. Serve with hot dogs, hamburgers, and any other picnic food. These beans are also great for a potluck.

Note: If you like soupy beans, do not drain the beans before adding them to the cooker. If you prefer a drier outcome, drain all beans before pouring into cooker.

Partytime Beans
Beatrice Martin
Goshen, IN

Makes 14-16 servings

1 1/2 cups ketchup
1 onion, chopped
1 green pepper, chopped
1 sweet red pepper, chopped
1/2 cup water
1/2 cup packed brown sugar
2 bay leaves
2-3 tsp. cider vinegar
1 tsp. ground mustard
1/8 tsp. pepper
16-oz. can kidney beans, rinsed and drained
15 1/2-oz. can Great Northern beans, rinsed and drained
15-oz. can lima beans, rinsed and drained
15-oz. can black beans, rinsed and drained
15 1/2-oz. can black-eyed peas, rinsed and drained

1. Combine first 10 ingredients in slow cooker. Mix well.
2. Add remaining ingredients. Mix well.
3. Cover. Cook on low 5-7 hours, or until onion and peppers are tender.
4. Remove bay leaves before serving.
5. Serve with grilled hamburgers, tossed salad or veggie tray, chips, fruit, and cookies.

Slow Cooker Kidney Beans

Jeanette Oberholtzer
Manheim, PA

Makes 12 servings

2 30-oz. cans kidney beans, rinsed and
  drained
28-oz. can diced tomatoes, drained
2 medium-sized red bell peppers, chopped
1 cup ketchup
½ cup brown sugar
¼ cup honey
¼ cup molasses
1 Tbsp. Worcestershire sauce
1 tsp. dry mustard
2 medium red apples, cored, cut into
  pieces

1. Combine all ingredients, except apples,
in slow cooker.
2. Cover. Cook on low 4-5 hours.
3. Stir in apples.
4. Cover. Cook 2 more hours.

Tasty, meatless eating!

Red Beans and Pasta

Naomi E. Fast
Hesston, KS

Makes 6-8 servings

3 15-oz. cans chicken, or vegetable, broth
½ tsp. ground cumin
1 Tbsp. chili powder
1 garlic clove, minced
8 ozs. uncooked spiral pasta
half a large green pepper, diced
half a large red pepper, diced
1 medium onion, diced
15-oz. can red beans, rinsed and drained
chopped fresh parsley
chopped fresh cilantro

1. Combine broth, cumin, chili powder, and
garlic in slow cooker.
2. Cover. Cook on high until mixture comes
to boil.
3. Add pasta, vegetables, and beans. Stir
together well.
4. Cover. Cook on low 3-4 hours.
5. Add parsley or cilantro before serving.

Menu Idea

Red Beans and Pasta
Cheese Cubes of many kinds
Crusty Multi-Grain Bread
Fresh Fruit Salad

Hosting Idea

Use name cards at plates with Bible
verses on backs of cards. Have all at the
table read their verses. That can take
the place of grace.

Other Main Dish Favorites

Lamb Stew

Dottie Schmidt
Kansas City, MO

Makes 6 servings

2 lbs. lamb, cubed
1/2 tsp. sugar
2 Tbsp. oil
2 tsp. salt
1/4 tsp. pepper
1/4 cup flour
2 cups water
3/4 cup red cooking wine
1/4 tsp. powdered garlic
2 tsp. Worcestershire sauce
6-8 carrots, sliced
4 small onions, quartered
4 ribs celery, sliced
3 medium potatoes, diced

1. Sprinkle lamb with sugar. Brown in oil in skillet.

2. Remove lamb and place in cooker, reserving drippings. Stir salt, pepper, and flour into drippings until smooth. Stir in water and wine, until smooth, stirring until broth simmers and thickens.

3. Pour into cooker. Add remaining ingredients and stir until well mixed.

4. Cover. Cook on low 8-10 hours.

5. Serve with crusty bread.

Lamb Chops

Shirley Sears
Tiskilwa, IL

Makes 6-8 servings

1 medium onion, sliced
1 tsp. dried oregano
1/2 tsp. dried thyme
1/2 tsp. garlic powder
1/4 tsp. salt
1/8 tsp. pepper
8 loin lamb chops (1 3/4-2 lbs.)
2 garlic cloves, minced
1/4 cup water

1. Place onion in slow cooker.
2. Combine oregano, thyme, garlic powder, salt, and pepper. Rub over lamb chops. Place in slow cooker. Top with garlic. Pour water down along side of cooker, so as not to disturb the rub on the chops.
3. Cover. Cook on low 4-6 hours.

Venison Roast

Colleen Heatwole
Burton, MI

Makes 6-8 servings

3-4-lb. venison roast
1/4 cup vinegar
2 garlic cloves, minced
2 Tbsp. salt
1/2 cup chopped onions
15-oz. can tomato sauce
1 Tbsp. ground mustard
1 pkg. brown gravy mix
1/2 tsp. salt
1/4 cup water

1. Place venison in deep bowl. Combine vinegar, garlic, and salt. Pour over venison. Add enough cold water to cover venison. Marinate for at least 8 hours in refrigerator.
2. Rinse and drain venison. Place in slow cooker.
3. Combine remaining ingredients and pour over venison.
4. Cover. Cook on low 10-12 hours.
5. Serve with a green salad, potatoes, and rolls to make a complete meal.

Note: The sauce on this roast works well for any meat.

This is an easy meal to have for a Saturday dinner with guests or extended family. There is usually a lot of sauce, so make plenty of potatoes, noodles, or rice.

Venison in Sauce

Anona M. Teel
Bangar, PA

Makes 12 sandwiches

3-4-lb. venison roast
1/2 cup vinegar
2 garlic cloves, minced
2 Tbsp. salt
cold water
oil
large onion, sliced
half a green pepper, sliced
2 ribs celery, sliced
1-2 garlic cloves, minced
1 1/2-2 tsp. salt
1/4 tsp. pepper
1/2 tsp. dried oregano
1/4 cup ketchup
1 cup tomato juice

1. Combine vinegar, garlic cloves, and 2 Tbsp. salt. Pour over venison. Add water until meat is covered. Marinate 6-8 hours.

2. Cut meat into pieces. Brown in oil in skillet. Place in slow cooker.

3. Mix remaining ingredients together; then pour into cooker. Stir in meat.

4. Cover. Cook on low 8-10 hours.

5. Using two forks, pull the meat apart and then stir it through the sauce.

6. Serve on sandwich rolls, or over rice or pasta.

Note: This recipe can be made in larger quantities to freeze and then reheat when needed.

This barbecue recipe was made in large quantities and served at the concession stand for our farm machinery sale in 1987. They used ice cream dippers to scoop the meat into the sandwich rolls.

Company Seafood Pasta

Jennifer Yoder Sommers
Harrisonburg, VA

Makes 4-6 servings

2 cups sour cream
3 cups shredded Monterey Jack cheese
2 Tbsp. butter or margarine, melted
1/2 lb. crabmeat, or imitation flaked
  crabmeat
1/8 tsp. pepper
1/2 lb. bay scallops, lightly cooked
1 lb. medium shrimp, cooked and peeled

1. Combine sour cream, cheese and butter in slow cooker.

2. Stir in remaining ingredients.

3. Cover. Cook on low 1-2 hours.

4. Serve immediately over linguine. Garnish with fresh parsley.

Beef-Venison Barbecue

Gladys Longacre
Susquehanna, PA

Makes 8 servings

1 1/2 lbs. ground beef
1/2 lb. ground venison
oil, if needed
1 onion, chopped
1/2 cup chopped green peppers
1 garlic clove, minced
1 tsp. salt
1/4 tsp. pepper
1/2 tsp. dried thyme
1 tsp. dried oregano
1 tsp. dried basil
1/4 cup brown sugar
1/4 cup vinegar
1 Tbsp. dry mustard
1 cup ketchup
1/2-1 Tbsp. hickory-smoked barbecue sauce
8 hamburger rolls

1. Brown meat in skillet, in oil if needed. Place in slow cooker.

2. Add remaining ingredients. Mix well.

3. Cover. Cook on high 1 hour or low 2-3 hours.

4. Serve barbecue in hamburger rolls.

Curried Shrimp

Charlotte Shaffer
East Earl, PA

Makes 4-5 servings

1 small onion, chopped
2 cups cooked shrimp
1 tsp. curry powder
10¾-oz. can cream of mushroom soup
1 cup sour cream

1. Combine all ingredients except sour cream in slow cooker.
2. Cover. Cook on low 4-6 hours.
3. Ten minutes before serving, stir in sour cream.
4. Serve over rice or puff pastry.

Variation: Add another ½ tsp. curry for some added flavor.

Tuna Noodle Casserole

Ruth Hofstetter
Versailles, Missouri

Makes 8 servings

2½ cups dry noodles
1 tsp. salt
½ cup finely chopped onion
6- or 12-oz. can tuna, according to your
    taste preference
10¾-oz. can cream of mushroom soup
half a soup can of water
¼ cup almonds, optional
½ cup shredded Swiss or sharp cheddar
    cheese
1 cup frozen peas

1. Combine all ingredients in slow cooker, except peas.
2. Cover. Cook on high 2-3 hours or on low 6-8 hours, stirring occasionally.
3. Twenty minutes before end of cooking time, stir in peas and reduce heat to low if cooking on high.

Oriental Shrimp Casserole

Sharon Wantland
Menomonee Falls, WI

Makes 10 servings

4 cups cooked rice
2 cups cooked or canned shrimp
1 cup cooked or canned chicken
1-lb. can (2 cups) Chinese vegetables
10¾-oz. can cream of celery soup
½ cup milk
½ cup chopped green peppers
1 Tbsp. soy sauce
can of Chinese noodles

1. Combine all ingredients except noodles in slow cooker.
2. Cover. Cook on low 45 minutes.
3. Top with noodles just before serving.

Macaroni and Cheese

Sherry L. Lapp
Lancaster, PA

Makes 8 servings

8-oz. pkg. elbow macaroni,
  cooked al dente
13-oz. can evaporated milk
1 cup whole milk
1/4 cup butter, melted
2 large eggs, slightly beaten
4 cups grated sharp cheddar cheese,
  divided
1/4-1/2 tsp. salt, according to your taste
  preferences
1/8 tsp. white pepper
1/4 cup grated Parmesan cheese

1. In slow cooker, combine lightly cooked macaroni, evaporated milk, whole milk, melted butter, eggs, 3 cups cheddar cheese, salt, and pepper.

2. Top with remaining cheddar and Parmesan cheeses.

3. Cover. Cook on low 3 hours.

Crockpot Macaroni

Lisa F. Good
Harrisonburg, VA

Makes 6 servings

1 1/2 cups dry macaroni
3 Tbsp. butter
1 tsp. salt
1/2 lb. Velveeta cheese, sliced
1 qt. milk

1. Combine macaroni, butter, and salt.

2. Layer cheese over top.

3. Pour in milk.

4. Cover. Cook on high 3-4 hours, or until macaroni are soft.

Slow and Easy Macaroni and Cheese

Janice Muller
Derwood, MD

Makes 6-8 servings

1 lb. dry macaroni
1/2 cup butter or margarine
2 eggs
12-oz. can evaporated milk
10 3/4-oz. can cheddar cheese soup
1 cup milk
4 cups shredded cheddar cheese, divided
1/8 tsp. paprika

1. Cook macaroni al dente. Drain and pour hot macaroni into slow cooker.

2. Slice butter into chunks and add to macaroni. Stir until melted.

3. Combine, eggs, evaporated milk, soup, and milk. Add 3 cups cheese. Pour over macaroni and mix well.

4. Cover. Cook on low 4 hours. Sprinkle with remaining cheese. Cook 15 minutes until cheese melts.

5. Sprinkle with paprika before serving.

Variation: Add 12-oz. can drained tuna to Step 3.

Macaroni and Cheese

Leona Yoder
Hartville, OH

Makes 8-10 servings

2-3 Tbsp. butter or margarine
1 qt. milk
1 lb. mild cheese, grated, or Velveeta
   cheese, cubed
1/2 tsp. salt
1/8 tsp. pepper
1 lb. macaroni, cooked al dente and rinsed

1. Melt margarine in large saucepan. Add milk. Heat slowly but do not boil.
2. When very hot, stir in cheese, salt, and pepper. Stir until cheese is melted.
3. Stir in macaroni.
4. Pour into greased slow cooker.
5. Cover. Cook on high 15 minutes, then on low 30 minutes.

This recipe is an oven-saver.

Fifty-sixty children eat this delightedly—in fact, it's one of their favorite meals—at the day school where I cook.

Menu Idea

Macaroni and Cheese
Lil' Smokie Sausages,
Applesauce
Fresh Veggies with Dip
Steamed Green Beans

Macaroni and Cheese

Arlene Groff
Lewistown, PA

Makes 5 servings

8 cups cooked macaroni
1 1/4 cups milk
1 lb. (1/2 block) Velveeta cheese, cubed
1/4 cup melted butter

1. Place macaroni in greased slow cooker.
2. Layer cheese over top. Pour milk and butter over all.
3. Cover. Cook on low 4 hours, stirring once halfway through cooking time.

Easy Stuffed Shells

Rebecca Plank Leichty
Harrisonburg, VA

Makes 4-6 servings

20-oz. bag frozen stuffed shells
15-oz. can marinara or spaghetti sauce
15-oz. can green beans, drained

1. Place shells around edge of greased slow cooker.
2. Cover with marinara sauce.
3. Pour green beans in center.
4. Cover. Cook on low 8 hours or on high 3 hours.
5. Serve with garlic toast and salad.

Variation: *Reverse Steps 2 and 3. Double the amount of marinara sauce and pour over both the shells and the beans.*

Cheese Souffle Casserole

Vicki Dinkel
Sharon Spring, KS

Makes 4 servings

14 slices fresh bread, crusts removed, divided
3 cups grated sharp cheese, divided
2 Tbsp. butter or margarine, melted, divided
6 eggs
3 cups milk, scalded
2 tsp. Worcestershire sauce
1/2 tsp. salt
paprika

1. Tear bread into small pieces. Place half in well-greased slow cooker. Add half the grated cheese and half the butter. Repeat layers.
2. Beat together eggs, milk, Worcestershire sauce, and salt. Pour over bread and cheese. Sprinkle top with paprika.
3. Cover. Cook on low 4-6 hours.

Arroz Con Queso

Nadine L. Martinitz
Salina, KS

Makes 6-8 servings

14.5-oz. can whole tomatoes, mashed
15-oz. can Mexican style beans, undrained
1 1/2 cups uncooked long grain rice
1 cup grated Monterey Jack cheese
1 large onion, finely chopped
1 cup cottage cheese
4.25-oz. can chopped green chili peppers, drained
1 Tbsp. oil
3 garlic cloves, minced
1 tsp. salt
1 cup grated Monterey Jack cheese

1. Combine all ingredients except final cup of cheese. Pour into well greased slow cooker.
2. Cover. Cook on low 6-9 hours.
3. Sprinkle with remaining cheese before serving.
4. Serve with salsa.

Minestra Di Ceci

Jeanette Oberholtzer
Manheim, PA

Makes 4-6 servings

1 lb. dry chickpeas
1 sprig fresh rosemary
10 leaves fresh sage
2 Tbsp. salt
1-2 large garlic cloves, minced
olive oil
1 cup small dry pasta, your choice of
  shape, or dry penne

1. Wash chickpeas. Place in slow cooker. Soak for 8 hours in full pot of water, along with rosemary, sage, and salt.
2. Drain water. Remove herbs.
3. Refill slow cooker with water to 1" above peas.
4. Cover. Cook on low 5 hours.
5. Saute garlic in olive oil in skillet until clear.
6. Puree half of peas, along with several cups of broth from cooker, in blender. Return puree to slow cooker. Add garlic and oil.
7. Boil pasta in saucepan until al dente, about 5 minutes. Drain. Add to beans.
8. Cover. Cook on high 30-60 minutes, or until pasta is tender and heated through, but not mushy.

Variation: Add 1/2 tsp. black pepper to Step 1, if you like.

Easy Wheatberries

Elaine Vigoda

Rochester, NY
Makes 4-6 servings

1 cup wheatberries
1 cup couscous, or small pasta like orzo
14 1/2-oz. can broth
1/2-1 broth can of water
1/2 cup dried craisins

1. Cover wheatberries with water and soak 2 hours before cooking. Drain. Spoon wheatberries into slow cooker.
2. Combine with remaining ingredients in slow cooker.
3. Cover. Cook on low until liquid is absorbed and berries are soft, about 2 hours.

Notes:
1. If craisins are unavailable, use raisins.

2. This is a satisfying vegetarian main dish, if you use vegetable broth.

Soups

Black Bean Soup

Sue Tjon
Austin, TX

Makes 6 servings

1-lb. bag black beans
2 10-oz. cans rotel tomatoes
1 medium onion, chopped
1 medium green bell pepper, chopped
1 Tbsp. minced garlic
14½-oz. can chicken or vegetable broth
water
Cajun seasoning to taste

1. Cover beans with water and soak for 8 hours or overnight. Drain well. Place beans in slow cooker.
2. Add tomatoes, onions, pepper, garlic, and chicken or vegetable broth. Add water just to cover beans. Add Cajun seasoning.
3. Cover. Cook on high 8 hours. Mash some of the beans before serving for a thicker consistency.
4. Serve over rice or in black bean tacos.

Note: Leftovers freeze well.

Many-Bean Soup

Trudy Kutter
Corfu, NY

Makes 12 servings

20-oz. pkg. dried 15-bean soup mix,
    or 2¼ cups dried beans
5 14½-oz. cans chicken or vegetable broth
2 cups chopped carrots
1½ cups chopped celery
1 cup chopped onions
2 Tbsp. tomato paste
1 tsp. Italian seasoning
½ tsp. pepper
14½-oz. can diced tomatoes

1. Combine all ingredients except tomatoes in slow cooker.
2. Cover. Cook on low 8-10 hours, or until beans are tender.
3. Stir in tomatoes.
4. Cover. Cook on high 10-20 minutes, or until soup is heated through.
5. Serve with bread and salad.

Crockpot Bean Soup

Betty B. Dennison
Grove City, PA

Makes 6 servings

3 15-oz. cans pinto beans, undrained
3 15-oz. cans Great Northern beans,
   undrained
4 cups chicken or vegetable broth
3 potatoes, peeled and chopped
4 carrots, sliced
2 celery ribs, sliced
1 large onion, chopped
1 green pepper, chopped
1 sweet red pepper, chopped, optional
2 garlic cloves, minced
1 tsp. salt, or to taste
1/4 tsp. pepper, or to taste
1 bay leaf, optional
1/2 tsp. liquid barbecue smoke, optional

1. Empty beans into 6-qt. slow cooker, or divide ingredients between 2 4- or 5-qt. cookers.
2. Cover. Cook on low while preparing vegetables.
3. Cook broth and vegetables in stockpot until vegetables are tender-crisp. Transfer to slow cooker.
4. Add remaining ingredients and mix well.
5. Cover. Cook on low 4-5 hours.
6. Serve with tossed salad, Italian bread or cornbread.

Note:
1. You can add the broth and vegetables to the cooker without cooking them in advance. Simply extend the slow-cooker cooking time to 8 hours on low.

2. This is a stress-free recipe when you're expecting guests, but you're not sure of their arrival time. Slow Cooker Bean Soup can burble on low heat for longer than its appointed cooking time without being damaged.

3. Make a tossed salad and have the dressing ready to go. Add dressing to salad as your guests make their way to the table.

Southwestern Bean Soup with Cornmeal Dumplings

Melba Eshleman
Manheim, PA

Makes 4 servings

15 1/2-oz. can red kidney beans, rinsed and
   drained
15 1/2-oz. can black beans, pinto beans, or
   Great Northern beans, rinsed and
   drained
3 cups water
14 1/2-oz. can Mexican-style stewed
   tomatoes
10-oz. pkg. frozen whole-kernel corn,
   thawed
1 cup sliced carrots
1 cup chopped onions
4-oz. can chopped green chilies
2 Tbsp. instant beef, chicken, or vegetable
   bouillon granules
1-2 tsp. chili powder
2 cloves garlic, minced

Dumplings:
1/3 cup flour
1/4 cup yellow cornmeal
1 tsp. baking powder
dash of salt
dash of pepper
1 egg white, beaten
2 Tbsp. milk
1 Tbsp. oil

1. Combine 11 soup ingredients in slow cooker.

2. Cover. Cook on low 10-12 hours or high 4-5 hours.

3. Make dumplings by mixing together flour, cornmeal, baking powder, salt, and pepper.

4. Combine egg white, milk, and oil. Add to flour mixture. Stir with fork until just combined.

5. At the end of the soup's cooking time, turn slow cooker to high. Drop dumpling mixture by rounded teaspoonfuls to make 8 mounds atop the soup.

6. Cover. Cook for 30 minutes (do not lift cover).

Garbanzo Souper

Willard E. Roth
Elkhart, IN

Makes 6 servings

1 lb. dry garbanzo beans
4 ozs. raw baby carrots, cut in halves
1 large onion, diced
3 ribs celery, cut in 1" pieces
1 large green pepper, diced
½ tsp. dried basil
½ tsp. dried oregano
½ tsp. dried rosemary
½ tsp. dried thyme
2 28-oz. cans vegetable broth
1 broth can of water
8-oz. can tomato sauce
8 ozs. prepared hummus
½ tsp. sea salt

1. Soak beans overnight. Drain. Place in bottom of slow cooker.

2. Add carrots, onion, celery, and green pepper.

3. Sprinkle with basil, oregano, rosemary, and thyme.

4. Cover with broth and water.

5. Cover. Cook on high 6 hours.

6. Half an hour before serving, stir in tomato sauce, hummus, and salt. Cook until hot.

7. Serve with Irish soda bread and lemon curd.

A fine meal for vegetarians on St. Patrick's Day!

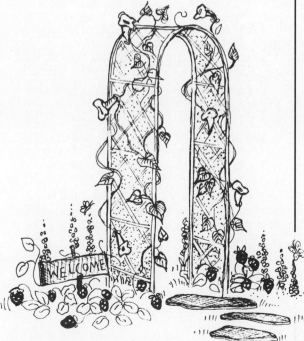

Hearty Bean and Vegetable Soup

Jewel Showalter
Landisville, PA

Makes 6-8 servings

2 medium onions, sliced
2 garlic cloves, minced
2 Tbsp. olive oil
8 cups chicken or vegetable broth
1 small head cabbage, chopped
2 large red potatoes, chopped
2 cups chopped celery
2 cups chopped carrots
4 cups corn
2 tsp. dried basil
1 tsp. dried marjoram
1/4 tsp. dried oregano
1 tsp. salt
1/2 tsp. pepper
2 15-oz. cans navy beans

1. Saute onions and garlic in oil. Transfer to large slow cooker.
2. Add remaining ingredients, mixing together well.
3. Cover. Cook on low 6-8 hours.

Variation: Add 2-3 cups cooked and cut-up chicken 30 minutes before serving if you wish.

I discovered this recipe after my husband's heart attack. It's a great nutritious soup using only a little fat.

Menu Idea

Hearty Bean and Vegetable Soup
Homemade Bread
Cheese Cubes and Crackers
Fruit
Cookies

Blessing Soup

Alix Nancy Botsford
Seminole, OK

Makes 8-10 servings

2 cups mixed dried beans (10-18 different kinds)
2-2 1/2 qts. water
1 cup diced ham
1 large onion, chopped
1 garlic clove, minced
juice of 1 lemon
14.5-oz. can Italian tomatoes, chopped
1/2 cup chopped sweet red pepper
1/2 cup chopped celery
2 carrots, thinly sliced
1 tsp. salt
1 tsp. pepper

1. Sort and wash beans. Cover with water and soak several hours or overnight. Drain.
2. Place beans in cooker and add 2-2 1/2 quarts water. Cook on high for 2 hours.
3. Combine all ingredients with beans in slow cooker.
4. Add more water so that everything is just covered.
5. Cover. Cook on high 4-6 hours or low 8-12 hours.

One January that was especially dismal, I invited many friends, most of whom didn't know each other, to my home. I put on a video about rose gardens around the world. Then I made this soup and a fresh bread crouton that could be eaten on top of the soup and tossed a large salad.

Mexican Rice and Bean Soup

Esther J. Mast
East Petersburg, PA

Makes 6 servings

½ cup chopped onions
⅓ cup chopped green peppers
1 garlic clove, minced
1 Tbsp. oil
4-oz. pkg. sliced or chipped dried beef
18-oz. can tomato juice
15½-oz. can red kidney beans, undrained
1½ cups water
½ cup long-grain rice, uncooked
1 tsp. paprika
½-1 tsp. chili powder
½ tsp. salt
dash of pepper

1. Cook onions, green peppers, and garlic in oil in skillet until vegetables are tender but not brown. Transfer to slow cooker.
2. Tear beef into small pieces and add to slow cooker.
3. Add remaining ingredients. Mix well.
4. Cover. Cook on low 6 hours. Stir before serving.
5. Serve with relish tray and cornbread, home-canned fruit, and cookies.

This is a recipe I fixed often when our sons were growing up. We have all enjoyed it in any season of the year.

Polish Sausage Bean Soup

Janie Steele
Moore, OK

Makes 10 servings

1-lb. pkg. dried Great Northern beans
28-oz. can whole tomatoes
2 8-oz. cans tomato sauce
2 large onions, chopped
3 cloves garlic, minced
1 tsp. salt
¼-½ tsp. pepper, according to your taste preference
3 celery ribs, sliced
bell pepper, sliced
large ham bone or ham hock
1-2 lbs. smoked sausage links, sliced

1. Cover beans with water and soak for 8 hours. Rinse and drain.
2. Place beans in 6-qt. cooker and cover with water.
2. Combine all other ingredients, except sausage, in large bowl. Stir into beans in slow cooker.
3. Cover. Cook on high 1-1½ hours. Reduce to low. Cook 7 hours.
4. Remove ham bone or hock and debone. Stir ham pieces back into soup.
5. Add sausage links.
6. Cover. Cook on low 1 hour.

Note: For enhanced flavor, brown sausage before adding to soup.

Black Bean Soup

Janie Steele
Moore, OK

Makes 5-6 quarts, or about 18 servings

4 cups dry black beans
5 qts. water
ham bone, ham pieces, or ham hocks
3 bunches of green onions, sliced thin
4 bay leaves
1 Tbsp. salt
1/4-1/2 tsp. pepper
3 cloves minced garlic
4 celery ribs, chopped
3 large onions, chopped
10 1/2-oz. can consomme
1/2 cup butter
2 1/2 Tbsp. flour
1/2 cup minced parsley
1 cup Madeira wine, optional
chopped parsley

1. In 6-qt. slow cooker, soak beans in 5 qts. water for 8 hours. Rinse. Drain. Pour beans back into slow cooker, or divide between 2 4- or 5-qt. cookers.

2. Add ham, green onions, bay, salt, pepper, garlic, celery, and onions. Pour in consomme. Add water to cover vegetables and meat.

3. Cover. Cook on high 1 1/2-2 hours. Reduce heat to low and cook for 6-8 hours.

4. Remove ham bones and bay leaves. Cut ham off bones and set meat aside

5. Force vegetable mixture through sieve, if you wish.

6. Taste and adjust seasonings, adding more salt and pepper if needed. Return cooked ingredients and cut-up ham to cooker.

7. In saucepan, melt 1/2 cup butter. Stir in flour until smooth. Stir into soup to thicken and enrich.

8. Prior to serving, add wine to heated soup mixture. Garnish with chopped parsley.

Party Bean Soup

Jo Haberkamp
Fairbank, IA

Makes 9 servings

1 cup dry navy beans
1 qt. water
1 lb. smoked or plain ham hocks
1 cup chopped onions
1/2 cup chopped celery
1 garlic clove, minced
8-oz. can tomatoes, cut up
2 14 1/2-oz. cans chicken broth
1/8 tsp. salt
1/8 tsp. pepper
1 cup (4 ozs.) shredded cheddar cheese
1 Tbsp. dried parsley flakes

1. Place beans and water in slow cooker.

2. Cover. Cook on low for 12 hours.

3. Add ham hocks, onions, celery, garlic, tomatoes, chicken broth, salt, and pepper.

4. Cover. Cook on low 8-10 hours.

5. Add cheese and parsley. Stir until cheese is melted.

Hostess Idea

Buy 10-18 different kinds of dried beans. Mix them together in a large bag or jar. Scoop them into small bags (8-oz. is a good size). Top each with a dried bay leaf to discourage bugs, tie them shut, and present them to the friends who have just eaten from your buffet table.

A bag full of these dried beans is also a welcome and interesting addition to a gift basket.

—Alix Nancy Botsford

Navy Bean Soup

Lucille Amos
Greensboro, NC

Makes 8 servings

2 cups navy beans
1 cup chopped onions
1 bay leaf
1 tsp. salt
1 tsp. pepper
1/2 lb. ham, chopped

1. Soak beans in water overnight. Drain.
2. Combine ingredients in slow cooker. Add water to cover.
3. Cover. Cook on low 10-12 hours or on high 5-6 hours.
4. Remove bay leaf and serve.

Navy Bean and Bacon Chowder

Ruth A. Feister
Narvon, PA

Makes 6 servings

1 1/2 cups dried navy beans
2 cups cold water
8 slices bacon, cooked and crumbled
2 medium carrots, sliced
1 rib celery, sliced
1 medium onion, chopped
1 tsp. dried Italian seasoning
1/8 tsp. pepper
46-oz. can chicken broth
1 cup milk

1. Soak beans in 2 cups cold water for 8 hours.
2. After beans have soaked, drain, if necessary, and place in slow cooker.
2. Add all remaining ingredients, except milk, to slow cooker.
3. Cover. Cook on low 7-9 hours, or until beans are crisp-tender.
4. Place 2 cups cooked bean mixture into blender. Process until smooth. Return to slow cooker.
5. Add milk. Cover and heat on high 10 minutes.
6. Serve with crusty French bread and additional herbs and seasonings for diners to add as they wish.

Cassoulet Chowder

Miriam Friesen
Staunton, VA

Makes 8-10 servings

1¼ cups dry pinto beans
4 cups water
12-oz. pkg. brown-and-serve sausage links,
  cooked and drained
2 cups cubed cooked chicken
2 cups cubed cooked ham
1½ cups sliced carrots
8-oz. can tomato sauce
¾ cup dry red wine
½ cup chopped onions
½ tsp. garlic powder
1 bay leaf

1. Combine beans and water in large saucepan. Bring to boil. Reduce heat and simmer 1½ hours. Refrigerate beans and liquid 4-8 hours.
2. Combine all ingredients in slow cooker.
3. Cover. Cook on low 8-10 hours or on high 4 hours. If the chowder seems too thin, remove lid during last 30 minutes of cooking time to allow it to thicken.
4. Remove bay leaf before serving.

Grandma's Barley Soup

Andrea O'Neil
Fairfield, CT

Makes 10-12 servings

2 smoked ham hocks
4 carrots, sliced
4 potatoes, cubed
1 cup dried lima beans
1 cup tomato paste
1½-2 cups cooked barley
salt, if needed

1. Combine all ingredients in slow cooker, except salt.
2. Cover with water.
3. Cover. Simmer on low 6-8 hours.
4. Debone ham hocks and return cut-up meat to soup.
5. Taste before serving. Add salt if needed.

Note: If you want to reduce the amount of meat you eat, this dish is flavorful using only 1 ham hock.

Green Bean Soup

Loretta Krahn
Mountain Lake, MN

Makes 6 servings

1 meaty ham bone, or 2 cups cubed ham
1½ qts. water
1 large onion, chopped
2-3 cups cut-up green beans
3 large carrots, sliced
2 large potatoes, peeled and cubed
1 Tbsp. parsley
1 Tbsp. summer savory
½ tsp. salt
¼ tsp. pepper
1 cup cream or milk

1. Combine all ingredients except cream in slow cooker.
2. Cover. Cook on high 4-6 hours.
3. Remove ham bone. Cut off meat and return to slow cooker.
4. Turn to low. Stir in cream or milk. Heat through and serve.

Green Bean Soup

Bernita Boyts
Shawnee Mission, KS

Makes 5-6 servings

1 medium onion, chopped
2 carrots, sliced
2 ribs celery, sliced
1 Tbsp. olive oil
5 medium potatoes, cubed
10-oz. pkg. frozen green beans
2 14½-oz. cans chicken broth
2 broth cans water
⅓ lb. link sausage, sliced, or bulk sausage, browned
2 Tbsp. chopped fresh parsley
   (2 tsp. dried)
1-2 Tbsp. chopped fresh oregano
   (1-2 tbsp. dried)
1 tsp. Italian spice
salt to taste
pepper to taste

1. Saute onion, carrots, and celery in oil in skillet until tender.
2. Combine all ingredients in slow cooker.
3. Cover. Cook on high 1-2 hours and then on low 6-8 hours.
4. Serve with freshly baked bread or cornbread.

Variation: *If you like it hot, add ground red pepper or hot sauce just before serving.*

Hostess Idea

It's fun to type up questions from the "Ungame" onto small pieces of paper, roll them up, and tie each with a colorful ribbon. Place one by each place-setting, or put them in a small basket on the table. As an after-dinner activity and as a way to learn to know each other, take turns opening the "scrolls" and answering the questions.
—Esther J. Mast

Broccoli, Potato, and Cheese Soup

Ruth Shank
Gridley, IL

Makes 6 servings

2 cups cubed or diced potatoes
3 Tbsp. chopped onion
10-oz. pkg. frozen broccoli cuts, thawed
2 Tbsp. butter or margarine, melted
1 Tbsp. flour
2 cups cubed Velveeta cheese
1/2 tsp. salt
5 1/2 cups milk

1. Cook potatoes and onion in boiling water in saucepan until potatoes are crisp-tender. Drain. Place in slow cooker.
2. Add remaining ingredients. Stir together.
3. Cover. Cook on low 4 hours.

Cheesy Broccoli Soup

Dede Peterson
Rapid City, SD

Makes 4 servings

1 lb. frozen chopped broccoli, thawed
1 lb. Velveeta cheese, cubed
10 3/4-oz. can cream of celery soup
14 1/2-oz. can chicken or vegetable broth
dash of pepper
dash of salt

1. Combine ingredients in slow cooker.
2. Cover. Cook on low 5-6 hours.

Curried Carrot Soup

Ann Bender
Ft. Defiance, VA

Makes 6-8 servings

1 garlic clove, minced
1 large onion, chopped
2 Tbsp. oil
1 Tbsp. butter
1 tsp. curry powder
1 Tbsp. flour
4 cups chicken or vegetable broth
6 large carrots, sliced
1/4 tsp. salt
1/4 tsp. ground red pepper, optional
1 1/2 cups plain yogurt, or light sour cream

1. In skillet cook minced garlic and onion in oil and butter until limp but not brown.
2. Add curry and flour. Cook 30 seconds. Pour into slow cooker.
3. Add chicken broth and carrots.
4. Cover. Cook on high for about 2 hours, or until carrots are soft.
5. Puree mixture in blender. Season with salt and pepper. Return to slow cooker and keep warm until ready to serve.
6. Add a dollop of yogurt or sour cream to each serving.

Corn Chowder

Mary Rogers
Waseca, MN

Makes 12 servings

1 lb. bacon
4 cups diced potatoes
2 cups chopped onions
2 cups sour cream
2 1/2 cups milk
2 10 3/4-oz. cans cream of chicken soup
2 15 1/4-oz. cans corn, undrained

1. Cut bacon into 1" pieces. Cook for 5 minutes in large skillet.
2. Add potatoes and onions and a bit of water. Cook 15-20 minutes, until tender, stirring occasionally. Drain. Transfer to slow cooker.
3. Combine sour cream, milk, chicken soup, and corn. Place in slow cooker.
4. Cover. Cook on low for 2 hours.
5. Serve with homemade biscuits or a pan of steaming cornbread fresh from the oven.

Green Chile Corn Chowder

Kelly Evenson
Pittsboro, NC

Makes 8 servings

16-oz. can cream-style corn
3 potatoes, peeled and diced
2 Tbsp. chopped fresh chives
4-oz. can diced green chilies, drained
2-oz. jar chopped pimentos, drained
1/2-3/4 cup chopped cooked ham
2 10 1/2-oz. cans chicken broth
salt to taste
pepper to taste
Tabasco sauce to taste
1 cup milk
shredded Monterey Jack cheese

1. Combine all ingredients except milk and cheese in slow cooker.
2. Cover. Cook on low 7-8 hours or until potatoes are tender.
3. Stir in milk. Heat until hot.
4. Top individual servings with cheese. Serve with homemade bread.

Corn and Shrimp Chowder

Naomi E. Fast
Hesston, KS

Makes 6 servings

4 slices bacon, diced
1 cup chopped onions
2 cups diced, unpeeled red potatoes
2 10-oz. pkgs. frozen corn
1 tsp. Worcestershire sauce
1/2 tsp. paprika
1/2 tsp. salt
1/8 tsp. pepper
2 6-oz. cans shrimp
2 cups water
2 Tbsp. butter or margarine
12-oz. can evaporated milk
chopped chives

1. Fry bacon in skillet until lightly crisp. Add onions to drippings and saute until transparent. Using slotted spoon, transfer bacon and onions to slow cooker.
2. Add remaining ingredients to cooker except milk and chives.
3. Cover. Cook on low 3-4 hours, adding milk and chives 30 minutes before end of cooking time.
4. Serve with broccoli salad.

I learned to make this recipe in a 7th grade home economics class. It made an impression on my father who liked seafood very much. The recipe calls only for canned shrimp, but I often increase the taste appeal with extra cooked shrimp.

I frequently use frozen hash brown potatoes for speedy preparation. There is no difference in the taste.

Elijah's Cucumber Soup

Shirley Unternahrer Hinh
Wayland, IA

Makes 8 servings

1 lb. ground pork
2 Tbsp. fish sauce
1/4 tsp. black pepper
4 large cucumbers, peeled
2 qts. boiling water
2 green onions, chopped
1/8 tsp. black pepper
4 Tbsp. fish sauce
salt to taste

1. Combine pork, 2 Tbsp. fish sauce, and 1/4 tsp. black pepper in mixing bowl.
2. Cut peeled cucumbers in half and scoop out seeds, creating a channel in each cuke. Stuff pork mixture into cucumbers.
3. Form remaining meat into 1" balls. Drop balls into stockpot with 2 qts. boiling water. Boil until a layer of foam develops on the water. Skim off foam and discard.
4. Drop stuffed cucumbers into boiling water. Simmer for 15 minutes. Transfer cucumbers and pork balls into slow cooker. Add hot liquid from stockpot.
5. Add green onions, 1/8 tsp. black pepper, and 4 Tbsp. fish sauce.
6. Cover. Cook on high 11/2-2 hours.
7. Serve over rice in bowl, along with lemon juice and chili sauce.

This dish was brought into our family's recipe collection by my husband, Hai. Hai came to the United States, from Vietnam, 23 years ago.

We eat this soup quite often at our house. Many of our friends and family have enjoyed it over the years and we've had many requests for it.

Oriental Pork Soup

Judi Manos
West Islip, NY

Makes 6 servings

1 lb. ground pork, chicken, or turkey
1 garlic clove, minced
2 medium carrots, cut into julienne strips
4 medium green onions, cut into 1″ pieces
1 garlic clove, minced
¼ cup soy sauce
½ tsp. gingerroot, chopped
⅛ tsp. pepper
49½-oz. can chicken broth
1 cup sliced mushrooms
1 cup bean sprouts

1. Cook meat with garlic in skillet until brown. Drain.
2. Combine all ingredients except mushrooms and sprouts in slow cooker.
3. Cover. Cook on low 7-9 hours or high 3-4 hours.
4. Stir in mushrooms and bean sprouts.
5. Cover. Cook on low 1 hour.

Variation: For added flavor to the meat, add ⅛ tsp. five-spice blend to Step 1.

Lentil Soup with Ham Bone

Rhoda Atzeff
Harrisburg, PA

Makes 6-8 servings

1 lb. lentils, washed and drained
1 celery rib, chopped
1 large carrot, grated
½ cup chopped onions
1 bay leaf
¼ tsp. dried thyme
7-8 cups water
1 ham bone, thinly sliced kielbasa, or hot smoked sausage
¼-½ tsp. crushed red hot pepper flakes
pepper to taste
salt to taste

1. Combine all ingredients except pepper and salt in slow cooker.
2. Cover. Cook on low 8-9 hours. Remove bay leaf and ham bone. Dice meat from bone and return to cooker.
3. Season to taste with pepper and salt.
4. Serve alone, or over rice with grated cheese on top.

Russian Red-Lentil Soup

Naomi E. Fast
Hesston, KS

Makes 8 servings

1 Tbsp. oil
1 large onion, chopped
3 cloves garlic, minced
1/2 cup diced, dried apricots
1 1/2 cups dried red lentils
1/2 tsp. cumin
1/2 tsp. dried thyme
3 cups water
2 14 1/2-oz. cans chicken or vegetable broth
14 1/2-oz. can diced tomatoes
1 Tbsp. honey
3/4 tsp. salt
1/2 tsp. coarsely ground black pepper
2 Tbsp. chopped fresh mint
1 1/2 cups plain yogurt

1. Combine all ingredients except mint and yogurt in slow cooker.
2. Cover. Heat on high until soup starts to simmer, then turn to low and cook 3-4 hours.
3. Add mint and dollop of yogurt to each bowl of soup.

Menu Idea

Russian Red Lentil Soup
Pita Bread Triangles
Waldorf Salad
Platter of Fresh Veggies—radishes,
  celery, cauliflower, carrots, and
  pickles

Onion Soup

Rosemarie Fitzgerald
Gibsonia, PA

Makes 6-8 servings

3 medium onions, thinly sliced
1/4 cup butter
1 tsp. salt
1 Tbsp. sugar
2 Tbsp. flour
1 qt. beef or vegetable broth
1/2 cup dry white wine
slices of French bread
Swiss or Parmesan cheese, grated

1. Saute onions in butter in covered skillet until soft. Uncover. Add salt and sugar. Cook 15 minutes. Stir in flour. Cook 3 more minutes.
2. Combine onions, broth, and wine in slow cooker.
3. Cover. Cook on low 6-8 hours.
4. Toast bread. Sprinkle with grated cheese and then broil.
5. Dish soup into individual bowls; then float a slice of broiled bread on top of each serving of soup.

Lentil Soup

Tina Snyder
Manheim, PA

Makes 10 servings

4 cups hot water
14 1/2-oz. can tomatoes
1/4 cup tomato juice
3 medium potatoes, peeled and diced
3 carrots, thinly sliced
1 onion, chopped

1 rib celery, sliced
1 cup dry lentils
2 garlic cloves, minced
2 bay leaves
4 tsp. curry powder
1½ tsp. salt
sour cream

1. Combine all ingredients except sour cream in slow cooker.
2. Cover. Cook on low 8 hours.
3. Serve with sour cream on top of individual servings and crusty bread as a go-along.

Potato Soup

Deborah Santiago
Lancaster, PA

Makes 6 servings

6 potatoes, peeled and cubed
2 onions, chopped
1 carrot, sliced
1 rib celery, sliced
4 chicken or vegetable bouillon cubes
1 Tbsp. parsley flakes
5 cups water
¼ tsp. pepper
1 Tbsp. salt
⅓ cup butter, melted
13-oz. can evaporated milk

1. Combine all ingredients except evaporated milk in slow cooker.
2. Cover. Cook on high 3-4 hours or low 10-12 hours.
3. Stir in evaporated milk during last hour of cooking time.
4. Serve with sandwiches, crackers, and beverage.

Potato Soup

Zona Mae Bontrager
Kokomo, IN

Makes 4 servings

½ cup chopped onions
1 tsp. butter
14½-oz. can beef, chicken, or vegetable broth
1 potato, chopped
1 carrot, shredded
1 rib celery, chopped
½-¾ tsp. salt
⅛-¼ tsp. pepper
2 cups mashed potatoes
½ cup shredded mild cheese, optional

1. Saute onions in butter in skillet.
2. Stir in broth, 1 potato, carrot, celery, and seasonings. Cook until vegetables are tender. Pour into hot slow cooker.
3. Add mashed potatoes and cheese. Stir well.
4. Cover. Heat on low until ready to serve.

Hostess Idea

Present any new recipe without apologies. Offer new foods and tastes as a wonderful experience.
—Naomi E. Fast

Potato Cheddar-Cheese Soup

Marla Folkerts
Holland, OH

Makes 4 servings

6-10 potatoes, peeled and cubed
½ cup vegetable broth
1 cup water
1 large onion, finely chopped
½ tsp. garlic powder
⅛ tsp. white pepper
2 cups milk, heated
1 cup shredded sharp, or extra sharp,
   cheddar cheese
paprika

1. Place potatoes, broth, water, onions, and garlic powder in slow cooker.
2. Cover. Cook on low 7-9 hours, or on high 4-6 hours.
3. Mash potatoes, leaving them a bit lumpy. Stir in pepper and milk a little at a time. Add cheese. Cook until cheese has melted, about 5 minutes. Add more milk if you'd like a thinner or creamier soup.
4. Garnish each serving with paprika.
5. Serve with homemade bread, salad, and fruit.

Ham and Potato Chowder

Penny Blosser
Beavercreek, OH

Makes 5 servings

5-oz. pkg. scalloped potatoes
sauce mix from potato pkg.
1 cup cooked ham, cut into narrow strips
4 cups chicken broth
1 cup chopped celery
⅓ cup chopped onions
salt to taste
pepper to taste
2 cups half-and-half
⅓ cup flour

1. Combine potatoes, sauce mix, ham, broth, celery, onions, salt, and pepper in slow cooker.
2. Cover. Cook on low 7 hours.
3. Combine half-and-half and flour. Gradually add to slow cooker, blending well.
4. Cover. Cook on low up to 1 hour, stirring occasionally until thickened.

Aunt Thelma's Homemade Soup

Janice Muller
Derwood, MD

Makes 10-12 servings

7 cups water
4 chicken or vegetable bouillon cubes
1 cup thinly sliced carrots
1-lb. pkg. frozen peas
1-lb. pkg. frozen corn
1-lb. pkg. frozen lima beans
1 bay leaf
1/4 tsp. dill seed
28-oz. can whole tomatoes
1 cup diced raw potatoes
1 cup chopped onions
2-3 tsp. salt
1/2 tsp. dried basil
1/4 tsp. pepper
2 Tbsp. cornstarch
1/4 cup cold water

1. Combine all ingredients except cornstarch and 1/4 cup water in slow cooker.
2. Cover. Simmer on high 4 hours, or until vegetables are tender.
3. Thirty minutes before end of cooking time, mix cornstarch and cold water together until smooth. Remove 1 cup broth from cooker and mix with cornstarch-water. When smooth, stir into soup. Cover and continue cooking another half hour.
4. A loaf of fresh Italian bread goes well with a hot bowl of this soup.

My aunt always makes this in the winter and freezes an extra batch for unexpected guests.
I converted the recipe to crockpot-use a few years ago, but I think of her whenever I make it.

Diet Soup Unlimited

Eileen Lehman
Kidron, OH

Makes 6 servings

4 cups water
2 cups tomato juice
2 beef or vegetable bouillon cubes
1 Tbsp. soy sauce, optional
1 tsp. sweetener, optional
1 cup sliced cabbage
2 carrots, sliced
1 celery rib, sliced
1 onion, sliced
2 cups frozen green beans
1 tsp. salt
pepper to taste

1. Combine all ingredients in slow cooker.
2. Cover. Cook on low 4-8 hours.

Variation: Add mushrooms, if you like, after the first 2 hours of cooking.

After the holidays this tasty, low-calorie soup is a welcome meal. It improves in flavor the longer it cooks.

Minestrone

Bernita Boyts
Shawnee Mission, KS

Makes 8-10 servings

1 large onion, chopped
4 carrots, sliced
3 ribs celery, sliced
2 garlic cloves, minced
1 Tbsp. olive oil
6-oz. can tomato paste
14½-oz. can chicken, beef, or vegetable broth
24-oz. can pinto beans, undrained
10-oz. pkg. frozen green beans
2-3 cups chopped cabbage
1 medium zucchini, sliced
8 cups water
2 Tbsp. parsley
2 Tbsp. Italian spice
1 tsp. salt, or more
½ tsp. pepper
¾ cup dry acini di pepe
  (small round pasta)
grated Parmesan or Asiago cheese

1. Saute onion, carrots, celery, and garlic in oil until tender.
2. Combine all ingredients except pasta and cheese in slow cooker.
3. Cover. Cook 4-5 hours on high or 8-9 hours on low, adding pasta 1 hour before cooking is complete.
4. Top individual servings with cheese.

The Soup

Joanne Kennedy
Plattsburgh, NY

Makes 8 servings

2 14½-oz. cans vegetable broth
2 vegetable boullion cubes
4 cups water
1 qt. canned tomatoes
3-4 garlic cloves, minced
1 large onion, chopped
1 cup chopped celery
2 cups chopped carrots
1 small zucchini, cubed
1 small yellow squash, cubed
2 tsp. fresh basil
1 tsp. fresh parsley
pepper to taste
3 dashes Tabasco sauce

1. Combine ingredients in slow cooker.
2. Cover. Cook on low 9 hours.

Variation: Add cooked pasta after soup is done.

Homemade Vegetable Soup

Audrey Romonosky
Austin, TX

Makes 10-12 servings

1 lb. stewing meat, cut into pieces
1 bay leaf
1 small onion, diced
3 carrots, sliced
2 ribs celery, sliced
2-3 potatoes, diced
14½-oz. can stewed tomatoes, cut up
8-oz. can tomato sauce

¼ cup frozen corn
½ cup frozen green beans
¼ cup frozen peas
¼ cup chopped cabbage
salt to taste
pepper to taste

1. Combine all ingredients in slow cooker. Add water to fill pot.
2. Cover. Cook on low 6-8 hours.

Beef Dumpling Soup

Barbara Walker
Sturgis, SD

Makes 5-6 servings

1 lb. beef stewing meat, cubed
1 envelope dry onion soup mix
6 cups hot water
2 carrots, peeled and shredded
1 celery rib, finely chopped
1 tomato, peeled and chopped
1 cup buttermilk biscuit mix
1 Tbsp. finely chopped parsley
6 Tbsp. milk

1. Place meat in slow cooker. Sprinkle with onion soup mix. Pour water over meat.
2. Add carrots, celery, and tomato.
3. Cover. Cook on low 4-6 hours, or until meat is tender.
4. Combine biscuit mix and parsley. Stir in milk with fork until moistened. Drop dumplings by teaspoonfuls into pot.
5. Cover. Cook on high 30 minutes.

Variation: Increase the flavor of the broth by adding 2 cloves garlic, ½ tsp. dried basil, and ¼ tsp. dill weed to Step 2.

Easy Vegetable Soup

Winifred Paul
Scottdale, PA

Makes 8-10 servings

1 lb. ground beef, browned
1 cup chopped onions
15-oz. can kidney beans or butter beans, undrained
1 cup sliced carrots
¼ cup rice, uncooked
1 qt. stewed tomatoes
3½ cups water
5 beef bouillon cubes
1 Tbsp. parsley flakes
1 tsp. salt
⅛ tsp. pepper
¼ tsp. dried basil
1 bay leaf

1. Combine all ingredients in slow cooker.
2. Cover. Cook on low 8-10 hours.

Note: Add more herbs and additional seasonings for zestier flavor.

Easy Veggie-Beef Soup

Rebecca Plank Leichty
Harrisonburg, VA

Makes 6-8 servings

1 lb. browned ground beef, or 2 cups
    stewing beef
2 cups sliced carrots
1 lb. frozen green beans, thawed
14½-oz. can corn, drained,
    or 16-oz. bag frozen corn, thawed
28-oz. can diced tomatoes
3 cups beef or veggie broth
3 tsp. instant beef bouillon
2 tsp. Worcestershire sauce
1 Tbsp. sugar
1 Tbsp. minced onion
10¾-oz. can cream of celery soup

  1. Place meat in bottom of slow cooker.
  2. Add remaining ingredients except celery
soup. Mix well.
  3. Stir in soup.
  4. Cover. Cook on low 7-8 hours or high
4 hours.
  5. If using stewing meat, shred and mix
through soup just before serving.
  6. Serve with freshly baked bread and
homemade jam.

*Two modern-day conveniences—the slow
cooker and bread machine—allow me to prepare
tasty meals without too much last-minute dashing
around. Utilizing both gives me time to plan table
settings and decorations, too.*

Hamburger Soup

Naomi Ressler
Harrisonburg, VA
Kay Magruder
Seminole, OK

Makes 8 servings

1½ lbs. ground beef, browned
1 medium onion, chopped
1 cup sliced carrots
1 cup sliced celery
1 cup sliced cabbage
6-oz. can tomato paste
2 tsp. Worcestershire sauce
2-3 cups beef broth, depending upon how
    thick or thin you like your soup

  1. Combine beef, onions, carrots, celery,
and cabbage in slow cooker.
  2. Combine tomato paste, Worcestershire
sauce, and broth. Pour into slow cooker. Mix to
blend.
  3. Cover. Cook on low 8-10 hours or on
high 3-4 hours.

*Variation: Stir in ¼ tsp. black or cayenne pepper
and 2 bay leaves in Step 2 for added flavor.*

Ground Beef Soup

Nadine L. Martinitz
Salina, KS

Makes 6-8 servings

1 lb. ground beef
1 medium onion, chopped
1 Tbsp. oil
15.8-oz. can Great Northern Beans,
    undrained
15-oz. can tomato sauce
1 1/2-2 tomato-sauce cans water
2 large potatoes, cubed
14.5-oz. can tomatoes
1 tsp. salt

1. Brown ground beef and onions in oil in skillet. Drain. Place in slow cooker.
2. Add remaining ingredients.
3. Cook on high 1 hour, then low 6-8 hours.
4. Serve with grilled cheese sandwiches.

Hamburger Vegetable Soup

Joyce Shackelford
Green Bay, WI

Makes 8-10 servings

1 lb. ground chuck
1 onion, chopped
2 garlic cloves, minced
4 cups V8 juice
14 1/2-oz. can stewed tomatoes
2 cups cole slaw mix
2 cups frozen green beans
2 cups frozen corn
2 Tbsp. Worcestershire sauce

1 tsp. dried basil
1/2 tsp. salt
1/4 tsp. pepper

1. Brown beef, onion, and garlic in skillet. Drain and transfer to slow cooker.
2. Add remaining ingredients to slow cooker and combine.
3. Cover. Cook on low 8-9 hours.

Taco Soup

Suzanne Slagel
Midway, OH

Makes 6-8 servings

1 lb. ground beef
1 large onion, chopped
16-oz. can Mexican-style tomatoes
16-oz. can ranch-style beans
16-oz. can whole-kernel corn, undrained
16-oz. can kidney beans, undrained
16-oz. can black beans, undrained
16-oz. jar picante sauce
corn or tortilla chips
sour cream
shredded cheddar cheese

1. Brown meat and onions in skillet. Drain.
2. Combine with all other vegetables and picante sauce in slow cooker.
3. Cover. Cook on low 4-6 hours.
4. Serve with corn or tortilla chips, sour cream, and shredded cheese as toppings.

Taco Soup
Sue Tjon
Austin, TX

Makes 8 servings

1 lb. ground beef
1 envelope dry ranch dressing mix
1 envelope dry taco seasoning mix
3 12-oz. cans rotel tomatoes, undrained
2 24-oz. cans pinto beans, undrained
24-oz. can hominy, undrained
14.5-oz. can stewed tomatoes, undrained
1 onion, chopped
2 cups water

1. Brown meat in skillet. Pour into slow cooker.
2. Add remaining ingredients. Mix well.
3. Cover. Cook on low 4 hours.

Notes:
1. Increase or decrease the amount of water you add to make the dish either stew-like or soup-like.

2. A serving suggestion is to line each individual soup bowl with tortilla chips, ladle taco soup on top, and sprinkle with grated cheese.

Ruth's Ground Beef Vegetable Soup
Ruth Ann Penner
Hillsboro, KS

Makes 6 servings

1 lb. ground beef
1½ qts. water
¾ cup chopped celery
1 cup chopped carrots
1 large onion, chopped
2 cups cubed potatoes
1½ tsp. salt
½ cup uncooked rice
¼ tsp. pepper
10¾-oz. can tomato soup

1. Crumble ground beef in slow cooker. Add water.
2. Add remaining ingredients except soup. Mix together well.
3. Cover. Cook on low 8-10 hours.
4. Add soup 30 minutes before serving and stir through.

Menu Idea

Ruth's Ground Beef Vegetable Soup
Fresh Bread or Biscuits
Pie

Beef Barley Soup

Michelle Showalter
Bridgewater, VA

Makes 10-12 servings

1 lb. ground beef, browned
1½ qts. water
1 qt. canned tomatoes, stewed, crushed, or whole
3 cups sliced carrots
1 cup diced celery
1 cup diced potatoes
1 cup diced onions
¾ cup quick-cooking barley
3 tsp. beef bouillon granules, or 3 beef bouillon cubes
2-3 tsp. salt
¼ tsp. pepper

1. Combine ingredients in slow cooker.
2. Cover. Cook on low 8-10 hours or high 4-5 hours.
3. Serve with fresh bread and cheese cubes.

Variation: You may use pearl barley instead of quick-cooking barley. Cook it according to package directions and add halfway through cooking time of soup.

Easy Vegetable Soup

Dawn Day
Westminster, CA

Makes 6-8 servings

4 cups vegetable, beef, or chicken stock
4 cups vegetables (use any or all of corn, peas, carrots, broccoli, green beans, cauliflower, mushrooms), either fresh or frozen
leftover meat, cut in small pieces, or 1 lb. cubed beef, browned in oil in skillet
15-oz. can chopped tomatoes
1 bay leaf
¼ cup uncooked rice or barley, or ½ cup cooked orzo or small shells

1. Combine all ingredients in slow cooker except pasta.
2. Cover. Cook on low 6 hours, adding pasta ½ hour before serving.
3. Serve with rolls and a salad for a great comfort meal.

Everyone's Hungry Soup

Janie Steele
Moore, OK

Makes 20-25 servings

6 thick slices bacon
3 lbs. boneless beef stewing meat, cubed
1 lb. boneless pork, cubed
3 14.5-oz. cans tomatoes
10-oz. can rotel tomatoes and chilies
3 celery ribs, chopped
3 large onions, chopped
garlic to taste
salt to taste
pepper to taste
1/2 cup Worcestershire sauce
2 Tbsp. chili powder
2 cups water
6-8 medium potatoes, peeled and cubed
1 lb. carrots, sliced
15-oz. can English peas, undrained
14 1/2-oz. can green beans, undrained
15.25-oz. can corn, undrained
1 lb. cut-up okra, optional

1. Fry bacon in skillet until crisp. Remove bacon, but reserve drippings. Crumble bacon and divide between 2 large (6 qt. or larger) slow cookers.

2. Brown stewing beef and pork in skillet in bacon drippings.

3. Combine all ingredients and divide between slow cookers.

4. Cover. Cook on low 8-10 hours.

5. Serve with loaves of homemade bread or pans of cornbread.

Hamburger Sausage Soup

Esther Becker
Gordonville, PA

Makes 4-6 servings

1 lb. ground beef
1 lb. Polish sausage, sliced
1/2 tsp. seasoning salt
1/4 tsp. dried oregano
1/4 tsp. dried basil
1 pkg. dry onion soup mix
6 cups boiling water
16-oz. can diced tomatoes
1 Tbsp. soy sauce
1/2 cup sliced celery
1/4 cup chopped celery leaves
1 cup pared, sliced carrots
1 cup uncooked macaroni

1. Brown ground beef and sausage in skillet. Drain. Place in slow cooker.

2. Add seasoning salt, oregano, basil, and onion soup mix to cooker.

3. Stir in boiling water, tomatoes, and soy sauce.

4. Add celery, celery leaves, and carrots. Stir well.

5. Cover. Cook on low 8-10 hours.

6. One hour before end of cooking time, stir in dry macaroni.

7. Serve with cornbread or corn muffins.

Hosting Idea

A simple meal of a tasty soup and a few other make-ahead items sets an atmosphere for relaxed hosting. Setting the table with my best china, in spite of the simplicity of the meal, helps to make the event special.
—Esther Becker

Delicious Sausage Soup

Karen Waggoner
Joplin, MO

Makes 4 servings

5½ cups chicken broth
½ cup heavy cream
3 carrots, grated
4 potatoes, sliced or cubed
4 cups kale, chopped
1 lb. spicy Italian sausage, browned
½ tsp. salt
½ tsp. crushed red pepper flakes

1. Combine broth and cream in slow cooker. Turn on high.
2. Add carrots, potatoes, kale, and sausage.
3. Sprinkle spices over top.
4. Cover. Cook on high 4-5 hours, stirring occasionally.

Spicy Sausage Soup

Janie Steele
Moore, OK

Makes 8-10 servings

1 lb. ground beef
1 lb. bulk spicy sausage (casings removed)
half a large onion, chopped
2 cups chopped carrots
2 cups chopped celery
1 green or red bell pepper, chopped, optional
2 tsp. salt, or to taste
¼ tsp. pepper, or to taste
1 tsp. dried oregano, or to taste
2 or 3 garlic cloves, minced
14½-oz. can stewed tomatoes with chilies
14½-oz. can green beans
¼ tsp. chili powder
1 cup instant rice, uncooked

1. Combine beef, sausage, and onions. Form into balls. Place in slow cooker.
2. Add all remaining ingredients, except rice. Stir gently so as not to break up the meatballs.
3. Cover. Cook on low 6-8 hours. Stir in rice 20 minutes before serving.
4. Serve with rolls or cornbread.

Sauerkraut-Sausage Bean Soup

Bonnie Goering
Bridgewater, VA

Makes 8-10 servings

3 15-oz. cans white beans, undrained
16-oz. can sauerkraut, drained and rinsed
1 lb. link sausage, sliced
¼ cup brown sugar
½ cup ketchup

1. Combine all ingredients in slow cooker.
2. Cover. Cook on high 2-3 hours.
3. Serve with cornbread, applesauce, or coleslaw.

Note: You may add tomato juice or water if you prefer a thinner soup.

Pixie's Chicken Stew

Janice Muller
Derwood, MD

Makes 8-10 servings

2-3-lb. chicken
2 qts. water
1 pkg. dry chicken noodle soup
2 chicken bouillon cubes
15-oz. can whole-kernel corn, undrained
1 Tbsp. onion flakes
½ tsp. dried thyme, or according to your taste preference

1. Place chicken in slow cooker. Add water.
2. Cover. Cook on high 3-4 hours. Cool.
3. Strain liquid into container and save. Debone chicken. Return cut-up meat and strained broth to slow cooker.
4. Stir in remaining ingredients.
5. Cover. Cook on high 2 hours.

Note: I make this a day ahead so that it can sit overnight in the refrigerator making it easier to skim fat off the top.

Pixie would invite friends in for soup after long walks in the snow. She always served this with fresh bread in front of a roaring fire. Pixie finished these meals by offering us a plate of chocolate fudge. Life couldn't get any better.

Chicken Noodle Soup

Jennifer J. Gehman
Harrisburg, PA

Makes 6-8 servings

2 cups cubed chicken
15¼-oz. can corn, or 2 cups frozen corn
1 cup frozen peas or green beans
10 cups water
10-12 chicken bouillon cubes
3 Tbsp. bacon drippings
½ pkg. dry Kluski (or other very sturdy) noodles

1. Combine all ingredients except noodles in slow cooker.
2. Cover. Cook on high 4-6 hours or low 6-8 hours. Add noodles during last 2 hours.
3. Serve with potato rolls and butter or grilled cheese sandwiches.

Santa Fe Chicken Soup

Sherry Conyers
McPherson, KS

Makes 6-8 servings

4 whole chicken breasts, cooked and
  shredded
1 small onion, diced
15 1/4-oz. can whole-kernel corn, undrained
24-oz. can pinto beans, undrained
14 1/2-oz. can diced tomatoes, undrained
10-oz. can rotel tomatoes, undrained
1/2 lb. mild Velveeta cheese, cubed
1/2 lb. regular Velveeta cheese, cubed
1/4 cup milk

1. Place chicken and onions in slow cooker.
2. Add corn, beans, tomatoes, cubed cheese,
and milk.
3. Cover. Cook on low 3-4 hours, or until
cheese is melted. Try not to let soup boil.

Matzoh Ball Soup

Audrey Romonosky
Austin, TX

Makes 6 servings

2 eggs
2 Tbsp. oil
2 Tbsp. water
1/2 cup matzoh meal*
1 tsp. salt, optional
1 1/2 qts. water
32-oz. can chicken broth

1. Lightly beat eggs, oil, and 2 Tbsp. water
together.
2. Add matzoh meal and salt. Mix well.
3. Cover and refrigerate for 20 minutes.
4. Bring 1 1/2 qts. water to boil in saucepan.
5. Wet hands. Roll matzoh mixture into
1" balls. Drop into boiling water and cook for
20 minutes. Remove from water. (Cooked balls
can be stored in refrigerator for up to 2 days.)
6. Pour chicken broth into slow cooker. Add
matzoh balls.
7. Cover. Cook on high 2-3 hours or on low
5-6 hours.

* *Finely crushed matzoh may be substituted.*

*I made this soup for an ethnic luncheon at
work. Everyone enjoyed it. Matzoh ball soup is
traditionally served on the Jewish holiday of
Passover. It is also known as "Jewish penicillin,"
and I make it all year-round.*

Lidia's Egg Drop Soup

Shirley Unternahrer Hinh
Wayland, IA

Makes 8 servings

2 14 1/2-oz. cans chicken broth
1 qt. water
2 Tbsp. fish sauce
1/4 tsp. salt
4 Tbsp. cornstarch
1 cup cold water
2 eggs, beaten
1 chopped green onion
pepper to taste

1. Combine broth and water in large saucepan.
2. Add fish sauce and salt. Bring to boil.
3. Mix cornstarch into cold water until smooth. Add to soup. Bring to boil while stirring. Remove from heat.
4. Pour beaten eggs into thickened broth, but do not stir. Instead, pull fork through soup with 2 strokes.
5. Transfer to slow cooker. Add green onions and pepper.
6. Cover. Cook on low 1 hour. Keep warm in cooker.
7. Eat plain or with rice.

One day when the kids were sledding I surprised them with something other than hot cocoa when they came in. "Mmmmm," was all I heard, and, "This tastes great!" "You're the best, Mom!" They finished all the egg drop soup and wondered if I'd make more.

Buffalo Chicken Wing Soup

Anna Stoltzfus
Honey Brook, PA

Makes 8 servings

6 cups milk
3 10 3/4-oz. cans cream of chicken soup
3 cups shredded cooked chicken
1 cup sour cream
1/4-1/2 cup hot pepper sauce (or if you're timid, use 2 Tbsp.)

1. Combine ingredients in slow cooker.
2. Cover. Cook on low 4-5 hours.

White Chicken Chili

Jewel Showalter
Landisville, PA

Makes 6-8 servings

2 whole skinless chicken breasts
6 cups water
2 chopped onions
2 garlic cloves, minced
1 Tbsp. oil
2-4 4-oz. cans chopped green chilies
1-2 diced jalapeno peppers
2 tsp. ground cumin
1 1/2 tsp. dried oregano
1/4 tsp. cayenne pepper
1/2 tsp. salt
3-lb. can navy beans, undrained
1-2 cups shredded cheese
sour cream
salsa

1. Place chicken in slow cooker. Add 6 cups water.

2. Cover. Cook on low 3-4 hours, or until tender.

3. Remove chicken from slow cooker. Cube and set aside.

4. Saute onions and garlic in oil in skillet. Add chilies, jalapeno peppers, cumin, oregano, pepper, and salt. Saute 2 minutes. Transfer to broth in slow cooker.

5. Add navy beans.

6. Cover. Cook on low 30-60 minutes.

7. Right before serving add chicken and cheese.

8. Serve topped with sour cream and salsa. Cornbread or corn chips are good go-alongs with this chili.

Variation: If you want to use dried beans, use 3 cups navy beans and cover with water in saucepan, soaking overnight. In the morning, drain and cover with fresh water. Cook in saucepan on low 7-8 hours, or until tender. Drain of excess moisture and stir into chicken and broth.

White Chili

Rebecca Plank Leichty
Harrisonburg, VA

Makes 6-8 servings

15-oz. can chickpeas or garbanzo beans, undrained
15-oz. can small Northern beans, undrained
15-oz. can pinto beans, undrained
1 qt. frozen corn, or 2 1-lb. bags frozen corn
1 1/2 cups shredded cooked chicken
2 Tbsp. minced onion
1 red bell pepper, diced
3 tsp. minced garlic
3 tsp. ground cumin
1/2 tsp. salt
1/2 tsp. dried oregano
2 15-oz. cans chicken broth

1. Combine all ingredients in slow cooker.

2. Cover. Cook on low 8-10 hours, or high 4-5 hours.

3. Serve with warmed tortilla chips topped with melted cheddar cheese

Variations: For more zip, add 2 tsp. chili powder, or one or more chopped jalapeno peppers, to Step 1.

Pumpkin Black-Bean Turkey Chili

Rhoda Atzeff
Harrisburg, PA

Makes 10-12 servings

1 cup chopped onions
1 cup chopped yellow bell pepper
3 garlic cloves, minced
2 Tbsp. oil
1 1/2 tsp. dried oregano
1 1/2-2 tsp. ground cumin
2 tsp. chili powder
2 15-oz. cans black beans, rinsed and drained
2 1/2 cups chopped cooked turkey
16-oz. can pumpkin
14 1/2-oz. can diced tomatoes
3 cups chicken broth

1. Saute onions, yellow pepper, and garlic in oil for 8 minutes, or until soft.

2. Stir in oregano, cumin, and chili powder. Cook 1 minute. Transfer to slow cooker.

3. Add remaining ingredients.

4. Cover. Cook on low 7-8 hours.

Turkey Chili

Reita F. Yoder
Carlsbad, NM

Makes 6-8 servings

2 lbs. ground turkey
16-oz. can pinto, or kidney, beans
2 cups fresh or canned tomatoes, chopped
2 cups tomato sauce
1 garlic clove, minced
1 small onion, chopped
16-oz. can rotel tomatoes
1-oz. pkg. Williams chili seasoning

1. Crumble ground turkey in bottom of slow cooker.
2. Add remaining ingredients. Mix well.
3. Cover. Cook on low 6-8 hours.

Chilly-Chili

Alix Nancy Botsford
Seminole, OK

Makes 6-8 servings

2 cups dried beans
1 tsp. salt
2 Tbsp. olive oil
1 large onion, chopped
1 lb. ground turkey
2 tsp. minced garlic
oil
1 tsp. salt
2 celery ribs, chopped
1 green pepper, diced
10-oz. can tomatoes and green chilies

1. Sort, wash, and cover beans with water. Soak 6-8 hours. Drain.

2. Place beans in slow cooker. Cover with fresh water. Add 1 tsp. salt.
3. Cover. Cook on high 2-3 hours, or until a bean can be crushed with a fork. Drain off all but 1-2 cups liquid.
4. Brown onion, turkey, and garlic in oil in skillet. Add 1 tsp. salt, celery, and green pepper. Cook until vegetables have started to soften. Add tomatoes. Place in slow cooker.
5. Cover. Cook on low 1-8 hours.
6. Serve with slices of cheese and crackers.

This is a good meal for guests—or when we're all working outdoors and need our meal to be ready when we come in, like early spring when we're getting the garden ready.

Three-Bean Chili

Chris Kaczynski
Schenectady, NY

Makes 8-10 servings

2 lbs. ground beef
2 medium onions, diced
16-oz. jar medium salsa
2 pkgs. dry chili seasoning
2 16-oz. cans red kidney beans, drained
2 16-oz. cans black beans, drained
2 16-oz. cans white kidney, or garbanzo, beans drained
28-oz. can crushed tomatoes
16-oz. can diced tomatoes
2 tsp. sugar

1. Brown beef and onions in skillet.
2. Combine all ingredients in 6-qt. slow cooker, or in 2 4- or 5-qt. cookers.
3. Cover. Cook on low 8-10 hours.
4. Serve with chopped raw onion and/or shredded cheddar cheese.

Note: This recipe can be cut in half without injuring the flavor, if you don't have a cooker large enough to handle the full amount.

Hearty Chili
Joylynn Keener
Lancaster, PA

Makes 8 servings

1 onion, chopped
2 ribs celery, chopped
1 lb. ground beef
2 14-oz. cans kidney beans, undrained
14-oz. can pinto beans, undrained
14-oz. can diced tomatoes
2 14-oz. cans tomato sauce
1 green pepper, chopped
1 Tbsp. sugar
1 tsp. salt
1 tsp. dried thyme
1 tsp. dried oregano
1 Tbsp. chili powder, or to taste

1. Brown onion, celery, and beef in skillet. Pour into slow cooker.
2. Add remaining ingredients. Mix well.
3. Cover. Cook on low 8 hours.

Slow-Cooker Chili
Kay Magruder
Seminole, OK

Makes 8-10 servings

3 lbs. stewing meat, browned
2 cloves garlic, minced
1/4 tsp. pepper
1/2 tsp. cumin
1/4 tsp. dry mustard
7 1/2-oz. can jalapeno relish
1 cup beef broth
1-1 1/2 onions, chopped, according to your taste preference
1/2 tsp. salt
1/2 tsp. dried oregano
1 Tbsp. chili powder
7-oz. can green chilies, chopped
14 1/2-oz. can stewed tomatoes, chopped
15-oz. can tomato sauce
2 15-oz. cans red kidney beans, rinsed and drained
2 15-oz. cans pinto beans, rinsed and drained

1. Combine all ingredients except kidney and pinto beans in slow cooker.
2. Cover. Cook on low 10-12 hours or on high 6-7 hours. Add beans halfway through cooking time.
3. Serve with Mexican cornbread.

So-Easy Chili

Sue Graber
Eureka, IL

Makes 4 servings

1 lb. ground beef
1 onion, chopped
15-oz. can chili, with or without beans
14.5-oz. can diced tomatoes with green
chilies, or with basil, garlic, and
oregano
1 cup tomato juice
chopped onion
grated cheddar cheese

1. Brown ground beef and onion in skillet. Drain and put in slow cooker.
2. Add chili, diced tomatoes, and tomato juice.
3. Cover. Cook on low 4-6 hours.
4. Serve with onion and cheese on top of each individual serving.

Note: This chili is of a good consistency for serving over rice. For a thicker chili, add 4-6 ozs. tomato paste 20 minutes before end of cooking time.

Extra Easy Chili

Jennifer Gehman
Harrisburg, PA

Makes 4-6 servings

1 lb. ground beef or turkey, uncooked
1 pkg. dry chili seasoning mix
16-oz. can chili beans in sauce
2 28-oz. cans crushed or diced tomatoes
seasoned with garlic and onion

1. Crumble meat in bottom of slow cooker.
2. Add remaining ingredients. Stir.
3. Cover. Cook on high 4-6 hours or low 6-8 hours. Stir halfway through cooking time.
4. Serve over white rice, topped with shredded cheddar cheese and chopped raw onions.

I decided to make this chili recipe one year for Christmas. Our family was hosting other family members—and we had had guests for about a week prior to Christmas. Needless to say, I was tired of cooking so this seemed easy enough. It was so nice to put the ingredients in the slow cooker and let it cook all day long. Not only did the chili warm us up on a cold day, but it was a welcomed change from the traditional Christmas meal. It has been my tradition ever since!

Menu Idea

Extra Easy Chili
Baked Potatoes
Buttered Macaronis
Cornbread Muffins

Grandma's Chili

Beverly (Flatt) Getz
Warriors Mark, PA

Makes 8 servings

1 large onion, chopped
2 lbs. ground beef
28-oz. can stewed tomatoes
16-oz. can dark kidney beans, undrained
15-oz. can Hormel chili with beans
10¾-oz. can tomato soup
1 tsp. K.C. Masterpiece BBQ sauce
¼ tsp. garlic salt
¼ tsp. garlic powder
¼ tsp. onion salt
¼ tsp. chili powder
pinch of sugar

1. Brown onion and beef in skillet, leaving meat in larger chunks. Place in slow cooker.

2. Add remaining ingredients. Stir.

3. Cover. Cook on high 4 hours.

4. Serve with crackers, rolls, butter, and apple crisp with whipped topping.

When the grandchildren come to visit from five different states, they always ask for Grandma's Chili. I just made up the recipe. Now I'm afraid to change it!

Chili Soup

Fannie Miller
Hutchinson, KS

Makes 12-15 servings

4 lbs. ground beef
1 large onion, diced
2 cups cold water
2 Tbsp. brown sugar
2 Tbsp. chili powder
2 tsp. salt
2 tsp. dried oregano
1/2 tsp. garlic salt
1/4 tsp. ground coriander

1. Brown hamburger and onion in skillet. Drain and transfer to slow cooker.

2. Add remaining ingredients. Mix well.

3. Cover. Cook on low 4-6 hours.

Our Favorite Chili

Ruth Shank
Gridley, IL

Makes 10-12 servings

1 1/2 lbs. ground beef
1/4 cup chopped onions
1 rib celery, chopped
29-oz. can stewed tomatoes
2 15.5-oz. cans red kidney beans, undrained
2 16-oz. cans chili beans, undrained
1/2 cup ketchup
1 1/2 tsp. lemon juice
2 tsp. vinegar
1 1/2 tsp. brown sugar
1 1/2 tsp. salt
1 tsp. Worcestershire sauce
1/2 tsp. garlic powder
1/2 tsp. dry mustard powder
1 Tbsp. chili powder
2 6-oz. cans tomato paste

1. Brown ground beef, onions, and celery in skillet. Drain. Place in slow cooker.

2. Add remaining ingredients. Mix well.

3. Cover. Cook on low 8-10 hours or high 4-5 hours.

4. Serve with fresh warm cornbread and slices of Colby or Monterey Jack cheese.

Slow-Cooked Chili

Jean A. Shaner
York, PA

Makes 10 servings

2 lbs. ground beef, browned
2 16-oz. cans kidney beans, rinsed and
   drained
2 14½-oz. cans diced tomatoes
8-oz. can tomato sauce
2 onions, chopped
1 green pepper, chopped
2 garlic cloves, minced
2 Tbsp. chili powder
2 tsp. salt
1 tsp. pepper
shredded cheddar cheese

1. Combine all ingredients except cheese in slow cooker.
2. Cover. Cook on low 8-10 hours.
3. Ladle chili into individual bowls and top with cheese just before serving.

Chili Soup

Glenna Fay Bergey
Lebanon, OR

Makes 5 quarts

3 lbs. ground beef
¾ cup chopped onions
2 Tbsp. celery flakes
2 tsp. salt
1 Tbsp. chili powder, or more, according to taste
3 15-oz. cans kidney beans
1 qt. tomato juice
2 10¾-oz. cans tomato soup
1 cup ketchup
¼ cup brown sugar

1. Brown meat, onions, and seasonings in large skillet. Transfer to large bowl and stir in remaining ingredients.
2. Divide between 2 4- or 5-qt. slow cookers (this is a large recipe!).
3. Cover. Cook on high 2 hours or low 4-6 hours.
4. Serve with cornbread.

Country Auction Chili Soup

Clara Newswanger
Gordonville, PA

Makes 20 servings

1 1/2 lbs. ground beef
1/4 cup chopped onions
1/2 cup flour
1 Tbsp. chili powder
1 tsp. salt
6 cups water
2 cups ketchup
1/3 cup brown sugar
3 15.5-oz. cans kidney beans, undrained

1. Brown ground beef and onions in skillet. Drain. Spoon meat mixture into slow cooker.
2. Stir flour into meat and onions. Add seasonings.
3. Slowly stir in water. Add ketchup, brown sugar, and beans.
4. Cover. Cook on high 4 hours or low 8 hours.

The Chili Connection

Anne Townsend
Albuquerque, NM

Makes 6 servings

1 1/2 lbs. ground beef
1 cup chopped onions
28-oz. can tomatoes, chopped
15-oz. can kidney beans, undrained
1 Tbsp. brown or granulated sugar
2-4 tsp. chili powder, according to your taste preference
1 tsp. salt

1. Brown ground beef and onions in skillet.
2. Combine all ingredients in slow cooker.
3. Cover. Cook on low 3-5 hours.

Variation: In order to have a thicker chili, stir in a 6-oz. can of tomato paste in Step 2.

Notes:
1. An assortment of toppings can take the place of a salad with this chili. I usually offer chopped onions, tomatoes, grated cheddar cheese, picante sauce, and, when avocados are in season, guacamole. Cornbread or refrigerated twist rolls sprinkled with garlic salt are delicious. Either chocolate or apple cake with ice cream makes a happy ending.

2. This is a fun informal party dish which connects the guests as they get involved in selecting their favorite toppings.

3. As a frequently enjoyed dish, this recipe has stood the test of time. Our children thought it was delicious when they were young and now they enjoy preparing it for their own families.

Hot and Good Chili

Rose Hankins
Stevensville, MD

Makes 12 servings

1 lb. ground beef
1 cup chopped onions
1 cup chopped celery
1 cup chopped green peppers
28-oz. can tomatoes
14-oz. can tomato sauce
2 14-oz. cans kidney beans, undrained
2 Tbsp. chili powder
1 Tbsp. garlic powder
1 Tbsp. hot sauce

1. Brown beef in skillet. Reserve drippings and transfer drained beef to slow cooker.
2. Saute onions, celery, and green peppers in drippings. Drain and transfer to slow cooker.
3. Stir in remaining ingredients.
4. Cover. Cook on high 4-5 hours or on low 8-10 hours.

Slowly Cooked Chili

Beatrice Martin
Goshen, IN

Makes 6-8 servings

2 lbs. ground beef or turkey, browned in skillet
15½-oz. can kidney beans, undrained
3 cups tomato juice
3 Tbsp. chili powder
1 tsp. minced garlic
1 pkg. dry onion soup mix
½-1 tsp. salt, according to taste
¼ tsp. pepper

1. Combine all ingredients in slow cooker.
2. Cover. Cook on low 10-12 hours or on high 5-6 hours.
3. Serve in soup bowls with crackers, or over rice.

Note: This chili freezes well.

Hearty Potato Chili

Janice Muller
Derwood, MD

Makes 8 servings

1 lb. ground beef
½ cup chopped onions, or 2 Tbsp. dried minced onions
½ cup chopped green peppers
1 Tbsp. poppy seeds (optional)
1 tsp. salt
½ tsp. chili powder
1 pkg. au gratin or scalloped potato mix
1 cup hot water
15-oz. can kidney beans, undrained
16-oz. can stewed tomatoes
4-oz. can mushroom pieces, undrained

1. Brown ground beef in skillet. Remove meat and place in slow cooker. Saute onions and green peppers in drippings until softened.
2. Combine all ingredients in slow cooker.
3. Cover. Cook on high 4 hours, or until liquid is absorbed and potatoes are tender.

Spicy Chili
Deborah Swartz
Grottoes, VA

Makes 4-6 servings

½ lb. sausage, either cut in thin slices or
    removed from casings
½ lb. ground beef
½ cup chopped onions
½ lb. fresh mushrooms, sliced
⅛ cup chopped celery
⅛ cup chopped green peppers
1 cup salsa
16-oz. can tomato juice
6-oz. can tomato paste
½ tsp. sugar
½ tsp. salt
½ tsp. dried oregano
½ tsp. Worcestershire sauce
¼ tsp. dried basil
¼ tsp. pepper

1. Brown sausage, ground beef, and onion
in skillet. During last 3 minutes of browning,
add mushrooms, celery, and green peppers.
Continue cooking; then drain.
2. Add remaining ingredients. Pour into
slow cooker.
3. Cover. Cook on high 2-3 hours.

Variations:
Add any or all of the following to Step 2:
    1 tsp. chili powder
    1 tsp. ground cumin
    15-oz. can black beans, undrained
    15-oz. can whole-kernel corn,
        undrained

M&T's Chili
Sherry Conyers
McPherson, KS

Makes 4 servings

1 lb. ground beef, browned
½ lb. sausage links, sliced and browned
1 pkg. Williams chili seasoning
2 10-oz. cans Mexican tomatoes
15-oz. can chili with no beans
2 10-oz. cans rotel tomatoes
1-lb. can refried beans
¼ cup diced onions

1. Combine ingredients in slow cooker.
2. Cover. Cook on low 5-6 hours.

*Variations: If you want a soupier, and less spicy,
chili, add a 1-lb. can of stewed tomatoes or 2 cups
tomato juice.*

Wintertime Vegetable Chili

Maricarol Magill
Freehold, NJ

Makes 6 servings

1 medium butternut squash, peeled and
    cubed
2 medium carrots, peeled and diced
1 medium onion, diced
3 tsp.—3 Tbsp. chili powder, depending
    upon how hot you like your chili
2 14-oz. cans diced tomatoes
4-oz. can chopped mild green chilies
1 tsp. salt, optional
1 cup vegetable broth
2 16-oz. cans black beans, drained and
    rinsed
sour cream, optional

  1. In slow cooker, layer ingredients in order
given—except sour cream.
  2. Cover. Cook on low 6-8 hours, or until
vegetables are tender.
  3. Stir before serving.
  4. Top individual servings with dollops of
sour cream.
  5. Serve with crusty French bread.

Black Bean Chili Con Carne

Janie Steele
Moore, OK

Makes 18 1-cup servings

1 lb. black beans
3 lbs. ground beef
oil, if needed
2 large onions, chopped
1 green pepper, chopped
3 cloves garlic, minced
2 tsp. salt
1 tsp. pepper
6-oz. can tomato paste
3 cups tomato juice, or more
1 tsp. celery salt
1 Tbsp. Worcestershire sauce
1 tsp. dry mustard
cayenne pepper to taste
cumin to taste
3 Tbsp. chili powder

  1. Soak beans 8 hours or overnight. Rinse
and drain.
  2. Brown ground beef in batches in large
skillet, in oil if needed.
  3. Combine all ingredients in 6-qt. or larger
slow cooker, or divide between 2 smaller
cookers.
  4. Cover. Cook on low 8 hours.
  5. Serve over salad greens or wrapped in
tortillas, topped with lettuce and grated cheese.

Norma's Vegetarian Chili

Kathy Hertzler
Lancaster, PA

Makes 8-10 servings

2 Tbsp. oil
2 cups minced celery
1½ cups chopped green pepper
1 cup minced onions
4 garlic cloves, minced
5½ cups stewed tomatoes
2 1-lb. cans kidney beans, undrained
1½-2 cups raisins
¼ cup wine vinegar
1 Tbsp. chopped parsley
2 tsp. salt
1½ tsp. dried oregano
1½ tsp. cumin
¼ tsp. pepper
¼ tsp. Tabasco sauce
1 bay leaf
¾ cup cashews
1 cup grated cheese, optional

1. Combine all ingredients except cashews and cheese in slow cooker.
2. Cover. Simmer on low for 8 hours. Add cashews and simmer 30 minutes.
3. Garnish individual servings with grated cheese.

Menu Idea

Norma's Vegetarian Chili
Cornbread
Plate of Crudites
Chocolate Chip Cookies

Easy Cheese Soup

Nancy Wagner Graves
Manhattan, KS

Makes 4 servings

2 10¾-oz. cans cream of mushroom or
　cream of chicken soup
1 cup beer or milk
1 lb. cheddar cheese, grated
1 tsp. Worcestershire sauce
¼ tsp. paprika
croutons

1. Combine all ingredients except croutons in slow cooker.
2. Cover. Cook on low 4-6 hours.
3. Stir thoroughly 1 hour before serving, to make sure cheese is well distributed and melted.
4. Serve topped with croutons or in bread bowls.

Wonderful Clam Chowder

Carlene Horne
Bedford, NH

Makes 4-6 servings

2 12-oz. cans evaporated milk
1 evaporated milk can of water
2 6-oz. cans whole clams, undrained
6-oz. can minced clams, undrained
1 small onion, chopped
2 small potatoes, diced
2 Tbsp. cornstarch
¼ cup water

1. Combine all ingredients except cornstarch and ¼ cup water in slow cooker.
2. Cover. Cook on low 6-7 hours.
3. One hour before end of cooking time, mix cornstarch and ¼ cup water together. When smooth, stir into soup. Stir until soup thickens.

Clam Chowder

Ruth Shank
Gridley, IL

Makes 8-12 servings

2 10¾-oz. cans cream of potato soup
10¾-oz. can cream of celery soup
2 6½-oz. cans minced clams, drained
3 slices bacon, diced and fried
1 soup can of water
1 small onion, minced
1 Tbsp. fresh parsley
dash of dried marjoram
1 Tbsp. Worcestershire sauce
pepper to taste
2 soup cans of milk

1. Combine all ingredients, except 2 soup cans of milk, in slow cooker.
2. Cover. Cook on low 6-8 hours.
3. Twenty minutes before end of cooking time, stir in milk. Continue cooking until heated through.

Vegetables

Easy Flavor-Filled Green Beans

Paula Showalter
Weyers Cave, VA

Makes 10 servings

2 qts. green beans, drained
1/3 cup chopped onions
4-oz. can mushrooms, drained
2 Tbsp. brown sugar
3 Tbsp. butter
pepper to taste

1. Combine beans, onions, and mushrooms in slow cooker.
2. Sprinkle with brown sugar.
3. Dot with butter.
4. Sprinkle with pepper.
5. Cover. Cook on high 3-4 hours. Stir just before serving.

Green Bean Casserole

Brenda S. Burkholder
Port Republic, VA

Makes 6-8 servings

1 qt. cooked green beans
1/2 tsp. sugar
10 3/4-oz. can cream of mushroom soup
3/4 cup grated cheddar cheese

1. Combine ingredients in slow cooker.
2. Cover. Cook on low 3-4 hours.

If I ask my husband what to make for a company meal, he quite frequently asks for these beans.

Green Bean Casserole

Mary Sommerfeld
Lancaster, PA

Makes 6 servings

2 lbs. fresh green beans, cut up,
  or 4 10-oz. pkgs. frozen beans
10³/₄-oz. can cream of mushroom soup
3-oz. can French-fried onion rings
1 cup grated cheddar cheese
8-oz. can water chestnuts, thinly sliced
slivered almonds, optional
salt to taste
pepper to taste
1 cup water

1. In slow cooker, layer one-third of ingredients, except water, in order given. Repeat 2 times, saving a few onion rings for top.
2. Pour water into slow cooker.
3. Cover. Cook on high 4-5 hours or on low 8-10 hours. Sprinkle reserved onion rings on top 20 minutes before serving.

Green Bean Casserole

Jane Meiser
Harrisonburg, VA

Makes 4-5 servings

14¹/₂-oz. can green beans, drained
3¹/₂-oz. can French fried onions
1 cup grated cheddar cheese
8-oz. can water chestnuts, drained
10³/₄-oz. can cream of chicken soup
¹/₄ cup white wine or water
¹/₂ tsp. curry powder
¹/₄ tsp. pepper

1. Alternate layers of half the beans, half the onions, half the cheese, and half the water chestnuts in slow cooker. Repeat.
2. Combine remaining ingredients. Pour over vegetables in slow cooker.
3. Cover. Cook on low 6-7 hours or high 3-4 hours.

Green Bean Casserole

Vicki Dinkel
Sharon Springs, KS

Makes 9-11 servings

3 10-oz. pkgs. frozen, cut green beans
2 10¹/₂-oz. cans cheddar cheese soup
¹/₂ cup water
¹/₄ cup chopped green onions
4-oz. can sliced mushrooms, drained
8-oz. can water chestnuts, drained and
  sliced (optional)
¹/₂ cup slivered almonds
1 tsp. salt
¹/₄ tsp. pepper

1. Combine all ingredients in lightly greased slow cooker. Mix well.
2. Cover. Cook on low 8-10 hours or on high 3-4 hours.

Creamy Cheesy Bean Casserole

Martha Hershey
Ronks, PA

Makes 5 servings

16-oz. bag frozen green beans, cooked
3/4 cup milk
1 cup grated American cheese
2 slices bread, crumbled

1. Place beans in slow cooker.
2. Combine milk and cheese in saucepan. Heat, stirring continually, until cheese melts. Fold in bread cubes and pour mixture over beans.
3. Cover. Heat on high 2 hours.

Variation: Use 15-oz. container of Cheez Whiz instead of making cheese sauce. Mix crumbled bread into Cheez Whiz and pour over beans. Proceed with Step 3.

Au Gratin Green Beans

Donna Lantgen
Rapid City, SD

Makes 8 servings

2 16-oz. cans green beans, drained
1/4 cup diced onions
1/2 cup cubed Velveeta cheese
1/4 cup evaporated milk
1 tsp. flour
1/2 tsp. salt
dash of pepper

1. Combine all ingredients in slow cooker.
2. Cover. Cook on low 4 hours.
3. Garnish with sliced almonds at serving time, if you wish.

Green Bean Casserole

Darla Sathre
Baxter, MN

Makes 8 servings

4 14 1/2-oz. cans French-style green beans, drained
2 10 3/4-oz. cans cream of celery soup
6-oz. can French-fried onion rings
2 cups shredded cheddar cheese
2 tsp. dried basil
5-oz. can evaporated milk

1. In greased slow cooker, layer half of each ingredient, except milk, in order given. Repeat. Pour milk over all.
2. Cover. Cook on low 6-10 hours.

Super Creamed Corn

Ruth Ann Penner
Hillsboro, KS
Alix Nancy Botsford
Seminole, OK

Makes 8-12 servings

2-3 lbs. frozen corn
8-oz. pkg. cream cheese, cubed
1/4 cup butter or margarine, melted
2-3 Tbsp. sugar or honey
2-3 Tbsp. water, optional

1. Combine ingredients in slow cooker.
2. Cover. Cook on low 4 hours.
3. Serve with meat loaf, turkey, or hamburgers.

A great addition to a holiday that is easy and requires no last-minute preparation. It also frees the stove and oven for other food preparation.

Corn Pudding

Lizzie Weaver
Ephrata, PA

Makes 3-4 servings

2 eggs, beaten slightly
1/4 cup sugar
1 tsp. salt
1/8 tsp. pepper
2 Tbsp. melted butter
2 Tbsp. flour
1/2 cup milk
16-oz. can cream-style corn

1. Combine all ingredients except corn. Pour into slow cooker.
2. Add corn. Mix well.
3. Cover. Cook on low 4 hours.

Variation: Add 1/2 cup grated cheese to Step 2.
—**Brenda S. Burkholder, Port Republic, VA**

This recipe frees your oven space for other dishes. It's perfect, too, for Sunday lunch if you've been gone all morning.

Baked Corn

Velma Stauffer
Akron, PA

Makes 8 servings

1 qt. corn, frozen or fresh
2 eggs, beaten
1 tsp. salt
1 cup milk
1/8 tsp. pepper
2 tsp. oil
3 Tbsp. sugar
3 Tbsp. flour

1. Combine all ingredients well. Pour into greased slow cooker.
2. Cover. Cook on high 3 hours and then on low 45 minutes.

Note: If you use home-grown sweet corn, you could reduce the amount of sugar.

Scalloped Corn
Rebecca Plank Leichty
Harrisonburg, VA

Makes 6 servings

2 eggs
10¾-oz. can cream of celery soup
⅔ cup unseasoned bread crumbs
2 cups whole-kernel corn, drained, or
  cream-style corn
1 tsp. minced onion
¼-½ tsp. salt, according to your taste
  preference
⅛ tsp. pepper
1 Tbsp. sugar
2 Tbsp. melted butter

1. Beat eggs with fork. Add soup and bread crumbs. Mix well.
2. Add remaining ingredients and mix thoroughly. Pour into greased slow cooker.
3. Cover. Cook on high 3 hours or on low 6 hours.

Hosting Idea

Because not all guests enjoy the same vegetable, I usually prepare two or three different ones. By utilizing my slow cooker for a vegetable dish, as well as the oven and stove-top, I have alot of freedom to plan and make a desirable variety.

— Rebecca Plank Leichty

Scalloped Corn and Celery
Darla Sathre
Baxter, MN

Makes 8 servings

2 16-oz. cans whole-kernel corn, drained
2 16-oz. cans cream-style corn
2 cups chopped celery
40 saltine crackers, crushed
⅛-¼ tsp. pepper
2 Tbsp. butter
12-oz. can evaporated milk

1. Layer in greased slow cooker, half of whole-kernel corn, cream-style corn, celery, crackers, pepper, and butter. Repeat. Pour milk over all.
2. Cover. Cook on low 8-12 hours.

Baked Corn and Noodles
Ruth Hershey
Paradise, PA

Makes 6 servings

3 cups noodles, cooked al dente
2 cups fresh or frozen corn, thawed
¾ cup grated cheddar cheese, or cubed
  Velveeta cheese
1 egg, beaten
½ cup butter, melted
½ tsp. salt

1. Combine all ingredients in slow cooker.
2. Cover. Cook on low 6-8 hours or on high 3-4 hours.

Mexican Corn

Betty K. Drescher
Quakertown, PA

Makes 8-10 servings

2 10-oz. pkgs. frozen corn, partially
  thawed
4-oz. jar chopped pimentos
1/3 cup chopped green peppers
1/3 cup water
1 tsp. salt
1/4 tsp. pepper
1/2 tsp. paprika
1/2 tsp. chili powder

1. Combine all ingredients in slow cooker.
2. Cover. Cook on high 45 minutes, then on low 2-4 hours. Stir occasionally.

Variations: For more fire, add 1/3 cup salsa to the ingredients, and increase the amounts of pepper, paprika, and chili powder to match your taste.

Confetti Scalloped Corn

Rhoda Atzeff
Harrisburg, PA

Makes 6-8 servings

2 eggs, beaten
1 cup sour cream
1/4 cup butter or margarine, melted
1 small onion, finely chopped, or 2 Tbsp.
  dried chopped onion
11-oz. can Mexicorn, drained
14-oz. can cream-style corn
2-3 Tbsp. green jalapeno salsa, regular
  salsa, or chopped green chilies
8 1/2-oz. pkg. cornbread mix

1. Combine all ingredients. Pour into lightly greased slow cooker.
2. Cover. Bake on high 2-2 1/2 hours, or until corn is fully cooked.

Cornbread Casserole

Arlene Groff
Lewistown, PA

Makes 8 servings

1 qt. whole-kernel corn
1 qt. creamed corn
1 pkg. corn muffin mix
1 egg
2 Tbsp. butter
1/4 tsp. garlic powder
2 Tbsp. sugar
1/4 cup milk
1/2 tsp. salt
1/4 tsp. pepper

1. Combine ingredients in greased slow cooker.
2. Cover. Cook on low 3 1/2-4 hours, stirring once halfway through.

Cheesy Hominy

Michelle Showalter
Bridgewater, VA

Makes 12-14 servings

2 cups cracked hominy
6 cups water
2 Tbsp. flour
1½ cups milk
4 cups sharp cheddar cheese, grated
1-2 tsp. salt
¼ tsp. pepper
4 Tbsp. butter

1. Combine hominy and water in 5-6 qt. slow cooker.
2. Cover. Cook on high 3-4 hours or on low 6-8 hours.
3. Stir in remaining ingredients.
4. Cover. Cook 30-60 minutes.

Cheesy Hominy is a nice change if you're tired of the same old thing. It's wonderful with ham, slices of bacon, or meatballs. Add a green vegetable and you have a lovely meal. Hominy is available at bulk-food stores.

Hosting Idea

The most important thing to remember when hosting is to relax and be yourself. This will make your company feel at home.
—Michelle Showalter

Southwest Posole

Becky Harder
Monument, CO

Makes 6 servings

2 12-oz. pkgs. dry posole
1 garlic clove, minced
2 14-oz. cans vegetable or chicken broth
2 10-oz. cans rotel Mexican diced tomatoes
4-oz. can diced green chilies, optional
salt to taste

1. Soak posole for 4-8 hours. Drain water.
2. Combine ingredients in slow cooker.
3. Cover. Cook on high 3 hours; then turn to low for 2 hours.
4. Serve with enchiladas, black beans, Spanish rice, and chopped lettuce with black olives and tomatoes.

Note: Dry posole can be found in the Mexican food department of the grocery store. If you cannot find dry posole, you can used canned hominy and skip to Step 2.

Fruited Wild Rice with Pecans

Dottie Schmidt
Kansas City, MO

Makes 4 servings

1/2 cup chopped onions
2 Tbsp. margarine
6-oz. pkg. long-grain and wild rice
seasoning packet from wild rice pkg.
1 1/2 cups hot water
2/3 cup apple juice
1 large tart apple, chopped
1/4 cup raisins
1/4 cup coarsely chopped pecans

1. Combine all ingredients except pecans in greased slow cooker.
2. Cover. Cook on high 2-2 1/2 hours.
3. Stir in pecans. Serve.

Menu Idea

Grilled Chicken Breasts
Fruited Wild Rice with Pecans
Tossed Salad

Mjeddrah

Dianna Milhizer
Brighton, MI

Makes 20-24 servings

10 cups water
4 cups dried lentils, rinsed
2 cups uncooked brown rice
1/4 cup olive oil
2 tsp. salt

1. Combine ingredients in large slow cooker
2. Cover. Cook on high 8 hours, then on low 2 hours. Add 2 more cups water, if needed, to allow rice to cook and to prevent dish from drying out.
3. This is traditionally eaten with a salad with an oil-and-vinegar dressing over the lentil-rice mixture, similar to a tostada without the tortilla.

Broccoli Casserole

Dorothy Van Deest
Memphis, TN

Makes 4-6 servings

10-oz. pkg. frozen chopped broccoli
6 eggs, beaten
24-oz. carton small-curd cottage cheese
6 Tbsp. flour
8 ozs. mild cheese of your choice, diced
1/4 cup butter, melted
2 green onions, chopped
salt to taste

1. Place frozen broccoli in colander. Run cold water over it until it thaws. Separate into pieces. Drain well.
2. Combine remaining ingredients in large bowl and mix until well blended. Stir in broccoli. Pour into greased slow cooker.
3. Cover. Cook on high 1 hour. Stir well, then resume cooking on low 2-4 hours.

Quick Broccoli Fix

Willard E. Roth
Elkhart, IN

Makes 6 servings

1 lb. fresh or frozen broccoli, cut up
10¾-oz. can cream of mushroom soup
½ cup mayonnaise
½ cup plain yogurt
½ lb. sliced fresh mushrooms
1 cup shredded cheddar cheese, divided
1 cup crushed saltine crackers
sliced almonds, optional

1. Microwave broccoli for 3 minutes. Place in greased slow cooker.
2. Combine soup, mayonnaise, yogurt, mushrooms, and ½ cup cheese. Pour over broccoli.
3. Cover. Cook on low 5-6 hours.
4. Top with remaining cheese and crackers for last half hour of cooking time.
5. Top with sliced almonds, for a special touch, before serving.

Broccoli and Rice Casserole

Deborah Swartz
Grottoes, VA

Makes 4-6 servings

1 lb. chopped broccoli, fresh or frozen, thawed
1 medium onion, chopped
¼ cup butter or margarine
1 cup minute rice, or 1½ cups cooked rice
10¾-oz. can cream of chicken or mushroom soup
¼ cup milk
1⅓ cups Velveeta cheese, cubed, or cheddar cheese, shredded
1 tsp. salt

1. Cook broccoli for 5 minutes in saucepan in boiling water. Drain and set aside.
2. Saute onion in butter in saucepan until tender. Add to broccoli.
3. Combine remaining ingredients. Add to broccoli mixture. Pour into greased slow cooker.
4. Cover. Cook on low 3-4 hours.

Squash Medley

Evelyn Page
Riverton, WY

Makes 8 servings

8 summer squash, each about 4″ long,
   thinly sliced
1/2 tsp. salt
2 tomatoes, peeled and chopped
1/4 cup sliced green onions
half a small sweet green pepper, chopped
1 chicken bouillon cube
1/4 cup hot water
4 slices bacon, fried and crumbled
1/4 cup fine dry bread crumbs

   1. Sprinkle squash with salt.
   2. In slow cooker, layer half the squash,
tomatoes, onions, and pepper. Repeat layers.
   3. Dissolve bouillon in hot water. Pour into
slow cooker.
   4. Top with bacon. Sprinkle bread crumbs
over top.
   5. Cover. Cook on low 4-6 hours.

*Variation: For a sweeter touch, sprinkle 1 Tbsp.
brown sugar over half the layered vegetables.
Repeat over second half of layered vegetables.*

Baked Acorn Squash

Dale Peterson
Rapid City, SD

Makes 4 servings

2 acorn squash
2/3 cup cracker crumbs
1/2 cup coarsely chopped pecans
1/3 cup butter or margarine, melted
4 Tbsp. brown sugar
1/2 tsp. salt
1/4 tsp. ground nutmeg
2 Tbsp. orange juice

   1. Cut squash in half. Remove seeds.
   2. Combine remaining ingredients. Spoon
into squash halves. Place squash in slow cooker.
   3. Cover. Cook on low 5-6 hours, or until
squash is tender.

Apple Walnut Squash

Michele Ruvola
Selden, NY

Makes 4 servings

1/4 cup water
2 small acorn squash
1/4 cup packed brown sugar
1/4 cup butter, melted
3 Tbsp. apple juice
1 1/2 tsp. ground cinnamon
1/4 tsp. salt
1 cup toasted walnuts
1 apple, chopped

   1. Pour water into slow cooker.
   2. Cut squash crosswise in half. Remove
seeds. Place in slow cooker, cut sides up.

3. Combine brown sugar, butter, apple juice, cinnamon, and salt. Spoon into squash.

4. Cover. Cook on high 3-4 hours, or until squash is tender.

5. Combine walnuts and chopped apple. Add to center of squash and mix with sauce to serve.

6. Serve with a pork dish.

Stuffed Acorn Squash

Jean Butzer
Batavia, NY

Makes 6 servings

3 small carnival or acorn squash
5 Tbsp. instant brown rice
3 Tbsp. dried cranberries
3 Tbsp. diced celery
3 Tbsp. minced onion
pinch of ground or dried sage
1 tsp. butter, divided
3 Tbsp. orange juice
1/2 cup water

1. Slice off points on the bottoms of squash so they will stand in slow cooker. Slice off tops and discard. Scoop out seeds. Place squash in slow cooker.

2. Combine rice, cranberries, celery, onion, and sage. Stuff into squash.

3. Dot with butter.

4. Pour 1 Tbsp. orange juice into each squash.

5. Pour water into bottom of slow cooker.

6. Cover. Cook on low 2½ hours.

7. Serve with cooked turkey breast.

Note: To make squash easier to slice, microwave whole squash on high for 5 minutes to soften skin.

Tzimmes

Elaine Vigoda
Rochester, NY

Makes 6-8 servings

1-2 sweet potatoes
6 carrots, sliced
1 potato, peeled and diced
1 onion, chopped
2 apples, peeled and sliced
1 butternut squash, peeled and sliced
1/4 cup dry white wine or apple juice
1/2 lb. dried apricots
1 Tbsp. ground cinnamon
1 Tbsp. apple pie spice
1 Tbsp. maple syrup or honey
1 tsp. salt
1 tsp. ground ginger

1. Combine all ingredients in large slow cooker, or mix all ingredients in large bowl and then divide between 2 4- or 5-qt. cookers.

2. Cover. Cook on low 10 hours.

This is a special dish served primarily on Jewish holidays, such as Rosh Hashana and Passover. The sweetness of the vegetables and fruit signifies wishes for a sweet year.

Stewed Tomatoes

Michelle Showalter
Bridgewater, VA

Makes 10-12 servings

2 qts. canned tomatoes
1/3 cup sugar
1 1/2 tsp. salt
dash of pepper
3 Tbsp. butter
2 cups bread cubes

1. Place tomatoes in slow cooker.
2. Sprinkle with sugar, salt, and pepper.
3. Lightly toast bread cubes in melted butter. Spread over tomatoes.
4. Cover. Cook on high 3-4 hours.

Variation: If you prefer bread that is less moist and soft, add bread cubes 15 minutes before serving and continue cooking without lid.

Stuffed Mushrooms

Melanie L. Thrower
McPherson, KS

Makes 4-6 servings

8-10 large mushrooms
1/4 tsp. minced garlic
1 Tbsp. oil
dash of salt
dash of pepper
dash of cayenne pepper
1/4 cup grated Monterey Jack cheese

1. Remove stems from mushrooms and dice.
2. Heat oil in skillet. Saute diced stems with garlic until softened. Remove skillet from heat.
3. Stir in seasonings and cheese. Stuff into mushroom shells. Place in slow cooker.
4. Cover. Heat on low 2-4 hours.

Variations:
1. Add 1 Tbsp. minced onion to Step 2.

2. Use Monterey Jack cheese with jalapenos.

Easy Olive Bake

Jean Robinson
Cinnaminson, NJ

Makes 8 servings

1 cup uncooked rice
2 medium onions, chopped
1/2 cup butter or margarine, melted
2 cups stewed tomatoes
2 cups water
1 cup black olives, quartered
1/2-3/4 tsp. salt
1/2 tsp. chili powder
1 Tbsp. Worcestershire sauce
4-oz. can mushrooms with juice
1/2 cup grated cheese

1. Wash and drain rice. Place in slow cooker.
2. Add remaining ingredients except cheese. Mix well.
3. Cover. Cook on high 1 hour, then on low 2 hours, or until rice is tender but not mushy.
4. Add cheese before serving.
5. This is a good accompaniment to baked ham.

Caponata

Katrine Rose
Woodbridge, VA

Makes 8-10 servings

1 medium eggplant, peeled and cut into
   1/2" cubes
14-oz. can diced tomatoes
1 medium onion, chopped
1 red bell pepper, cut into 1/2" pieces
3/4 cup salsa
1/4 cup olive oil
2 Tbsp. capers, drained
3 Tbsp. balsamic vinegar
3 garlic cloves, minced
1 1/4 tsp. dried oregano
1/3 cup chopped fresh basil, packed in
   measuring cup
toasted, sliced French bread

1. Combine all ingredients except basil and
bread in slow cooker.
2. Cover. Cook on low 7-8 hours, or until
vegetables are tender.
3. Stir in basil. Serve on toasted bread.

Baked Sweet Potatoes

Shari Mast
Harrisonburg, VA

Makes 6-8 servings

6-8 medium-sized sweet potatoes

1. Scrub and prick sweet potatoes with fork.
Wrap each in tin foil and arrange in slow
cooker.
2. Cover. Cook on low 6-8 hours or high
4-5 hours, or until each potato is soft.

3. Remove from foil and serve with butter
and salt.

Sweet Potato Casserole

Jean Butzer
Batavia, NY

Makes 8 servings

2 29-oz. cans sweet potatoes, drained and
   mashed
1/3 cup (5 1/3 Tbsp.) butter, melted
2 Tbsp. sugar
2 Tbsp. brown sugar
1 Tbsp. orange juice
2 eggs, beaten
1/2 cup milk
1/3 cup chopped pecans
1/3 cup brown sugar
2 Tbsp. flour
2 tsp. butter, melted

1. Combine sweet potatoes, 1/3 cup butter,
2 Tbsp. sugar, and 2 Tbsp. brown sugar.
2. Beat in orange juice, eggs, and milk.
Transfer to greased slow cooker.
3. Combine pecans, 1/3 cup brown sugar,
flour, and 2 tsp. butter. Spread over sweet
potatoes.
4. Cover. Cook on high 3-4 hours.

Meal Idea

Ham in Foil or a Bag (page 85)
Sweet Potato Casserole
Asparagus

Glazed Sweet Potatoes

Martha Hershey
Ronks, PA

Makes 8 servings

10 medium-sized sweet potatoes
½ cup butter, melted
¼ cup brown sugar
½ cup orange juice
½ tsp. salt

1. Cook sweet potatoes until just soft. Peel and cut in half.
2. Combine remaining ingredients. Pour over potatoes.
3. Cover. Cook on high 2½-3 hours, or until tender but not mushy.

Note: The sweet potatoes can be cooked and peeled ahead of time, and frozen in a single layer. Defrost before putting in slow cooker.

These are great to serve with Thanksgiving dinner.

Orange Yams

Gladys Longacre
Susquehanna, PA

Makes 6-8 servings

40-oz. can yams, drained
2 apples, cored, peeled, thinly sliced
3 Tbsp. butter, melted
2 tsp. orange zest
1 cup orange juice
2 Tbsp. cornstarch
½ cup brown sugar
1 tsp. salt
dash of ground cinnamon and/or nutmeg

1. Place yams and apples in slow cooker.
2. Add butter and orange zest.
3. Combine remaining ingredients and pour over yams.
4. Cover. Cook on high 1 hour and on low 2 hours, or until apples are tender.

Variation: Substitute 6-8 medium-sized cooked sweet potatoes, or approximately 4 cups cubed butternut squash, for yams.

Apples n' Yams

Rebecca Plank Leichty
Harrisonburg, VA

Makes 8-10 servings

1 Tbsp. lemon juice or lemonade
6 apples, peeled and sliced
6 large yams or sweet potatoes,
    peeled and thinly sliced
¼ cup apple juice
1 Tbsp. butter, melted

1. Toss sliced apples and yams in lemon juice.
2. Combine apple juice and butter. Pour over apples and sweet potatoes. Pour into greased slow cooker.
3. Cover. Cook on high 4 hours or low 6 hours.

This is a tasty vegetable dish to add to a meal when serving children. The apples smell wonderful when cooking and truly moisten the potatoes when served together. It is a well-rounded and easy way to serve sweet potatoes.

Sweet Potatoes and Apples

Bernita Boyts
Shawnee Mission, KS

Makes 8-10 servings

3 large sweet potatoes, peeled and cubed
3 large tart and firm apples, peeled and
    sliced
1/2-3/4 tsp. salt
1/8-1/4 tsp. pepper
1 tsp. sage
1 tsp. ground cinnamon
4 Tbsp. (1/2 stick) butter, melted
1/4 cup maple syrup
toasted sliced almonds or chopped pecans,
    optional

1. Place half the sweet potatoes in slow cooker. Layer in half the apple slices.
2. Mix together seasonings. Sprinkle half over apples.
3. Mix together butter and maple syrup. Spoon half over seasonings.
4. Repeat layers.
5. Cover. Cook on low 6-8 hours or until potatoes are soft, stirring occasionally.
6. To add a bit of crunch, sprinkle with toasted almonds or pecans when serving.
7. Serve with pork or poultry.

Sweet Potatoes with Applesauce

Judi Manos
West Islip, NY

Makes 6-8 servings

6 medium-sized sweet potatoes or yams
1 1/2 cups applesauce
2/3 cup packed brown sugar
3 Tbsp. butter, melted
1 tsp. ground cinnamon
1/2 cup chopped toasted nuts

1. Peel sweet potatoes and cut into 1/2" cubes. Place in slow cooker.
2. Combine remaining ingredients, except nuts. Spoon over potatoes.
3. Cover. Cook on low 6-7 hours or until potatoes are very tender.
4. Sprinkle with nuts.

Variation: If you prefer a less sweet dish, cut the sugar back to 1/3 cup.

Meal Idea

Turkey Breast (pages 125-127)
Sweet Potatoes with Applesauce
Green Salad

Barbecued Black Beans with Sweet Potatoes

Barbara Jean Fabel
Wausau, WI

Makes 4-6 servings

4 large sweet potatoes, peeled and cut into
   8 chunks each
15-oz. can black beans, rinsed and drained
1 medium onion, diced
2 ribs celery, sliced
9 ozs. Sweet Baby Ray's Barbecue Sauce

1. Place sweet potatoes in slow cooker.
2. Combine remaining ingredients. Pour over sweet potatoes.
3. Cover. Cook on high 2-3 hours, or on low 4 hours.

Mashed Potatoes

Mrs. Audrey L. Kneer
Williamsfield, IL

1-2 medium-sized potatoes per person
3 Tbsp. milk per potato
1/2 Tbsp. butter per potato, melted
1/8 tsp. salt per potato

1. Peel and boil potatoes until soft. Mash.
2. While mashing potatoes, heat milk to scalding. Then add hot milk, butter, and salt to mashed potatoes, stirring in well.
3. Put in slow cooker a couple of hours before serving. Set cooker on low. Stir once in a while. These will be the same as fresh mashed potatoes.

Note: This saves needing to mash potatoes at the last minute.

Garlic Mashed Potatoes

Katrine Rose
Woodbridge, VA

Makes 6 servings

2 lbs. baking potatoes, unpeeled
   and cut into 1/2" cubes
1/4 cup water
3 Tbsp. butter, sliced
1 tsp. salt
3/4 tsp. garlic powder
1/4 tsp. black pepper
1 cup milk

1. Combine all ingredients, except milk, in slow cooker. Toss to combine.
2. Cover. Cook on low 7 hours, or on high 4 hours.
3. Add milk to potatoes during last 30 minutes of cooking time.
4. Mash potatoes with potato masher or electric mixer until fairly smooth.

Company Mashed Potatoes

Eileen Eash
Carlsbad, NM

Makes 12 servings

15 medium-sized potatoes
1 cup sour cream
1 small onion, diced fine
1 tsp. salt
1/8-1/4 tsp. pepper, according to your taste
    preference
1-2 cups buttermilk
1 cup fresh, chopped spinach, optional
1 cup grated Colby or cheddar cheese,
    optional

1. Peel and quarter potatoes. Place in slow cooker. Barely cover with water.
2. Cover. Cook on low 8-10 hours. Drain water.
3. Mash potatoes. Add remaining ingredients except cheese.
4. Cover. Heat on low 4-6 hours.
5. Sprinkle with cheese 5 minutes before serving.

Buttermilk gives mashed potatoes a unique flavor that most people enjoy. I often serve variations of this recipe for guests and they always ask what I put in the potatoes.

Notes:
l. I save the water drained from cooking the potatoes and use it to make gravy or a soup base.

2. Small amounts of leftovers from this recipe add a special flavor to vegetable or noodle soup for another meal.

Refrigerator Mashed Potatoes

Deborah Swartz
Grottoes, VA

Makes 8-10 servings

5 lbs. potatoes
8-oz. pkg. cream cheese, softened
1 cup sour cream
1 tsp. salt
1/4 tsp. pepper
1/4 cup crisp bacon, crumbled
2 Tbsp. butter

1. Cook and mash potatoes.
2. Add remaining ingredients except butter. Put in slow cooker. Dot with butter.
3. Cover. Cook on low 2 hours.

Variations:
1. These potatoes can be made several days ahead and refrigerated. Cook refrigerated potatoes on low for 5 hours.

2. If you wish, sprinkle 1 cup cheddar cheese over the top of the potatoes during their last half hour in slow cooker.

3. Substitute chopped ham for the bacon.

4. Add 2 Tbsp. chopped fresh chives to Step 2.

Hosting Idea

My mom always prepared mashed potatoes for any get-togethers at my grandmother's house. She made them ahead of time, put them in her slow cooker, and transported them, turning on the cooker when we arrived. The potatoes were always hot, steamy, and wonderful whenever we got around to eating.

— Lucille Amos

Creamy Mashed Potatoes
Brenda S. Burkholder
Port Republic, VA

Makes 10-12 servings

2 tsp. salt
6 Tbsp. (3/4 stick) butter, melted
2 1/4 cups milk
6 7/8 cups potato flakes
6 cups water
1 cup sour cream
4-5 ozs. (approximately half of a large
   pkg.) cream cheese, softened

1. Combine first five ingredients as directed on potato box.
2. Whip cream cheese with electric mixer until creamy. Blend in sour cream.
3. Fold potatoes into cheese and sour cream. Beat well. Place in slow cooker.
4. Cover. Cook on low 3-5 hours.

Sunday Dinner Potatoes
Ruth Ann Penner
Hillsboro, KS

Makes 8 servings

4 cups cooked, sliced potatoes
1/3 cup margarine
1/4 cup flour
2 cups milk
1 tsp. salt
pepper to taste
1 tsp. onion powder

1. Place potatoes in slow cooker.
2. Melt butter in small skillet. Add flour and stir. Slowly add milk, stirring constantly.

3. Add salt, pepper, and onion powder. When smooth and thickened, pour over potatoes.
4. Cover. Cook on high 2-3 hours or low 4-5 hours.

Swiss-Irish Hot Sauce
Jo Haberkamp
Fairbank, IA

Makes 6-8 servings

2 medium onions, diced
5 garlic cloves, minced
1/4 cup oil
1-lb. can tomatoes, pureed
15-oz. can tomato sauce
12-oz. can tomato paste
2 Tbsp. parsley, fresh or dried
1/2 tsp. red pepper
1/2 tsp. black pepper
1 tsp. chili powder
1 tsp. dried basil
2 tsp. Worcestershire sauce
2 tsp. Tabasco sauce
1/4 cup red wine

1. Saute onions and garlic in oil in skillet.
2. Combine all ingredients in slow cooker.
3. Cover. Cook on low 4 hours.
4. This is a flavorful sauce for eating over pasta or baked potatoes. Serve with French bread and a tossed salad.

Herbed Potatoes
Jo Haberkamp
Fairbank, IA

Makes 6 servings

1½ lbs. small new potatoes
¼ cup water
¼ cup butter or margarine, melted
3 Tbsp. chopped fresh parsley
1 Tbsp. lemon juice
1 Tbsp. chopped fresh chives
1 Tbsp. dill weed
¼-½ tsp. salt, according to your taste
   preference
⅛-¼ tsp. pepper, according to your taste
   preference

1. Wash potatoes. Peel a strip around the center of each potato. Place in slow cooker.
2. Add water.
3. Cover. Cook on high 2½-3 hours. Drain well.
4. In saucepan, heat butter, parsley, lemon juice, chives, dill, salt, and pepper. Pour over potatoes.
5. Serve with ham or any meat dish that does not make gravy.

Onion Potatoes
Donna Lantgen
Rapid City, SD

Makes 6 servings

6 medium potatoes, diced
⅓ cup olive oil
1 pkg. dry onion soup mix

1. Combine potatoes and olive oil in plastic bag. Shake well.
2. Add onion soup mix. Shake well.
3. Pour into slow cooker.
4. Cover. Cook on low 6 hours or high 3 hours.

Variations: Add more zest to the potatoes by stirring in 1 small onion, chopped; 1 bell pepper, chopped; ½ tsp. salt; and ¼ tsp. black pepper, after pouring the potatoes into the slow cooker. Continue with Step 4.

Potatoes Perfect
Naomi Ressler
Harrisonburg, VA

Makes 4-6 servings

¼ lb. bacon, diced and browned until
   crisp
2 medium-sized onions, thinly sliced
6-8 medium-sized potatoes, thinly sliced
½ lb. cheddar cheese, thinly sliced
salt to taste
pepper to taste
2-4 Tbsp. butter or margarine

1. Layer half of bacon, onions, potatoes, and cheese in greased slow cooker. Season to taste.
2. Dot with butter. Repeat layers.
3. Cover. Cook on low 8-10 hours or on high 3-4 hours, or until potatoes are soft.

Pete's Scalloped Potatoes

Dede Peterson
Rapid City, SD

Makes 8-10 servings

5 lbs. red potatoes, peeled and sliced
2 cups water
1 tsp. cream of tartar
1/4 lb. bacon, cut in 1" squares, browned until crisp, and drained
dash of salt
1/2 pt. whipping cream
1 pt. half-and-half

1. Toss potatoes in water and cream of tartar. Drain.
2. Layer potatoes and bacon in large slow cooker. Sprinkle with salt.
3. Mix whipping cream and half-and-half. Pour over.
4. Cover. Cook on low 6-7 hours.

Variations: For added flavor, cut one large onion into thin rings. Saute in bacon drippings; then layer onion along with potatoes and bacon. Sprinkle each layer of potatoes with salt and pepper. Continue with Step 3.

Scalloped Potatoes

Zona Mae Bontrager
Kokomo, IN

Makes 10 servings

5-oz. box scalloped potatoes
5.25-oz. box au gratin potatoes
6 hot dogs, sliced, or 1 cup cubed pre-cooked ham
1/4 tsp. pepper, optional

1. Mix both potatoes per package instructions. Combine in slow cooker.
2. Cover. Cook on high 30 minutes.
3. Add meat. Reduce heat to low and cook on low for 4-5 hours.

I often fix this for church dinners, and I always bring home an empty slow cooker. The children love it with hot dogs. A quick dish to prepare and forget.

Lotsa Scalloped Potatoes

Fannie Miller
Hutchinson, KS

Makes 20-25 servings

5 lbs. potatoes, cooked and sliced
2 lbs. cooked ham, cubed
1/4 lb. butter
1/2 cup flour
2 cups cream or milk
1/4 lb. mild cheese (your favorite), shredded
1 1/2 tsp. salt
1/4-1/2 tsp. pepper

1. Place layers of sliced potatoes and ham in very large (or two smaller) slow cooker(s).

2. Melt butter in saucepan on stove. Stir in flour. Gradually add milk to make a white sauce, stirring constantly until smooth and thickened.

3. Stir in cheese, salt, and pepper. Stir until cheese is melted. Pour over potatoes and ham.

4. Cover. Cook on low 2-3 hours.

Note: A great way to free up oven space.

Cheese Potatoes

Joyce Shackelford
Green Bay, WI

Makes 10 servings

6 potatoes, peeled and cut into ¼" strips
2 cups sharp cheddar cheese, shredded
10¾-oz. can cream of chicken soup
1 small onion, chopped
4 Tbsp. butter or margarine, melted
1 tsp. salt
1 tsp. pepper
1 cup sour cream
2 cups seasoned stuffing cubes
3 Tbsp. butter or margarine, melted

1. Toss together potatoes and cheese. Place in slow cooker.

2. Combine soup, onion, 4 Tbsp. butter, salt, and pepper. Pour over potatoes.

3. Cover. Cook on low 8 hours.

4. Stir in sour cream. Cover and heat for 10 more minutes.

5. Meanwhile, toss together stuffing cubes and 3 Tbsp. butter. Sprinkle over potatoes just before serving.

Company Potatoes

Deborah Swartz
Grottoes, VA
Julia A. Fisher
New Carlisle, OH

Makes 6-8 servings

6 medium-sized potatoes, cooked, cooled, and shredded
2 cups shredded cheddar cheese
⅓ cup finely chopped onions
¼ cup butter or margarine, melted
1 tsp. salt
¼ tsp. pepper
1½-2 cups sour cream
butter

1. Combine potatoes, cheese, onions, melted butter, salt, pepper, and sour cream in slow cooker. Dot with butter.

2. Cover. Cook on low 4 hours.

Variations:
1. Use garlic salt instead of regular salt.

2. Add ½ tsp. chopped parsley to Step 1.

3. Use 1 cup milk and 1 cup sour cream instead of 2 cups sour cream.
　　　—Kim Stoltzfus, New Holland, PA

Creamy Scalloped Potatoes

Sara Kinsinger
Stuarts Draft, VA

Makes 6 servings

6 large potatoes, peeled and thinly sliced
1 small onion, thinly sliced
1/4 cup flour
1 tsp. salt
1/4 tsp. pepper
2 Tbsp. butter, melted
1/4 cup milk
10 3/4-oz. can cream of mushroom soup
4 slices American cheese, or 1 cup grated
　cheddar cheese

1. Place half of potatoes in slow cooker. Top with half of onion, flour, salt, and pepper. Repeat layers.
2. Mix together butter, milk, and soup. Pour over potato layers.
3. Cover. Cook on low 6-9 hours, on high 3-4 hours, or until potatoes are soft.
4. Add cheese 30 minutes before serving.

Variation:
Eliminate 1/4 cup milk. Simply top seasoned and layered vegetables with chunks of butter and then pour soup over top.

I make this recipe often when I'm having company for lunch after church. (For that, I cook the dish on high.) Using a slow cooker for the potatoes allows you to have more room in your oven for other dishes on the menu.
　　　—Ruth Hershey, Paradise, PA

Cheese Scalloped Potatoes

Mary Jane Musser
Manheim, PA
Miriam Nolt
New Holland, PA

Makes 6-10 servings

6-8 good-sized potatoes
3 Tbsp. butter
2 Tbsp. flour
3 cups milk
2 Tbsp. chopped onion
1 tsp. salt
1/8 tsp. pepper
1 tsp. parsley
1 1/2 cups diced mild cheese

1. Cook potatoes in saucepan until tender. Peel and refrigerate. When thoroughly cooled, shred.
2. Melt butter in saucepan. Stir in flour. Gradually add milk, stirring constantly until smooth and thickened.
3. Stir in onions, seasonings, and cheese, a half cup at a time. Continue stirring over heat until cheese melts.
4. Combine potatoes and sauce in slow cooker.
5. Cover. Cook on low 4 hours.

Note: Cook and shred the potatoes the day before serving them. That will relieve the pressure on the day you're having guests.

Hash Brown Potato Casserole

Michelle Strite
Goshen, IN

Makes 8-10 servings

26-oz. pkg. frozen shredded hash browns
3 Tbsp. oil
2 cups chopped ham, optional
2 10¾-oz. cans cream of potato soup
½ cup grated Parmesan cheese
16-oz. container sour cream
8 ozs. shredded cheddar cheese

1. Brown hash browns in oil in skillet. Transfer to slow cooker.
2. Add remaining ingredients and stir well.
3. Cover. Cook on low 3 hours.

Meal Idea

Ham Balls (page 94)
Hash Brown Potato Casserole
Apple Crisp or Baked Apples
(pages 221-225)

Shredded Potatoes with Canadian Bacon

Carol Eberly
Harrisonburg, VA

Makes 8 serving

32-oz. bag frozen hash browns
6-8 thin slices of Canadian bacon, or fully cooked ham
1 cup shredded sharp cheese
2 cups shredded mild cheddar cheese
¾ cup chopped onions
salt to taste

pepper to taste
10¾-oz. can cream of mushroom soup
10¾-oz. can cream of chicken soup

1. Layer half of potatoes, meat, cheeses, and onions in slow cooker. Season with salt and pepper. Repeat layers.
2. Combine soups. Pour over top.
3. Cover. Cook on low 5 hours.

We used this recipe, minus the meat, for our daughter's wedding reception meal. We made 12 slow-cookers-full. We put the recipe together the night before, put the mixture in the refrigerator overnight, and got up at 4 a.m. to plug in the cookers. They were ready for lunch.

Hot German Potato Salad

Judi Manos
West Islip, NY

Makes 6 servings

5 medium-sized potatoes, cut ¼" thick
1 large onion, chopped
⅓ cup water
⅓ cup vinegar
2 Tbsp. flour
2 Tbsp. sugar
1 tsp. salt
½ tsp. celery seed
¼ tsp. pepper
4 slices bacon, cooked crisp and crumbled
chopped fresh parsley

1. Combine potatoes and onions in slow cooker.
2. Combine remaining ingredients, except bacon and parsley. Pour over potatoes.
3. Cover. Cook on low 8-10 hours.
4. Stir in bacon and parsley.
5. Serve warm or at room temperature with grilled bratwurst or Polish sausage, dilled pickles, pickled beets, and apples.

Mushroom Stuffing

Laverne Stoner
Scottdale, PA

Makes 7-8 cups stuffing

1/2 cup butter or margarine
1 cup finely chopped onions
1 cup finely chopped celery
8-oz. can sliced mushrooms, drained
1/4 cup chopped parsley
11/2-2 tsp. poultry seasoning
1/2 tsp. salt
1/8 tsp. pepper
12 cups toasted bread cubes*
2 eggs, well beaten
11/2 cups chicken broth

1. Saute onion and celery in butter in skillet until cooked. Stir in mushrooms and parsley.
2. Combine seasonings and sprinkle over bread cubes.
3. Gently add remaining ingredients. Spoon lightly into slow cooker.
4. Cover. Cook on high 1 hour, then reduce to low and cook 1-2 hours.

Toast 18-22 slices of bread for 15 minutes at 300°.

Note: This is not as much a time-saver as it is a space-saver. If your oven is full, make your stuffing in your slow cooker.

Slow Cooker Stuffing

Allison Ingels
Maynard, IA

Makes 10-12 servings

12-13 cups dry bread cubes
    (equal to a 20-oz. loaf of bread)
1/4 cup dried parsley
2 eggs, beaten
giblets, cooked and chopped (reserve
    broth)
1 tsp. salt
1/4 tsp. pepper
1/2 tsp. sage
11/2 tsp. poultry seasoning
31/2-41/2 cups turkey broth (from cooking
    giblets)
2 chicken bouillon cubes
2 cups finely chopped celery
1 cup finely chopped onion
1 cup butter or margarine

1. Combine bread cubes and parsley in slow cooker.
2. Add eggs, giblets, and seasonings.
3. Dissolve bouillon in turkey broth. Add to slow cooker.
4. Saute celery and onion in butter in skillet. Stir into bread mixture.
5. Cover. Cook on high 1 hour and then on low 2 hours, stirring occasionally.

Note: A convenient way to free up oven space— or keep your kitchen cool.

Poultry Stuffing

Evelyn L. Ward
Greeley, CO

Makes 8 servings

1 cup butter, melted
2 cups chopped celery
½ cup chopped onions
1 tsp. poultry seasoning
½ tsp. sage
1 tsp. salt
2 eggs, beaten
4 cups chicken broth
12 cups fresh bread crumbs, slightly dried

1. Combine everything but crumbs. Mix well. Add crumbs. Stir to blend.
2. Place in 5- or 6-qt. lightly greased slow cooker.
3. Cover. Cook on high 45 minutes, then on low 4-6 hours.

Slow Cooker Dressing

Marie Shank
Harrisonburg, VA

Makes 16 servings

2 boxes Jiffy Cornbread mix
8 slices day-old bread
4 eggs
1 onion, chopped
½ cup chopped celery
2 10¾-oz. cans cream of chicken soup
2 cups chicken broth
1 tsp. salt
½ tsp. pepper
1½ Tbsp. sage or poultry seasoning
½-¾ cup butter or margarine

1. Prepare cornbread according to package instructions.
2. Crumble cornbread and bread together.
3. In large bowl combine all ingredients except butter and spoon into 6-qt. greased slow cooker, or 2 smaller cookers. Dot top with butter.
4. Cover. Cook on high 2-4 hours or on low 3-8 hours

Variations:
1. Prepare your favorite cornbread recipe in an 8"-square baking pan instead of using the cornbread mix.

2. For a more moist dressing, use 2 14½-oz. cans chicken broth instead of 2 cups chicken broth.

3. You may reduce the butter to 2 Tbsp.

Serve with roast chicken or turkey drumsticks.
—Helen Kenagy, Carlsbad, NM

Mashed Potato Filling

Betty K. Drescher
Quakertown, PA

Makes 8-10 servings

1/2 cup diced onions
1 cup diced celery
1/2 cup butter
2 1/2 cups milk
4 large eggs, beaten
8 ozs. bread cubes
4 cups mashed potatoes
1 1/2 tsp. salt
1/4 tsp. pepper

1. Saute onions and celery in butter in skillet for 5-10 minutes, or until vegetables are tender.
2. Combine onions and celery, milk, and eggs. Pour over bread cubes. Mix lightly to absorb liquid.
3. Stir in potatoes and seasonings. Pour into greased slow cooker.
4. Cover. Cook on low 4 hours.

Variation: For more flavor, add the packet of seasoning from the bread cube package in Step 3.

Sweet Potato Stuffing

Tina Snyder
Manheim, PA

Makes 8 servings

1/2 cup chopped celery
1/2 cup chopped onions
1/4 cup butter
6 cups dry bread cubes
1 large sweet potato, cooked, peeled, and cubed
1/2 cup chicken broth
1/4 cup chopped pecans
1/2 tsp. poultry seasoning
1/2 tsp. rubbed sage
1/2 tsp. salt
1/4 tsp. pepper

1. Saute celery and onion in skillet in butter until tender. Pour into greased slow cooker.
2. Add remaining ingredients. Toss gently.
3. Cover. Cook on low 4 hours.

Sweets

Boston Brown Bread

Jean Butzer
Batavia, NY

Makes 3 loaves

3 16-oz. vegetable cans, cleaned and
  emptied
1/2 cup rye flour
1/2 cup yellow cornmeal
1/2 cup whole wheat flour
3 Tbsp. sugar
1 tsp. baking soda
3/4 tsp. salt
1/2 cup chopped walnuts
1/2 cup raisins
1 cup buttermilk*
1/3 cup molasses

1. Spray insides of vegetable cans, and one
side of 3 6"-square pieces of foil, with nonstick
cooking spray. Set aside.
2. Combine rye flour, cornmeal, whole
wheat flour, sugar, baking soda, and salt in a
large bowl.
3. Stir in walnuts and raisins.

4. Whisk together buttermilk and molasses.
Add to dry ingredients. Stir until well mixed.
Spoon into prepared cans.
5. Place one piece of foil, greased side
down, on top of each can. Secure foil with
rubberbands or cotton string. Place upright in
slow cooker.
6. Pour boiling water into slow cooker to
come halfway up sides of cans. (Make sure foil
tops do not touch boiling water).
7. Cover cooker. Cook on low 4 hours, or
until skewer inserted in center of bread comes
out clean.
8. To remove bread, lay cans on their sides.
Roll and tap gently on all sides until bread
releases. Cool completely on wire racks.
9. Serve with butter or cream cheese, and
bowls of soup.

** To substitute for buttermilk, pour 1 Tbsp. lemon
juice into 1-cup measure. Add enough milk to fill
the cup. Let stand 5 minutes before mixing with
molasses.*

Date and Nut Loaf

Jean Butzer
Batavia, NY

Makes 16 servings

1½ cups boiling water
1½ cups chopped dates
1¼ cups sugar
1 egg
2 tsp. baking soda
½ tsp. salt
1 tsp. vanilla
1 Tbsp. melted butter
2½ cups flour
1 cup walnuts, chopped
2 cups hot water

1. Pour 1½ cups boiling water over dates. Let stand 5-10 minutes.
2. Stir in sugar, egg, baking soda, salt, vanilla, and butter.
3. In separate bowl, combine flour and nuts. Stir into date mixture.
4. Pour into 2 greased 11.5-oz. coffee cans or one 8-cup baking insert. If using coffee cans, cover with foil and tie. If using baking insert, cover with its lid. Place cans or insert on rack in slow cooker. (If you don't have a rack, use rubber jar rings instead.)
5. Pour hot water around cans, up to half their height.
6. Cover slow cooker tightly. Cook on high 3½-4 hours.
7. Remove cans or insert from cooker. Let bread stand in coffee cans or baking insert 10 minutes. Turn out onto cooling rack. Slice. Spread with butter, cream cheese, or peanut butter.

Banana Loaf

Sue Hamilton
Minooka, IL

Makes 6-8 servings

3 very ripe bananas
½ cup margarine, softened
2 eggs
1 tsp. vanilla
1 cup sugar
1 cup flour
1 tsp. baking soda

1. Combine all ingredients in an electric mixing bowl. Beat 2 minutes or until well blended. Pour into well greased 2-lb. coffee can.
2. Place can in slow cooker. Cover can with 6 layers of paper towels between cooker lid and bread.
3. Cover cooker. Bake on high 2-2½ hours, or until toothpick inserted in center comes out clean. Cool 15 minutes before removing from pan.

Cheery Cherry Bread

Shirley Sears
Tiskilwa, IL

Makes 6-8 servings

6-oz. jar maraschino cherries
1½ cups flour
1½ tsp. baking powder
¼ tsp. salt
2 eggs
¾ cup sugar
¾ cup coarsely chopped pecans

1. Drain cherries, reserving ⅓ cup syrup. Cut cherries in pieces. Set aside.

2. Combine flour, baking powder, and salt.

3. Beat eggs and sugar together until thickened.

4. Alternately add flour mixture and cherry syrup to egg mixture, mixing until well blended after each addition.

5. Fold in cherries and pecans. Spread in well greased and floured baking insert or 2-lb. coffee can. If using baking insert, cover with its lid; if using a coffee can, cover with 6 layers of paper towels. Set in slow cooker.

6. Cover cooker. Cook on high 2-3 hours.

7. Remove from slow cooker. Let stand 10 minutes before removing from pan.

8. Cool before slicing.

Gingerbread with Lemon Sauce

Jean Butzer
Batavia, NY
Marie Shank
Harrisonburg, VA

Makes 8 servings

½ cup butter or margarine, softened
½ cup sugar
1 egg, lightly beaten
1 cup sorghum molasses
2½ cups flour
1½ tsp. baking soda
1 tsp. cinnamon
2 tsp. ground ginger
½ tsp. ground cloves
½ tsp. salt
1 cup hot coffee or hot water
½ cup powdered sugar
2 tsp. cornstarch
pinch of salt
juice of 2 lemons
½ cup water

1 Tbsp. butter
powdered sugar for garnish

1. Cream together ½ cup butter and sugar.

2. Add egg. Mix well.

3. Add molasses. Mix well.

4. Sift together flour, baking soda, cinnamon, ginger, cloves, and salt. Stir into creamed mixture.

5. Add coffee or water. Beat well.

6. There are two ways to bake the gingerbread:

a. If you have a baking insert, or a 2-lb. coffee can, grease and flour the inside of it. Pour in batter. Place in slow cooker. Pour water around insert or coffee can. Cover insert with its lid, or cover coffee can with 6-8 paper towels.

b. Cut waxed paper or parchment paper to fit bottom of slow cooker. Place in bottom of cooker. Spray paper and sides of cooker's interior with nonstick cooking spray. Pour batter into preheated slow cooker.

7. Cover cooker with its lid slightly ajar to allow excess moisture to escape. Cook on high 1¾-2 hours, or on low 3-4 hours, or until edges are golden and knife inserted in center comes out clean.

8. If you used a baking insert or coffee can, remove from cooker. Cool on cake rack. Let stand 5 minutes before running knife around outer edge of cake and inverting onto serving plate.

If you baked the gingerbread directly in the cooker, cut the cake into wedges after allowing it to cool for 30 minutes, and carefully lift the wedges out of the cooker onto serving plates.

9. In saucepan, mix together ½ cup powdered sugar, cornstarch, and salt. Add lemon juice and water, stirring with each addition. Cook over medium heat until thick and bubbly, about 1 minute. Remove from heat. Stir in butter.

10. If gingerbread has been cooling on a rack, cut it into wedges. To serve, top with sauce and sprinkle with powdered sugar.

Hot Fruit Salad

Sharon Miller
Holmesville, OH

Makes 16 servings

25-oz. jar chunky applesauce
21-oz. can cherry pie filling
20-oz. can pineapple chunks
15½-oz. can sliced peaches
15½-oz. can apricot halves
11-oz. can mandarin oranges
½ cup packed brown sugar
1 tsp. ground cinnamon

1. Combine fruit in slow cooker, stirring gently.
2. Combine brown sugar and cinnamon. Sprinkle over mixture.
3. Cover. Bake on low 3-4 hours.

Variation: If you prefer a less sweet dish, reduce amount of brown sugar to ¼ cup, or to 2 Tbsp.

Baked Fruit

Paula Showalter
Weyers Cave, VA

Makes 8-10 servings

4 cups sliced peaches, drained
4 cups sliced apples
2 cups crushed pineapple, drained
1½ tsp. ground cinnamon
½ tsp. ground nutmeg
1½ cups sugar
2 Tbsp. cornstarch

1. Combine fruit in slow cooker.
2. Sprinkle with spices.

3. Combine sugar and cornstarch. Add to fruit. Mix well.
4. Cover. Cook on high 2 hours or low 4 hours.
5. Serve as a side dish with the main meal, or as a topping for vanilla ice cream.

Curried Fruit

Jane Meiser
Harrisonburg, VA

Makes 8-10 servings

1 can peaches, undrained
1 can apricots, undrained
1 can pears, undrained
1 large can pineapple chunks, undrained
1 can black cherries, undrained
½ cup brown sugar
1 tsp. curry powder
3-4 Tbsp. quick-cooking tapioca,
    depending upon how thickened you'd
    like the finished dish to be
butter or margarine, optional

1. Combine fruit. Let stand for at least 2 hours, or up to 8, to allow flavors to blend. Drain. Place in slow cooker.
2. Add remaining ingredients. Mix well. Top with butter, if you want.
3. Cover. Cook on low 8-10 hours.
4. Serve warm or at room temperature.

Fruit Dessert Topping

Lavina Hochstedler
Grand Blanc, MI

Makes 6 cups

3 tart apples, peeled and sliced
3 pears, peeled and sliced
1 Tbsp. lemon juice
1/2 cup packed brown sugar
1/2 cup maple syrup
1/4 cup butter or margarine, melted
1/2 cup chopped pecans
1/4 cup raisins
2 cinnamon sticks
1 Tbsp. cornstarch
2 Tbsp. cold water

1. Toss apples and pears in lemon juice in slow cooker.
2. Combine brown sugar, maple syrup, and butter. Pour over fruit.
3. Stir in pecans, raisins, and cinnamon sticks.
4. Cover. Cook on low 3-4 hours.
5. Combine cornstarch and water until smooth. Gradually stir into slow cooker.
6. Cover. Cook on high 30-40 minutes, or until thickened.
7. Discard cinnamon sticks. Serve over pound cake or ice cream.

We also like this served along with pancakes or an egg casserole. We always use Fruit Topping for our breakfasts at church camp.

Dried Fruit

Janet Roggie
Lowville, NY

Makes 3-4 servings

2 cups mixed dried fruit
1/4 cup water

1. Place dried fruit in slow cooker. Add water.
2. Cover. Cook on low 4-8 hours.
3. Serve warm with a spoonful of sour cream on each individual serving and a dash of ground nutmeg.

Variations and Notes:

1. To do more than plump the fruit, and to increase juiciness, increase water to 1/2 cup.

2. This is a good alternative to fresh fruit in the wintertime.

3. Use a single dried fruit, or put together your own choice of mixed fruits.

Zesty Pears

Barbara Walker
Sturgis, SD

Makes 6 servings

6 fresh pears
1/2 cup raisins
1/4 cup brown sugar
1 tsp. grated lemon peel
1/4 cup brandy
1/2 cup sauterne wine
1/2 cup macaroon crumbs

1. Peel and core pears. Cut into thin slices.
2. Combine raisins, sugar, and lemon peel. Layer alternately with pear slices in slow cooker.
3. Pour brandy and wine over top.
4. Cover. Cook on low 4-6 hours.
5. Spoon into serving dishes. Cool. Sprinkle with macaroons. Serve plain or topped with sour cream.

Southwest Cranberries

Bernita Boyts
Shawnee Mission, KS

Makes 8 servings

16-oz. can whole berry cranberry sauce
10 1/2-oz. jar jalapeno jelly
2 Tbsp. chopped fresh cilantro

1. Combine ingredients in slow cooker.
2. Cover. Cook on low 2-3 hours.
3. Cool. Serve at room temperature.
4. Serve these spicy cranberries as a side dish or as a marinade for poultry or pork.

Slow-Cooker Spoon Peaches

Jeanette Oberholtzer
Manheim, PA

Makes 6 servings

1/3 cup sugar
1/2 cup brown sugar
3/4 cup buttermilk baking mix
2 eggs
2 tsp. vanilla
2 tsp. butter or margarine, melted
half a 12-oz. can evaporated milk
2 cups mashed peaches, fresh, frozen, or canned (if canned, drain slightly)
3/4 tsp. cinnamon

1. Combine sugar, brown sugar, and baking mix.
2. Add eggs and vanilla. Mix well.
3. Add margarine and milk. Mix well.
4. Add peaches and cinnamon. Mix well. Pour into greased slow cooker.
5. Cover. Cook on low 6-8 hours.
6. Serve warm with whipped cream or vanilla ice cream.

This is a great warm dessert for a cold winter evening.

Cranberry Baked Apples

Judi Manos
West Islip, NY

Makes 4 servings

4 large cooking apples
⅓ cup packed brown sugar
¼ cup dried cranberries
½ cup cran-apple juice cocktail
2 Tbsp. butter, melted
½ tsp. ground cinnamon
¼ tsp. ground nutmeg
chopped nuts, optional

1. Core apples. Fill centers with brown sugar and cranberries. Place in slow cooker.
2. Combine cran-apple juice and butter. Pour over apples.
3. Sprinkle with cinnamon and nutmeg.
4. Cover. Cook on low 4-6 hours.
5. To serve, spoon sauce over apples and sprinkle with nuts.
6. This is a great accompaniment to vanilla ice cream.

This was one of our favorite recipes while growing up. When it's cooking, the house smells delicious. I'm suddenly full of memories of days gone by and a much more relaxing time. My mother passed away in October and I re-found this recipe among her collection of favorites.

Baked Apples

Donna Lantgen
Rapid City, SD

Makes 4 servings

4 baking apples, cored and unpeeled
1 tsp. cinnamon
¼ cup brown sugar
4 Tbsp. butter

1. Place apples in slow cooker.
2. Combine cinnamon and brown sugar. Stuff into apples.
3. Top each apple with 1 Tbsp. butter.
4. Cover. Cook on low 4-5 hours.
5. Delicious as a side dish served warm, or as a topping for waffles, pancakes, or ice cream.

Wagon Master Apple-Cherry Sauce

Sharon Timpe
Mequon, WI

Makes 12-15 servings

2 21-oz. cans apple pie filling
2-3 cups frozen tart red cherries
1 Tbsp. butter or margarine
1/2 tsp. ground cinnamon
1/2 tsp. ground nutmeg
1/8 tsp. ground ginger
1/8 tsp. ground cloves

1. Combine all ingredients in slow cooker.
2. Cover. Heat on low 3-4 hours, until hot and bubbly. Stir occasionally.
3. Serve warm over vanilla ice cream, pudding, pound cake, or shortcake biscuits. Top with whipped cream.

Spiced Apples

Michelle Showalter
Bridgewater, VA

Makes 8-10 servings

2 qts. peeled, sliced apples
2 1/2 cups water
1/4 cup cinnamon candy
1/2-3/4 cup sugar, according to your taste
    preference
1/3 cup Therm-flo or Clearjell
1/2 tsp. ground cinnamon
1/8 tsp. salt
1/8 tsp ground nutmeg

1. Place apples in slow cooker.
2. Combine remaining ingredients and stir until thickening agent dissolves. Pour over apples.
3. Cover. Cook on high 3 hours.
4. Serve hot with your main meal, or chill and serve with whipped cream and chopped pecans, or as a topping for ice cream, or as a base for apple crisp.

Hosting Idea

"End of the Trail Cook-Out"

To help create a casual setting I use large bandanas as napkins. I also tie bandanas around pots of flowering plants for centerpieces and add small cowboy hats and horse shoes on the table. I use spattered enamel-ware dishes. If it is a large party I switch to aluminum pie plates for dishes.
—Sharon Timpe

Caramel Apples

Becky Harder
Monument, CO
Jeanette Oberholtzer
Manheim, PA

Makes 8-10 servings

2 14-oz. bags of caramels
1/4 cup water
8-10 medium apples
sticks
waxed paper
granulated sugar

1. Combine caramels and water in slow cooker.
2. Cover. Cook on high for 1-1½ hours, stirring every 5 minutes.
3. Wash and dry apples. Insert a stick into stem end of each apple. Turn cooker to low. Dip apple into hot caramel, turning to coat entire surface.
4. Holding apple above cooker, scrape off excess accumulation of caramel from bottom of apple.
5. Dip bottom of caramel-coated apple in granulated sugar to keep it from sticking. Place apple on greased waxed paper to cool.

This is a good recipe for Fall/Harvest/Halloween parties. Children won't forget the hands-on experience of dipping their own apples. Room mothers can make the caramel mix ahead of time and bring into the classroom. This recipe is also a fun intergenerational activity for church groups or family reunions.

In the late 1950s and early 1960s, my sister and I were rewarded with a store-bought caramel apple, only after our Saturday night baths and our Sunday school lessons had been completed. I remember that the waxed paper wrapped around each apple had colorful clowns printed on it, and they sold for less than 50¢ each.
—Becky Harder

Apple Caramel Dessert

Jeanette Oberholtzer
Manheim, PA

Makes 7 servings

2 medium apples, peeled, cored, and cut in wedges
1/2 cup apple juice
7 ozs. caramel candy
1 tsp. vanilla
1/8 tsp. ground cardamom
1/2 tsp. ground cinnamon
1/3 cup creamy peanut butter
7 slices angel food cake
1 qt. vanilla ice cream

1. Combine apple juice, caramel candies, vanilla, and spices. Place in slow cooker.
2. Drop peanut butter, 1 tsp. at a time, into slow cooker. Stir.
3. Add apple wedges.
4. Cover. Cook on low 5 hours.
5. Stir well.
6. Cover. Then cook 1 more hour on low.
7. Serve 1/3 cup warm mixture over each slice of angel food cake and top with ice cream.

Hosting Idea

For those times when you can't have everything done, don't spend a lot of time apologizing. It might actually make your guests feel more comfortable if there are a few toys on the floor.
—Michelle Showalter

Apple Schnitz

Betty Hostetler
Allensville, PA

Makes 6-8 servings

1 qt. dried apples
3 cups water
1 cup sugar
1 tsp. ground cinnamon
1 tsp. salt

1. Combine apples, water, sugar, cinnamon, and salt in slow cooker.
2. Cover. Cook on low 6 hours or on high 2½ hours.
3. Serve warm as a side dish with bean soup, or as filling for Half Moon Pies (see below).
4. For pie filling, remove apples from slow cooker. Mash until smooth with potato masher or put through food mill. Cool.

Pie Crust:
   4 cups flour
   2 tsp. salt
   4 Tbsp. shortening
   ¼ cold water, or more

1. Combine flour and salt. Cut in shortening until mixture resembles small peas.
2. Add ¼ cup cold water to dough, adding more by tablespoonfuls as needed to make a soft pie dough.
3. Pinch off small pieces of dough, each about the size of a large walnut. Roll into round pieces, each about 8″ in diameter.
4. Jag one half of the circle a few times with a sharp fork to create holes for the steam to escape while baking. On the other half place a heaping tablespoon of apple filling. Fold one-half of dough up over the half holding the pie filling, shaping the pie like a half moon. Press edges of dough together. Cut off remaining dough and crimp edges.
5. Bake at 350° for 30 minutes.

On a cold winter day, Mother would prepare dried beans to make soup. After the beans were soft, she added milk to the soup pot. She heated the mixture to the boiling point, then added rivels. While the beans were cooking, she cooked dried apples until they were soft. She served these Half Moon Pies as a side dish/dessert with the soup.

Menu Idea

Bean Soup (pages 149-156)
Cheese Cubes
Sour Pickles
Celery and Carrot Sticks
Half Moon Pies

Apple Crisp

Michelle Strite
Goshen, IN

Makes 6-8 servings

1 qt. canned apple pie filling, or
   ⅔ cup sugar
   1¼ cups water
   3 Tbsp. cornstarch
   4 cups sliced, peeled apples
   ½ tsp. ground cinnamon
   ¼ tsp. ground allspice
¾ cup quick oatmeal
½ cup brown sugar
½ cup flour
¼ cup butter or margarine, at room
   temperature

1. Place pie filling in slow cooker. If not using prepared filling, combine ⅔ cup sugar, water, cornstarch, apples, cinnamon, and allspice. Place in cooker.
2. Combine remaining ingredients until crumbly. Sprinkle over apple filling.
3. Cover. Cook on low 2-3 hours.

Applescotch Crisp ✓

Mary Jane Musser
Manheim, PA

Makes 6 servings

4 cups cooking apples, peeled and sliced
2/3 cup brown sugar
1/2 cup flour
1/2 cup quick-cooking oats
3 1/2-oz. pkg. cook-n-serve butterscotch pudding mix
1 tsp. ground cinnamon
1/2 cup cold butter or margarine

1. Place apples in slow cooker.
2. Combine remaining ingredients. Cut in butter until mixture resembles coarse crumbs. Sprinkle over apples.
3. Cover. Cook on low 5-6 hours.
4. Serve with ice cream.

Variation: For a less-sweet dish, use only 1/4 cup brown sugar.

Steamed Chocolate Pudding

Evelyn L. Ward
Greeley, CO

Makes 8 servings

1/2 cup butter, softened
3/4 cup sugar
3/4 cup flour
3 Tbsp. cocoa powder
1/4 tsp. salt
3 eggs
1/2 tsp. vanilla
1/4 cup half-and-half

1. Cream together butter and sugar in electric mixer.
2. Sift together flour, cocoa powder, and salt. Add alternately with eggs to creamed mixture. Beat well.
3. Add vanilla and half-and-half. Beat well.
4. Spoon into greased and floured slow cooker baking insert*. Cover tightly with lid or double layer of foil. Place insert on a rack in slow cooker. Add boiling water to slow cooker, halfway up sides of insert.
5. Cover slow cooker. Cook on high 2 1/2 hours.
6. Remove insert from cooker. Cool 2 minutes. Unmold.
7. Slice and serve with frozen whipped topping, thawed, or ice cream.

Hint: A coffee can that fits inside your slow cooker serves as a good pudding mold. You can use a jar ring for a rack under the can or baking insert.

225

Steamed Carrot Pudding

Evelyn L. Ward
Greeley, CO

Makes 12 servings

1/2 cup butter, softened
3/4 cup sugar
1 tsp. ground cinnamon
1 tsp. ground nutmeg
1/2 tsp. ground cloves
1 1/2 cups day-old bread crumbs
1 cup grated carrots
1 cup grated cooked potatoes
1 cup raisins
1/2 cup chopped nuts

Lemon Sauce:
1/2 cup sugar
1 1/2 Tbsp. cornstarch
1/8 tsp. salt
1 cup boiling water
2 Tbsp. butter, at room temperature
3 Tbsp. lemon juice
1 tsp. grated lemon rind

1. Cream together butter and sugar. Stir in spices.
2. Add remaining ingredients, mixing well.
3. Fill a greased baking insert 2/3 full. Cover tightly with lid or double layer of foil. Place on rack or rubber jar rings in slow cooker. Pour boiling water into cooker, so that it comes halfway up sides of baking insert.
4. Cover cooker. Steam 3-4 hours on high.
5. Remove insert and uncover. Let stand 5 minutes, then unmold. Serve warm with Lemon Sauce.
6. To make lemon sauce, mix together dry ingredients in saucepan. Add boiling water. Cook over medium heat until thickened, stirring constantly. Remove from heat.
7. Add butter, lemon juice, and rind. Mix together well. Serve hot over pudding.

Note: A 11.5-oz. coffee can, if it fits into your slow cooker, is a good pudding mold.

Fifty-two years ago I was a guest at a Christmas luncheon, and the hostess served this dessert "flaming." She had soaked sugar cubes in lemon extract, placed one on each serving and lighted it.

Dried Cranberry Pudding

Evelyn L. Ward
Greeley, CO

Makes 8 servings

1/4 cup butter, softened
1/2 cup brown sugar
1/2 cup molasses
1 egg
1/2 tsp. baking soda
1/2 cup hot water
1 1/2 cups flour, divided
1 tsp. baking powder
1/2 cup dried cranberries

Butter Sauce:
1/2 cup sugar
1 Tbsp. flour
1/2 cup water
pinch salt
1 Tbsp. butter
2 tsp. vanilla

1. Cream together butter, sugar, and molasses.
2. Add egg. Beat well.
3. Dissolve baking soda in hot water. Stir into creamed mixture until well mixed.
4. Beat in 1 cup flour and baking powder.
5. Combine cranberries with 1/2 cup flour. Stir into batter.
6. Pour into well-greased baking insert. Cover tightly with lid or double layer of foil. Place on rack in slow cooker.

7. Pour boiling water into cooker, halfway up the sides of the insert.

8. Cover cooker. Steam 3 hours on high.

9. Remove insert from water. Cool 2 minutes. Run knife around edge of insert, turn upside down, and unmold.

10. Serve with hot Butter Sauce.

11. To make butter sauce, combine sugar, flour, water, and salt in saucepan. Cook over medium heat, stirring constantly until thickened. Remove from heat. Stir in butter and vanilla. Serve hot.

Hint: A coffee can that fits your slow cooker works as a good pudding mold. You can use a jar ring as a rack under the mold.

Deluxe Tapioca Pudding

Michelle Showalter
Bridgewater, VA

Makes 16 servings

2 qts. milk
3/4 cup dry small pearl tapioca
1 1/2 cups sugar
4 eggs, beaten
2 tsp. vanilla
**3-4 cups whipped cream, or frozen
   whipped topping, thawed**
chocolate candy bar

1. Combine milk, tapioca, and sugar in slow cooker.

2. Cook on high 3 hours.

3. Add a little of the hot milk to the eggs. Stir. Whisk eggs into milk mixture. Add vanilla.

4. Cover. Cook on high 20-30 minutes.

5. Cool. Chill in refrigerator. When fully chilled, beat with hand mixer to fluff the pudding.

6. Stir in whipped cream or whipped topping. Garnish with chopped candy bar.

Rice Pudding

Vera Schmucker
Goshen, IN

Makes 4-6 servings

2 1/2 cups cooked rice
1 1/2 cups evaporated milk, or scalded milk
2/3 cup sugar
2 tsp. butter or margarine, melted
1/2-1 tsp. ground nutmeg
whipped cream
maraschino cherries

1. Combine all ingredients. Pour into lightly greased slow cooker.

2. Cover. Cook on high 2 hours or on low 4-6 hours. Stir after first hour.

3. Serve topped with whipped cream and maraschino cherries.

Slow-Cooker Rice Pudding

Dede Peterson
Rapid City, SD

Makes 5 servings

1 pkg. vanilla cook-and-serve pudding mix
1 cup cooked white rice
1 cup raisins
1 tsp. cinnamon
2 tsp. vanilla
3 cups half-and-half or milk

1. Combine ingredients in slow cooker.
2. Cover. Cook on low 3-4 hours.

Chocolate Rice Pudding

Michele Ruvola
Selden, NY

Makes 4 servings

4 cups cooked white rice
3/4 cup sugar
1/4 cup baking cocoa powder
3 Tbsp. butter, melted
1 tsp. vanilla
2 12-oz. cans evaporated milk
whipped cream
sliced toasted almonds
maraschino cherries

1. Combine first 6 ingredients in greased slow cooker.
2. Cover. Cook on low 2 1/2-3 1/2 hours, or until liquid is absorbed.
3. Serve warm or chilled. Top individual servings with a dollop of whipped cream, sliced toasted almonds, and a maraschino cherry.

Simple Bread Pudding

Melanie L. Thrower
McPherson, KS

Makes 6-8 servings

6-8 slices of bread, cubed
2 cups milk
2 eggs
1/4 cup sugar
1 tsp. ground cinnamon
1 tsp. vanilla

Sauce:
6-oz. can concentrated grape juice
1 Tbsp. cornstarch

1. Place bread in slow cooker.
2. Whisk together milk, eggs, sugar, cinnamon, and vanilla. Pour over bread.
3. Cover. Cook on high 2-2 1/2 hours, or until mixture is set.
4. Combine cornstarch and concentrated juice in saucepan. Heat until boiling, stirring constantly, until sauce is thickened. Serve drizzled over bread pudding.
5. This is a fine dessert with a cold salad main dish.

Home-Style Bread Pudding

Lizzie Weaver
Ephrata, PA

Makes 4-6 servings

2 eggs, beaten
2 1/4 cups milk
1/2 tsp. cinnamon
1/4 tsp. salt
1/2 cup brown sugar
1 tsp. vanilla
2 cups 1" bread cubes
1/2 cup raisins or dates

1. Combine all ingredients in bowl. Pour into slow cooker baking insert. Cover baking insert. Place on metal rack (or rubber jar ring) in bottom of slow cooker.
2. Pour 1/2 cup hot water into cooker.
3. Cover slow cooker. Cook on high 2-3 hours.
4. Serve pudding warm or cold topped with cherry pie filling and whipped topping.

Apple-Nut Bread Pudding

Ruth Ann Hoover
New Holland, PA

Makes 6-8 servings

8 slices raisin bread, cubed
2-3 medium-sized tart apples, peeled and sliced
1 cup chopped pecans, toasted
1 cup sugar
1 tsp. ground cinnamon
1/2 tsp. ground nutmeg
3 eggs, lightly beaten
2 cups half-and-half
1/4 cup apple juice
1/4 cup butter or margarine, melted

1. Place bread cubes, apples, and pecans in greased slow cooker and mix together gently.
2. Combine sugar, cinnamon, and nutmeg. Add remaining ingredients. Mix well. Pour over bread mixture.
3. Cover. Cook on low 3-4 hours, or until knife inserted in center comes out clean.
4. Serve with ice cream.

Peach or Pineapple Upside Down Cake

Vera M. Kuhns
Harrisonburg, VA

Makes 10 servings

½ cup butter or margarine, melted
1 cup brown sugar
1 medium-sized can pineapple slices,
   drained, reserving juice
6-8 maraschino cherries
1 box yellow cake mix

1. Combine butter and brown sugar. Spread over bottom of well greased cooker.
2. Add pineapple slices and place cherries in the center of each one.
3. Prepare cake according to package directions, using pineapple juice for part of liquid. Spoon cake batter into cooker over top fruit.
4. Cover cooker with 2 tea towels and then with its own lid. Cook on high 1 hour, and then on low 3-4 hours.
5. Allow cake to cool for 10 minutes. Then run knife around edge and invert cake onto large platter.

No Fat Apple Cake

Sue Hamilton
Minooka, IL

Makes 8 servings

1 cup flour
1 cup sugar
2 tsp. baking powder
1 tsp. ground cinnamon
¼ tsp. salt
4 medium-sized cooking apples, chopped
2 eggs, beaten
2 tsp. vanilla

1. Combine flour, sugar, baking powder, cinnamon, and salt.
2. Add apples, stirring lightly to coat.
3. Combine eggs and vanilla. Add to apple mixture. Stir until just moistened. Spoon into lightly greased slow cooker.
4. Cover. Bake on high 2½-3 hours.
5. Serve warm. Top with frozen whipped topping, thawed, or ice cream and a sprinkle of cinnamon.

Variation: Stir ½ cup broken English or black walnuts, or ½ cup raisins, into Step 2.

The slow cooker is great for baking desserts. Your guests will be pleasantly surprised to see a cake coming from your slow cooker.

Creamy Orange Cheesecake
Jeanette Oberholtzer
Manheim, PA

Makes 10 servings

Crust:
3/4 cup graham cracker crumbs
2 Tbsp. sugar
3 Tbsp. melted butter

Filling:
2 8-oz. pkgs. cream cheese, at room
    temperature
2/3 cup sugar
2 eggs
1 egg yolk
1/4 cup frozen orange juice concentrate
1 tsp. orange zest
1 Tbsp. flour
1/2 tsp. vanilla

1. Combine crust ingredients. Pat into 7" or 9" springform pan, whichever size fits into your slow cooker.
2. Cream together cream cheese and sugar. Add eggs and yolk. Beat for 3 minutes.
3. Beat in juice, zest, flour, and vanilla. Beat 2 minutes.
4. Pour batter into crust. Place on rack in slow cooker.
5. Cover. Cook on high 2½-3 hours. Turn off and leave stand for 1-2 hours, or until cool enough to remove from cooker.
6. Cool completely before removing sides of pan. Chill before serving.
7. Serve with thawed frozen whipped topping and fresh or mandarin orange slices.

Carrot Cake
Colleen Heatwole
Burton, MI

Makes 6-8 servings

1/2 cup salad oil
2 eggs
1 Tbsp. hot water
1/2 cup grated raw carrots
3/4 cup flour
3/4 cup sugar
1/2 tsp. baking powder
1/8 tsp. salt
1/4 tsp. ground allspice
1/2 tsp. ground cinnamon
1/8 tsp. ground cloves
1/2 cup chopped nuts
1/2 cup raisins or chopped dates
2 Tbsp. flour

1. In large bowl, beat oil, eggs, and water for 1 minute.
2. Add carrots. Mix well.
3. Stir together flour, sugar, baking powder, salt, allspice, cinnamon, and cloves. Add to creamed mixture.
4. Toss nuts and raisins in bowl with 2 Tbsp. flour. Add to creamed mixture. Mix well.
5. Pour into greased and floured 3-lb. shortening can or slow cooker baking insert. Place can or baking insert in slow cooker.
6. Cover insert with its lid, or cover can with 8 paper towels, folded down over edge of slow cooker to absorb moisture. Cover paper towels with cooker lid. Cook on high 3-4 hours.
7. Remove can or insert from cooker and allow to cool on rack for 10 minutes. Run knife around edge of cake. Invert onto serving plate.

Dump Cake

Janice Muller
Derwood, MD

Makes 8-10 servings

20-oz. can crushed pineapple
21-oz. can blueberry or cherry pie filling
18½-oz. pkg. yellow cake mix
cinnamon
½ cup butter or margarine
1 cup chopped nuts

1. Grease bottom and sides of slow cooker.
2. Spread layers of pineapple, blueberry pie filling, and dry cake mix. Be careful not to mix the layers.
3. Sprinkle with cinnamon.
4. Top with thin layers of butter chunks and nuts.
5. Cover. Cook on high 2-3 hours.
6. Serve with vanilla ice cream.

Variation: Use a pkg. of spice cake mix and apple pie filling.

Lemon Poppy Seed Upside-Down Cake

Jeanette Oberholtzer
Manheim, PA

Makes 8-10 servings

1 pkg. lemon poppy seed bread mix
1 egg
8 ozs. light sour cream
½ cup water

Sauce:
1 Tbsp. butter
¾ cup water
½ cup sugar
¼ cup lemon juice

1. Combine first four ingredients until well moistened. Spread in lightly greased slow cooker.
2. Combine sauce ingredients in small saucepan. Bring to boil. Pour boiling mixture over batter.
3. Cover. Cook on high 2-2½ hours. Edges will be slightly brown. Turn heat off and leave in cooker for 30 minutes with cover slightly ajar.
4. When cool enough to handle, hold a large plate over top of cooker, then invert.
5. Allow to cool before slicing.

Chocolate Peanut Butter Cake

Ruth Ann Gingerich
New Holland, PA

Makes 6-8 servings

2 cups (half a package) milk chocolate
  cake mix
1/2 cup water
6 Tbsp. peanut butter
2 eggs
1/2 cup chopped nuts

1. Combine all ingredients. Beat 2 minutes
in electric mixer.
2. Pour into greased and floured 3-lb.
shortening can. Place can in slow cooker.
3. Cover top of can with 8 paper towels.
4. Cover cooker. Bake on high 2-3 hours.
5. Allow to cool for 10 minutes. Run knife
around edge and invert cake onto serving
plate. Cool completely before slicing and
serving.

Graham Cracker Cookies

Cassandra Ly
Carlisle, PA

Makes 8 dozen cookies

12-oz. pkg. (2 cups) semi-sweet chocolate
  chips
2 1-oz. squares unsweetened baking
  chocolate, shaved
2 14-oz. cans sweetened condensed milk
3¾ cups crushed graham cracker crumbs,
  divided
1 cup finely chopped walnuts

1. Place chocolate in slow cooker.
2. Cover. Cook on high 1 hour, stirring
every 15 minutes. Continue to cook on low
heat, stirring every 15 minutes, or until
chocolate is melted (about 30 minutes).
3. Stir milk into melted chocolate.
4. Add 3 cups graham cracker crumbs,
1 cup at a time, stirring after each addition.
5. Stir in nuts. Mixture should be thick but
not stiff.
6. Stir in remaining graham cracker crumbs
to reach consistency of cookie dough.
7. Drop by heaping teaspoonfuls onto
lightly greased cookie sheets. Keep remaining
mixture warm by covering and turning the
slow cooker to warm.
8. Bake at 325° for 7-9 minutes, or until
tops of cookies begin to crack. Remove from
oven. Cool 1-2 minutes before transferring to
waxed paper.

Note: These cookies freeze well.

*This delectable fudge-like cookie is a family
favorite. The original recipe (from my maternal
grandmother) was so involved and yielded so few
cookies that my mom and I would get together to
make a couple of batches only at Christmas-time.
Adapting the recipe for using a slow cooker,
rather than a double boiler, allows me to prepare
a double batch without help.*

Chocolate Fondue

Vera Schmucker
Goshen, IN
Vicki Dinkel
Sharon Springs, KS

Makes 8-10 servings

1 Tbsp. butter
16 1-oz. chocolate candy bars with
  almonds, broken
30 large marshmallows
1⅓ cups milk, divided

1. Grease slow cooker with butter. Turn to high for 10 minutes.
2. Add chocolate, marshmallows, and ⅓ cup milk.
3. Cover. Turn to low. Stir after 30 minutes; then continue cooking for another 30 minutes, or until melted and smooth.
4. Gradually add additional milk.
5. Cover. Cook on low 2-6 hours.
6. Bring the cooker to the table, along with cubes of angel food cake, strawberries, chunks of pineapple, bananas, apples, and oranges, and pretzels for dipping.

Chocolate Covered Pretzels

Beth Maurer
Harrisonburg, VA

Makes 10-12 servings

1 lb. white chocolate bark coating
2 blocks chocolate bark coating
1 bag pretzel rods

1. Chop white chocolate into small chunks. Place in slow cooker.
2. Cover. Heat over low setting, stirring occasionally until melted. Turn off cooker.
3. Using a spoon, coat ¾ of each pretzel rod with chocolate. Place on waxed paper to cool.
4. Chop chocolate bark into small chunks. Microwave on high for 1½ minutes. Stir. Microwave on high for 1 minute. Stir. Microwave on high in 30-second intervals until chocolate is smooth when stirred. (Do not allow chocolate to get too hot or it will scorch.)
5. Put melted chocolate in small bag. Snip off corner of bag. Drizzle chocolate over white chocolate-covered pretzels.

These are easy to make; they taste wonderful and are good holiday gifts when placed in small gift bags!

Appetizers, Snacks, and Spreads

Hot Artichoke Dip
Mary E. Wheatley
Mashpee, MA

Makes 7-8 cups dip

2 14¾ oz. jars marinated artichoke hearts,
   drained
1 cup mayonnaise
1 cup sour cream
1 cup water chestnuts, chopped
2 cups grated Parmesan cheese
¼ cup finely chopped scallions

1. Cut artichoke hearts into small pieces.
Add mayonnaise, sour cream, water chestnuts,
cheese, and scallions. Pour into slow cooker.
2. Cover. Cook on high 1-2 hours or on low
3-4 hours.
3. Serve with crackers or crusty French
bread.

Red Pepper-Cheese Dip
Ann Bender
Ft. Defiance, VA

Makes 12-15 servings

2 Tbsp. olive oil
4-6 large red peppers, cut into 1″ squares
½ lb. feta cheese
crackers or pita bread

1. Pour oil into slow cooker. Stir in peppers.
2. Cover. Cook on low 2 hours.
3. Serve with feta cheese on crackers.

Chili Con Queso

Arlene Leaman Kliewer
Lakewood, CO

Makes 12-16 servings

2 Tbsp. oil
1 medium onion, chopped
2 4-oz. cans chopped green chilies
14½-oz. can Mexican-style stewed
   tomatoes, drained
1 lb. Velveeta cheese, cubed

1. In skillet saute onion in oil until
transparent. Add chilies and tomatoes. Bring to
boil.
2. Add cheese. Pour into slow cooker on
low. Cook for 2 hours.
3. Keep warm in slow cooker, stirring
occasionally.
4. Serve with tortilla chips.

Chili Bean Dip

Glenna Fay Bergey
Lebanon, OR

Makes 10 appetizer servings

15-oz. can chili
1 small green or red sweet pepper, diced
8-oz. jar Cheese Whiz
1 lb. cheddar cheese, cubed

1. Combine all ingredients in slow cooker.
2. Cover. Cook on high 45-60 minutes, or
until cheese is melted. Turn cooker to low for
up to 6 hours.
3. Serve dip warm from the cooker with
nacho chips.

Hot Chili Dip

Lavina Hochstedler
Grand Blanc, MI
Anna Stoltzfus
Honey Brook, PA
Kathi Rogge
Alexandria, IN

Makes 2 cups

24-oz. jar hot salsa
15-oz. can chili with beans
2 2¼-oz. cans sliced ripe olives, drained
12 ozs. mild cheese, cubed

1. Combine all ingredients in slow cooker.
2. Cover. Cook on low 1-2 hours, or until
cheese is melted, stirring halfway through.
3. Serve with tortilla chips.

Chili Dip

Sue Tjon
Austin, TX

Makes 8 servings

1 large can chili without beans
8-oz. pkg. cream cheese
10-oz. pkg. jalapeno Jack cheese, shredded
tortilla chips

1. Pour chili into slow cooker.
2. Cut cream cheese into chunks and add to
chili.
3. Add shredded cheese. Stir well.
4. Cover. Cook on low 4 hours.
5. Serve with tortilla chips.

*This is best served warm, so I keep it in the
slow cooker to serve. You can refrigerate leftovers
and reheat them.*

Cheesy Hot Bean Dip

John D. Allen
Rye, CO

Makes 4-5 cups dip

16-oz. can refried beans
1 cup salsa
2 cups (8 ozs.) shredded Jack and cheddar
　cheeses, mixed
1 cup sour cream
3-oz. pkg. cream cheese, cubed
1 Tbsp. chili powder
1/4 tsp. ground cumin
tortilla chips

1. Combine all ingredients except chips in slow cooker.
2. Cover. Cook on high 2 hours. Stir 2-3 times during cooking.
3. Serve warm from the cooker with chips.

This bean dip is a favorite. Once you start on it, it's hard to leave it alone. We have been known to dip into it even when it's cold.

Mexican
Bean and Cheese Dip

Mary Sommerfeld
Lancaster, PA

Makes about 5 cups dip

15-oz. can refried beans
8-oz. jar taco sauce
1 lb. Velveeta cheese, cubed
1 pkg. dry taco seasoning

1. Combine ingredients in slow cooker.
2. Cover. Cook on low 2-3 hours, or until cheese is melted.
3. Serve warm from the cooker with tortilla chips.

Note: If you're cautious about salt, choose minimally salted chips.

Mexican Meat Dip

Deborah Swartz
Grottoes, VA

Makes 20 servings

1 lb. ground beef
3/4-1 cup chopped onions
15-oz. can refried beans
1 pkg. dry taco seasoning mix
1 cup sour cream
1 1/2 cups grated mozzarella cheese

1. Brown ground beef and onions in skillet. Drain. Place meat and onions in slow cooker.
2. Add beans and taco seasoning mix. Mix together well.
3. Spread sour cream over mixture. Sprinkle cheese over top.
4. Cover. Cook on low 1 1/2 hours or on high 3/4 hour.
5. Serve warm from the cooker with tortilla chips.

Hamburger Cheese Dip

Carol Eberly
Harrisonburg, VA

Makes about 6 cups dip

1 2-lb. box Velveeta cheese, cubed
1 lb. ground beef
1 onion, chopped
10³/4-oz. can cream of mushroom soup
14.5-oz. can diced tomatoes with green
  chilies

1. While cutting up cheese, brown beef and onions in skillet. Drain meat mixture and place in slow cooker.
2. Place all remaining ingredients in slow cooker and combine.
3. Cover. Cook on low 2 hours, or until cheese is melted, stirring occasionally.
4. Serve over baked potatoes or with tortilla chips.

Variation: For more snap, add 4.5-oz. can green chilies in Step 2.

Hot Hamburger Dip √

Kristi See
Weskan, KS

Makes 10-12 servings

1 lb. ground beef
1 small onion, chopped
1 lb. Velveeta cheese, cubed
8-oz. can green chilies and tomatoes
2 tsp. Worcestershire sauce
1/2 tsp. chili powder
1 tsp. garlic powder
1/2 tsp. pepper

10³/4-oz. can tomato soup
10³/4-oz. can cream of mushroom soup

1. Brown ground beef and onions in skillet. Drain and place in slow cooker.
2. Add remaining ingredients and stir well.
3. Cover. Simmer until cheese is melted.
4. Serve with corn chips and little barbecue smokies.

TNT Dip √

Sheila Plock
Boalsburg, PA

Makes 8 cups

1 1/2 lbs. ground beef, browned
10³/4-oz. can cream of mushroom soup
1/4 cup butter, melted
1 lb. Velveeta, cubed
1 cup salsa
2 Tbsp. chili powder

1. Combine all ingredients in slow cooker.
2. Cover. Cook on high 1-1 1/4 hours, or until cheese is melted, stirring occasionally.
3. Serve with tortilla chips, corn chips, or party rye bread.

Variation: To change the balance of flavors, use 1 lb. browned ground beef and 1 1/2 cups salsa.

My son has hosted a Super Bowl party for his college friends at our house the past two years. He served this dip the first year, and the second year it was requested. His friends claim it's the best dip they've ever eaten. With a bunch of college kids it disappears quickly.

Nacho Dip ✓

Beth Maurer
Harrisonburg, VA

Makes 10-12 servings

2 lbs. ground beef, browned
1 lb. sausage, browned
16-oz. jar medium-hot salsa
1 pkg. dry taco seasoning mix
2-lb. box Velveeta cheese, cubed
10¾-oz. can cream of mushroom soup

1. Stir salsa and seasoning mix into meat. Then spread in bottom of slow cooker.
2. Cover and cook on high one hour.
3. Stir in cheese and soup.
4. Cover. Cook on low 3-4 hours, until ingredients are hot and cheese and soup are melted.
5. Serve with unsalted chips, tortilla or nacho chips, pita wedges, chopped tomatoes, refried beans, onions, and sour cream.

This is a delight at any party or get-together. We serve it at every Christmas party.

Hot Beef Dip

Paula Showalter
Weyers Cave, VA

Makes about 3 cups dip

2 8-oz. pkgs. cream cheese, softened
8 ozs. mild cheddar cheese, grated
1 green pepper, chopped fine
1 small onion, chopped fine
¼ lb. chipped dried beef, shredded

1. Combine cheeses.
2. Fold in onions, peppers, and beef.
3. Place in slow cooker.
4. Cover. Cook on low 2-3 hours.
5. Serve hot with crackers.

Variation: For more kick, add a few finely diced chili peppers to Step 2.

Hearty Beef Dip Fondue

Ann Bender
Ft. Defiance, VA
Charlotte Shaffer
East Earl, PA

Makes 2½ cups dip

1¾ cups milk
2 8-oz. pkgs. cream cheese, cubed
2 tsp. dry mustard
¼ cup chopped green onions
2½ ozs. sliced dried beef, shredded or
    torn into small pieces
French bread, cut into bite-sized pieces,
    each having a side of crust

1. Heat milk in slow cooker on high.
2. Add cheese. Stir until melted.
3. Add mustard, green onions, and dried beef. Stir well.
4. Cover. Cook on low for up to 6 hours.
5. Serve by dipping bread pieces on long forks into mixture.

Variations: Add ½ cup chopped pecans, 2 Tbsp. chopped olives, or 1 tsp. minced onion in Step 3.

I make this on cold winter evenings, and we sit around the table playing games.

Menu Idea

Hearty Beef Dip Fondue
French Bread Cubes
Tossed Salad with a variety of greens,
    slivered almonds, mandarin oranges,
    and purple onion rings, topped with
    a Vidalia Onion Dressing
Strawberry Rhubarb Custard Pie

Cheesy Sausage Dip

Reba Rhodes
Bridgewater, VA

Makes 12-14 servings

1 lb. smoked sausage, chopped
1 lb. Velveeta cheese, cubed
1¼ cups salsa

1. Brown sausage in skillet. Drain and place in slow cooker.
2. Add cheese. Pour salsa over top.
3. Cover. Cook on low 1½-2 hours.
4. Serve with tortilla chips or party rye bread.

Sausage Cheese Dip

Fannie Miller
Hutchinson, KS

Makes 20 servings

1 lb. sausage, either sliced thin, or with
    casings removed and crumbled
1 medium onion, chopped
1 green pepper, chopped
2 lbs. Velveeta or American cheese, cubed
16-oz. jar medium salsa

1. Brown sausage and onions in skillet. Drain of drippings and transfer meat and onions to slow cooker.
2. Add remaining ingredients to slow cooker and stir well.
3. Cover. Cook on low 4-5 hours.
4. Serve warm from cooker with tortilla chips.

Barbara Jean's Pizza Dip

Barbara Jean Fabel
Wausau, WI

Makes 8-10 servings

4 ozs. mozzarella cheese, shredded
4 ozs. cheddar cheese, shredded
1 green pepper, minced
5-oz. can sliced black olives
5-oz. jar sliced stuffed green olives
4 ozs. sliced mushrooms
1 cup mayonnaise
pepperoni slices, cut up

1. Combine all ingredients except pepperoni in slow cooker.
2. Top with pepperoni.
3. Cover. Cook on low 2 hours.
4. Stir well before bringing to the buffet or table.
5. Serve with snack crackers, or pour over steamed cauliflower and broccoli.

Slow Cooker Reuben Dip

Allison Ingels
Maynard, IA

Makes 8-12 servings

8-oz. carton sour cream
2 8-oz. pkgs. cream cheese, softened
8-oz. can sauerkraut, drained
3 2¹/2-oz. pkgs. dried corned beef, finely chopped
6-oz. pkg. shredded Swiss cheese

1. Combine ingredients in slow cooker.
2. Cover. Heat on low 3-4 hours, or until cheeses are melted.

3. Serve from cooker with rye crackers or rye party bread.

Reuben Appetizer

Joleen Albrecht
Gladstone, MI

Makes 12 servings

¹/2 cup mayonnaise
10 ozs. Swiss cheese, shredded
¹/2 lb. chipped or thinly sliced corned beef
16-oz. can sauerkraut, drained and cut up
sliced party rye bread

1. Combine all ingredients except bread in slow cooker.
2. Heat until cheese is melted.
3. Serve hot on rye bread.

Black-Eyed Pea Dip

Audrey Romonosky
Austin, TX

Makes 12 snack-sized servings

8 ozs. Velveeta cheese, cubed
15.5-oz. can black-eyed peas, drained
4.5-oz. can chopped green chilies
1/2 cup (1 stick) butter, melted
4 chopped green onions
tortilla chips

1. Combine cheese, peas, chilies, butter, and onions in slow cooker.
2. Cover. Cook on low, stirring occasionally, until cheese melts. Cook an additional 1 1/2 hours on low.
3. Serve warm from cooker with tortilla chips.

Cheese and Crab Dip

Donna Lantgen
Rapid City, SD

Makes 10-12 servings

3 8-oz. pkgs. cream cheese, at room
   temperature
2 6-oz. cans crabmeat, drained
1 can broken shrimp, drained
6 Tbsp. finely chopped onions
1 tsp. horseradish
1/2 cup toasted almonds, broken

1. Combine all ingredients in slow cooker.
2. Cover. Cook on low 2 hours.
3. Serve with crackers or bread cubes.

Hot Crab Dip

Cassandra Ly
Carlisle, PA
Miriam Nolt
New Holland, PA

Makes 15-20 servings

1/2 cup milk
1/3 cup salsa
3 8-oz. pkgs. cream cheese, cubed
2 8-oz. pkgs. imitation crabmeat, flaked
1 cup thinly sliced green onions
4-oz. can chopped green chilies
assorted crackers or bread cubes

1. Combine milk and salsa. Transfer to greased slow cooker.
2. Stir in cream cheese, crabmeat, onions, and chilies.
3. Cover. Cook on low 3-4 hours, stirring every 30 minutes.
4. Serve with crackers or bread.

Crab Dip

Rebecca Plank Leichty
Harrisonburg, VA

Makes 8-10 servings

2 eggs, beaten
1 green pepper, diced
2 Tbsp. diced pimento
1/2 tsp. ground mustard
1/8 tsp. pepper
1 tsp. salt
10¾-oz. can cream of celery soup
1-lb. can white crabmeat, or imitation crabmeat
toasted bread crisps

1. Beat eggs with whisk in greased slow cooker.
2. Add green pepper, pimento, seasonings, and soup. Mix well.
3. Fold in crabmeat.
4. Cover. Cook on high 3 hours.
5. Serve with toasted bread crisps for dipping.

Note: To make bread crisps, cut crusts off bread slices. Cut remaining bread into triangles. Toast on baking sheet in 350° oven. Turn once to brown evenly.

This is an easy way to serve an appetizer before a meal.

Liver Paté

Barbara Walker
Sturgis, SD

Makes 1½ cups paté

1 lb. chicken livers
1/2 cup dry wine
1 tsp. instant chicken bouillon
1 tsp. minced parsley
1 Tbsp. instant minced onion
1/4 tsp. ground ginger
1/2 tsp. seasoning salt
1 Tbsp. soy sauce
1/4 tsp. dry mustard
1/4 cup soft butter
1 Tbsp. brandy

1. In slow cooker, combine all ingredients except butter and brandy.
2. Cover. Cook on low 4-5 hours. Let stand in liquid until cool.
3. Drain. Place in blender or food grinder. Add butter and brandy. Process until smooth.
4. Serve with crackers or toast.

Pear Butter

Betty Moore
Plano, IL

Makes 2-3 pints

10 large pears (about 4 lbs.)
1 cup orange juice
2½ cups sugar
1 tsp. ground cinnamon
1 tsp. ground cloves
½ tsp. ground allspice

1. Peel and quarter pears. Place in slow cooker.
2. Cover. Cook on low 10-12 hours. Drain and then discard liquid.
3. Mash or puree pears. Add remaining ingredients. Mix well and return to slow cooker.
4. Cover. Cook on high 1 hour.
5. Place in hot sterile jars and seal. Process in hot water bath for 10 minutes. Allow to cool undisturbed for 24 hours.

Snack Mix √

Yvonne Boettger
Harrisonburg, VA

Makes 10-14 servings

8 cups Chex cereal, of any combination
6 cups from the following: pretzels, snack crackers, goldfish, Cheerios, nuts, bagel chips, toasted corn
6 Tbsp. butter or margarine, melted
2 Tbsp. Worcestershire sauce
1 tsp. seasoning salt
½ tsp. garlic powder
½ tsp. onion salt
½ tsp. onion powder

1. Combine first two ingredients in slow cooker.
2. Combine butter and seasonings. Pour over dry mixture. Toss until well mixed.
3. Cover. Cook on low 2 hours, stirring every 30 minutes.

Beverages

Hot Apple Cider

Joan Rosenberger
Stephens City, VA

Makes 21 servings

4 qts. cider
4 sticks cinnamon
2 tsp. whole cloves

1. Combine ingredients in 6-qt. slow cooker.
2. Cover. Cook on high 2 hours. Turn to low and simmer until ready to serve.

Spicy Hot Cider

Marcia S. Myer
Manheim, PA

Makes 16 servings

1 gallon cider
4 cinnamon sticks
2 Tbsp. ground allspice
1/2 cup brown sugar

1. Combine all ingredients in slow cooker.
2. Cover. Cook on low 3 hours.

Red Hot Apple Cider

Allison Ingels
Maynard, IA

Makes 16 servings

1 gallon apple cider or apple juice
1¼ cups cinnamon candy hearts
4-5 cinnamon sticks

1. Combine ingredients in slow cooker.
2. Cover. Cook on low 1½-2 hours.
3. Serve hot with a cinnamon stick in each cup.

Our family enjoys this recipe on cold winter evenings and especially Christmas Eve. The smell creates a very relaxing atmosphere.

Matthew's Hot Mulled Cider

Shirley Unternahrer Hinh
Wayland, IA

Makes 12 servings

2 qts. apple cider
¼-½ cup brown sugar, according to your
    taste preference
½ tsp. vanilla
1 cinnamon stick
4 cloves

1. Combine ingredients in slow cooker.
2. Cover. Cook on low 5 hours. Stir.

Our kids just tried hot mulled cider for the first time this past Christmas. They loved it. It's fun to try new old things.

Cider Snap

Cathy Boshart
Lebanon, PA

Makes 12-16 servings

2 qts. apple cider or apple juice
4 Tbsp. red cinnamon candies
at least 16 apple slices
at least 16 cinnamon sticks

1. Combine cider and cinnamon candies in slow cooker.
2. Cover. Cook on high for 2 hours until candies dissolve and cider is hot.
3. Ladle into mugs and serve with apple slice floaters and cinnamon stick stirrers.

This is a cold-winter-night luxury. Make it in the morning and keep it on low throughout the day so its good fragrance can fill the house.

Menu Idea

Cider Snap
Ginger Cookies
Popcorn
Cheeseball and Crackers

Maple Mulled Cider

Leesa Lesenski
Wheately, MA

Makes 8-10 servings

½ gallon cider
3-4 cinnamon sticks
2 tsp. whole cloves
2 tsp. whole allspice
1-2 Tbsp. orange juice concentrate,
   optional
1-2 Tbsp. maple syrup, optional

1. Combine ingredients in slow cooker.
2. Cover. Heat on low for 2 hours. Serve warm.

Serve at Halloween, Christmas caroling, or sledding parties.

Deep Red Apple Cider

Judi Manos
West Islip, NY

Makes 8-9 servings

5 cups apple cider
3 cups dry red wine
¼ cup brown sugar
½ tsp. whole cloves
¼ tsp. whole allspice
1 stick cinnamon

1. Combine all ingredients in slow cooker.
2. Cover. Cook on low 3-4 hours.
3. Remove cloves, allspice, and cinnamon before serving.

Variation: You can use 8 cups apple cider and no red wine.

Hot Spicy Cider for a Crowd

Lydia A. Yoder
London, OH

Makes 32 servings

1 gallon apple cider
1 cup sugar
2 tsp. ground cloves
2 tsp. ground allspice
2 3"-long cinnamon sticks
2 oranges studded with cloves

1. Combine all ingredients in slow cooker.
2. Cover. Cook on low 5-6 hours or on high 2-3 hours.

Variation: You can replace apple cider with apple juice, especially if cider is out of season, and ¼ cup orange juice for the oranges.

Orange Cider Punch

Naomi Ressler
Harrisonburg, VA

Makes 9-12 6-oz. servings

1 cup sugar
2 cinnamon sticks
1 tsp. whole nutmeg
2 cups apple cider or apple juice
6 cups orange juice
fresh orange

1. Combine ingredients in slow cooker.
2. Cover. Cook on low 4-10 hours or high 2-3 hours.
3. Float thin slices of an orange in cooker before serving.

Wassail ✓

Virginia Bender
Dover, DE

Makes 16-18 servings

1 gallon cider
6-oz. container orange juice concentrate
6-oz. container lemonade concentrate
½-1 cup brown sugar
1 tsp. whole nutmeg
1 Tbsp. whole cloves
1 Tbsp. whole allspice
orange slices
cinnamon sticks

1. Combine cider, orange juice and lemonade concentrates, and brown sugar. Mix well.
2. Place nutmeg, cloves, and allspice in cheesecloth bag or spice ball. Add to juices in slow cooker.
3. Cover. Cook on low 2-8 hours.
4. Float orange slices and cinnamon sticks on top. Ladle from slow cooker to serve.

Wassail Hot Cider ✓

Ruth Hershey
Paradise, PA

Makes 18 6-oz. servings

3 tea bags, your choice of flavors
1 qt. boiling water
2 qts. cider
1 qt. cranberry juice
2 cups orange juice
½ cup sugar
3 cinnamon sticks
12 whole cloves
thin orange slices, optional

1. Steep tea in boiling water for 5 minutes. Remove tea bags and pour tea into cooker.
2. Combine all remaining ingredients in slow cooker.
3. Cover. Cook on low 4 hours.
4. Float orange slices in cider when ready to serve. Keep warm in cooker while serving.

Hot Cranberry Cider

Kristi See
Weskan, KS

Makes 10-12 servings

2 qts. apple cider or apple juice
1 pt. cranberry juice
½-¾ cup sugar, according to your taste preference
2 cinnamon sticks
1 tsp. whole allspice
1 orange, studded with whole cloves

1. Put all ingredients in slow cooker.
2. Cover. Cook on high 1 hour, then on low 4-8 hours. Serve warm.
3. Serve with finger foods.

Note: To garnish wassail with an orange, insert 10-12 ½"-long whole cloves halfway into orange. Place studded orange in flat baking pan with ¼ cup water. Bake at 325° for 30 minutes. Just before serving, float orange on top of wassail.

I come from a family of eight children, and every Christmas we all get together. We eat dinner, and then set around playing games and drinking Hot Cranberry Cider.

Fruity Wassail

Kelly Evenson
Pittsboro, NC

Makes 20 cups

6 cups apple cider
1 cinnamon stick
¼ tsp. ground nutmeg
¼ cup honey
3 Tbsp. lemon juice
1 tsp. grated lemon rind
46-oz. can pineapple juice

1. Combine ingredients in slow cooker.
2. Cover. Cook on low 1-2 hours.
3. Serve warm from slow cooker.

Variation: Use 3 cups cranberry juice and reduce the amount of pineapple juice by 3 cups, to add more color and to change the flavor of the wassail.

Johnny Appleseed Tea ✓
Sheila Plock
Boalsburg, PA

Makes 8-9 cups

2 qts. water, divided
6 tea bags of your favorite flavor
6 ozs. frozen apple juice, thawed
¼ cup, plus 2 Tbsp., firmly packed
  brown sugar

1. Bring 1 quart water to boil. Add tea bags.
Remove from heat. Cover and let steep
5 minutes. Pour into slow cooker.
2. Add remaining ingredients and mix well.
3. Cover. Heat on low until hot. Continue
on low while serving from slow cooker.

*I serve this wonderful hot beverage with
cookies at our Open House Tea and Cookies
afternoon, which I host at Christmas-time for
friends and neighbors.*

Hot Fruit Tea
Kelly Evenson
Pittsboro, NC

Makes 20 servings

5-6 tea bags, fruit flavor of your choice
2 cups boiling water
1¾ cups sugar
2 cinnamon sticks
2½ qts. water
1¼ tsp. vanilla
1¼ tsp. almond extract
juice of 3 lemons
juice of 3 oranges

1. Steep tea bags in boiling water for
5 minutes.
2. Bring tea water, sugar, cinnamon sticks,
and 2½ qts. water to boil in saucepan. Remove
from heat and add remaining ingredients.
3. Pour tea into slow cooker and keep warm
there while serving.

Variation: Float thinly cut fresh lemon and/or
orange slices in tea.

Spicy Autumn Punch

Marlene Bogard
Newton, KS

Makes 16 servings

2 oranges
8 whole cloves
6 cups apple juice
1 cinnamon stick
1/4 tsp. ground nutmeg
3 Tbsp. lemon juice
1/4 cup honey
2 1/4 cups pineapple juice

1. Press cloves into oranges. Bake at 350° for 30 minutes.
2. Meanwhile, combine apple juice and cinnamon stick in slow cooker.
3. Cover. Cook on high 1 hour.
4. Add remaining ingredients except oranges.
5. Cover. Cook on low 2-3 hours. Add oranges at end, either whole or in quarters.

Hot Buttered Lemonade

Janie Steele
Moore, OK

Makes 5-6 servings

4 1/2 cups water
3/4 cup sugar
1 1/2 tsp. grated lemon peel
3/4 cup lemon juice
2 Tbsp. butter
6 cinnamon sticks

1. Combine water, sugar, lemon peel, lemon juice, and butter in slow cooker.
2. Cover. Cook on high for 2 1/2 hours, or until well heated through.
3. Serve very hot with a cinnamon stick in each mug.

Fruity Hot Punch

Evelyn L. Ward
Greeley, CO

Makes 12 servings

2 16-oz. cans cranberry sauce, mashed
4 cups water
1 qt. pineapple juice
3/4 cup brown sugar
1/4 tsp. salt
1/4 tsp. ground nutmeg
3/4 tsp. ground cloves
1/2 tsp. ground allspice
12 cinnamon sticks
butter, optional

1. Combine all ingredients in slow cooker.
2. Cover. Heat on low 4 hours.
3. Serve in mugs with cinnamon stick stirrers. Dot each serving with butter if you wish.

My daughter is a teacher and has served this at faculty meetings when it's her turn to treat.

Hot Cranberry Punch

Janie Steele √
Moore, OK

Makes 15-16 8-oz. servings

1 cup water
1 1/4 cups brown sugar
3/8 tsp. salt
3/8 tsp. nutmeg
3/8 tsp. cinnamon
3/4 tsp. allspice
1 1/8 tsp. cloves
46-oz. can unsweetened pineapple juice
64-oz. bottle cranberry juice
rum flavoring, optional
red food coloring, optional
15-16 cinnamon sticks

1. Combine water and sugar in slow cooker. Bring to boil.
2. Place salt and spices in bag or tea ball. Add spice ball to cooker.
3. Cover. Cook on high 1 hour.
4. Add juices, and rum flavoring and food coloring, if desired.
5. Cover. Cook on high 2-3 hours until hot.
6. Serve in cups, each with a cinnamon-stick stirrer.

Christmas Wassail

Dottie Schmidt
Kansas City, MO

Makes 6-8 servings

2 cups cranberry juice
3¼ cups hot water
⅓ cup sugar
6-oz. can lemonade concentrate
1 stick cinnamon
5 whole cloves
2 oranges, cut in thin slices

1. Combine all ingredients except oranges in slow cooker. Stir until sugar is dissolved.
2. Cover. Cook on high 1 hour. Strain out spices.
3. Serve hot with an orange slice floating in each cup.

Hot Chocolate

Colleen Heatwole
Burton, MI

Makes 10-12 servings

8 cups water
3 cups dried milk
⅓ cup non-dairy coffee creamer
1 cup instant hot chocolate mix (the kind you mix with milk, not water)
marshmallows

1. Pour water into slow cooker.
2. Gradually stir in dried milk until blended.
3. Cover and cook on high 2-3 hours, or until milk is hot.
4. Stir in coffee creamer and hot chocolate mix.
5. Turn on low until serving time, up to 3-4 hours.
6. Serve in mugs topped with marshmallows.

Hot Chocolate with Stir-Ins

Stacy Schmucker Stoltzfus
Enola, PA

Makes 12 6-oz. servings

9½ cups water
1½ cups hot chocolate mix
Stir-ins:
    smooth peanut butter
    chocolate-mint candies, chopped
    candy canes, broken
    assorted flavored syrups: hazelnut,
        almond, raspberry, Irish creme
    instant coffee granules
    cinnamon
    nutmeg
whipped topping
candy sprinkles

1. Pour water into slow cooker. Heat on high 1-2 hours. (Or heat water in tea kettle and pour into slow cooker.) Turn cooker to low to keep hot for hours.
2. Stir in hot chocolate mix until blended.
3. Arrange stir-ins in small bowls.
4. Instruct guests to place approximately 1 Tbsp. of desired stir-in in mug before ladling hot chocolate in. Stir well.
5. Top with whipped topping and candy sprinkles.

Crockery Cocoa ✓

Betty Hostetler
Allensville, PA

Makes 9-12 servings, depending on size of mugs

½ cup sugar
½ cup unsweetened cocoa powder
2 cups boiling water
3½ cups nonfat dry milk powder
6 cups water
1 tsp. vanilla
marshmallows
1 tsp. ground cinnamon

1. Combine sugar and cocoa powder in slow cooker. Add 2 cups boiling water. Stir well to dissolve.
2. Add dry milk powder, 6 cups water, and vanilla. Stir well to dissolve.
3. Cover. Cook on low 4 hours or high 1-1½ hours.
4. Before serving, beat with rotary beater to make frothy. Ladle into mugs. Top with marshmallows and sprinkle with cinnamon.

Variations:
1. Add ⅛ tsp. ground nutmeg, along with ground cinnamon in Step 4.

2. Mocha-style—Stir ¾ tsp. coffee crystals into each serving in Step 4.

3. Coffee-Cocoa—Pour half-cups of freshly brewed, high quality coffee; top with half-cups of Crockery Cocoa.

Breakfast Dishes

Breakfast Skillet

Sue Hamilton
Minooka, IL

Makes 4-5 servings

3 cups milk
5.5 oz. box au gratin potatoes
1 tsp. hot sauce
5 eggs, lightly beaten
1 Tbsp. prepared mustard
4-oz. can sliced mushrooms
8 slices bacon, fried and crumbled
1 cup cheddar cheese, shredded

　1. Combine milk, au gratin-sauce packet, hot sauce, eggs, and mustard.
　2. Stir in dried potatoes, mushrooms, and bacon.
　3. Cover. Cook on high 2½-3 hours or on low 5-6 hours.
　4. Sprinkle cheese over top. Cover until melted.

Menu Idea

For Brunch: Breakfast Skillet
Toast or Muffins

Western Omelet Casserole

Mary Louise Martin
Boyd, WI

Makes 10 servings

32-oz. bag frozen hash brown potatoes
1 lb. cooked ham, cubed
1 medium onion, diced
1½ cups shredded cheddar cheese
12 eggs
1 cup milk
1 tsp. salt
1 tsp. pepper

　1. Layer one-third each of frozen potatoes, ham, onions, and cheese in bottom of slow cooker. Repeat 2 times.
　2. Beat together eggs, milk, salt, and pepper. Pour over mixture in slow cooker.
　3. Cover. Cook on low 8-9 hours.
　4. Serve with orange juice and fresh fruit.

Mexican-Style Grits

Mary Sommerfeld
Lancaster, PA

Makes 10-12 servings

1½ cups instant grits
1 lb. Velveeta cheese, cubed
½ tsp. garlic powder
2 4-oz. cans diced chilies
½ cup (1 stick) butter or margarine

1. Prepare grits according to package directions.
2. Stir in cheese, garlic powder, and chilies, until cheese is melted.
3. Stir in butter. Pour into greased slow cooker.
4. Cover. Cook on high 2-3 hours or on low 4-6 hours.

Menu Idea

Mexican-Style Grits
Fried or Scrambled Eggs
Bacon or Sausage
Toast

Cornmeal Mush ✓

Betty Hostetler
Allensville, PA

Makes 15-18 servings

2 cups cornmeal
2 tsp. salt
2 cups cold water
6 cups hot water

1. Combine cornmeal, salt, and cold water.
2. Stir in hot water. Pour into greased slow cooker.
3. Cover. Cook on high 1 hour, then stir again and cook on low 3-4 hours. Or cook on low 5-6 hours, stirring once every hour during the first 2 hours.
4. Serve hot with butter as a side dish.

Variations:

1. Pour cooked cornmeal mush into loaf pans. Chill until set. Cut into ½-inch slices. Coat with flour and fry in butter.

2. Serve warm with milk, butter, and syrup or chili.

3. Serve slices for breakfast with maple syrup, bacon, sausage, or ham and eggs.

When we lived on the farm, Mother would prepare boiled mush for the evening meal. The rest she poured into pans and fried for supper the next evening. I adapted this recipe for the slow cooker several years ago when Mother was living with us and I needed to go to work.

Slow Cooker Oatmeal
Betty B. Dennison
Grove City, PA

Makes 2 servings

1 cup uncooked rolled oats
2 cups water
salt
1/3-1/2 cup raisins
1/4 tsp. ground nutmeg
1/4 tsp. ground cinnamon

1. Combine ingredients in slow cooker.
2. Cover. Cook on low 6-8 hours.
3. Eat with milk and brown sugar.

Peanut Butter Granola
Dawn Ranck
Harrisonburg, VA

Makes 16-20 servings

6 cups dry oatmeal
1/2 cup wheat germ
1/2 cup toasted coconut
1/2 cup sunflower seeds
1/2 cup raisins
1 cup butter
1 cup peanut butter
1 cup brown sugar

1. Combine oatmeal, wheat germ, coconut, sunflower seeds, and raisins in large slow cooker.
2. Melt together butter, peanut butter, and brown sugar. Pour over oatmeal in cooker. Mix well.
3. Cover. Cook on low 1½ hours, stirring every 15 minutes.

4. Allow to cool in cooker, stirring every 30 minutes or so, or spread onto cookie sheet. When thoroughly cooled, break into chunks and store in airtight container.

Hot Wheatberry Cereal
Rosemarie Fitzgerald
Gibsonia, PA

Makes 4 servings

1 cup wheatberries
5 cups water
butter
milk
honey

1. Rinse and sort berries. Cover with water and soak all day (or 8 hours) in slow cooker.
2. Cover. Cook on low overnight (or 10 hours).
3. Drain, if needed. Serve hot with honey, milk, and butter.

Variations and Notes:
1. Eat your hot wheatberries with raisins and maple syrup as a variation.

2. Wheatberries can also be used in pilafs or grain salads. Cook as indicated, drain and cool.

Breakfast Apple Cobbler

Anona M. Teel
Banga, PA

Makes 6-8 servings

8 medium apples, cored, peeled, sliced
1/4 cup sugar
dash of cinnamon
juice of 1 lemon
1/4 cup (1/2 stick) butter, melted
2 cups granola

1. Combine ingredients in slow cooker.
2. Cover. Cook on low 7-9 hours (while you sleep!), or on high 2-3 hours (after you're up in the morning).

Hot Applesauce Breakfast

Colleen Konetzni
Rio Rancho, NM

Makes 8 servings

10 apples, peeled and sliced
1/2-1 cup sugar
1 Tbsp. ground cinnamon
1/4 tsp. ground nutmeg

1. Combine ingredients in slow cooker.
2. Cover. Cook on low 8-10 hours.

Variations and Notes:
1. Yummy over oatmeal or with vanilla yogurt. Or serve it over pancakes or waffles.

2. Add chopped nuts for an extra treat.

Breakfast Prunes

Jo Haberkamp
Fairbank, IA

Makes 6 servings

2 cups orange juice
1/4 cup orange marmalade
1 tsp. ground cinnamon
1/4 tsp. ground cloves
1/4 tsp. ground nutmeg
1 cup water
12-oz. pkg. pitted dried prunes (1 3/4 cups)
2 thin lemon slices

1. Combine orange juice, marmalade, cinnamon, cloves, nutmeg, and water in slow cooker.
2. Stir in prunes and lemon slices.
3. Cover. Cook on low 8-10 hours, or overnight.
4. Serve warm as a breakfast food, or warm or chilled as a side dish with a meal later in the day.

Variation: If you prefer more citrus flavor, eliminate the ground cloves and reduce the cinnamon to 1/2 tsp. and the nutmeg to 1/8 tsp.

Dulce Leche (Sweet Milk)

Dorothy Horst
Tiskilwa, IL

Makes 2½ cups

2 14-oz. cans sweetened condensed milk

1. Place unopened cans of milk in slow cooker. Fill cooker with warm water so that it comes above the cans by 1½-2 inches.
2. Cover cooker. Cook on high 2 hours.
3. Cool unopened cans.
4. When opened, the contents should be thick and spreadable. Use as a filling between 2 cookies or crackers.

When on a tour in Argentina, we were served this at breakfast time as a spread on toast or thick slices of bread. We were also presented with a container of prepared Dulce Leche as a parting gift to take home. This dish also sometimes appears on Mexican menus.

Breakfast Wassail ✓

Lori Berezovsky
Salina, KS

Makes 4 quarts

64-oz. bottle cranberry juice
32-oz. bottle apple juice
12-oz. can frozen pineapple juice concentrate
12-oz. can frozen lemonade concentrate
3-4 cinnamon sticks
1 qt. water, optional

1. Combine all ingredients except water in slow cooker. Add water if mixture is too sweet.
2. Cover. Cook on low 3 hours.

Even though the name of this recipe conjures up thoughts of Christmas, it is the perfect breakfast substitute for juice, especially when entertaining a houseful of overnight guests.

Index

Index

Index

Index

Z

Notes

About the Authors

Phyllis Pellman Good and Dawn J. Ranck collaborated on the highly successful *Fix-it and Forget-It Cookbook* which has been the topselling cookbook throughout the country and has appeared for months on *The New York Times* bestseller list.

Good has been part of many cookbook projects, authoring *The Best of Amish Cooking* and *The Festival Cookbook*, and co-authoring *Recipes from Central Market, Favorite Recipes with Herbs, The Best of Mennonite Fellowship Meals*, and *From Amish and Mennonite Kitchens.*

Good and her husband, Merle, live in Lancaster, Pennsylvania, and are co-directors of The People's Place, a heritage interpretation center in the Lancaster County village of Intercourse, Pennsylvania.

Ranck has been a convinced slow-cooker user for years. She, along with her many friends, have been lining up their various-sized cookers on their kitchen counters before they set off each morning—and coming home to richly flavored full dinners.

Ranck, who lives in Harrisonburg, Virginia, is the co-author of *A Quilter's Christmas Cookbook* and *Favorite Recipes with Herbs.*